500 Treasured Country Recipes

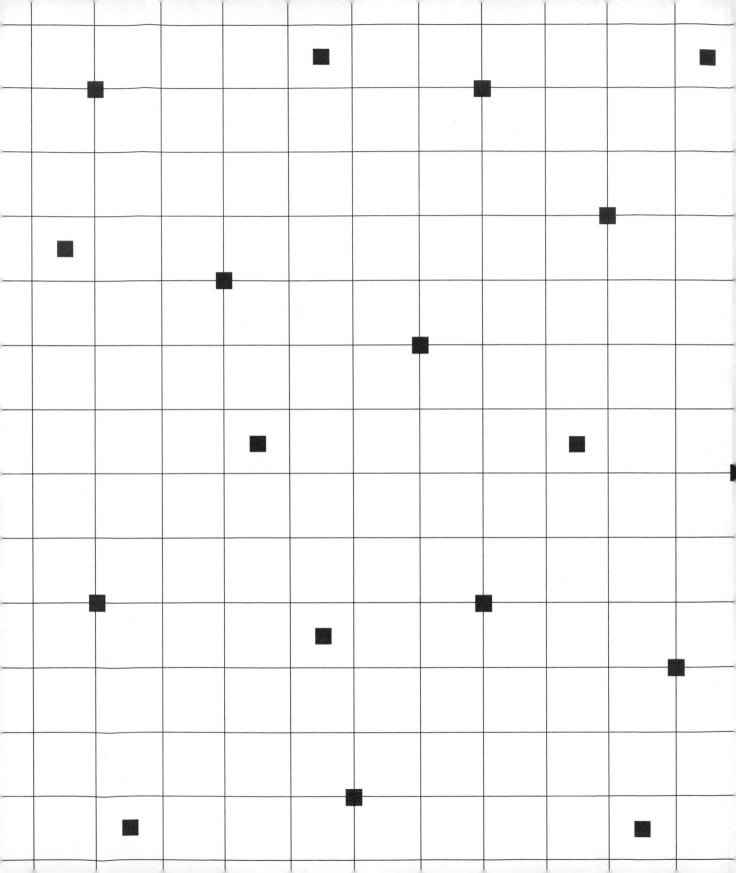

500 TREASURED
COUNTRY
RECIPES

MOUTHWATERING, TIME-HONORED, TRIED & TRUE, HANDED-DOWN, SOUL-SATISFYING DISHES

from
MARTHA STOREY & FRIENDS

STOREY
BOOKS

Schoolhouse Road
Pownal, Vermont 05261

*The mission of Storey Communications is to serve our customers
by publishing practical information that encourages personal
independence in harmony with the environment.*

Edited by Dianne M. Cutillo
Additional editing by Sally Patterson
Cover design by Lisa Hollander
Cover photographs: cherry pie, fried chicken, gingerbread, and rolling pin
    by Artville; muffins by Eyewire; canning jars and author photo
    by Giles Prett; and turkey and ice cream © Stockfood
Text design by Lisa Hollander and Erin Lincourt
Text production by Erin Lincourt
Production assistance by Deborah Daly, Susan Bernier, and
    Jennifer Jepson Smith
Illustrations edited by Ilona Sherratt
Recipe credits and a list of illustrators appear on pages 505 to 508. Photos by
    Giles Prett and Martha Storey.
Indexed by Nan Badgett/Word•a•bil•i•ty

Storey books are available for special premium and promotional uses and for customized editions. For further information, please call Storey's Custom Publishing Department at 1-800-793-9396.

Printed in the United States by R.R. Donnelley
10 9 8 7 6 5 4 3 2

Library of Congress Cataloging-in-Publication Data

500 Treasured country recipes from Martha Storey and friends / by
    Martha Storey.
       p. cm.
     ISBN 1-58017-291-1 (pbk.) — ISBN 1-58017-352-7
     1. Cookery, American. I. Storey, Martha, 1944-
    TX715 .T6827 2000
641.5-dc21   00-041317

Dedication

This book is lovingly dedicated to my mother,
Elizabeth Mullendore, known as "Mimi" to her 11 grandchildren and
15 great-grandchildren. She has taught me not only how to cook but
how to be a strong partner in a marriage, how to build a warm and
comfortable home, and how to raise a loving and happy family. She is
an example of boundless creative energy.
Best of all, she is my friend.

My mother in her kitchen

CONTENTS

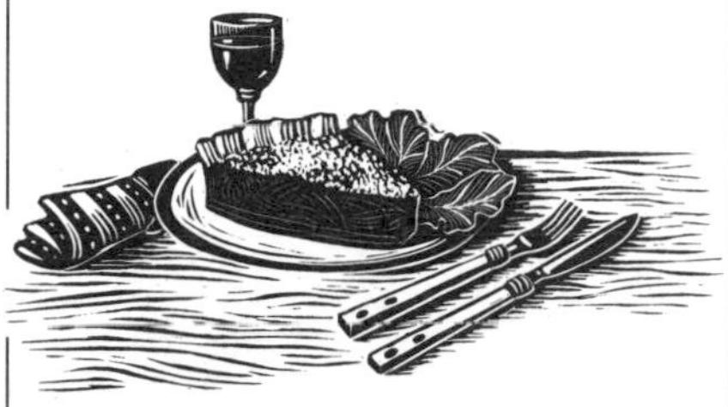

❀❀❀❀❀❀❀❀❀❀
PART FOUR:
ARTS OF THE COUNTRY
KITCHEN

❁❁❁❁❁❁❁❁❁❁❁❁❁
PART FIVE:
ARTS OF THE COUNTRY
HOME

Welcome to My Kitchen

Some of the regulars in my kitchen join me for a photo. Daughter Jessica Dils, her sons Tommy and Sam, and, at right, her daughter, Miranda, trying not to smile.

Nothing brings family and friends together more easily and genuinely than the sharing of a meal. My family has always made taking the time to slow down and break bread together a high priority. But as the pace of modern life has quickened, many find that fast food is replacing "slow food," and home-cooked meals become exceptional rather than routine.

While pulling my favorite family recipes together for this book, I found that they evoked special feelings as I re-discovered them. Wonderful moments from the past came flooding back when I talked with my relatives. Each recipe sparked a different vivid memory — the smell of a gar-lic-laced roast lamb took me back to many Easter Sundays; the wafting aroma of fresh

bread baking reminded me of the Texas home of my child-hood; and the toasty scent of corn bread browning trans-ported me to summer at the farm.

One great joy of prepar-ing this book was that I found myself sharing memories more frequently with Mother, who now lives in Georgia. I speak by telephone with her every Sunday night, but as I

John, my husband, picking apples on our farm with grandson Matthew.

gathered recipes, I began consulting with her several times a week and, as we neared the end of the project, several times a day. As a result, Mother and I have never been closer. We laughed out loud when we remembered the time that my brother Joe was in such a hurry to get home for dinner that he walked directly into the lamppost in front of our house and knocked himself out cold! We fondly recalled Daddy shaving every last morsel off the Thanksgiving turkey carcass for delicious sandwiches and then making soup that lasted for days. In these conversations, we revived family lore that otherwise I would not have passed along to my children, Jennifer, Jessica, and Matthew.

My project and our reminiscing got Mother talking more about her own mother, Nora Carter Minchey, who taught her to cook in the early part of the 20th century. Now it is my pleasure to pass on third-generation recipes to my grandchildren at the beginning of the 21st century.

Over the years, I've also learned about my husband John's favorite foods from his mother, Helen Frances Huntsberger, who was a great cook. Her handwritten recipe cards remain treasures in my country kitchen in our home in Williamstown, Massachusetts.

The family recipe collection, which includes favorites titled after my children's names for their grandparents — on my side, Mimi and Grandpa, and on John's side, MomMom and PopPop — has expanded as each generation has grown up and started its own homes and food traditions. My sister, Margie, and brothers, Charles and Joe; John's sisters, Helen and Judy; and our children's spouses have all given me recipes that have found their way onto my family's table and into this compendium.

Some may find this cookbook a bit old-fashioned. It's

Our daughter Jennifer Storey Gillis shares a smile with three of her children, Charlie, Sara, and Matthew.

Taking a break from chores in the garden at the farm with Jessica and Jennifer.

whether we are creating special foods and preserves for ourselves or as gifts. And each season brings a different opportunity: the first asparagus stalks pushing up in the spring; the unforgettable aroma of campfire cooking in the summer; a cider pressing in the fall with apples picked from our own trees; ice fish pulled from Lake Champlain, near our farm in New York's Champlain valley, in the winter.

❂ ❂ ❂

meant to be. I strongly believe that passing along the arts, crafts, and skills of country cooking is an obligation, lest our heritage be lost as memories fade. Do-it-yourself techniques — making cheese, churning homemade ice cream, and tapping trees for making maple syrup — are certainly not necessary today. In most places, one can run out to a store; buy cheese, ice cream, or maple syrup; and be home in a matter of minutes. But slowing down, using nearly forgotten implements, and sharing the processes with family and friends bring us remarkable satisfaction,

In this book, we offer you dozens of family recipes. But this project couldn't have happened without an even larger circle: coworkers, neighbors, and personal friends whose culinary creations have made their way into my collection over the years.

I've also chosen for inclusion in this book many of my favorite recipes, tips, and techniques from the talented authors and experts whom we have been fortunate to find over the years to share their knowledge with readers of Storey books. John and I founded our company, known today as Storey

Matthew, Charlie, and Sara patiently awaiting a cookout.

Communications, Inc., in 1983 to bring to others our passion for country living. It has been a labor of love made easier by the quality of the authors and employees who have been a part of Storey. You may read about many of the authors whose work is included in Contributors, page 500.

Son Matt and his wife — yes, another Jessica — getting ready for summer picnics on the porch.

The food and menus you'll find in this book may not be as chic and trendy as those that appear on the cover of the latest food magazines. I read, respect, and admire these contemporary creations, but I find it soul-satisfying to go back to the family classics. It's both exciting and comforting to pull out that dog-eared recipe for sticky buns one more time, and to know without doubt that those warm cinnamon buns will be the best that can be made.

I hope you'll discover or rediscover recipes in these pages that will become classics in your family's kitchen. Let me know what you like and what else you'd like to see in future editions. There's a handy reply card bound into the book that you can use or, if you prefer, send an e-mail message to martha.storey@storey.com. I'll be sure to get back to you.

With John at the farm.

I feel privileged to think that my family's cookbook is in your hands and hope that it will inspire your own hospitality while you create memories of family gatherings for years to come.

Happy cooking from the Storey family to yours
— Martha

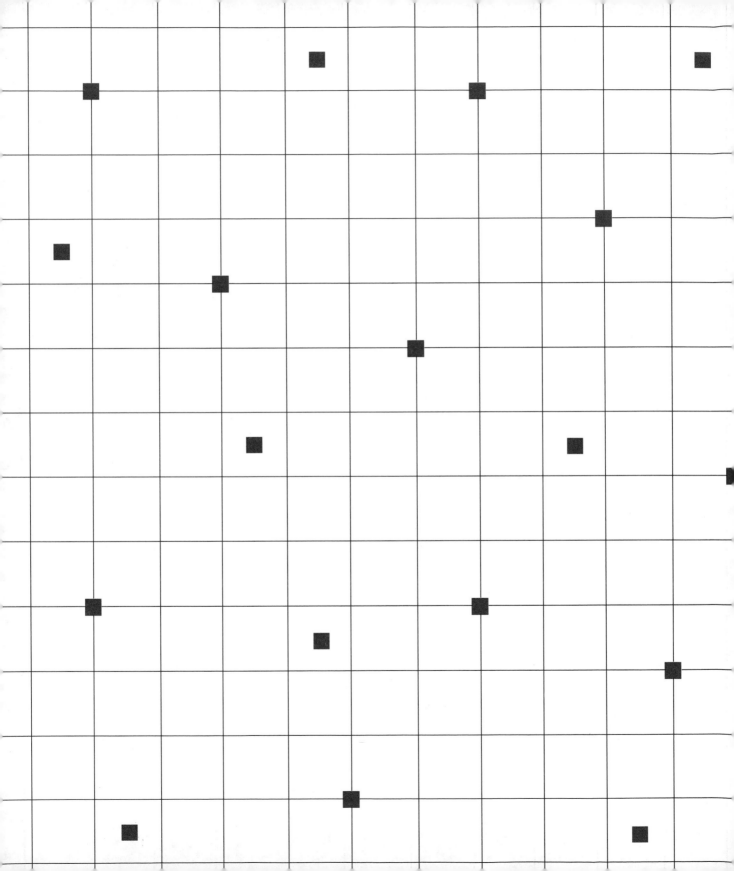

PART ONE

THE WELL-STOCKED COUNTRY KITCHEN

KITCHEN KNOW-HOW

My mother was a good cook but an even better teacher. She was so patient with me as I experimented in her country kitchen, learning the basics of cooking: baking bread, frying chicken, mashing potatoes, and making meat loaf. I also had an inspiring teacher for high-school home economics, a course that one doesn't easily find these days. Cooking came naturally to me, but learning some of the science behind what makes food taste good was illuminating. I hope that this chapter will become dog-eared, a sign that it has become a trusted reference in your kitchen — almost like having your mom at your elbow.

■ ■ ■ ■ ■ ■
Contributors to this chapter are Janet Ballantyne;
Janet B. Chadwick; Geri Harrington; and
Alexandra Nimetz, Jason Stanley, and Emeline Starr.

> MEASUREMENTS
> & METRICS
> ·············
> EQUIVALENTS
> & SUBSTITUTIONS
> ·············
> TECHNIQUES & TERMS

MEASUREMENTS & METRICS

Many early recipe collections relied on the cook's experience to judge quantities in the kitchen. Such terms as "a pinch," "a wineglass," "a goodly handful," "until just right," and "a lump the size of a walnut" were as specific as it got. For some recipes you can "eyeball" amounts — do you know anyone who measures how many cups of tomato or lettuce go into the salad bowl? But in many recipes, measuring accurately is essential to ensure consistent quality and reliable results.

To Measure Accurately and Easily

Dry ingredients. Use a metal or plastic measuring cup that fills to the top. Dip the cup into the dry ingredient (but not if you're measuring flour) or fill the cup by using a spoon. You should not dip the cup into flour, because you could pack it down and get too much flour, which could affect the success of a recipe. Spoon the flour lightly into the cup instead. Do not pack unless the recipe specifies that you should. Set the cup on a level surface and smooth off the excess with a knife so that the top is level. For measuring out less than 1 cup, use the size of cup appropriate to the amount specified or fill to the correct mark in a larger cup and shake slightly to level.

KITCHEN WISDOM

....

"A pint's a pound the world around."

Liquid ingredients. Use a glass measuring cup with a pouring spout and clearly marked lines indicating cup increments. Check measurements at eye level; ideally, you should set the cup on a flat surface and bend down so that your eye is level with the mark.

Solid ingredients. To measure solid ingredients in a liquid measuring cup, fill the cup with an amount of water equal to the amount of the solid ingredient your recipe calls for. Then add the dry ingredient until the water measures twice the amount. For example, to measure ½ cup shortening, pour in ½ cup water, then add shortening until the water reaches the 1-cup mark.

measuring spoons

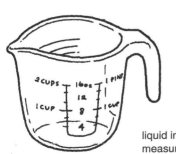

liquid ingredient measuring cup

dry ingredient measuring cups

U.S. Measurement Equivalents

Measurement	Equivalent
A few grains/pinch/dash, etc. (dry)	Less than ⅛ teaspoon
A dash (liquid)	A few drops
3 teaspoons	1 tablespoon
½ tablespoon	1½ teaspoons
1 tablespoon	3 teaspoons
2 tablespoons	1 fluid ounce
4 tablespoons	¼ cup
5⅓ tablespoons	⅓ cup
8 tablespoons	½ cup
8 tablespoons	4 fluid ounces
10⅔ tablespoons	⅔ cup
12 tablespoons	¾ cup
16 tablespoons	1 cup
16 tablespoons	8 fluid ounces
⅛ cup	2 tablespoons
¼ cup	4 tablespoons
¼ cup	2 fluid ounces
⅓ cup	5 tablespoons plus 1 teaspoon
½ cup	8 tablespoons
1 cup	16 tablespoons
1 cup	8 fluid ounces
1 cup	½ pint
2 cups	1 pint
2 pints	1 quart
4 quarts (liquid)	1 gallon
8 quarts (dry)	1 peck
4 pecks (dry)	1 bushel

Other Useful Measurements

U.S. Can Sizes

Average Weight of Contents	Approximate Cup Equivalents
4 ounces	½ cup
8 ounces	1 cup
10½ ounces	1¼ cups
14–16 ounces	1¾–2 cups
16–17 ounces	2 cups
20 ounces	2½ cups
29 ounces	3½ cups
46 ounces	5¾ cups
106 ounces	13 cups

Metric Conversion

Unless you have finely calibrated measuring equipment, conversions between U.S. and metric measurements will be inexact. It's important to convert the measurements for all of the ingredients in a recipe to maintain the same proportions as in the original. With these caveats, we provide the following tables as a convenience to our readers.

General Formula for Metric Conversion

Ounces to grams	multiply ounces by 28.35
Grams to ounces	multiply grams by 0.035
Pounds to grams	multiply pounds by 453.5
Pounds to kilograms	multiply pounds by 0.45
Cups to liters	multiply cups by 0.24
Fahrenheit to Celsius	subtract 32 from Fahrenheit temperature, multiply by 5, then divide by 9
Celsius to Fahrenheit	multiply Celsius temperature by 9, divide by 5, then add 32

Approximate Metric Equivalents by Volume

U.S.	METRIC
¼ cup	60 milliliters
½ cup	120 milliliters
1 cup	230 milliliters
1¼ cups	300 milliliters
1½ cups	360 milliliters
2 cups	460 milliliters
2½ cups	600 milliliters
3 cups	700 milliliters
4 cups (1 quart)	0.95 liter
1.06 quarts	1 liter
4 quarts (1 gallon)	3.8 liters

METRIC	U.S.
50 milliliters	0.21 cup
100 milliliters	0.42 cup
150 milliliters	0.63 cup
200 milliliters	0.84 cup
250 milliliters	1.06 cups
1 liter	1.06 quarts

Approximate Metric Equivalents by Weight

U.S.	METRIC
¼ ounce	7 grams
½ ounce	14 grams
1 ounce	28 grams
1¼ ounces	35 grams
1½ ounces	40 grams
2½ ounces	70 grams
4 ounces	112 grams
5 ounces	140 grams
8 ounces	228 grams
10 ounces	280 grams
15 ounces	425 grams
16 ounces (1 pound)	454 grams

METRIC	U.S.
1 gram	0.035 ounce
50 grams	1.75 ounces
100 grams	3.5 ounces
250 grams	8.75 ounces
500 grams	1.1 pounds
1 kilogram	2.2 pounds

Approximate Metric Equivalents by Length

U.S.	METRIC
¼ inch	0.6 centimeter
1 inch	2.5 centimeters
2 inches	5.08 centimeters
4 inches	10.16 centimeters
5 inches	13 centimeters
6 inches	15.24 centimeters
12 inches	30.48 centimeters
36 inches	91.44 centimeters

Wine Bottle Capacities

SIZE	U.S. OUNCES	METRIC EQUIVALENT
Split	6.3	187 milliliters
Half bottle	12.7	375 milliliters
Standard bottle	25.4	750 milliliters
Liter	33.8	1 liter
Magnum	50.7	1½ liters

EQUIVALENTS & SUBSTITUTIONS

How many times have you wanted to make a recipe and found that you are short an ingredient? Often, you can successfully substitute something you do have on hand. Keep in mind, however, that the result may not be exactly the same, especially if you are substituting a dried or packaged ingredient for a fresh or homemade one. Still, these guidelines are handy in a pinch.

IF YOUR RECIPE CALLS FOR	YOU MAY SUBSTITUTE
1 teaspoon baking powder	¼ teaspoon baking soda plus ½ teaspoon cream of tartar
½ cup bread crumbs	½ cup cracker crumbs
1 cup beef or chicken broth	1 cup water (or part water and part wine) plus 2 teaspoons *powdered* beef or chicken bouillon; reduce salt in the recipe by 1 teaspoon
1 cup butter	1 cup margarine
butter, margarine, or oil	equivalent amount of meat drippings (pork, beef, bacon, chicken, ham, or turkey); especially good in gravies and stir-fried dishes
1 ounce semisweet chocolate	1 ounce chocolate chips

IF YOUR RECIPE CALLS FOR	YOU MAY SUBSTITUTE
1 ounce unsweetened chocolate	3 tablespoons unsweetened cocoa plus 1 tablespoon butter or shortening
1 cup cream	1 cup whole milk plus ⅓ cup powdered dry milk and 1 tablespoon butter
	1 cup double-strength reconstituted dry milk plus 2 tablespoons butter
	1 cup evaporated milk
8 ounces cream cheese	8 ounces well-drained ricotta cheese
1 egg	2 egg yolks or 2 egg whites plus 1 teaspoon vegetable oil
1 cup fish stock	1 cup bottled clam juice; reduce salt in recipe, if necessary
1 cup all-purpose flour	1 cup unbleached white flour
	1 cup rye or whole-wheat flour (texture may change)
	1 cup plus 2 tablespoons cake flour
1 cup cake flour	⅞ cup (1 cup minus 2 tablespoons) all-purpose flour plus 2 tablespoons cornstarch
1 tablespoon flour for thickening	½ tablespoon cornstarch (use for recipes that will not require reheating, since cornstarch breaks down quickly when reheated)
	2 tablespoons quick-cooking tapioca
	1 tablespoon granular tapioca
	2 tablespoons granular cereal
	½ tablespoon arrowroot

If your recipe calls for	You may substitute
1 fresh clove of garlic	½ teaspoon garlic powder (not garlic salt)
1 teaspoon fresh ginger	½ teaspoon ground ginger
1 tablespoon chopped fresh herbs	1 teaspoon dried herbs
1 cup fresh milk	½ cup evaporated milk plus ½ cup water
	¼ cup dry milk plus ¾ cup water
1 cup sour milk or buttermilk	scant 1 cup fresh milk with 1 tablespoon lemon juice or vinegar
	1 cup water mixed with 4 tablespoons dry buttermilk powder
1 cup white rice	1 cup brown rice; allow more liquid and longer cooking time
1 can condensed soup	1½ cups thick homemade cream soup of a similar type
1 cup sour cream	1 cup yogurt
	1 cup nonbutterfat sour cream substitute
	1 cup cottage cheese plus 2 teaspoons lemon juice, blended until smooth (works best in uncooked recipes)
1 cup sugar	¾ cup honey plus a pinch of baking soda
	1 cup firmly packed brown sugar
	1 cup molasses plus ½ teaspoon baking soda; omit ¼ cup liquid from the recipe
	1½ cups maple syrup; omit ½ cup liquid from the recipe

If your recipe calls for	You may substitute
1 cup tomato sauce	1 cup canned tomato sauce
	2 cups tomato juice; cook until reduced by half
	4 ounces tomato paste plus 4 ounces water; ½ teaspoon dried basil and ¼–½ teaspoon salt
1 teaspoon vinegar	2 teaspoons lemon juice
1 cup white sauce	1 cup cream of chicken or cream of celery soup

ABOUT BAKING ON THE LIGHTER SIDE

Following are some health-related tips to make your baked goods just a little lighter.

- Use low-fat or skim milk.
- Replace 1 egg with 2 egg whites or ¼ cup egg substitute.
- Replace part (not all!) of the butter or oil with an equal amount of plain yogurt or apple-sauce.
- Replace 1 cup of sour cream with 1 cup whole milk plus 1 tablespoon lemon juice (let stand 5 minutes before using).
- Replace 1 ounce unsweetened chocolate with 3 tablespoons cocoa powder and 1 tablespoon light oil.

TECHNIQUES & TERMS

Every cook needs to know the basic techniques covered in this section. Most are not complicated, but it is important to understand the difference between stir and fold, or sauté and braise. The list is divided into three main sections: preparing and mixing, stovetop techniques, and oven techniques. Master these concepts, and you'll be ready to cook almost anything.

Preparing and Mixing

Beat. To stir rapidly with a spoon, fork, wire whisk or electric mixer to add air to a mixture and to get all the ingredients evenly distributed. When beating, be sure to reach all parts of the bowl, scraping up from the bottom in a circular motion.

Blanch. To dip fruits, vegetables, or nuts into boiling water briefly so that you can peel them easily. (For another meaning of blanch, see the Stovetop Techniques section below.)

Blend. To mix two or more ingredients together so that they are evenly distributed throughout the mixture. Sometimes this is accomplished by stirring, some-times by beating or folding. Sometimes an electric blender or food processor is used for this purpose.

Bread. To coat with cracker or bread crumbs. Sometimes the food is first dipped in milk or a beaten egg.

Butter. (*See* **Grease**) To smear or spread with butter.

Chiffonade. A cutting term reserved for greens and herbs. Stack leaves, roll them up, and slice them to make uniform thin ribbons or shreds.

chiffonade

Chop. To cut into pieces, usually to allow uniform, faster cooking time. Chopping often produces randomly shaped, small pieces. (*See also* **Cube**, **Dice**, and **Mince**)

Cream. To soften butter or shortening by pressing it against the side of a bowl, preferably with a wooden spoon, until it is soft and smooth. Sometimes the butter is worked with sugar, as in making a cake. An electric mixer set on very low speed may also be used.

Crisp. 1. To make vegetables crunchy by soaking them briefly in ice water and refrigerating them. Such vegetables as carrot strips and celery respond well to this process.

2. To create a crunchy outer shell on food by heating it in the oven or under the broiler.

Cube. To cut into cubes that are uniformly about 1 inch to a side.

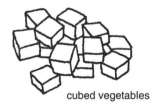

cubed vegetables

Cut. 1. To separate food into pieces by using scissors or a knife.

2. To combine butter or shortening with dry ingredients by working with two knives or a pastry blender. The action is basically a cutting action, but the purpose is to mix the ingredients evenly and finely.

Degrease. To remove fat from the surface of liquids. The best way to degrease is to chill the dish until the fat solidifies on top and can be lifted off. With this method, you can save the fat for later use, if desired. Another method is to drop in a couple of ice cubes, then remove them immediately; the fat will congeal on them. Brush a lettuce leaf or paper towel across the surface; the fat will adhere to it. Or, since fat always floats on top of liquid, you can remove it by just skimming the surface.

Devil. To mix a food — for example, hard-cooked egg yolks — with mustard or another hot seasoning.

Diagonal Cut. To cut with the knife held at an angle to the food; this maximizes the cut surface for quicker cooking. It also looks attractive.

Dice. To cut into cubes that are about ½ inch on a side.

Dot. To put small dabs of butter here and there over the top of the food before baking or broiling it. As the butter melts, it keeps the surface of the food from drying out.

Dredge. To coat something with flour, cornmeal, finely ground nuts, or the like. An easy method is to put the food and the dredging material into a bag and shake. (*See also* **Bread**)

Dust. To sprinkle flour, sugar, or any powdered ingredient lightly over the surface of food.

Eggs, beaten. Sometimes recipes will call for eggs beaten in various ways. It is usually important to beat them in the specified manner.

Lightly beaten. Beat just enough to blend the yolks and whites.

Well beaten. As you continue from the lightly beaten stage, the eggs will become frothy and full of air.

Egg whites, very stiff. Separate the whites from the yolks. A simple way to do this is to carefully break the egg in half over the edge of a custard cup. Do not break the yolk; whites will not beat if there is even a drop of yolk in them. Pass the yolk back and forth from shell half to shell half over the cup, letting the white drip down into the cup. Let the whites warm to room temperature and beat with a whisk or electric mixer until they stand up in peaks. The points of the peaks should not droop when the beater is removed. The surface of the whipped whites should look glossy but not dry. Use beaten egg whites right away, or they will liquefy and you will have to start over again with new egg whites.

Yolks, well beaten. Separate from the whites as directed above. Beat the yolks until they are slightly thickened and paler yellow.

Fold. To incorporate two or more ingredients by gently lifting and turning. This method is used to combine fragile ingredients, such as egg whites or whipped cream. If you simply stir, the mixture will collapse. Put the more fragile ingredient on top of the sturdier ingredient; then, using a spoon or rubber spatula, gently cut down through the mixture and bring up some of the bottom ingredient over the top. Repeat this folding action until the ingredients are well blended.

Grate. To shred food into particles with a grater. Graters come in various gauges for finer or coarser results.

Grease. To rub a pan or grill with butter, oil, or other fat so that food will not stick to it

diagonal-cut asparagus

and it will be easier to clean. To grease a pan rapidly and keep your hands clean, put the butter or oil in the pan and rub it around with a piece of wax paper.

Grind. 1. To crush into very small particles or powder by using a mortar and pestle, a food processor, or a grinder.

2. To reduce meat or fowl into crumbled shreds for hamburger, meat loaf, or the like.

Julienne. To cut into thin strips like matchsticks, about ¼ inch on each side.

julienned vegetables

Knead. To make dough elastic by pressing into it with the heel of your hand until it is stretched and smooth. This is accomplished by repeatedly lifting the dough, folding it over, and pressing it down. Kneading is essential to most breadmaking.

Leavening. A substance, such as yeast or baking powder, that expands and aerates dough and causes it to rise.

Lyonnaise. To have added chopped onions to a dish, as in "potatoes Lyonnaise," for instance.

Marinate. To soak food in a seasoned liquid (such as oil, vinegar, lemon juice, or wine), usually for several hours to overnight. The marinade flavors and tenderizes whatever is in it. Tough cuts of meat and some vegetables respond well to marinating.

Mince. To cut into very fine pieces. Foods are often minced for sprinkling or so that they will be well distributed throughout a dish.

minced food

Pare. To use a knife or vegetable peeler to remove the outer skin or covering of a vegetable or fruit.

Punch down. To flatten raised dough by punching it with your fist. This action allows gas that has been formed by yeast to escape and allows a fresh supply of oxygen to reach the yeast.

Purée. To mash into a very smooth consistency. A blender is good for puréeing, or you can press soft food through a sieve. Many vegetables and fruits must be cooked before they can be puréed.

Rise. To let leavened dough sit in a warm place so that the yeast can work to increase the volume of the dough mass, usually to double its bulk.

Roll cut. To cut food on a diagonal, then roll it a half turn, or 90 degrees, so that the next diagonal is at a right angle to the first, making a triangle-shaped piece of food.

Scallop. To arrange food in layers in a casserole dish, then cover with sauce and flour or bread crumbs and bake.

Shred. To tear, cut, or grate into long, flat, narrow pieces by using a knife, grater, or shredder. Shredded foods cook faster than chopped foods because they are thinner.

Skim. To remove the top surface, such as the fat from chicken soup, the foam from boiling jelly, or the cream from raw milk.

Stock. The strained liquid in which anything has been cooked, such as meat or vegetables. Seasoned vegetable, meat, chicken, and fish stocks can be used as bases for many soups, stews, and casseroles.

Toss. To mix by lifting the bottom ingredients to the top. Tossing should be done by using two large spoons or a large spoon and a large fork; take care not to bruise the ingredients.

Whip. To beat air into ingredients so that they increase in volume and become light or fluffy. Heavy cream should be cold when it is whipped, whereas egg whites should be at room temperature.

Stovetop Techniques

Blanch. To cook something in boiling water for a very short time to merely soften it a little. (For another meaning of blanch, see the Preparing and Mixing section.)

Boil. To cook liquid food, usually over high heat, until bubbles break the surface.
Racing boil. Water is bubbling as fast as it can.
Slow boil. Bubbles break the surface in a regular sort of pattern.

Braise. To cook food in a small amount of butter, oil, or stock. The pot is kept tightly closed so that the food is continually basted with the juices that condense on the lid.

Brown. To cook food rapidly in a small amount of hot fat until the outside begins to darken and turn brown. The inside is not cooked through at this point. Browning adds caramelized flavor to vegetables and seals in the juices of meat or fowl.

Clarify. To remove solids or food particles from liquid so that it becomes clear.
To clarify stock. Add egg white, egg shells, or raw hamburger and simmer uncovered for 15–20 minutes. Strain.
To clarify butter. Melt and heat until foamy. Spoon off the foam and carefully pour the clear yellow butter into a container, being careful not to include the white solids at the bottom. Clarified butter can be heated to a much higher temperature without burning and is therefore better for sautéing than regular butter.

Deep-fat frying. Also called French frying. (*See* **Fry**)

Deglaze. To remove solids that are stuck to the bottom of a skillet or roasting pan by adding wine, water, or other liquid and simmering while scraping up the loosened bits with a wooden spoon. It cleans the pan and provides an intensely flavored liquid for sauce or gravy.

Fry. To cook in hot fat in a pan on top of the stove. If you use no oil or very little, you are *grilling* or *pan-broiling*. If you use a little oil or butter, you are *sautéing*. If you use a lot of oil in a deep pan, you are *deep-fat frying* or *French frying*.

In all frying methods, it is important to get the oil hot enough so that the food will cook quickly, forming a crisp outer crust and absorbing as little oil as possible.

If you are frying with butter, it is hot enough for cooking when the foam begins to subside. After that, the butter will brown and then burn if food is not added.

When pan-broiling fatty meats, keep pouring off excess fat or the food will be greasy.

skillet

Nonreactive. Cookware made of or coated with metals that are not sensitive to the acids in foods. Porcelain-clad cast iron, flameproof glass, Teflon, enamel, stainless steel, silver, and tin are nonreactive surfaces. Reactive cookware, such as copper, aluminum and cast iron, can affect the color and flavor of food. Some food acids can also discolor aluminum.

Poach. To cook pieces of food in gently simmering liquid. Poaching is generally used to cook foods that would break up under rougher treatment (such as fish or eggs). Sometimes food must be wrapped in parchment or cheesecloth to keep it whole.

Reduce. To decrease the volume of food by simmering or boiling. Reducing lessens the amount of liquid and intensifies its flavor.

Render. To melt fat into liquid. Use very low heat and strain out the solids.

Sauté. *See* **Fry.**

Scald. 1. To heat (usually milk) to just below the boiling point, until tiny bubbles form around the edge of the pot. Milk can easily be scalded in the microwave if you have a temperature probe; set it for 180°F. When scalding milk in a saucepan, rinse the pan first in cold water for easier cleanup.
2. To dip in boiling water. (*See* **Blanch**)

Simmer. To cook liquid, usually over low or moderate heat, so that bubbles rise and break just under the surface. A simmer is like a boil, but much more subdued.

Steam. To cook food in a perforated container over, but not in, boiling water. The pot is kept tightly closed so that the hot steam does the cooking. Steaming keeps food, especially vegetables, from becoming watery.

Steep. To extract flavor by soaking in a liquid, as when making tea.

Stew. To cook in simmering liquid until tender, usually after an initial browning. Stewing is a slow-cooking method; if the mixture boils, flavor and tenderness will be lost.

Stir-fry. To quickly fry small pieces of food in a large pan over very high heat while constantly and quickly stirring it. This method uses less fat than other frying techniques.

Oven Techniques

Bake. To cook using dry heat in an oven or similar enclosed space.

Barbecue. To cook on a spit or grill or under a broiler. Food is usually basted with a seasoned sauce to flavor it and keep it moist.

Baste. To moisten food while cooking by spooning or brushing melted butter, pan juices, or sauces over it.

Broil. To cook under the broiler unit in your oven or on an outdoor grill. Broiling is used for a final browning on cooked dishes or as a primary cooking method for vegetables or meat. Food is usually placed on a rack so that fat and juices will drain off; only one side of the food is heated at a time. With a ridged grill pan, you can approximate "broiling" on the stovetop.

Drippings. Just what they sound like — the fat and juice that drip from meat as it cooks. Drippings are used to enrich gravies, soups, casseroles, and sauces. Store in the refrigerator.

Gratinée, Gratin. To bake food in a sauce, often sprinkled with grated cheese or buttered crumbs. A great way to dress up leftovers.

Grill. (*See* **Broil**) Grilling and broiling are almost the same; grilling often refers to outdoor cooking and broiling to indoor cooking.

Preheat. To heat the oven or broiler to cooking temperature before putting in the food to be cooked. Preheating is a very important step that should not be skipped if it is called for, especially in baking. Cooking times are based on the time at which the food enters a preheated oven; always preheat unless the recipe specifies a cold oven.

Roast. (*See* **Bake**) Roasting and baking are essentially the same thing; roasting usually means cooking meats or vegetables, not casseroles, breads, sweets, or pastries.

Toast. To crisp and brown by applying dry heat, either on a flat pan in the oven or in a toaster.

Using an Oven

The following chart tells you what recipes mean when they specify a "slow," "moderate," or "hot" oven.

very slow oven	250–275°F
slow oven	300–325°F
moderate oven	350–375°F
hot oven	400–450°F
very hot oven	475°F and up

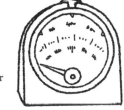

oven thermometer

Check the thermostat of an oven that you are using for the first time. Buy an inexpensive portable oven thermometer (available in hardware and department stores) and set it on the middle oven rack. Turn your oven on to 350°F. When your oven indicator tells you it's preheated (some ovens have an indicator light that turns off; some make a beeping sound — check the manufacturer's instructions), quickly check the reading on the portable thermometer. It should read 350°F. If it does not, make a note of the discrepancy and adjust your oven setting accordingly whenever you cook in it. Many perfectly good ovens are about 50°F off their thermostat settings. If your oven is temperamental, use an oven thermometer regularly instead of relying on the thermostat.

For cooking roasts, a meat thermometer or instant-read thermometer gives you the most reliable temperature control; inserted into the thickest part of the meat (but not touching bone), it gives an accurate reading of the internal temperature, no matter what size and shape your roast is.

The placement of the oven rack can affect the way your food cooks. Unless specified otherwise, place the rack in the middle of the oven for the greatest circulation of heat. If you have several pans in the oven at once, you may need to increase the cooking time; rotating the pans helps ensure even cooking.

Using a Microwave Oven

Microwave ovens can be a great time-saver in everything from defrosting to cooking to reheating. Because models vary widely in power, it is advisable to follow the instructions that come with your appliance. Here are some general tips for all microwave ovens.

• When using the microwave, make sure that all items put inside are microwave safe. Never use any metal, including aluminum foil or twist ties.

It is preferable to use paper, glass, or microwave-safe ceramics in the microwave. Plastic containers may melt slightly, pick up stains, or (some believe) release toxic substances into the food.

• Cover food with a microwave-safe paper towel, paper plates, or plastic wrap. Poke a tiny hole in the plastic to vent steam.

• A sheet of wax paper on the microwave tray makes cleaning up easier.

• Because microwaves cook food from the inside out, food will not brown attractively; basting or saucing food can compensate for this.

• Microwaves are great for precooking meats for the grill. The insides will cook first, so the grilling time will be shorter. This means less chance of burned or dried-out foods or underdone centers.

• Microwaves are ideal for melting small amounts of butter or chocolate.

• Foods cooked in the microwave without a carousel should be stirred or rotated for uniform cooking.

TOOLS FOR THE COUNTRY COOK

While I was on a recent visit with my mother, we spent a rainy afternoon going through her kitchen cupboards and drawers. We found some wonderful old kitchen tools, many older than I am. She still uses the aluminum pots that she received as a wedding present 67 years ago, an old-fashioned coffee percolator (the kind that you just set on the stove), a manual meat grinder, a food mill that she still uses for applesauce, and a great old sifter that she taps with the heel of her right hand, like a tambourine player, while squeezing the handle with her left. My mother still enjoys all of these things for their simple efficiency. We're fortunate to have modern conveniences and tools, but most are fashioned after the tried-and-true utensils from generations past.

Contributors to this chapter are Janet Ballantyne; Janet B. Chadwick; and Alexandra Nimetz, Jason Stanley, and Emeline Starr.

THE BASIC KITCHEN
....
THE WELL-STOCKED KITCHEN
....
THE COMPLETE KITCHEN
....
GRANDMA'S GADGETS

14

THE BASIC KITCHEN

For the beginning cook or someone setting up a kitchen for the first time, the array of equipment can seem bewildering. But when you think of what our ancestors worked with — a big kettle, a bowl or two (one of which might have been made from a dried gourd), a knife, and maybe a big spoon or fork — it clearly doesn't take much to get going. The following list outlines the basic ware for the modern cook's startup kitchen and each makes a great gift.

Equipment & Utensils

❑ **Bottle opener.**
❑ **Can opener.** Handheld, wall-mounted, or electric.
❑ **Colander.** Metal, mesh, or sturdy plastic, for draining.
❑ **Cutting boards.** Preferably made of hardwood.
❑ **Grater.** A four-sided grater with different-sized cutting holes is a good place to start.
❑ **Knives.** Chef's, paring, serrated, carving; preferably stainless steel, because carbon steel can discolor many foods.
❑ **Ladle.** For handling soups and sauces.
❑ **Measuring cups.** Dry (flat-topped) and liquid (lipped).

❑ **Measuring spoons.** Preferably metal, graded sizes.
❑ **Mixing bowls (nesting or assorted sizes).** Stainless steel is preferred for all-purpose use, glass or ceramic for good looks or to double as serving ware.
❑ **Rubber spatula.** For scraping food efficiently from bowls and jars and for folding.
❑ **Salad bowl and tossers.** Preferably wooden; get a bigger bowl than you think you'll need.
❑ **Salt and pepper shakers.**
❑ **Scrub brush.** For vegetables.
❑ **Sifter.** For dry ingredients.

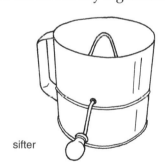

sifter

❑ **Slotted spoon.** For lifting food out of liquids.

slotted spoon

❑ **Spatula or pancake turner.** For turning and flipping.
❑ **Strainer.** Fine mesh.
❑ **Tongs.** For picking up almost anything hot; especially handy for grilling.

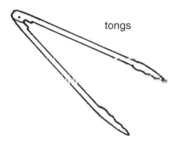

tongs

❑ **Vegetable peeler.** Handheld, preferably with a wide blade and soft handle.
❑ **Wire whisks and whips.** For easy mixing.
❑ **Wooden spoons.** For stirring in any kind of pan.

SUPPLIES IN STOCK

Versatile kitchen helpers that you will want to keep on hand include toothpicks, aluminum foil, kitchen string, plastic wrap, wax paper, resealable plastic bags in various sizes, vegetable cooking spray, muffin papers, bamboo skewers, parchment paper, paper doilies, and straws.

Appliances

❑ **Coffeemaker.** Take your pick! We like a simple electric drip pot.

❑ **Electric mixer.** Handheld, for beating things that take more than a whisk.

A WORD TO THE WISE

Beware of appliances that serve as several appliances in one, such as a food processor with whippers, blenders, and dough hooks; a slow-cooker that serves as a grill and deep-fat fryer as well; or a combination microwave/convection oven. Very often they don't work as efficiently as well-designed single-purpose equipment.

Cookware

❑ **Heavy covered kettle or Dutch oven.** An enamel or Calphalon one is preferable, if your budget can support it.

❑ **Saucepans.** Large and small, with lids.

❑ **Scissors.** For everything from snipping chives to cutting parchment to line baking pans.

❑ **Skillets.** Medium and large, at least one with a nonstick coating.

❑ **Stockpot.** 8 to 10 quarts.

❑ **Tea kettle.** One that whistles, unless you have a good memory.

Ovenware

❑ **Baking sheets.** The kind with a layer of air in them is best.

❑ **Cake pans, round.** 8- or 9-inch diameter, preferably metal.

❑ **Casserole or deep baking dish.** Glass or ceramic; 1½ to 2 quarts is a good size, if you have only one.

❑ **Cooling racks.**

❑ **Loaf pan.** For breads and meat loaves.

❑ **Pie pans.** 9- or 10-inch diameter, preferably glass or ceramic.

❑ **Roasting pan.** With cover.

Soft Stuff

❑ **Aprons.** Chef's or decorative; they really save your clothing.

❑ **Cheesecloth.** For fine straining and dripping.

❑ **Dishrags.** Even if you use sponges, dishrags come in handy.

❑ **Oven mitts.** At least one per hand.

❑ **Potholders.**

❑ **Tea cozy.** Like a sleeping bag for the teapot, useful and fun.

❑ **Tea towels.** Cotton or linen.

❑ **Terry towels.**

THE SELF-SUFFICIENT COOK'S KITCHEN

Whether you grew up amid the tools and crafts of a country kitchen or acquired a passion for greater self-sufficiency later in life, you will want to build a collection of specialized tools for preserving the harvest and creating truly homemade food and drink.

❑ **Bottle capper.** For home-bottled beverages. (page 428)

❑ **Brewing or winemaking equipment.** (page 428)

❑ **Canning funnel.** (page 382)

❑ **Canning jars and lids.** (page 382)

❑ **Canning thermometer.**

❑ **Food dehydrator.**

❑ **Freezer.** A major investment, so shop wisely; look for an energy-efficient label, a bottom drain, baskets for bulk items, a light that indicates that the freezer is running properly, and an alarm that sounds if freezer temperature increases.

❑ **Grain mill.** For do-it-yourself flours and grits.

❑ **Jar lifter.** (page 382)

❑ **Maple syrup taps.**

❑ **Meat grinder.** For grinding your own burgers and sausage.

❑ **Pressure canner.** (page 386)

❑ **Water-bath canner.** (page 384)

THE WELL-STOCKED KITCHEN

If you've been cooking for a while now and are ready for making more daring recipes, you might try your hand at making pastry, boning a chicken, or cooking for a dinner party. The following pieces of equipment will help you move up your culinary skills a notch or two.

Equipment & Utensils

❏ **Apple corer.**

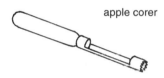

apple corer

❏ **Baked-potato nails.** Thick metal skewers, sometimes in a rack, that conduct heat to the center of the spud for quick, even baking.
❏ **Boning knife.** Thin-bladed for delicate work.

boning knife

❏ **Bottle brush.**
❏ **Bulb baster.** Especially helpful when roasting poultry.
❏ **Cake tester.** Toothpicks are a good substitute.

❏ **Citrus juicer.** Look for a wooden reamer, a reamer or strainer that fits on a measuring cup, or a glass reamer with a bowl for catching juice.
❏ **Cleaver.** For cutting up meat and for tenderizing.

cleaver

❏ **Corkscrew.** Take your pick from dozens of models.
❏ **Food mill.** For perfectly textured mashes and purées.

food mill

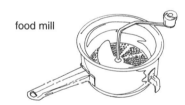

❏ **Funnel.** Plastic or metal; one with a built-in sieve is nice.
❏ **Garlic press.**
❏ **Ice bucket.**
❏ **Ice cream scoop.**
❏ **Kitchen scale.**
❏ **Kitchen shears.**
❏ **Kitchen timer.**
❏ **Knife sharpener.**
❏ **Melon baller.** Handy for making neat cores in fruit such as pears, too.

❏ **Nutcracker.**
❏ **Pastry bag.** With an assortment of tips for special effects.
❏ **Pastry brush.**
❏ **Pepper mill.** Made of wood, metal, or Lucite; buying a cheap one is false economy.
❏ **Potato masher or ricer.**

potato masher

❏ **Rolling pin.** Hardwood or marble.
❏ **Rotary cheese grater.** For hard cheeses; a must for serving fresh Parmesan at the table.

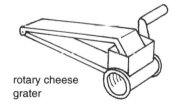

rotary cheese grater

❏ **Salad spinner.**
❏ **Skewers.** Metal or bamboo.
❏ **Thermal carafe.** Wonderful for buffet and at-table serving, not to mention for breakfast in bed!

Appliances

❑ **Blender.** Incredibly versatile. If I had only one small appliance, this would be it. I've used my trusty blender so long that I'm on my third set of replacement blades.

❑ **Microwave oven.** Avoid buying one that is built into a range — if one breaks down you'll have to replace both — and look for at least two power levels, a defrost cycle, and a carousel. Clocks, timers, and temperature probes are convenient extras.

❑ **Stand mixer.** With dough hook; a great time-saver, especially if you like to bake.

❑ **Toaster or toaster oven.** The toaster oven has the advantage of allowing you to bake or reheat small batches in an energy-efficient way.

Cookware

❑ **Double boiler.**
❑ **Griddle.**
❑ **Pan insert steamer.** The folding "umbrella" kind that fits almost any pan.

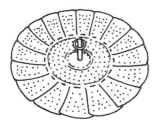

pan insert steamer

Ovenware

❑ **Jelly-roll pan.** Looks like a cookie sheet with low sides.

❑ **Meat thermometer or instant-read thermometer.** The latter is not left in the meat as it roasts but is used for an on-the-spot reading. It's useful for measuring the temperature of the warm water added to yeast or the perfect serving temperature for wine.

❑ **Muffin tins.** Regular and/or miniature.

❑ **Oven thermometer.**

❑ **Springform pan.** 9- or 10-inch, has removable sides so that you don't have to invert delicate cakes and pastries.

springform pan

❑ **Square baking pan.** Metal or glass.

❑ **Tart pan with removable bottom.** For elegant, straight-sided tarts and quiches.

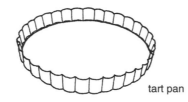

tart pan

❑ **Tube pan.** Plain or fluted.

ABOUT COOKWARE

If you can afford stainless steel or lined copper cookware, buy it. Stainless steel is robust and very easy to clean. Lined copper pots are excellent heat conductors and the choice of many professional chefs; however, they require polishing to look their best.

Enamelware is great for cooking and handsome for serving, but it may chip, leaving the base iron exposed. Even enameled cast-iron ware will eventually wear out. Cast iron is useful and sturdy, but must be seasoned before it is used (page 21).

If you like the ease and health benefits of nonstick pans, invest in high-quality ones; the coating on cheaper ones tends to scratch off quickly.

Aluminum or uncoated ironware taints or discolors many vegetables and sauces.

When you are selecting pots, it is handy to have some small ones for melting butter, heating milk, etc., but, generally, it is good to purchase large pans. You'll find you're always growing out of them.

THE COMPLETE KITCHEN

*O*nce you really know your way around the kitchen, have a repertoire of classic dishes, and are ready to tackle whatever kitchen project takes your fancy, you can increase your enjoyment of cooking with all sorts of gadgets that each do one thing very well. You may not ever need everything on the following list, but for the projects that appeal to you the most, having just the right tools will truly be a delight.

Equipment & Utensils

❏ **Candy thermometer.**
❏ **Chafing dish.** For elegant at-table serving.
❏ **Citrus zester.** A handheld, shallow grater that makes perfect strands of zest.

citrus zester

❏ **Cookie press.** For fancy-shaped cookies.
❏ **Copper bowl.** For beating egg whites.
❏ **Lobster cracker.** So much neater and more elegant than a hammer and tongs.
❏ **Marble slab.** For candy-making and rolling dough.
❏ **Meat mallet.** For tenderizing; heavy metal is best.

❏ **Mortar and pestle.** For grinding your own spices.

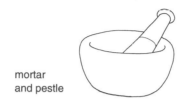

mortar and pestle

❏ **Mushroom brush.** For the gentlest cleaning.
❏ **Nutmeg grater.** For the freshest of flavors.

nutmeg grater

❏ **Offset spatula.** For icing and decorating.
❏ **Oil mister.** For spraying oil sparingly.
❏ **Pastry scraper.** Has a flat blade for smearing with butter and for scraping together stray bits of pastry.
❏ **Shrimp deveiner.** Peels and deveins in one motion.
❏ **Spaghetti fork.** For easy handling of long pasta.
❏ **Spoon rest.**
❏ **Strawberry huller.** A favorite of mine, for plucking out the green part without cutting away a lot of delicious berry or staining your fingertips.
❏ **Trivets.** For keeping hot pots off tabletops.

Appliances

❏ **Bread machine.** Commercial bread machines do the mixing, kneading, raising, and baking for you. If you are busy, this can be a great time-saver.
❏ **Coffee grinder.** Get two if you plan to use one for spices.
❏ **Deep-fat fryer.**
❏ **Electric hot trays.** Great for entertaining.
❏ **Electric knife.** For carving like a pro.
❏ **Espresso maker.**
❏ **Fondue pot.** For a slower-paced meal. Don't forget the Sterno.
❏ **Food processor.** It slices, minces, purées, chops, and even kneads dough.
❏ **Juicer.** A manual one-armed squeezer or an electric version.
❏ **Pasta maker.** Can be a food processor or stand-mixer attachment or a separate appliance.
❏ **Slow-cooker.** Look for a model that has the heating coil wrapped around the crockery liner, not underneath it.

Cookware

❏ **Bamboo steamer.** For Chinese vegetables or dumplings.
❏ **Ridged grill pan.** For healthful indoor grilling.
❏ **Wok.** Lots of metal surface means very quick cooking for extra freshness.

Ovenware

❏ **Baking stone.** For making crisp-bottomed European-style breads and pizza.

❏ **Bundt pan.** A wide, fluted tube pan for decorative cakes and breads.

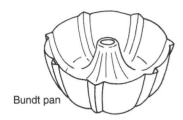

Bundt pan

❏ **Custard cups.**

❏ **French bread pan.** Has holes for air circulation to make a crisp crust.

❏ **Gratin dishes.** Low ceramic bakers for sauced dishes.

❏ **Miniature tart pans.**

❏ **Pizza pan.**

❏ **Popover pans.**

❏ **Ramekins.**

❏ **Soufflé dishes.** In several sizes; straight-sided white porcelain is classic.

Just for Fun

Besides some of the single-purpose items in The Complete Kitchen, consider starting a collection of favorites that make food preparation and serving a bit more fun.

❏ **Apple cutter.** Looks like a wheel; the center circle cuts out the core, while the outer spokes cut neat wedges.

❏ **Assorted baskets.** For serving, keeping fruit, carrying produce from the garden, and pure decoration.

❏ **Bean pot.** A heavy earthenware crock for mellow, slow-baked beans.

❏ **Cookie stamp.** For decorative cookies.

❏ **Corn holders.** Look like large pushpins and come in pairs — one for each end of the cob — to avoid burned fingers. They're often made to look like miniature corncobs.

❏ **Crinkle cutter.** A zigzag or scalloped blade for cutting fancy fries. It's not just decorative; it creates more surface area for faster, lighter frying.

❏ **Egg slicer.** Nothing beats this little wire gadget for cutting eggs into tidy rounds.

egg slicer

❏ **Gelatin Molds.** Make beautiful creations out of the jiggly stuff.

gelatin mold

❏ **Ice cream freezer.** Hand-cranked, electric, or freezer tub, an ice cream freezer is a favorite with young and old.

Pan Sizes

....

It is sometimes necessary or desirable to substitute one pan for another in cooking. While the size and shape of the pan does affect the texture and baking time, the critical feature is the volume — how much the dish will hold. This chart gives the approximate volume of many standard pans. If you have an heirloom or odd-sized pan, measure it yourself; simply fill it to the brim with water, measuring as you go.

Cake pans			Loaf pans	
round	8 x 1½"	4 cups	9 x 5 x 3"	8 cups
	9 x 2"	6 cups	8½ x 4½ x 2½"	6 cups
square	8 x 2"	6 cups		
	9 x 2"	10 cups	**Pie pans**	
rectangular	13 x 9 x 2"	15 cups	8 x 1½"	3 cups
tube	9 x 3"	12 cups	9 x 1½"	4 cups
	10 x 4"	18 cups	9 x 2" (deep dish)	6 cups
Bundt	10"	14 cups		
			Casseroles	
Cupcake tins			various sizes	2 to 10 cups
	standard	⅓ cup	**Ramekins**	
	mini	2 tablespoons	3 x 1½"	½ cup

GRANDMA'S GADGETS

❑ **Apple peeler/corer.** This old-time crank-operated gadget turns the apple efficiently against a blade while reaming out the core.

❑ **Bean frencher.** Put beans in whole, and they come out in thin, quicker-cooking strips.

❑ **Butter curler.** A serrated, looped blade for making fancy butter curls; also handy for scooping seeds and pulp from melons and squash.

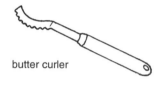

butter curler

❑ **Butter stamps.** For making decorative impressions or cameos in your homemade butter.

❑ **Cherry pitter.** Simply pushes the pits out.

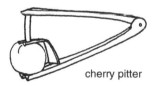

cherry pitter

❑ **Cookie jar.** I recall a capacious ceramic container with a never-ending supply of the best home-baked goodies.

❑ **Pantry crocks.** Once meant for cool storage and brining, earthenware crocks are used for decorative purposes — holding utensils, arrangements of flowers. It is not recommended that old chipped ones be used for culinary purposes.

❑ **Pastry wheel.** For cutting zigzag-edged pastry strips.

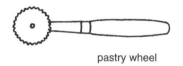

pastry wheel

❑ **Pea sheller.** Quickly removes peas from their pod.

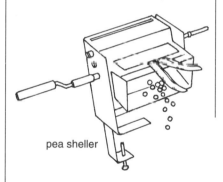

pea sheller

❑ **Pickle fork.** A decorative two-pronged fork for spearing pickles.

❑ **Squeezo strainer.** A clamp-on grinder/strainer that skins and seeds apples, tomatoes, and the like for making quick, easy sauces and purées; hard to find, so keep your eyes peeled at yard sales or in your great-aunt's attic.

❑ **Sugar tongs.** When lump sugar was *de rigueur* for tea, little silver tongs were used to pick up "one lump or two."

❑ **Waffle iron.** While cast-iron ones have been replaced by modern electric ones, the old-fashioned taste of fresh waffles has never lost its popularity.

ABOUT SEASONING CAST IRON

Cast-iron pots and skillets must be seasoned before using. Scrub the pan and dry thoroughly, rub it lightly with unsalted shortening or grease, inside and out, and bake for 1 hour at 350°F. This gives the pan a natural nonstick finish. To clean, wipe gently with a paper towel or soft cloth. If you must scrub, do so gently with a plastic scrubber. Dry very thoroughly and rub on a thin film of oil to prevent rust. If you use harsh abrasives or detergents on your seasoned pan, you'll have to repeat the seasoning process.

In the Pantry

The pantry at our farmhouse is my pride and joy. It's large, light, airy, and special for at least two reasons. First, it's actually a second kitchen; it has a sink and loads of cupboard space for extra kitchen supplies and utensils, and it's big enough for a second refrigerator that takes the "company's coming" pressure off my primary kitchen. Second, an entire wall consists of open shelving where I keep everything from peanut butter to popcorn to paper towels. This is where I store the food that John and I have grown and preserved — jams, jellies, relishes, ketchup, applesauce, tomatoes — lined up in full view. I am proud of our harvest, and the pantry is a showcase for the fruits of our labor.

■ ■ ■ ■ ■ ■ ■ ■ ■ ■

Contributors to this chapter are Liz Anton and Beth Dooley, Janet Ballantyne, Joanne Barrett, Charlene Braida, Janet B. Chadwick, Carol Costenbader, Gail Damerow, and Ken Haedrich.

STAPLES
....
DAIRY FOODS
....
MEAT, POULTRY & FISH
....
VEGETABLES
....
FRUIT

STAPLES

Perhaps because they are so easy to store, dried foods — flours, grains, nuts, and pastas — are the cornerstone of the pantry. They can be pulled out at a moment's notice to fill out or showcase whatever fresh produce or meat is on the menu. If stored away from heat and humidity, such foods will keep for months.

FLOURS

Flours are grains that are finely ground for easy incorporation into recipes.

Flour should be stored in airtight containers. All-purpose white flour keeps for 10 to 12 months; whole-grain flours, which contain fat from the germ, will keep only about half as long, but they may be frozen for up to 1 year in airtight wrapping.

Some flours are best suited to one particular purpose. Cake or pastry flour is made from softer wheat, which results in more delicate baked goods. Bread flour is higher in protein and makes a denser, less crumbly loaf. Nutritious whole-grain flours may be substituted for one third to one half of the white flour in most recipes; the resulting baked goods will be somewhat coarser in texture.

GRAINS

Grains are the dried seeds of cereal plants; examples are oats, barley, corn, millet, quinoa, buckwheat groats, and triticale. They are high in nutrition and easy to store in bags or in glass or plastic containers. To reduce cooking time, long-cooking grains can be soaked for several hours in the liquid in which they'll later be cooked.

RICE

Many varieties of rice are available. The primary distinction between brown and white rice is that white rice has had the hull or bran removed. Long-grain rice cooks into fluffier, individual grains, whereas short-grain rice is stickier and chewier. For such dishes as risotto, short-grain rice, preferably arborio, is essential. White rice cooks considerably faster than brown, but brown rice is more nutri-

tious. For nutrition and convenience, brown rice may be cooked in bulk and then frozen in 2- or 4-cup batches for quick meals.

Wild rice, a dark, nutty-tasting delicacy, is actually a grass. It is more expensive than other types of rice and is often combined in rice blends.

PASTA

"Pasta" refers to spaghetti plus a host of noodles in various shapes and sizes. It is commonly available in dried form, but fresh pasta can be found in most supermarkets and is easy to make at home with a food processor. Pasta made with semolina or durum wheat has the best flavor and texture when cooked. Dried pasta will keep almost indefinitely as long as it is not exposed to air or humidity.

Pasta should be cooked in plenty of salted water to keep it from sticking together; a tablespoon or two of oil in the water will further reduce sticking. Pasta is best when cooked just to the point where it is tender but still firm to the bite; it should be drained well but not rinsed before sauce is added. Plan on using about 2 cups of sauce per pound of pasta.

DRIED LEGUMES

Beans and legumes add meatless protein to soups, casseroles, and salads. There are a great many beans to choose from, including pink and red kidney beans, black beans, white and Great Northern beans, limas, pink or brown lentils, split peas, and chickpeas. Many legumes may be bought in cans, but home-cooked beans usually have better texture and are more economical. Dried beans, chickpeas, and lentils may be purchased in bulk from a bin or packaged in bags. Stored in airtight glass or plastic containers out of direct light, they will keep indefinitely.

Beans and legumes should be picked over carefully before soaking. They absorb a great deal of water; if you soak them overnight, it is important to cover them with enough water that they will still be submerged the following morning. Drain the beans, place them in a pan, and cover with fresh, *unsalted* water. Bring to a boil, cook over a brisk heat for 5 minutes, cover, and reduce to a simmer. Most beans will probably take nearly 1 hour to cook, but check them after 30 minutes and then every 10 minutes; add water if necessary. Salt the beans just 5 or 10 minutes before you think they will be tender. Drain but do not rinse the cooked beans.

NUTS

Nuts add flavor, texture, and protein to many dishes. The most economical way to buy nuts is in bulk. Nuts may be stored in sealed containers for 1 or 2 months at room temperature; in hot weather or for longer storage, keep them in the freezer. Popular nuts to keep on hand are almonds, cashews, hazelnuts (filberts), peanuts, pecans, sunflower seeds, and walnuts. Pistachios, pine nuts (for pesto), macadamia nuts, and Brazil nuts are more expensive and best purchased in small quantities.

Roasting makes nuts crispier and enhances the flavor. To roast any nut, spread the nuts in a single layer and place in a 300°F oven. Roast, turning or shaking frequently, until the nuts are slightly browned, 10 to 15 minutes.

SWEETENERS

Sweeteners are important for flavoring and preserving foods; they keep well for extended periods of time.

Sugars

Sugars are usually made from sugarcane or sugar beets. They may be white, light brown, or dark brown, depending on the amount of molasses left in during processing. White sugar is best stored in an airtight canister; brown sugars keep best in heavy plastic bags. If brown sugar begins to harden, add a slice of apple to the bag to soften it. Confectioners' sugar has been ground into a powder for use in icings and glazes; superfine is good in drinks and uncooked recipes, as it dissolves rapidly and completely.

Honey

Honey, a versatile sweetener, is available in the comb, just as the bees store it, or removed from the comb as a liquid. Honey can be stored in the wax combs and eaten wax and all. Liquid honey is the most commonly used form for cooking. Liquid honey that is bottled may crystallize after a while on the shelf; this makes it ideal for spreading. To liquefy it again, simply set it in a pan of very hot water, or microwave it in the jar, 15 seconds at a time, until melted. Do not allow the honey to boil.

Following are a few helpful things to know when cooking with honey.

• Substitute honey for sugar cup for cup, but decrease the amount of liquid in the recipe by ¼ cup. If you find that this proportion is too sweet, substitute ¾ cup of honey per 1 cup of sugar and reduce the

SWEET TOOTH SATISFIED

I never have to make an emergency trip to the supermarket when I need something sweet for family, friends, or a bake sale. I always keep on hand flour, sugar, chocolate chips, vanilla, brown sugar, baking soda, baking powder, and butter — that is, all of the ingredients for baking chocolate-chip cookies. I usually measure out a second set of the dry ingredients for a batch and keep it in a jar for an easy homemade mix.

amount of the liquid by 2 to 3 tablespoons.

- Measure out the honey in a cup that has been used to measure the oil or fat in a recipe, or coat the cup or spoon with oil. This keeps the honey from sticking to the cup.
- Honey is acidic. In baked goods in which as much as 1 cup of honey is being substituted for sugar and in which no baking soda is called for, add ½ teaspoon of baking soda.

Maple Syrup

Maple syrup is simply reduced maple sap. It lends wonderful flavor and sweetness to food. Commercial maple-flavored syrups just don't have the same taste. If you can't get the real stuff, it's better to use brown sugar than to use artificially flavored "maple" syrup. One cup of sugar is equivalent to ¾ cup of maple syrup; in baking, you will have to increase the liquid in the recipe by about 3 tablespoons for every cup of syrup substituted.

Maple syrup is usually graded for color and texture (see page 455). Grade A syrup is lighter and more delicate — well suited for use on pancakes and waffles — but for cooking, grade B is more economical and gives a fuller maple flavor.

Pure maple syrup should be stored in the refrigerator after opening; it will keep for about 1 year.

Molasses

Molasses is the syrup left from boiling sugar cane when the sugar crystals are separated out. Brown sugar stays brown because some of the molasses is still present. Molasses may be light, dark, or "blackstrap," depending on how long it is boiled. It may be processed with sulfur for a lighter taste; unsulfured molasses is often available in health food stores.

CANNED GOODS

Keeping a supply of canned goods on hand rescues many a last-minute meal. While many people prefer fresh or frozen vegetables to canned ones, tinned tomatoes, beans, fish, soups, and vegetable purées are very useful.

In general, high-acid canned foods, such as tomatoes, grapefruit, and pineapple, can be stored on the shelf for 12 to 18 months. Low-acid canned foods, such as meat, poultry, fish, and most vegetables, will keep 2 to 5 years if the can remains in good condition and has been stored in a cool, clean, dry place.

BAKING SUPPLIES

For baking, in addition to flours and sweeteners, keep a stock of butter, and shortenings and/or lard; baking powder, yeast, and baking soda for leavening; vanilla and other flavorings and extracts; squares of sweetened and unsweetened chocolate and chocolate chips; and unsweetened cocoa powder.

FREEZE-AHEAD IDEAS

- *Cheese. Freeze grated cheese for casseroles, pizza, and toppings.*

- *Toppings. Prepare bread and cracker crumbs for toppings and coatings and store in the freezer.*

- *Individual servings. Fix favorite foods or leftovers in individual foil or boilable-bag servings. Always chill any foods that have been precooked before packaging. Refrigerate for use within a day or so, or freeze for longer storage.*

- *Quick breakfasts. Make extra pancakes and waffles and tuck some away in the freezer. The kids can fix their own breakfast by warming the waffles and pancakes in the toaster.*

- *Ground beef. Cook several pounds of ground beef. Divide it among several containers to be tossed quickly into sauces and casserole dishes; cooked ground meats may be frozen for 2 to 3 months.*

- *Other meats. Meatballs, meat patties, fried chicken, and similar foods can be frozen on trays or baking sheets and then packed in plastic bags. By individually freezing the items on trays first, they do not clump together and, at mealtime, you can take out the number of servings needed.*

Dried fruits, such as raisins and cranberries, and coconut are also useful.

CONDIMENTS

What's salad without its dressing, a hot dog without its mustard? Condiments are part of every cook's repertoire. As marinade or sauce, they enhance foods, bringing out their best flavor. Sometimes they're just for accent; other times they are essential to the cooking process. Modern markets offer all sorts of interesting imported condiments to try in addition to the basics.

Oils

Oils are used for cooking, marinating, and flavoring food. They should be stored in jars in a cool, dark place. Oil is best when used within 1 or 2 months of purchase. Specialty oils may be stored in the refrigerator. Sniff or taste any oil before using. If it smells even slightly rancid, throw it out; it will mar the taste of your food.

Mild oils. Canola, corn, peanut, safflower, soy, and sunflower oils add little or no flavor to a dish but are fine for cooking.

Peanut oil adds a mild nuttiness to foods, and corn oil is economical for frying.

Flavored oils. Olive oil is easily digestible and brings out the best flavor in many dishes. Good olive oil has a clean, fruity flavor; it varies widely in strength and taste depending on where it is produced. Virgin olive oil from the first pressing is the best to use for dressings and dishes in which the olive oil flavor is highlighted. Sesame oil is a dark, smoky-flavored oil that is used in Asian cooking; it should be used sparingly or in combination with milder oils. Walnut and other nut oils are highly flavored and should be used with discretion.

A nutrition note: Monounsaturated fats are known to help reduce the levels of low-density lipoprotein, or LDL, cholesterol (the bad kind). Olive, canola, and peanut oils are high in monounsaturated fats. Polyunsaturated oils are relatively healthful as well; these include safflower, soybean, corn, and sesame oil.

Vinegar

For pickling, preserving, and adding a sour sharpness to foods and sauces, vinegar is essential. The vinegar spectrum ranges from fine balsamic, wine, sherry, and rice vinegars to less complex cider and distilled white vinegars. Herbs and berries are used to enhance many vinegars. Unopened vinegar keeps indefinitely. After opening, it will keep for 6 to 8 months.

Mustards

Prepared mustards are used as a condiment and a pungent ingredient in cooking. Bright yellow mustard is a hot-dog favorite, but the subtler dark mustards are preferable for sauces and dressings. Dijon mustard is made with white wine and spices. Mustards may be smooth or grainy with mustard seed. Dry mustard may be made into a strongly flavored paste with water, vinegar, or white wine.

Ketchup

Sweet, tangy tomato ketchup (or catsup, if you prefer) is a staple condiment throughout the country. It is not only beloved on burgers and fries, but serves as the base for many dressings, cocktail sauces, and barbecue bastes. Ketchup is usually available in classic glass bottles or in handy plastic squeeze bottles. It will keep indefinitely on the shelf; once opened, it may be kept in the refrigerator for about 3 months. The top of the bottle should be wiped before replacing the lid to keep it from getting dark and sticky.

Sauces

Every good cook keeps a few basic sauces on hand to dress up meals in a hurry. A jar of pasta sauce can be a lifesaver; also try Worcestershire sauce, hoisin sauce, curry pastes, tamari and other soy sauces, liquid smoke flavoring, sesame tahini, and hot pepper sauces. Sauces should be stored according to the manufacturer's instructions.

ABOUT PRODUCT DATING & FOOD SAFETY

Manufacturers stamp calendar dates on food products to help stores determine how long to display a product for sale. They also help purchasers know the time limit for purchasing or using a product while it is still at its best quality. It is not a safety date, according to the Food Safety and Inspection Service of the U.S. Department of Agriculture.

There are four types of dates:
• A *sell-by* date tells the store how long to display the product for sale. Buy the product before the date has passed.
• A *best-if-used-by* (or **before**) date is recommended for best flavor or quality. It is not a purchase or safety date.
• A *use-by* date is the last date recommended by the manufacturer for use of a product while at peak quality.
• *Closed* or *coded* dates are packing numbers for use by the manufacturer; they often appear on canned goods but cannot be used by consumers.

Seasonings

In the kitchen, seasonings (herbs, spices, roots, and salt) are truly "the spice of life." Well-balanced seasoning is often the "secret" that brings all the flavors in a dish together or lifts an ordinary dish to culinary stardom.

Seasonings have been prized throughout history; indeed, Columbus was looking for a shortcut to spice sources in the Far East when he stumbled upon the "New World"!

Following are some tips for choosing and storing some staples from my seasoning collection.

Ginger root. Fresh ginger root has a sharp, sweet ginger flavor that tastes fresher than ground ginger. It is available in most supermarkets. It is also available in Asian food stores. Choose ginger with smooth skin (wrinkled skin indicates that the root is dry and past its prime) and a fresh, spicy fragrance. Before mincing, peel the skin away from as much of the root as you will be using.

Unpeeled ginger root, tightly wrapped, can be refrigerated for up to 3 weeks. Ginger root will keep up to 3 months in the refrigerator if it is stored in ginger ale or dry sherry to cover. It will also keep for a few months if it is wrapped in a perforated plastic bag. Ginger root can be frozen for up to 6 months; to use frozen ginger, slice off a piece of the unthawed root and return the rest to the freezer.

Horseradish. Horseradish root adds a delightful, sharp piquancy to sauces and meats. While horseradish is usually purchased prepared, minced in vinegar or beet juice, it is not difficult to make your own. Wash and peel the root, then shred it or chop it into small pieces. In a blender or food processor, combine each cup of horse-

---

THE SPICE SHELF

....

Here's a checklist of herbs and spices for the well-stocked spice shelf:

- *Allspice*
- *Anise*
- *Basil*
- *Bay leaves*
- *Caraway seeds*
- *Cardamom, ground*
- *Cayenne*
- *Celery seeds*
- *Chili powder*
- *Cilantro*
- *Cinnamon, ground and sticks*

- *Cloves, ground and whole*
- *Coriander, ground*
- *Cumin, seeds and ground*
- *Curry powder*
- *Dill, seeds and weed*
- *Fennel, seeds and ground*
- *Ginger, ground*
- *Mace*
- *Marjoram*
- *Mint*

- *Mustard, ground and seeds*
- *Nutmeg, ground*
- *Oregano*
- *Paprika*
- *Pepper, black, white, and crushed red*
- *Rosemary*
- *Sage*
- *Savory*
- *Tarragon*
- *Thyme*
- *Turmeric*

radish with 3 to 4 tablespoons of water and 1 to 2 tablespoons of vinegar. Process until it reaches the desired consistency. You can add a few slices of raw beet to the horseradish. The flavor difference won't be noticeable, but the color will change from white to pink. Store the horseradish in sterilized jars in the refrigerator or freezer. It will keep for months, but it loses potency over time.

Salt. Salt is important in cooking both for flavor and for food preservation. Table salt is fine-grained and may be iodized. Pickling or kosher salt is coarser grained. Sea salt is retrieved from evaporated seawater and is rather expensive. Moisture is the enemy of salt, making it clump or become sticky. Keep salt in a dry place; a few grains of rice in your salt shaker will absorb moisture and keep the salt granular. Excessive amounts of salt are considered unhealthful. By using fresh herbs and lemon juice to enhance the flavor of vegetables, you can reduce salt intake without sacrificing flavor (see Salt-Free Herbal Blend, page 306).

THE "COMPANY" PANTRY

Keep a cupboard reserved (and known to be "hands-off") for snacks, special treats, or hors d'oeuvres to serve to spur-of-the-moment guests. Keep a few goodies in the freezer, too. You can be as creative as you like with this collection. Here are some of my favorite items:

- **SNACKS.** Popcorn, mixed nuts, chips, salsa, pretzels, herbal jelly, crackers, cheeses, olives, pickles, tea biscuits, dried apricots, biscotti, mints, small candies.

- **HORS D'OEUVRES.** Canned chickpeas, smoked oysters, sun-dried tomato spread, olive paste, canned salmon, chutney, jams, cream cheese, Parmesan cheese.

- **BEVERAGES.** Decaffeinated and regular coffee, herbal teas, cocoa, juices, soda, sparkling waters, beer, red and white wine, assorted liquors.

- **SUNDRIES.** Hot fudge and butterscotch sauces, barbecue sauce, consommé, balsamic vinegar, wild rice, dried wild mushrooms, specialty pasta, couscous.

- **FREEZER.** Peas, spinach, cheese tortellini, homemade pesto, boneless chicken breasts, berries, pound cake, cookies, baked pie shell, ice cream, frozen yogurt.

- **PRESERVED FOODS.** Some of my best jams, pickles, relishes, and vegetables are always reserved as gifts for my guests — a welcome reversal of the hostess-gift custom.

DAIRY FOODS

Dairy products, and their cousins made from soy milk, are important sources of protein. They are essential for baking and enrich many recipes. It used to be that dairy products were delivered and used up daily to ensure freshness. Nowadays we can keep them in the fridge or the freezer, always at the ready.

MILK

Whether you use whole milk, skim milk, or something in between is mostly a matter of personal preference. Soy milk, rice milk, and lactose-reduced milks are available to fulfill particular dietary needs. Tinned, evaporated, and condensed milks and powdered dry milk are handy to have in stock for emergencies. Milk should be kept in a closed container in the refrigerator for no more than 1 week.

CHEESE

Cheese is a delicious high-protein snack and a fine addition to vegetarian and meat entrées. Most cheese keeps for several weeks in the refrigerator. It should be wrapped well to prevent drying out or mingling flavors with other foods. Staple cheeses for cooking include cottage and cream cheeses, Swiss, Cheddar, Monterey Jack, and Parmesan. Feta and other cheeses made from goat's or sheep's milk are becoming increasingly popular because of their lower fat content and distinctive flavors. Hundreds of cheeses from around the world are also available in many larger supermarkets.

BUTTER

Butter is a naturally delicious product made by separating the fat in cream from the whey. It has a rich, sweet flavor that is unequaled for baking, for spreads, for enriching sauces, and for dressing vegetables. Butter may be salted or unsalted; unsalted butter does not keep as long as salted butter, but its mild flavor is preferred by many. It also tends to be of the best quality, since it must be very fresh. Butter is best stored in the refrigerator, away from strong-smelling foods, whose odors it can pick up; it may also be stored in the freezer for a month or two. Low-fat butters may have gelatin or oils added and will not reliably replace butter in baking.

EGGS

Whether you have your own hens or go to the market, eggs are one of nature's perfect foods. However, they require careful handling. Farm-fresh eggs should not be washed; fresh eggs may be brushed with a damp brush if they have debris clinging to them or they may be rinsed immediately before use. Washing before storing may remove a protective coating on the shell that prevents spoilage. Eggs are best stored wide end up in clean cartons in the refrigerator. (See page 31 "About Freezing Dairy Products" for information on freezing.)

Eggs are graded by size and quality. Most recipes anticipate the use of grade A large eggs. If your eggs are significantly larger or smaller, you may need to adjust quantities.

Salmonella bacteria can cause serious illness in humans and may be acquired from contaminated eggs. Cooking eggs and egg-rich foods to 160°F destroys *Salmonella* bacteria. Wash hands and utensils after handling raw eggs. Immediately cook or refrigerate foods prepared with raw or undercooked eggs, and promptly refrigerate leftovers.

IS THIS EGG FRESH?

To determine whether an egg is fresh, submerge it in water. A fresh egg will settle to the bottom of the container and rest horizontally. If it floats, don't use it. The U.S. Department of Agriculture advises that eggs may be safely used for 3 to 5 weeks after the date you purchase them, as long as you purchase the eggs before the expiration date printed on the carton.

Hard-cooked eggs

For hard-cooked eggs, stored or store-bought eggs are actually preferable, because fresh eggs are very difficult to peel. Eggs should be cooled down in cold water after cooking so that a gray-green film will not develop around the yolk. Always mark hard-cooked eggs before storing, so that you can distinguish them from raw ones.

Beating egg whites

Experts recommend beating egg whites only in a copper bowl; they react with the copper to keep their volume best. You can get similar results in a glass or stainless steel bowl by adding cream of tartar. In general, use about ⅛ teaspoon cream of tartar per egg white; if you're making meringue, use ⅛ teaspoon per 2 egg whites. To achieve the greatest volume, have egg whites at room temperature before beating; use clean beaters and take care not to get any yolk into the whites when you separate them.

ABOUT FREEZING DAIRY PRODUCTS

Most dairy products can be frozen if the proper procedure is followed. Thaw dairy products in the refrigerator and consume them within a few days.

- **Whole eggs.** Stir to mix whites with yolks, but don't whip in air. To each cup of whole eggs, add 1½ teaspoons of sugar (for use in sweet foods) or ½ teaspoon of salt (for use in savory foods or for scrambling) to prevent gumminess. Pour into container, allowing at least ½ inch of headroom; seal, label, and freeze.
- **Egg yolks.** Separate eggs; stir the yolks together. To each cup of egg yolks, add 2 teaspoons sugar (for use in sweet foods) or 1 teaspoon salt (for use in savory foods). Pour into container, allowing for headroom; seal, label, and freeze.
- **Egg whites.** Separate eggs; strain egg whites through a sieve. Do not stir or add sugar or salt. Pour into container, allowing headroom; seal, label, and freeze.
- **Butter and cheeses.** In vapor- and moistureproof wrapping, butter and some cheeses freeze well; as a rule, firm cheeses freeze better than soft ones. Like most foods, they should be thawed in the refrigerator. Cheese that has been frozen has a slightly changed texture and crumbles more easily, but when used for cooking, there is no discernible difference. Freeze in small blocks or portions, 1 pound or less, and no more than 1 inch thick.
- **Cream.** Pasteurized cream that is at least 40 percent butterfat may be frozen whipped or unwhipped; however, unwhipped cream that has been frozen and thawed will not whip well. To freeze liquid cream, heat it in a saucepan to 170°F for 10 to 15 minutes. For each quart, add ⅓ cup of sugar. Pour into containers, allowing headroom; seal, label, and freeze.

MEAT, POULTRY & FISH

Although modern diets often emphasize a reduction in consumption of meat, poultry, and fish, these foods are still a major source of protein and a central component of many people's diets. Selecting and handling these foods carefully will ensure that you get the most enjoyment and nutrition from whatever amount you choose to eat.

MEATS

When choosing meat, keep in mind that its flavor and tenderness are influenced by the amount of fat it contains, which varies according to type of animal and cut. Tenderness is also influenced by the animal's age and activity level, as well as by the way the meat is cooked. The parts of the animal that have been most active, such as the neck, shoulder, and legs, tend to be less tender than the loin and rib areas. Cook tougher cuts of meat slowly in liquids such as wine, juice, or water for longer periods of time. More tender cuts can be grilled, roasted, broiled, or panfried.

The three main grades of meat are "prime," "choice," and "good." Almost all prime cuts are sold to restaurants. Choice cuts are widely available to the public in markets.

Beef

For grilling or broiling, choose U.S.D.A. Choice or Select beef that has a good rosy color and is well marbled with fat. Sometimes beef is aged for several days before being marketed, which adds to its tenderness and flavor. Beef may be stored in the refrigerator or the freezer. Cooked dishes made with beef, such as barbecued ribs, take-out Chinese dishes, or fast-food burgers, should be hot when purchased and eaten within 2 hours.

Quantity to buy. For bone-in rib beef roasts, buy ¾ pound per serving; boneless, ⅓ to ½ pound per serving.

For bone-in pot roast and steaks, buy ½ to ¾ pound per serving; boneless pot roast and steaks, ⅓ to ½ pound per serving.

For ground beef, buy ⅓ to ½ pound per serving.

HOME STORAGE OF BEEF PRODUCTS

If the beef product has a use-by date, follow that date. If it has a sell-by date or no date, cook or freeze the product according to the times on the following chart.

PRODUCT	REFRIGERATOR 40°F	FREEZER 0°F
Fresh beef roast, steaks, chops, or ribs	3 to 5 days	6 to 12 months
Fresh beef liver or variety meats	1 to 2 days	3 to 4 months
Home-cooked beef; soups, stews, or casseroles	3 to 4 days	2 to 3 months
Store-cooked convenience meals	1 to 2 days	2 to 3 months
Cooked beef gravy or beef broth	1 to 2 days	2 to 3 months
Beef hot dogs or lunch meats, sealed in package	2 weeks (or 1 week after a use-by date)	1 to 2 months

Veal

Veal is the meat of calves 5 to 12 weeks old. Milk-fed veal is very pale and the tenderest of all; when calves have fed on grass, there is a rosier tinge to the veal.

Quantity to buy. For bone-in roast veal loin or rib, buy ¾ to 1 pound veal per serving; boneless, ⅓ to ½ pound.

For scallopine, allow ¼ to ⅓ pound per serving.

Pork

Pork is sold fresh or processed as ham, bacon, or sausage. When selecting fresh pork, choose well-marbled meat that has a whitish-pink color. The pinker the meat, the older the animal. Pork must be fully cooked to ensure the destruction of any harmful organisms. The juices should run absolutely clear when pork is cooked.

Bacon may be frozen in the package. If you require only a small amount, cut off a piece and return the rest to the freezer. Two slices of bacon equal about ¼ cup, diced or crumbled.

Quantity to buy. For a bone-in pork roast, buy ¾ to 1 pound per serving; boneless, ⅓ to ½ pound.

For spareribs, buy ¾ to 1 pound per serving, though 1 pound of country-style ribs will serve two.

For a ham roast with a large bone, buy ¾ to 1 pound per serving; with a small bone, ⅓ to ½ pound per serving. For boneless ham, buy ¼ to ⅓ pound per serving.

HOME STORAGE OF HAM PRODUCTS

If the ham product has a use-by date, follow that date. If it has a sell-by date or no date, cook or freeze the product according to the times on the following chart.

PRODUCT	REFRIGERATOR 40°F	FREEZER 0°F
Fresh (uncured) ham, uncooked	3 to 5 days	6 months
Fresh (uncured) ham, cooked	3 to 4 days	3 to 4 months
Cured ham, cook-before-eating; uncooked	5 to 7 days	3 to 4 months
Cured ham, cook-before-eating; after consumer cooks it	3 to 5 days	1 to 2 months
Fully cooked ham, vacuum sealed at plant, *undated*; unopened	2 weeks	1 to 2 months
Fully cooked ham, vacuum sealed at plant, *dated*; unopened	use-by date	1 to 2 months
Country ham, uncooked, cut	2 to 3 months	1 month
Prosciutto, Parma, or Serrano ham, dry Italian or Spanish type, cut	2 to 3 months	1 month

HOME STORAGE OF FRESH PORK

If the pork product has a use-by date, follow that date. If it has a sell-by date or no date, cook or freeze the product according to the times on the following chart.

PRODUCT	REFRIGERATOR 40°F	FREEZER 0°F
Fresh pork roast, steaks, chops, or ribs	3 to 5 days	4 to 6 months
Fresh pork liver or variety meats	1 to 2 days	3 to 4 months
Home-cooked pork; soups, stews, or casseroles	3 to 4 days	2 to 3 months

Lamb

Lamb is usually tender because it comes from animals less than 1 year old. "Baby" lamb and "spring" lamb are usually from animals less than 5 months old; the meat is paler and extra tender. Look for good marbling (white flecks of fat throughout the meat) and meat that is fine textured and firm. The meat should be pink and the fat should be firm, white, and not too thick. The U.S.D.A. quality grades are reliable guides.

- Raw lamb roasts and chops can be refrigerated for 3 to 5 days (ground lamb, 1 to 2 days); cooked lamb keeps for 3 to 4 days in the refrigerator.
- If the product has a use-by date, follow that date.
- If the product has a sell-by date or no date, cook or freeze it according to the times recommended above.
- For best quality, use frozen lamb roasts and chops within 6 to 9 months; ground lamb, 3 to 4 months.

Quantity to buy. For a bone-in roast leg or shoulder, buy ¾ to 1 pound per serving; boneless, ⅓ to ½ pound per serving.

For a rack or rib roast, 1 rack makes 2 servings. Allow 2 ribs per serving for a crown roast.

Game

Popular game meats include venison, elk, rabbit, and pheasant. Fresh game should be cleaned and either cured or frozen as soon as possible. Most game in supermarkets is already frozen; use it or return it (unthawed) to the freezer as soon as possible.

Poultry

Chicken is usually classified according to age. Young chickens — those 7 or 8 weeks old and up to 4 pounds — are tender enough for broiling or frying. Plump roasters are older and somewhat fatter, whereas chickens older than 8 months are generally suitable only for stewing or making into stock. Turkeys are primarily sold for roasting. Tom turkeys tend to be larger than hens. Turkey breasts, legs, cutlets, and ground turkey are increasingly available in markets and make a good alternative to red meats.

HOME STORAGE OF POULTRY PRODUCTS

If the poultry has a use-by date, store and use according to that date. If it has a sell-by date or no date, cook or freeze it according to the times on the following chart.

PRODUCT	REFRIGERATOR 40°F	FREEZER 0°F
Fresh chicken, giblets, or ground chicken	1 to 2 days	3 months
Cooked chicken	3 to 4 days	1 month
Chicken broth or gravy	1 to 2 days	3 months
Cooked chicken dishes or soup	3 to 4 days	6 months
Cooked chicken pieces, covered with broth or gravy	1 to 2 days	6 months
Fried chicken	3 to 4 days	4 months
Chicken salad	3 to 5 days	do not freeze
Fresh whole turkey	1 to 2 days	12 months
Fresh turkey parts	1 to 2 days	9 months
Ground turkey, giblets	1 to 2 days	3 to 4 months
Cooked turkey	3 to 4 days	4 months
Cooked turkey dishes	3 to 4 days	4 to 6 months
Turkey broth or gravy	1 to 2 days	2 to 3 months
Cooked turkey dishes	3 to 4 days	4 to 6 months
Turkey broth or gravy	1 to 2 days	2 to 3 months

When selecting poultry, look for U.S.D.A.-inspected, fresh, Grade A chicken. It should have a clean scent, firm flesh, and bright, even color.

Quantity to buy. For a whole chicken, allow ¾ pound per serving. For chicken parts, ½ to ⅔ pound per serving.

For a whole turkey under 12 pounds, allow ¾ pound per serving. For a bird 12 pounds or over, ½ to ¾ pound per serving.

Fish

If the fish is whole, its eyes should be clear and should bulge a little. Only a few fish, such as walleye, have naturally cloudy eyes. Fresh whole fish and fillets should have firm and shiny flesh. The whole fish should also have bright red gills that are free from slime. If the flesh doesn't spring back when pressed, the fish isn't fresh. One of the best tests for fresh fish is the nose test: Fish should smell fresh and mild, not "fishy" or ammonia-like. Below are some buying tips:

• Buy only from reputable sources.
• Buy only fresh seafood that is refrigerated or iced.
• Don't buy cooked seafood, such as shrimp, crabs, or smoked fish, if displayed in the same case as raw fish. Cross-contamination can occur.
• Don't buy frozen seafood if the package is open, torn, or crushed on the edges. Look for signs of frost or ice crystals. This could mean that the fish has been stored for a long time or thawed and refrozen.
• Immediately after buying seafood, put it on ice, in the refrigerator, or in the freezer.

ABOUT SAFE HANDLING OF MEAT, POULTRY, AND FISH

For safe handling, make your meat, poultry, and fish selections at the very end of your shopping. Wrap them in extra plastic bags and bag them apart from other foods. In very hot weather, it is a good idea to carry a picnic cooler in the trunk of your car for keeping perishables cool on your way home.

Store all meat and fish in the refrigerator or freezer as soon as possible. For freezing, an overwrap of freezing paper or plastic helps prevent dry patches on the meat ("freezer burn"). Once thawed, raw meat and fish should never be refrozen.

When handling meat, be sure that knives, counters, cutting boards and utensils are scrupulously cleaned before and after use.

The U.S. Department of Agriculture warns that no meat, poultry, or fish should be thawed at room temperature. There are three safe ways to defrost food: in the refrigerator, in cold water, and in the microwave.

Refrigerator. Defrosting in the refrigerator requires planning, because food may take a day or more to thaw fully. After thawing in the refrigerator, foods should be used within 1 or 2 days.

Cold water. Thawing in cold water is faster than thawing in the refrigerator but requires more attention. The food must be in a leakproof plastic bag. It should be submerged in cold tap water, and the water should be changed every 30 minutes. Small packages of meat may thaw in 1 hour or less; for larger items, such as a whole turkey, estimate 30 minutes per pound. After thawing, food should be refrigerated if it is not cooked promptly.

Microwave. Food that is thawed in the microwave should be used at once, because the thawing process is sometimes uneven and part of the food may become warm before the rest is unfrozen. Thawing times vary greatly according to the power of the microwave; use the defrost setting and follow the manufacturer's instructions.

VEGETABLES

Buy your vegetables garden-fresh from local producers or, better still, grow them yourself. Supermarket vegetables are usually of good quality, especially if the vegetable is in season. Out-of-season vegetables are often lower in quality and higher in price, making them a questionable luxury. Vegetables should be stored unwashed to prevent dampness, which is conducive to sogginess or mold; wash them in plenty of cool water just before use. Plastic bags that are perforated to allow air flow are best for storing most vegetables.

Artichokes, globe. Globe artichokes are in season from October to June but are most plentiful and of the best quality in April and May. Spring artichokes should be green; in fall and winter, they may be bronzed by frost. Select compact, fleshy artichokes without black spots or withered leaves. Refrigerate and use within 2 days.

Asparagus. The short asparagus season runs from spring to early summer. Choose asparagus with tight heads. Thickness depends on variety rather than age; when cooking, pencil-thin stalks may be snapped off at the bottom, whereas thicker asparagus should be peeled from the middle down. Asparagus may be kept in the refrigerator for up to 3 days; stand the stalks in a container with an inch of water in the bottom.

Avocados. The alligator-skinned California Haas avocados are most plentiful from December to June. Green Florida avocados peak from November to January. Buy avocados unripe and store them in a warm room for a few days until they give when pressed with a finger. Do not buy fruit with cracked, sunken, or badly bruised skins.

Beans, green and yellow (wax). Green and yellow beans are plentiful in local markets during the summer and in supermarkets year-round. Choose small, firm beans of equal size for uniform cooking. Store unwashed for 2 to 3 days.

Beets. Beets are best small and tender; buying them with their greens attached allows you to gauge how fresh they are and gives you great greens, too. When red-veined beet greens wilt, they turn red at the tips instead of yellow. Leave 2 inches of stem when trimming greens so that the color won't leach out of the beets during cooking. Beets will keep in the refrigerator for about 1 week.

Broccoli. Broccoli is available year-round but is best from midsummer to mid-autumn. Choose compact, bright heads that do not have yellow flowers. Store for 4 to 5 days in perforated plastic bags in the refrigerator. Look also for broccoli cousins — leafy, slightly bitter broccoli rabe and the recent broccoli/asparagus crosses. These are delicious steamed or stir-fried like greens.

Cabbage. Red and white cabbages are available year-round; crinkle-leaved Savoy cabbages are plentiful from late autumn to early spring. Look for cabbages with outer leaves that are fresh and unwithered; store for up to 2 weeks in the refrigerator.

Carrots. Carrots are available year-round. Look for bright, unbroken roots. Bagged baby carrots are a convenience, but they often lack the flavor of the longer ones. Carrots keep in the refrigerator for 1 week to 10 days.

Cauliflower. Cauliflower from local farmers is available in most of the United States from late summer through early fall, after which the western and southern crops take over until early spring. Choose heavy, white heads that have not turned grayish at the tips. Store in the refrigerator no more than 4 or 5 days.

Celeriac. Also called celery root, this relatively rare root vegetable is available from autumn through spring. Choose medium-sized roots without deep pits or crevices. Store for up to 4 days in the refrigerator. Peel before using, and drop into acidulated water (2 tablespoons of vinegar per quart) or blanch it if it is not dressed immediately. Once celeriac has been peeled and cut, it must immediately be placed in acidulated water, or it will discolor.

Celery. Celery is best from October to April. Look for plump, crisp stalks; refrigerate for up to 1 week in a perforated plastic bag. Use leaves for stock.

Corn, sweet. Corn should be eaten the day it is picked. Choose corn with fresh, green husks and brittle, browned silk. If you buy more corn than you can eat at once, cook it all and cut the remaining kernels from the cob for use in salads and soups or as a side dish.

Cucumbers. Cucumbers are best during the summer season, but they are available and good year-round. Choose firm, dark green fruit of medium size. If the peel is waxed, it must be removed. Cucumbers keep about 5 days in the refrigerator; long English cucumbers may keep for a week.

Eggplants. Choose glossy, unblemished specimens with good fresh stems; use within 2 days. The size of the eggplant does not usually affect its flavor, but the smaller ones will be fleshier and less seedy. When cutting and cooking eggplant, do not use carbon steel or aluminum utensils; they will discolor eggplant.

Fennel. Bulb fennel, with its delicate anise flavor, is available in markets from late summer through most of the winter. Choose firm, unspotted bulbs with fresh-looking ferny greens.

Garlic. Look for plump, tightly closed heads without sprouting. Store for up to 2 weeks in open air, out of direct light. For easy peeling, crush the individual cloves gently with the flat side of a knife until the skin cracks slightly.

Greens. Cooking greens, such as chard, kale, bok choy, and spinach, should be crisp and bright, without woody stems or yellowing leaves. Store in perforated bags in the refrigerator for no more than 3 days; wash only just before use.

Leeks and scallions. Leeks and scallions are more delicate in late spring and summer, larger and thicker in autumn and winter. They should be cylindrical at the bottom, not bulbous, and the greens should not look withered. Store them in the refrigerator for 3 to 5 days.

Mushrooms. Because most mushrooms — even the widely available exotic varieties — are commercially grown, they are available throughout the year. Choose mushrooms with smooth, unblemished skins. Loosely cover them and refrigerate for 2 to 3 days. When you are ready to use them, trim the bottoms and gently brush the tops. If it is absolutely necessary to wash them, rinse quickly and dry on paper towels.

Okra. Choose young okra pods that are firm enough to snap. Store in the refrigerator for no more than 2 days.

Onions and shallots. Onions are available year-round, but they vary widely in taste and pungency. Common or yellow onions are best used for cooking, whereas milder or sweeter Spanish, Vidalia, and red onions are tasty raw or cooked. Tiny white or pearl onions are splendid in stews or vegetable mélanges. Do not store onions in the refrigerator; keep them in a cool, dark place in a well-aired basket or net bag. Most onions will keep for 2 months or more; however sweet, moist varieties, such as Vidalia and Empire, should be used within 2 weeks.

Parsnips. Parsnips are like broad-shouldered, ivory-skinned carrots with a sweet, nutty flavor. They should be peeled and cut into uniform sticks for cooking. They will keep for up to 2 weeks in the refrigerator.

Peas. Peas fall into three main categories: shell peas, snow peas, and sugar snap peas. Select crisp, bright green peas that are not too large. Shell peas should be eaten the day they are picked; snow and snap peas, which have edible pods, may be stored for 2 days in the refrigerator.

Peppers, hot (chilies). Dozens of varieties of hot chili peppers are available. They range in heat from the milder Anaheims and banana peppers to the scorching hot serranos and Scotch bonnets. The most familiar is probably the jalapeño pepper. Buy hot peppers in small quantities (a little goes a long way). Handle cut peppers with gloves or wash hands immediately to avoid skin and eye irritation. Most fresh chili peppers will keep up to 2 weeks in a paper bag in the refrigerator.

Peppers, sweet. Peppers are freshest in the late summer but are available all the year round. Red, orange, and yellow peppers are mellower and usually more expensive than green peppers. Select firm, shiny fruit; store in the refrigerator for no more than 5 days.

Potatoes. Potatoes come in many varieties: Red or brown-skinned all-purpose potatoes, waxy boiling potatoes, and dry, floury bakers are but a few. Whatever type you purchase, avoid potatoes that are sprouting or that have greenish skin or black spots. New potatoes are thin-skinned and should be eaten right away; potatoes with thicker, dry skins will keep for several months if they are stored in a cool, dry place. Do not store potatoes in the refrigerator or near onions, which cause them to soften and rot.

Radishes. Radishes range from red to white in color and from small and round to long and cylindrical in shape. Look for firm, bright roots; if the leaves are still attached, they can help you determine freshness. Overly large radishes tend to be woody, except for daikon radishes, but even these are best when no more than 1 inch thick. Store radishes for 5 to 7 days in the refrigerator; set them in ice water to crisp for a few hours if eating them raw.

Sprouts. Available year-round, sprouts are useful for salads, sandwiches, and stir-frys. Look for alfalfa, radish, pea, and sunflower sprouts in addition to bean sprouts. Store in the refrigerator for no more than 3 days in their perforated plastic containers.

Squash, summer. Zucchini, yellow, crookneck, and patty-pan are the main summer squashes. Because they are so plentiful in the summer, gardeners joke about the lengths that they will go to in trying to give away their harvest. Although huge squashes are funny to look at, they are seedy and poor in flavor. Choose fairly small, tender-skinned, and unwithered fruits, and store them in the refrigerator for only 3 to 4 days. For a gourmet treat, try tiny, baby squash or squash blossoms (page 198).

Squash, winter. Winter squashes, such as acorn, Hubbard, butternut, and pumpkins, keep well and have great nutritional value. Choose uncracked, unblemished squashes that feel heavy in the hand. In a cool, dry place, they will keep up to 3 months.

Tomatoes. You've heard it before, but it bears repeating: There is nothing like a sun-ripened, fresh-picked tomato. Enjoy them to the fullest when they are in season and canned or in sauces when they are not. Choose tomatoes for their purpose — larger varieties for all-purpose eating and cooking; smaller cherry or pear tomatoes for salads or grilling; and fleshy, plum-shaped tomatoes for sauce. Tomatoes should be eaten within a day or two of ripening. For best flavor, do not refrigerate tomatoes; if you must do so, let them return to room temperature before eating. To peel a tomato, dip it into boiling water for about 15 seconds, drain, and slip off the skin.

FRUIT

Almost everyone loves the natural sweetness of fruit. It is wonderful raw and in all kinds of salads, baked goods, and preserves. If fruit is to be eaten raw, it should be at its peak ripeness. If underripe, it should usually be allowed to ripen at room temperature. It should then either be eaten at once or be refrigerated, to be eaten as soon as possible. Remember that when several fruits are stored together — in a bag, fruit bowl, or refrigerator bin — they will ripen faster.

Apples. There are hundreds of varieties of apples for eating and cooking (page 222). One of the best ways to get them is to pick your own at an orchard. Otherwise, look for mature, ripe fruit without spots or blemishes. Store in a cool place for 1 week or more.

Apricots. Ripe apricots are a delicacy, and fairly expensive, too, so be sure to buy them when they are ready to eat — plump, sweet, but just soft to the touch. They may be refrigerated for about 3 days.

Bananas. We like to buy some fully ripe bananas and some slightly green. The green ones will ripen by the time we finish the first bunch. Store bananas in open air. If they ripen faster than you can eat them, peel and freeze them for smoothies or for baking.

Cherries. Both sweet eating cherries and tart sour cherries for baking are delicious. Choose plump, shiny fruit; store in the refrigerator for up to 5 days.

Citrus fruit. Oranges, tangerines, clementines, grapefruit, lemons, limes, and kumquats are available year-round. Store citrus in a very cool place or in the refrigerator for up to 2 weeks. If a recipe calls for lemon or lime juice, use fresh juice; it provides truer flavor without bitterness or an off taste. To get the most juice from a lemon or lime, roll it under your palm on the countertop until it feels soft. Citrus fruits do not generally need to be washed unless you are using the zest or peel.

Kiwifruit. The kiwifruit, once considered exotic, is now a mainstream item. If it gives a little when pressed, it is ready to eat. It will keep for 1 week or more in the refrigerator. The fuzzy outer peel is usually removed and the fruit sliced to show its beautiful green interior.

Mangoes and papayas. These delicious tropical fruits are gaining in popularity and availability. Buy fruit that is beginning to soften, with unblemished skin; the mango may have a red blush, and the papaya will ripen to yellow. Store them in bags in the refrigerator for up to 4 days, or at room temperature for 1 or 2 days.

Melons. Pick a melon that feels full and heavy for its size. When it's pressed, the flesh should give a little, especially at the stem end, and the melon should have a good scent. Store a melon for up to 2 days at room temperature; a cut melon should be wrapped in plastic and refrigerated.

Peaches and nectarines. Enjoy peaches and nectarines in the summer, when they are in season. Green peaches and nectarines will not ripen at home, but ones that are slightly hard should soften in a day or so at room temperature. Store ripe fruit in the refrigerator. If you are using the peaches for cooking, try the varieties labeled "freestone" to be sure that pitting them won't be such a chore.

Pears. Popular pears include Bartlett, Anjou, Bosc, and Comice. Most can be used interchangeably in recipes. To to use pears at the peak of ripeness, buy them slightly underripe and then wait until they soften slightly, usually in 3 to 5 days. Dip peeled pears in acidulated water (*see* **Celeriac,** page 37) to prevent discoloration.

Pineapples. Hawaiian pineapples are the largest, juiciest, and sweetest. They are most plentiful from late autumn through the winter and early spring. Pineapples from South America and the Caribbean are available year-round.

Plums. Plums should be smooth and somewhat soft when ripe. Buy ripe red, purple, bluc, blue-black, and even green plums when they appear in the markets, and eat them as soon as possible. Ripen firm plums at room temperature; refrigerate ripe plums for 2 to 3 days.

Pomegranates. Pomegranates are mostly available in the autumn; choose a fruit that is pink to red, without brown or withered spots. Cut through the leather peel carefully and fold the edges back to remove the ruby kernels.

BERRIES

··············

These little gems of the fruit world are great favorites for their color and intense, fragrant taste. Unless you grow or pick them yourself, they tend to be fairly expensive, so treat them as a delicacy and use them as fresh as possible, unless you plan to freeze or preserve them.

Berries should be washed in cold, running water just before use. If they are stored damp, thcy will quickly become moldy. Most berries cannot be stored for more than a day or two, and keep best if spread on paper towels on a baking sheet or plate, then covered lightly in plastic wrap.

- **Blackberries.** Purple-black with a deep wine flavor, blackberries should be harvested when they are sweet and ready to drop off the bush at the slightest touch. Most varieties bear fruit in mid- to late summer.
- **Blueberries.** Lowbush or wild blueberries are the tiny sweet berries enjoyed by hikers and mountain climbers. Highbush blueberries, which are larger and sturdier, are cultivated for commercial use. Blueberries are in season from mid- to late summer but are available throughout much of the year. They keep longer than most berries, up to 1 week in the refrigerator if they are kept dry and tightly covered.
- **Cranberries.** A cousin of the blueberry, cranberries are very high in vitamin C. Cranberries are usually available between October and December, but they may be frozen right in the bag for up to 6 months.
- **Currants.** Black, red, and white currants are usually available fresh only during the summer. They should be used within a day or two of purchase. The easiest way to remove currants from their twiggy stalks is to comb them off by using the tines of a fork.
- **Raspberries.** Red and black raspberries have been cultivated for the past 400 years. Golden raspberries are relative newcomers. Raspberries are best picked fresh or found at farm stands, as they don't hold up well when shipped. In the market, look for raspberries with a brilliant color, and check carefully for signs of fuzzy gray mold. Use as soon as possible.

Strawberries. Off the vine, strawberries will deepen in color but will not ripen further. They should be bought or picked when the fruit is fully bright red and shiny. The stem should be intact. Do not stem strawberries until after they are rinsed, or they may get watery inside. Strawberries should be used within a day or two of purchase; they will keep slightly longer if sliced and sprinkled with sugar and lemon juice.

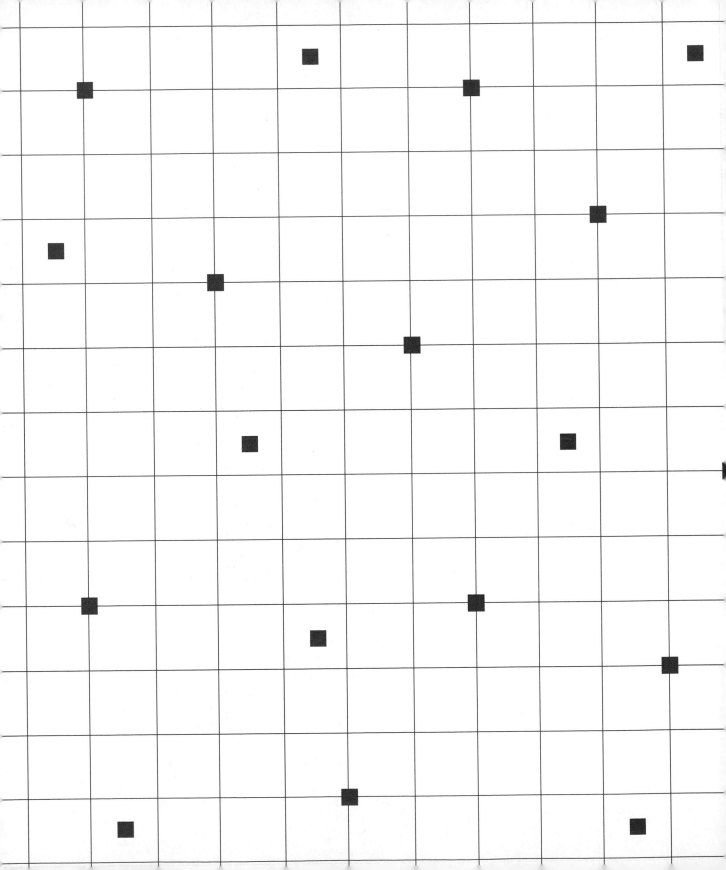

PART TWO
COUNTRY
COOKING

GREAT STARTS: BREAKFASTS

We've all heard that breakfast is the most important meal of the day, but I'm sure that my mother was the first to discover that fact. We never missed breakfast, and Daddy was her trusted partner in the early-morning feast. "Time to wake up — breakfast is ready!" he'd holler at 6 A.M. without fail. We'd roll sleepily out of bed and scramble down the stairs to a table of warm baking-powder biscuits, homemade strawberry jam, crispy bacon, and eggs scrambled to perfection. Breakfast was hot, hearty, and happy . . . a great start to our day.

■ ■ ■ ■ ■ ■ ■

Contributors to this chapter are Glenn Andrews; Liz Anton and Beth Dooley; Janet Ballantyne; Ruth Bass; Jane Cooper; Ken Haedrich; Phyllis Hobson; Dorothy Parker; Phyllis V. Shaudys; Edith Stovel and Pamela Wakefield; and Olwen Woodier.

CEREALS & GRAINS

·············

EGG DISHES

·············

PANCAKES & COMPANY

·············

BERRIED DELIGHTS
& OTHER FRUITY
PLEASURES

·············

MISCELLANEOUS
BREAKFAST
CONCOCTIONS

MARTHA'S FAVORITES

Apple Sausage Bake

❈ ❈ ❈

This is the perfect choice for Sunday morning breakfast when you've taken your weekend guests apple picking on Saturday.

1 pound sausage links, cut in half (use turkey breakfast sausage if you find one you like)
6 tart apples, cored and sliced but not peeled
salt and freshly ground black pepper
1 tablespoon lemon juice
3 tablespoons brown sugar

1. Preheat oven to 350°F. Coat a 2-quart casserole with vegetable cooking spray.

2. In a skillet, brown the sausage; drain off grease. Toss apples and sausage pieces together and transfer to a casserole. Sprinkle with salt, pepper, lemon juice, and brown sugar.

3. Cover and bake for 45 minutes. Remove from oven, uncover, and let stand 10 minutes before serving.

Yield: 6 servings

Maple-Nut Oatmeal

❈ ❈ ❈

Loaded with vitamins, high in fiber, and naturally sweet, thanks to the pure maple syrup, oatmeal is a "stick-to-your-ribs" way to start the day.

3½ cups skim milk
2 cups old-fashioned oats
1 tablespoon butter
⅛ teaspoon salt
¼ cup maple syrup
½ cup raisins
½ cup chopped walnuts
1 cup chopped, unpeeled apple

1. Bring milk to a low boil; stir in oats. Add butter and salt and cook for about 5 minutes over medium heat, stirring occasionally.

2. Remove from heat and add maple syrup, raisins, walnuts, and apple. Mix well. Serve in individual bowls with warm milk and a tablespoon of maple syrup or brown sugar on top.

Yield: 4–6 servings

TOOLS

- Spatula
- Egg beater
- Grinder
- Food mill
- Cast-iron pans of different sizes
- Cutting board
- Chef's knife

BREAKFAST MAKINGS

- *Whole-grain cereals*
- *Whole-grain baked goods (or their makings)*
- *Fresh milk, butter, and yogurt*
- *Fresh fruit and juices*
- *Dried or preserved fruits*
- *Eggs*
- *Natural sweeteners: honey, maple syrup, brown sugar, cinnamon*
- *Potatoes (white and sweet)*
- *Onions*
- *Coffee*
- *Teas*

CEREALS & GRAINS

I have friends who grew up eating only prepared, packaged cereals from the supermarket. It's a special treat to introduce them to some of these hearty and wholesome cereals. I hope you will enjoy them as much as we do.

A Gallon of Granola

✺ ✺ ✺

Every Christmas, Ken Haedrich likes to prepare large batches of this granola for his friends and family. "It makes a great stocking stuffer," he says.

- 8 cups old-fashioned oats
- 2 cups coarsely chopped nuts (cashews, pecans, or almonds)
- 2 cups raw (untoasted) sunflower seeds
- 1 cup sesame seeds
- 1 cup shredded unsweetened coconut (available in health food stores)
- 1 teaspoon salt
- ¾ cup maple syrup
- ¾ cup light-tasting vegetable oil, such as sunflower oil
- 2 cups chopped dried fruit (raisins, currants, and dates are good)

1. Preheat oven to 350°F. In a large mixing bowl, toss together the oats, nuts, sunflower seeds, sesame seeds, coconut, and salt.

2. Warm the maple syrup and oil in a saucepan. Pour over the dry ingredients. Stir with a wooden spoon, then roll up your sleeves and work the mixture with your hands until everything is damp.

3. Spread on baking sheets — no more than about ½ inch thick — and roast for 30 to 40 minutes, stirring occasionally, until golden. When the granola has cooled, stir in the dried fruit. Store in jars or plastic bags.

VARIATION: Instead of all oats, use other grain flakes; bran or untoasted wheat germ can replace some of the seeds.

Yield: 1 gallon

COOKED CEREALS

Delicious cereals can be made from whole grains and water. Set the pot on the back of the woodstove or in the oven at night, and breakfast will be waiting in the morning. This is the way many a farm family would start the day.

Glorious Granola

✺ ✺ ✺

Some consider granola too high in calories and fat to be used as an everyday breakfast cereal, though it's delicious that way. We also love to use it as a topping for fruit and yogurt. Pack some of this granola into an attractive glass jar: It makes a great hostess gift.

- 6 cups old-fashioned oats
- 1 cup wheat germ
- 1 cup skim milk powder
- ½ cup sliced almonds
- ½ cup chopped hazelnuts
- ½ cup shelled sunflower seeds
- ½ cup sesame seeds
- 2 teaspoons cinnamon
- 1 cup honey
- 1 cup canola oil
- 2 teaspoons vanilla extract
- ¾ cup golden raisins
- ¾ cup dark raisins
- ½ cup dried cherries
- ½ cup dried cranberries

1. Preheat oven to 325°F. In a large bowl, toss together the oats, wheat germ, milk powder, nuts, sunflower and sesame seeds, and cinnamon.

2. In a heavy saucepan, heat the honey and oil until hot but not boiling. Remove pan from heat; stir in vanilla.

3. Pour the honey–oil mixture over the oats mixture and toss to coat thoroughly. Spread evenly in three 9- by 13-inch baking pans, or two roasting pans.

4. Bake for approximately 45 minutes, stirring every 15 minutes until mixture is golden.

5. Cool thoroughly; mix in the raisins, cherries, and cranberries.

Yield: About 10 cups

Oatmeal and Apples

❈ ❈ ❈

We enjoy this recipe most on those first crisp fall mornings. It's especially warming when it's made with apples from our own orchard!

> 1 cup rolled oats
> 2 cups cold water
> ½ teaspoon salt
> 2 tart apples, cored, peeled and grated
> ½ teaspoon cinnamon

1. Combine oats, water, and salt and bring to a boil. Cover pan and let simmer slowly for about 10 minutes.

2. Stir in apple and cinnamon; cover and cook 10 minutes longer. Serve with honey and milk.

Yield: 2 servings

GOOD GRAINS

....

Cereals are simply plants (grasses) that yield starchy, edible grains. They are good sources of protein and carbohydrates. Besides the common corn and oats, there are many other varieties to enjoy. Some of our favorites:

GRITS: Many people think only of hominy when they hear "grits." Hominy is dried white or yellow corn kernels, but the term *grits* includes any coarsely ground grain. Try soy, rye, and buckwheat grits.

STEEL-CUT OATS: Unlike the old-fashioned or rolled oats more common in American kitchens, these oat groats are less processed. They take longer to cook and have a chewy texture, but we love their heartiness. They are also called Scotch oats, Irish oatmeal, and, in our house, porridge.

TRITICALE: A blend of wheat and rye, this grain has more protein and less gluten than wheat. It has a nutty-sweet flavor.

Ground Grain Cereal

❈ ❈ ❈

Jane Cooper advocates grinding your own grains: They will be fresher longer, and thus better tasting and more nutritious.

> 1 cup ground grains
> 2–4 cups water
> ½ teaspoon salt

1. Put grains in a large pot; add water and salt. Bring water to a boil, stir, and cook for about 3 minutes.

2. On a woodstove, move pot so that the water slowly simmers and cook 20 minutes longer. On a stovetop, reduce heat to low and simmer 20 minutes. If preparing the night before, push pot to the back of the stove, or set in the oven. The heavier the pot, such as cast iron or earthenware, the better it will retain heat.

Note: Grains to choose from are steel-cut oats, old-fashioned oats, cornmeal, brown rice, grits, millet, soy grits, rye grits, buckwheat grits, and wheat grits.

Cinnamon-Fried Cornmeal Mush

❈ ❈ ❈

One of my favorite things about Ken Haedrich's *Maple Syrup Cookbook* is the evocative descriptions he writes of his recipes, such as this one:

"I love corny things, and these luscious slices — dredged in cinnamon-spiked cornmeal, delicately fried in butter, then doused with maple syrup — are high on my list of breakfast favorites. They're perfect with breakfast meats and eggs, or with applesauce, berries, or yogurt on the side. A few other things to know: You must start this the night before. This will last in the refrigerator for several days, so you can slice and fry anytime. And be sure to use fresh, stone-ground cornmeal, available in health food stores."

4 cups water
1 teaspoon salt
2 cups coarsely ground cornmeal
about 3 tablespoons unsalted butter
1½ teaspoons cinnamon maple syrup

1. Butter a large, shallow casserole, measuring either 8 by 12 inches or 9 by 13 inches. Heat the water in a large, heavy-bottomed pot. Add the salt. As the water heats, sprinkle in 1½ cups of the cornmeal, a little at a time, whisking all the while.

2. When the mixture reaches a boil, switch to a wooden spoon. Reduce the heat to medium low and cook the mush, stirring continuously, for 15 minutes; the mixture will become quite thick. Stir in 1 tablespoon of the butter until melted, then remove from the heat. Immediately scrape the mush into the prepared casserole and flatten the top as best as you can with a spatula. Cool to room temperature, cover, and refrigerate overnight.

3. The next morning, stir the cinnamon into the remaining ½ cup cornmeal. Cut the chilled cornmeal mush into serving-sized pieces; roughly 2 by 3 inches is a good size, but anywhere around there is fine.

4. Melt about 2 tablespoons of the butter in a cast-iron skillet over medium-low heat. Dredge the slices in the cinnamon mix, then fry them in the butter, without crowding, 3 to 4 minutes on each side. Serve hot, drizzled with maple syrup.

Yield: 8 servings

Whole-Wheat Flakes

❈ ❈ ❈

I wholeheartedly believe that homemade breakfast cereals are more delicious and far more nutritious than many commercially made ready-to-eat cereals. Well worth the time and effort.

2 cups finely ground dried wheat (approximately)
1 teaspoon ground cinnamon
1 teaspoon ground nutmeg
½ teaspoon salt
½ teaspoon baking soda
¼ cup warm water
½ cup molasses

WHAT'S FOR BREAKFAST?

The heartiness of a traditional country breakfast is more akin to breakfast in England than elsewhere in Europe.

If your menu includes fruit or juice, eggs, bacon or other meat, cereal, baked goods, jam, and tea, it would qualify as an "English breakfast," though breakfast in America is more likely to include coffee than tea.

A "continental breakfast" includes bread and a beverage: toast, a muffin, a croissant, a bagel, or pastry, and coffee, tea, or other drink.

1. Combine 1 cup of the wheat with the cinnamon, nutmeg, and salt.

2. Dissolve the baking soda in water and stir quickly into the molasses. Add the flour mixture, then enough of the remaining wheat to make a very stiff dough. Roll very thin and cut into strips.

3. Dry according to your preferred method.

Dehydrator: Lay strips on trays without overlapping. Dry at highest setting until crisp, about 4 to 6 hours. Remove and cool. Crumble into small, flaky pieces. Spread over trays again and dry at highest setting for 2 hours longer, or until very crisp.

Sun: Lay strips over trays and dry in full sun where there is good air circulation. Dry until crisp, about 6 to 8 hours, turning once. Crumble into small pieces and spread over trays. Continue drying for 2 to 4 hours longer, stirring occasionally. Take trays inside at night, if necessary.

Oven or homemade dryer: Lay strips on trays. Dry at 150°F for 4 to 6 hours with door ajar until crisp. Remove from oven or dryer and crumble, then return to trays and dry for 2 to 4 hours longer, or until very crisp.

4. Store dried cereal in an airtight container. Serve with sugar and milk as a ready-to-eat cereal.

Yield: 10 servings

Carrot Cereal

❂ ❂ ❂

With this tasty home-dried cereal, you can use fresh bounty from your garden. It tastes great with milk as a ready-to-eat cereal or alone as a snack.

2   cups finely ground dried wheat
½   cup firmly packed brown sugar
¼   cup old-fashioned oats
1½   teaspoons baking powder
½   teaspoon salt
1   dried pasteurized egg
1   cup cooked, mashed, and cooled carrots
1   teaspoon vanilla extract

1. Combine wheat, brown sugar, oats, baking powder, salt, egg, carrots, and vanilla. Beat well.

2. Cover trays with plastic wrap; thinly spread batter over plastic.

3. Dry according to your preferred method.

Dehydrator: Spread batter on plastic-covered trays and dry at highest setting for 4 to 6 hours, or until top is firm and batter can be peeled away from plastic easily. Invert onto another tray and peel off and discard plastic wrap. Continue drying batter until it is hard and crisp, about 6 to 8 hours longer. Cool and crumble, then spread over trays again and dry until very crisp, about 2 to 3 hours longer.

Sun: Spread batter on plastic-covered trays and dry in full sun in a well-ventilated area. Dry for 4 to 6 hours, or until batter can be pulled away from plastic. Invert onto another tray and peel off and discard plastic. Dry batter until hard, about 4 to 6 hours longer. Take trays inside at night. In the morning, crumble and spread over trays to dry until very crisp, about 3 to 4 hours longer.

Oven or homemade dryer: Spread batter on plastic-covered trays. Dry at 150°F for 6 to 8 hours with door ajar, or until batter can be peeled away from plastic. Invert onto another tray, peel off plastic and discard. Return batter to oven or dryer and dry until hard, about 6 to 8 hours longer. Crumble and spread flakes over uncovered trays. Dry for 3 to 4 hours longer, or until very crisp.

4. Store in small batches in airtight containers.

Yield: 10 servings

EGG DISHES

Though there's nothing quite like a farm-fresh egg prepared simply and with little embellishment, we also enjoy dressing up eggs in casseroles, omelettes, frittatas, and stratas.

Creamy Scrambled Eggs

※ ※ ※

This recipe is a favorite for brunches and of college kids coming home for the weekend. Its richness makes them forget cafeteria scrambled eggs at first bite.

10 *eggs*
 4 *egg whites*
 ¼ *cup skim milk*
 1 *package (8 ounces) light cream cheese, diced*
 ¼ *cup chopped fresh basil, or 1 teaspoon dried*
 ¼ *cup chopped fresh parsley*
 1 *teaspoon dried oregano*
 1 *teaspoon unsalted butter*

1. In a large bowl, whisk eggs and egg whites together. Beat in milk, cream cheese, basil, parsley, and oregano.

2. Melt butter in a heavy skillet, add the egg mixture, and cook over low heat for about 5 minutes, stirring constantly. Serve immediately.

Yield: 8 servings

Pam's Baked Eggs

Pam Art has been a friend and colleague since we started our publishing business. Her baked eggs are a fast favorite for casual morning entertaining.

12 *eggs, slightly beaten*
 1 *cup milk*
 1 *teaspoon dry mustard*
 1 *teaspoon dried minced onion*
 2 *cups chopped ham*
 2 *cups Cheddar cheese, grated*
   salt and freshly ground black pepper

1. Preheat oven to 350°F and grease a 9- by 13-inch baking pan.

2. In a large bowl, beat the eggs and mix in the milk, mustard, and onion. Add the ham, cheese, and salt and pepper to taste. Pour into the pan and bake for 30 to 35 minutes, or until puffed and a knife inserted in the center comes out clean.

Yield: 8 servings

SUNDAY BREAKFAST

....

Assorted juices

....

Creamy Scrambled Eggs (this page)

....

Tamarack Blueberry Muffins (page 121)

....

Coffee

Poached Eggs with Tomato Hash on Toasted Egg Bread

✿ ✿ ✿

These are poached eggs with flair. They require a little extra effort, but some of the work can be done in advance. The result is so delicious that you'll be glad you did it. Show it off with something green as a garnish: asparagus tips, watercress, or even a sprig or two of flat-leaf parsley.

1 egg
2 egg whites
¼ cup skim milk
6 1-inch slices egg bread
1 teaspoon butter

Hash

4 ounces turkey breakfast sausage
2 tablespoons minced shallots
2 cups seeded and chopped fresh tomatoes
2 tablespoons finely chopped sun-dried tomatoes (packed in oil and drained)
½ teaspoon rubbed sage
salt and freshly ground black pepper

Eggs

¼ cup vinegar
6 eggs
3 tablespoons freshly grated Parmesan cheese

1. Whisk together the egg, egg whites, and milk. Dip slices of bread in egg mixture and set aside. Melt butter in a large nonstick skillet and pan-toast the bread slices until they are golden brown on both sides. Arrange on a foil-covered baking sheet and set aside.

2. Make the hash filling by cooking the sausage in the same skillet, breaking it up as finely as possible while it lightly browns. Remove from the pan onto paper towels and wipe out the pan.

3. Add shallots and fresh tomatoes to the pan and cook for a few minutes. Next, add sun-dried tomatoes and cook a few minutes longer. Finally, add sausage and seasonings and cook briefly. This can be done ahead and stored, covered, in the refrigerator.

4. Preheat broiler.

5. Prepare a large saucepan for cooking eggs by adding the vinegar to 4 inches of water; bring to a simmer. Crack each egg into a small dish and slip it into the simmering water. Poach for 2 to 4 minutes to desired doneness; remove with a slotted spoon and place on a paper towel to drain.

6. Spoon about 3 tablespoons tomato-sausage filling onto each piece of toast, leaving a small depression for the egg. Slip the egg into the hot filling.

7. Sprinkle the Parmesan over the tops of the eggs. Broil 6 inches from heating element for 30 seconds and serve immediately.

Yield: 6 servings

EGGS IN DIFFERENT GUISES

....

FRITTATA: The ingredients are mixed in with the eggs rather than being folded inside. It's an Italian omelette.

OMELETTE: Eggs and seasonings, and sometimes water or milk, are mixed and cooked in butter or fat until firm; filled with various items, such as herbs, cheese, meat, or vegetables; and, finally, rolled or folded.

QUICHE: A pastry shell filled with a custard made of eggs, cream, seasonings, and often meat and vegetables.

STRATA: A layered casserole of bread, eggs, and cheese. May include meat or vegetables.

Basic Herbed Omelette

❈ ❈ ❈

This family-sized omelette has several variations to suit anybody's taste. I love it with basil, savory, and tarragon.

8   eggs
4   tablespoons milk
4   tablespoons butter or bacon fat
½   cup shredded Cheddar cheese
1   teaspoon marjoram
½   teaspoon salt

1. Whisk eggs and milk together. In a small bowl, combine Cheddar, marjoram, and salt.

2. Heat a large omelette pan or nonstick skillet over medium-high heat. Add butter, swirling to coat pan. Add the egg mixture to the pan.

3. With one hand, shake the pan back and forth. Stir the eggs with your other hand, using a fork held flat so that you don't break through the bottom of the omelette. When the eggs begin to form curds and set along the bottom, stop stirring. With the back of the fork, spread the eggs evenly around the pan.

4. Spoon the filling across the middle of the omelette. Let cook another minute or so.

5. Tilt the pan up and use the fork to roll the top third of the omelette onto the filling. If you want the omelette lightly browned, let it sit for a few seconds.

6. Tilt the pan over a serving platter; make a second fold by sliding the omelette out of the pan, seam side down, onto the platter. Serve hot.

Yield: 4–6 servings

VARIATION: Omit the cheese; instead of Cheddar, marjoram, and salt, try 2 teaspoons chives, 2 teaspoons parsley, and 1 teaspoon marjoram, or 1 teaspoon each of basil, savory, and tarragon.

Sausage & Apple Omelette

❈ ❈ ❈

Sausage and apples is one of my favorite combinations of meat and fruit. The flavors make a great omelette.

4   ounces sausage meat
3   scallions, including the green tops, sliced
1   medium apple (Granny Smith, Baldwin, Rhode Island Greening)
freshly ground black pepper
1   tablespoon unsalted butter
4   large eggs

Making the perfect omelette

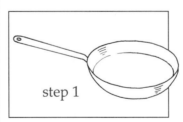

step 1

For individual omelettes, use a 7- or 8-inch omelette pan or non-stick skillet.

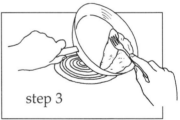

step 3

Tilt the pan up and use the fork to roll the top third of the omelette onto the filling.

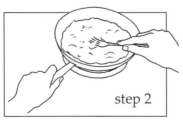

step 2

With one hand, shake the pan back and forth while stirring the eggs with your other hand. Use a fork held flat so as not to break through the bottom of the omelette.

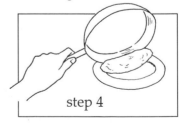

step 4

Tilt the pan over a serving platter and make a second fold by sliding the omelette out of the pan, seam side down, onto the platter.

1. In a medium-sized skillet, brown the sausage meat, breaking it up and turning it as it cooks, for about 8 minutes. Drain off most of the fat and push the meat to one side.

2. Sauté the scallions for 2 minutes in the sausage skillet.

3. Peel, core, and chop the apple. Stir into the sausage meat and scallions, add pepper to taste; cook over low heat for 5 minutes. Remove from the heat and cover to keep warm.

4. Beat the eggs until light.

5. Heat a medium omelette pan or nonstick skillet over medium-high heat. Add the butter, swirling to coat pan. Add the eggs to the pan.

6. With one hand, shake the pan back and forth while stirring the eggs with your other hand. Stir, using a fork held flat so as not to break through the bottom of the omelette. When the eggs begin to form curds and set along the bottom, stop stirring. With the back of the fork, spread the eggs evenly around the pan.

7. Spoon the sausage mixture across the middle of the omelette. Let cook another minute or so.

8. Tilt the pan up and use the fork to roll the top third of the omelette onto the filling. If you want the omelette lightly browned, let it sit for a few seconds.

9. Tilt the pan over a serving platter and make a second fold by sliding the omelette out of the pan, seam side down, onto the platter. Serve immediately.

Yield: 2 servings

Greek Omelette

❂ ❂ ❂

The feta cheese makes a nice change from the rich creaminess of other popular omelette cheeses.

>   2   tablespoons olive oil
>   3   tomatoes, chopped (fresh or canned)
>   1   tablespoon minced onion
>   1   cup crumbled feta cheese
>   ½   teaspoon dried marjoram, or 1 teaspoon fresh
>   8   eggs
>   ½   cup milk
>   salt and freshly ground black pepper
>   3   tablespoons butter

1. Heat oil in a skillet. Sauté tomatoes and onions or scallions until soft, stirring occasionally (3 or 4 minutes). Remove from heat and stir in cheese and marjoram. Set aside.

2. Beat the eggs until light. Blend in milk and salt and pepper to taste.

3. Heat a large omelette pan or nonstick skillet over medium-high heat. Add the butter, swirling to coat pan. Add the eggs to the pan.

4. With one hand, shake the pan back and forth while stirring the eggs with your other hand. Stir, using a fork held flat so as not to break through the bottom of the omelette. When the eggs begin to form curds and set along the bottom, stop stirring. With the back of the fork, spread the eggs evenly around the pan.

5. Spoon the tomato mixture across the middle of the omelette. Let cook another minute or so.

6. Tilt the pan up and use the fork to roll the top third of the omelette onto the filling. If you want the omelette lightly browned, let it sit for a few seconds.

7. Tilt the pan over a serving platter and make a second fold by sliding the omelette out of the pan, seam side down, onto the platter. Serve immediately.

Yield: 4 servings

Tomato Omelette
with Marjoram
❂ ❂ ❂

Ruth Bass, who wrote a series of books celebrating the use of herbs in cooking, says there are two ways to mingle tomato, marjoram, and eggs. You can cut cherry tomatoes in half, heat a little olive oil in a small skillet, put them in cut side down, and then serve them sprinkled with fresh marjoram next to eggs. Or you can turn out this omelette, which combines tomatoes, marjoram, and farmer cheese.

2   *tablespoons extra virgin olive oil*
3   *fresh ripe tomatoes, chopped*
3   *large shallots, minced*
1   *cup farmer cheese, crumbled*
2   *teaspoons minced fresh marjoram*
8   *eggs*
¼   *cup water*
   salt and freshly ground black pepper
4   *tablespoons butter*

1. Heat the oil in a skillet. Add the tomatoes and shallots and cook until soft, stirring frequently. Remove the pan from the heat and stir in the cheese and marjoram. Set aside.

2. Beat the eggs with a fork until they are light and well blended. Add the water and salt and pepper to taste.

3. Heat a large omelette pan or nonstick skillet over medium-high heat. Add the butter, swirling to coat pan. Add the eggs to the pan.

4. With one hand, shake the pan back and forth while stirring the eggs with your other hand. Stir, using a fork held flat so as not to break through the bottom of the omelette. When the eggs begin to form curds and set along the bottom, stop stirring. With the back of the fork, spread the eggs evenly around the pan.

5. Spoon the tomato mixture across the middle of the omelette. Let cook another minute or so.

6. Tilt the pan up and use the fork to roll the top third of the omelette onto the filling. If you want the omelette lightly browned, let it sit for a few seconds.

7. Tilt the pan over a serving platter and make a second fold by sliding the omelette out of the pan, seam side down, onto the platter. Serve immediately.

Yield: 4 servings

VARIATION: For a **scallion omelette**, use only 2 tomatoes and add ½ cup chopped scallions. Try substituting feta cheese for the farmer cheese.

Individual Omelettes
❂ ❂ ❂

I like the idea of giving my guests just what they crave, so I really love DeeDee Stovel and Pam Wakefield's suggestion that you select two or three willing guests to take turns as chefs to make individual omelettes. Prepare the omelette fillings ahead of time and keep them covered in small serving bowls in the refrigerator. When ready to cook, arrange fillings attractively and encourage guests to make imaginative combinations.

ABOUT FARMER CHEESE

Slightly tart, slightly tangy, farmer cheese is a form of cottage cheese from which most of the liquid has been pressed. It's sold in loaves and is firm enough to slice or crumble.

2–3 *eggs*
  1 *tablespoon water*
salt and freshly ground black
  pepper
  1 *tablespoon butter or*
  vegetable cooking spray
fillings (see note)

1. In a small bowl, whisk together the eggs, water, and salt and pepper to taste.

2. Heat a 7- or 8-inch omelette pan or nonstick skillet over medium-high heat. Add butter, swirling to coat pan. Add the eggs to the pan.

3. With one hand, shake the pan back and forth while stirring the eggs with your other hand. Stir, using a fork held flat so as not to break through the bottom of the omelette. When the eggs begin to form curds and set along the bottom, stop stirring. With the back of the fork, spread the eggs evenly around the pan.

4. Spoon the filling across the middle of the omelette. Let cook another minute or so.

5. Tilt the pan up and use the fork to roll the top third of the omelette onto the filling. If you want the omelette lightly browned, let it sit for a few seconds.

6. Tilt the pan over a serving platter and make a second fold by sliding the omelette out of the pan, seam side down, onto the platter. Serve immediately.

Yield: 1 omelette

Note: Omelette Filling Ideas:
- Shredded low-fat cheese: Cheddar, Swiss, Monterey Jack, or crumbled feta or goat cheese
- Chopped tomatoes, scallions, peppers, spinach, or avocado
- Sautéed chopped onions, zucchini, or sliced mushrooms
- Chopped parsley
- Alfalfa sprouts
- Caviar
- Snipped fresh herbs

Potato Cheese Soufflé

❂ ❂ ❂

A versatile dish suitable for breakfast, brunch, or even dinner. This soufflé is a lighter version of the dish, which traditionally is made with heavy cream and more whole eggs.

  3 *or 4 large potatoes*
    (about 2 pounds)
  1 *medium onion*
  3 *tablespoons watercress*
  1 *egg yolk*
  4 *tablespoons butter*
  3 *tablespoons yogurt*
  3 *tablespoons sour cream*
  ½ *cup crumbled goat cheese*
  ½ *teaspoon pepper*
  ½ *teaspoon paprika*
  ½ *teaspoon cumin*
  4 *egg whites*

1. Scrub the potatoes, halve them, and boil for about 20 minutes, or until they are tender. While they are boiling, peel and quarter the onion, then mince it. Mince the watercress. Beat the egg yolk lightly. Melt the butter and let it cool.

2. Drain, cool, and peel the potatoes. Mash or put them through a ricer. In a large bowl, add to the potatoes the minced onion, watercress, egg yolk, and butter, blending well. Stir in the yogurt, sour cream, cheese, and spices, again mixing well.

3. Preheat oven to 350°F. Lightly butter a soufflé or baking dish.

4. Beat the egg whites until stiff. Fold them into the potato mixture. Pour or spoon the soufflé mixture into the dish. Bake for 40 to 45 minutes — until the soufflé is puffed up and pretty; serve immediately.

Yield: 5–6 servings

Tomato Pesto Frittata

Omelettes are fun, versatile, and tasty, in Ruth Bass's opinion. But, she says, frittatas are elegant. You pull that puffed-up, golden dish out of the oven, and oohs and aahs are yours. For a special breakfast or a quick but out-of-the-ordinary supper, put this frittata with pesto together in a very few minutes.

- 4 *tablespoons extra virgin olive oil*
- 2 *onions, sliced*
- *salt*
- 3 *ripe tomatoes, peeled, seeded, and chopped*
- 1 *clove of garlic, minced*
- 5 *eggs*
- *freshly ground black pepper*
- 2 *tablespoons chopped fresh basil*
- ¼ *cup chopped fresh parsley*
- 2 *tablespoons grated Parmesan cheese*
- 1 *teaspoon finely chopped pine nuts*
- 2 *tablespoons butter*

1. In a large skillet, heat the oil and add the onions and a little salt. Cover the pan and simmer over low heat for 5 minutes. Uncover and cook until the onions are soft and golden.

2. Add the tomatoes and the garlic, stirring to coat all ingredients. Let simmer for 15 minutes, then drain off the oil. Set the vegetables aside.

3. Preheat the oven to 350°F. In a large bowl, beat the eggs; add the tomato and onion mixture, pepper to taste, basil, parsley, Parmesan, and pine nuts. Combine well.

4. Place the butter in a 10-inch layer cake pan and put it into the oven until the butter melts. Swirl the butter to cover the sides of the pan. Pour in the frittata mixture. Bake for about 15 minutes or until the eggs are no longer runny.

5. Loosen the edges and slide the frittata onto a serving plate, or serve from the pan, cutting wedge-shaped pieces.

Yield:* *4 servings

Apple Frittata

The spices in this recipe are surprising, but delicious.

- 2 *tablespoons vegetable or olive oil*
- 1 *medium onion, chopped*
- 1 *red or green bell pepper, chopped*
- 1 *clove of garlic, minced*
- 1 *medium apple (Granny Smith)*
- 4 *eggs*
- 2 *tablespoons water*
- ½ *teaspoon dried sage*
- ¼ *teaspoon ground mace*
- ⅛ *teaspoon freshly ground black pepper*
- ½ *cup grated Cheddar, Monterey Jack, or mozzarella cheese*

1. Heat the oil in a medium-sized skillet. Add the onion, pepper, and garlic, and cook over low heat until the onion is tender, about 15 minutes.

2. Peel, core, and thinly slice the apple. Add to the vegetables and cook for 5 minutes.

3. Beat the eggs with the water, sage, mace, and pepper. Pour over the vegetables. Sprinkle with the cheese.

4. Cover the pan and cook over low heat for 10 minutes, until the eggs are set and the cheese has melted. Serve at once.

Yield:* *2–4 servings

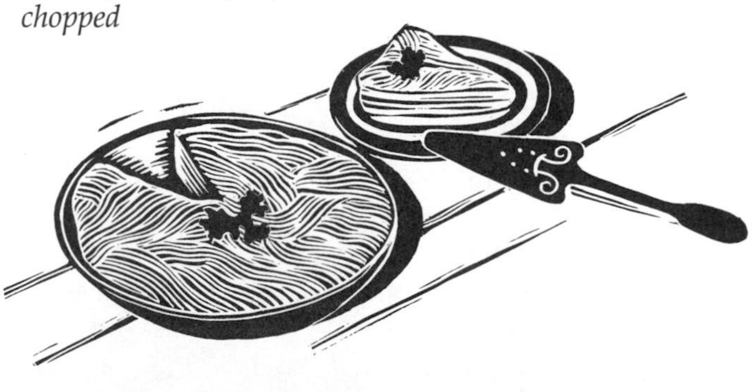

Tomato Strata

☒ ☒ ☒

A strata makes a wonderful breakfast when you have guests, because the dish is assembled the day before.

12 slices sourdough or regular French bread, cut in ½-inch diagonal slices
3 medium ripe tomatoes, sliced
½ cup sliced sun-dried tomatoes (packed in oil and drained)
1 cup shredded fresh basil leaves
1–2 tablespoons olive oil
2 cups mixed grated Fontina and Gruyère cheeses
4 eggs
2 egg whites
3 cups evaporated skim milk
1 teaspoon dried oregano
¼ teaspoon salt
freshly ground black pepper
¼ cup freshly grated Parmesan cheese

1. Lightly coat a 2-quart casserole dish with vegetable cooking spray; line the dish with six slices of the bread. Arrange the tomato slices and sun-dried tomatoes over the bread; scatter the basil leaves on top, drizzle with olive oil, and sprinkle Fontina and Gruyère over all. Lay the remaining bread slices over the cheese and press down.

2. In a large bowl, whisk the eggs and egg whites together until they are foamy. Add the milk, oregano, salt, and pepper and mix well. Pour this mixture over the bread. Cover the casserole with plastic wrap and let sit in the refrigerator overnight.

3. Preheat oven to 350°F. Sprinkle the strata with the Parmesan. Bake for 45 minutes to 1 hour, or until puffy and golden brown.

Yield: 6 servings

SHIRRED EGGS

....

A shirred, or baked, egg is a lovely old-fashioned treat. Grease a ramekin or small casserole; carefully break an egg into it. Sprinkle with salt and a teaspoon or so of cream or melted butter. Put the ramekins into a pan of hot water and bake at 350°F for about 7 minutes. The egg white will be firm, but the yolk still soft.

Zucchini Strata

☒ ☒ ☒

I make note of recipes, like this, that feature zucchini for those summer days when the garden can't seem to stop producing it.

8 large slices Italian semolina bread or French bread
2 cups grated zucchini
2 sweet Italian sausages, casings removed, and browned, crumbled, and well drained to remove excess fat (use turkey sausage if you find one you like)
1 medium onion, chopped
2 cups grated sharp Cheddar or Gruyère cheese
4 eggs
2 egg whites
3 cups evaporated skim milk
1 teaspoon dried thyme
¼ teaspoon dry mustard
¼ teaspoon salt
¼ teaspoon white pepper
2 tablespoons freshly grated Parmesan cheese

1. Lightly coat a shallow 2-quart casserole dish with vegetable cooking spray and line with four slices of the bread. Scatter the zucchini and sausage over the bread; sprinkle with onions and Cheddar. Lay the remaining bread slices over the cheese.

2. In a large bowl, whisk the eggs and egg whites together until foamy. Add the milk, thyme, mustard, salt, and pepper and mix well; pour mixture over the bread. Cover the casserole with plastic wrap and let sit in the refrigerator overnight.

3. Preheat oven to 350°F. Sprinkle strata with Parmesan. Bake for 45 minutes to 1 hour or until puffy and golden brown.

Yield: 6 servings

PANCAKES & COMPANY

Fire up your griddle (or a nonstick pan) for rural America's favorite breakfast. Whether you call them pancakes, flapjacks, or hotcakes, you can't beat a short stack with real maple syrup to make your family happy and your guests feel "at home." Waffles, French toast, and crêpes are also griddle greats that everyone loves.

Whole-Wheat Pancakes

❈ ❈ ❈

I can't beat Ken Haedrich's words in describing this recipe to you: "These pancakes are like home to me. After I've been spinning off all sorts of pancake variations for a while, they're comforting to come back to. They have an honest, grainy flavor, just the right amount of crunch and a pleasant, cakey texture."

    1   cup cornmeal, preferably
        stone-ground
    1½ cups whole-wheat flour
    ½   teaspoon salt
    1   tablespoon baking powder
    3   eggs
    1¾ cups milk
    2   tablespoons molasses
    ¼   cup oil or melted butter

1. Stir together the cornmeal, flour, salt, and baking powder.

2. In a separate bowl, beat the eggs well and blend in the milk and molasses.

3. Make a well in the dry ingredients, then pour in the liquids, including the oil, and stir just until smooth. Let stand for several minutes before cooking on a hot griddle.

Note: Whole-grain flours vary widely in their absorptive capabilities, so the batter may have to be thinned with a little milk to reach the proper consistency.

Yield: 14 four-inch pancakes

Buckwheat Pancakes

❈ ❈ ❈

A diner not far from our company's Massachusetts office serves buckwheat pancakes that people rave about, but there's nothing like hot and homemade. For international flair, serve silver-dollar-sized buckwheats Slavic style by topping them with caviar and sour cream.

    2   teaspoons active dry yeast
    2   cups milk, scalded and
        cooled to lukewarm
    2   cups buckwheat flour
    ½   teaspoon salt

THE GREADEAL

....

The griddle, or girdle, is one of our simplest and oldest cooking utensils — centuries ago the Gaels used hot stones called *greadeals* — and it is still used to make traditional baked goods in Great Britain, France, and the United States.

There are many traditional griddle cakes, which vary from region to region. They come in the form of hotcakes, johnnycakes, hoecakes, fritters, scones, tea pancakes, bannocks, flapjacks, and crumpets — to list just a few.

Griddle cakes are speedy and easy to make, which makes them a great breakfast favorite. In Europe, though, they're also eaten for afternoon tea and supper.

Ideally, the griddle or skillet should be of cast iron or heavy aluminum to allow the cakes to brown without burning as they are baked on a moderately hot burner.

2 tablespoons molasses
½ teaspoon baking soda, dissolved in ¼ cup lukewarm water
1 egg
¼ cup vegetable oil

1. In a mixing bowl, combine yeast and milk, stirring to dissolve. Stir in flour and salt until mixture is smooth. Cover with a cloth and let stand at room temperature overnight.

2. Before cooking, stir in molasses, soda, egg, and oil. Grease a skillet lightly and spoon on batter. Cook until bubbles begin to form around edges, 2 to 3 minutes. Turn pancakes over and continue cooking until browned.

Yield: 4 servings

Orange Whole-Wheat Pancakes

❈ ❈ ❈

These pancakes are delicious topped with a dollop of applesauce, orange-flavored whipped cream, or Honey Orange Butter (page 285).

1 cup whole-wheat flour
1 cup orange juice
½ teaspoon salt
1 teaspoon baking soda
½ cup vegetable oil
2 eggs plus 2 egg whites, whisked together
1 cup blueberries (optional)

1. In a medium-sized bowl, blend together flour, juice, salt, and soda. Slowly add the oil, mixing thoroughly. Blend in the eggs.

2. Coat a skillet with vegetable cooking spray and heat to medium high. Pour on batter; sprinkle with blueberries if desired. Lower heat to medium and cook for about 2 to 3 minutes; turn pancakes over and continue cooking for another 2 to 3 minutes, until golden brown.

Yield: 10 large pancakes

Power-Packed Pancakes

❈ ❈ ❈

Light, healthful, and delicious! The wheat germ is full of vitamins, minerals, and protein.

1 cup all-purpose white flour
¼ cup whole-wheat pastry flour
¼ cup wheat germ
½ teaspoon baking powder
½ teaspoon baking soda
¼ teaspoon salt
1 tablespoon sugar
1 egg

2 egg whites
1 cup buttermilk
1 tablespoon vegetable oil

1. In a small bowl, mix together the flours, wheat germ, baking powder, soda, salt, and sugar.

2. In a large bowl, whisk the egg and egg whites until they are light and frothy. Pour some of the flour mixture into the eggs and stir well. Add some of the buttermilk and stir again. Repeat steps until all of the flour mixture and buttermilk is mixed into the eggs. Add the oil and mix again.

3. Place a large skillet or griddle over medium heat for a few minutes.

4. Spoon enough batter for one pancake onto the hot griddle. Let each pancake cook for several minutes, until bubbles form on the top and the bottom is golden brown, before turning.

5. Serve with maple syrup, butter, yogurt, jam, or whatever pleases you.

Yield: 4 servings

SIZZLING HOT

Test the temperature of the skillet or griddle by splashing a few drops of water onto the surface. If the water "dances," the skillet is the right temperature for cooking pancakes.

Jeanne's Oatmeal Pancakes

✖ ✖ ✖

As Ken Haedrich tells it, "This comes from my friend Jeanne Lemlin, author of *Vegetarian Pleasures* . . . known far and wide for her inspired vegetarian cooking. She makes my kind of hotcakes, grainy and nicely textured. You'll want to make these often, once you've tried them." I have. Ken's right.

  1 cup old-fashioned oats
  1 cup unbleached white or all-purpose flour
  ½ cup whole-wheat flour
  2½ teaspoons baking powder
  1 teaspoon salt
  2 large eggs
  2 cups milk
  2 tablespoons brown sugar
  5 tablespoons butter, melted

1. Whirl the oats in a blender until they become a fine powder; a few traces of flakes are fine.

2. Pour into a large bowl, then mix in the flours, baking powder, and salt. Set aside.

3. In a medium-sized bowl, beat the eggs lightly, then whisk in the milk and sugar.

4. Make a well in the dry ingredients, pour in the liquids, and stir briefly. Add the melted butter and blend just until no traces of dryness are visible. Let the batter sit for several minutes, then cook on a hot griddle.

Yield: 14 four-inch cakes

Apple Pancakes

✖ ✖ ✖

Use this batter for soul-satisfying waffles as well as tasty pancakes.

  2   cups sifted all-purpose flour
  1½ teaspoons baking powder
  1   teaspoon baking soda
  1   teaspoon ground cinnamon
  ¼   cup sugar or honey
  ¼   cup apple juice or cider
  ¼   cup vegetable oil or melted unsalted butter
  2   cups sour cream or 1½ cups plain yogurt
  2   large eggs
  2   medium apples (McIntosh, Golden Delicious, Empire)
  shortening for frying

1. In a large mixing bowl, blender, or food processor, combine flour, baking powder, soda, cinnamon, honey, apple juice, oil, sour cream, and eggs until smooth. The batter will be very thick. Allow it to rest for 30 to 60 minutes.

2. Core and grate the apples. Stir into the batter.

3. Heat a heavy skillet over medium-high heat and grease with about 1 teaspoon of shortening. Drop the batter onto the hot griddle a few tablespoons at a time (for large pancakes, measure out ¼ cup of batter per pancake).

4. When bubbles appear on top (after about 2 minutes), turn and brown the other sides. Serve with butter, lemon juice, and sugar.

Yield: 4–6 servings

BANANA PANCAKES

Use mashed bananas for all or part of the liquid in your pancakes. The result is moist pancakes with wonderful flavor. For two bananas, use 1 egg, ½ cup milk, ½ cup flour, and 1 teaspoon baking powder. Top them with a fruit syrup or purée.

Stuffed French Toast

✖ ✖ ✖

Stuffing French toast makes it more fun to eat.

  4–6 large fresh apples, peeled, cored, and sliced
  1   teaspoon plus 1 tablespoon butter
  2   tablespoons sugar
  1   teaspoon ground cinnamon
  2   eggs, slightly beaten
  1   egg white
  ½   cup skim milk
  ¼   teaspoon salt
  12   slices whole-wheat bread pure maple syrup and applesauce

1. In a large skillet, sauté the apples in the teaspoon of butter until they are slightly soft, about 10 minutes. Mix the sugar and cinnamon in a small bowl and add to the apples. Cook 1 minute or until sugar melts.

2. In a deep-dish pie plate, whisk the eggs, egg white, milk, and salt together until smooth.

3. Dip the slices of bread into the egg mixture; lay six of them out on a cutting board. Spread the apple mixture over the bread and cover with remaining slices to make "sandwiches." Press down slightly.

4. Melt half of the tablespoon of butter in a large skillet or griddle. When butter is hot but not brown, add three of the sandwiches and cook until the bottoms are lightly browned. Turn them and lightly cook the other sides.

5. Cook remaining French toast sandwiches with remaining butter. Serve with maple syrup and applesauce.

Yield: 6 servings

Orange French Toast

✿ ✿ ✿

Your family will feel like royalty when you serve this treat. Challah can be substituted for the Swiss braided bread.

4 eggs
4 egg whites
¼ teaspoon salt
1 tablespoon grated orange zest
½ cup orange juice
1 loaf Swiss braided bread, cut into 12 slices (page 107)

Orange Syrup

1½ cups orange juice
1 teaspoon sugar

1. To make the orange syrup, combine the orange juice and sugar in a small saucepan over medium heat. Bring to a boil and cook for 1 minute; keep warm.

2. In a large glass pie plate, whisk together the eggs and egg whites. Add salt, zest, and juice; mix well. Dip slices of bread in egg mixture; transfer to a platter.

3. Heat a nonstick griddle or a large skillet brushed lightly with butter. Brown the bread; keep on a warm serving plate in a 200°F oven until ready to serve. Serve with the warm orange syrup.

Yield: 6 servings

Overnight Oven French Toast

✿ ✿ ✿

The night-before assembly of this dish decreases morning chaos. I recommend it for a first-day-of-school breakfast.

2 tablespoons butter
8 slices raisin bread, sliced 1 inch thick
4 eggs
4 egg whites
1½ cups milk
¼ cup sugar
½ teaspoon ground cinnamon
2 tablespoons maple syrup
1 teaspoon vanilla extract
½ teaspoon salt
confectioners' sugar

1. Butter a large shallow baking pan and arrange the bread slices in a single layer.

2. In a large bowl, beat together the eggs, egg whites, milk, sugar, cinnamon, syrup, vanilla, and salt. Pour mixture over bread; turn slices to coat.

3. Cover with plastic wrap and refrigerate overnight.

4. Preheat oven to 400°F. Bake bread 20 minutes or until tester inserted into center comes out clean. Turn bread over; bake until golden, about 4 minutes longer.

5. Transfer cooked toast to warm plates; sprinkle with confectioners' sugar.

Yield: 8 servings

Whole-Wheat and Hearty Corn Waffles

❈ ❈ ❈

These wholesome waffles have a wonderful crunch and a deep, grainy flavor. They're great topped with apple or pumpkin butter, or with plain yogurt on the side.

 1½ cups whole-wheat flour
 ½ cup cornmeal, preferably stone-ground
 2 tablespoons sugar
 4 teaspoons baking powder
 ¾ teaspoon salt
 2 eggs
 2⅓ cups milk
 ½ cup (1 stick) unsalted butter, melted and cooled

1. Preheat waffle iron. Combine the flour, cornmeal, sugar, baking powder, and salt in a large mixing bowl and toss to mix.

2. In a separate bowl, beat the eggs lightly. Whisk in the milk and butter. Make a well in the dry ingredients, then pour in the liquids. Whisk briefly, just until blended. Let the batter sit for several minutes.

3. Cook on a hot waffle iron according to the manufacturer's directions.

Yield: 4 servings

Corny Yogurt Waffles

❈ ❈ ❈

The lightness of a waffle with the flavor of corn bread. Top with a slice of ham and a poached egg or some chili and salsa for a hearty breakfast-inspired meal any time of day.

 1 cup all-purpose flour
 3 teaspoons baking powder
 1 teaspoon baking soda
 ½ teaspoon salt
 1 cup yellow cornmeal
 4 eggs, separated
 2 cups yogurt
 1 cup (2 sticks) butter, melted and cooled

1. Preheat waffle iron. Sift together flour, baking powder, soda, and salt. Add cornmeal.

2. In a separate bowl, beat egg yolks, yogurt, and butter. Stir the egg-yolk mixture into the flour mixture. Beat egg whites until stiff; fold into batter.

3. Cook on a hot waffle iron according to the manufacturer's directions.

Yield: 4 servings

Lightweight Waffles

❈ ❈ ❈

No need to pass on the waffles; this makes a delicate crispy waffle with only two eggs and no butter at all. Freeze extras to heat up in the toaster for a fast weekday treat.

 2 cups all-purpose flour
 1 teaspoon baking soda
 ½ teaspoon salt
 2 eggs, separated
 2 cups milk, sour milk or buttermilk
 1 cup oil

1. Preheat waffle iron. Sift flour, soda, and salt into mixing bowl. Stir in egg yolks, milk, and oil. Beat egg whites until stiff; fold into the batter. For interest, add chopped nuts, diced banana, or berries.

2. Cook on a hot waffle iron according to the manufacturer's directions.

Yield: 4 servings

TIP ON BEATING EGG WHITES

A sure way to test whether egg whites are sufficiently beaten to form stiff peaks is to turn the bowl upside down — with stiff peaks, the egg whites won't slide out of the bowl. It is best to do this test gradually.

Sour Cream Waffles

✿ ✿ ✿

Good recipes always get passed along, as this one did: from Walter Goodridge of Conway, Massachusetts, to Jane Cooper to me, and now to you. Try these full-flavored waffles with a sifting of confectioners' sugar or with warmed honey mixed with a bit of fresh orange juice.

1   cup whole-wheat pastry
    flour
2   teaspoons baking powder
¼   teaspoon salt
1   teaspoon baking soda
1   tablespoon honey
3   eggs, separated
2   cups sour cream
1   teaspoon grated orange or
    lemon zest

1. Preheat waffle iron. Sift flour, baking powder, salt, and soda into mixing bowl.

2. Stir in honey, egg yolks, sour cream, and zest. Beat egg whites until stiff; fold into batter.

3. Cook on a hot waffle iron according to directions.
Yield: 2–3 servings

Paul's Waffles

✿ ✿ ✿

Named after Paul Falcone from East Randolph, Vermont, this recipe makes classic golden waffles.

3   eggs, separated
1½ cups unbleached
    all-purpose flour
3   teaspoons baking powder
½   teaspoon salt

6   tablespoons melted butter
1   cup milk
1   tablespoon sugar

1. Preheat waffle iron. Beat egg whites until stiff.

2. In another bowl, combine flour, baking powder, salt, butter, milk, and sugar and stir only until moistened. Fold in egg whites.

3. Cook on a hot waffle iron according to directions.
Yield: 2–3 servings

WAFFLES FOR LUNCH, DINNER, OR DESSERT

Waffles aren't just for breakfast. Use them instead of toast or rice with creamed foods or make sandwiches with them.

For dessert, substitute waffles for shortcake with strawberries, make ice-cream sandwiches, or use them as a base for sundaes.

WAFFLES ON A WOODSTOVE

Nonelectric waffle irons come in many designs and metals, but they're all used in basically the same way. Grease the two halves and set the waffle iron over the hottest lid. When the bottom half is very hot — indicated when drops of water sprinkled on the surface sizzle and steam — turn the iron over and heat the second half to the same temperature. Just before baking, turn the waffle iron so that the hot side is on top and pour in the batter, adding only enough to cover about the middle two-thirds of the surface; when the halves are closed, the batter will be pressed out to the sides. Bake 1 minute on each side, continuing to cook and turn until steam is no longer puffing out the sides. After removing the cooked waffle, flip the waffle iron over and add more batter.

Crêpes

❂ ❂ ❂

Basic crêpes can be filled for many uses.

1 cup unbleached
   all-purpose flour
4 eggs
4 tablespoons butter, melted
½ teaspoon salt
1¾ cups milk
1 teaspoon butter

1. Combine the flour, eggs, melted butter, salt, and milk in a food processor or blender and process until smooth. Add more milk if necessary; the batter should have the consistency of light cream. Chill for at least 30 minutes.

2. Heat a small, nonstick skillet or omelette pan. Melt the teaspoon of butter in the pan; spread the butter to cover the bottom and part of the sides of the pan.

3. Pour a little less than ¼ cup of batter into the pan and quickly tip the pan, moving it in a circular fashion to evenly spread the batter over the bottom and sides. Cook over medium heat for about 2 minutes. Flip the crêpe; continue cooking for 30 seconds. Remove to a plate and fill.

Yield: 24–26 crêpes

Note: Freeze crêpes, unfilled, for later use. Place wax paper between layers of crêpes before freezing.

Crêpes with Herbed Wild Mushrooms

❂ ❂ ❂

Fresh herbs and mushrooms make a delicious filling for crêpes, and this recipe makes brunch or lunch special.

12 Crêpes (this page)

Filling

¼ pound crimini mushrooms
½ pound shiitake mushrooms
¼ cup butter
2 teaspoons minced fresh
   thyme
2 teaspoons minced fresh
   rosemary
½ teaspoon light soy sauce
   juice of ½ lemon
   salt and freshly ground black
   pepper

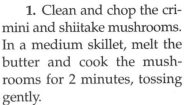

1. Clean and chop the crimini and shiitake mushrooms. In a medium skillet, melt the butter and cook the mushrooms for 2 minutes, tossing gently.

2. As the mushrooms start to color, add the thyme, rosemary, soy sauce, lemon juice, and salt and pepper to taste. Remove from heat while making the sauce.

Sauce

3 tablespoons butter
3 tablespoons unbleached
   all-purpose flour
3 cups chicken broth
1 clove of garlic on a
   toothpick
½ cup light cream
¼ cup Marsala wine

1. In a saucepan, brown the butter and flour, stirring them together. Stir in the broth and whisk to remove all lumps. Add the garlic and, over low heat, cook covered for 20 minutes, stirring occasionally. When the liquid is reduced to about 2 cups, add the cream and wine.

2. Preheat the broiler and lightly grease a broiler pan.

3. Divide the filling among the crêpes and roll them up. With the seam side down, place the crêpes in the pan.

4. Pour the sauce over the tops and broil for 2 minutes or less, until the sauce bubbles.

Yield: 6 servings (12 crêpes)

Breakfast Sausage Crêpes with Apples

❈ ❈ ❈

These crêpes give you a tasty way to use your canned apple slices.

    2   cups canned apple slices
        (page 388), drained
    ½   teaspoon ground mace
    ½   teaspoon ground
        cinnamon
    3   tablespoons unsalted
        butter
    8   link sausages, 5–6 inches
        long
    8   crêpes (page 64)
        pure maple syrup

1. Sprinkle the apple slices with the mace and cinnamon.

2. Heat the butter in a medium-sized skillet and sauté the apples for about 15 minutes, or until soft and golden. Keep warm.

3. Prick the sausages and cook over low heat in a greased skillet for about 10 minutes. Keep warm in a low oven or covered on top of the stove.

4. Roll the crêpes around the sausages, top with sautéed apples, and serve hot with maple syrup.

Yield: 4 servings

APPLE TIPS

· · · · · · · · · · ·

When cooking with apples, it's handy to know that:

• **1 pound of apples yields 4 cups when chopped or sliced and 1½ cups of applesauce.**

• **1 pound of apples may contain 4 small, 3 medium-sized, or 2 large apples.**

BREAKFAST AT YOUR HOUSE

· ·

I don't know why people think "dinner party" or "cocktail party" when they think about entertaining. If you invite people for breakfast or brunch, you'll have the rest of the day to spend the way you want! Here are some good tips so that you don't have to get up two hours early to do it.

Host a cereal bar with an assortment of fresh-cut fruit and berries, a pot of oatmeal on the stove, five or six kinds of boxed cereal, regular and skim milk, juice, coffee (regular and decaffeinated), tea, and hot cocoa.

For brunch, have a make-your-own buffet.

Besides a cereal and juice bar, set out a bagel and cream cheese bar, Bloody Marys and mimosas, salads, sandwich makings, baked potatoes, and sundaes. Everyone can make his or her own.

Pancake batter can be partially made ahead (keep the liquids separate from the dry ingredients). Or make an overnight buckwheat batter. A large griddle that covers two burners at once is great for feeding a crowd. Make some pancakes ahead of time and keep them warm under a clean, damp towel in a low oven.

BERRIED DELIGHTS & OTHER FRUITY PLEASURES

Blueberries in the pancakes, raisins in the toast, raspberries in the muffins, and all's right with the world. Little nuggets of fruit goodness, fresh or dried, add color, flavor, and nutrition to all sorts of breakfast classics.

Blueberry & Green Grape Jewels

❈ ❈ ❈

The only problem with this delicious dish is deciding the best time to serve it. We enjoy it at lazy Sunday brunches on the farm, especially if our guests helped pick the berries. It's equally wonderful for dessert, served in pretty glass dishes so the "jewels" glisten through.

- 2   cups light sour cream
- ¼   cup brown sugar, firmly packed
- 1   teaspoon vanilla extract
- 2   cups blueberries
- 2   cups seedless green grapes

1. Stir together the sour cream, sugar, and vanilla. Chill at least 30 minutes for flavors to blend.

2. Set aside ¼ cup of the blueberries. In a large serving bowl or individual dessert dishes, combine blueberries and grapes, then top with the sour cream mixture. Garnish with reserved blueberries.

Yield: 6–8 servings

Blackberry Gingerbread Waffles

❈ ❈ ❈

Blackberries and ginger combine for a dark, spicy waffle with lots of character. Serve with extra berries and a pouf of whipped or sour cream.

- 2   cups all purpose flour
- 3   teaspoons baking powder
- 1½   teaspoons ground ginger
- 3   eggs
- 4   tablespoons butter, melted
- 1   cup buttermilk
- 4   tablespoons molasses
- ½   cup blackberries

1. Preheat waffle iron. In a large bowl, mix flour, baking powder, and ginger.

2. In a separate bowl, beat eggs, butter, buttermilk, and molasses. Stir the egg mixture into the flour mixture and mix just until moistened.

3. Fold in berries. Pour mixture onto seasoned waffle iron and cook until steam no longer rises.

Yield: 6 servings

BLACKBERRY WINTER

....

"Blackberry winter" is an English term for a cold early May, when blackberries first come into bloom. "Blackberry summer" is a period of fine weather in late September and early October.

Blueberry Cinnamon Doughnuts

❈ ❈ ❈

Our grandchildren enjoy these treats the day after we've all been berrying, because they helped pick!

2 *eggs*
1½ *cups sugar*
1 *cup buttermilk*
4 *cups all-purpose flour*
1 *teaspoon baking powder*
½ *teaspoon baking soda*
½ *teaspoon salt*
½ *teaspoon ground nutmeg*
4 *teaspoons ground cinnamon*
2 *tablespoons butter, melted*
½ *cup blueberries, rinsed*
vegetable oil for frying

1. Beat together the eggs, 1 cup of the sugar, and the buttermilk. Sift together the flour, baking powder, soda, salt, nutmeg, and 2 teaspoons of the cinnamon; stir into the egg mixture. Add butter. Fold in the blueberries.

2. Roll or pat out dough on a floured board to ½ inch thick. Using a well-floured cutter, cut shapes and allow them to rest on a floured surface for 5 minutes.

3. Heat enough oil to fill 3 inches of a frying kettle. When oil is 365°F on a deep-fat thermometer, drop in 3 or 4 doughnuts. As soon as they float to the surface and hold their shape, turn them. Fry until golden on both sides (approximately 3 minutes). Drain on absorbent paper. Combine the remaining cinnamon and sugar and sprinkle on doughnuts while warm.

Yield: 30 doughnuts

Blueberry Sour Cream Pancakes

❈ ❈ ❈

If you get lucky on a summer hike, you can pick wild blueberries for these pancakes; but cultivated berries, fresh or even frozen, are also delicious.

1⅓ *cups all-purpose flour*
½ *teaspoon baking soda*
1 *teaspoon salt*
1 *tablespoon brown sugar*
½ *teaspoon ground nutmeg*
1 *tablespoon cinnamon*
1 *egg, beaten*
1 *cup sour cream*
1 *cup whole or skim milk*
1 *cup blueberries, rinsed*

1. Stir the flour, soda, salt, sugar, nutmeg, and cinnamon together thoroughly. Combine the egg, sour cream, and milk and add to the dry ingredients, stirring just enough to combine.

2. Add the blueberries carefully, blending just enough to mix them in. Drop the batter by ¼ cupfuls onto a hot, greased griddle. Cook until the surface is covered with bubbles; turn and cook until the other sides are well browned.

Yield: 18 four-inch pancakes

GUIDELINES FOR BUYING THE BEST BERRIES

Select berries that are plump and shiny, true to their variety's color. Stick with berries in season or purchase frozen. In late November, strawberries have traveled too far and have been stored too long to be anything but a disappointment.

Avoid purchasing leaky or stained cartons that tell of damaged berries. Peek around and under the container to be sure that the choice berries have not just been strategically placed on top. Avoid moldy berries or those with a white, cottonlike appearance. It's best if you can select the berries yourself from an open bin.

Nectarine and Apple Salsa

❖ ❖ ❖

Glenn Andrews, who has written quite a few of our Country Wisdom Bulletins, says you can use nectarines or peaches in this recipe; however, she insists that you use only fresh fruit. She likes this recipe as a morning treat with toast or bagels and cottage cheese, but it's also great with grilled pork chops or chicken.

> 3 large nectarines or
>   peaches
> 1 tart cooking apple, peeled,
>   cored, and chopped
> ½ cup chopped fresh cilantro
> ¼ cup honey
> 2 tablespoons freshly
>   squeezed lime juice
> ¼ teaspoon ground allspice
> ¼ teaspoon ground cinnamon

1. Skin the nectarines by dipping them for 30 seconds into a saucepan of boiling water, then plunging them into a bowl of ice water. The skins will come right off. Chop the nectarines.

2. Mix nectarines and apples in a nonreactive bowl; add cilantro, honey, juice, allspice, and cinnamon. Stir to combine; chill at least 1 hour.
Yield: About 1½ cups

Strawberry Blintzes

❖ ❖ ❖

Our son Matt has a fine strawberry patch. We look forward all year to his first June berries. Feather-light blintzes, with their creamy filling, are a perfect way to celebrate their arrival.

> 12 crêpes (page 64)
> 4 tablespoons (2
>   ounces) cream cheese
> 1 egg yolk
> ⅛ teaspoon salt
> 1 teaspoon vanilla extract
> 1 tablespoon lemon juice
> 1 teaspoon grated lemon
>   zest
> ¼ cup sugar
> 1½ cups cottage cheese
> ¼ cup ricotta cheese
> 4 cups sliced strawberries

1. Preheat oven to 350°F. Prepare the crêpes and set aside.

2. Combine the cream cheese, egg yolk, salt, vanilla, juice, zest, and sugar in a food processor or mixing bowl; process until well blended. Add the cottage cheese and ricotta. Using the pulsing action on the processor, process for 3 short pulses; in a mixing bowl, mix gently until the cheese is just blended but not soupy. If you have used a food processor, remove the cheese mixture and stir in 2 cups of the strawberries.

3. Spoon ¼ cup of the cheese mixture onto each crêpe. Fold in the sides of the crêpe to make an envelope that completely encloses the filling. Place seam side down in a greased baking dish big enough to hold all the blintzes in a single layer. Cover the dish with foil and bake for 20 minutes or until the blintzes are hot.

4. Remove the blintzes from the oven and sprinkle with the remaining strawberries. Serve at once.
Yield: 6 servings

VARIATION: Replace the strawberries with raspberries and the lemon juice with 1 teaspoon of balsamic vinegar; omit the lemon zest.

MISCELLANEOUS BREAKFAST CONCOCTIONS

Sometimes it's the go-withs that make the meal. Hash browns, popovers, and home-made hash are all side dishes that bring out the best in break-fast or brunch.

Apple Fritters

❋ ❋ ❋

These apple ring fritters taste good at any time of the day. Try them for breakfast, snacks, and desserts.

1¼ cups sifted all-purpose
      flour
  1 cup beer
  1 tablespoon vegetable oil
  1 tablespoon sugar
  2 eggs, separated
  5 large apples (Rome
      Beauty, Mutsu)
2–4 cups vegetable oil for deep
      frying
  ¼ cup all-purpose flour
      confectioners' sugar

Apple-Maple Sauce

  2 cups applesauce
  ⅓ cup pure maple syrup
  1 teaspoon ground cinnamon

1. Combine the flour, beer, 1 tablespoon vegetable oil, sugar, and egg yolks in a blender or food processor. Whirl until smooth. Cover and leave at room tempera-ture for at least 1 hour.

2. Core and slice the apples into ½-inch rings.

3. Pour at least 2 inches of oil into a wok or large skil-let. Heat to 375°F.

4. Beat the egg whites in a large bowl until stiff. Stir the batter and fold in the egg whites.

5. Dip the apple rings first in the ¼ cup flour to coat both sides, then in the batter. Fry a few at a time in the hot oil for 2 to 3 minutes on each side, until golden brown. Drain on absorbent paper.

6. To make the sauce, blend the applesauce with the maple syrup and cinna-mon. Serve immediately.

7. Serve the fritters with the Apple-Maple Sauce.

Yield: 4–6 servings

Summer Squash Fritters

❋ ❋ ❋

Little ones in our family who balk at eating their squash come back for seconds and thirds of these tasty fritters.

4–5 small yellow squash,
      grated
  3 eggs, beaten
  4 tablespoons all-purpose
      flour
  ½ teaspoon ground cinnamon
  ½ teaspoon salt
  ¼ teaspoon allspice
      vegetable oil for frying

1. Pat squash dry with paper towels. In a large bowl, combine squash, eggs, flour, cinnamon, salt, and allspice.

2. Heat ½ inch of oil in a large skillet until drops of water sprinkled on it bounce.

3. Drop batter by table-spoonfuls into the oil and cook until brown. Turn frit-ters over and continue cook-ing until brown. Serve with maple syrup.

Yield: 4 servings

Lacy Sweet Potato Breakfast Patties

❈ ❈ ❈

These savory pancakes are designed to be served with just a drizzle of maple syrup, so they're a good choice when you're not in the mood for an overly sweet breakfast. They go well with almost any egg dish, a side of applesauce, breakfast meats, toast, and biscuits. The pancake mixture isn't terribly cohesive, but as long as you handle the patties gently and make them about 3 to 4 inches across, they'll hold together just fine.

  1 *large sweet potato (about*
     ¾ pound)
  ¼ *teaspoon salt*
  1 *large egg*
  2 *tablespoons heavy cream*
  1 *tablespoon cornmeal*
  ½ *cup minced ham or*
     Canadian bacon
  1 *tablespoon minced onion*
    salt and freshly ground black
     pepper
  1 *tablespoon oil*
  1 *tablespoon butter*
    oil and butter for frying

1. Wash the potato and remove any bad spots; grate it into a bowl. Mix in the salt and set aside for 5 minutes.

2. Beat the egg lightly, then whisk in the cream and cornmeal. Using your hands, squeeze the moisture out of the grated potato, then add to the egg mixture. Stir in the ham, onion, and a pinch of salt and pepper.

3. Heat the oil in a heavy skillet over medium heat. Add the butter, let it melt, and then spoon about ¼ cup of the patty mixture per pancake into the skillet. Don't crowd the pancakes. Spread and flatten the patties with a fork to a thickness of about ¼ inch. They should be no wider than your spatula.

4. Fry for 3 to 4 minutes per side, flipping only once; they'll be dark and crusty on the outside. Serve hot. The patties will hold up for a little while in a hot oven, in case you want to serve them all at once.

Yield: 3 to 4 servings

Corned Beef Parsnip Hash

❈ ❈ ❈

I replaced the potatoes with parsnips in this old family favorite.

  5 *cups finely diced or shred-*
     ded cooked corned beef
6–7 *cups diced or grated*
     parsnips
  2 *cups diced onions*
  ½ *cup cream or milk*
    salt and freshly ground black
     pepper
1–2 *tablespoons vegetable oil*

1. Combine the corned beef, parsnips, onions, and cream. Season to taste with salt and pepper.

2. Cover the bottom of a large frying pan with oil and fry the hash until it is

WAYS TO MAKE A BRUNCH SPECIAL

- Calico or woven napkins and cloth
- A pitcher of daisies or other field flowers
- Carafes of fresh juices in an ice-filled casserole
- Baskets and more baskets
- Butter cut from a block with a fresh flower on the plate
- A selection of mini-breads
- A choice of toppings for cereal or yogurt — nuts, sliced or diced fruit, granola, cinnamon sugar, coconut, dried cranberries, or golden raisins
- Homemade herb butter or herbed cream cheese

browned on one side. Turn the hash over and fry on the other side. Serve hot.

Yield: 8 servings

Big Breakfast Popover

❁ ❁ ❁

This is a cross between a BIG popover and an oven pancake. It makes a spectacular appearance and is very easy to put together. The pan you use is important. If you have a paella pan or an attractive, large shallow casserole dish, use it. I have relied on my old faithful Pyrex glass baking dish. Just don't choose a deep-sided dish. Determine the capacity of your pan with premeasured cups of water before you start filling it. The pan must hold 3 to 4 quarts.

5   tablespoons unsalted
    butter
4   eggs
1   cup skim milk
1   cup whole-wheat pastry
    or all-purpose flour, or a
    combination of the two
1¼ teaspoons cinnamon

Optional Toppings

*powdered sugar with a spritz
    of lemon juice
warm maple syrup
sliced seasonal fruit*

1. Preheat oven to 425°F. Place butter in a 3- or 4-quart casserole and put in hot oven to melt.

2. Beat eggs at high speed in a medium mixing bowl. Reduce speed; slowly add milk, then flour and cinnamon. Beat until thoroughly mixed.

3. Remove pan from oven and pour in batter. Return to oven and bake 20 to 25 minutes or until puffed and golden brown. Cut in wedges and serve immediately on warm plates with toppings of your choice.

Yield: 4–6 servings

Home Sweet Home Fries

❁ ❁ ❁

Janet Ballantyne says that her search for the perfect home fries has led her to many enjoyable breakfasts at diners throughout the country. Here's how she tells the story: "Most people rate a diner by the coffee. For me, it's the home fries. There are many styles of home fries. The potatoes can be preboiled, or not. They can be sliced, diced, cubed, or grated. The fries can be cooked in butter, oil, or bacon grease. In some diners, paprika is added to the frying oil to give the potatoes the funny orange color. The potatoes can be cooked almost as a cake and flipped once. Or they can be stirred frequently. Then there are onions or no onions. The possibilities are great."

Here's her formula for the perfect home fries — crispy on the outside, soft on the inside, flavored with sweet, nearly burned onions.

6   cups cubed (1-inch
    pieces) potatoes
2   tablespoons vegetable
    oil
2   cups diced onions
    salt and freshly ground
    black pepper

1. Parboil potatoes for 5 minutes, until barely tender. Drain.

2. Heat oil in a heavy skillet and sauté onions until limp, 3 to 5 minutes. Add the potatoes and continue cooking. Rather than stir, flip frequently with a spatula so that potatoes brown evenly. The onions will get quite brown, which makes the flavor sweeter.

3. Season to taste with salt and pepper.

Yield: 6–8 servings

SOUPS AND STARTERS

S unday has, for the past 35 years, been "Soup Day" in our home. The process of chopping, slicing, dicing, sautéing, and slowly simmering is simple but satisfying. Our home gradually takes on a new aroma, bringing back memories for some of us, creating new ones for others. My family is the beneficiary of my pleasure. With a hot, hearty soup, such as Chicken Gumbo, I serve a crusty loaf of freshly baked bread, a selection of Italian or French cheeses, and fruit. Family and friends have shared their favorite recipes with me. I'm more than happy to share them with you.

■ ■ ■ ■ ■ ■ ■ ■ ■ ■ ■ ■

Contributors to this chapter are Glenn Andrews; Janet Ballantyne; Ruth Bass; Marjorie Page Blanchard; Charlene Braida; Betty Cavage; Gail Damerow; Ken Haedrich; Phyllis Hobson; Alexandra Nimetz, Jason Stanley, and Emeline Starr; Nancy C. Ralston and Marynor Jordan; Charles G. Reavis; Phyllis V. Shaudys; Edith Stovel and Pamela Wakefield; Olwen Woodier; and Adriana and Rochelle Zabarkes.

STOCKS & BROTHS
....
SOUPS
....
CREAM SOUPS
....
CHOWDERS
....
GUMBO & CHILI
....
CHILLED SOUPS
....
DIPS & SPREADS
....
CHEESE, PLEASE
....
PASTRY BITES
....
MEAT, POULTRY
& SEAFOOD BITES
....
FRUIT &
VEGETABLE BITES

MARTHA'S FAVORITES

Decibel Dip

❈ ❈ ❈

My friend Lynda Scofield told me this dip was named after a singing group she had belonged to in Connecticut. She shared it with me when we first moved to Williamstown. It's easy to vary — try adding peas or herbs — and it's pretty when served in a glass bowl.

2   avocados, peeled, chopped, and drizzled with lemon juice
1   red bell pepper, finely chopped
1   green bell pepper, finely chopped
1   cup sour cream
1   jar (11 ounces) salsa, mild or hot
½   pound Monterey Jack or Cheddar cheese, grated
8–10 scallions (1 large bunch), chopped

1. In a large, shallow glass bowl, layer avocado, red pepper, green pepper, sour cream, salsa, cheese, and scallions.

2. Chill 1 hour or overnight; serve with taco chips.

Yield: 8 servings

Phyllis's Chicken & Dumpling Stew

❈ ❈ ❈

Succulent chicken and garden vegetables make this stew a supper favorite. Topped with tender, fluffy dumplings, it is a true-blue classic of home cooking.

5   tablespoons vegetable oil
1   3–4-pound stewing chicken, cut up
1   medium onion, chopped
1   clove of garlic, minced
2   cups tomato juice or purée
2   cups water
salt and freshly ground black pepper
2   cups fresh or frozen peas
3   tablespoons plus 2 cups unbleached all-purpose flour
½   cup cold water
4   teaspoons baking powder
1   teaspoon salt
1   cup low-fat milk

1. In a large soup pot, heat 3 tablespoons of the oil and brown the chicken parts. Add the onion and garlic and sauté for 5 minutes, stir-ring frequently. Drain off the fat. Add the juice and 2 cups water. Simmer, covered, for 2 to 2½ hours, or until the chicken is tender.

2. Remove the chicken and set aside. Strain the broth into a shallow container and chill to congeal fat. Lift off hardened fat and discard. Return broth to the soup pot.

3. Remove the skin and bones from the reserved chicken and discard. Cut the meat into bite-size pieces and add to the soup pot. Add the salt, pepper, and peas and simmer for 10 minutes.

4. In a small bowl, blend the 3 tablespoons flour with the ½ cup cold water to make a thin paste. Add the paste to the soup pot and cook until thickened, stirring frequently.

5. In a large bowl, sift together the 2 cups flour, baking powder, and 1 teaspoon salt. In a small bowl, blend together the milk and the remaining oil. Add the milk mixture to the flour mixture, all at once, stirring quickly to form a soft dough.

6. Drop the dough by spoonfuls onto the hot soup. Simmer, covered, for 15 minutes, without removing the cover. Serve.

Yield: 4–6 servings

STOCKS & BROTHS

The cornerstone of a great homemade soup is the stock or broth with which it's made. Homemade stock is not tricky to make. It is a simple matter of simmering aromatic vegetables, meats or fish, bones, herbs, and spices with water until a full-flavored liquid is produced. Stock recipes are actually just guidelines; in a traditional kitchen, everything from potato peelings to last night's ham bone goes into the stockpot.

STOCKS

Nothing ensures the success of a homemade soup like a rich, full-flavored stock. So easy to prepare and store, stocks are full of wholesome goodness and, depending on how you season them, can be low in salt. Nevertheless, you need to know how to take advantage of that goodness by ridding the stock or soup of fat.

Greasy soup is high in cholesterol and calories. To remove as much of the fat as possible from stocks and soups, yet make use of the less-expensive fatty meats, you can remove every trace of fat with one of these simple methods:

1. For larger amounts of fat, chill the liquid and lift off the congealed fat.

2. Float a paper towel on the surface of the liquid. When the paper towel has absorbed as much of the grease as possible, discard it. Repeat if necessary.

3. Use a meat baster with a bulb end to suction the grease from the liquid.

Brown Stock

❂ ❂ ❂

For a rich, dark brown stock, the beef is seared before it is simmered. Aromatic vegetables, herbs, and spices round out the flavor for use in soups, sauces, or gravy.

    2 tablespoons vegetable oil
    1 pound lean beef, cut into
       1½-inch cubes
    5 pounds beef bones
    5 quarts cold water
    4 stalks of celery, chopped
    2 medium carrots, chopped
    1 medium onion, chopped
    1 medium turnip, chopped
   10 whole peppercorns
    6 whole cloves
    1 bay leaf
    ½ cup chopped fresh parsley
       salt to taste

1. In a medium-sized skillet, heat the oil and brown the beef on medium heat. In a large soup pot, cover the beef and bones with water. Let stand for 1 hour.

2. Add the vegetables. Tie the peppercorns, cloves, bay leaf, and parsley in a cheesecloth bag and add to the soup pot. Simmer for 3 to 4 hours partially covered.

3. Remove the meat, bones, and vegetables and discard the bones and vegetables. The meat may be used in other dishes. Strain the stock into a shallow container and chill to congeal fat. Lift off hardened fat and discard.

4. Return the stock to the soup pot. Add the salt. Store in the refrigerator and use within 4 days, or freeze (see page 78).

Yield: 3–4 quarts

Chicken Broth

❂ ❂ ❂

This light golden broth is simple and elegant. Vary it by using leeks or shallots, or use garlic in place of the onion and lovage or other fragrant herbs in place of the celery. If you want a stronger poultry flavor, make it with turkey.

1 4–5-pound stewing
  chicken, cut up
6 cups cold water
1 medium carrot, chopped
1 medium onion, chopped
2 stalks of celery, chopped
sliced zest of ½ lemon
1 bay leaf
salt and freshly ground black
  pepper

1. In a large soup pot, cover the chicken parts with the water. Let stand for 1 hour. Add the carrot, onion, celery, and zest. Simmer, covered, for 2 hours. Add the bay leaf and simmer for 15 minutes longer.

2. Remove the chicken, vegetables, and bay leaf. Discard the vegetables and bay leaf; the meat may be used in other dishes. Strain the broth into a shallow container and chill to congeal fat. Lift off hardened fat; discard.

3. Return the broth to the soup pot and reheat. Add the salt and pepper to taste and serve.

Yield: 1 quart

SOUP TOOLS

....

- **SOUP POT.** For a one-meal quantity of soup, a 4- to 6-quart stainless steel or enameled pot is ideal. For two-meal or larger quantities, an 8- to 10-quart stainless steel or enameled pot will hold all the ingredients, yet can be stored easily in the refrigerator.
- **CHEESECLOTH.** Cheesecloth is used in many recipes to strain soup liquid and to make small bags containing herbs and spices for seasoning the soup. One package of cheesecloth usually contains four square yards — plenty for your needs.
- **BLENDER OR FOOD PROCESSOR.** Most of the recipes call for chopping vegetables. Most vegetables can be quickly chopped in a blender or food processor. Or, after cooking, the vegetables may be puréed. The possible exceptions are tough or stringy vegetables, such as celery or asparagus, whose fibers will sometimes survive even metal blades.
- **METAL COLANDER OR FOOD MILL.** Many of the recipes contain the instructions: "Purée in a blender or food processor or force through a metal colander or food mill." If you do not have a blender or food processor, you will need a metal colander (with or without a wooden pestle) or a food mill to extract the pulp of vegetables and remove the tougher portions.
- **SLOW COOKER (CROCK-POT).** If you have enjoyed the convenience a slow cooker can provide, you might want to use it often for making soups, since most of the recipes in this book may be made in a slow cooker. First set the dial on high for 1 hour, then lower the temperature for the duration of the cooking time. Cream soups and soups that require a larger-capacity pot should not be made in a slow cooker.

SUMMER STOCK

During the summer, when barbe-cued chicken is in demand, I stock up on soup stock. Before grilling the chicken, I parboil the chicken pieces in just enough water to cover them for 20 minutes. This ensures that the chicken will be cooked evenly, while cutting down on barbecuing time, and giving me the base for soup stock.

After I remove the chicken from the cooking water, I add onions, celery, carrots, and a few bay leaves to the cooking liquid and cook to reduce the stock to a strongly flavored broth. Then I strain the stock, skim off the fat, and freeze in 2-cup and 3-cup batches for later use.

Vegetable Stock

❂ ❂ ❂

Fresh homemade stock provides a distinct background of flavor to soups and other dishes. Although some consider vegetable stock to be less rich in flavor than meat-based stocks, this version stands up well.

 2 tablespoons vegetable oil
 1 cup chopped onions
 ½ cup chopped carrots
 2 cups chopped celery
 1 cup shredded lettuce
 ¼ cup chopped turnips
 ½ teaspoon sugar
3 ½ quarts cold water
    salt and freshly ground black pepper
    cayenne pepper

1. In a small skillet, heat the oil and sauté the onions until transparent, but not browned.

2. In a large soup pot, cover the onions, carrots, celery, lettuce, turnips, and sugar with the water. (Add any leftover vegetables and cooking water.) Simmer, covered, for 2 hours.

3. Remove the vegetables and discard. Strain the stock through a fine-mesh sieve or three thicknesses of cheesecloth. Return the stock to the soup pot. Add the salt, pepper, and cayenne to taste. Store in the refrigerator and use within 4 days, or freeze.

Yield: 2 quarts

Fish Stock

❂ ❂ ❂

This stock makes Catfish Soup or Fish Chowder tastier. You could even use it instead of water in clam chowder.

 4 pounds white–fleshed fish with bones
 ½ cup chopped carrots
 ½ cup chopped celery
 ½ cup chopped onions
 ½ cup chopped fresh parsley
 2 cloves of garlic, minced
 2 whole cloves
2 ½ quarts cold water
 ½ teaspoon dried thyme
    salt and freshly ground black pepper

1. In a large soup pot, cover all the ingredients except the thyme, salt, and pepper with the water. Simmer, covered, for 2 hours. Add the thyme and simmer, covered, for 15 minutes longer.

2. Remove the fish, bones, and vegetables and discard the bones and vegetables. The fish may be used in other dishes. Strain the stock through three thicknesses of cheesecloth. Return the stock to the soup pot. Add the salt and pepper. Store in the refrigerator and use within 4 days, or freeze.

Yield: 2 quarts

SOUPS

A loaf of bread, a bowl of soup, and a good companion is a recipe for contentment. Whether served in china plates at the start of dinner or in a stoneware mug on the porch swing, soup is one of the true comforts from the kitchen.

Martha's Chicken Noodle Soup

❖ ❖ ❖

Simple and simply delicious, this low-fat soup is just the ticket for grumbly bellies. My grandson Matthew says, "It tastes like MomMom hugs," and I think he's right.

8 cups water
4 boneless, skinless chicken-breast halves
4 large carrots, diced
2 stalks of celery, diced
1 medium onion, chopped
6 chicken bouillon cubes
3 cups cooked elbow macaroni
2 teaspoons dried basil
freshly ground black pepper
grated Parmesan cheese

1. In a large pot, heat water. Add chicken breasts, carrots, celery, onion, and bouillon cubes. Bring to a low boil, then simmer on low for 15 to 20 minutes or until breasts are cooked through.

2. Remove breasts to a plate and cut into bite-size pieces. Return chicken to the pot; add macaroni. Season with basil and pepper to taste. Reheat if necessary (avoid overcooking, which may cause pasta to get mushy). Serve with grated cheese.

Yield: 8–10 servings

Family Soup

❖ ❖ ❖

Leftovers taste like a brand-new dish when they are artfully disguised in a hearty soup. This soup has enough heft to make a great hearthside supper.

bones and leftover beef from beef roast
2 quarts cold water
1 medium onion, chopped
2 stalks of celery, chopped
½ cup barley
4 medium carrots, chopped
2 medium turnips, chopped
1½ cups sliced celery
2 cups tomato juice or purée
salt and freshly ground black pepper

1. In a large soup pot, cover the bones and beef with the water. Let stand for 1 hour. Add the onion and chopped celery. Simmer, covered, for 2 hours.

2. Remove the beef and bones. Discard the bones and set aside the beef. Strain the broth into a shallow container and chill to congeal fat. Lift off hardened fat and discard. Return the broth to the soup pot.

3. Cut the reserved beef into bite-size pieces and add to the soup pot. Add the barley and simmer for 1 hour. Add the carrots, turnips, sliced celery, and juice. Simmer for 20 minutes, or until the vegetables are tender. Add salt and pepper to taste and serve.

Yield: 6 servings

Turkey & Mushroom Soup

❊ ❊ ❊

After the holiday turkey has been picked for salad and sandwiches, we toss the bones into the soup kettle for this deeply flavored soup. We make it with fresh turkey wings the rest of the year.

2 turkey wings (or bones
     from leftover roast turkey)
2 quarts cold water
1 medium carrot, chopped
1 stalk of celery, chopped
1 small onion, chopped
¼ cup uncooked white rice
2 tablespoons butter
2 tablespoons unbleached
     all-purpose flour
1 cup low-fat milk
¼ pound mushrooms, sliced
1 cup half-and-half
   salt and freshly ground black
     pepper

1. In a large soup pot, cover the turkey wings with the water. Let stand for 1 hour. Add the carrot, celery, and onion. Simmer, covered, for 2 to 3 hours.

2. Remove the turkey and set aside. Strain the broth into a shallow container and chill to congeal fat. Lift off hardened fat and discard. Return the broth to the soup pot.

3. Remove the skin and bones from the reserved turkey and discard. Add meat to the soup pot. Bring the broth to a boil and add the rice. Simmer, covered, for 30 minutes or until the rice is tender.

4. In a small saucepan, melt the butter and blend in the flour. Gradually add the milk and cook until thickened, stirring frequently.

5. Add the flour mixture and mushrooms to the soup pot and simmer for 5 minutes, stirring frequently. Add the half-and-half and salt and pepper to taste. Stir well and reheat. Serve.

Yield: 4–5 servings

FREEZING SOUPS

· · · · · · · · · · · · · · · · · · · ·

The convenience, economy, and good flavor that come from making soups in large quantities cannot be underrated. The method is simple: Make a full pot of soup, serve, and freeze the surplus. Better still, when you have an unexpected amount of spare time, double or triple the soup recipe, then store for use on those days when you have no time to prepare a hot meal.

Just complete the recipe, cool the soup, then freeze it in freezer-safe plastic containers or resealable plastic freezer bags at 0°F.

Some soups don't freeze well, including cream soups; bisques; chowders; chilled soups; and fruit and sweet soups containing milk, milk products, or potatoes as the main ingredient. Milk tends to curdle when thawed, and potatoes become grainy. If you plan to freeze the soup you are preparing, do not add salt and pepper. Season the soup after it is thawed and reheated.

To serve frozen soup, thaw and reheat, or reheat over hot water without thawing.

Note: This soup should not be frozen, because it includes milk and half-and-half.

· · · · · · · · · · · · · · · · · · · ·

DRESSING UP YOUR SOUP

· · · · · · · · · · · · · · ·

Float minced fresh chives, scallions, dill, or parsley atop bowls of soup for a brightly accented garnish. Lavender flowers or squash, basil, or chive blossoms will add a touch of elegance. Want a splash of color? Float a nasturtium atop your soup.

· · · · · · · · · · · · · · · · · · · ·

Overnight Hearty Bean Soup

❈ ❈ ❈

This recipe was adapted from a column by Rosemarie Vassalluzzo in *Bucks County Kitchen*. It was passed from friend to friend before it found its permanent home in my recipe file.

1½ cups dried navy beans
 6 cups cold water
 ¼ pound bacon, cut into 1-inch cubes
 1 teaspoon salt
 2 tablespoons olive oil
 ½ pound mushrooms, sliced
 1 large onion, chopped
 2 cups sliced carrots
 2 cups sliced celery
 1 clove of garlic, finely chopped
 3 cups tomatoes
 1 teaspoon each sage, thyme, oregano
 1 bay leaf
 2 cups elbow macaroni
 parsley
 freshly ground black pepper
 grated Parmesan cheese

1. In a large pot, combine the beans and water. Refrigerate overnight.

2. Add the bacon and salt to the beans and water; simmer for 2 hours, covered.

3. Meanwhile, heat the olive oil and gently sauté the mushrooms, onion, carrots, celery, and garlic. Do not brown. Add the tomatoes, sage, thyme, oregano, and bay leaf. Stir to blend, then add to bean mixture.

4. Cook the macaroni, drain, and add to the soup. Simmer gently. Add parsley, pepper, and Parmesan to taste before serving.

Yield: 8–10 servings

Spring Onion Soup

❈ ❈ ❈

The success of this fresh-tasting soup depends on the bright color and crisp texture of the new vegetables. It must be served immediately and should not be reheated.

2 tablespoons butter
2 cups (about 3 bunches) sliced scallions, including some green tops
2 teaspoons minced ginger root

3 tablespoons light soy sauce or tamari
½ cup dry white wine
6 cups chicken broth
 salt
1 cup snow pea pods, strings removed, sliced diagonally in thirds

1. Melt the butter in a soup pot and sauté the scallions and ginger for 2 minutes. Add the soy sauce, wine, chicken broth, and salt to taste. Cook just long enough to soften the scallions, 1 or 2 minutes. Add the pea pods and simmer 1 minute longer. Serve immediately.

Yield: 6 servings

SOUP PARTY

Have a fall harvest soup buffet. Borrow three or four Crock-Pots and make a variety of hearty soups 2 days before your gathering. Pick up fresh breads at a local bakery. Make a salad using the convenient packed lettuce varieties. Serve the soups right in the Crock-Pots, and your buffet is complete! Or, better yet, ask three friends to bring their favorite soups in their own Crock-Pots, and you have to make only one.

Great American Beer Pumpkin Soup

❁ ❁ ❁

This unique soup recipe was developed by Candy Schermerhorn, teacher, author of the *Great American Beer Cookbook*, and TV cooking personality on NBC's affiliate in Phoenix, Arizona. For this soup, Candy recommends using any full-bodied beer that doesn't have a high hops content (in other words, isn't extremely bitter).

1   medium yellow onion
6   cloves of garlic
⅔   cup pecans or walnuts
¼   teaspoon ground ginger
¼   teaspoon ground allspice
1   cup amber lager
4   cups chicken or vegetable
       stock simmered until
       reduced to 2 cups
1½ cups pumpkin purée
1   cup sour cream
1   extra-large egg
½   cup milk
       salt and freshly ground black
          pepper

1. Preheat oven to 350°F. On a baking sheet, roast the unpeeled onion until it's softened like a baked potato, 40 minutes. Bake the unpeeled garlic and the pecans on a baking sheet for 15 minutes.

2. Cool the onion and garlic thoroughly before peeling them.

3. In a food processor, combine the onion, garlic, pecans, ginger, and allspice. Process until fairly smooth.

4. Heat together the lager, stock, and pumpkin. Stir in the puréed mixture. Simmer 15 minutes.

5. Stir in the sour cream.

6. Beat together the egg and milk. Stirring constantly, pour slowly into the soup. Without boiling, heat 10 minutes longer.

7. Season to taste with salt and pepper. Serve hot.

Yield: 6 servings

FOR TASTIER SOUPS

....

Deglazing the pan after sautéing is one of the secrets to a better-tasting soup or stew. Add some liquid to the pan, scrape up the rich residue, and combine with the remaining ingredients.

A. J.'s "Peasant Food" Lentil Soup

❁ ❁ ❁

A longtime friend and a fabulous cook, A. J. Meehan calls this soup "peasant food" because it is cheap and simple, and her Italian mother made it often when times were tough. It is truly delicious, thick, and hearty. We top it with fresh Parmesan and pepper, and serve it with a crusty loaf of bread and a good glass of wine.

1   large head of escarole
½   pound dried lentils
6   cloves of garlic
       salt and freshly ground black
          pepper
¼   cup olive oil

1. Coarsely chop the escarole and steam it with a little water until it becomes limp. Remove the greens and set aside. Add lentils to the pot; add more water until you have 2 to 3 inches of cover.

2. Chop the garlic; add to the lentils. Simmer until the lentils are soft, about 20 to 35 minutes.

3. Return the greens to the pot; add salt and pepper to taste. Pour olive oil over the top before serving.

Yield: 4 servings

Catfish Soup

✵ ✵ ✵

A soup Huck Finn might have enjoyed, this is a perfect use for a lazy day's catch. Use another firm, white fish if you can't find catfish.

6 small catfish, skinned, cleaned, and cut into fillets
1½ pounds cooked lean ham, cut into 1-inch cubes
¼ cup chopped fresh parsley
1 teaspoon dried marjoram
3 stalks of celery, coarsely chopped
2 quarts cold water
4 tablespoons butter, softened
4 tablespoons unbleached all-purpose flour
4 cups low-fat milk
2 egg yolks, slightly beaten
salt and freshly ground black pepper

1. In a large soup pot, cover the catfish, ham, parsley, marjoram, and celery with the water. Simmer, covered, for 30 minutes, or until the fish is tender but not overcooked.

2. Strain the soup stock through three thicknesses of cheesecloth; return the stock to the soup pot. Return the fish and ham to the soup pot. Discard the cooked herbs and celery. Reheat the stock.

3. In a large saucepan, melt the butter and blend in the flour. Gradually add the milk and cook until thickened, stirring frequently. Add the egg yolks and cook on low heat, stirring, for 2 minutes. Add the egg mixture to the fish and ham mixture. Stir well and reheat. Add salt and pepper to taste and serve.

Yield: 6–8 servings

Note: This soup should not be frozen.

SOUP'S ON

....

BISQUE: A thick, smooth soup of puréed vegetables, seafood, or chicken with a cream base.

CHOWDER: A chunky soup made with a milk or stewed-tomato base. Commonly made with seafood, often with vegetables as well.

CONSOMMÉ: A clarified meat or fish broth that can be served hot or cold and is sometimes used as a soup or sauce base.

COULIS: When referring to soup, a thick, puréed shellfish soup. Otherwise, a thick purée.

GUMBO: A thick, stewlike soup made with spicy sausage, shellfish, and a variety of vegetables, usually including okra. In fact, the name "gumbo" is derived from an African word for okra.

PURÉE: A thick, smooth mass of mashed or strained vegetables or other foods; purées are often used to thicken soups. Cooked vegetables may be puréed in a food mill, blender, or food processor.

ROUX: A mixture of flour and butter, cooked until smooth, that is used to thicken liquids.

STOCK: Vegetables, meat, poultry, or fish and seasonings cooked in water to make a flavored broth as the base for soups and stews.

CREAM SOUPS

Cream soups have a velvety smoothness that endears them to children and grown-ups alike. Whether the mixture gets its creamy texture from rich milk, heavy cream, or a buttery roux, the resulting soup will feel like indulgence.

Cream of Tomato Soup

✠ ✠ ✠

This soup is best made in the late summer when the tomatoes are abundant in the garden, but canned tomatoes can be used as well. Double the recipe for a great camp meal, served straight from the pot with cuts from an oversize sandwich.

4   cups chopped fresh tomatoes
1   onion, chopped
4   whole cloves
6   peppercorns
1   teaspoon brown sugar
1   teaspoon salt

4   sprigs parsley
3   tablespoons butter
3   tablespoons flour
1½ cups chicken broth
1   cup heavy cream

1. Simmer the tomatoes, onion, cloves, peppercorns, sugar, salt, and parsley together for 10 minutes. Run through a food mill.

2. Melt the butter; add flour and stir until golden. Pour in chicken broth and stir until thickened. Add the tomato mixture and simmer 5 minutes; cool slightly before adding cream. Heat through, but do not boil.

Yield: 6 servings

VARIATION: Omit the salt and parsley, and use light cream instead of heavy. Cook 2 slices of chopped bacon with the onions, cloves, and peppercorns; stir in the brown sugar, then the tomatoes. Simmer 10 to 15 minutes. Proceed as directed.

SIMPLEST CREAM SOUP

You can easily turn your favorite vegetable into a creamy, delectable soup. Simply purée the vegetable, then add a few cups of milk or cream, and you have a cream soup. Or just serve the purée piping hot with a pat of butter on top, and you have an elegant side dish.

Cream of Broccoli Soup

✠ ✠ ✠

MomMom Storey persuaded chef Albert Stockley, whom she met on a visit to Connecticut's Stonehenge Restaurant in the early 1970s, to give her this recipe. She greatly enjoyed meeting him, and our family requests this soup often.

1   tablespoon butter
2   slices bacon, chopped
1   medium onion, chopped
1   small leek or 2 scallions, chopped
1   stalk of celery, chopped
1   tablespoon all-purpose flour
4   cups chicken or beef stock
    florets from 1 large head of broccoli, chopped
½   teaspoon salt
    freshly ground black pepper
    dash of ground nutmeg
1   cup light cream

1. Melt butter. Sauté bacon, then add onion, leek, and celery. Cook until heated through.

2. Add flour and stir until well combined. Stir in stock; simmer for 15 minutes.

3. Add broccoli; simmer for 15 minutes. Pour into

blender and purée. Return to pot and season with salt, pepper, and nutmeg. Stir in cream and cook until heated through; do not boil.

Yield: 4–6 servings

VARIATION: Make it spinach soup. Use chicken stock and substitute 1 pound well-washed spinach with tough stems removed for the broccoli. Simmer 8 minutes after adding the spinach.

Squashyssoise (Squash Soup)

❈ ❈ ❈

This is a sensational takeoff on traditional leek and potato vichyssoise. Summer squash and onions are blended into a creamy potage.

4   *medium onions, minced*
2   *tablespoons butter*
2   *cups summer squash*
4   *cups chicken broth or bouillon*
1   *cup milk or cream*
    salt and freshly ground black pepper

1. In a medium skillet, sauté the onions in butter until translucent. Remove onions and set aside.
2. Sauté the squash until soft. Add 1 cup of the chicken broth.

3. Pour this mixture gradually with the reserved onions into a blender or food processor with the motor running; blend until smooth. Return to a large saucepan along with the remaining broth, milk, and salt and pepper to taste. Serve hot or cold.

Yield: 4 servings

Sweet Potato, Bacon & Maple Bisque

❈ ❈ ❈

What a wonderful cold-weather soup this is! The maple lifts the sweetness and flavor of the sweet potatoes, while the bacon and onion add depth and contrast. Serve this with corn bread or corn muffins and a mixed-greens salad topped with a mustardy vinaigrette.

4   *cups peeled, diced sweet potatoes*
4   *cups water*
6   *slices bacon*
1   *small onion, minced*
1½ *cups light cream or milk*
    salt
¼   *cup pure maple syrup*
¼   *teaspoon ground cinnamon*

1. Combine the potatoes and water in a large, heavy-bottomed soup pot. Bring to a boil; cover and reduce heat to a simmer. Cook for

about 20 minutes, until the potatoes are very tender. Remove from heat; do not drain.
2. While the potatoes are cooking, fry the bacon in a skillet until crisp. Remove from the pan and blot with paper towels. Pour out all but about 3 tablespoons of the fat, then add the onion and sauté for 5 minutes. Remove from heat.
3. Working in batches, purée the potatoes and cooking water in a blender or food processor. (Always be careful when puréeing hot liquids in the blender. Never fill the container more than one-third full to avoid the risk of the lid's blowing off.) Return the purée to the soup pot; stir in the onion, cream, salt to taste, maple syrup, and cinnamon.
4. Crumble the bacon into bits and add to the pot. Heat, but do not boil, and serve piping hot. Put a small dollop of sour cream in each bowl, if that sounds good.

Yield: 4–6 servings

VARIATION: Use ham instead of bacon, in which case you would simply sauté the onion in some butter.

CHOWDERS

Chowder gets its name from a French word for "soup pot," chaudière, *which in turn derives from* chaud, *meaning "hot." The lure of a tureen of steaming chowder is as enticing today as it must have been for colonial fishermen returning from the sea on a cold evening.*

Aunt Helen's Manhattan Clam Chowder

Aunt Helen serves this during the summer when we visit the beach with her family. It's best made with fresh clams and ripe garden tomatoes, but canned will do.

- 6 *slices bacon, diced*
- 1 *large onion, chopped*
- 2 *large potatoes, diced*
- 1 *bottle (8 ounces) clam juice*
- 20 *fresh clams or 2 cans (8 ounces each) minced clams*
- 1 *pound tomatoes, peeled and coarsely chopped*
- 1 *teaspoon salt*
- *freshly ground black pepper*
- ½ *teaspoon thyme*

1. Sauté the bacon and onion together. Add the potatoes and clam juice. Simmer, covered, for 15 minutes or until potatoes are tender.

2. Stir in the clams, with their juice if using canned, and tomatoes. Simmer until bubbly and season with salt, pepper to taste, and thyme.

Yield: 4–6 servings

New England Clam Chowder

If fresh clams are not available, substitute three 6½-ounce cans of whole or chopped clams with liquid.

- 24 *fresh clams in the shell*
- 4 *cups boiling water*
- 2 *tablespoons butter*
- 1 *small onion, chopped*
- 2 *slices lean bacon, cooked and crumbled*
- 4 *medium potatoes, thinly sliced*
- 4 *cups water*
- 1 *quart milk or half-and-half*
- *salt and freshly ground black pepper*

1. Clean the clams thoroughly with a vegetable brush. In a large soup pot, cover the unopened clams with the boiling water. As each shell opens, remove the clam and set aside. Pour the liquor from each shell into the soup pot.

2. Remove the thin skin from each reserved clam and cut off the black end and discard. Chop the tough parts of the clams and leave the soft parts whole. Set aside.

3. In a small saucepan, melt 1 tablespoon of the butter and sauté the onion until transparent. Add the onion, bacon,

About Fresh Clams

Fresh clams should be tightly closed with unbroken shells. To prepare for cooking, scrub the shells and then soak the clams in cold salted water (⅓ cup salt to each gallon of water) to remove sand and grit. Some people sprinkle the water with cornmeal when soaking. Discard any clams that float. Open clams by inserting a knife between the shells. For easier opening, set the clams on a tray in the freezer for about 40 minutes; they will begin to open slightly. Clams should be cooked on low heat to keep them from getting tough.

potatoes, and the water to the soup pot. Simmer, covered, for 25 minutes, or until the potatoes are tender.

4. Add the reserved clams, milk, and remaining butter and simmer for 10 minutes. Add salt and pepper to taste and serve with crackers.

Yield: 8–10 servings

Herbed Corn Chowder

❁ ❁ ❁

My son Matt's favorite, this is a soup I keep warm in my slow cooker (on low) when family and friends are coming in from out of town. It's a great way to provide a soothing "welcome home."

    6 slices bacon
    1 medium onion, chopped
    1 medium green bell pepper,
       diced (or ½ cup frozen
       green pepper)
    2 cans (16 ounces each)
       cream-style corn
    2 cans (10¾ ounces each)
       potato soup
    2 cans milk

    1 tablespoon snipped fresh
       chives
    1 tablespoon finely chopped
       fresh parsley
    1 teaspoon chopped fresh
       dill or thyme

1. Cook the bacon in a large pan. Add the onion and pepper and sauté in the bacon fat until softened. Add the corn, potato soup, and milk to the pan; stir until smooth and hot, about 10 minutes.

2. While the chowder is warming up, add the chives, parsley, and dill.

Yield: 8–10 servings

Fish Chowder

❁ ❁ ❁

Asked what kind of fish was in her delicious chowder, a Nova Scotia fisherman's wife answered that she just went to the freezer and took out whatever was available. The fish chunks were all very white, and the broth was white and sweet, something like this filling soup.

    1½ pounds white fish fillets
    2   cups water
    3   medium potatoes
    2   scallions
    ¼   cup diced salt pork
    1   onion, chopped
    1   teaspoon chopped fresh
        thyme

    ½ cup chopped fresh parsley
    3 cups milk
    1 tablespoon chopped fresh
       tarragon
    salt and freshly ground black
    pepper

1. Cut the fish into chunks and put it into a pot with the water. Simmer over medium heat for 3 or 4 minutes. Remove the pot from the burner and set aside.

2. Peel the potatoes and cut into paper-thin slices. Cut the scallions into 1-inch pieces and shred.

3. In a large soup pot, cook the salt pork until it is golden brown. Remove the browned pieces with a slotted spoon and place on a double thickness of paper towels to drain.

4. Drain from the pot all but 2 tablespoons of the pork fat. Add the onion, thyme, and half the parsley. Cook for 2 or 3 minutes until softened. Pour the fish cooking liquid into the pot. Add the potatoes, scallions, salt pork, and enough water to cover. Boil until the potatoes are cooked, about 10 minutes.

5. Add the fish, milk, tarragon, and salt and pepper to taste. Heat thoroughly, but don't boil. Ladle the soup into bowls and sprinkle the remaining parsley over the top of each serving.

Yield: 4–5 servings

GUMBO & CHILI

America's melting pot of cultures has greatly enriched the contents of its soup kettles. My family grew up on fiery Texas chili, with its Spanish influences, and heady Creole gumbo from neighboring Louisiana.

Knock-Your-Socks-Off Chili

❈ ❈ ❈

Folks up North consider this a chili with personality. Westerners may deem it a little on the tame side and perk it up with additional chili powder or jalapeño peppers. Whatever your taste preference — spicy, spicier, or spiciest — it's an all-time favorite.

- 2 pounds lean ground beef
- 1 pound lean pork, cut into ½-inch cubes
- 4 cups coarsely chopped onion
- 3 cloves of garlic, minced
- 1 cup chopped green bell pepper
- 3 tablespoons chili powder (or to taste)
- ½ cup beer
- 4 cups tomato purée
- ¾ cup tomato paste
- 4 ripe tomatoes, peeled and coarsely chopped
- 1 teaspoon ground cumin
- 1 bay leaf
- ½ teaspoon freshly ground black pepper
- 1 teaspoon oregano
- 4 cups cooked red kidney beans
- 1 cup shredded Monterey Jack or Cheddar cheese
- 2 flour tortillas, cut into wedges

1. Brown the beef and pork in a large soup kettle. Stir in the onions, garlic, and bell pepper. Cook until tender.

2. Add the chili powder, beer, tomato purée and paste, chopped tomatoes, cumin, bay leaf, black pepper, and oregano. Mix well. Simmer slowly for 1½ hours, stirring occasionally.

3. Add the kidney beans and cook 30 minutes longer. Remove and discard the bay leaf. Ladle the chili into bowls. Sprinkle generously with the cheese. Serve piping hot with tortilla wedges.

Yield: 6–8 servings

Vegetable Chili

❈ ❈ ❈

This is a hot dish for a cold day. Make up a large batch over the weekend to freeze for quick meals throughout the week. Try serving it with corn chips or squares of warm corn bread and a bottle of hot sauce for the die-hards.

- 1 yellow onion, diced
- 2 green bell peppers, diced
- 2 cans (14½ ounces each) stewed whole tomatoes
- 2 cans (15 ounces each) black beans
- 1 can (16 ounces) cooked corn
- 1 can (15 ounces) kidney beans

THINK SOUP

Think "soup" all during the week as you prepare meals. Almost any freshly cooked meat or vegetable can provide an ingredient for the soup pot. Save the cooking water from fresh vegetables and the liquid from canned vegetables. Scrub vegetables well before peeling; add parings to the stockpot or store them in a plastic bag in the refrigerator for a few days. Reserve celery leaves, spinach stems, and the trimmed parts of asparagus, broccoli, scallions, and other vegetables. Simmer leftover bones from cooked meats to make stock; label and freeze surplus.

½ tablespoon chili powder
1 teaspoon cayenne pepper
½ teaspoon cinnamon
   salt and freshly ground black
   pepper
2 fresh tomatoes, diced
2 cups shredded low-fat
   Cheddar cheese (optional)

1. Spray a large pot with vegetable cooking spray. Over medium heat, sauté the onion and peppers until they just begin to brown.

2. Add the tomatoes, black beans, corn, kidney beans, and the liquid from all six cans, as well as the chili powder, cayenne, and cinnamon to the pot. Bring to a boil, reduce heat, and simmer for at least 30 minutes, or until the mixture reaches desired consistency. Season with salt and pepper.

3. Ladle into bowls, topping with diced tomatoes and Cheddar, if desired.

Yield: 10 servings

Chicken Gumbo

❈ ❈ ❈

A pot of this gumbo may transport you to the Mississippi delta. There are thousands of variations, but it's the okra that gives gumbo its characteristic flavor and texture.

¼ cup vegetable oil
1 4–5-pound stewing
   chicken, cut up
¾ pound lean veal, cut into
   1½-inch cubes
1 small onion, sliced
7 cups boiling water
1 cup fresh or frozen whole-
   kernel corn
1 quart okra, cut into
   ½-inch slices
   salt and freshly ground black
   pepper
½ teaspoon filé powder or
   1 bay leaf, crushed

1. In a large skillet, heat the oil and brown the chicken and veal. Add the onion. Cook, covered, for 10 minutes, stirring occasionally. Drain off the fat.

2. Place the meat and onion in a large soup pot. Add the water. Simmer, covered, for 2 hours. Remove the skin and bones from the chicken and discard. Return the chicken to the soup pot.

3. Add the corn and okra and cook on medium heat for 15 minutes. Add salt and pepper to taste.

4. Before serving, add the filé powder and stir well.

Yield: 8–10 servings

- - - - - - - - - - - - - - - - - -

TOPPERS

· · · · · · · · · · · · · · · ·

Add croutons and other toppers to enhance your soups. Grated cheese, diced bell peppers, chopped parsley, sliced olives, and paprika add color; small crackers, chow mein noodles, toasted nuts, crumbled French-fried onion rings, and broken corn chips add crunch; chopped chives or mint, grated Parmesan cheese, diced cucumbers, and thinly sliced lemons or grated lemon zest add flavor. For simple croutons, spread white or whole-wheat bread slices with garlic butter or butter and grated cheese. Cut slices into small squares. Broil for 2 to 3 minutes until golden brown.

- - - - - - - - - - - - - - - - - -

CHILLED SOUPS

One great thing about chilled soups is that they actually taste better if they are made ahead, so they are ideal for effortless entertaining. A side benefit is that they are such a refreshing way to eat your vegetables — or fruit!

Bubbie's Borscht

❁ ❁ ❁

Originally from Russia and Poland, borscht is a favorite in many families and recipes for it are frequently passed along. Ruth Bass got this recipe from her mother-in-law, then passed it beyond her own circle of family and friends by sharing it in her book *Herbal Soups*. The elder Mrs. Bass served it with boiled new potatoes, which she plunked hot into the soup plate for a contrast to the cool soup.

½ pound beets with tops
2 large carrots
2 medium onions, chopped
3 cups water
2 cups vegetable stock
1 cup shredded cabbage
2 cloves of garlic, minced
1 bay leaf
2 tablespoons lemon juice

salt and freshly ground black pepper
low-fat sour cream

1. Cut off beet tops, leaving 2 inches of stem. In a large soup pot, cover the whole beets, whole carrots, and onions with the water. Simmer, covered, for about 20 minutes.

2. Remove the beets, slip off skins, and return the beets to the soup pot. Add the stock, cabbage, garlic, and bay leaf. Simmer, covered, for 15 minutes. Remove the bay leaf and discard.

3. Purée the vegetables in a blender or food processor, or force through a metal colander or food mill. Return the vegetable mixture to the soup pot. Add the lemon juice and salt and pepper to taste. Stir well; chill several hours or overnight.

4. Garnish each serving with a dollop of the sour cream.

Yield: 8 servings

Note: Borscht also may be served hot.

Leftover-Salad Soup

❁ ❁ ❁

Don't toss that leftover salad; whirl it into a quick chilled soup. You may find yourself making salad just for the soup, it's so good.

4 cups leftover dressed green salad
1 cup buttermilk
½ cup yogurt
¼ cup sour cream
1 tablespoon lemon juice
1 clove of garlic, minced
1 tablespoon minced fresh dill
6 tablespoons water
¾ cup diced tomatoes

1. Purée the salad in a food processor or blender.

2. Add the buttermilk, yogurt, sour cream, lemon juice, garlic, dill, and water. Purée until smooth.

3. Pour into a serving bowl and stir in tomatoes. Serve chilled.

Yield: 3–4 servings

Note: Vary the amount of liquid according to the amount of leftover salad that you have. Add more lemon juice if it wasn't dressed with a vinaigrette dressing.

Gazpacho

❖ ❖ ❖

Of Spanish heritage, this soup has become a cool summer staple. And no wonder! It's like eating a garden in a bowl, and so refreshing on a sultry day.

 1 cup chopped onions
 1 cup chopped green bell pep-
    pers (2–3 medium peppers)
 4 cloves of garlic, finely
    chopped
 3 tablespoons chopped fresh
    parsley
 4 tablespoons vegetable oil
 2–3 cucumbers, chopped
    (2 cups)
 5–6 ripe red tomatoes (2 cups
    peeled and chopped)
 6 ounces tomato paste
 2 teaspoons vinegar
 ½ teaspoon salt
 ¼ teaspoon freshly ground
    black pepper
    dash of lemon juice
    dash of crushed red pepper
    pinch of sugar

1. Sauté the onions, peppers, garlic, and parsley in 3 tablespoons of the oil for about 5 minutes, just until the vegetables are a bit soft.

2. Combine the sautéed vegetables with the cucumbers and tomatoes in a blender. Process until well blended.

3. In a large bowl, combine the vegetables with the tomato paste, the remaining 1 tablespoon of oil, and the vinegar. Season with the salt, pepper, lemon juice, crushed red pepper, and sugar to taste. Refrigerate for at least 4 hours. Stir before serving.

Yield: 4 servings

Sour Cherry Soup

❖ ❖ ❖

Cooked, puréed fruit combined with cream, milk, water, wine, or a light stock makes a Scandinavian specialty, a fruit soup. These soups are most often served cold, like this sweet-and-sour specialty, and make fine first courses or desserts.

 2 pounds sour cherries,
    pitted
 1½ cups sugar
 2 cups water
 2 tablespoons cornstarch
 4 cups low-fat milk

1. In a large soup pot, combine the cherries, sugar, and water. Simmer, covered, for 20 minutes.

2. Purée the cherries in a blender or food processor, or force through a metal colander or food mill. Return the cherry mixture to the soup pot.

3. In a small bowl, dissolve the cornstarch in 2 tablespoons of the milk and add to the soup pot. Cook until thickened, stirring frequently. Add the remaining milk and blend well. Chill for at least 1 hour. Serve.

Yield: 2 quarts

VARIATION: Substitute blueberries for the cherries.

Chilled Strawberry Soup

❖ ❖ ❖

An ice-cold fruit soup in a chilled bowl tames the midsummer heat. Look for strawberries that are ripe but firm. If you're picking the berries yourself, harvest them in the afternoon, when they've gained sweetness from the sun.

 1 quart fresh strawberries
 1 cup sugar
 1 cup plain yogurt
 2 teaspoons minced fresh
    mint
 4 cups ice water
 ¾ cup dry white wine

1. Chop the strawberries in a food processor, and then force them through a sieve. In a large bowl, combine the strawberries, sugar, yogurt, and mint.

2. Add the ice water and white wine; sample for sweetness, adding more sugar if needed. Chill for at least 2 hours before serving.

Yield: 8 servings

DIPS & SPREADS

There is something innately pleasing about sharing a communal bowl of food with family and friends. Add to that the fun of "hands-on" eating, and you can account for the popularity of dips and spreads. For good health's sake, provide crudités — raw veggies — along with the breads, crackers, and chips.

Garlicky Mushroom Spread

❈ ❈ ❈

For a tasty appetizer, make this mushroom spread ahead of time. Several hours of chilling will allow the flavors of the rosemary and shiitakes to blend. Take it out of the refrigerator half an hour before serving.

    1 whole bulb of garlic
  2–3 tablespoons extra virgin
         olive oil
    4 large shallots, finely
         chopped
   ½ cup chicken broth
    1 pound shiitake mush-
         rooms, wiped clean, stems
         discarded
    1 teaspoon minced fresh
         rosemary
    2 teaspoons minced fresh
         Italian flat-leaf parsley
    1 tablespoon Marsala wine

    6 black olives, pitted
       salt and freshly ground black
         pepper

1. Preheat oven to 350°F. Slice a thin layer off the top of the bulb of garlic. Brush a little oil in a small ovenproof pan, add the unpeeled garlic bulb, and drizzle 1 tablespoon of the oil over the top. Roast for 15 minutes.

2. In a large skillet, heat the rest of the oil and cook the shallots over low heat, stirring frequently, for about 10 to 12 minutes, or until they are soft. Add the broth, increase the heat, and cook another minute. With a slotted spoon, transfer the shallots to a food processor or blender, leaving all the liquid in the pan.

3. Add the mushrooms to the skillet and cook over medium heat, stirring often. Add the rosemary and parsley and continue cooking until the mushrooms are tender.

4. Pop the roasted cloves of garlic out of their skins and into the food processor or blender. Add the mushrooms, wine, and olives to the processor or blender. Process until creamy. Season with

salt and pepper to taste and chill. Serve on plain crackers or rye rounds.
Yield: 1½ cups

Salsa Ranchero

❈ ❈ ❈

Here's a country salsa, more informal than most. It's a cooked salsa with just a touch of heat. For a southwestern breakfast treat, *huevos rancheros,* poach eggs in this salsa, or use it to dress up fried eggs.

   ¾ cup minced onion
   ½ teaspoon minced garlic
    1 jalapeño pepper, minced
    1 pound tomatoes, peeled,
         seeded, and chopped
   ¼ cup water
   ½ teaspoon dried oregano
   ½ teaspoon sugar
   ¼ teaspoon salt

1. Put all of the ingredients into a medium-sized nonreactive saucepan. Bring to a boil, then turn the heat down and simmer for 15 minutes, or until the onions and tomatoes are soft. For a smooth sauce, run it in a blender or food processor. This salsa will keep for weeks if refrigerated.
Yield: About 2 cups

Ginger Dip

❈ ❈ ❈

This Asian-style dip is a personal favorite. Serve it with a pleasing platter of zucchini and carrot strips, raw snow or sugar snap peas, trimmed scallions, sliced white radish, sliced mushrooms, and perhaps some steamed shrimp.

1 cup mayonnaise
4 tablespoons soy sauce
1 teaspoon ground ginger
2 teaspoons grated onion
1 teaspoon cider vinegar
2 tablespoons milk
(optional)

1. Combine the mayonnaise, soy sauce, ginger, onion, and vinegar. Add milk if the dip is too thick.

2. Cover and chill at least 2 hours.

Yield: 1½ cups

Hummus

❈ ❈ ❈

John's sister Helen is a great cook, who shared this recipe and others during one of our Thanksgiving gatherings at her home near Cape Cod, Massachusetts. Helen says that this one can't have too much lemon or garlic, so follow the recipe loosely!

1 can (16 ounces) chickpeas, drained and rinsed
¼ cup lemon juice (juice of 2 lemons)
3 cloves of garlic, minced
3 tablespoons tahini
3 tablespoons water
salt and freshly ground black pepper

1. In a food processor, process the chickpeas, lemon juice, garlic, and tahini. Add water, one tablespoon at a time, if needed to achieve a creamy consistency. Add salt and pepper to taste; add more garlic or lemon juice if desired. Serve with wedges of pita bread, toasted or not.

Yield: About 2 cups

VARIATION: Add ½ teaspoon ground cumin.

Dilly of a Dip

❈ ❈ ❈

Quick and easy, this dip can be made on the spot for last-minute guests, though its flavors blend and the taste improves if you chill it for a few hours.

⅔ cup sour cream or low-fat sour cream
⅔ cup mayonnaise or low-fat mayonnaise
2 tablespoons minced onion or chives
1 tablespoon minced celery, or ½ teaspoon celery seeds
1 tablespoon minced fresh dill, or 1 teaspoon dried dillweed

1. Combine the sour cream, mayonnaise, onion, celery, and dill in a small bowl. Cover and refrigerate overnight.

2. Serve with raw or lightly blanched vegetables or crackers.

Yield: About 1½ cups

VARIATIONS: Add 1 tablespoon horseradish. For a spicier version, add 1 tablespoon chili sauce, 1 clove of garlic, minced, and ½ teaspoon dry mustard.

HOW MUCH DO I NEED?

....

When serving hors d'oeuvres, a good rule of thumb is to plan for 8 pieces per person if you are also serving dinner, 12 pieces per person if you are serving only hors d'oeuvres.

CHEESE, PLEASE

*C*heese is the basis of many classic snacks. It turns the goodness of milk into all sorts of tantalizing flavors and textures. It melts, it slices, it crumbles, and it spreads. And it is a good choice if you're serving drinks, because its fat content slows the absorption of alcohol.

Sage Cheese Spread

❈ ❈ ❈

*S*age and mustard add depth to this easy cheese spread. It takes only minutes to prepare, and it makes a lovely hostess gift.

1 cup dry or small curd cottage cheese
½ cup extra-sharp Cheddar cheese, grated and at room temperature
4 teaspoons chopped fresh sage, or 2 teaspoons dried
1 teaspoon prepared mustard

1. Mix all ingredients in a blender or food processor until smooth and creamy. Store in a crock in the refrigerator at least 24 hours before serving.

Yield: 1½ cups

Corn Cheese Puffs

❈ ❈ ❈

*T*hese golden puffs of corn and cheese are almost like a baked corn fritter; they make a great "finger food" for a party.

¼ cup butter
1 cup milk
½ teaspoon salt
1 cup unbleached all-purpose flour
4 eggs
1 cup grated Swiss cheese
½ teaspoon chili powder
1 teaspoon minced fresh basil, or ¼ teaspoon dried
⅛ teaspoon cayenne pepper
2 cups corn kernels

- - - - - - - - - - - - - - - - -

CHEESE AND . . .

. . . .

One of the easiest and best-loved snacks of all is a board of cheese and fruit. You can add biscuits or crackers and a pot of raspberry mustard, if you like. Some classic combinations include blue cheeses, such as Stilton or Gorgonzola, with pears, Cheddar or Havarti with apples, Cheddar or Brie with grapes, and chèvre with strawberries.

- - - - - - - - - - - - - - - - -

1. Preheat oven to 375°F. In a small saucepan, combine the butter, milk, and salt. Bring to a boil and remove the pan from the heat.

2. Add the flour and stir well. The dough will form a ball, rolling off the sides of the pan. Return the pan to the heat and cook for about 1 minute to dry out the dough, stirring constantly.

3. Remove the pan from the heat and stir in the eggs, one at a time. Add the cheese, chili powder, basil, cayenne, and corn; stir well.

4. Grease a baking sheet and drop teaspoons of dough onto it, leaving at least 2 inches between each puff. Bake for 25 minutes or until puffy and browned. Serve hot.

*Yield: 20–24 puffs
(6–8 servings)*

Bacon Cheese Ball

❈ ❈ ❈

*P*ut some unpeeled apple slices on the platter along with an assortment of crackers and cocktail breads when you serve this zippy cheese ball.

1 pound low-fat cream cheese

½ pound lean bacon,
    browned and crumbled
4 scallions, finely diced
1 medium green tomato,
    finely chopped
1 cup finely chopped walnuts

1. In a small bowl, mix cream cheese, bacon, scallions, and tomato. Cover with the walnuts. Chill for at least 1 hour before serving.

Yield: 8–10 servings

Pimiento Cheese Spread

❉ ❉ ❉

So-called "Paminna" cheese is a staple in most southern homes, and there are as many recipes as there are ways to eat it. My mother keeps hers simple, and though it "lasts forever," it's never around long.

1 pound Velveeta cheese
1 jar (4 ounces) roasted
    pimientos, chopped
½ cup mayonnaise

1. Cut cheese into ¼-inch chunks. Add chopped pimientos with their juice. Add mayonnaise; mix until thoroughly blended. Add more mayon-

naise if needed to achieve spreading consistency.

2. Store, tightly covered, in the refrigerator. Spread on crackers, raw vegetables, sandwiches, or toast.

Yield: About 3½ cups

Pub-Style Cheese Spread

❉ ❉ ❉

An all-time favorite in English pubs, this spicy spread is best if aged at least a week in the refrigerator.

½ cup beer
1 pound white Cheddar
    cheese, grated
4 tablespoons butter, softened
2 tablespoons snipped fresh
    chives
2 tablespoons finely chopped
    fresh parsley
1 tablespoon grated sweet
    onion
1 teaspoon lemon juice
½ teaspoon dry mustard
3 cloves of garlic, peeled and
    halved

1. In a blender or food processor, combine the beer, Cheddar, butter, chives, parsley, onion, lemon juice, and mustard. Process until blended and smooth.

2. Spoon one-third of the mixture into a crock or jar with an airtight cover. Push 2 garlic halves into the mix-

ture. Add another one-third of the mixture. Insert 2 more garlic halves. Fill the crock with the remaining cheese mixture and garlic.

3. Cut a circle of wax paper to the size of the crock top; cover the cheese mixture with the wax paper. Seal the crock tightly. Age the spread in the refrigerator and remove garlic cloves before serving.

Yield: 2 cups

VARIATION: For a Club-Style Cheese Spread, substitute ½ cup brandy or cognac for the beer.

. . . .

FUN SPREAD IDEAS

. . . .

- Cream cheese and chopped olives
- Pimiento cheese spread (jalapeño or mild)
- Chopped nuts, raisins, dates, or prunes moistened with mayonnaise and lemon
- Potted ham with pickle relish, Dijon mustard, and cream cheese
- Sautéed mushrooms and onions mixed with cottage cheese
- Chicken livers sautéed with onions and garlic salt, mashed, and mixed with mayonnaise
- Peanut butter, honey, and raisins

. . . .

PASTRY BITES

Sometimes we want to go all out for a special occasion. That is when we go the extra step to make special appetizer pastries. Prepared phyllo dough and puff pastry make such delicacies much easier than they look!

Savory Vegetable Turnovers

⧇ ⧇ ⧇

Phyllo pastry makes easy, melt-in-your mouth turnovers. Use green or wax beans in the filling; even mature beans or canned beans can be used.

½ pound yellow or green
    beans, diced
¼ cup olive oil
1 cup diced onion
½ pound mushrooms, sliced
½ cup chopped walnuts
¼ cup minced fresh basil
1 cup grated Parmesan
    cheese
⅓ cup heavy cream
¾ pound phyllo dough
½ cup melted butter

1. Preheat oven to 350°F.
2. Steam the beans until tender crisp, about 3 minutes.
3. Heat the oil in a sauté pan, and sauté the onion and mushrooms until browned,

3 to 5 minutes. Mix the onion, mushrooms, beans, walnuts, basil, Parmesan, and cream.

4. On a dry surface, lay out two sheets of phyllo dough on top of each other and brush the top sheet with melted butter. Fold the dough in half lengthwise. Place about ½ cup of the filling on one end of the dough. Fold one end of dough over the filling; brush the dough adjacent to the filled triangle with butter; fold the triangle up onto the dough. Continue folding to the end of the dough, brushing on butter between each fold. (You are folding as you would a flag.)
5. Place the turnover on a greased cookie sheet. Repeat to make six turnovers. Bake for 35 minutes or until golden brown.

Yield: 6 servings

Baked Brie with Fresh Fruit

⧇ ⧇ ⧇

A wrapping of phyllo pastry and a short stint in the oven give Brie a buttery crisp exterior and a warm oozy interior. A perfect complement to cool fresh fruit.

1 package (1 pound) phyllo
    dough
½ cup (1 stick) butter, melted
1½ pounds Brie, cut into
    8 wedges
    grapes
    strawberries
    apple wedges

1. Unroll the phyllo sheets and keep them covered with plastic wrap to prevent them from drying out. Remove two sheets of phyllo and brush the top one with butter.

PUFF PASTRY

....

Puff pastry gets its meltingly flaky texture from thin layers of butter folded into it; as the butter melts during baking, steam pockets form, causing the pastry to puff up. Puff pastry is excellent for rich little appetizers with savory fillings. Frozen puff pastry sheets are a real time-saver and very easy to use.

2. Place a wedge of the Brie diagonally on the phyllo sheet, about 2 inches from one corner. Fold the phyllo to cover the cheese and continue to roll the Brie up in the phyllo sheet. Fold the ends in when half of the phyllo is used up. Finish rolling until the whole sheet is used and the Brie is neatly packaged. Brush the outside with butter to prevent flaking. Repeat the process until all the Brie is used. Chill the wrapped Brie for 30 minutes. (It can be refrigerated, wrapped tightly with plastic wrap, for a day.)

3. Preheat oven to 400°F. Bake the phyllo on a baking sheet for 10 to 12 minutes or until golden brown.

4. Line a basket with a napkin; gently place baked Brie in it. Arrange the fruit around it and serve.

Yield: 8 servings

Leeks & Sausage in Puff Pastry

❂ ❂ ❂

These are heaven — savory filling in puff pastry. Tiny ones make elegant appetizers, but for a memorable brunch or lunch, prepare the larger version and indulge.

- 1 *package (17¼ ounces) frozen puff pastry sheets*
- 1 *pound lean bulk pork sausage, crumbled*
- 2 *tablespoons butter*
- 3 *leeks, cleaned, trimmed, and sliced, with some of the green part*
- 2 *shallots, chopped*
- ½ *cup cream*
- ¼ *cup sour cream*

1. Thaw the puff pastry. Unfold the sheets. Divide the dough into eight equal squares with a sharp knife. Preheat oven to 400°F.

2. In a large, heavy skillet, cook the sausage until brown. Remove with a slotted spoon; drain on paper towels. Discard pan drippings.

3. Melt the butter and sauté the leeks and shallots slowly until tender; do not brown. Add the cream and cook until it is absorbed. Remove from the heat. Stir in the sausage. Cool slightly. Add sour cream; mix well.

4. Lightly moisten the edges of the pastry squares with water. Spoon the sausage mixture into the center of each square, dividing it equally. Fold over one half of each pastry square to form a triangle. Using a fork, press the edges together to seal. Prick the tops in several places.

5. Using a spatula, transfer the turnovers to an ungreased baking sheet. Bake for 20 minutes or until puffy and golden brown. Serve immediately.

Yield: 8 servings

APPETIZER PARTY

INFORMAL GATHERING:
Garlicky Mushroom Spread (page 90) and Sage Cheese Spread (page 92)

· · · · · · · · · · · · · · · ·

Assorted crackers, bread sticks, and fresh vegetables

· · · · · · · · · · · · · · · ·

A platter of Barbecued Wings (page 96)

· · · · · · · · · · · · · · · ·

An assortment of cold beer, ale, and soft drinks

• • • • • • • • •

ELEGANT OCCASION:

Asian vegetables and cocktail shrimp or grilled scallops with Ginger Dip (page 91)

· · · · · · · · · · · · · · · ·

Luscious wedges of Baked Brie with Fresh Fruit (page 94)

· · · · · · · · · · · · · · · ·

Leeks & Sausage in Puff Pastry (this page) or Shrimp & Beef Fondue (page 96) with sauces for dipping

· · · · · · · · · · · · · · · ·

Accompany with red and white wine or chilled champagne. For non-drinkers, sweetened lime juice and tonic

MEAT, POULTRY & SEAFOOD BITES

For a hearty approach, pack some protein into your snacks. These tasty bites are great after a tramp in the woods, a day of city sightseeing, or an active afternoon at the swimming hole, when invigorated appetites won't wait until dinner.

Barbecued Wings

❊ ❊ ❊

When you want a crowd-pleasing appetizer or a novel supper, wing it! Be sure to supply plenty of napkins for these finger-lickin' favorites.

- 12 chicken wings
- 1 cup tomato sauce
- 3 tablespoons brown sugar
- 1 tablespoon tamari or soy sauce

1. Preheat oven to 400°F. In a shallow baking pan, arrange the chicken wings so they do not touch each other. Bake for 30 minutes.

2. In a small saucepan, combine the tomato sauce, sugar, and tamari; cook until the sugar has dissolved.

3. After the chicken wings are cooked, thickly spread the sauce over the wings and bake for 30 to 40 minutes longer or until browned and very tender. Serve warm.

Yield: 4 servings

Shrimp & Beef Fondue

❊ ❊ ❊

Six to eight people is a good number for one fondue pot. This recipe makes a congenial, interactive meal. Give each person two long fondue forks for cooking beef and shrimp. At least three different sauces provide a nice variety of flavors for dipping. Try Horseradish Sauce (page 264), Mustard Sauce (page 266), and ginger-soy sauce.

- 4 cups peanut oil
- 1½–2 pounds boneless beef tenderloin, sirloin, or filet of beef, cut into 1-inch cubes
- 1½ pounds fresh shrimp (large or jumbo), shelled

1. At the table, pour peanut oil into a fondue pot with sides that curve inward to avoid spattering. Heat to a temperature at which a piece of shrimp dropped in cooks quickly.

2. Arrange the raw beef on one platter and the raw shrimp on another; pass around the table. Serve the sauces in small bowls.

3. When the oil is hot, have each person spear the food of choice and cook it in the hot oil; eat with one of the sauces. A leisurely pace is recommended to avoid competitive cooking.

Yield: 6–8 servings

Ghina's Cheese and Sausage Roll

❊ ❊ ❊

Ghina is a friend of a friend, and this is a recipe that makes friends quickly. Sausage and cheese encased in golden dough: hospitable food in the best Italian tradition.

Dough

- 1 package (¼ ounce) active dry yeast
- ¾ cup plus ½ cup warm water
- salt to taste
- 3 cups all-purpose flour
- 1 tablespoon olive oil

Filling

1 pound sweet Italian-style
  sausage, removed from
  casing and crumbled
1 recipe dough or packaged
  pizza dough
  olive oil
½ pound mozzarella or
  Swiss cheese, grated

1. For the dough, mix the yeast into ¾ cup of water and allow to sit for 15 minutes, until bubbles form. Add salt to flour, if desired (a little salt helps improve the texture of the dough). Gradually add the yeast and water and the oil. Working on a floured surface, gradually add the ½ cup of water and knead the dough for about 10 minutes. Place the dough in a lightly greased bowl, cover, put it in a warm place, and let it double in size.

2. Preheat oven to 375°F. Crumble the sausage into a skillet and sauté over medium heat until lightly browned, about 10 minutes. Remove the meat with a slotted spoon and set aside.

3. Roll out the dough into a rectangle about 12 by 18 inches and about ¼ inch thick. Brush the dough with olive oil, leaving a 1-inch border all around.

4. Spread the sausage evenly on the dough and top with the cheese.

5. Roll up the dough jelly-roll fashion, being careful to tuck in the ends and seal the edges.

6. Place the roll carefully on a cookie sheet, seam side down, and bake 30 to 45 minutes or until the crust is crispy and golden brown.

7. Cool about 20 minutes and slice into ½-inch-thick serving pieces.

Yield: 8–10 servings

Steak & Onion Kabobs

❈ ❈ ❈

Once you've experienced the fun of kabobbing, you'll be hooked forever. Remember that skillful skewery is just a matter of selecting flavors, textures, and colors to complement one another and choosing a marinade that brings out the best in the foods. Allow 8 hours of marinating time for this recipe.

2 pounds beef chuck, cut
  into 1½-inch cubes
Zesty Beer Marinade (page
  278)
12 small (1-inch) pearl
  onions, unpeeled
12 large mushroom caps
12 red or green bell pepper
  chunks, or a combination
½ pound uncooked bacon
  slices
½ cup large pimiento-stuffed
  olives

1. In a glazed ceramic, glass, or stainless steel bowl, combine the beef and the marinade. Toss well to coat the meat. Cover and refrigerate for 8 hours. Stir occasionally.

2. Parboil the unpeeled onions until tender crisp. Cool and peel. Blanch the mushroom caps and pepper chunks in boiling water for 30 seconds to prevent splitting. Drain and set aside. Drain the beef and pat dry, reserving the marinade.

3. Using long metal skewers, thread the bacon slices between alternating pieces of steak, onion, mushroom, pepper, and olive. Thread the onions and olives crosswise to prevent the centers from popping out.

4. Grill to desired doneness 4 to 6 inches above glowing coals. Baste frequently with marinade to keep moist.

Yield: 6 servings

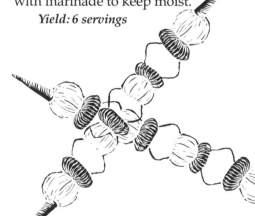

FRUIT & VEGETABLE BITES

The garden and the orchard are always great sources for snack makings. Raw fruits and vegetables, skewered or artfully arranged in napkin-lined wicker baskets, are nearly perfect foods, but sometimes it's fun to dress them up and present them in a novel way.

Spicy Potato Chips

❈ ❈ ❈

It is actually better to serve these as a snack than as an appetizer. They're so addictive that your guests might not leave room for dinner if you offered them before the meal.

2 sweet potatoes, peeled and sliced ⅛ inch thick

2 Idaho potatoes, peeled and sliced ⅛ inch thick
peanut oil for frying
3 tablespoons Jamaican Blend (page 309) or Cajun or taco seasoning
½ cup blue cheese, crumbled
Tabasco

1. Soak the sweet potatoes and Idaho potatoes in separate bowls of ice water in the refrigerator for 4 hours.

2. Preheat the oven to 250°F. Heat oil in a deep fryer to 370°F. Drain the potatoes and pat dry with paper towels. Fry the potatoes in small batches until nicely browned. Bring the oil back to temperature before frying the next batch. Drain the chips on brown paper bags or paper towels and sprinkle with Jamaican Blend. As you finish each batch, place chips in a single layer on a baking sheet in the oven to keep warm and crisp.

3. When all of the chips are fried, crumble the blue cheese on top and heat in the oven for 5 minutes, or until the cheese is soft. Serve with Tabasco on the side.

Yield: 6 servings

Hot Olive Cheese Puffs

❈ ❈ ❈

Judy Madden is one of the first friends we made in Williamstown. She and I met at the elementary school where her husband, Jack, was the superintendent of schools, and she was active in just about everything. Judy happens to be a great cook, and these little treats are absolutely scrumptious.

1 cup grated sharp Cheddar cheese
3 tablespoons butter, softened
½ cup all-purpose flour
¼ teaspoon salt
½ teaspoon paprika
24 pimiento-stuffed olives

1. Preheat oven to 400°F. To make dough, blend the cheese with the butter. Stir in

---

ANTIPASTO PLATTERS

∙∙∙∙∙∙∙∙∙∙∙∙∙∙∙∙∙∙∙∙∙∙∙∙∙∙∙∙∙∙

Antipasto is not so much a recipe as a concept: a platter of small snacks to whet the appetite "before the pasta." Select traditional Italian tidbits, such as smoked meats and sausages, cheeses, anchovies, olives, pickled peppers, fresh and marinated vegetables. Go Scandinavian with herring, pickled beets, smoked salmon, onions, Havarti cheese with good rye bread, and horseradish or dill butter. Give it a Greek twist with stuffed grape leaves, olives, feta cheese, chickpeas, and shrimp. Or simply raid your larder for cold cuts, cheeses, pickles, dilly beans, or what have you.

the flour, salt, and paprika. Mix well. Wrap 1 teaspoon of dough around each olive, covering completely.

2. Bake until lightly browned, 12 to 15 minutes. Can be made in advance and frozen, covered tightly with plastic wrap, before baking.

Yield: 12 servings

Pumpkin Tempura

❁ ❁ ❁

Cinnamon, nutmeg, and a trace of sugar play up the natural sweetness of the vegetable in this delightfully different appetizer. Consider serving this treat to celebrate the first lighting of your Halloween jack-o'-lantern: It's a tasty way to use the pumpkin you scooped out.

1 *cup all-purpose flour*
⅓ *teaspoon sugar*
⅓ *teaspoon salt*
⅓ *teaspoon ground cinnamon*
   pinch of ground nutmeg
1 *egg, beaten*
2 *tablespoons vegetable oil*
   vegetable oil for frying
1 *pound pumpkin or winter squash, cut into bite-size cubes*

1. In a medium-sized bowl, combine flour, sugar,

salt, cinnamon, nutmeg, egg, and vegetable oil.

2. In a deep-fat fryer or a large, heavy saucepan, heat 2 inches of oil to 365°F on a deep-fat thermometer.

3. Dip cubes of pumpkin in the batter, then fry in hot oil until golden brown, about 5 minutes. Drain on paper towels; serve hot.

Yield: 4 servings

Hot Fruit

❁ ❁ ❁

A light fruit salad becomes satisfying comfort food in this warming concoction. Kids love it as a pick-me-up between school and dinner, and it hits the spot after the exertion of cross-town commuting, cross-country skiing, or chopping wood.

1 *large grapefruit, peeled and the skin removed from each segment, or 1 can (about 10 ounces) grapefruit segments, drained*
1 *apple (Granny Smith, Golden Delicious)*
1 *banana*
2 *tablespoons raisins*
¼ *cup apple juice or cider*
1 *tablespoon honey*

1. Place the grapefruit segments in a medium-sized saucepan.

2. Core and chop the apple. Add to the grapefruit.

3. Peel the banana and slice into ½-inch slices. Mix with the grapefruit and apple.

4. Add the raisins, apple juice, and honey and warm over low heat for about 10 minutes. The mixture should be hot enough to eat without scalding the mouth.

Yield: 4 servings

APPLE RINGS

Forget the bread, crackers, and cookies — serve apple rings instead. Topped with a variety of spreads, cheeses, and meats, they bring a welcome change to the hors d'oeuvre platter. They are particularly successful with children and weight-conscious adults. Simply wash and core the apples and cut into ¼- to ½-inch slices. Choose from the following toppings, or invent your own:

- **Cream cheese with raisins and chopped nuts**
- **Cream cheese with onion slices and smoked salmon or sardines**
- **Cream cheese with chopped fresh chives**
- **Cream cheese and chutney**
- **Cream cheese, cinnamon, and honey**
- **Cream cheese with diced ham or bologna, curry powder, and chutney**
- **Liverwurst**
- **Refried beans or mashed baked beans**
- **Mashed blue cheese**
- **Canned corned beef with a slice of pickle**

BREADS AND MUFFINS

For our family, a meal just isn't complete without a fresh loaf of bread. My mother says that having bread baking in the oven is the best way to say "I love you" to your family. It welcomes you home even before you open the front door. It may be the least expensive way to sell your house, since that wonderful aroma is impossible to resist! And the process of kneading bread dough is so therapeutic it reduces tension. Plain or fancy, yeast or quick, biscuits or muffins, bread on the table is the staff of life.

Contributors to this chapter are Glenn Andrews; Janet Ballantyne; Ruth Bass; Miriam Jacobs; Ellen Foscue Johnson; Barbara Karoff; Edith Stovel and Pamela Wakefield; and Maggie Stuckey.

MomMom's Sticky Buns

❈ ❈ ❈

John's mother was born into a Pennsylvania Dutch family and had four brothers. Her mother taught her how to knead dough as a five-year-old. She mastered these "best-in-the-world" cinnamon (sticky) buns over the next seven decades, passing the precious recipe along to her daughters Helen and Judy, and to me. I deliver dozens to our friends on Christmas Eve.

Buns

½ cup (1 stick) margarine
½ cup sugar
3 eggs
1 cup scalded milk, slightly cooled (easy in the microwave)
1 package (¼ ounce) active dry yeast, dissolved in ¼ cup warm water
4 cups all-purpose flour
½ teaspoon salt

Topping

½ cup (1 stick) butter
1⅓ cups brown sugar

Filling

½ cup (1 stick) butter, softened
1 cup brown sugar
1 cup raisins
4 teaspoons ground cinnamon

1. In a large bowl, cream the margarine and sugar. Add eggs and beat well. Add milk and whisk. Add yeast. Mix in flour and salt. Cover with plastic wrap and a clean towel. Let rise until double in size, then pat down. Cover again; refrigerate overnight.

2. The next day, prepare topping in the baking pans. Preheat oven to 350°F. In each of four pie plates, melt 2 tablespoons of the butter and ⅓ cup of the brown sugar in the oven; set aside. Divide dough into four quarters.

3. On a floured surface, pat one quarter of the dough into a long rectangle, approximately 12 by 5 inches. Spread the dough with one-quarter of the butter, brown sugar, raisins, and cinnamon. Fold dough over lengthwise several times to form a long roll. Slice the roll into 12 equal pieces. Place slices, cut side up and slightly touching, in a pie pan. Repeat with remaining quarters of dough.

4. Bake for 15 to 20 minutes or until lightly browned. Line four plates with foil. Remove buns from oven and carefully turn onto the prepared plates; cool.

Yield: 4 dozen

Popovers

❈ ❈ ❈

Growing up, we always called these Dutch Babies, though I've never known why. To everyone else, they are popovers, the light, puffy breads that are an essential part of the menu with roast beef in England.

5 tablespoons butter
4 eggs
1 cup flour
1 cup milk

1. Preheat oven to 425°F. Divide the butter among 10 cups in a popover pan or large muffin pan and melt it in the oven.

2. In a blender, beat eggs on medium speed until foamy; add flour and milk. Blend for 1 minute.

3. Pour the batter into muffin cups, filling them three-quarters full.

4. Bake for 10 minutes. Reduce oven temperature to 350°F; bake for 10 minutes longer. Don't open the oven door during baking. Serve immediately.

Yield: 10 servings

BASICS OF MAKING YEAST BREADS

Making bread is not difficult. Like other activities that we soon enough take for granted (such as driving a car or planting a garden), several steps must be linked together in sequence. That sequence, however, is somewhat flexible. There are few rules in baking, few measurements that must be precise. Making bread intimidates people because the behavior of yeast mystifies them (they don't quite trust it) and the number of steps seems long and complex. But after you have done it a few times, you will assimilate this process until you can make bread with a light heart and confidence.

Let's take one good, simple bread from start to finish, elaborating each step so as to banish awe. These instructions are given in detail; but the procedure is quite simple and is applicable to almost every yeast bread.

BREAD-MAKING SUPPLIES & EQUIPMENT

NECESSITIES
- Yeast or some other leavener (usually)
- Water
- Flour
- Bowl or other container
- Wooden or similar strong spoon
- Two knives and a fork (for some kinds of mixing)
- Surface for kneading
- Something to bake on or in (pan, cookie sheet, tile, coffee can)
- Something to cover dough (towel, shirt, pillow case, plastic wrap)
- Oven (stovetop, fireplace, outdoor fire)
- Measuring cup
- Measuring spoons

HELPFUL TO HAVE
- A second bowl
- Electric mixer or hand beater
- Loaf pans
- Sharp knife

- Rubber spatula
- Single-edged razor for slashing loaves
- Pancake turner
- Pastry scraper
- Pastry brush
- Wire rack
- Reliable oven and/or good oven thermometer
- Instant-read thermometer
- Pastry blender

OPTIONS & FRILLS
- Two pastry brushes: one for melted butter, one for glazes
- Bread pans in many sizes, a variety of casseroles, soufflé dishes, tube pan, fluted molds, special French bread pan
- A large, convenient surface to use solely for kneading bread
- Heavy-duty electric mixer with dough hook
- Plant mister for spraying

ABOUT YEAST

Baker's yeast is usually available in one of two forms.

ACTIVE YEAST: Granulated yeast that must be activated in water. 1 packet = 1 tablespoon

COMPRESSED YEAST: Moist, live yeast sold in small cakes. Must be used within 2 weeks. 1 cake = 1 packet of dry yeast

Laura's Easy, Basic, and Good White Bread

❈ ❈ ❈

It is advisable to assemble all the ingredients close at hand before starting.

2 cups warm water
2 tablespoons honey
1 tablespoon active dry yeast
2 tablespoons light oil
2 teaspoons salt
5–6 cups unbleached all-purpose flour
2 tablespoons raw wheat germ
½ cup nonfat dry milk

Proofing Yeast

1. The most critical judgment you make comes at the very beginning, when you test the temperature of the water in which you dissolve your yeast. It should be warm, not tepid and not hot — around 100°F. If you have a thermometer, use it. If not, run the water over your wrist; if it feels definitely but not uncomfortably warm, it's okay.

2. Put 2 cups warm water in a large mixing bowl. Add the honey and the dry yeast. Stir together. Set aside for a few minutes; it will take about 3 to 15 minutes, depending on the temperature of the water. As the grains of yeast activate, they begin to foam.

Combining Ingredients

1. When the yeast is bubbly, add the oil, salt, and 2 cups of the flour. Beat this mixture extremely well; this stimulates early development of gluten, the magic ingredient in the flour that gives your bread lightness and a fine texture. If you have an electric mixer, use it to beat the mixture on medium speed for 2 minutes or longer. Otherwise, beat it with a wooden spoon, at least 200 strokes. When you have finished beating, the surface of the dough may have a glossy look — a good sign.

2. Add the wheat germ and dry milk and mix them in. Then add 2 to 3 cups more of the flour, a little at a time, mixing with a wooden spoon until the dough is too stiff to stir and pulls away from the sides of the bowl.

Kneading

1. Kneading is like dancing — most any way you do it will be okay. A delicate touch is fine, but it will take longer to produce a state of elasticity. Energy and decisiveness will get you there more quickly. If you have a heavy-duty mixer with a dough hook, you can use it to knead. If you are kneading by hand, choose a kneading surface (bread board, tabletop, or other clean surface) that is about the level of your wrists when your arms are hanging at your sides. Anything higher will tire your shoulders.

2. Sprinkle the kneading surface with flour. Dip your hands in flour. Dump the dough out of the bowl onto the surface. Turn the dough around and over to coat the outside with flour, patting it into a cohesive mass. Begin to knead.

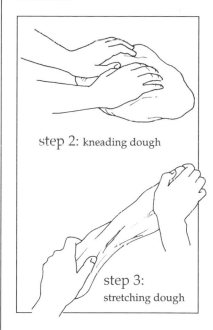

step 2: kneading dough

step 3: stretching dough

3. Take the far side of the dough and fold it toward you, stretching dough and then folding it as though you were folding a sheet of paper. With the heels of your (floury) hands, push the folded portion down and away from you. Give the whole piece of dough a quarter-turn, fold, and push. Repeat. Each time you will be folding and pushing a different segment of the dough. Do it over and over. Ten minutes is a good ballpark figure. The dough will be rough and sticky at first. You may have to keep dipping your hands and sprinkling flour onto the dough and onto the board; add only as much flour as you need to keep the dough from being too sticky to work with. Too much flour makes a dry loaf; you should end up with a dough that is smooth but still soft and pliable. When you push it, it springs back. Eventually, it will become smooth and satiny.

First Rise

1. Rub a large bowl with soft butter, or brush it with melted butter. (Oil tends to be absorbed by the dough, which then sticks to the bowl.) Place the dough in the bowl and turn until all sides are coated with a thin layer of fat, or brush the top of the dough with melted butter. Cover the bowl with a kitchen towel.

2. Place the bowl in a warm, draft-free place. Many people recommend the inside of the oven. If your oven has no pilot light, pre-heat it for half a minute, turn it off, and put the bowl inside. Or put the bowl in the oven with a pan of hot water on the shelf below.

3. Let the dough rise until it has doubled in size. You can test it by poking a finger into the top of the dough, about an inch down. If the hole you have made remains, it has risen enough. This can take anywhere from 45 minutes to several hours. If the dough gets away from you and rises to much greater than double, it's best to punch it down and let it rise again in the bowl before you proceed.

Punching Down

1. Give the dough a good sock with your fist. This is called punching down the dough. Take the dough over to your lightly floured work surface and dump or pull it out of the bowl. Knead it a few times to press out gas bubbles, then take a sharp knife and cut the dough into two equal pieces. Cover them with your towel and do something else for 5 to 15 minutes while the dough rests.

Preparing Pans

1. Grease two 8- or 9-inch loaf pans. Use soft or melted butter, preferably unsalted. If you don't have loaf pans or prefer free-form loaves, grease a baking sheet and sprinkle it lightly with cornmeal.

Shaping

1. Take one piece of dough, pat it with your hands into a rough ball, and flatten it to a size about twice as wide as your loaf pan and slightly longer. Fold the two

BREAD INGREDIENTS

- *Salt*
- *Milk*
- *Eggs*
- *Butter and oil*
- *Several kinds of flour*
- *Several kinds of sweeteners*
- *Fruits, nuts, seeds*
- *A variety of flours and meals*
- *Nonfat dry milk or evaporated milk*
- *Liquors and liqueurs (occasionally)*

long sides under so that they meet in the middle of the bottom. Tuck the two short ends under. Gently press the loaf against the board to help folded dough stick to itself. Place the shaped dough in a loaf pan or on the baking sheet. It should fill the pans no more than half full. Repeat this process with the remaining piece of dough. Brush the tops of the loaves with soft or melted butter.

Second Rise and Baking

1. Cover the pans or baking sheet with the towel and put the loaves in a draft-free place to rise again until they double in size, usually 45 minutes to 1 hour. Meanwhile, preheat the oven to 375°F.

2. Place pans in the oven and bake about 25 to 30 minutes. Resist the impulse to open the oven door and peek during the first 15 to 20 minutes.

Testing for Doneness

1. When the bread has baked almost the minimum baking time, take a look. If the loaves are well browned and the sides have shrunk slightly from the sides of the pan, remove from the oven.

Tap bottom of pan to release a loaf. Turn the loaf out into your other, oven-gloved hand. Give the bottom of the loaf a tap; if it makes a hollow sound, it is done. If it makes a dull thud, bake a few minutes longer.

Finishing the Bread

1. When done, turn out the loaves on a wire rack to cool. If you like a softer crust, brush the loaves with melted butter or cover the loaves with a towel as they cool on the rack.

2. Bread doesn't slice well when it's hot, but the suspense may be too strong to let you wait. Don't be disappointed if it's a bit doughy inside. The texture will improve as the bread cools. In any event, be sure to wait until the bread is thoroughly cool before wrapping it. Happy eating!

Yield: 2 loaves

Note: Whole-wheat and rye flours make dough that is stickier and less elastic than white-flour dough. It has been kneaded enough when it feels resilient. When rising whole-wheat and rye dough, covering with a dampened towel helps prevent a crust from forming on the top.

TYPES OF BREAD

Yeast bread may be the first thing that comes to mind when you think of homemade bread, but there are many other types of bread worth trying and tasting as you explore and expand your bread-making skills.

BATTER: Batter bread is beaten, not kneaded. With a heavy-duty mixer, you can make superb breads with little effort. They have a coarse crumb, a chewy texture, and a cratered surface like a lava flow; they have a yeasty flavor (they need more yeast because the gluten that supports rising is not completely developed by kneading).

QUICK: Quick breads are almost effortless. Most are sweeter than most yeast breads, contain fruit and/or nuts, and are leavened with baking powder and/or baking soda. They have a crumbly, often crunchy texture.

SOURDOUGH: Yeast-leavened breads are relatively recent. For thousands of years, people leavened bread by tearing off a piece of dough and using it to start the next day's batch. These breads, which require use of a sourdough starter, are coarser and chewier and have a heavier crust than yeast breads.

YEAST BREADS

The smell of yeast dissolving in warm water is delicious. It tells me that something wonderful is about to happen, and indeed it is. The miracle of rising bread dough is topped only by the fragrance of baking bread, or perhaps by the taste of that first warm slice

Zesty Whole-Wheat Sourdough French Bread

❈ ❈ ❈

This crusty and individualistic bread can be shaped into traditional loaves or free-form rounds; its flavor is amiable and not too sour. And it adds the nutrition of whole wheat to whatever meal it accompanies.

> 1 cup sourdough starter (this page)
> 2 cups unbleached all-purpose white flour
> 3 cups whole-wheat flour, preferably stone-ground
> 1½ cups warm water
> 2 tablespoons honey
> ½ tablespoon dry yeast
> 2 teaspoons salt
> ⅓ cup wheat germ

1. In a glass or pottery bowl, mix together the starter, 1 cup each of the white and whole-wheat flours, 1 cup of the water, and 1 tablespoon of the honey. Cover with plastic wrap and let sit in a warm, draft-free place overnight or for up to 24 hours.

2. In a large mixing bowl, dissolve the yeast in the remaining ½ cup of water with the remaining honey. When bubbly, add the starter mixture, salt, and the remaining white flour and beat thoroughly, 2 minutes with an electric mixer or at least 200 strokes by hand. Mix in the wheat germ.

3. Gradually add enough whole-wheat flour to make a dough that clings together and leaves the sides of the bowl. Turn the dough out onto a floured board and knead until smooth and elastic, sprinkling with a little more whole-wheat flour if it remains too sticky.

4. Place the dough in a buttered bowl, turn to coat all sides, cover with a damp towel, and let rise until double in bulk. Punch the dough down and, if you have time, let it rise again in the bowl. Punch the dough down again, turn it out onto a lightly floured board, and knead a few times. Cut in half, cover, and let rest 10 minutes.

SOURDOUGH STARTER

··

Starters are available in some health food and specialty stores, but it's easy to make your own. There are several ways. Dissolve 1 tablespoon dry yeast and 2 tablespoons honey in 2 cups warm water in a glass, plastic, or crockery bowl. Stir in 2 cups unbleached white flour; cover with a towel and let sit in a warm place for several days, or until foamy and soured. Store in a covered jar in the refrigerator.

Warning: Use a bowl big enough to contain what may be a startling degree of expansion.

If you don't use your starter for a week, you'll need to feed it. First, remove ½ to 1 cup of the original starter. Throw it away, give it away, or use it. Stir in a mixture of 1 cup flour, 1 cup warm liquid (milk or water), and a little sugar (optional). Let sit at room temperature for a few hours; stir and refrigerate.

5. Using a rolling pin, roll one half of the dough into a long rectangle. Starting with a long side, roll the dough into a tight tube. Tuck the ends under, pinch them to seal, and place, seam side down, on a greased baking sheet that has been dusted with cornmeal. Repeat with the other piece of dough. With a sharp knife, make long diagonal slashes in the tops of the loaves. Brush the tops with melted butter, cover with a light cloth, and let rise until not quite double in size.

6. Preheat the oven to 400°F. Place a shallow pan of boiling water on the bottom of the oven. Using a clean plant mister or other spray bottle, spray loaves with cold water. Put into oven immediately. Bake 5 minutes, remove loaves, and spray again with cold water. Return to oven. Repeat after another 5 minutes. Remove the pan of water and continue baking 15 to 25 minutes longer (25 to 35 minutes in all) or until the bottoms of the loaves sound hollow when tapped. Cool loaves on a rack.

Yield: 2 loaves

Swiss Braided Bread

❁ ❁ ❁

Braided bread is easy to make, and the attractive loaves make wonderful gifts. The recipe may be doubled for giving or freezing.

1 tablespoon active dry yeast
1 cup warm water
⅓ cup nonfat dry milk
2 tablespoons sugar
1 teaspoon salt
2 tablespoons butter
1 egg
3 cups all-purpose flour, plus ½ cup if needed

Glaze

1 egg yolk, beaten and mixed with 1 tablespoon water

1. In a large bowl, sprinkle the yeast into the water; stir until dissolved. Add the milk powder, sugar, salt, butter, and egg; mix well to break the butter into small pieces.

2. Add 2 cups of the flour and beat the mixture with a wooden spoon until smooth. Gradually add the remaining 1 cup of flour and continue to stir with the wooden spoon. Remember, it is easy to add more flour as needed, but it is impossible to remove flour if the dough becomes too stiff.

3. Scrape the dough out of the bowl and knead it on a floured surface for 5 to 10 minutes, until it is smooth and elastic. Add more flour if the dough becomes unmanageably sticky.

4. Place the smooth ball of dough into a large, lightly greased bowl. Cover it with a damp towel and let it rise in a warm spot for 1 hour, or until double in bulk. Make a fist and punch down the dough. Divide the dough in two, making one half slightly bigger than the other. Divide the larger half into six equal pieces. Roll each piece into a 10- to 12-inch strand. Separate into two groups of three strands and make two braids. Repeat process with the smaller half to make two slightly smaller braids. Place the smaller braids on top of the larger ones to make two double-decker braided loaves.

5. Coat a large baking sheet with vegetable cooking spray. Arrange the loaves on the sheet, at least 6 inches apart. Cover with a towel and let the dough rise for about 1 hour.

6. Preheat oven to 400°F. Brush each loaf with the glaze. Bake the loaves for 40 to 50 minutes, or until lightly browned. Remove from the pan immediately and cool on a wire rack.

Yield: 2 large loaves

Triticale Bread

❋ ❋ ❋

Triticale flour may be the wave of the future. A hybrid of wheat and rye, it has been called the first man-made cereal grain. Although it was developed in the late nineteenth century, triticale has only recently begun to be grown in any volume in the United States. Its star quality is its high protein content (one-third more than that of whole wheat). It's also nice to work with and has a lovely flavor.

  1 cup milk, scalded
  4 tablespoons unsalted butter
  ¼ cup plus 1 teaspoon honey
  ¼ cup unsulfured molassses
  2 teaspoons salt
  2 tablespoons active dry yeast
  1 cup warm water
  1 egg
  3 cups unbleached
     all-purpose flour
  ⅔ cup sunflower kernels
  3½ cups triticale flour, approx-
     imately

1. In a medium-sized bowl, combine the milk, butter, ¼ cup honey, molasses, and salt. Cool to lukewarm.

2. In a large mixing bowl, dissolve the yeast in the water with the teaspoon of honey. When bubbly, add the milk mixture, egg, and all-purpose flour; beat at least 2 minutes with an electric mixer or at least 200 strokes by hand.

3. Mix in the sunflower kernels. Gradually add the triticale flour, as much as it takes to make a dough that clings together and leaves the sides of the bowl.

4. Turn the dough out onto a floured surface and knead until smooth and elastic, adding a little more triticale flour if the dough remains persistently sticky. Be patient and try not to add more than necessary; given time, the dough will become more pliant.

5. Place the dough in a buttered bowl, turn over to coat all sides. Cover with a towel and let rise until double in bulk.

HOMEMADE MACHINE-MADE BREAD

Some people cringe at the very thought of anything but wholly handmade — mixed, kneaded, and oven-baked — bread. Others swear by the dough hook on their heavy-duty mixer, their food processor, or their bread machine. For every purist who insists on the old-fashioned way, there is a busy person who finds that assistance from machinery is the only way they can make their bread at home and thus control the quality of ingredients and, therefore, of the finished product.

Your food processor or bread machine guide will tell you how to use your particular machine to save you time and allow you to serve your family homemade bread.

Adapting recipes to use in a bread machine takes some trial and error. You need to make sure your machine has the capacity to accommodate the recipe you want to use. Your bread machine's capacity should be listed in pounds. If the recipe you want to convert does not give the yield in pounds, a rough guide is 1 pound for every 2½ cups of flour in the recipe. You may also need to decrease the total amount of liquid.

Some people use their bread machines just to mix and knead the dough if they want to make a recipe that has not been formulated for the bread machine. After mixing and kneading, they remove the dough from the machine to shape it, let it rise, then bake it. With this method, you can control the rising and baking times (for some non-machine recipes, the times that are preprogrammed in the machines don't work well).

If it's a choice between store-bought and machine-made at home, even purists should agree that homemade is better!

5. Punch the dough down, turn it out onto a lightly floured surface, knead a few times to press out air bubbles. Divide the dough in half, cover with a towel, and let rest for about 10 minutes.

6. Form the dough into oblong shapes and place them in two buttered medium to large loaf pans. Brush the tops with melted butter and let rise again, covered with the towel, until almost double in size.

7. Preheat oven to 350°F. Bake about 40 minutes or until the bottoms of the loaves sound hollow when tapped. Remove loaves from the pans and cool on a rack.

Yield: 2 loaves

Cheese Bread

❁ ❁ ❁

A rich cheese bread is one of our favorites for toasting. Letting it rise three times lightens the texture.

1	cup milk
1	tablespoon unsalted butter
¼	cup honey
1	tablespoon active dry yeast
¼	cup warm water
½	teaspoon sugar or honey
1½	teaspoons salt
1	egg
4	cups unbleached all-purpose flour, approximately
2	cups grated sharp Cheddar cheese

1. Scald the milk in a small saucepan; add the butter and honey, and let the mixture sit until lukewarm. In a large mixing bowl, dissolve the yeast in the water with the ½ teaspoon sugar. Wait until the mixture is frothing. Add the lukewarm milk mixture to the yeast mixture, along with the salt and egg; beat all together. Add 1½ cups of the flour and beat 2 minutes with an electric mixer, or at least 200 strokes by hand. Mix in the cheese and gradually add more flour until the dough leaves the sides of the bowl and is stiff enough to knead.

2. Turn the dough out onto a floured surface and knead until smooth and elastic, sprinkling with a little more flour if it remains sticky. Put the dough into a buttered bowl; turn it over or brush the top with melted butter. Cover with a towel and let rise until double in size. Punch it down in the bowl and, if you have time, allow it to rise again. (It will rise faster this time.)

3. Grease an oval or round casserole and shape the dough to fit. It should fill half the pan. Put the dough into the pan, brush the top with melted butter, cover with the towel, and let rise again until almost double in size.

4. You can preheat the oven to 350°F or put this bread into a cold oven, turn it on to 350°F, bake 40 to 45 minutes, and then take the bread out of the pan and put it directly on the oven rack for a final 5 minutes. It is done when the bottom sounds hollow when tapped. Cool on a rack.

Yield: 1 large loaf

MAKING ROLLS

Any of the basic white or whole-wheat doughs can be formed into rolls. If you haven't made rolls before, a good kind to start with is the cloverleaf. Just make small balls of dough (about the size of large marbles) and stick three of them in each cup of a greased standard-sized muffin pan. Cover loosely and allow to rise until double in size, then bake in a preheated 350°F oven for about 20 minutes, or until lightly browned.

Don't try this with any of the batter bread doughs or with rye dough, which is usually too soft and sticky. However, those doughs, as well as all the basic ones, can be baked in miniature loaf pans; be sure to adjust the baking time.

Anadama Batter Bread

❈ ❈ ❈

Legend has it that this bread was invented long ago by a New England farmer who came home to find his wife out and nothing but cornmeal mush for supper. He cried, "Anna, damn her!" as he tossed molasses, flour, and yeast into a pot and proceeded to make this wonderful bread.

  1 *package (¼ ounce) active dry yeast*
  ¼ *cup warm water*
  ¾ *cup boiling water*
  ½ *cup yellow cornmeal*
  3 *tablespoons butter, softened*
  ¼ *cup molasses*
1½ *teaspoons salt*
  1 *egg*
2¾ *cups all-purpose flour*

1. In a small bowl, proof the yeast in the warm water.

2. In a large bowl (preferably one that goes with an electric mixer), combine the boiling water, cornmeal, butter, molasses, and salt, then add the egg.

3. Add 1½ cups of the flour and beat until well combined, either by machine or by hand (or in a food processor). Add the rest of the flour and beat again.

4. Spoon the dough into a greased 9-inch bread pan. Let rise until it reaches about 1 inch from the top of the pan. Preheat oven to 375°F. Bake for about 35 minutes.

Yield: 1 large loaf

Batter Brown Bread

❈ ❈ ❈

This is a compact loaf with a finer crumb than most batter breads have. It is a fine accompaniment to a vegetarian feast fresh from the garden.

  2 *tablespoons active dry yeast*
  ½ *cup water*
  1 *teaspoon sugar or honey*
  2 *teaspoons salt*
  ⅓ *cup molasses*
1½ *cups warm water*
  2 *eggs*
  2 *cups unbleached all-purpose white flour*
  4 *cups whole-wheat flour, approximately, preferably stone-ground*
  ¼ *cup yellow cornmeal, preferably stone-ground*

1. In a large bowl, dissolve the yeast in the ½ cup water with the sugar. When the mixture is bubbling, add the salt, molasses, warm water, and eggs; beat well to mix.

2. Add the white flour and 1 cup of the whole-wheat flour; beat very thoroughly for 5 to 10 minutes. Add the cornmeal and, gradually, about 3 more cups whole-wheat flour, stirring vigorously until the dough clings together and leaves the sides of the bowl.

3. Cover and let the dough rise in its bowl until it has doubled in size.

SUBSTITUTE INGREDIENTS

··

When making bread, it's easy to substitute ingredients:

• If you don't have honey, use sugar. (Use ¼ cup additional liquid for each cup of sugar.)

• If you don't have oil, use melted butter or margarine.

• If you don't have wheat germ, leave it out.

• If you don't have dry milk, use 1 cup whole or skim milk in place of 1 cup of the water.

• If you don't have unbleached white flour, use bleached, but know that your bread will taste and be better when you have unbleached flour. Or use whole-wheat flour and increase the yeast to 1½ tablespoons.

• If you don't have yeast, maybe you'd better wait for another day. Or make a quick bread or some muffins. Or read about sourdough.

4. Punch the dough down and, if you have time, let it rise again in the bowl. Stir it down with a wooden spoon and divide it equally between two buttered medium (about 8- by 5-inch) loaf pans. Cover the pans and let the dough rise until it reaches or almost reaches the tops of the pans.

5. Preheat oven to 375°F. Bake about 25 minutes or until the loaves sound hollow when thumped on the bottom. Cool on a rack.

Yield: 2 loaves

Soft Pretzels

❂ ❂ ❂

My son-in-law Blair Dils loves to make these with his kids. He thinks it encourages their young creative minds, but the kids think they just plain taste good. While the traditional pretzel shape is always fun to make, they love to make snakes and letters of the alphabet; dip them in salsa, mustard, or even peanut butter; then eat them while they are still warm from the oven.

> 1 package (¼ ounce) active dry yeast
> 1¼ cups warm water
> ⅓ cup corn syrup
> 1¾ cups all-purpose white flour
> 1 cup whole-wheat flour
> ¼ teaspoon salt
> 1 egg
> 2 teaspoons water
> 2 tablespoons coarse salt
> 3 tablespoons melted butter

1. Generously oil a large bowl; set aside. In another large bowl, dissolve the yeast in the warm water. Add corn syrup, flours, and salt. Using an electric mixer and paddle, mix ingredients until moistened. Change to the dough hook and mix until the dough forms a ball.

2. On a floured surface, flatten the dough ball into a ½-inch-thick circle. Knead the dough for approximately 10 minutes, adding flour to the work surface, until the dough is smooth and no longer sticky.

3. Form the dough into a ball, put it into the well-oiled bowl, and turn it over to coat it with oil. Cover the bowl with plastic wrap, then a clean cloth towel, and let it rise for about 45 minutes or until it expands to almost double its original size.

4. Preheat oven to 400°F; oil a baking sheet. Divide the dough into 12 balls of equal size, then roll each one into a skinny rope about 12 to 14 inches long. Form a U with the rope, then cross the ends to form a traditional pretzel shape. Put the pretzels on the baking sheet.

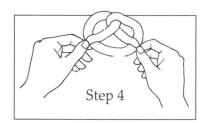

Step 4

5. In a small bowl, beat the egg with the water to make an egg wash. Brush each pretzel with egg wash and sprinkle with coarse salt. Bake about 25 minutes, or until light brown. Remove from oven and brush with melted butter.

Yield: 12 pretzels

FREEZING DOUGH

Yeast dough can be frozen before baking, so why not make up a double batch of dough when you are making bread? Let the dough rise once, then punch it down and shape it. Line the pan you would bake the dough in with a large piece of plastic wrap, lightly oiled, and wrap the dough. Freeze the dough in the pan until it is solid. Remove it from the pan and double wrap it in foil or place it in a resealable plastic freezer bag. The dough can be frozen for up to 2 months. Before thawing, unwrap the dough and place it into a greased pan. Thaw, covered, overnight in the refrigerator. The next day, cover the dough with a kitchen towel and let rise until doubled in size. Bake according to the recipe's instructions.

Yankee Grits Bread

❈ ❈ ❈

I n spite of its name, this bread reminds me of my Texas childhood. It's made with bacon, eggs, milk, and grits; from a southern point of view, that's a complete breakfast in every slice.

1½   tablespoons active dry yeast
½   cup warm water
1   teaspoon sugar or honey
½   cup water
⅓   cup honey
1   egg
3   tablespoons bacon grease or light oil
2   teaspoons salt
6–7   cups unbleached all-purpose flour
1½   cups warm grits, cooked without salt
¾   cup nonfat dry milk
2   tablespoons melted butter

1. In a large bowl, dissolve the yeast in the warm water with the teaspoon sugar. When bubbling, add the second ½ cup water, honey, egg, bacon grease, salt, and 2 cups of the flour. Beat 2 minutes with an electric beater or 200 strokes by hand. Add the grits and dry milk. Gradually add about 4 cups flour, or enough to make a dough that is too stiff to beat and pulls away from the sides of the bowl.

2. Turn dough out onto a floured surface and knead until smooth and elastic. Fortify yourself for a long haul — this dough takes a lot of kneading and will try to thwart you by remaining persistently sticky. Add a little more flour as necessary. When dough is properly elastic, it will be a bit tacky. Put it in a buttered bowl and turn to coat all sides; cover with a towel and let rise until double in bulk.

3. Punch dough down and, if time permits, let it rise a second time in the bowl. Punch it down again and turn out onto a floured board.

Knead a few times to press out air bubbles. Cut in half, cover, and let rest 10 minutes. Shape each half into a loaf and put into 9-inch buttered loaf pans. Brush the tops with melted butter. Cover and let rise until not quite double in size.

4. Preheat oven to 375°F. Bake for about 40 minutes or until the bottoms of the loaves sound hollow when tapped.

5. Remove from pans and cool on a rack. Crusty, chewy, a little sweet, and good.

Yield: 2 generous loaves

YOUR FAVORITE PAN

••

If you don't have the pan called for in a recipe or want to make individual portions of quick bread, use a different container; porcelain, earthenware, and metal will work. The times are meant as a guide. Watch the bread carefully.

PAN SIZE/TYPE	APPROXIMATE BAKING TIME
1-cup porcelain ramekin	15 to 20 minutes
3-cup pie pan	15 to 20 minutes
9- by 5-inch loaf pan	about 1 hour
5½- by 3-inch loaf pan	30 to 40 minutes
1-quart casserole	40 to 50 minutes

QUICK BREADS

Company coming and time running short? Quick breads are the perfect way to say "welcome" with bread fresh from the oven. Quick breads, risen with baking powder or soda instead of yeast, are fun to make and, because they are so easy, lend themselves to experimentation. Bake them fruit-studded and herb-scented as tea loaves, or whip up some savory dinner breads with shredded vegetables, sausage, and peppers. Leftovers, spread with unsalted butter or cream cheese, make wonderful breakfast or lunchbox treats.

Buckwheat Apple Bread

❉ ❉ ❉

Buckwheat flour has a distinctive and rather old-fashioned flavor that pairs beautifully with tart apples.

1 ⅓ cups buckwheat flour
⅔ cup unbleached all-purpose white flour
1 teaspoon salt
½ teaspoon baking soda
2 tablespoons baking powder
4 tablespoons sugar
1 egg

1 ¼ cups buttermilk
½ cup vegetable oil
1 cup tart apples, peeled, cored, and chopped

1. Preheat oven to 375°F; grease 2 loaf pans. In a large bowl, combine the buckwheat flour, white flour, salt, soda, baking powder, and sugar. In another bowl, combine the egg, buttermilk, oil, and apples and add them quickly to the dry ingredients.

2. Spoon the batter into the pans and bake at 375°F until a tester comes out clean. Cool in the pans for 10 minutes and remove to a rack to cool completely.

Yield: 2 loaves

Basic Quick Bread

❉ ❉ ❉

This is a basic recipe to which you can add different flours, spices, nuts, seeds, and fruits. It is not very interesting as it stands, so use it as a basic guide to create your own special breads.

1 ½ cups all-purpose flour
½ tablespoon baking powder
½ teaspoon salt
¼ cup butter or margarine, softened
½ cup sugar
1 egg
¾ cup milk

In a large bowl, combine the flour, baking powder, and salt. In another bowl, cream the butter and sugar. Stir in the egg and mix well. Stir in the milk and add the liquid mixture quickly to the dry ingredients. Stir just enough to moisten completely. Spoon the mixture into a greased 9- by 5-inch loaf pan and bake at 350°F until a tester comes out clean. Cool in the pan for 10 minutes and then remove to a wire rack to cool completely.

Yield: 1 loaf

ADDITIONS: Be creative! Stir in fresh or dried fruit and nuts. If you use fruit purée, use a little less fat. If you add or substitute an acidic ingredient, such as applesauce or buttermilk, compensate for it by adding ½ teaspoon baking soda.

Banana Lemon Bread

❈ ❈ ❈

For mellow banana flavor, use bananas that are too ripe for any other purpose. Tart lemon balm perks up the sweetness of the bananas, but grated lemon zest will work if you can't find the herb.

1¾ cups unbleached all-
     purpose white flour
¼   cup whole-wheat flour
1   teaspoon baking soda
½   teaspoon salt
4   tablespoons butter, softened
½   cup granulated sugar
½   cup light brown sugar
2   eggs, beaten
3   very ripe medium
     bananas, mashed
1   teaspoon minced fresh
     lemon balm or grated
     lemon zest
⅓   cup milk

1. Preheat oven to 350°F. Butter a 4- by 8-inch loaf pan and line with wax paper.

2. Sift together the flours, baking soda, and salt.

3. In a large bowl, cream the butter and sugars together. Blend in the eggs, bananas, and lemon balm. Add half of the flour mixture and half of the milk, stirring. Add the remaining milk and then the remaining flour mixture, and blend well. Pour into the loaf pan.

4. Bake for 1 hour or until a toothpick inserted in the center comes out clean.

Yield: 1 loaf

Carrot Bread

❈ ❈ ❈

Like a cross between tea bread and carrot cake, this bread is terrific with cream cheese. It was one of Mom-Mom's "top-secret" recipes that she shared only with family and friends. I hope you'll do the same.

¾   cup vegetable oil
1   cup sugar
2   eggs, beaten well
1½ cups grated raw carrot
½   cup chopped nuts
1½ cups all-purpose flour
1   teaspoon baking soda
1   teaspoon ground cinnamon
½   teaspoon salt
½   cup golden raisins
     (optional)

1. Grease one standard-sized or two small loaf pans. Preheat oven to 350°F.

2. Blend the oil and sugar; add eggs and mix well. Stir in the carrots, nuts, flour, soda, cinnamon, salt, and raisins, if desired; mix well. Pour batter into prepared pan.

3. Bake for 45 minutes or until a tester inserted in center comes out clean.

Yield: 1 loaf

MomMom's Batter Bread

❈ ❈ ❈

John's mother liked to make this wonderful recipe to serve alongside a roast. It is similar to a warm spoon bread or soft polenta. John likes it with a pat of butter and warm maple syrup on top, so I serve it in soup bowls next to the plate.

1   cup white cornmeal
     (yellow cornmeal works
     okay, too) mixed with
     ½ cup cold water
¾   teaspoon salt
2   tablespoons butter
2½ cups boiling water
½   cup milk
2   eggs, beaten
2   tablespoons
     all-purpose flour
2   tablespoons sugar
2   teaspoons baking powder

1. Preheat oven to 400°F. Grease a casserole dish.

2. In a large bowl, combine the cornmeal, salt, and butter. Slowly pour water over the mixture, mixing until it is a paste. Let cool.

3. Add milk, eggs, flour, sugar, and baking powder; stir until combined. Pour into the prepared dish.

4. Bake for 45 minutes, until raised and slightly browned on top. Serve warm.

Yield: 6 servings

Zucchini Parmesan Jalapeño Flatbread

❖ ❖ ❖

When you discover yet another zucchini in the garden, this is what to do with it. Everyone will applaud this novel use of that ubiquitous vegetable, here livened with jalapeño.

1 cup all-purpose flour
1 teaspoon baking powder
½ teaspoon vegetable broth mix
2 egg whites, or 4 teaspoons pasteurized dried egg whites plus ¼ cup water
1 cup shredded zucchini
¼ cup nonfat plain yogurt
½ jalapeño pepper, minced
2 tablespoons grated Parmesan cheese

1. Preheat oven to 350°F. Coat a 9-inch-square nonstick baking pan with cooking spray.

2. In a large bowl, sift the flour, baking powder, and broth mix.

3. In a medium-sized bowl, beat the egg whites until frothy. Add the zucchini, yogurt, jalapeño, and Parmesan, and blend well. Stir the zucchini mixture into the flour mixture and combine well.

4. Spread the dough on the prepared pan and smooth the top. Bake for 40 minutes, or until a tester inserted in the center comes out clean.

Yield: 6 servings

Dill Corn Bread with Sausage

❖ ❖ ❖

Hot sausage spices up this corn bread for an unusual brunch item or supper dish. Sweet sausage works fine, too, if you don't want the heat; in fact, the bread can be made without any sausage at all.

2 tablespoons butter
3 medium onions, thinly sliced
½ pound hot Italian sausage
2 cups unbleached all-purpose flour
1 cup yellow cornmeal
¼ cup sugar
½ teaspoon baking soda
2 eggs
¼ cup vegetable oil
1¾ cups plain low-fat yogurt
¼ cup snipped dill
salt and freshly ground black pepper

1. Preheat oven to 400°F, and grease a 10-inch round baking dish that is at least 1½ inches deep.

2. Melt the butter in a medium-sized skillet and sauté the onions until they are soft and golden. Set aside.

3. Remove the casings from the sausage. Slice the sausage about ¼ inch thick and bake in a shallow pan for 15 minutes. Drain off the fat, turn the oven down to 350°F, and spread the sausage in the baking dish.

4. Combine the flour, cornmeal, sugar, and baking soda in a large bowl.

5. In a small bowl, beat 1 of the eggs and combine with the oil, 1 cup of the yogurt, and the dill. Blend into the dry ingredients until everything is just mixed. Pour over the sausage slices.

6. Spread the onions on top of the batter. Combine the remaining yogurt, the remaining egg, and a dash of salt and pepper, and pour over the onion layer.

7. Bake for 25 to 30 minutes or until a toothpick inserted near the center comes out clean.

Yield: 8–10 servings

COFFEETIME TREATS

Make a fresh pot of coffee (or tea), collect a friend or two, and take a little time out for a chat and a chuckle. A plate of warm scones or a just-baked coffeecake will make it even more special.

Whole-Wheat Granola Coffeecake

✖ ✖ ✖

Rich but not too sweet. A robust treat for Sunday breakfasts.

- ½ cup unbleached all-purpose white flour
- 1 teaspoon baking soda
- ½ teaspoon salt
- 1¼ cups whole-wheat flour, preferably stone-ground
- 1 egg
- 1 cup buttermilk or sour milk
- ¼ cup unsalted butter, melted
- ½ cup maple syrup (Honey may be substituted, but the texture will not be as nice. Or use brown sugar and reduce the whole-wheat flour to 1 cup.)

Topping:

- ¼ cup whole-wheat flour
- ¼ cup brown sugar, firmly packed
- ¾ cup granola (homemade, or the best and freshest you can buy)
- ½ cup chopped pecans or walnuts
- 1 teaspoon cinnamon
- 4 tablespoons (½ stick) unsalted butter, melted

1. Preheat oven to 375°F. Sift together the white flour, baking soda, and salt. Mix in the whole-wheat flour with a fork. In a large bowl, beat the egg until very light; add the buttermilk, butter, and maple syrup and beat well to blend. Add the flour mixture and fold in gently until just combined. Spread batter smoothly in a buttered 8-inch square pan or its equivalent.

2. To make the topping, toss the flour, sugar, granola, pecans, and cinnamon with a fork. Drizzle the butter over the mixture and toss again. Sprinkle over the batter.

3. Bake the coffeecake about 25 minutes or until a toothpick inserted into the cake part comes out clean. Serve warm from the pan with unsalted butter. To reheat, cover with foil.

Yield: 9 servings

Basic Scones

✖ ✖ ✖

For slight sweetness in the dough, add ¼ cup of sugar with the flour. For richness, use cream instead of milk or add 1 egg and decrease the milk to ½ cup.

- 2 cups flour
- 2½ teaspoons baking powder
- ¼ teaspoon salt
- 4 tablespoons (½ stick) butter
- ¾ cup milk

1. Preheat oven to 400°F.
2. Sift together the flour, baking powder, and salt. Cut in the butter until the mixture is crumbly (a food processor helps here). Add the milk and blend well; the finished dough should be sticky.
3. Flour a flat work space and knead the dough for about half a minute. Roll

it out to about a ½-inch thickness and cut into whatever shape you like (triangles are traditional). Bake for 15 minutes.

Yield: About 12 scones, depending on size

VARIATIONS:

Herb Scones: Follow the recipe for basic scones, but add about 3 tablespoons fresh (or 1 tablespoon dried) herbs (basil, thyme, or oregano). Serve with softened herbed butter and a dash of lemon juice.

Raisin Scones: To the basic scone recipe, add 3 tablespoons sugar and ½ cup raisins. Serve with lemon curd.

Raspberry Nut Scones: To the basic scone recipe, carefully fold in 1 cup fresh or frozen raspberries and ½ cup chopped nuts. Blend raspberry jam into softened butter for a spread.

Citrus Scones: To the basic scone recipe, add 1 teaspoon orange or lemon zest.

Ginger Scones

❖ ❖ ❖

Ginger scones go equally well with a hot cup of tea or a hot bowl of soup.

1 ¼ cups all-purpose flour
1 tablespoon sugar
2 teaspoons pasteurized dried egg whites
1 teaspoon baking powder
½ teaspoon baking soda
¼ teaspoon salt
¾ cup nonfat vanilla yogurt
1 tablespoon minced crystallized ginger

1. Preheat oven to 425°F. Coat a nonstick baking sheet with cooking spray.

2. In a large mixing bowl, sift all but 1 tablespoon of the flour, the sugar, egg whites, baking powder, soda, and salt. Mix well.

3. In a small bowl, combine the yogurt and ginger.

4. Add the wet ingredients to the dry ingredients, and stir until just combined. Sprinkle the remaining table-spoon of flour onto a work surface and turn out the dough. Flip it over once so that the flour will coat both sides. Lightly pat the dough into a 12-inch circle and cut the circle into eight wedges. Transfer them with a spatula onto the baking sheet.

5. Bake the scones for 12 to 15 minutes, or until golden brown.

Yield: 8 scones

VARIATION: If you like, you can replace the ginger with the more traditional currants: Add ¼ cup of currants to the flour mixture before adding the yogurt.

ABOUT CRYSTALLIZED GINGER

· · · · · · · · · · · ·

Like candied fruit, crystallized ginger gets its extra sweetness by being boiled or dipped in sugar syrup and then dried. Sometimes, it's also rolled in granulated sugar. It adds flavor to baked goods and is a great garnish.

LITTLE BREADS

Sometimes all a menu needs is a little something from the oven: a biscuit, a popover, a square of savory cheese bread. These make up quickly but last long in the memory of a good meal.

Mother's Sunday Dinner Rolls

❂ ❂ ❂

Sunday dinner was the most important meal in our home, and Mother served only the best. That meant homemade dinner rolls, hot from the oven. I've continued the tradition in my own home, making the dough the night before and letting it rise a second time overnight in the refrigerator. Then I bake these rolls just before we sit down to our family feast.

- ½ cup (1 stick) butter
- ½ cup sugar
- 3 eggs
- 1 cup scalded milk, slightly cooled
- 1 package (¼ ounce) active dry yeast, dissolved in ¼ cup warm water
- 4 cups all-purpose flour
- ½ teaspoon salt

1. In a large bowl, cream together the butter and sugar. Add the eggs and beat well with a wire whisk. Add milk and yeast. Using a wooden spoon, mix in the flour and salt. Cover with plastic wrap and a clean towel.

2. Let rise until double in bulk, then pat down. Recover tightly and place in the refrigerator overnight.

3. The next day, preheat oven to 350°F. Grease three 12-cup muffin pans. Divide the dough into three equal balls and place on a floured surface. Pat each ball into a long loaf and cut it into 12 equal parts. With your fingers, pinch each dough ball into three small balls and place into each muffin cup. Brush tops with melted butter and let rise once more.

4. Bake for 15 minutes or until lightly browned.

Yield: 3 dozen

Baking Powder Biscuits

❂ ❂ ❂

These light and fluffy biscuits were a staple in our home as I grew up. Biscuits and homemade jam are terrific, but we preferred to stuff a warm baking powder biscuit with melted butter and a teaspoon of sugar. Sheer heaven!

- 2 cups all-purpose flour
- 5 teaspoons baking powder
- 1 teaspoon salt
- 2 tablespoons butter or vegetable shortening
- ¾ –1 cup cold milk, preferably skim

1. Preheat oven to 450°F. Sift the flour, baking powder, and salt into a medium-sized bowl. Work the butter into the flour mixture with your fingers or a pastry blender.

2. Gradually add the milk, mixing gently until just blended. Turn onto a floured board and roll out to approximately ½-inch thick. Cut biscuits with a round biscuit cutter and place on a greased cookie sheet; bake until light brown, 12 to 15 minutes.

Yield: 16 biscuits

VARIATION: For a different treat, add a teaspoon of your favorite fresh or dried herbs, such as rosemary, thyme, oregano, basil, or chives, to the dry ingredients.

Easy Pickin' Blueberry Drop Biscuits

❊ ❊ ❊

Wonderfully fresh for a summer meal, especially if you have spent an hour gathering your own wild blueberries. Actually, it takes much less than an hour to get a cup of berries, but you need to take into account the number that will disappear into your mouth. These biscuits are not sweet. Serve with butter and honey.

- 2 cups unbleached all-purpose flour
- 1 tablespoon baking powder
- ½ teaspoon salt
- 3 tablespoons cold unsalted butter
- 1 cup cold milk
- 1 cup fresh blueberries, washed and drained on a towel, then tossed with 2 tablespoons sugar

1. Preheat oven to 375°F. Sift together the flour, baking powder, and salt. Cut in the butter with a pastry blender or two knives until the mixture is coarsely textured.

2. Pour in the milk and mix gently with a fork. Before completely mixed, add the berries and continue mixing with a large spoon — gingerly, so as not to bruise the berries.

3. Drop the batter by spoonfuls onto a buttered baking sheet. If you wish, sprinkle a little more sugar over the biscuits before baking.

4. Bake for 20 to 25 minutes or until lightly browned. The time will depend on their size. Break one open to test. Serve immediately.

Yield: 12 large biscuits

THE BEAUTY OF BISCUITS

....

Even folks who love to spend lots of time in the kitchen sometimes appreciate the quickness with which biscuits can be made. You can lightly roll and cut out for symmetrical shapes or drop by spoonfuls onto baking sheets. Rolled or dropped, they taste great.

Cheesy Bread with Thyme

❊ ❊ ❊

Herbs, poppy seeds, and a nippy topping of cheese transform basic baking powder biscuit dough into a flavorful dinner bread. Cut in generous squares and serve hot.

- ½ cup (1 stick) butter
- 1 large yellow onion, chopped (½ cup)
- 1 egg, lightly beaten
- ½ cup buttermilk
- 1½ cups unbleached all-purpose flour
- 2 teaspoons baking powder
- 1 cup shredded sharp Cheddar cheese
- 3 tablespoons minced fresh thyme
- 1 tablespoon poppy seeds

1. Preheat oven to 350°F and grease an 8-inch square pan.

2. In a small skillet, melt 1 tablespoon of the butter and sauté the onion until it is soft and golden.

3. Combine the egg and buttermilk in a large bowl.

4. In a separate bowl, sift together the flour and baking powder, and cut in 5 tablespoons of the butter. Blend into the egg and buttermilk mixture.

5. Add the onion and ½ cup of the cheese.

6. Melt the remaining 2 tablespoons of butter and combine with the remaining cheese, the thyme, and the poppy seeds. Spread the dough in the pan and pour the cheese mixture over the top.

7. Bake for 20 to 25 minutes, cut into squares, and serve hot.

Yield: 16 squares

MUFFINS

Nestle a batch of warm muffins into a napkin-lined basket and watch the family smile. Muffins go way beyond breakfast at our house; they're also for lunchboxes, teatime, and a friendly accompaniment to lunch or dinner.

Apple Muffins

❈ ❈ ❈

This basic recipe is delicious with most any fruit, including dried dates, figs, or even cut-up prunes.

    2 cups all-purpose flour
    1 cup apples, cored and
       chopped but not peeled
    1 cup milk
    1½ cups (3 sticks) butter, melted
    ¼ cup sugar
    1 egg
    3 teaspoons baking powder
    1 teaspoon ground cinnamon
    ¼ teaspoon ground nutmeg
    ½ teaspoon salt

1. Preheat oven to 400°F. Grease 12 muffin cups or line with paper liners.

2. Mix all ingredients together using a wooden spoon. Batter will be lumpy. Fill muffin cups ⅔ full. Bake for 20 to 25 minutes or until a tester inserted in the center of a muffin comes out clean.

Yield: 1 dozen

Sunny Morning Muffins

❈ ❈ ❈

A great start for a beautiful day, these muffins are full of the natural sweetness of coconut, pineapple, and raisins, and a healthy addition of carrot or zucchini keeps them moist.

    1½ cups unbleached all-
       purpose white flour
    ½ cup whole-wheat flour
    ¾ cup sugar
    2 teaspoons ground cinnamon
    2 teaspoons baking soda
    ½ teaspoon salt
    3 eggs, lightly beaten
    ¾ cup vegetable oil
    2 cups grated carrots or
       zucchini, or a combination
    ½ cup coconut
    ½ cup chopped pecans
    ½ cup undrained crushed
       pineapple
    ½ cup golden raisins

1. Preheat oven to 350°F. Sift the flours with the sugar, cinnamon, soda, and salt into a large bowl. In a small bowl, mix the eggs and oil and add to the flour mixture. Stir the batter just until the dry ingredients are moistened.

2. Fold the carrots, coconut, pecans, pineapple, and raisins into the batter. Stir until blended.

3. Pour the batter into greased muffin pans and bake for 25 to 30 minutes, or until a tester inserted in the center of a muffin comes out clean. Cool the muffins in the pans on a wire rack for 10 minutes.

Yield: 15 muffins

Eternal Bran Muffins

❈ ❈ ❈

We've dubbed these moist tender muffins "eternal" because the batter can be stored in the refrigerator for up to two weeks without losing flavor. Bake them as you need them.

    6 cups 100-percent bran
       cereal
    2 cups boiling water
    1 cup canola oil
    1 cup granulated sugar
    1 cup brown sugar
    4 eggs, beaten
    1 quart buttermilk
    5 cups whole-wheat pastry
       flour or all-purpose flour
    5 teaspoons baking soda
    2 teaspoons salt
    2 cups fruit and/or nuts of
       your choice

1. Preheat oven to 375°F. Coat the cups of muffin pans with vegetable cooking spray.

2. Put 2 cups of the bran cereal in a medium-sized bowl and cover with the water. Mix in oil; let cool.

3. In a large bowl, mix together the rest of the cereal, the granulated and brown sugars, eggs, and buttermilk. Add flour, soda, and salt. Combine all ingredients except fruit and/or nuts. If you are using all the batter, add the fruits and nuts now; if not, add only a proportional amount. (At this point, you may transfer the mixture to a tightly covered container and store in the refrigerator until you are ready to add remaining fruit and bake.)

4. Spoon the batter into muffin cups until they are about three-quarters full. Bake for 15 to 20 minutes, or until tester inserted into center of a muffin comes out clean.

Yield: 48 muffins

Sweet Potato Muffins

❈ ❈ ❈

Sweet potato gives these muffins a rich tawny color and a flavor that is reminiscent of Thanksgiving candied yams.

1½ cups unbleached
      all-purpose flour

½ cup sugar
½ teaspoon baking powder
2 teaspoons baking soda
½ teaspoon salt
1 teaspoon ground cinnamon
1 teaspoon ground nutmeg
½ cup vegetable oil
½ cup pure maple syrup
2 eggs, beaten
1 teaspoon vanilla extract
1½ cups cooked mashed sweet
      potatoes
1½ cups well-packed grated
      raw zucchini
¼ cup chopped walnuts

1. Preheat oven to 375°F. Sift together the flour, sugar, baking powder, soda, salt, cinnamon, and nutmeg. Beat together the oil, maple syrup, eggs, and vanilla.

2. Stir the sweet potatoes and zucchini into the oil mixture. Add the dry ingredients and walnuts, mixing just until blended.

3. Grease two 12-cup muffin pans. Fill the muffin cups two-thirds full. Bake on the top rack of the oven for 20 to 25 minutes, or until brown.

Yield: 24 muffins.

Tamarack Blueberry Muffins

❈ ❈ ❈

Camp Tamarack was a summer day camp run by our friends Marvin and Mary Gangemi. They gave the recipe

for these muffins to our daughters Jennifer and Jessica, who now bake them for their own children.

2½ cups all-purpose flour
2½ teaspoons baking powder
1 cup sugar
¼ teaspoon salt
1 cup milk
½ cup (1 stick) butter, melted
2 eggs
1½ cups blueberries

1. Preheat oven to 400°F. Grease 18 muffin cups or line with paper liners.

2. Sift together the flour, baking powder, sugar, and salt.

3. Make a well in the middle of the flour mixture and add milk, butter, and eggs.

4. Mix with a wooden spoon. When ingredients are well blended, fold in the blueberries. Spoon batter into cups.

5. Sprinkle tops with sugar; bake for 20 minutes, or until light brown.

Yield: 22 muffins

ideal muffin   oven too cool

oven too hot   batter over-beaten

SALADS

Early in the spring, our first gardening effort goes into preparing and planting a salad garden just steps from the kitchen. We plant many kinds of lettuce, onions, scallions, radishes, carrots, and spinach. These early birds are a welcome addition to mealtime — their crisp freshness perks up any lunch or dinner, particularly after a long winter of supermarket greens. But as you will see in this chapter, there are many creative additions to salads, including citrus, berries, nuts, fish, and meats, that go beyond traditional greens. Have fun with them and use your imagination to mix flavors, textures, and colors.

Contributors to this chapter are Janet Ballantyne; Ruth Bass; Charlene Braida; Betty Cavage; Miriam Jacobs; Alexandra Nimetz, Jason Stanley, and Emeline Starr; Maggie Oster; Dorothy Parker; Sara Pitzer; Nancy C. Ralston and Marynor Jordan; Phyllis V. Shaudys; and Edith Stovel and Pamela Wakefield.

GREEN SALADS
....
SLAWS
....
CHEESY SALADS
....
VEGETABLE SALADS
....
POTATO SALADS
....
RICE & GRAIN SALADS
....
PASTA SALADS
....
LUNCHEON SALADS
....
FRUIT & MOLDED SALADS
....
MAIN DISH SALADS
....
VINAIGRETTES & DRESSINGS

Waldorf Salad

❊ ❊ ❊

New York City's Waldorf Hotel took the bounty of a country orchard, dressed it in style, and created a true American classic. We published Olwen Woodier's version in her *Apple Cookbook*, and, in the best tradition of country cooks, I made a few changes of my own. Here's my version.

3   medium apples (Jonagold, Cortland, Northern Spy, Granny Smith)
3   stalks of celery, diced
½   cup chopped toasted walnuts
½   cup dried cherries or cranberries
½   cup green grapes, halved
2   tablespoons lemon juice
1   teaspoon sugar
½   teaspoon ground nutmeg
½   teaspoon ground white pepper
¾   cup heavy cream
8   mint leaves or 2 tablespoons chopped fresh parsley
1   head Boston lettuce

1. Chill a medium-sized bowl for beating the cream.

2. Core and dice the apples. Place in a large bowl. Add the celery, walnuts, cherries, and grapes.

3. Beat the lemon juice, sugar, nutmeg, pepper, and cream together in the chilled bowl. When the cream is thick and stands in soft mounds, stir into the apple mixture.

4. Tear the mint leaves into small pieces and sprinkle on the top. Serve on Boston lettuce leaves.

Yield: 4 servings

TEAR, DON'T CUT

·····················

Gently tear the leaves of salad greens into smaller pieces. If you cut the leaves, you will find that they bleed and collapse quickly. The heavy, ribbed leaves of romaine lettuce can be cut along the rib without ill effect.

Frosted Lettuce Wedges

❊ ❊ ❊

Head lettuces have been somewhat ignored lately in favor of more exotic leafy greens. This simple salad of lettuce wedges in sensational blue cheese and herb dressing is so good, it may spark a comeback!

1   cup crumbled blue cheese
2   tablespoons lemon juice
2   tablespoons wine vinegar
3   tablespoons minced scallions
2   tablespoons minced fresh parsley
½   cup vegetable oil
½   cup heavy cream, beaten until stiff
1   head iceberg lettuce, cut into 8 wedges

1. Combine cheese, lemon juice, vinegar, scallions, and parsley in a blender or food processor. Process until well mixed. With the machine running, slowly pour in the oil. Transfer to a bowl and fold in the cream.

2. Using a spatula, spread the dressing over the lettuce wedges. Chill for 1 hour before serving.

Yield: 8 servings

GREEN SALADS

In my mother's day, salad greens consisted primarily of iceberg lettuce for the bowl, Boston lettuce for lining plates, watercress for a daring departure, and parsley or chives, used mainly as a garnish. How much richer is the variety now that we are rediscovering older varieties of lettuce and using the field greens and leafy herbs that our great-grandmothers used to grow. Here are some of our favorites:

Arugula: Also called Rocket, a peppery green and a good foil for beans and strongly flavored dressings.

Borage: Tender leaves are chopped for cucumber accents; sky-blue flowers add edible beauty.

Boston: Also called Bibb, buttery-soft leaves in loosely packed heads with pale yellow centers.

Belgian Endive (Witloof): Compact ovate heads of white leaves with pale green edges; very crisp.

Black-Seeded Simpson: A green leafy garden lettuce, easy to grow for repeated cuttings.

Burnet (Salad Burnet): Small scalloped leaves on long stalks; mild cucumber flavor.

Chicory: Deeply curled leaves with a strong flavor; use in mixed greens.

Curly Endive: Slightly bitter leaves with curled edges.

Dandelion: Use very young shoots for an interesting, bitter accent.

Escarole: Broad, lightly curled green leaves.

Frisée: Finely curled, feathery leaves, beautiful in mesclun or mixed greens.

Green Leaf: Large, ruffled green leaves with mild flavor.

Iceberg: Crisp, head lettuce with pale green leaves and very mild flavor.

Mesclun: Also called salad mix, this is simply a combination of young small salad greens.

Mizuna: Pungent, ferny leaves, related to mustard; often used in mesclun.

Oak Leaf: A delicate garden lettuce with distinctive lobed leaves.

Radicchio: Small, compact heads of gorgeous deep red leaves with white veins; slightly bitter.

Romaine: Rich flavor and plenty of crunch; especially nice in Caesar salads.

Ruby: Large leaves tinged dark red; adds color interest.

Spinach: Dark green leaves with distinctive flavor; young flat-leafed varieties preferable.

Watercress: Very pungent leaves on crisp stems.

WASHING & DRYING TIPS

Wash lettuce and greens by dunking in lukewarm water and lifting out of the water. Inspect each leaf to be sure it's dirt-free before tearing it into the salad.

We like our lettuce and greens bone-dry when we add them to a salad. Use a salad spinner to remove the water clinging to the leaves — it works! In the old days, folks used to stuff a pillowcase with wet lettuce and greens and spin the pillowcase in the air until all the water had spun off the leaves. I've even heard of folks who use linen tablecloths to dry big batches of greens. Same principle, but more work.

Just-the-Greens Salad

❈ ❈ ❈

Especially in summer, when gardeners can pick their greens just before dinner and nongardeners can choose the finest greens from a favorite farm stand or produce store, a simple salad is best. We use four or five types of greens in our summer salads. Go easy on dressing: You want the flavor of the greens to come through.

1 pound lettuce or salad greens (a single type or an assortment)

1. Thoroughly wash and dry the lettuce. Tear it into small pieces.

2. Place greens into a large salad bowl and toss with vinaigrette or dressing just before serving. Or place greens on individual, chilled glass salad plates and serve dressing on the side.

Yield: 6 servings

HOW MUCH DO I NEED?

....

1 pound fresh lettuce or greens equals 24 cups salad-sized pieces or 12 cups chiffonade (shredded).

Spinach, Fennel, Apple, and Walnut Salad

❈ ❈ ❈

These fresh, crisp flavors go well together and are nicely sparked by the lemon dressing.

5 cups fresh baby spinach leaves
juice of 1 lemon
½ cup olive oil
1 teaspoon sugar
¼ teaspoon salt
1 teaspoon dried basil
freshly ground black pepper
1 fennel bulb, thinly sliced
2 scallions, chopped
1 Granny Smith apple, with peel, cored and sliced
½ cup toasted walnuts
Parmesan cheese shavings

1. Wash the spinach, dry thoroughly, and arrange on 4 individual salad plates.

2. In a medium-sized bowl, combine the lemon juice, olive oil, sugar, salt, basil, and pepper to taste; whisk until well blended.

3. Add to the dressing the fennel, scallions, and apples; coat well. Arrange on top of the spinach leaves. Top with walnuts and a few shavings of fresh Parmesan.

Yield: 4 servings

SEVEN SALAD TIPS

....

- *Lettuce and greens should be torn into bite-size pieces. Cutting lettuce at the table with a fork and knife should not be necessary.*

- *To prevent soggy salads, dress them at the table. Toss and serve.*

- *The proportion of oil to vinegar in a salad dressing is a matter of taste. Everything from an equal proportion of oil to vinegar or lemon juice to 4 parts oil to 1 part vinegar is acceptable. For more salad dressing recipes, see pages 142–143.*

- *Make dressings ahead of time for the sake of convenience and to ensure a good blending of flavors.*

- *Edible flowers are delightful in salads. Favorites are calendula, nasturtium, opal basil, rose petals, borage blossoms, daylilies, squash blossoms, chive blossoms, thyme blossoms, pansies, mint blossoms, chamomile, and marigolds.*

- *Fresh herbs are excellent in salads. See page 305 for more ideas.*

- *Young Swiss and ruby chard are good in salads, too.*

SLAWS

When our Dutch ancestors settled in America, they brought with them a taste for koolsla, or cabbage salad. It was a taste that rapidly caught on; coleslaw is now one of the universal favorites.

Confetti Coleslaw

❈ ❈ ❈

This colorful slaw is so pretty, and the apple and parsnip add a distinctive, mellow sweetness.

    3   cups shredded green cabbage
    1   cup shredded red cabbage
    ½   cup peeled, cored, and diced apple
    ½   cup grated carrot
    ½   cup chopped red onion
    ½   cup grated peeled parsnip
    ½   cup chopped green bell pepper
    ½   cup plain yogurt
    ¾   cup mayonnaise
    1   tablespoon honey
    3   tablespoons lemon juice
    ¼   cup heavy cream
    ½   teaspoon mustard seeds
    ¼   cup chopped peanuts

    1. In a large bowl, combine the green and red cabbage, apple, carrot, onion, parsnip, and bell pepper.
    2. Whisk together the yogurt, mayonnaise, honey, lemon juice, cream, and mustard seeds. Fold into the slaw mixture. Toss well to mix.
    3. Refrigerate for at least 1 hour.
    4. Sprinkle the slaw with the chopped peanuts and serve immediately.
    Yield: 6–8 servings

CRISPEST SLAWS

....

If you want your slaw to be crisp, plan ahead when making it. Shred the cabbage, then immerse it in ice water for 1 hour. Drain it well and dry it thoroughly. You can make the recipe at this point, or refrigerate the crisped cabbage in a tightly sealed container or plastic bag.

Janet's Favorite Coleslaw

❈ ❈ ❈

This coleslaw is for people with a sweet tooth. Add other vegetables, fruits, and nuts as desired. Try caraway or celery seeds for contrast.

    1½   cups mayonnaise
    ¼   cup pure maple syrup
    ¼   cup lemon juice
    ¾   teaspoon nutmeg
    6–8 cups chopped red or green cabbage

    1. Whisk together mayonnaise, maple syrup, lemon juice, and nutmeg. Combine the dressing with the cabbage and allow the salad to sit for at least 1 hour before serving.
    Yield: 4–6 servings

Zucchini Slaw

❈ ❈ ❈

Yet another delicious way to use abundant garden zucchini. The dark green skin adds color contrast to this slaw.

    1   medium zucchini, julienned
    1   medium carrot, julienned
    1   stalk of celery, chopped
    ½   medium green bell pepper, chopped
    ½   small head green or red cabbage, grated
    ⅓   cup olive oil
    2   tablespoons lemon juice
    1   teaspoon Dijon mustard
        salt and freshly ground black pepper

    1. Toss the zucchini, carrot, celery, pepper, and cabbage in a large bowl.
    2. In a small mixing bowl, whisk together the oil, lemon juice, mustard, and salt and pepper to taste; pour over vegetables.
    Yield: 2 servings

CHEESY SALADS

Cheese is wonderful in salads, adding richness, texture, and flavor contrast to crisp greens and vegetables. Think of blue cheese in dressings, Swiss in a chef's salad, feta in Greek salads, and warm goat cheese with mesclun. Perfect mates!

Tomato, Basil, & Mozzarella Salad

❊ ❊ ❊

Save this recipe for the summertime, when tomatoes are vine-ripe and full of flavor from the sun.

4 slices tomato
4 leaves fresh basil
4 slices low-fat mozzarella
freshly ground black pepper

1. Place the tomatoes on a plate. Top with the basil and mozzarella; season with pepper to taste.

Yield: 2 servings

Greek Salad

❊ ❊ ❊

How lucky that our cooking is influenced by so many diverse cultures! Greek salad is an example of an ethnic classic we've embraced as our own.

2 heads romaine lettuce
½ red onion, chopped
1 cucumber, chopped
1 green bell pepper, seeded and chopped
1 tomato, cut into wedges
¼ cup crumbled feta cheese
⅓ cup sliced black olives
2 tablespoons extra virgin olive oil
2 tablespoons lemon juice
1 tablespoon red wine vinegar
1 clove of garlic, minced
1 teaspoon chopped fresh oregano, or ½ teaspoon dried
salt and freshly ground black pepper

1. In a large bowl, toss together the lettuce, onion, cucumber, green pepper, tomato, feta, and olives.

2. In a separate bowl, whisk together the oil, lemon juice, vinegar, garlic, oregano, and salt and pepper to taste.

3. Pour the dressing over the salad and toss. Serve immediately.

Yield: 4 servings

ABOUT OLIVES

....

Olives are a fixture in Greek salads, and they can be used in many other combinations as well. In addition to the familiar seedless black olives and pimiento-stuffed green olives, look for their stronger-flavored, briny cousins from the deli. Huge, fleshy, green olives; coal-black, oil-cured, tangy kalamatas; and tiny niçoise olives add interest to salads.

To pit a ripe olive, press on it firmly with the flat side of a knife until it splits; the pit should come out cleanly.

VEGETABLE SALADS

When my family thinks of salad, we think of much more than greens. We raid the garden for whatever is freshest, dress leftover steamed asparagus or green beans in a light vinaigrette, cut corn from the cob for hearty, Southwest-style salads, and never tire of that old standby — Three-Bean Salad.

SALADS DON'T HAVE TO BE TOSSED

....

You can make a composed salad by arranging vegetables on a bed of greens on a platter or in a bowl. Try several different patterns — rows of vegetables, concentric circles, V-shaped rows, alternating half-circles. The vegetables should be chopped or sliced in fairly uniform-sized pieces for visual harmony.

Three-Bean Salad

❈ ❈ ❈

For color and for speed of preparation, it's hard to beat this salad, which is a great addition to any picnic or buffet.

> 2 cups cooked chickpeas or 1 can (16 ounces), drained
> 2 cups green beans, cooked until tender crisp, or 1 can (16 ounces), drained
> 2 cups cooked red kidney beans or 1 can (16 ounces), drained
> 1 sweet onion, peeled and sliced paper-thin
> 2–4 cloves of garlic, minced
> 2 tablespoons finely chopped fresh oregano
> salt and freshly ground black pepper
> ⅔ cup olive oil
> ¼ cup vinegar

1. In a large bowl, combine the chickpeas, green beans, kidney beans, and onion.

2. Mix the garlic, oregano, salt and pepper to taste, oil, and vinegar and pour over the bean mixture. Toss gently. Let stand at room temperature for at least 30 minutes. Serve immediately or chill before serving.

Yield: 8 servings

Herbed Vegetable Salad

❈ ❈ ❈

For a colorful salad that you can make hours before dinnertime, try this mélange of vegetables and fresh herbs.

> 5 cups carrots, green beans, cauliflower, and broccoli in any combination, cut into bite-size pieces
> 1 red onion, thinly sliced
> ½ cup vegetable oil
> ½ cup cider vinegar
> 2 tablespoons lemon juice
> 1 teaspoon minced fresh oregano
> 1 teaspoon minced fresh basil
> 1 teaspoon minced fresh rosemary
> 1 clove of garlic, minced
> ½ cup minced fresh parsley

1. Cook the carrots, green beans, cauliflower, and broccoli until crisp tender but not soft. Drain, place in a bowl, and toss gently.

2. Separate the onion slices into rings and arrange on top of the other vegetables.

3. Blend the oil, vinegar, lemon juice, oregano, basil, rosemary, garlic, and parsley and pour over the vegetables. Chill for several hours.

Yield: 6–8 servings

Peas and Carrots Salad

❈ ❈ ❈

Wonderful cook and good friend Connie McGlynn shared this easy recipe with me many years ago when our kids were small. It proved to be a sure way to get healthful vegetables into all of them!

    2   cups freshly shelled peas
    2   cups diced carrots
    3   large carrots, sliced
    3   stalks of celery, diced
    1   medium green bell pepper,
        diced
    1   cup mayonnaise
    2   tablespoons cider vinegar
    1   tablespoon sugar
    salt and freshly ground black
        pepper

1. Blanch the peas and carrots until just tender. Drain and run under cold water to stop the cooking. Toss with the celery and bell pepper.

2. In a separate small bowl, whisk the mayonnaise, vinegar, sugar, and salt and pepper to taste until well blended. Toss with the vegetables and chill until ready to serve. Can be made a day ahead.

Yield: 8 servings

Note: Two 10-ounce packages frozen peas and carrots may be substituted for the diced peas and carrots.

Corn and Tomato Salad

❈ ❈ ❈

At the end of the summer, when the corn goes from field to kettle in minutes and the tomatoes are nearly falling off their vines, this salad is incomparably good.

    4   cups fresh corn kernels
    2   cups diced tomatoes
    ¼   cup minced fresh parsley
    ½   cup diced red onion
    2   tablespoons lime juice
    2   tablespoons vegetable oil
    2   teaspoons minced fresh
        cilantro
    salt and freshly ground black
        pepper

1. Blanch the corn in boiling water for 3 to 4 minutes and drain. Run under cold water to cool, and drain again.

2. In a salad bowl, combine the corn, tomatoes, parsley, and onion.

3. Whisk together the lime juice, oil, and cilantro. Pour over the salad. Toss to coat. Season to taste with salt and pepper. Chill the salad for at least 1 hour before serving.

Yield: 4–6 servings

VARIATION: For a sturdier salad, add a can of rinsed, well-drained black beans; increase the lime juice and oil to 3 tablespoons each and the cilantro to ¼ cup.

SALAD COMBOS

Creating your own salad combinations is part of the fun of country cooking. Here are some ideas to get you started.

- **MEXICAN:** Avocados, red bell peppers, chickpeas, cooked corn, green bell peppers
- **FARM-STYLE:** Carrots, green bell peppers, cucumbers, kohlrabi
- **FRENCH:** Mushrooms, parsley, peas
- **ASIAN:** Broccoli, water chestnuts, cashews, soy sauce or tamari

POTATO SALADS

I love my mom's potato salad (see Mimi's Picnic Potato Salad in "Country Carryouts," page 314) so much that I make it year-round, but I also like trying new recipes. Hot German Potato Salad is terrific with bratwurst and beer, and Sweet Potato Tarragon Salad is definitely a keeper in my recipe file.

Hot German Potato Salad

❁ ❁ ❁

When piquant dressing hits hot potatoes, just enough is absorbed to give the potatoes irresistible savor. The crumble of crisp bacon on top is the crowning touch.

6 cups diced potatoes
¼ pound bacon, diced
¾ cup diced scallions
½ cup diced dill pickle
¼ cup pickle juice
¼ cup wine vinegar
1 teaspoon caraway seeds
1 teaspoon sugar
½ teaspoon celery seeds
salt and freshly ground black pepper

1. Boil the potatoes until tender, about 10 minutes.

2. Meanwhile, brown the bacon and remove it from the pan. Drain off the bacon fat, reserving ¼ cup. Combine the reserved bacon fat, scallions, pickle, pickle juice, vinegar, caraway seeds, sugar, and celery seeds in the pan. Simmer for 3 minutes.

3. When the potatoes are cooked, drain and place in a large bowl. Pour the dressing over the potatoes and toss to coat. Add the bacon. Season to taste with salt and pepper. Serve immediately.

Yield: 6–8 servings

Red Potato Salad with Fresh Peas

❁ ❁ ❁

Our friend DeeDee Stovel started us putting fresh peas into our potato salad. This is especially tasty with baby red potatoes and tiny, just-shelled peas.

2 pounds small red potatoes, unpeeled, washed and cut into halves or quarters (about 8 cups)
1 medium Vidalia or sweet onion, chopped
¼ cup cider vinegar
½ teaspoon salt
2 tablespoons mayonnaise
1 tablespoon Dijon mustard
¼ cup plain yogurt
freshly ground black pepper
4 leaves fresh mint, chopped, or 1 tablespoon minced fresh dill
1 pound fresh peas, shelled

1. Bring a large pot of salted water to a boil. Add the potatoes and cook for 15 minutes or until they are tender when pierced with a sharp knife. Drain the potatoes and place them in a large bowl with the onion, 2 tablespoons of the vinegar, and the salt. Gently stir the potatoes to combine all the ingredients. Cover the bowl with plastic wrap and let it sit unrefrigerated for 30 minutes to blend the flavors.

2. In a small bowl, whisk together the remaining vinegar, the mayonnaise, mustard, yogurt, and pepper to taste just until smooth. Pour this dressing over the marinated potatoes and stir to blend. Sprinkle the mint over the salad and scatter the peas over all. Refrigerate for at least 2 hours; serve cold.

Yield: 8 servings

Sweet Potato Tarragon Salad

❈ ❈ ❈

Sweet potatoes give a whole new take on potato salad. The lemon-tarragon dressing offsets them perfectly.

    4   cups julienned peeled
        sweet potatoes
    ⅓   cup vegetable oil
    5   tablespoons lemon juice
    1   tablespoon minced fresh
        tarragon
        salt and freshly ground black
        pepper

1. Parboil the julienned potatoes for 3 to 5 minutes, until just tender. Plunge into cold water and put into a medium-sized bowl. Drain immediately.

2. In a small bowl, combine the oil, lemon juice, tarragon, and salt and pepper to taste. Pour over the potatoes and toss to coat. Refrigerate for at least 2 hours to allow the flavors to mingle. Serve cold.

Yield: 4–6 servings

Spicy Black-and-White Potato Salad

❈ ❈ ❈

Olives and raisins make a striking color contrast with the potatoes in this salad; the flavor is out-of-the-ordinary, too, with its generous kick of spices.

 4 or 5   medium-sized new pota-
          toes (about 2 pounds)
    2   tablespoons butter
    1   tablespoon olive oil
  4–6   scallions, chopped
    ½   teaspoon chili powder
    ½   teaspoon ground
          coriander
    ¼   teaspoon ground allspice
    ¼   teaspoon ground cumin
    ¼   teaspoon ground ginger
    1   large stalk of celery,
          including leaves,
          chopped
 4 or 5   green olives, chopped
    ½   cup raisins, chopped
    ½   ripe avocado, peeled
          and mashed
    1   cup plain yogurt

1. Chill a serving bowl. Cook the potatoes, unpeeled, in boiling water for 20 minutes, or until just tender. Drain and cool them, then peel and cut into 1-inch dice.

2. In a large skillet, melt the butter over medium heat; add the olive oil. Sauté the scallions, stirring, for a minute or two, until they are softened. Add the chili powder, coriander, allspice, cumin, and ginger; turn off the heat. Stir in the potatoes and the celery; toss to coat. Transfer the potato mixture to the chilled bowl.

3. In a small bowl, combine the olives, raisins, and avocado. Stir in the yogurt and blend well.

4. Stir the yogurt sauce into the potato mixture; blend well.

Yield: 4–6 servings

SHORT ON TIME?

Homemade is best, but once in a while everyone is just too pressed for time. In that case, consider buying potato salad at a good deli and personalizing it. Add finely chopped bell peppers, cucumbers, carrots, pickles, summer squash, zucchini, or herbs. Basil, dill, or parsley would do well. With your added touch, it's homemade!

RICE & GRAIN SALADS

Salad becomes a balanced meal when it incorporates wholesome grains along with fresh produce. Experiment with any leftover grain or starch — brown or white rice, barley, quinoa, hominy, bulgur, wild rice, or millet.

Red Bean and Rice Salad

◉ ◉ ◉

Red beans and rice are widely eaten throughout the southern United States. When I moved north, I brought the dish with me. This salad is a fun variation and great to serve with barbecue.

- ½ pound smoked low-fat turkey sausage in casings
- 1 cup plus 3 tablespoons garlic red wine vinegar
- 1 can (16 ounces) red beans, drained and rinsed
- 1 cup cooked brown or white rice
- ½ cup peeled, seeded and diced cucumber
- ½ cup diced red bell pepper
- ¼ cup diced celery
- ¼ cup thinly sliced scallions (about 3 or 4 scallions)
- 1 tablespoon extra virgin olive oil

- 2 tablespoons coarse-grain mustard
- 1 tablespoon minced fresh thyme
- 1 clove of garlic, minced
- ½ teaspoon hot red pepper sauce
- salt and freshly ground black pepper

1. Combine the sausage and 1 cup vinegar in a nonreactive saucepan and bring to a boil over medium heat. Cover, reduce heat to low, and simmer for 5 minutes, or until sausage is cooked through. Remove sausage from vinegar, cut into 1-inch pieces, and set aside.

2. In a large nonreactive bowl, combine the beans, rice, cucumber, bell pepper, celery, scallions, and sausage.

3. In a small nonreactive bowl, whisk together the 3 tablespoons of vinegar, the oil, mustard, thyme, garlic, hot pepper sauce, and salt and pepper to taste. Pour over the bean mixture and toss until all ingredients are coated. Cover and refrigerate for several hours before serving to allow the flavors to blend.

Yield: 4 servings

Brown Rice Salad

◉ ◉ ◉

Since brown rice takes a long time to cook, we always make enough to get two meals from one pot.

- 6 cups cooked brown rice (about 1½ cups uncooked)
- 1 medium green bell pepper, seeded and chopped
- 1 medium red onion, thinly sliced
- ¾ cup dried currants
- 1 Granny Smith or other tart apple, cored and chopped
- ¼ cup capers
- ½ teaspoon peeled and grated fresh ginger root
- ½ cup toasted slivered almonds

Dressing

- ½ cup white wine tarragon vinegar
- 1 tablespoon sugar
- ½ teaspoon salt
- freshly ground black pepper
- 2 teaspoons curry powder, or garam masala (available in gourmet or natural food stores)
- 1 teaspoon dry mustard
- ½ teaspoon ground cardamom
- ½ teaspoon ground mace
- ¼ teaspoon cayenne pepper
- ¼ teaspoon ground cinnamon
- ¾ cup vegetable oil

1. Mix the rice, bell pepper, onion, currants, apple, capers, ginger root, and almonds together in a large bowl.

2. In a food processor or blender, combine the vinegar, sugar, salt, pepper to taste, curry powder, mustard, cardamom, mace, cayenne, and cinnamon until blended. With the processor running, slowly pour the oil through the feed tube until it is incorporated and the mixture is creamy. Pour the dressing over the salad; chill for several hours. This salad can be served at room temperature.

Yield: 8 servings

Tabbouleh
❈ ❈ ❈

Throughout the Middle East, this minty salad is made with many variations. The key ingredients, however, are the bulgur (cracked wheat), parsley, and mint. This regional version adds ½ cup cooled cooked peas.

    2 cups boiling water
    ½ cup bulgur
    ½ cup peas
    3 ripe tomatoes
    1 cucumber, peeled and seeded
    5 scallions
    4 tablespoons olive oil
    juice of one lemon
    1 large bunch mint (about 8 ounces), finely chopped
    1 large bunch Italian parsley (about 8 ounces), finely chopped
    salt and freshly ground black pepper

1. In a large bowl, pour the boiling water over the bulgur. Cover; let stand for at least 30 minutes, until all the water is absorbed.

2. Cook peas until tender but not soft, about 4 minutes. Drain; set aside to cool.

3. Dice the tomatoes and cucumber into small pieces. Thinly slice the scallions and add to the tomato mixture.

4. In a small bowl, combine the oil and lemon juice.

5. Combine the bulgur with the peas and the tomato mixture and stir gently. Add the mint, parsley, and salt and pepper to taste and toss with the oil and lemon juice. Set in a cool place for about 1 hour to let the flavors develop.

Yield: 6–8 servings

Tuna Rice Salad
❈ ❈ ❈

Years ago, Lynn Doll made all of us busy moms feel like queens when we went to her home for lunch. The kids got tuna sandwiches; we were served this salad with a deviled egg, sliced homegrown tomatoes, and fresh strawberries. It's an elegant but easy way to dress up a can of tuna.

    1 can (6 ounces) tuna, drained and flaked
    3 cups cold cooked rice
    6 pimiento-stuffed olives, sliced
    ⅓ cup pickle relish
    1½ cups finely chopped celery
    2 tablespoons minced fresh parsley
    ¼ cup mayonnaise
    ¼ cup sour cream
    2 tablespoons lemon juice
    ½ teaspoon salt
    ¼ teaspoon pepper
    2 pimientos, diced

1. Combine the tuna, rice, olives, relish, celery, and parsley; toss lightly.

2. In a separate small bowl, combine the mayonnaise, sour cream, lemon juice, salt, and pepper.

3. Toss the dressing with the rice mixture; gently stir in the pimientos. Chill until ready to serve.

Yield: 4 servings

SIMPLE GRAIN SALAD

Packaged couscous can become a refreshing side-dish salad in 15 minutes or less. Add your favorite dried fruit and citrus zest, then toss with a little olive oil and fruit vinegar. Chill at least 1 hour to blend flavors. We like dried cranberries, orange zest, and wildflower vinegar — or raisins, lemon zest, and raspberry vinegar.

PASTA SALADS

There's a pasta salad to please almost every taste — from picnic macaroni salad to elegant combinations of shaped pastas with shellfish, pesto, vegetables, nuts, and you name it.

Macaroni Salad

⊠ ⊠ ⊠

Macaroni salad is always a favorite with the little ones. This version is enhanced with hard-cooked eggs, grated carrot, and celery.

    2   cups elbow macaroni
    2   quarts boiling, lightly
        salted water
    ½   cup mayonnaise
    1   tablespoon oil
  2–2½ teaspoons vinegar
    1   clove of garlic, chopped
    3   hard-cooked eggs, chopped
    1   carrot, grated
    1   heaping teaspoon
        chopped onion
    ½   cup chopped celery
    1   tablespoon chopped fresh
        parsley
    4   tablespoons pickle relish
        salt and freshly ground
        black pepper

1. Add the macaroni to the water. Boil for 6 to 8 minutes. Do not overcook; macaroni should be al dente. Drain. Rinse in cold water; drain again.

2. Combine the mayonnaise with the oil and vinegar. Pour over the macaroni. Add the garlic, hard-cooked eggs, carrot, onion, celery, parsley, relish, and salt and pepper to taste. Mix well and serve.

Yield: 6–8 servings

Country Weekend Pasta Salad

⊠ ⊠ ⊠

Developed by a former Manhattan resident who now lives in the Berkshires, this pasta salad is a cinch for an easy homemade dish during a busy country weekend. Adapt it to what you have on hand or what looks good at the farmer's market: Try cilantro instead of parsley, or pine nuts instead of walnuts.

    8   ounces shell-shaped
        pasta
    2   tablespoons chopped
        walnuts
    1   tomato, chopped
    1   scallion, minced
    4   black olives, sliced
    ¼   cup minced fresh parsley

Dressing

    2   tablespoons sour cream
    1   tablespoon balsamic vinegar
    1   teaspoon Dijon mustard
    1   teaspoon grated Parmesan
        cheese

1. Cook the pasta as the package directs for al dente. Rinse under cold water to stop the cooking; drain.

2. In a large bowl, combine the walnuts, tomato, scallion, olives, and parsley. Mix well; add the cooled pasta and stir completely.

SPECIAL LUNCHES

....

For a special occasion luncheon or an everyday lunch when you want to make family feel special, spend an extra few minutes on how you present your salads. Spoon them into hollowed-out vegetables, such as a colorful red cabbage or bell peppers. For a salad on the sweet side, use a melon as a serving container. Or line a pretty platter with greens, mound the salad on top, and garnish with radish or tomato roses.

3. In a small bowl, thoroughly combine the sour cream, vinegar, and mustard.

4. Just before serving, pour the dressing over the salad, mix well, and sprinkle the Parmesan on top.

Yield: 2 servings

Pesto, Pasta, and Tomato Salad

❈ ❈ ❈

This refreshing dish is very different, and it is equally good served hot or cold. The pesto ingredients may be mixed and frozen for later use with tomatoes and orzo.

> 1   cup chopped fresh basil leaves
> 1   cup chopped fresh lemon basil leaves
> ½   cup light olive oil
> ½   cup balsamic vinegar
> 4   large cloves of garlic
> salt and freshly ground black pepper
> 8   large fresh tomatoes, peeled and quartered
> 1   pound orzo

1. In a food processor, blend the basils, oil, vinegar, garlic, and salt and pepper to taste. Add the tomatoes, and chop coarsely.

2. Transfer mixture to a covered bowl and chill.

3. Cook the orzo according to package instructions.

Drain. While still hot, gently toss with the chilled pesto-tomato mixture. Serve warm or chilled.

Yield: 6–8 servings as a main dish; 8–10 servings as a side dish

Hot and Cold Sesame Noodles

❈ ❈ ❈

Here's an Asian-style pasta salad with a great interplay of sesame and scallion.

> ¾   pound good-quality Italian spaghetti
> 1   tablespoon sesame oil
> 1–2   teaspoons hot chili oil
> 6   scallions (about 1 bunch), trimmed, cut on a diagonal into 1-inch pieces, and sliced in half lengthwise

Sauce

> 1   teaspoon cornstarch
> ½   cup chicken broth
> 3   tablespoons rice vinegar
> 3   tablespoons soy sauce
> 3   tablespoons Dijon mustard
> 1   tablespoon toasted sesame oil

1. In a large kettle of boiling salted water, cook the spaghetti until al dente, about 8 minutes. Drain and toss with the sesame and chili oils; let cool. Add the scallions and toss.

2. For the sauce, cook the cornstarch and broth in a small saucepan over medium heat, stirring until the mixture thickens. Whisk in the rice vinegar, soy sauce, mustard, and sesame oil and pour over the pasta. For a spicier mix, add more hot chili oil. Serve at room temperature.

Yield: 6–8 servings

Note: If you can't find sesame oil, toss the pasta with vegetable oil, and use 2 tablespoons of peanut butter in place of the sesame oil in the sauce.

OVEN-ROASTED TOMATOES

Oven-roasted tomatoes are moister than sun-dried tomatoes but denser and more concentrated in flavor than fresh ones. Serve as a side dish with a sprinkling of herbs, on pasta salads, or on pizza or focaccia. Cut plum tomatoes in half lengthwise or slice crosswise into three or four rounds. Place on an oiled baking sheet and brush with additional oil; salt and pepper lightly, if desired. Bake at 200°F, for 2 to 3 hours, until much of the moisture has evaporated and the tomatoes are reduced by about half. Refrigerate for up to 2 weeks if not using immediately.

LUNCHEON SALADS

These salads range from lunch-counter specials — egg, tuna, and the like — to modern vegetarian meal salads, such as Tomatoes Stuffed with Herbed Lentils and hearty Taco Salad.

The Best Egg Salad

❈ ❈ ❈

There are two tricks to making great egg salad. My mother says you should always add some good mustard. My good friend Connie McGlynn says to mix the yolks separately, and completely, with all of your flavorings, then add the chopped egg whites. This egg salad is "the best," since I do both!

IS THIS EGG COOKED?

An easy way to tell whether an egg is already hard-cooked is to spin it on a flat surface. A cooked egg will spin quickly and evenly; a raw egg will slowly wobble.

EASY-TO-PEEL COOKED EGGS

For easy-to-peel hard-cooked eggs, try the following: Cover eggs in a pan with cold water at least an inch above the eggs. Bring the water to a rolling boil, remove the pan from the heat, cover, and let stand for 15 to 20 minutes. Drain, then cool the eggs thoroughly in cold water. Roll the egg on a hard surface to loosen the shell, then peel from the large end of the egg. The shells should come off easily.

- 6 large eggs, hard-cooked
- ¼ cup mayonnaise
- 2 tablespoons Dijon mustard
- ½ teaspoon dried minced onion
- ¼ teaspoon dried dillweed
  salt and freshly ground black pepper

1. Separate the egg yolks from the egg whites and place them in separate bowls. Chop the egg whites; set aside.

2. Mash the egg yolks thoroughly. Add the mayonnaise, mustard, onion, dill, and salt and pepper to taste. Blend until smooth.

3. Add the chopped egg whites to the yolk mixture; adjust seasonings.

Yield: 4 servings

VARIATION: For a lower-fat version, replace the mayonnaise with nonfat yogurt.

Tuna Salad

❈ ❈ ❈

Serve on greens or in a sandwich; this low-fat salad is tasty either way. Makes great leftovers.

- 1 can (6 ounces) white tuna in water, drained
- 2 tablespoons nonfat plain yogurt
- ½ teaspoon Dijon mustard
- 2 tablespoons grated carrot
  salt and freshly ground black pepper

1. Combine all the ingredients and stir well, using a fork. Refrigerate or serve immediately.

Yield: 2 servings

VARIATION: For a richer, more traditional salad, use mayonnaise in place of all or part of the yogurt.

Tomatoes Stuffed with Herbed Lentils

✖ ✖ ✖

Tomatoes and lentils star in this colorful dish. The tomatoes must be large and ripe, and while uncooked lentils are specified, any leftover lentil salad will do just fine. You may also substitute chopped parsley or basil if cilantro isn't available.

½ cup lentils, uncooked
1 cup water
1 small onion, minced
1 bay leaf
1½ teaspoons minced fresh thyme, or ½ teaspoon dried
¼ teaspoon paprika
¼ teaspoon salt
4 large tomatoes
2 tablespoons minced fresh cilantro

1. In a small saucepan, combine the lentils, water, onion, bay leaf, thyme, paprika, and salt. Bring to a boil, reduce the heat, and simmer uncovered for 20 minutes, or until the lentils are soft.

2. Pour the lentils into a colander and let them drain for 10 minutes.

3. Meanwhile, cut the tops off the tomatoes and, with a melon baller or small spoon, scoop out the seeds and membranes, leaving the shells of the tomatoes intact. Drain the tomatoes upside down for 30 minutes.

4. When the lentils are drained and cool, fill the tomato shells. Top with the cilantro.

Yield: 4 servings

Taco Salad

✖ ✖ ✖

Southwestern flavors find fans all over the country. Use mild or hot salsa to flavor it the way you like it.

½ pound lean ground beef
  cayenne pepper
  chili powder
  salt and freshly ground black pepper
24 baked corn chips
¼ head of lettuce, shredded
1 tomato, sliced
¼ green bell pepper, finely chopped
3 tablespoons finely chopped red onion
⅓ cup salsa
4 olives, thinly sliced

1. In a small skillet over medium heat, brown the beef. Season with the cayenne, chili powder, salt, and pepper to taste.

2. Line the edges of four serving bowls with the chips. Add the lettuce and top with the meat, followed by the tomato, bell pepper, onion, a dollop of salsa, and olives.

Yield: 4 servings

TOMATO BASKET

························

For whimsical stuffed tomatoes, make a tomato basket. Use only large firm tomatoes and an extra-sharp serrated knife.

1. Looking down at the top of the tomato (the stem end), slice into the tomato just right of the stem scar. Draw your knife halfway down into the tomato, stop, and bring the knife back up. Make another cut, parallel to the first on the other side of the stem scar, about 1 inch from the first slice.

2. Make two more cuts into the sides of the tomatoes so that these cuts meet the slices you made in Step 1. Remove the wedges of tomato you just cut. What remains is the basket handle and basket.

3. Carefully remove pulp and seed from the handle; leave as much flesh as possible so the handle stays firm. Remove seed and pulp from the basket and stuff it with a cold salad.

4. Garnish with a parsley "ribbon."

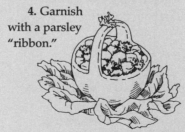

FRUIT & MOLDED SALADS

Choose a fruit salad for a refreshing side dish or a light dessert. It can be a simple mélange of fresh fruit and berries or a more elaborate, molded salad.

Cider Salad Mold

❂ ❂ ❂

The fall flavors in this molded salad are wonderful and make a terrific side to a dinner of roast chicken or pork.

- 4   cups apple cider
- 4   whole cloves
- 1   cinnamon stick (4 inches)
- 2   packages (3 ounces each) lemon flavored gelatin
- 1   orange, peeled and sectioned
- 1   tart apple, with peel, cored and diced

1. In a saucepan, combine the cider, cloves, and cinnamon. Simmer, covered, for 15 minutes. Strain.

2. Dissolve the gelatin in the hot cider and pour 2 cups of cider mixture into a cup ring mold. Chill until partially set. Keep the remaining cider mixture at room temperature.

3. When the first layer of gelatin is set, arrange the orange sections on top. Chill until almost firm.

4. Chill the remaining gelatin until partially set, then fold in the apples. Pour apple gelatin on top of the orange layer. Chill until firm.

5. Carefully unmold, and serve on a bed of crisp lettuce.

Yield: 6 servings

Fresh Fruit Bowl Kaleidoscope

❂ ❂ ❂

Nothing beats a light, colorful bowl of fruit for brightening a table. If you don't have all the fruits listed, don't worry; just about any combination will work.

- 2   nectarines, pitted and cut into 1-inch chunks
- 3   peaches, pitted and cut into 1-inch chunks
- 1   pint blueberries
- 2   Granny Smith apples, washed, cored, and cut into ½-inch cubes
- 1   small cantaloupe, peeled, seeded, and cut into ½-inch cubes
- 2   pounds watermelon, peeled, seeded, and cut into ½-inch cubes
- 1   cup green or red seedless grapes
- 2   tablespoons sugar
- ¼   cup Grand Marnier liqueur
- 1   cup raspberries

Dressing

- 1   cup plain yogurt
- 2   tablespoons lemon juice
- 2   tablespoons sugar

1. In a large bowl, mix the nectarines, peaches, blueberries, apples, cantaloupe, watermelon, grapes, and sugar. Pour the Grand Marnier over all and stir gently. Put the fruit into a glass serving bowl and sprinkle the raspberries

over the top. Serve at room temperature.

2. To make the dressing, combine the yogurt, lemon juice, and sugar in a small bowl. Serve with the fruit.

Yield: 8 servings

Cool Cucumber Salad

❈ ❈ ❈

I was in high school the first time I made this salad. Some friends were coming for dinner before a big game, and I wanted things to be perfect. They were, except that, as I unmolded my prize salad, it slid off the plate and went down the drain in one loud swoosh!

1 package (3 ounces) lime gelatin
¾ cups boiling water
¼ cup lemon juice
1 cup finely chopped unpeeled cucumber
1 cup sour cream

1. Stir the gelatin into the water until it is completely dissolved.

2. Add the lemon juice, cucumber, and sour cream; blend well. Pour into a mold.

3. Chill overnight, or until very firm.

4. To unmold, dip the mold in very hot water for 10 seconds to loosen the gelatin. Invert onto a plate.

Yield: 6 servings

Southern Strawberry Salad

❈ ❈ ❈

Citrus and strawberries are accented by fresh garden greens in this refreshing salad.

Dressing

1 tablespoon chopped fresh oregano, or 1 teaspoon dried
1 tablespoon chopped fresh basil, or 1 teaspoon dried
2 tablespoons chopped fresh parsley, or 1 tablespoon dried
1 teaspoon salt
1 clove of garlic, peeled
⅔ cup vegetable oil
½ cup grapefruit juice
2 teaspoons grated grapefruit zest
2 tablespoons strawberry purée

Salad

3 cups spinach leaves, torn into bite-size pieces
3 cups romaine, torn into bite-size pieces
3 cups watercress, with large stems removed
1 grapefruit, peeled and sectioned
2 oranges, peeled and sectioned
3 cups whole fresh strawberries, washed and hulled
½ cup chopped celery
½ cup chopped green bell pepper
¼ cup slivered almonds, toasted

1. In a shaker jar, combine the oregano, basil, parsley, salt, garlic, oil, grapefruit juice, grapefruit zest, and purée. Chill while making the salad.

2. Toss the spinach, romaine, and watercress lightly in a large bowl. Arrange the grapefruit, oranges, strawberries, celery, and bell pepper in an attractive pattern on top of the greens. Sprinkle on the almonds.

3. When ready to serve, remove the garlic from the dressing and pour it sparingly over the salad. Serve the remaining dressing in a pitcher to allow diners to add more, if desired.

Yield: 6–8 servings

MAIN DISH SALADS

Roast Beef Salad

✵ ✵ ✵

Meat lovers enjoy this tasty salad, which travels well for picnics.

4   cups cold cooked London broil or flank steak, thinly sliced and julienned
1   small red onion, thinly sliced
6   sun-dried tomatoes, julienned
¼   cup balsamic vinegar
1   tablespoon olive oil
2   tablespoons sesame oil, or additional olive oil
2   teaspoons prepared horseradish
¼   teaspoon salt
    freshly ground black pepper

1. Mix the beef, onion, and tomatoes in a large bowl.
2. In a small bowl, whisk together the vinegar, olive and sesame oils, horseradish, salt, and pepper to taste. Pour over beef mixture and combine well.

Yield: 4 servings

Crab-Cucumber Salad

✵ ✵ ✵

Remember this quick, company-worthy salad for an informal lunch when friends are coming by. Serve it with rolls and butter or a selection of crackers, toasts, and bread sticks.

8   ounces frozen or canned crabmeat, drained and picked over
1   tablespoon lemon juice
1   tablespoon chopped fresh dill
1   tablespoon snipped fresh chives
    salt and freshly ground black pepper
¾   cup sour cream
1   cucumber, cubed
4   tomatoes

1. Gently mix together the crabmeat, lemon juice, dill, chives, salt and pepper to taste, sour cream, and cucumber. Chill. Serve on sliced tomatoes or in tomato cups.

Yield: 4 lunch servings or 2 dinner servings

Caesar Salad

✵ ✵ ✵

Hats off to all the chefs who take credit for creating this beloved salad! Whatever its true origins, it is an all-time winner. We top it with sliced grilled chicken breast or shrimp to expand it into an easy, light meal.

1   egg (see note)
2   anchovy fillets

- -

CHEF'S SALAD

- -

The nicest thing about a recipe called "Chef's" is that the chef can choose whatever he or she wants to put in it. To prepare the classic chef's salad, make a bed of greens and top with julienne-sliced ham, turkey, roast beef, and Swiss cheese. Garnish with wedges of hard-cooked eggs and dress with your favorite dressing.

- -

2   cloves of garlic
4   tablespoons lemon juice
½   cup grated Parmesan
    cheese
½   cup olive oil
salt and freshly ground black
    pepper
1   head romaine lettuce, torn
    into bite-size pieces
croutons
anchovy fillets (optional)

1. To make the dressing, combine the egg, anchovies, garlic, lemon juice, and Parmesan in a blender or food processor. With the motor running, slowly pour in olive oil. Season to taste with salt and pepper.

2. Pour the dressing over the lettuce and croutons. Top with anchovy fillets, if desired.

Yield: 4–6 servings

Note: Gently boiling the egg before making the dressing helps thicken the dressing and should be done if you are concerned about egg safety (see Egg Caution, page 365).

Mediterranean Chicken Salad

❂ ❂ ❂

This is a favorite summer salad. It's flexible — you can adjust the quantities depending on what you like best.

8   chicken breast halves,
    skinned
1   medium green bell pepper,
    seeded and cut into ½-
    inch chunks
1   small red bell pepper,
    seeded and cut into ½-
    inch chunks
1   medium red onion, cut
    into ¼-inch chunks
½   cup pitted black olives
¼   cup artichoke hearts
4   leaves fresh basil, chopped
freshly ground black pepper
6   tablespoons balsamic
    vinegar
6   tablespoons corn oil
6   tablespoons olive oil

1. Place chicken in a large pot and barely cover with cold water. Bring water to a boil. Reduce heat and simmer for 20 minutes or until chicken is cooked through. Let it cool slightly in the liquid.

2. When chicken can be handled, remove meat from bones and cut into 1-inch chunks. Place in a large serving bowl.

3. Add the green and red bell peppers, onion, olives, artichoke hearts, basil, and pepper to taste and stir well.

4. In a small bowl, combine vinegar with corn and olive oils; pour over salad and stir gently. Chill for at least 30 minutes and serve.

Yield: 8 servings

STORING GREENS

....

Folks lucky enough to have a garden harvest their salad greens as they need them. If you find yourself with extra lettuce or greens, or purchase yours at the market, wrap them unwashed in a damp paper towel and place in a perforated plastic bag in the refrigerator. They should keep for 3 to 4 days. Or store them in your salad spinner in the refrigerator after drying them.

VINAIGRETTES & DRESSINGS

Homemade dressings are good and so easy to prepare from natural ingredients that let your fresh lettuces and vegetables shine through. Many can be used as marinades as well. Herbal vinegars and dressings in pretty bottles make wonderful gifts.

VINAIGRETTE

....

Vinaigrettes are particularly tasty on salads made of mixed vegetables. If you heat vinaigrette and combine it with still-warm par-boiled vegetables, the vegetables will absorb the flavors best. Of course, vinaigrettes are good on green salads, too.

Basic Herb-Vinegar Salad Dressing

❂ ❂ ❂

Try dried basil, tarragon, dill, oregano, chervil, chives, or parsley, alone or in combination. By all means, add snippets of fresh herbs, too, if you have them in your garden.

   1 cup oil, preferably olive oil
½–1 cup herb vinegar of choice
   2 tablespoons dried herbs, or the herbs preserved in the vinegar
      salt and freshly ground black pepper

1. Combine all ingredients in a glass cruet and shake to mix before using.
Yield: 2 cups

Lemon Vinaigrette

❂ ❂ ❂

This makes an excellent marinade for vegetables.

   1 cup vegetable or olive oil
   ¼ cup lemon juice
   1 teaspoon Dijon mustard
   ¼ teaspoon white pepper
      salt

1. Whisk together the oil, lemon juice, mustard, and pepper. Season to taste with salt. Pour over salads. To use as a marinade, pour over par-boiled vegetables and marinate for 1 to 2 hours. Serve chilled.
Yield: 1¼ cups

Green Goddess Dressing

❂ ❂ ❂

Named for a popular play from the 1920s, this dressing has been starring in salads ever since.

   ½ cup mayonnaise
   ⅓ cup vegetable oil
   2 cloves of garlic, minced
   ¼ cup minced fresh parsley
   ¼ cup chopped scallion greens
   1 tablespoon minced fresh chives
   1 tablespoon white vinegar
   2 tablespoons lemon juice
      salt and freshly ground black pepper, to taste

1. Combine all ingredients in a food processor or blender and process until smooth.
Yield: 1¼ cups

French-Style Dressing

❈ ❈ ❈

If you like bottled French dressings, wait till you taste this fresh-tomato version!

½ cup chopped tomatoes
2 tablespoons lemon juice
1 tablespoon red wine vinegar
⅓ cup vegetable or olive oil
1 tablespoon tomato paste
1 clove of garlic, minced
salt and freshly ground black pepper, to taste

1. Combine all ingredients in a blender or food processor and blend until smooth.

Yield: 1 cup

....

LEFTOVER SALAD?

....

I try to plan just the right amount to avoid leftover salad, but sometimes I guess wrong. Leftover salad, particularly if it's already dressed, does not store well. But it makes a great soup (page 88). Next time you have leftovers, try it.

....

Caroline's Salad Dressing

❈ ❈ ❈

Caroline Burch works with me at Storey in the production department. When she brought a salad with this dressing to a Storey picnic one summer, it was so good I asked her to share her recipe. Not hard, and it tastes just right on a fresh green salad.

5 tablespoons oil
2 tablespoons vinegar
½ teaspoon salt
⅛ teaspoon pepper
⅛ teaspoon dried thyme
¼ teaspoon paprika
½ teaspoon sugar
½ teaspoon dried parsley
onion flakes (optional)

1. Combine all ingredients in a large, covered salad-dressing cruet or jar. Shake until well combined.

Yield: ½ cup

Brasserie Dressing

❈ ❈ ❈

The Brasserie was a good little restaurant at the Bennington (Vermont) Potter's Yard. My colleagues and I used to enjoy our working lunches there. This dressing was inspired by their wonderful house salads, which consisted of a whole baby head of buttercrunch lettuce.

¼ cup tarragon vinegar
⅓ cup fresh tarragon, or 2 tablespoons dried
1–1½ tablespoons lemon juice
1 tablespoon Dijon mustard
1½ teaspoons crushed garlic
1½ teaspoons dry mustard
1 teaspoon freshly ground black pepper
¾ teaspoon salt
1½ cups vegetable oil

1. Combine the vinegar, tarragon, lemon juice, mustard, garlic, dry mustard, pepper, and salt; blend well.

2. Gradually whisk in oil, whisking until the dressing reaches the desired consistency.

Yield: About 2 cups

ENTRÉES

Each of us has a "most favorite" family dish that, no matter how many times it's served, always makes us feel special. That's how I feel about the recipes in this chapter. Spinach Cannelloni, for instance, brings my family closer together and reminds us of our most wonderful journey ever. Macaroni and Cheese says basic, but it also suggests slowing down and simplifying our lives a bit. Coquilles St. Jacques transports us to the seaside and makes us feel elegant. Special entrées can, for everyone around your table, feed the soul as well as the body.

MEAT
....
POULTRY
....
FISH & SHELLFISH
....
GAME
....
PASTA
....
CHEESE
....
GRAINS & LEGUMES
....
DINNER IN A POT
....
CASSEROLES
....
FARMHOUSE FAVORITES
....
SANDWICHES

Contributors to this chapter are Janet Ballantyne; Ruth Bass; Marjorie Page Blanchard; Charlene Braida; Betty Cavage; Janet B. Chadwick; Jane Cooper; Ken Haedrich; Geri Harrington; Phyllis Hobson; Miriam Jacobs, Alexandra Nimetz, Jason Stanley, and Emeline Starr; Sara Pitzer; Nancy Ralston and Marynor Jordan; Charles G. Reavis; Phyllis V. Shaudys; Edith Stovel; Nancy Van Leuven; Olwen Woodier; and Adriana and Rochelle Zabarkes.

Mimi's Sunday Pot Roast

❖ ❖ ❖

Every Sunday morning, my mother would prepare this pot roast before we headed off to church. By the time we arrived home it was done, the entire neighborhood smelled delicious, and Sunday dinner was on the table in no time flat.

2½–3 pounds boneless chuck beef roast with fat removed
1½ teaspoons salt
1 teaspoon freshly ground black pepper
½ teaspoon paprika
6–8 large potatoes, peeled and quartered
8 large carrots, peeled and quartered
4 large onions, peeled and quartered
1 can (16 ounces) stewed tomatoes
1 cup water or beef broth
½ cup ketchup
1 tablespoon prepared mustard
1 tablespoon Worcestershire sauce
1 cup dry red wine

1. Preheat oven to 350°F. Rub meat with salt, pepper, and paprika. Place in a large roasting pan and surround with potatoes, carrots, and onions.

2. Mix the tomatoes, water, ketchup, mustard, and Worcestershire in a bowl. Pour over the vegetables. Cover and bake for 2½ to 3 hours or until fork tender.

3. Remove the meat and vegetables from the pan; arrange on a large serving platter. Add the wine to the pan juices; simmer over medium heat until slightly thickened. Use the pan sauce for gravy.

Yield: 8 servings

Daddy's Banana Pudding

❖ ❖ ❖

If my father had a weekend specialty, this was it! His banana pudding was the best — smooth and creamy, with just the right amount of vanilla wafers. We clamored to eat it warm and freshly made, but it was even more delicious the next day, cold from the refrigerator.

2 cups milk
1 cup sugar
4 tablespoons all-purpose flour
2 eggs
½ teaspoon vanilla extract
pinch of salt
1 package (12 ounces) vanilla wafers
2–3 bananas, sliced
sweetened whipped cream

1. In a medium saucepan, heat milk to not quite boiling.

2. In a bowl, mix sugar, flour, eggs, vanilla, and salt; add to the milk. Continue to cook over medium heat, stirring constantly, until the pudding thickens.

3. Line the bottom of a 2-quart casserole with vanilla wafers. Top with a layer of bananas, then a layer of pudding. Repeat these layers two times, or until pudding is used up; be sure to end with bananas. Serve warm or cold with a dollop of whipped cream.

Yield: 6–8 servings

SUNDAY DINNER TRADITIONS

Sunday dinner means pot roast for my mother, but it's soup night for my kids. For others it's a roast chicken dinner. I know of a family that always has pizza on Sunday nights. But it isn't what's served that inspires people to speak fondly of Sunday dinners — it's being together as a family. If you don't have a Sunday dinner tradition, start one. It's what memories are made of.

MEAT

Although my family loves pasta and casseroles and vegetable dishes, meat is still a part of our diet. From plain roasts and grilled steaks to company hams and saucy entrées, we enjoy the taste and vigor of meat on the menu. We look to the garden and orchard for delicious herbal seasonings and for vegetable and fruit accompaniments.

WEEKNIGHT SUPPERS

Roast Beef with Herbs

✖ ✖ ✖

Phyllis Shaudys donated the herb blend she uses for her roasts to local bazaars and fairs, and she got many requests for it ever after. You'll love the good flavor it gives beef roasts.

Herb Seasoning

- 3 tablespoons dried parsley
- 2 tablespoons dried rosemary
- 2 tablespoons dried chives
- 1 tablespoon dried summer savory
- 1 tablespoon dried minced garlic
- 1 tablespoon dried thyme

Roast Beef

- 1 prime rib roast or any beef roast, 4–6 pounds

1. Combine the parsley, rosemary, chives, savory, garlic, and thyme. Mix well; seasoning can be

stored for up to 6 months in a covered jar.

2. Preheat oven to 325°F. Place the meat on a rack in a roasting pan.

3. About 1 hour before the end of the cooking time, remove the roast from the oven and spread 2 tablespoons of the seasoning on it. Finish cooking. Let meat stand 15 minutes before carving; temperature may rise another 5 to 10 degrees while standing. (For medium, a bone-in rib roast will take about 20 to 25 minutes per pound; a boneless roast about 13 to 15 minutes per pound.)

Yield: 8–12 servings

Grilled Beef Sirloin

✖ ✖ ✖

There is nothing like a good grilled steak. We like to top ours with herbed butter (page 285) or tarragon-flavored Béarnaise Sauce (page 266).

- 4 6-ounce boneless sirloin steaks
- 2 teaspoons peanut oil

1. Prepare a hot charcoal grill.

2. Lightly coat steaks with peanut oil. This will prevent them from sticking to the grill.

3. Grill steaks for approximately 8 to 10 minutes. Turn and grill for 6 to 8 minutes longer for a rare steak. Test by cutting into center of steak if necessary.

Yield: 4 servings

Beef Stroganoff

❈ ❈ ❈

Y ou don't need Russian ancestry to make this a family heirloom recipe. Its earthy mushroom and onion sauce has made it an all-American favorite, too. And it cooks up in very short order.

    ½ *pound egg noodles*
    1¼ *pounds top round beef,*
         cut into small chunks
    ¼ *cup sliced onion*
    1 *tablespoon flour*
    1 *clove of garlic, minced*
    8 *fresh mushrooms, sliced*
    ½ *cup chicken broth*
    ½ *cup sour cream*
       salt and freshly ground black
         pepper
       paprika

1. Bring a pot of water to a boil. Add the noodles and cook until tender, about 8 to 10 minutes. Drain and set aside.

2. In a skillet, cook the beef and onion over medium heat. As the beef begins to brown, stir in the flour and toss so that it coats the beef.

3. Stir in the garlic, mushrooms, broth, and sour cream. Cook until the sauce is an even consistency and the mushrooms are soft. Add salt and pepper to taste. Serve over the egg noodles, topped with a dash of paprika.

Yield: 6–8 servings

TESTING FOR DONENESS

....

Experienced chefs can usually tell when meat is done by how it feels when they press a finger against it. For steaks and chops, many cooks make a small slice in the center to look at the color, though the juices can be lost with that technique.

How long it takes a roast to cook depends on the temperature at which it's being cooked and the cut of meat. Generally, the more tender the cut, the shorter the cooking time.

The most reliable way to test for doneness is to use a meat thermometer or instant-read thermometer. Insert it into the thickest part of the roast; be sure that it does not touch bone. The U.S. Department of Agriculture recommends that meat be cooked to the following internal temperatures:

Meat	Type	Temperature
Fresh beef, veal, and lamb	Ground	160°F
Fresh beef, veal, and lamb	Roasts, steaks, and chops	
	Medium rare	145°F
	Medium	160°F
	Well done	170°F
Fresh pork	All types	
	Medium	160°F
	Well done	170°F
Fresh ham	Raw	160°F
	Fully cooked (to reheat)	140°F

Note that the temperature may rise 5 to 10 degrees as the meat rests before carving!

meat thermometer

Moussaka

❈ ❈ ❈

For this Greek specialty, do not rely on packaged pre-ground lamb. Select an attractive cut, such as a portion of the shoulder, and ask your butcher to trim the fat and grind the meat just for you.

  2 *large eggplants*
    vegetable oil
  ¾ *cup chopped onions*
  2 *cloves of garlic, finely*
    chopped
  1 *tablespoon fresh parsley,*
    chopped
3–4 *tablespoons vegetable oil*
  1 *pound ground lamb*
  1 *teaspoon salt*
  ¼ *teaspoon freshly ground*
    black pepper
    dash of cinnamon
  ½ *cup tomato sauce*
  ½ *cup cornflake crumbs*
  ½ *cup grated Parmesan*
    cheese
  2 *tablespoons butter*
  2 *tablespoons*
    all-purpose flour
  1 *cup milk*
  ½ *cup ricotta cheese*
  1 *egg, beaten*
    dash of nutmeg

1. Preheat oven to 425°F. Peel the eggplants and cut them into ¼-inch-thick slices.

2. Cover the surface of a cookie sheet with a thin film of vegetable oil. Put the cookie sheet into the oven for a minute or two to heat the oil. Add the eggplant slices to the cookie sheet and bake for 7 to 10 minutes, until soft. Add more oil as needed. Remove from the oven; drain eggplant in a colander, then on paper towels. Reduce oven temperature to 350°F.

3. Meanwhile, sauté the onions, garlic, and parsley in 3 to 4 tablespoons vegetable oil for 3 to 5 minutes, until the onions are tender. Add the lamb. Season with salt, pepper, and cinnamon. When browned, add the tomato sauce and, if too dry, some water; simmer for 5 minutes. Remove from heat.

4. Layer the eggplant and the ground lamb mixture alternately in a medium-sized casserole dish, finishing with an eggplant layer. Top the casserole with cornflake crumbs and grated Parmesan.

5. Melt the butter in a saucepan. When it begins to bubble, add the flour all at once; stir quickly to avoid lumps. Add the milk, a little at a time, to keep the mixture smooth. Allow it to reach a slow boil and to thicken somewhat. Remove from heat and cool slightly; then add ricotta and egg. Season mixture with nutmeg and pour over the eggplant. Bake for 30 to 40 minutes. Cover loosely with foil if the top gets too brown.

Yield: 8 servings

Veal Scallopine
with Sage

❈ ❈ ❈

We happen to live very near a shiitake farm, but these and other wild mushrooms are increasingly available in supermarkets. Enjoy this veal and mushroom feast with linguine tossed in garlicky olive oil and a salad of fresh greens, thinly sliced cucumbers, parsley, and diced oranges.

  3 *tablespoons unbleached*
    all-purpose flour
    freshly ground black pepper
  ¾ *pound veal scallops,*
    pounded thin
  2 *tablespoons extra virgin*
    olive oil
  4 *shallots, chopped*
  ¼ *pound shiitake or crimini*
    mushrooms, sliced
  2 *tablespoons butter*
  2 *teaspoons chopped fresh*
    sage
  ¼ *cup chopped fresh parsley*
    juice of 1 lemon
  ½ *cup dry white wine*

1. Mix the flour with pepper to taste. Dredge the veal in the seasoned flour.

2. In a large, heavy skillet, heat the oil until quite hot (drops of water will bounce when flicked into the pan). Quickly brown the veal scallops, cooking them 1 to 2 minutes on each side. Remove them to a plate.

3. Add the shallots to the pan and cook them for about 1 minute, stirring constantly. Add the mushrooms, cooking them for 2 minutes.

4. Add the butter, and when it's melted, return the veal and any juice from the plate to the pan, turning the veal scallops to coat them with butter. Add the sage, parsley, lemon juice, and wine. Cook until the veal scallops are hot and the sauce is brown and thickened.

Yield: 4 servings

Baked Ham
with Pineapple Glaze

❂ ❂ ❂

Of the many ways that my colleague Dianne Cutillo has prepared a baked ham, this is the one that she says her family requests most often. Serve this with a pitcher of Mustard Sauce (page 266) on the side.

1 8- to 10-pound ham
2 *tablespoons whole cloves*
2 *cups apple juice or cider*

1 *cup hot honey mustard or Dijon mustard*
2 *8¼-ounce cans crushed pineapple in syrup*
⅔ *cup honey*
½ *teaspoon ground ginger*

1. Preheat oven to 325°F. Place the ham on a rack in a roasting pan; insert cloves into ham in a diamond pattern with rows 3 to 4 inches apart. Pour juice into the bottom of the pan. Heat on the stovetop until the juice boils; then place the pan in the oven. Cook until the internal temperature of the ham reads 160°F, about 20 minutes per pound.

2. For the glaze, combine mustard, pineapple (with its juice), honey, and ginger in a saucepan. Bring to a boil over medium heat; reduce heat and simmer 5 minutes, stirring occasionally.

3. About 40 minutes before the ham is ready, score the surface in diamond shapes and spread the glaze over the surface. Return the ham to the oven and baste with the glaze every 10 minutes.

Yield: 8–12 servings

Ham Steaks
in Rum Raisin Sauce

❂ ❂ ❂

Sweet rum raisin sauce gives simple ham steaks a festive air. This sauce is an interesting twist on a classic — the raisins are puréed to thicken the sauce.

1 *pound ham steak*
1 *cup apple cider*
¼ *cup plus 2 tablespoons pure maple syrup*
¼ *cup dark rum*
2–3 *tablespoons orange juice*
½ *cup raisins*

1. Preheat oven to 350°F. Put the ham steak in a shallow casserole slightly larger than the steak. Set aside. Combine the cider, ¼ cup of the maple syrup, the rum, orange juice, and raisins in a small saucepan; bring to a near boil. Remove from heat; cover and let sit for 10 minutes. Remove the raisins with a slotted spoon, put them into a small bowl, and spoon enough of the hot liquid over them to cover completely. Pour the remaining liquid over the ham and bake for 1 hour.

2. When the ham has baked for 1 hour, combine the raisins and their soaking liquid in a blender with several tablespoons of the casserole juice and the remaining 2 tablespoons of maple syrup. Process briefly — a little roughness is good — and pour it directly over the ham. Run the ham under the broiler for just a few moments, until it sizzles and browns; keep a close eye on it. Serve hot.

Yield: 2–3 servings

Roast Pork and Oven-Browned Potatoes

The center-cut pork loin is one of the best cuts of pork for roasting — it is tender, meaty, and flavorful. The garlic treatment gives this meat-and-potatoes dinner a very special savor.

- 4–5 *pounds pork loin roast (with the bone)*
- 2 *large cloves of garlic, sliced*
- ¼ *teaspoon paprika*
- ¼ *teaspoon freshly ground black pepper*
- ⅛ *teaspoon ground thyme*
- 2–3 *tablespoons vegetable oil*
- 4–6 *white potatoes, unpeeled*
- *salt*

1. Using a sharp knife, make several ½-inch-deep slits in the top and sides of the pork roast and stuff with the garlic slices. Mix the remaining spices with the vegetable oil and rub over the roast.

Cover with plastic wrap and refrigerate for 12 to 24 hours.

2. The next day, preheat oven to 325°F and bake the roast uncovered for 2 hours, or until a meat thermometer reads 165 to 170°F.

3. While the roast is cooking, boil the potatoes for 20 minutes, or until tender. Drain, slice lengthwise into halves, and add to the roasting pan 20 to 30 minutes before the roast is done. Baste the potatoes with the meat juices and turn occasionally until crisp and golden. Serve with the roast.

Yield: 4–6 servings

Roasting Tenderloins

If you don't want to grill a pork tenderloin, bake it at 400°F for 40 to 45 minutes (for a 2-pound roast).

Grilled Pork Tenderloin
with Cranberry Sauce

Our good friend and colleague Megan Kuntze made this wonderful dish for us and kindly shared the recipe. The tangy sauce is outstanding with the mellow pork.

- 1 *can (16 ounces) whole cranberry sauce*
- ½ *cup brown sugar, firmly packed*
- ½ *cup soy sauce*
- ¼ *cup mustard (Be creative: Use honey mustard, horseradish mustard, Vidalia onion mustard, Dijon mustard, or another favorite.)*
- 2 *tablespoons orange juice*
- 2 *pork tenderloins, 1½–2 pounds each*
- *oil*
- *salt and freshly ground black pepper*

1. Prepare the sauce by mixing the cranberry sauce, brown sugar, soy sauce, mustard, and orange juice in a saucepan and simmering until hot. This sauce may be made well ahead of time and reheated when you need it; it also freezes well.

2. Prepare grill. Rub the tenderloins with oil and season with salt and pepper to taste.

3. Grill for approximately 10 minutes on each side, or until cooked to desired doneness.

4. Let pork sit for 5 minutes before slicing. Slice pork into medallions and cover with cranberry sauce.

Yield: 4 servings

THE ORIGINS OF ROAST PORK

According to an ancient Chinese folk tale, Bo-Bo, a clumsy adolescent peasant boy, discovered the joys of roast pork when he accidentally burned down his father's pigsty. As Charles Lamb relates in his Dissertation Upon Roast Pig, *"Imitators were soon building and burning down pigsties at a terrifying rate."*

Pork Chops and Peaches

❂ ❂ ❂

My grandmother used to put up quarts and quarts of spiced peaches. This recipe always reminds me of her kitchen. Peaches are lovely with pork, and a touch of garlic livens up the sauce and keeps it from tasting too sweet. Select center-cut loin chops, which are among the tastiest cuts of pork.

3 tablespoons all-purpose flour
½ teaspoon salt
¼ teaspoon freshly ground black pepper
4 large pork chops
5 tablespoons butter
1 tablespoon vegetable oil
1 clove of garlic, chopped
¼ teaspoon ground cloves
¼ teaspoon ground ginger
⅛ teaspoon ground nutmeg
4 tablespoons peach preserves
1 cup sliced peaches (drained if canned)

1. Preheat oven to 350°F.

2. Combine the flour with the salt and pepper; coat the chops with this mixture. In a large skillet, heat 3 tablespoons of the butter and the oil and sauté the garlic. Do not allow the garlic to darken. Brown the chops briefly in the garlicky oil. Remove the chops from the pan and season with cloves, ginger, and nutmeg. Reserve the pan drippings.

3. Add the pan drippings and the remaining 2 tablespoons butter to a baking dish. Add the chops. Bake for about 20 minutes; cover the dish with foil for the first 10 minutes. Turn the chops once. Top with the preserves and peach slices during the last 5 minutes of baking time. Do not overcook. Serve hot.

Yield: 4 servings

SIMPLE EMBELLISHMENTS FOR CHOPS

PORK CHOPS:

- Applesauce mixed with cranberry sauce
- Apples sautéed with a pinch of sage
- Herbal Jelly (page 104)

VEAL CHOPS:

- Sautéed onions and green olives
- Drained, warmed mandarin orange sections
- Minced parsley and lemon wedges

LAMB CHOPS:

- Natural Mint Jelly (page 303)
- Rhubarb Chutney (page 212) or Apricot Salsa (page 215)
- Puréed turnips

POULTRY

Scarcely a week goes by that I don't serve poultry in some form; it is quintessential country food, providing a light alternative to red meats and a wonderful base for soups, fricassees, bakes, and casseroles. Fried chicken — hot or cold — is a classic for community suppers and picnics. Fowl is incredibly adaptable, starring in everything from humble potpie to elegant coq au vin or braised duck with apples.

Garlicky Roast Chicken

❈ ❈ ❈

We love garlic so much that we keep a braid of it in the kitchen, both for decoration and for making such dishes as this garlicky chicken. Don't worry if it seems like a lot; after a lengthy time in the oven, the garlic becomes soft and sweet.

 1 5-pound roasting chicken
 4 tablespoons butter
 1 teaspoon crushed fresh rosemary leaves
 1 teaspoon ground sage
 1½ teaspoons ground thyme
    salt and freshly ground black pepper
 20 whole cloves of garlic, peeled

 3 tablespoons lemon juice
 ½ cup water

1. Preheat oven to 375°F.

2. Rinse the chicken in cold water. Drain and pat dry.

3. Soften the butter and season it with the rosemary, sage, and thyme. Place the chicken in a roasting pan and rub it with the seasoned butter. Sprinkle with salt and pepper to taste. Place the garlic cloves in and around the chicken. Add the lemon juice to the chicken cavity. Add the water to the pan.

4. Cover pan tightly with aluminum foil. Bake for 45 minutes, or until the chicken is tender. Raise the oven temperature to 425°F, remove the foil, and cook for 15 more minutes to brown the skin. Serve.

Yield: 4–6 servings

- - - - - - - - - - - -

THE WHOLE BIRD

· · · · · · · · · · · ·

I am from a big family where nothing ever went to waste. After a chicken supper, we'd pick the rest of the meat for chicken salad or pies and then cover the carcass with water, add a few aromatic vegetables, and make a simple chicken broth base.

- - - - - - - - - - - -

Coq au Vin

❈ ❈ ❈

Perhaps the best legacy of a summer working in the French countryside was discovering coq au vin. The tiniest bistros with their open kitchens allowed us to witness the work in progress. The chefs were liberal with their use of a good French Burgundy. But I use what I have on hand, from Italian Chianti to American cabernets.

 1 5-pound roasting chicken cut into serving-sized pieces
 4 slices bacon, cut into 1-inch pieces
 4 tablespoons olive oil
 1 onion, finely chopped
 2 cloves of garlic, minced
 ½ cup sliced carrots
 2 tablespoons flour
 1 tablespoon finely chopped fresh parsley
 1 tablespoon finely chopped fresh marjoram
 1 teaspoon finely chopped fresh thyme
 2 cups dry red wine
 1 cup sliced mushrooms
    salt and freshly ground black pepper
    sprigs of fresh parsley, marjoram, and/or thyme

1. Wash the chicken and pat dry. In a large, heavy skillet, cook the bacon until lightly browned, then add the oil. Add the onion, garlic, and carrots and sauté until onion is translucent but not browned.

2. Add the chicken pieces; brown well on all sides. When chicken is browned, move everything to one side of the skillet and blend in the flour, parsley, marjoram, and thyme. Spread the chicken and vegetables out again, pour in the wine, and scrape bits from the bottom of the pan. Simmer, covered, for about 45 minutes, turning the chicken once or twice.

3. When the chicken is tender, add the mushrooms; simmer for 5 to 7 minutes. Correct the seasoning with salt and pepper to taste. Serve the chicken and its sauce directly from the skillet or from a low casserole onto plates garnished with parsley, marjoram, and/or thyme.

Yield: 6 servings

Southern Fried Chicken Livers

❈ ❈ ❈

Southern fried anything is wonderful, but southern fried chicken livers are so delectable they truly melt in your mouth. My mother always fried them in bacon fat, but these days we use vegetable oil for a healthful alternative. You can make gravy from the pan juices, or simply serve the livers with ketchup.

1 pound chicken livers
½ cup all-purpose flour
1 teaspoon garlic salt
freshly ground black pepper
¼ cup vegetable oil

1. Rinse the chicken livers in cool water, pat dry, and cut into bite-size pieces.

2. Place the livers in a resealable plastic bag with the flour, garlic salt, and pepper to taste. Shake until all the pieces are coated with flour and spices.

3. Heat the oil in a skillet; when quite hot (drops of water will bounce when flicked into the pan), arrange the livers in the skillet so that they are not touching one another. Fry on one side until lightly browned, about 3 minutes, then turn to brown on the other side. Remove from pan and drain on paper towels. Serve immediately.

Yield: 4 servings

ABOUT ROAST CHICKEN

Buy a roasting chicken; it will be meatier and more succulent than a broiler or fryer.

Choose the best all-natural or free-range chicken you can find.

For the crispiest skin, store the chicken uncovered in the refrigerator for several hours or overnight, so the skin dries slightly. Another way to crisp the skin is to roast the chicken in high heat (about 450°F) for about 15 minutes, then lower the temperature to 350°F for the remaining time.

To infuse more flavor into your bird, loosen the skin and tuck seasonings under it.

Roast chicken for about 20 minutes per pound at 350°. Stuffed chickens require about 20 minutes longer in the oven than do unstuffed ones.

Roast chicken is done when an instant-read thermometer inserted into the thickest part of the thigh reads 180°F or when the leg joint moves freely in its socket and the juices run clear when a thigh is pricked deeply with a fork.

Southern-Style Fried Chicken

❁ ❁ ❁

Whenever our family goes on a picnic, someone takes this fried chicken. A classic, it always says "family gathering" to me. Served with fresh coleslaw, potato salad, and sliced tomatoes, it's a winner.

2½–3 pounds chicken pieces
    3 cups milk or buttermilk
   ¼ teaspoon Tabasco sauce
    1 cup all-purpose flour
    1 teaspoon salt
   ½ teaspoon paprika
   ½ teaspoon freshly ground
       black pepper
 1–2 cups vegetable shorten-
       ing or vegetable oil

1. Wash and dry chicken pieces. Pour milk and Tabasco into a medium-sized bowl and soak chicken pieces in it for 20 to 30 minutes. Remove and pat dry.

2. In a large plastic bag, combine flour, salt, paprika, and pepper. Add chicken pieces, a few at a time, and shake to coat well. Set aside on a plate.

3. In a large, heavy skillet, heat oil until it reaches 360°F on a deep-fat thermometer. With long tongs, carefully place a few pieces of flour-coated chicken into the hot oil. Do not crowd it. Turn the chicken when nicely browned on one side (about 5 to 8 minutes), and continue to cook and brown on the other side for about 10 to 15 minutes. Remove chicken and drain on a rack set over paper towels.

4. Bring oil back up to 360°F, and continue frying chicken in batches until it is all cooked.

Yield: 4 servings

Chicken Potpie
with Sugar Snap Peas

❁ ❁ ❁

I love making potpie with sliced sugar snap peas, which don't get lost in the sauce as shelled peas do. The crust on this pie is spooned over the filling rather than rolled out.

    1 stewing hen (7–8 pounds)
       water
    1 stalk of celery, sliced in
       2-inch pieces
    1 carrot, cubed
    1 medium onion, quartered
    1 bay leaf
    2 tablespoons butter
    1 cup diced onion
 1½ teaspoons chopped fresh
       thyme, or ½ teaspoon
       dried
 1½ cups light cream
 2¾ cups unbleached
       all-purpose flour
    2 cups sliced sugar snap peas

       salt and freshly ground black
       pepper
    1 teaspoon salt
    1 tablespoon baking powder
    1 teaspoon baking soda
    2 tablespoons minced fresh
       parsley
    2 teaspoons crumbled dried
       sage
    2 teaspoons vegetable short-
       ening
   ¾ cup buttermilk

1. Place the chicken in a large stockpot and cover with water. Add the celery, carrot, onion, and bay leaf. Bring the water to a boil. Skim off any foam, reduce the heat, and simmer gently for 1 hour.

2. Remove the chicken from the pot. Strain the broth and save; reserve 3 cups for this recipe. Let the chicken cool enough to handle, then remove the meat from the bones. Dice the meat into 1-inch pieces. Measure out 2 cups of chicken meat for this recipe. Reserve the extra meat for another meal.

3. In a large sauté pan, melt the butter and sauté the onion and thyme until the onion is limp, 3 to 5 minutes. Add the 3 cups of chicken broth and the cream. Simmer until the sauce is reduced by half, 15 to 20 minutes. Sprinkle 3 to 4 tablespoons of the flour over the liquid and blend. Add the chicken.

4. Parboil the peas until they turn bright green, about 1 minute. Add the peas to the chicken and season to taste with salt and pepper.

5. Preheat oven to 400°F. Place the chicken mixture in a greased 2-quart casserole dish.

6. Sift together the remaining 2½ cups flour, the salt, baking powder, and soda. Add the parsley and sage. Cut in the shortening until the mixture resembles gravel and sand. Stir in the buttermilk, using just enough to moisten the mixture. Spoon the dough topping onto the chicken. Bake for 20 minutes or until the top is golden brown. Serve hot.

Yield: 6 servings

Lemon Chicken Marcella

❋ ❋ ❋

In his later years, PopPop loved this dish that his wife, Marcella, would make for him. It's tangy and makes a nice sauce that is good with rice.

3 lemons
all-purpose flour
salt
4 boneless, skinless chicken breasts, split

2 tablespoons olive oil
3 tablespoons light brown sugar
1 can (14½ ounces) chicken broth

1. Preheat oven to 375°F. Squeeze the juice of two of the lemons into a shallow bowl. In another shallow bowl, season enough flour for dredging with salt to taste. Dip the chicken breasts into the lemon juice, then dredge them in the flour mixture.

2. Heat the oil in a sauté pan. Brown the chicken in the oil. Place the chicken breasts in a single layer in a casserole dish; sprinkle with the brown sugar. Cut the remaining lemon into very thin slices and place on chicken. Pour the broth over the chicken.

3. Bake the chicken for 1 hour or until it is tender and cooked through.

Yield: 4 servings

CHICKEN MAGIC

Boneless chicken breasts go from simple to supreme very easily. Try them broiled or grilled with just brushed-on olive oil and fresh herbs. Smother them in salsa or barbecue sauce and poach them in the liquid in the microwave; they'll be cooked in 5 to 10 minutes, depending on how powerful your microwave is. Place the breasts between two sheets of wax paper or in a resealable plastic bag, then flatten them with a meat mallet or rolling pin. Layer on cheese, stuffing, roasted red peppers, or even sliced fruit, roll them up, and fasten with a toothpick. Coat the rolls in breading and fry them or bake them, and you have an easy but elegant stuffed chicken breast entrée.

Turkey Cutlets
with Roasted Shallot Sauce

❈ ❈ ❈

We plant rows of shallots among our garden lettuces. Roasted shallot sauce spooned over turkey gives all the satisfaction of turkey with gravy — without the fat.

10 shallots
1 pound skinless turkey breast cutlets
salt and freshly ground black pepper
½ cup nonfat chicken broth
¼ cup white wine
1 tablespoon all-purpose flour
1½ teaspoons minced fresh thyme, or ½ teaspoon dried

1. Preheat oven to 350°F. Break the shallots apart, but do not remove their skins. Place in an ovenproof dish and bake for 20 minutes, or until soft when pierced. Cool and remove the skins.

2. Meanwhile, season the turkey cutlets with salt and pepper to taste.

3. Place the shallots, broth, wine, flour, and thyme in a food processor or blender and purée. Heat a nonstick skillet. Add the purée and stir constantly until thick. Simmer for 1 minute longer. Add salt and pepper to taste and keep warm.

4. Coat a second nonstick skillet with cooking spray and heat for 20 seconds. Add the seasoned turkey cutlets and sauté until brown and cooked through, 1 to 2 minutes per side. Spoon the hot shallot sauce over the cutlets and serve.

Yield: 4 servings

TURKEY CUTLETS

....

Cutlets are thin, tender cuts of meat or poultry that taste best when cooked quickly, such as by sautéeing, grilling, or broiling. Overcooking toughens cutlets. Turkey cutlets offer a quick way to enjoy the taste of turkey without cooking a big turkey dinner.

Game Hens
with Apricot Sauce

❈ ❈ ❈

My kids always liked game hens because they look like "teeny chickens." I like the fact that they make a glamorous presentation with a much shorter roasting time than a bigger bird. This apricot sauce keeps the meat moist and adds superb flavor.

2 Cornish game hens, each 1½–2 pounds, cut in half
salt and freshly ground black pepper
3 tablespoons butter
1 tablespoon lemon juice
1 cup apricot purée or preserves
½ cup orange juice
grated zest of ½ orange
1 teaspoon ground ginger
¼ cup honey
1 tablespoon grated onion
orange slices

1. Preheat broiler. Arrange the game hens, skin side up, on broiler pan. Sprinkle with salt and pepper to taste. Melt the butter with the lemon juice and brush birds with mixture. Broil 4 inches from heat until golden, basting with butter mixture. Turn and brush underside of hens with butter mixture. Broil until lightly browned.

2. In a saucepan, heat together apricot purée, juice, zest, ginger, honey, and onion, stirring until well blended. Heat oven to 350°F.

3. Transfer game hens, skin side up, to a buttered baking dish. Pour apricot sauce over them and cover the dish with foil. Bake for 40 minutes. Garnish with orange slices.

Yield: 4 servings

STUFFED HENS

Cornish game hens pair well with wild rice, fruity rice stuffings, or an herb-flavored bread stuffing.

Braised Duck

❊ ❊ ❊

We love duck but find it too fatty to eat very often. This delicious dish has a great advantage: Since it can be prepared two days ahead of time, almost all of the fat can be removed from the juices when the duck is chilled.

Braising Stock

- 1 *5½–6-pound duckling, including neck, gizzard, heart, and liver*
- 4 *cups duck or chicken stock or water*
- 1 *carrot, coarsely chopped*
- 1 *stalk of celery*
- 1 *small onion, halved*
- 4 *cloves of garlic, flattened*

Vegetable Seasoning

- 1 *large onion, chopped*
- 2 *medium carrots, chopped*
- 2 *medium stalks of celery, chopped*
- 2 *cloves of garlic, minced*
- 1 *teaspoon ground mace*
- 1 *teaspoon dried sage*
- 1 *teaspoon dried thyme*
- ½ *teaspoon ground allspice*
- ¼ *teaspoon freshly ground black pepper*
- ⅛ *teaspoon cayenne pepper*
- 1 *cup red wine*
- 2 *tablespoons cornstarch*
- 3 *apples (Granny Smith)*

1. For the braising stock, place the neck, gizzard, heart, and liver in a medium-sized saucepan and cover with stock. Add the carrot, celery, onion, and 2 of the cloves of garlic. Bring to a boil, reduce heat, place the lid askew, and simmer for 40 minutes.

2. Cut the duck into serving-sized pieces, removing any fat from around the neck and vent areas. Cut off the wing tips and parson's nose (stubby tailpiece); discard.

3. In a 4- or 5-quart Dutch oven, brown the duck pieces, skin side down (do not use any fat or oil) for 20 minutes to render the fat. Add the remaining 2 cloves of garlic to the pan during the browning. Transfer the duck pieces to a plate. Discard the garlic. Drain off all but 2 tablespoons of the fat and discard.

4. For the vegetable seasoning, add the onion, carrots, celery, and garlic to the 2 tablespoons of fat. Sprinkle with the mace, sage, thyme, allspice, black pepper, and cayenne. Sauté for 10 minutes.

5. Place the browned duck pieces, skin side up, on top of the vegetables in the Dutch oven.

6. Strain the stock and skim off the fat. (Use one of those fat jugs that allow fats to rise to the top. Or make the stock a day ahead of time and scrape the solid fat off the chilled liquid.)

7. Preheat oven to 325°F. Add the wine to the stock and pour over the duck and vegetables. Cover the Dutch oven and roast for 1¼ hours. Let cool.

8. Refrigerate the duck for a day or two, so that any remaining fat can solidify and be scraped off.

9. Preheat oven to 325°F. Place the Dutch oven on top of the stove and simmer for 15 minutes.

10. Remove the duck pieces to a dish, cover, and keep warm. Place the vegetables and liquid in a blender with the cornstarch. Purée until smooth and return to the Dutch oven with the duck pieces.

11. Peel, core, and cube the apples into ½-inch pieces. Stir into the duck, cover the pot, and return to the oven to bake for 30 minutes, or until the apples are tender.

Yield: 4 servings

FISH & SHELLFISH

There is hardly a more delightful way to take home supper than to spend a lazy day fishing. Whether from stream or pond or ocean, your own day's catch will seem the best fish ever. Even if you "catch" your fish at the market, you are in for a dinner treat that is high in protein, nutritious, and a real time-saver. Except for a large whole or stuffed fish, most fish can be on the table in 25 minutes or less.

Nutty Buttermilk Fish

❂ ❂ ❂

Our grandchildren "go nuts" for the coating. It is a bit more elaborate than ordinary oven-frying, but worth it!

½ cup (1 stick) butter
1 cup buttermilk
1 egg, beaten
1 cup whole-wheat flour
1 cup ground pecans or walnuts
⅓ cup sesame seeds
1 tablespoon paprika
3 pounds white fish pieces
⅔ cup pecan or walnut halves

1. Preheat oven to 350°F.
2. In a large roasting pan, melt the butter in the oven; set aside. In a bowl, combine the buttermilk and egg.

3. In another bowl, mix the flour, ground nuts, seeds, and paprika. Coat the fish in the buttermilk mixture and then roll in the flour mixture until it's covered.

4. Place fish in pan, turning to coat all sides in butter. Sprinkle on the nut halves and bake for 1½ hours.

Yield: 4 servings

Note: The coating works well with chicken, too.

Baked Lake Trout

❂ ❂ ❂

Our love affair with trout began in our first year of marriage, when we lived in the Italian countryside. Every Friday we'd stop at the fish vendor's for two *Lago di Garda trotta*, fresh from Lake Garda in northern Italy. Now we fish, with occasional success, on Lake Champlain, just below Vergennes, Vermont. Trout from Lake Champlain usually serve at least two people amply. Here's a simple recipe.

1 large trout, cleaned and gutted, with skin on
5 tablespoons butter
garlic salt
freshly ground black pepper
chopped fresh herbs, such as basil, oregano, marjoram, chives, parsley, or a combination
1 lemon, thinly sliced
2 tablespoons lemon juice
tartar sauce (page 265)

1. Preheat oven to 400°F. Place prepared fish on a baking sheet that has been covered with aluminum foil. Thinly slice 2 tablespoons of the butter. Open the cavity in the fish and sprinkle garlic salt, pepper, and herbs to cover the inside. Place the lemon and butter slices inside. Close and turn fish on its side.

2. Melt the remaining 3 tablespoons butter; combine with lemon juice. Pour the mixture on top of fish and bake for about 20 minutes. Serve with tartar sauce.

Yield: 2 servings

Baked Stuffed Fillet of Sole

❈ ❈ ❈

These rolled fish fillets are light and tasty. You can assemble them up to 24 hours in advance and refrigerate, covered, until baking time. Add 10 minutes to the baking time if they are refrigerated.

¼ cup diced celery
¼ cup diced mushrooms
¼ cup diced onions
1 tablespoon butter
6 tablespoons low-sodium chicken broth
¾ cup bread crumbs
1½ pounds fillet of sole, cut into large serving-sized pieces
1 teaspoon grated fresh lemon zest
2 tablespoons finely minced fresh parsley
paprika

1. Preheat oven to 350°F. Sauté celery, mushrooms, and onions in the butter until they are tender and the juices have evaporated.

2. Add the vegetables and 4 tablespoons of the broth to the bread crumbs and mix well. Let stand for 5 minutes.

3. Rinse the fish and pat dry.

4. Put a spoonful of the bread crumb mixture in the center of each fillet. Roll the fillet around the mixture.

5. Place the fish rolls, seam side down, in a baking dish sprayed with vegetable cooking spray.

6. Pour the remaining broth over the fish rolls.

7. Sprinkle the lemon zest, parsley, and paprika to taste over all.

8. Bake, uncovered, for 25 minutes.

Yield: 4 servings

ABOUT GRILLED OR BROILED FISH

Fish is best grilled over (or under) high heat, so that it cooks quickly without drying. Firm-fleshed fish steaks, such as salmon, tuna, and swordfish, are the best for grilling. Grill them skin side down for about 3 to 5 minutes. Turn and grill for about 3 minutes longer. More delicate fish is best broiled, since it is supported by a pan. A thin fillet won't even need turning. If it is a thicker cut, brush it with marinade or oil to keep it moist and broil a bit farther from the heat.

Grilled Tuna with Lime

❈ ❈ ❈

Fresh tuna is a wonderful, meaty fish with enough character to stand up to a strongly flavored sauce. Serve it with a side of colorful coleslaw or cold sesame noodles for a relaxed patio dinner.

2½–3 pounds tuna steaks
1 cup Sesame Lime Marinade (page 278)
2 limes, cut into wedges

1. Rinse the tuna and pat dry. Pour the marinade over the tuna, cover, and refrigerate 1 to 3 hours.

2. Prepare the grill for high heat. Grill the tuna over hot coals, 5 to 7 minutes on each side, or broil, brushing frequently with the marinade. Place the tuna on a serving platter and surround with the lime wedges.

Yield: 8 servings

Note: If you want to serve this at a picnic, rinse and dry the tuna before leaving the house. Allow the tuna to marinate in a low-sided container with a tight-fitting cover. Pack in a cooler, along with the lime wedges (in a plastic bag), and cook when ready.

Coquilles St. Jacques

❖ ❖ ❖

John's mom loved the Jersey shore from the time she was a young girl. One of her favorite things to do was taking us to the fish market down by the pier in Ocean City, where we could watch the boats come in and unload their day's catch. She would select the freshest fish of the day, then prepare a seafood classic for her family. She served this in large scallop shells, but small ramekins are fine.

1 *pound bay scallops, rinsed and dried*
2 *tablespoons all-purpose flour*
4 *tablespoons butter*
4 *scallions, diced*
½ *cup dry sherry*
½ *pound mushrooms, thinly sliced*
½ *cup light cream*
2 *tablespoons chopped fresh parsley*
salt and freshly ground black pepper
2 *tablespoons grated Swiss cheese*
nutmeg

1. Place the scallops and flour in a plastic bag and shake to coat. Melt the butter in a skillet and sauté the scallops and scallions until scallops are opaque. Add the sherry and mushrooms; simmer for 5 minutes.

2. Add the cream and parsley and simmer until the sauce thickens, about 3 to 4 minutes. Do not boil. Season to taste with salt and pepper.

3. Preheat broiler. Divide the mixture among individual scallop shells or ramekins; sprinkle lightly with cheese and nutmeg. Broil until lightly browned and bubbling.

Yield: 4 servings

Shrimp Scampi

❖ ❖ ❖

Somehow scampi always seems like a romantic dish. We like to accompany it with rice or a hot baguette to absorb the delicious, buttery juices. Steamed snow peas and a glass of chilled white wine make it a special dinner for two.

1 *pound shrimp, shelled and deveined*
2 *large cloves of garlic, finely chopped*
2 *heaping tablespoons chopped fresh parsley*
4 *tablespoons butter*
1 *tablespoon vegetable oil*
1–2 *tablespoons dry vermouth*
salt and freshly ground black pepper
1 *teaspoon all-purpose flour*
dash of lemon juice

1. Rinse the shrimp in cold water; dry on paper towels.

2. Sauté the garlic and parsley in the butter and oil for 1 to 2 minutes. Do not let the garlic brown. Add the vermouth.

3. Add the shrimp. Raise the heat to medium high and cook for 3 to 5 minutes, stirring frequently. Do not overcook. Season with salt and pepper. Stir in the flour to slightly thicken the garlic butter. Add the lemon juice during the last minute of cooking. Remove from heat and serve immediately.

Yield: 2–3 servings

VARIATION: Chicken, pork, and scallops are also delicious cooked in this sauce. Watch to be sure they are cooked through, but not overdone.

Seafood Newburg

❖ ❖ ❖

This recipe is actually a low-calorie version of lobster Newburg. You have to try it to believe how good it is. Use real butter and young, tender zucchini, peeled to prevent a green Newburg. The poaching liquid can be saved for fish soup, if you like.

1 pound any mixture of shellfish or thick-fleshed fish
 fillets, cut into 1-inch
 chunks
chicken broth, fish stock, or
 water to cover fish
dash of salt
¾ cup raw zucchini, peeled
 but not seeded, cut in
 chunks
2 tablespoons diced onion
dash of white pepper
⅔ cup chicken broth (may be
 canned)
1 tablespoon butter
¾ cup cubed Velveeta cheese
2 tablespoons grated
 Parmesan cheese
¼ cup sherry
¼ cup boiled potato, peeled
 and cut into chunks
dash of cayenne pepper

1. Place the fish in a skillet or saucepan and cover
with the broth and the salt.
Cover the pan and bring to a
boil. Remove from heat and
let stand, covered, for 5 to 8
minutes.

2. In a 1-quart saucepan,
cook the zucchini, onion, and
pepper in the ⅔ cup broth,
covered, until the zucchini is
mushy.

3. Pour the zucchini mixture into a blender with the
butter, Velveeta, Parmesan,
sherry, potato, and cayenne.
Purée until very smooth.

4. Pour the contents of
the blender back into the
saucepan. Heat through until
the sauce reaches the simmering point, stirring constantly (about 5 minutes).

5. Add the cooked fish
and heat through. Do not
boil. Serve over rice.

Yield: 4 servings

ABOUT SHRIMP

....

**Shrimp is sold according to the number per pound. A good size for
scampi is 20 to 25 per pound. Very large shrimp tend to be tough
and less flavorful when broiled. Fresh shrimp is usually marketed
headless and unshelled. The flesh is almost colorless, but the shells
may range in color from light brown to coral, depending on the
variety or origin of the shrimp. Fresh shrimp is very perishable, so most are frozen for market. Frozen shrimp should
be thawed slowly in the refrigerator just before cooking.**

Baked Stuffed Clams

❈ ❈ ❈

Lynn Doll gave me this recipe
when we were young moms
living in New Jersey. She was a
great cook and brought these to
some of our neighborhood block
parties. They didn't last long!

1 clove of garlic
1 tablespoon diced onion
1 teaspoon dried parsley
½ teaspoon dried oregano
2 tablespoons olive oil
¼ cup bread crumbs
1 can (6½ ounces) minced
 clams
¼ teaspoon salt
12 clam or scallop shells, cleaned
 grated Parmesan cheese
 lemon

1. Preheat oven to 375°F.
Sauté the garlic, onion, parsley,
and oregano in the oil for about
2 minutes. Add the bread
crumbs, mixing thoroughly.

2. When the garlic and
onion start to brown, remove
mixture from heat and mix with
the clams, their juice, and salt.

3. Spoon into shells.
Sprinkle tops lightly with
Parmesan.

4. Place on a baking sheet.
Bake for 25 to 30 minutes, until
crusty and lightly browned on
top. Serve with a squeeze of
lemon.

Yield: 12 clams

GAME

What country folks have known for years, restaurants and their patrons have discovered in recent times: *Game makes good eating.* If you don't hunt and don't have friends who do, it can be hard to find. But commercially grown pheasants and rabbits are often available (usually frozen) in specialty meat stores.

Venison Stew

❁ ❁ ❁

When friends who hunt bring us a piece of venison, we like to make a pot of this savory stew. The fresh crunch of green pepper on top complements the richly flavored, fork-tender meat and vegetables.

- ½ cup plus 3 tablespoons all-purpose flour
- 1 teaspoon salt
- ⅛ teaspoon freshly ground black pepper
- 2–3 pounds venison roast, cut into 1-inch cubes
- ¼ cup vegetable oil
- 2 cups boiling water
- 1 bay leaf
- 2 beef bouillon cubes
- 12 small whole onions, peeled
- 6 medium carrots, cut into 2-inch chunks
- 1 package frozen lima beans

- ½ cup cold water
- 2 large green bell peppers, seeded and cut into rings

1. Mix the ½ cup flour, the salt and pepper. Dredge the venison cubes in the flour. In a Dutch oven or large skillet, brown venison on all sides in the oil. Add the boiling water and bay leaf. Cover and simmer over low heat for 30 minutes. Discard the bay leaf. Add the bouillon cubes, onions, and carrots. Simmer 45 minutes longer. Stir in the lima beans and cook for an additional 15 minutes.

2. With a slotted spoon, remove the meat and vegetables to a serving dish, leaving the cooking liquid in the pan.

Blend the 3 tablespoons flour and the cold water in a cup; gradually add to the hot liquid. Cook, stirring constantly, until smooth and thickened. Pour over meat and vegetables. Top with pepper rings. Broil 5 minutes, until well browned on top.

Yield: 6 servings

Pheasant Baked in Foil

❁ ❁ ❁

A pheasant, simply cooked, makes a delightful departure from ordinary fare. The foil wrapping keeps the meat from drying out as it roasts. Roasted parsnips, stuffed

---

ABOUT THAT GAMY TASTE

....

The distinctive strong flavor of game is often an acquired taste. Most people look forward to it once they are accustomed to it. Here are a few tips to tone down the strong flavor of wild game for the uninitiated.

- Cover meat with a mixture of water and 3 tablespoons salt or 3 tablespoons vinegar. Soak for up to 30 minutes. Discard water.
- Parboil the meat. Simmer meat in water briefly before frying or baking. Discard water.
- Use a combination of half game and half beef or pork. Add aromatic vegetables or spicy sauce.
- Hunt early in the season. Late in the season, near mating time, game takes on a stronger taste.

squash, or a pilaf with wild rice is good alongside it.

- 1 pheasant (about 3½ pounds)
- 3 tablespoons butter, melted
- 1 teaspoon salt
- ⅛ teaspoon freshly ground black pepper
- ½ orange, unpeeled

1. Preheat oven to 450°F. Dry the pheasant and brush with the butter. Sprinkle inside and out with salt and pepper. Stuff orange half in cavity. Place the pheasant on a large sheet of aluminum foil; bring the edges together, and seal tightly.

2. Place in a roasting pan and bake for 1 hour. Open the foil, reduce heat to 350°F, and bake 20 minutes longer, until golden brown.

Yield: 3–4 servings

Country-Style Rabbit

❖ ❖ ❖

The flavor of rabbit is light and delicate, and the meat is low in fat and cholesterol. Wild rabbit may be used, but it tends to be less tender and not as meaty.

- 1 rabbit (2–2¼ pounds), dressed

- 3–4 slices uncooked bacon
- ¼ cup vegetable oil
- 1 teaspoon honey
- salt and freshly ground black pepper

Filling

- 2 cloves of garlic, chopped
- 3 tablespoons bread crumbs
- 1 tablespoon chopped onions
- 1 tablespoon grated Parmesan cheese
- 1 tablespoon raisins, finely chopped
- ½ teaspoon chopped fresh parsley
- 1 tablespoon milk
- 1 egg yolk

Sauce

- 1 tablespoon chopped onion
- 1 clove of garlic, chopped
- 2 tablespoons vegetable oil
- 1 teaspoon honey
- ¼ teaspoon chopped fresh parsley
- ⅛ teaspoon pepper
- 9 medium tomatoes, peeled
- 2 tablespoons white wine
- 1 tablespoon butter

1. Preheat oven to 400°F.

2. Rinse the rabbit in lukewarm, salted water. Drain and pat dry. Cut into parts.

3. Combine all ingredients for the filling. Using a sharp knife, make

pockets in the legs of the rabbit and stuff with the filling. If the pockets are especially large, double the filling recipe.

4. Place the rabbit parts in a baking dish. Top with bacon. Add the oil. Bake for 20 to 30 minutes, or until the rabbit is well browned. Turn once. Dribble the honey over the rabbit. Season lightly with salt and pepper to taste. Lower the oven temperature to 350°F.

5. Meanwhile, prepare the sauce. Sauté the onion and garlic in the oil; season with the honey, parsley, and pepper. Add the tomatoes and wine and cook at a low boil for about 30 minutes, until the sauce thickens. Pour over the browned rabbit (it should be completely submerged in the sauce). Bake in the oven, covered, for 30 to 60 minutes, or until the rabbit is very tender. Add the butter to the sauce 5 minutes before serving.

Yield: 3–4 servings

PASTA

Pasta has come a long way from the spaghetti and meatballs of my childhood. It is available in a multitude of shapes and sizes and is a perfect partner for sauces as well as vegetable, fish, or meat combinations. As a rule of thumb, creamy or smooth sauces pair best with straight or flat pastas, while chunkier sauces work better with the chunkier shapes. There are also large shapes for stuffing and tiny pastas for use in soup or broth.

Homemade Pasta

❈ ❈ ❈

Fresh pasta has a taste and texture so much richer than those of dried pasta that it's worth the extra time it takes to prepare it. For us, making fresh pasta always brings back the sights and sounds of Italy.

2¼   cups all-purpose flour
  3   large eggs
  ½   teaspoon salt, optional

1. Mound the flour on a smooth work surface or in a very large bowl and make a well in the center.

2. Beat the eggs and pour them into the center of the flour (adding salt, if desired). Using a fork or your hands, combine the mixture until it is blended and a ball forms.

3. Continue kneading until the dough is smooth and supple — about 5 minutes longer. (If the dough feels too sticky, sprinkle it with 1 tablespoon flour and knead the flour into the ball. If the dough feels too hard, add *1 drop at a time* of beaten egg or vegetable oil.)

4. Lightly grease a piece of plastic wrap with vegetable oil. Place the dough in the wrap, and let it rest for at least 30 minutes before rolling it out.

Mixing in a Food Processor

1. Place the flour in the food processor bowl and, with the motor running, add the eggs one at a time.

2. Process until the mixture forms a ball.

3. If the dough seems too sticky, add 1 tablespoon flour and process for 10 seconds until incorporated. Then process for 40 to 60 seconds longer.

4. Remove the dough and wrap it in greased plastic wrap. Allow the dough to rest for at least 15 minutes before rolling it out.

Rolling by Hand

1. To make the dough more manageable, divide it into four pieces and place them on a lightly floured surface.

2. Roll each piece into a rectangle. The dough should be ⅛ inch thick for noodles or 1/16 inch thick for ravioli, cannelloni, tortellini, lasagna, manicotti, and any other "stuffed" recipe. (If you lay the rectangle on a clean tea towel and you can see the design of the towel through the dough, the dough is approximately 1/16 inch thick.)

3. *To make noodles,* roll the rectangle lengthwise like a jelly roll and slice off ⅛-, ¼-, or ½-inch widths for noodles, or 2- to 4-inch widths for lasagna.

To make cannelloni or manicotti, cut the rectangle into 4-inch squares and drop them into a large pot of boiling water. When the squares come to the top, remove them immediately and place them on a clean towel. When the excess moisture has been removed, lay out the squares on a tablecloth and fold the cloth so that it comes between all the squares. They must not be touching. If the pasta is not going to be used during the next hour, place the folded tablecloth in a plastic bag and refrigerate the pasta for up to 2 days.

To make ravioli, cut the rectangle into 1½–2-inch squares, fill squares with a prepared stuffing, top with another square and crimp edges, and place them in a single layer on a lightly oiled or floured tray. Refrigerate until ready to use, or freeze. When they are frozen, pack them into plastic bags and seal. Cook in the frozen state.

Rolling by Machine

1. Cut the rested dough into four pieces; flatten and lightly flour each piece as required. Keep all but one piece wrapped in the plastic to prevent them from drying out.

2. Set the pasta machine at the widest setting and run a piece of the flattened dough through the machine. Repeat at this width four times, folding it in half each time.

3. The dough will now be thoroughly kneaded, and the rollers can be set closer together for each successive rolling to obtain the desired thickness.

4. Once the pasta has reached the desired thickness, allow the sheet to stiffen somewhat (without drying out) before running it through the cutter.

Yield: 1 pound

VARIATIONS

• Substitute semolina durum wheat flour for the whole amount of all-purpose flour and use 4 eggs.

• Use only 2 eggs and add ½ cup puréed vegetables, such as spinach, broccoli, beets, carrots, or red or yellow bell peppers. Combine the vegetables with the eggs before adding them to the flour.

• Substitute whole-wheat, buckwheat, triticale, rye, or semolina flour for 1 cup of the all-purpose flour and add ½ cup puréed vegetables.

• Omit the eggs and add ½ cup of puréed vegetables.

• Add ¼ to ½ cup chopped fresh herbs, such as parsley, basil, lemon thyme, or tarragon (a strong flavor — try 2 to 4 tablespoons the first time). If using dried herbs, add only 2 to 3 tablespoons.

COOKING PERFECT PASTA

Figure on ¼ pound of pasta per person. Use 4 to 6 quarts of water to every pound of pasta; cook in a large pot with room to spare. This prevents the pasta from sticking together and helps it cook faster. The addition of 1 teaspoon of oil will keep the strands from sticking.

Bring the water to a rolling boil over high heat (add 1 tablespoon of salt, if desired) and add the pasta all at once. Using a wooden fork, stir gently to separate the strands or shapes. Return water to a rolling boil; keep pot uncovered and lower the heat to medium to prevent its boiling over.

The pasta is done when it is tender but firm. The Italians call this *al dente* — firm to the bite. Cooking time varies according to the pasta: thick or thin, small or large, dried or fresh. If it's homemade (fresh or dried), it may take as little as 2 minutes, so check frequently. When commercial dried pasta is used, follow the directions on the package, but choose the shorter time listed and start testing (by tasting) several minutes before the end. This way, you'll be assured of getting perfectly cooked al dente pasta.

Drain pasta in a colander and serve immediately. When cooking manicotti, lasagna, or shells, drain and deposit on a clean tea towel to blot dry before use in a stuffed recipe. Do not rinse pasta unless it is to be chilled for a cold salad.

Spinach Cannelloni

❁ ❁ ❁

Our first year of marriage was spent outside Bologna, Italy, and our Italian neighbors were generous in sharing friendship and family recipes. We learned generations of old Italian cooking secrets. One of our favorites was Spinach Cannelloni. Everything was made from the freshest ingredients, bought daily in the local markets or grown in home gardens. Cannelloni became a standard in our home, and now with fresh pasta sheets available in most supermarkets, it's easier to make than ever.

Filling

3 tablespoons olive oil
2 cloves of garlic, minced
1 medium onion, minced
2 cups cooked spinach, squeezed dry and chopped
1 tablespoon butter
1 pound ground sirloin
2 tablespoons chopped fresh parsley
2 tablespoons chopped fresh oregano
1 tablespoon chopped fresh basil
1 large egg, beaten
⅔ cup grated Parmesan cheese
2 tablespoons light cream
¼ teaspoon ground nutmeg
¼ teaspoon salt
   freshly ground black pepper
   fresh spinach pasta sheets, or 12 cooked manicotti tubes
4–5 cups Italian Tomato Sauce (page 263)

Besciamella (White Sauce)

4 tablespoons butter
4 tablespoons all-purpose flour
2 cups light cream or half-and-half
½ teaspoon salt
¼ teaspoon ground nutmeg

1. To make the filling, in a large, heavy skillet, heat the oil. Sauté the garlic and onion until translucent but not brown. Add the spinach; cook until spinach mixture becomes dry, about 5 minutes. Remove to a large bowl.

2. In the same skillet, melt the butter and cook the sirloin until well browned. Add the browned meat to the bowl along with the parsley, oregano, basil, egg, ⅓ cup of the Parmesan, cream, nutmeg, salt, and pepper to taste. Mix well.

3. Preheat oven to 350°F. Cut pasta sheets into 5-inch squares and place 2 tablespoons of meat filling on top of each, then roll up (or stuff cooked manicotti tubes). Spread a thin layer of tomato sauce in the bottom of a 9- by 13-inch baking pan. Place cannelloni in the pan, seam side down.

4. When the pan is filled, top with a layer of tomato sauce, then a layer of *besciamella*. Sprinkle with the remaining ⅓ cup Parmesan; bake until bubbly and lightly browned on top, about 40 minutes.

Yield: 6–8 servings

Traditional Lasagna

❁ ❁ ❁

I frequently prepare lasagna ahead of time and either refrigerate it for a day or freeze it for a later date. From the refrigerator, it goes into a preheated 375°F oven for 45 minutes; from the freezer, it will need 1 to 1¼ hours. Cover it for the first half hour to keep the sauce from drying out.

½ pound Italian sausage meat
½ pound lean ground beef
2 cloves of garlic, crushed or minced
1 teaspoon dried basil
1 teaspoon dried oregano
¼ teaspoon coarsely ground black pepper
3 cups chopped tomatoes, or 1 can (28 ounces) crushed tomatoes
4 cups part-skim ricotta or dry cottage cheese
1¼ cups grated Parmesan cheese

2 large eggs, beaten
¼ cup low-fat milk
½ teaspoon ground mace
¼ teaspoon finely ground
    black pepper
1 pound part-skim moz-
    zarella cheese, grated
¼ cup chopped fresh parsley
12–16 lasagna noodles, cooked
    and drained as package
    directs

1. Preheat oven to 375°F and grease a 9- by 13-inch baking dish.

2. Break up and brown the sausage meat in a skillet over medium heat for 2 to 3 minutes; transfer to a bowl and drain off the excess fat.

3. Add the beef to the skillet, break it up, and brown for 2 to 3 minutes.

4. Add the garlic and stir for 1 minute.

5. Return the sausage meat to the skillet and add the basil, oregano, coarsely ground pepper, and tomatoes. Stir to combine; simmer for 15 to 20 minutes.

6. In a large bowl, combine the ricotta, 1 cup of the Parmesan, eggs, milk, mace, and finely ground pepper.

7. In a separate bowl, combine the mozzarella and parsley.

8. Place a layer of lasagna noodles in the baking dish and spread with one third of the ricotta mixture, followed by one third of the meat sauce, and one third of the mozzarella and parsley. Repeat two times, so that there are three layers. Sprinkle the remaining Parmesan over the top.

9. Bake for 30 minutes, or until the center is steaming.

Yield: 8–10 servings

Sausage and Rigatoni

❋ ❋ ❋

Every so often, the spirit moves us to make a batch of fresh sausage. Then we add it to a chunky pasta sauce and serve it with rigatoni for hearty homemade fare.

1 pound Sicilian-style
    Sweet Sausage (page 424)
1 tablespoon olive oil
1 small onion, chopped
1 small green bell pepper,
    cored, seeded, and chopped
4 cups tomato sauce
1 tablespoon chopped parsley
1 pound rigatoni, cooked
    and drained as package
    directs
1 12-ounce package moz-
    zarella cheese, shredded
½ cup Romano cheese, grated

1. In a large skillet, cook the sausages in the oil until they are lightly browned. Set the sausages aside to cool slightly and drain off all but 2 tablespoons of the drippings.

2. Sauté the onion and pepper until they are crisp-tender. Add the tomato sauce and parsley and simmer over medium heat until heated through.

3. Slice the sausages into 1-inch pieces and add to the sauce. Simmer for 10 minutes.

4. Preheat oven to 425°F. In a greased baking dish, arrange layers of sauce, rigatoni, and mozzarella. Sprinkle the Romano on top.

5. Bake, uncovered, until the sauce is bubbly and the top layer of cheese is slightly browned, about 20 minutes.

Yield: 4–6 servings

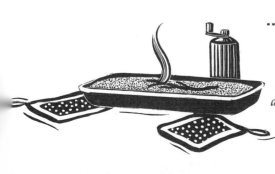

SIMPLY TOMATO SAUCE

Sometimes simple is best. With all the new sauces and combinations available, it bears remembering that pasta served with plain tomato sauce (page 390) and a fresh grating of cheese is hard to beat.

Meatballs
with Ziti

❁ ❁ ❁

Use ten of the twenty meatballs with the ziti and freeze the remainder for another meal. Or make some patties with the meat mixture and broil them for breakfast.

  1 *pound finely ground beef*
  1 *pound finely ground pork*
2–4 *cloves of garlic, crushed or minced*
  6 *scallions, including green, finely sliced*
  2 *teaspoons dried thyme*
  1 *teaspoon ground mace*
  1 *teaspoon crumbled leaf sage*
 ½ *teaspoon coarsely ground black pepper*
 ½ *teaspoon dried rosemary leaves*
  2 *cups fresh whole-grain bread crumbs (about 4 large slices of bread)*
 ¾ *cup liquid (tomato juice, stock, or wine)*
  1 *tablespoon vegetable oil*
    Italian Tomato Sauce (page 263)
  1 *pound ziti*

1. Place the beef, pork, garlic, scallions, thyme, mace, sage, pepper, rosemary, bread crumbs, and liquid in a large bowl. Mix with your hands or a fork.

2. Form the mixture into balls approximately 1 inch in diameter.

3. Heat the oil in a skillet and sauté 10 meatballs at a time for 1 to 2 minutes, rolling them around to sear them on all sides. Remove to a dish.

4. Simmer the meatballs in the Italian Tomato Sauce for at least 15 minutes. While the sauce is simmering, cook the ziti as the package directs. Drain and serve with the sauce and meatballs.

Yield: 4 servings

White Clam Sauce
with Thin Spaghetti

❁ ❁ ❁

I have not always lived so far inland. When I get a yearning for the sound and smell of the ocean, I make this simple pasta sauce and can almost taste the salt air.

  8 *ounces thin spaghetti (capellini or perciatelli)*
  2 *tablespoons butter*
  1 *clove of garlic, crushed or minced*
  2 *tablespoons cornstarch*
 ¼ *cup white wine, clam juice, or chicken stock*
  1 *can (10 ounces) whole baby clams in broth*
  1 *can (6½ ounces) chopped clams*
 ⅛ *teaspoon ground white pepper*
 ¼ *cup chopped fresh parsley*

1. Cook the spaghetti in boiling water as the package directs.

2. Melt the butter in a saucepan over low heat and sauté the garlic for 10 seconds. Add the cornstarch and stir for 1 minute. Drain clams, reserving the liquid.

3. Pour in the white wine and the liquid from the can of clams. Stir continuously until the sauce is smooth.

4. Add the baby clams, chopped clams, pepper, and parsley. Heat through for 5 minutes.

5. Drain the pasta and divide into two individual warm serving bowls. Top with the sauce and serve immediately.

Yield: 2 servings

HOW MUCH TO COOK

- *2 ounces of dry macaroni-type pasta = about 1¼ cups cooked*

- *8 ounces or 2 cups of dry macaroni-type pasta = 4½ to 5 cups cooked*

- *8 ounces of dry egg noodles = 4 cups cooked*

- *4 ounces or one 3½-inch bundle of dry spaghetti-type pasta = 2 to 2½ cups cooked*

- *8 ounces or one 4½-inch bundle of dry spaghetti-type pasta = 4 to 5 cups cooked*

- *12 ounces or one 5½-inch bundle of dry spaghetti-type pasta = 6½ to 7 cups cooked*

Peppers & Sun-Dried Tomatoes
with Pasta

❈ ❈ ❈

Peppers take the lead in this hearty sauce, while the sun-dried tomatoes play a small but intense supporting role. We like the sauce with sausage in it, but it is good without meat, too.

4 red bell peppers

4 tablespoons olive oil

2 Italian sausages, hot or sweet

4 cloves of garlic, peeled and sliced in half

1 pound spaghetti or linguini

2 tablespoons sun-dried tomatoes packed in oil, drained and chopped

3 tablespoons grated Romano cheese

¾ cup grated Parmesan cheese

3 tablespoons chopped fresh basil

3 tablespoons chopped fresh parsley

2 scallions, green and white parts, sliced

1. Preheat oven to 450°F. Roast the peppers in a baking pan, uncovered, on the lowest rack in the oven for about 30 minutes, or until they are blackened on all sides. Turn three or four times during roasting. When they are done, place them in a paper bag and roll the top closed. Leave for 10 minutes. Remove the peppers from the bag, peel, and let cool. Chop them coarsely.

2. In a skillet, heat the oil. Remove the casings from the sausages and crumble the meat into the pan. Add the garlic and cook, continuing to separate the sausage meat into crumb-sized pieces, until the sausage is brown and crisp. Remove the garlic and discard.

3. In the meantime, bring a large pot of water to a boil and cook the spaghetti as the package directs.

4. Combine the peppers, sausage, and sun-dried tomatoes. In a separate bowl, combine the Romano and ½ cup of the Parmesan with the basil, parsley, and scallions. When the pasta is cooked, drain it quickly and place in a large pasta bowl. Cover with the pepper mixture, then the cheese and herb mixture, and toss. Serve at once with the remaining Parmesan.

Yield: 4 servings

TYPES OF ITALIAN PASTA

··

PASTA	SUBSTITUTES
Spaghetti	Any long, thin, solid pasta: spaghettini, capellini, vermicelli, perciatelli, linguini, fusilli (curled), angel hair
Macaroni	Any short, cylindrical pasta: ziti, penne, elbows, mezzani, mezzanelli, bucatini, ditali, zitoni
Flat egg noodles	Tagliatelle, tagliarini, fettuccine, fettuccelle
Pasta for stuffing	Lasagna noodles, manicotti, tufoli, mafalde, cannelle, grooved rigatoni
Specialty shapes	Farfalle, farfallette, farfalloni, maruzze, maruzzelle, conchiglie, conchigliette, cavatelli
Stuffed pasta	Tortelli, tortellini, ravioli, ravioletti, raviolini, agnolotti, anolini, cappelletti, pansotti
Pasta for soups and side dishes	Acini di pepe, anelli, anellini, ditalini, tubetti, tubetini, stelle (stars), rotini (tiny wheels), rotelle (wheels), semi di melone (melon seeds), pasta grattingiate (grated fresh pasta), orzo, capelli d'angelo (angel hair), and many, many more

CHEESE

To me, main dishes featuring cheese are among the best comfort foods of all. Rich and creamy, cheese makes a great companion to macaroni, potatoes, eggs (as in quiche), meat, and poultry.

Crab and Broccoli Quiche

❁ ❁ ❁

At a ladies' lunch or family brunch, this quiche will be the star on your menu. Serve it with a tossed green salad, warm rolls, and a nice dry white wine or minted iced tea, and the picture is complete.

- 1 9-inch deep-dish piecrust, unbaked
- 1 cup shredded Swiss cheese
- 1 cup broccoli florets, cut small and steamed
- 1 can (6½ ounces) crabmeat, drained
- 2 scallions, diced
- 4 eggs
- 1½ cups light cream
- ½ teaspoon salt
- ½ teaspoon grated lemon zest
- ⅛ teaspoon ground mace

¼ teaspoon dry mustard
2 tablespoons sliced almonds
paprika

1. Preheat oven to 425°F. Sprinkle the cheese on the piecrust. Top with broccoli, crabmeat, and scallions.

2. In a medium-sized bowl, beat the eggs and whisk in the cream, salt, lemon zest,

---

QUICHE

....

Quiche is a pastry shell filled with a custard composed of eggs, cream or milk, cheese, seasonings, and other ingredients, such as vegetables, meat or shellfish, or herbs. *Quiche Lorraine* is the best-known pie of this kind; it's made with bits of crisply cooked bacon and Gruyère cheese. Many cooks use bits of leftover ham and vegetables to make quiche, which freezes well. Quiche is often prepared in mini-muffin pans to make appetizer-sized portions.

---

mace, and mustard. Pour over the crab mixture and top with the almonds and paprika.

3. Bake for 10 minutes. Reduce oven temperature to 325°F and cook for 50 minutes longer.

4. Remove from oven and let stand at least 10 minutes before serving.

Yield: 8 servings

Super-Quick Turkey Divan

❁ ❁ ❁

This is a workday dream; it is quick to assemble and can be prepared 24 hours ahead and refrigerated until baking time. We like it with chicken, too.

- 20 ounces frozen broccoli spears
- 2 ounces Cheddar cheese, grated (½ cup)
- 12 ounces sliced roast turkey
- 2 cans (10¾ ounces each) cream of chicken soup
- ¼ cup milk
- ¼ teaspoon ground nutmeg
- 1 cup biscuit mix
- 4 tablespoons cold butter, cut into chunks
- 2 tablespoons grated Parmesan cheese
paprika

1. Preheat oven to 400°F.

2. Rinse the broccoli under cold running water to thaw. Drain thoroughly. Arrange the broccoli in a 7- by 11- by 1½-inch baking dish sprayed with vegetable oil.

3. Sprinkle the Cheddar over the broccoli. Layer the turkey slices over the cheese.

4. Blend the soup, milk, and nutmeg. Pour over the turkey.

5. Measure the biscuit mix into a food processor bowl fitted with a steel cutting blade, add the butter and Parmesan, and process until crumbly. Sprinkle over the soup mixture. Top with paprika.

6. Bake, uncovered, for 25 minutes, or until golden brown.

Yield: 6 servings

Macaroni and Cheese

❉ ❉ ❉

Macaroni and cheese is a staple in most families, and there must be a thousand ways to prepare it. Mine has evolved over the years as the kids' tastes have developed. Now, with grandchildren, I've changed it yet again.

1 *pound macaroni*
  (I use rotelli)
3 *tablespoons butter*

3 *tablespoons all-purpose flour*
3 *cups skim milk*
2½ *cups grated sharp Cheddar cheese*
1 *tablespoon Dijon mustard*
½ *teaspoon garlic salt*
1 *teaspoon dried basil*
freshly ground black pepper

Topping

1 *cup dried seasoned stuffing*
3 4 *scallions, cut into small pieces*
1 *tablespoon butter*

1. Preheat oven to 350°F. Grease a 2-quart casserole dish. Cook the macaroni for a minute or two less than the package directs.

2. In a medium saucepan, melt the butter. Add the flour to make a roux; cook over low heat, whisking constantly, until the mixture is well blended and the color of straw. Add the milk and continue whisking until the mixture is slightly thickened and bubbly.

3. Stir in the Cheddar, mustard, garlic salt, basil, and pepper to taste until well blended. Remove from heat.

4. For the topping, blend the stuffing, scallions, and butter in a blender or food processor until thoroughly combined.

5. Toss the macaroni and cheese sauce together and place in the prepared casse-

role. Cover with the topping and bake, uncovered, for 30 minutes.

Yield: 6 servings

Scalloped Potatoes

❉ ❉ ❉

We discovered how easy it is to grow our own potatoes, and now we send the grandkids out almost nightly for "fresh spuds." When the potatoes are fresh and new, they don't require peeling — just scrub and slice!

6–8 *cups thinly sliced potatoes*
6–8 *scallions, diced*
2 *teaspoons chopped fresh thyme*
½ *teaspoon salt*
freshly ground black pepper
6–8 *tablespoons butter, cut into small pieces*
1¾ *cups light cream*

1. Preheat oven to 350°F. Grease a 9- by 13-inch pan or a 2-quart casserole.

2. Alternate layers of potatoes, scallions, thyme, salt, and pepper to taste, dotting each layer with butter.

3. Heat the cream and pour over the potatoes. Bake, uncovered, for 1 hour, until the top is lightly browned and the potatoes are very tender.

Yield: 6–8 servings

GRAINS & LEGUMES

Grains and legumes are economical and versatile; they can be served absolutely simply or adapted to endless casseroles and combinations. They are a feel-good part of eating — filling comfort food that bolsters the spirit and satisfies our desire for sound nutrition.

Paella

※ ※ ※

Paella, an elaborate Spanish rice dish, is a sensational choice for a gathering of friends. Seafood, chicken, and chorizo (page 424) add pizzazz to beautiful saffron-flavored rice and vegetables.

 1 *lobster (2 pounds)*
 1 *frying chicken (3 pounds)*
 ½ *cup olive oil*
 3 *cloves of garlic, finely minced*
 1 *large onion, chopped*
 1 *pound chorizo, cut into 1-inch pieces*
 1 *cup diced smoked ham*
 1 *green bell pepper, cored, seeded, and chopped*
 1 *teaspoon brined capers (do not use the salted variety)*
 2 *cups uncooked rice*
 2 *cups crushed tomatoes*
 2 *large pinches saffron*
 1 *cup water*
 1 *jar (2 ounces) pimientos*
 1 *teaspoon ground coriander*
 1 *teaspoon oregano*
 dash of cayenne pepper
 1 *pound cooked shrimp*
 1–2 *dozen fresh clams, well scrubbed and steamed*
 1 *cup fresh or frozen peas, cooked*

1. Boil or steam the lobster for 15 minutes. When the lobster is cool enough to handle, remove the meat from the shell.

2. Cut the chicken into serving pieces. In a large skillet, sauté the chicken in the oil until it is browned.

3. Add the garlic, onion, chorizo, ham, bell pepper, and capers to the pan with the chicken. Cook for 10 minutes, stirring.

4. Add the rice, tomatoes, saffron, water, pimientos, coriander, oregano, and cayenne. Mix well and cook, covered, for 20 minutes, or until the liquid is absorbed by the rice. Add the lobster, shrimp, clams, and peas. Heat through and serve.

Yield: 8 servings

ABOUT SAFFRON

....

Saffron strands are the stigma of a special crocus variety; it takes thousands of flowers to harvest an ounce of this highly prized seasoning. Fortunately, a little goes a long way, adding delicate flavor and beautiful yellow coloring to foods. Although turmeric is sometimes used as a substitute for the yellow coloring, this is undesirable; the strong flavor of turmeric overwhelms, whereas saffron is subtle.

Broccoli Rabe Risotto

※ ※ ※

Three essentials for perfect risotto are short-grain arborio rice, hot liquid to keep the pot from cooling, and the patience to work slowly, so that the rice will absorb the liquid without becoming mushy. The reward is a creamy, toothsome dish. This risotto's creaminess is balanced by the slightly bitter taste of the broccoli rabe.

 2 *cups water*

2 cups chopped broccoli rabe
2 cups vegetable or chicken broth
¼ cup chopped onion
¼ cup white wine
1 cup arborio rice
¼ cup grated Parmesan cheese

1. Place 1 cup of the water in a food processor or blender container with ½ cup of the broccoli rabe. Process until puréed. Add handfuls of broccoli rabe to the mix, processing until all of it is puréed. Set aside.

2. In a small saucepan, heat the broth to boiling. In a separate saucepan, combine the onion, wine, and rice and stir over medium heat until the wine is absorbed by the rice. Stirring continuously, over low heat add ¼ cup of the hot broth to the rice until it's absorbed. In this manner, gradually add 1 cup of the hot broth, stirring after each addition.

3. Add the broccoli rabe purée to the rice in three batches, stirring after each to absorb. Then gradually add the remaining 1 cup of broth in ¼-cup increments as outlined in Step 2. Taste the rice, which should by now be very soft. The broccoli rabe will have formed a thick creamy sauce around it.

4. Add the Parmesan and stir to combine. Serve on heated plates.

Yield: 4 servings

GOOD VEGETABLE AND SEASONING COMBINATIONS FOR RISOTTO

Risotto is one of those dishes that invite experiment. Here are some other vegetable and herb combinations to try:

- **Asparagus.** Basil and lemon zest
- **Carrots.** Marjoram
- **Celery.** Dill
- **Corn.** Cilantro, lime, tomato
- **Peas.** Mint, shallot
- **Peppers (red bell).** Leek, thyme
- **Shiitake mushrooms.** Oregano
- **Spinach or chard.** Ginger, sesame seeds
- **Winter squash or pumpkin.** Sage

BEANS

BABY LIMAS. Small dried limas are one of the faster-cooking dried beans.

BLACK BEANS. Small, elegant, dark beans that are traditionally used in Latin food. Once considered a gourmet rarity, they are gaining mainstream popularity in North America.

CHICKPEAS. Also called *garbanzos* or *ceci peas*, these roundish yellow beans are good for casseroles, salads, and spreads such as Hummus (page 91).

GREAT NORTHERN. These plump beans become very soft when cooked; they are good for baked beans or purées.

KIDNEY BEANS. Kidney beans may be red or pink; they are the popular choice for chili.

LENTILS. People have been eating lentils since biblical times. They are small and flat and may be brownish, green, or bright orange-red in color. Lentils take to many seasonings and are especially good in soups and salads.

NAVY BEANS. Also called *white beans* or *pea beans*, these are inexpensive, all-purpose beans.

PINTO BEANS. These are pale pink spotted with brown and are common in the Southwest.

Baked Beans

❁ ❁ ❁

An old Vermont family recipe, this is great for a woodstove or a slow oven. The long cooking time brings out the most delicious flavor and fills the house with good smells. If you are fond of ginger, add a little more.

    2 cups dry navy, Great
       Northern, or other white
       beans
    ¼ pound sliced salt pork
    1 small onion, sliced
    ⅓ cup molasses
    ½ cup brown sugar, firmly
       packed
    2 teaspoons salt
    2 teaspoons dry mustard
    ¼ teaspoon ground ginger
       dash of freshly ground black
       pepper

1. In a large bowl, cover the beans with about 6 cups water and let soak, covered, overnight. Drain the beans. Put into a large saucepan, cover with water, and bring to a boil; simmer until tender, about 30 minutes.

2. Preheat oven to 300°F. Drain the beans, reserving cooking water. Pour into a bean pot or a large greased casserole. Stir in the salt pork, onion, molasses, brown sugar, salt, mustard, ginger, and pepper.

3. Bake, covered, for 8 hours, stirring often. If the beans become dry, add a little of the reserved cooking water.

Yield: 6–8 servings

Note: You may also cook the beans in a Crock-Pot set on low.

Polenta

❁ ❁ ❁

A close Italian cousin to cornmeal mush and grits, polenta has become a popular and versatile dish. I make it simply and dress it up with different cheeses, meat sauce, or a spicy fresh tomato sauce; but this version is good enough to eat by itself with a garden salad.

    4 cups water
    1 cup yellow cornmeal
    1 teaspoon salt
    2 tablespoons butter or olive
       oil
    1 teaspoon dried oregano
    ½ cup grated Parmesan cheese
       freshly ground black pepper

1. In a small bowl, combine 1 cup of the water and the cornmeal. In a saucepan, bring the remaining 3 cups of water to a boil, then pour in the moistened cornmeal and salt, stirring constantly with a whisk so that lumps do not form. Cook over low heat until thickened and smooth. Remove from heat and cover for 5 minutes.

2. Add butter, oregano, and Parmesan, mixing well. Add pepper to taste and serve with your favorite sauce, or stir in other cheeses, such as fontina or sharp Cheddar.

PARADISE

....

Up in the hills above Tremezzo, Italy, there's a tiny family restaurant called La Fagurida on the Lago di Como. Everything served is homegrown and home-raised, and the olives and grapes are pressed by hand. On the evening we visited, we were greeted warmly and, without asking, were served homemade red wine and a warm bowl of polenta that had been cooked over the open fire. We'll never forget the combination of strong wine and smoky polenta. Our host watched with anticipation. "E come paradiso, no?" he said, smiling. Indeed, it was as close as we have yet come to paradise.

Spicy Lentils

❈ ❈ ❈

We like to make these spicy lentils ahead to let the flavors develop. They are great for a simple entrée or as a vegetarian option on a buffet table.

1 cup lentils
salt
2 tablespoons oil
1 clove of garlic, minced
1 medium onion, finely chopped
1 cup tomato purée
1 teaspoon ground cumin
salt and freshly ground black pepper
1 tablespoon vinegar
2 tablespoons chopped fresh chives
2 tablespoons chopped fresh parsley

1. In a medium saucepan, cover the lentils with water and salt to taste and bring to a boil. Simmer the lentils until just tender, about 20 to 25 minutes. Drain.

2. In a large skillet, heat oil and add garlic and onion. Sauté until soft. Stir in the tomato purée, cumin, and salt and pepper to taste. Add the lentils and cook for 10 minutes.

3. Transfer the mixture to a serving dish and stir in the vinegar. Stir in the chives and parsley and let stand 2 hours. Serve at room temperature.

Yield: 4 servings

Vegetable Barley

❈ ❈ ❈

Barley is often overlooked as a grain. We eat this tasty combination of grain and veggies hot for supper and pack the leftovers for a cold lunch the next day. Try adding other vegetables, too — whatever you have on hand.

2 cups water
2 cups tomato purée
1 cup barley

MEASURING DRIED BEANS

....

- 1 cup dried beans = 2 to 3 cups cooked beans
- 1 pound dried beans = 2¼ to 2⅓ cups dried beans
- 1 pound dried beans = 6 cups cooked beans

1 medium red bell pepper, chopped
1 medium onion, chopped
2 cloves of garlic, minced
1 tablespoon low-sodium soy sauce
1 tablespoon chopped fresh oregano
2 bay leaves
½ cup frozen peas

1. In a medium-sized saucepan, combine the water and tomato purée; stir.

2. Add the barley, bell pepper, onion, garlic, soy sauce, oregano, and bay leaves; bring to a boil. Reduce heat and simmer for 45 minutes. Mix in the frozen peas and heat through. Serve hot.

Yield: 4 servings

QUICK-SOAKING BEANS

....

It's best to soak beans overnight, but if you've forgotten or don't have time, here's a quick method.

Cover beans with cold water, bring to a boil, then reduce heat and simmer for 2 minutes. Remove from heat; let stand, covered, about 1 hour.

Preprocessed beans do not need soaking, but the processing robs them of some nutrients.

DINNER IN A POT

Dinner in a pot, especially a slow cooker, is wonderful for modern convenience, but it is hardly a new idea. Our great-great-grandmothers often had only one pot, which would bubble all day on the hearth; this blended flavors and cooked meat to succulent tenderness. No wonder some of the great country dishes from around the world are one-pot classics.

Boeuf Bourguignonne

⊠ ⊠ ⊠

Boeuf bourguignonne is great for making two meals from one, since it uses the leftovers from a roast beef dinner. This French classic is a simple dish of meat, mushrooms, and onions braised in red wine, but it will win you rave reviews.

1 large onion, diced
4 tablespoons olive oil
3 cups baby carrots
1 tablespoon all-purpose flour
1 cup red wine
4 cups canned beef broth
4 cups leftover beef, cut into bite-size cubes
2 tablespoons chopped fresh parsley
2 tablespoons chopped fresh rosemary
2 tablespoons chopped fresh sage
2 tablespoons chopped fresh thyme
garlic salt
freshly ground black pepper
½ pound mushrooms, sliced
2 cups leftover potatoes and onions

1. Sauté the onion in 3 tablespoons of the oil until translucent. Add the carrots and sauté 5 to 7 minutes longer. Sprinkle with flour and mix well. Add the wine and simmer, stirring well, until the wine is slightly reduced.

2. Add the broth, beef, and herbs, and add garlic salt and pepper to taste. Simmer for 20 minutes, until carrots are tender.

3. Meanwhile, sauté the mushrooms in the remaining oil until nicely browned.

4. After the stew has cooked, add the mushrooms and leftover potatoes and onions and heat through. Serve in large soup bowls over brown rice.

Yield: 6–8 servings

Cioppino

⊠ ⊠ ⊠

Fish and shellfish make this Italian one-pot specialty a heady stew. We take this recipe with us when we vacation by the shore and revel in the variety of fresh seafood.

½ cup vegetable oil
½ cup chopped onions
½ cup chopped scallions
1 green bell pepper, chopped
2 cloves of garlic, chopped
3 cups tomato purée
2 cups red wine
1 bay leaf
salt and freshly ground black pepper
2 pounds firm white fish, cut into large pieces
1 cooked lobster (2 pounds) or Dungeness crab, cut into pieces
1 pound shrimp, shelled
1 pint clams or mussels

1. In a deep, heavy saucepan, heat the oil. Add the onions, scallions, bell pepper, and garlic; cook until soft. Add the tomato purée and wine. Add the bay leaf and salt and pepper to taste. Bring to a boil and simmer for 10 minutes.

2. Add the fish, lobster and shrimp. Cook for 15 minutes. Add the clams and cook for 5 minutes, until shells open.

3. Serve very hot in deep bowls, with plenty of Italian bread and red wine.

Yield: 6 servings

Cassoulet

❖ ❖ ❖

Cassoulet sounds French and fancy, but it is simply an uncommonly good meat and bean stew. In France, it's usually made with duck, but this chicken version is delectable and more accessible to American kitchens.

2 cups Great Northern beans
1 cup water
6 cups chicken stock
3 cloves of garlic, minced
1 large onion, chopped
2 stalks of celery with
  leaves, chopped
2 tablespoons chopped fresh
  parsley
1 bay leaf
½ teaspoon dried thyme
½ teaspoon salt
¼ teaspoon freshly ground
  black pepper
1 bone from a cooked pork
  roast, or 3 pork chops,
  browned
½ cup dry white wine

10 chicken thighs, drumsticks, wings, or a combination
½ pound smoked sausage

1. In a large pot, cover beans with about 6 cups water and soak, covered, overnight. Drain the beans and put them into a kettle with the 1 cup fresh water, stock, garlic, onion, celery, parsley, bay leaf, thyme, salt, and pepper. Bring to a boil. Cover the pan, reduce the heat, and simmer for 1 hour. Add the pork bone. Simmer another 1½ hours, or until the beans are tender.

2. Preheat oven to 200°F. Transfer the beans to a large baking dish. Cut the pork from the bone into small pieces and add it to the beans. Pour in the wine. Arrange the chicken pieces on top of the beans, cover the casserole, and bake for about 6 hours. Check the beans occasionally to be sure that they have lots of liquid. If they appear to be drying out, add stock. Cassoulet should be almost soupy, not as thick as ordinary baked beans.

3. While the beans are baking, cut the sausage into small pieces and brown it in a skillet. Drain off as much fat as possible. About 30 minutes before you

want to serve the cassoulet, stir in the sausage, raise the oven heat to 350°F, and bake about 30 minutes with the cover removed to brown the top of the beans and chicken. Be sure to keep adding stock, if necessary, to keep the beans juicy.

Yield: 10 servings

SERVING SUGGESTION

....

One-pot cooking is great for one-bowl serving. Ladle stews into large soup bowls and pass a basket of dinner rolls, crusty bread, breadsticks, or corn bread. A salad of watercress and orange slices is good with meat dishes, and field greens and olives tossed with vinaigrette goes well with fish stews.

CASSEROLES

Casseroles have enduring popularity because they are easy to prepare, they can usually be made in advance, and they can easily be stretched to feed a crowd. They are fun to vary (I hardly ever make the same casserole exactly the same way twice) and a great way to turn unexciting leftovers into fresh new dinners.

Chicken and Mushroom Bake

❈ ❈ ❈

Here's a dish I rely on when I am having company but won't have time that day to prepare a meal. I serve it with rice pilaf (from a box!), steamed green beans, and bakery rolls. It always seems to hit the spot.

6 whole chicken breasts, skinned, boned, and halved
1 can (10¾ ounces) cream of mushroom soup
1½ cups sliced mushrooms
1 cup sour cream
1 cup dry white wine
2 teaspoons dried basil
freshly ground black pepper

1. Preheat oven to 350°F. Arrange the chicken breasts in a shallow 9- by 13-inch baking dish.

2. In a bowl, mix together the soup, mushrooms, sour cream, wine, and basil. Pour over chicken breasts. Sprinkle with pepper to taste.

3. Bake for 1 hour, or until the chicken is browned and cooked through. This dish can be made the day before and reheated.

Yield: 6 servings

Butternut-Turkey Casserole

❈ ❈ ❈

This is a wonderful dish for a potluck or a fall covered-dish supper. In fact, it is a wonderful dish anytime.

1 butternut squash (about 2 pounds)
¾ cup minced onions
2 tablespoons butter
2 cups toasted croutons
½ teaspoon poultry seasoning
½ teaspoon salt
freshly ground black pepper
1 cup chicken broth
2 cups cooked diced turkey or chicken
½ cup shredded Cheddar cheese

1. Preheat oven to 350°F. Grease a 1½-quart casserole.

2. Cut squash in half lengthwise and discard seeds. Bake, cut side down, in a baking pan for 50 to 60 minutes, until squash is tender. Scoop out pulp and mash.

3. Sauté onions in butter. Add croutons, poultry seasoning, salt, and pepper to taste. Add broth, mashed squash, and turkey. Place mixture in the casserole. Bake for 20 minutes. Sprinkle Cheddar on top and return to oven until cheese is melted.

Yield: 6 servings

Hungarian Goulash

❂ ❂ ❂

When I am in the mood for something different, I make this satisfying goulash. Someone always asks why we don't have it more often!

1 cup white wine (optional)
2 cans (1 pound each) sauerkraut, drained
3 tablespoons peanut oil
4 pounds stewing beef, cubed
4 cups thinly sliced onions
2 cups canned tomatoes, chopped
4 tablespoons paprika
1 tablespoon caraway seeds
salt
3 cups sour cream

1. Pour the wine, if desired, over sauerkraut, mix, and put aside.

2. Heat oil in a heavy pot or skillet and brown the beef on all sides. Add the onions, tomatoes, paprika, caraway seeds, and salt to taste. If too dry, add 1 cup of water. It may be necessary to add more later as the mixture cooks. Check every so often to make sure there is enough liquid for cooking and serving.

3. Simmer, covered, for about 1 hour, or until meat is tender. It is better to over-cook meat than to serve it tough. Remove from heat and stir in the sour cream. Cover and let stand to reheat. (If you put the pot back onto the heat and the liquid boils, the sour cream may curdle.)

Yield: 8–10 servings

SERVING IDEA

Goulash is traditionally served over egg noodles, but rice works fine if it is handier.

Creamy Broccoli Casserole

❂ ❂ ❂

Canned soup makes this a snap to prepare. If you have broccoli haters in your family, this yummy treatment just may convert them.

1½ pounds broccoli
2 tablespoons lemon juice
1 10¾-ounce can cream of chicken soup
¼ cup mayonnaise
2 teaspoons curry powder
1 pound mushrooms, sliced and sautéed
½ cup bread crumbs
2 tablespoons butter, melted

1. Preheat oven to 350°F. Cook and drain broccoli. Place broccoli in the bottom of a shallow, 2-quart baking dish and sprinkle with lemon juice.

2. Mix together the soup, mayonnaise, curry powder, and mushrooms. Pour over the broccoli.

3. Cover with bread crumbs and drizzle on the butter. Bake for 20 minutes.

Yield: 6–8 servings

CREATIVE TOPPINGS

Give your casserole a tasty topping that adds flavor contrast while keeping the food underneath moist during baking:

• Bread crumbs or croutons moistened with melted butter or drizzled with olive oil

• Crumbled potato chips, corn chips, or crackers

• Chopped peanuts, sliced almonds, or a sprinkling of wheat germ

• Crispy chow mein noodles or fried onion rings

• Miniature marshmallows (especially good on sweet potato or squash bakes)

FARMHOUSE FAVORITES

These are the dinners our kids looked forward to when they came home from college: no frills, nothing exotic, just plain home cooking around the family table. We all love meat loaf, and I alternate making savory mushroom meat loaf, and a moist meat loaf, with applesauce (page 211). Which is our favorite? The one we're having at the time!

Mushroom Meat Loaf

✦ ✦ ✦

I always try to bake extra meat loaf, so that there'll be some left over for sandwiches. An ordinary meat loaf becomes more flavorful when you mix ground veal or ground pork in with the usual ground beef. Mix the ingredients with your hands to ensure an even distribution of flavors.

½ cup chopped onion
1 clove of garlic, chopped
1 tablespoon butter
2 tablespoons vegetable oil
4 ounces mushrooms, chopped
4 slices day-old Italian bread
½–1 cup milk
1½ pounds ground veal, beef, and pork mixture
1½ teaspoons salt
¼ teaspoon freshly ground black pepper
2 tablespoons chopped fresh parsley
2 eggs, beaten
bread crumbs

1. Sauté the onion and garlic in the butter and oil for about 3 minutes, until the onion is transparent and soft. Remove the onion and garlic and set aside. Sauté the mushrooms in the butter and oil remaining in the pan for 3 to 5 minutes, drain, and set aside.

2. Soak the bread in milk until soft. Crumble the bread into small pieces; squeeze out excess milk. When moistened and crumbled into pieces, the bread should equal about 1 heaping cup.

3. Preheat oven to 400°F. Combine all ingredients, adding some bread crumbs if the mixture is too soft. Form the mixture into an oblong shape and place in a greased pan.

4. Bake, uncovered, for 45 to 60 minutes. Serve.

Yield: 6 servings

Baked Pork Chops with Herbs

✦ ✦ ✦

Serve this with baked sweet potatoes and vegetables topped with a pat of butter and sealed in foil and you have a delicious meal — all made at the same time and no work.

8 pork chops, not too thick
4 cups bread crumbs, freshly made or purchased
1½ cups chives, chopped
1 cup minced parsley
½ cup peanut or safflower oil
4 tablespoons garlic salt
3 tablespoons thyme
salt and pepper to taste

1. Preheat oven to 400°F. Trim excess fat from chops.

2. Combine all other ingredients and mix thoroughly. One by one, press pork chops down on breadcrumb mixture, coating both sides of chops.

3. Lay chops in a single layer on a foil-covered pan. If any bread crumbs are left when you finish, add them to the top of the pork chops, pressing the mixture onto the top of the chops.

4. Bake for 1 hour.

Yield: 4–8 servings

Oven Lamb Stew

❈ ❈ ❈

The beauty of this hearty dish is that it stews in the oven, requiring little of the cook's attention. Prepare it when other chores will keep you away from the kitchen.

2 tablespoons vegetable oil
2 pounds lean lamb, cut into 1-inch cubes
1 medium onion, sliced
2 cups water
1 tablespoon Worcestershire sauce
2 tablespoons unbleached all-purpose flour
2 tablespoons cold water
1 cup fresh or frozen peas
3 medium carrots, sliced
1 stalk of celery, sliced
salt and freshly ground black pepper

1. Preheat oven to 325°F. In a large heavy skillet, heat the oil and brown the lamb. Add the onion and sauté for 5 minutes, stirring frequently. Drain off the fat. Add the water and Worcestershire. Bake, covered, for 1½ hours.

2. Remove the skillet from the oven. In a small bowl, blend the flour with the water to make a thin paste. Add the paste to the skillet and blend well. Add the peas, carrots, celery, and salt and pepper to taste. Bake, covered, for 30 minutes longer. Serve.

Yield: 1½ quarts

....

DINER FAVORITES

....

Just for fun, have a "diner night" at home. Serve up a blue-plate special, such as meat loaf with mashed potatoes, green peas, and a side of applesauce. Set the table with paper napkins and a bottle of ketchup. Offer a choice of pudding or pie for dessert, and make a pot of coffee (with refills, of course).

....

Shepherd's Pie

❈ ❈ ❈

This is a simple way that English country folk use up leftover Sunday "joint" or roast beef dinner; this dish is typically eaten on a Monday. It's also made with lamb and corn, and even leftover chicken.

2 cups minced roast beef
1 cup cooked carrots
1 cup green peas
½ cup cooked onions
2 cups cooked mashed potatoes
1 cup Cheddar cheese, grated

1. Preheat broiler.

2. Combine the roast beef, carrots, peas, and onions.

3. Spread the beef mixture over the bottom of a 9-by 12-inch glass or ceramic dish. Then spread a thick layer of the mashed potatoes on top and, with a fork, draw lines down the pan.

4. Sprinkle the Cheddar on top and broil for about 10 minutes, or until the mashed potatoes are browned. Serve immediately.

Yield: 6 servings

SANDWICHES

During the Middle Ages, large slabs of flat bread were used as plates to hold whatever meat came from the spit. After eating the meat, one ate one's "plate," which was flavored with meat juices. Perhaps that was the earliest form of the sandwich. In any event, sandwiches are an ever-popular way to make an informal meal. Whether hot or cold, planned or foraged from whatever's in the refrigerator, they are great eating.

Real Sloppy Sloppy Joe

❂ ❂ ❂

Just because our kids are grown doesn't mean we can't have sloppy joes. This is a childhood classic dressed up a bit for an older crowd.

1½ pounds lean ground beef
½ yellow onion, finely chopped
1 clove of garlic, minced
½ cup ketchup
½ cup crushed tomatoes or tomato sauce
1 tablespoon red wine vinegar
2 tablespoons Worcestershire sauce

2 teaspoons hot sauce
salt and freshly ground black pepper
4–6 hamburger buns

1. In a nonstick skillet, brown the beef with the onion and garlic over medium heat. Drain excess fat.

2. Add ketchup, tomatoes, vinegar, Worcestershire, hot sauce, and salt and pepper to taste. Stir well and simmer for 5 minutes.

3. While the beef mixture is simmering, toast the hamburger buns.

4. Arrange the buns face-up on plates. Ladle a generous portion of the beef mixture over each and serve immediately.

Yield: 4–6 servings

Hidden Cheeseburger

❂ ❂ ❂

When we grill these outside-in cheeseburgers, the kids love the surprise element, and we love the taste of cheese. Our favorite is jalapeño Monterey Jack, but blue cheese is a close runner-up.

2 pounds ground beef round
1 brick (8 ounces) Monterey Jack cheese, plain or with jalapeño bits

1. Divide the beef into the number of burgers you want to make, then divide each in half again and form large thin patties. Slice cheese and place slices on half of the thin patties, then set another patty on top, trapping the cheese in between. Work the edges with your fingers to get a good seal.

2. Grill the burgers over high heat, uncovered, for about 1 minute to sear the outside of the burger. Then cover the grill to smoke the burgers. For burgers that weigh ⅓ of a pound, cook, covered, for about 5 minutes on each side to get rare burgers. For ½-pound burgers, cook 7 to 9 minutes on each side. Be careful not to flip the burgers too vigorously, or they may break open.

Yield: 6–8 servings

Turkey Burgers

❈ ❈ ❈

To make sure the burgers are fully cooked, cut one open to its middle. If it's still pink, keep cooking. Serve these burgers with lots of lettuce and tomato or with equal parts ketchup and cranberry sauce, well blended.

1½ pounds lean ground turkey
¼ cup whole-wheat bread crumbs
2 cloves of garlic, minced
1 teaspoon hot sauce (optional)
   freshly ground black pepper
1 teaspoon extra virgin olive oil

1. In a large bowl, combine the turkey, bread crumbs, garlic, hot sauce, if desired, and pepper to taste. Mix well with your hands. Form the mixture into four patties.

2. In a skillet, warm the oil over medium heat. Cook the burgers in the oil for 5 minutes per side, or until they're done.

Yield: 4 servings

VARIATIONS: Replace the hot sauce with Worcestershire sauce, soy or teriyaki sauce, or horseradish.

BURGER TIPS

....

In most recipes, ground turkey is a great substitute for ground beef. Lean ground turkey usually contains less fat than lean ground beef.

We don't use egg in our burgers, because we think it adds unnecessary cholesterol. But burgers with an egg or two (or just their whites) in the meat mixture are easier to handle.

When freezing leftover raw ground beef, mold it into hamburger patties first. You can then defrost only the amount you need for the particular meal you will be preparing.

Tuna Melt

❈ ❈ ❈

When my kids were active in sports at school, they'd come home hungry after practice. This was a quick appetite appeaser that kept them from raiding the cookie jar. If you have a toaster oven, use it to prepare this snack.

2 English muffins, split in half
1 6-ounce can tuna in water, drained
1½ tablespoons low-fat mayonnaise
   salt and freshly ground black pepper
¼ cup shredded low-fat Cheddar cheese

1. Preheat oven to 350°F. Toast the muffins.

2. Mix the tuna, mayonnaise, and salt and pepper to taste. Place ¼ of the mixture on each English muffin half. Press with a fork to flatten. Sprinkle the Cheddar evenly over the tops of the muffins.

3. Bake until the cheese is melted, about 5 minutes.

Yield: 4 servings

VARIATION: For the tomato lovers in your family, add a juicy slice before topping the sandwich with the cheese.

THE SANDWICH BOARD

Here are some of our lunchbox favorites:

- Turkey breast, melted Monterey Jack cheese, Russian dressing, and celery salt on rye bread
- Egg salad made with mayonnaise, Dijon mustard, dill, and sunflower seeds on wheat bread
- Toasted bagel with cream cheese, Dijon mustard, sliced cucumbers, and tomatoes
- Roast beef, cream cheese, red onions, horseradish, and tomatoes on pumpernickel bread
- Ham, Swiss cheese, sweet or hot mustard, and thinly sliced green apples on rye bread
- Chicken salad with green grapes on whole-wheat bread

- Turkey, ham, provolone, roast beef, and coleslaw on a roll
- BBLT — bacon, fresh basil, lettuce, and tomatoes on white toast
- Turkey with cranberry sauce or chutney on wheat toast
- Veggie — lettuce or sprouts, tomatoes, cucumbers, shredded carrots, Cheddar cheese, and Dijon mustard in a pita pocket
- Roasted vegetable—roasted eggplant, bell pepper, onion, and zucchini, herbed goat cheese, and balsamic vinaigrette on sourdough bread

Turkey Sandwiches

❈ ❈ ❈

One of the best things about Thanksgiving is the leftover turkey for making sandwiches. Our family competes to see who can be the most creative. Here are a few of the winning combinations.

Turkey, mayonnaise, leftover stuffing, and lettuce on whole-wheat bread

Turkey, gravy, and mashed potatoes on whole-wheat toast

Turkey, mayonnaise, and Aunt Ina's Relish (page 263) on whole-wheat bread

Turkey, Swiss cheese, mayonnaise, and ketchup on rye bread

Turkey, cranberry sauce, mayonnaise, and lettuce on a croissant

Turkey, provolone cheese, and coleslaw on rye bread

Turkey, sliced tomato, fresh basil leaves, and mayonnaise on sourdough bread

Turkey, leftover gravy, and leftover stuffing on sourdough bread, served open-faced

FOR THE KIDS

Thrill the littlest ones with sandwiches that tell them how much you love them. Make cream cheese and jelly or open-faced American cheese sandwiches and cut them into heart shapes with a cookie cutter. Our daughter Jennifer also cuts cheese into heart-shaped slices for her kids.

Traditional Club Sandwich

❈ ❈ ❈

Most restaurants offer this on the menu, but I think it's fun to serve these sandwiches at home. The key to a great club sandwich is the bread, of good quality and toasted to perfection, and tomatoes, ripe and juicy. Serve with a dill pickle and potato chips on the side.

3 slices fresh whole-wheat
   bread, toasted
mayonnaise
2 slices turkey
2 slices roast beef
2 slices crisp bacon
2 slices baked ham
2 slices Swiss cheese
2 slices tomato
1 large leaf lettuce

1. Lightly spread toast with mayonnaise, then assemble sandwich as follows: One slice toast, turkey, roast beef, bacon, toast, ham, cheese, tomato, lettuce, and toast. Place on a plate and cut into quarters, using a large toothpick to hold each quarter together.

Yield: 1 sandwich

Hero Sandwich

❈ ❈ ❈

Whether you call it a hero, a Dagwood, or a submarine, this sandwich is a meal in itself. The longer you make it, the more people it will feed. Use your imagination, and if you like an ingredient, pile it on the sandwich!

1 foot-long sandwich roll
mayonnaise
ketchup
Italian dressing
sweet pickle relish
¼ pound provolone cheese
   (or any sliced cheese)
¼ pound sliced ham
¼ pound sliced turkey
¼ pound sliced roast beef
1 red onion, thinly sliced
1 tomato, thinly sliced
shredded iceberg lettuce
freshly ground black pepper

1. Slice roll lengthwise, and spread mayonnaise, ketchup, dressing, and relish on both sides.

2. Layer the cheese, ham, turkey, roast beef, onion, tomato, and lettuce in the roll. Season with pepper to taste.

3. Close sandwich and slice into four pieces.

Yield: 4 servings

OUR HEROES

....

Long sandwiches are very popular. They can be a meal for one or cut into pieces for appetizers. No one seems to agree on what they're called — it depends on where you're from. Some choices (and how they originated) are:

HERO. Because of its heroic proportions.

SUBMARINE (OR SUB). Because it looks like one.

DAGWOOD. After the comic-strip character who loved to raid the icebox.

GRINDER. Something to grind your teeth on? (This derivation is not certain.)

POOR BOY. Bread and meat in a simple form.

HOAGIE. Who knows? But it tastes just as good as the others.

VEGETABLE DISHES

My mom and dad took great pride in their beautiful vegetable garden each summer. It didn't matter how much or how little space we had; there was always room for a garden. John and I feel the same way, and we have graduated from a window box in Brooklyn to a small farm in the Lake Champlain valley. The best way to eat most vegetables is to harvest them as late in the day as possible and serve them raw or cook them briefly so that they maintain that fresh-from-the-garden flavor. But even if you're preparing the best available vegetables from a farm stand or supermarket, it takes very little to add a special zip to them.

Contributors to this chapter are Glenn Andrews; Janet Ballantyne; Joanne Barrett; Marjorie Page Blanchard; Charlene Braida; Betty Cavage; Gail Damerow; Mary Anna Dusablon; Jennifer Storey Gillis; Phyllis Hobson; Matt Kelly; Alexandra Nimetz, Jason Stanley, and Emeline Starr; Penny Noepel; Maggie Oster; Dorothy Parker; Phyllis Shaudys; and Edith Stovel.

SPRING
··········
SUMMER
··········
AUTUMN
··········
WINTER

Baked Stuffed Tomatoes

❁ ❁ ❁

Colorful and easy, these tomatoes accompany most any meal beautifully. If you want to serve them as your main course, just give everyone two. Any medium-sized slicing tomato will do, but we're partial to Early Girls. For additional color, you might try a yellow tomato, such as a Lemon Boy.

4 medium tomatoes
4 slices bacon, cut into ½-inch pieces
1 tablespoon olive oil
3 cloves of garlic, minced
3 tablespoons chopped fresh parsley
1 teaspoon chopped fresh thyme
1 cup bread crumbs made from soft bread
freshly ground black pepper
1 tablespoon lemon juice

1. Cut tomatoes in half and scoop out enough of the pulp to form a small indentation. Chop the pulp; set aside.

2. In a skillet, sauté bacon until crisp; drain on paper towels. Discard fat. To the same pan, add olive oil; sauté garlic until soft. Add the chopped tomato pulp, parsley, thyme, bread crumbs, pepper to taste, and lemon juice, stirring quickly to combine. Remove from heat.

3. Preheat oven to 400°F. Stuff each tomato with the bread crumb mixture and place in a shallow baking dish. Bake for 15 minutes, or until tomatoes are soft and browned on top.

Yield: 4 servings

Fried Green Tomatoes

❁ ❁ ❁

Green tomatoes have a tart, almost lemony taste. If you don't have backyard tomatoes, ask at your local farm stand in late summer, and they'll probably be glad to get you some.

1 medium green tomato
flour
salt and freshly ground black pepper
cooking oil

1. Wash, core, and cut tomato into ⅓-inch-thick slices. Do not peel.

2. Dip each slice in flour; season to taste with salt and pepper. In a medium skillet, heat ¼ inch of oil until a few drops of water bounce on it. Fry the slices until golden, 1 to 2 minutes on each side.

Yield: 1 serving

Garden Fresh Tomatoes
with Basil and Balsamic Vinegar

❁ ❁ ❁

The pleasure of this simple, summer-only dish depends on sun-ripe garden tomatoes, fresh basil, and the rich taste of balsamic vinegar. Hothouse tomatoes that keep for a week in the supermarket cannot be substituted.

4 large fresh garden tomatoes
8 fresh basil leaves
½ cup balsamic vinegar

1. Cut the tomatoes into ¼- to ½-inch slices and arrange on a low dish. Chop the basil. Drizzle the vinegar over the tomatoes and sprinkle with the basil.

Yield: 8 servings

SPRING

*S*pring sees the table rejuvenated with lots of fresh green vegetables. The garden and markets oblige with asparagus and greens, artichokes and spring onions. And nothing is more lovely than spring peas — snow peas, sugar snaps, and shell peas straight from the pod.

Marinated Asparagus

❈ ❈ ❈

*T*he first signs of spring in our garden are the green asparagus shoots that peek out of the ground. The bed has been around for decades, and we feel like we have been given a gift when the stalks are finally big enough to eat. Simply steamed and served with lemon butter, they can't be beat. This easy marinated version is delicious, too.

¾ *cup olive oil*
¼ *cup balsamic vinegar*
1 *clove of garlic, crushed*
1 *tablespoon lemon juice*
freshly ground black pepper
1 *pound fresh asparagus*
1 *cup cherry tomatoes*
1 *cup crumbled feta cheese*

1. Combine the oil, vinegar, garlic, lemon juice, and pepper to taste in a jar. Cover and shake until well blended.

2. Steam the asparagus for 3 to 4 minutes, until crisp-tender. Drain; run under cold water to cool.

3. Arrange the asparagus on a platter and top with tomatoes and feta.

4. Sprinkle with dressing; serve at room temperature.

Yield: 4–5 servings

Asparagus Pie

❈ ❈ ❈

*M*uch like a quiche, this pie makes a terrific luncheon entrée or, cut into smaller portions, a starter for a spring feast.

½ *pound fresh asparagus*
2 *eggs*
4 *tablespoons melted butter*
1 *cup cottage cheese*
1 *cup sour cream*
¼ *cup flour*
½ *teaspoon baking powder*
¼ *teaspoon salt*
1 *tomato, thinly sliced*
¼ *cup grated Parmesan cheese*

1. Preheat oven to 350°F. Steam the asparagus until just tender, about 3 minutes. Arrange in a spoke design on the bottom of a buttered 9-inch pie plate.

2. Beat the eggs until frothy. Add the butter and cottage cheese; beat until almost smooth. Mix in the sour cream, flour, baking powder, and salt. Pour on top of the asparagus; decoratively arrange the tomato slices on top. Sprinkle with the Parmesan.

3. Bake for 30 minutes, or until set and lightly browned. Remove from oven and let stand for 10 minutes before serving.

Yield: 6–8 servings

ABOUT BALSAMIC TREASURE

Casks of balsamic vinegar are family heirlooms in northern Italy, where the vinegar is made from Trebbiano grape juice and aged in barrels over several years. Well-aged balsamic vinegars are priced like fine wines. Balsamic vinegar is available in gourmet shops, natural food stores, and many larger supermarkets. Some balsamic vinegar made in Modena, Italy, where it is a specialty, carries a seal certifying that it is of the highest quality.

ABOUT ARTICHOKES

....

The true artichoke is the bud of a large thistle. It is sometimes called a "globe" artichoke. Jerusalem artichokes are actually not artichokes at all, but a delicious root vegetable.

Steamed Artichokes

❊ ❊ ❊

Steamed artichokes are one of the great finger foods. Serve with melted butter, Hollandaise sauce, or a lemony mayonnaise for dipping the leaves. The hairy "choke" in the center can be easily scraped out with a spoon, leaving the tender "heart" at the base.

4 large artichokes
lemon juice

1. Use a knife to cut off the artichoke stalks and scissors to trim spiny tips of leaves.
2. Put the artichokes into boiling water with a little lemon juice (3 tablespoons to each quart of water) and cook for 35 to 40 minutes.
3. Serve one whole artichoke to each person.
Yield: 4 servings

Note: Artichokes are cooked when one of the leaves of the middle part is easily removed.

Purée of Jerusalem Artichokes

❊ ❊ ❊

The Jerusalem artichoke is a little gem of a vegetable that can be eaten raw, when it resembles water chestnuts, or cooked, when it resembles nothing but its own marvelous self. It's often called "sunchoke" in markets. This purée is a fantastically good dish and a fine introduction to the joys of the Jerusalem artichoke.

1 pound Jerusalem artichokes
6 tablespoons butter
6 tablespoons heavy cream
salt and freshly ground black pepper

1. Peel the artichokes and cut them into chunks. Boil in water to cover for 10 to 15 minutes, or until very tender.
2. Drain. Process the artichoke chunks in a food processor along with the butter and cream until smooth.
3. Reheat gently while stirring. Season to taste with salt and pepper.
Yield: 4 servings

....

VEGGIE GARNISHES

....

Here are some quick ways to dress up a dish of vegetables.

- *A spritz of fresh lemon juice*
- *A sprinkling of minced herbs*
- *Crisp onion rings*

- *Crumbled bacon*
- *Chopped peanuts or walnuts*
- *Sliced almonds*
- *Toasted sunflower seeds*
- *Herbed butter*
- *Hollandaise sauce*
- *White sauce with a dash of nutmeg*
- *Seasoned croutons*
- *Strips of orange or lemon zest*

....

Penne with Peas and Prosciutto

❈ ❈ ❈

Garden-fresh peas make the difference in this pasta dish. Half the fun can be in the quiet enjoyment of shelling, by yourself or with friends and family.

1 pound penne pasta
2 cups fresh peas
1 tablespoon butter
¼ pound prosciutto, cut into small pieces
½ cup light cream
2 tablespoons chopped fresh chives
½ cup freshly grated Parmesan cheese

ABOUT COOKING PEAS

....

The main thing to remember when cooking peas is not to cook them too long. A pinch of sugar added to the cooking water enlivens older or frozen peas.
STEAM: 3 to 4 minutes for shelled peas or sugar snaps, 2 to 3 minutes for snow peas
BLANCH: 2 to 4 minutes for shelled peas, 1 minute for sugar snaps and snow peas
STIR-FRY OR SAUTÉ: 2 to 3 minutes for all varieties

---

1 cup cherry tomatoes, cut in half
1 teaspoon dried basil
   salt and freshly ground black pepper

1. Cook the penne according to package directions. Add the peas during the last 3 to 4 minutes. Drain and set aside.

2. In a large skillet, melt butter and sauté the prosciutto until crisp. Add the cream, chives, Parmesan, tomatoes, and basil, stirring well to blend. Add the penne and peas and mix well. Season with salt and pepper to taste. Serve with more Parmesan.

Yield: 4–5 servings

Variation: Try this dish with whole, edible-podded peas, too.

Snow Peas with Herbs

❈ ❈ ❈

Tarragon and mint highlight the natural sweetness of delightfully crisp snow peas.

½ pound snow peas
2½ tablespoons peanut oil
1 tablespoon snipped spearmint
1 teaspoon snipped fresh tarragon
   pinch of cayenne pepper

1. Wash, drain, and devein the peas. Heat the oil in a pan over high heat. When hot, quickly stir-fry the peas and herbs for 1 minute. Season with cayenne, and serve.

Yield: 2 servings

Fresh Creamed Spinach

❈ ❈ ❈

So easy and so good, this creamed spinach will turn anyone in your family into Popeye! Available year-round at the market, spinach is also easy to grow in your own backyard; plant an early spring crop and a fall crop as well.

1 tablespoon olive oil
1 pound fresh spinach, washed and dried
2 teaspoons minced dried onion
¼ teaspoon ground nutmeg
4 ounces cream cheese, softened

1. Heat the oil in a large skillet and place the spinach on top. Sprinkle with onion and nutmeg; cover.

2. Steam on medium heat until spinach has just wilted, about 3 minutes. Stir in the cream cheese until melted.

Yield: 3–4 servings

SNOW PEA APPETIZERS

Split open blanched snow peas and pipe in a filling of herbed cream cheese.

Wrap parboiled snow peas around steamed shrimp and secure with a toothpick.

Add uncooked snow peas to a platter of vegetables and dip. Ginger Dip (page 91) makes an interesting Asian-style complement.

Spinach Soufflé

❈ ❈ ❈

This is a company-worthy spinach and cheese soufflé. If you don't have shallots, use the white and pale green parts of scallions.

- 2 minced shallots
- 3 tablespoons butter
- 3 tablespoons all-purpose flour
- ½ cup chicken broth
- ½ cup milk
- 1 teaspoon salt
- ½ teaspoon ground nutmeg
- ½ teaspoon freshly ground black pepper
- 5 egg yolks

- 1 cup well-drained chopped spinach
- ½ cup grated Parmesan cheese
- 6 egg whites

1. Preheat oven to 325°F. In a large saucepan, sauté the shallots in butter for about 1 minute. Stir in the flour and cook until golden and bubbly.

2. Add the broth and milk all at once; stir until smooth and thick. Stir in the salt, nutmeg, and pepper. Whisk in the egg yolks until well combined. Stir in the spinach and ¼ cup of the Parmesan.

3. Beat egg whites until stiff; fold into spinach mixture. Gently pour the mixture into a 1½-quart soufflé dish and sprinkle the remaining Parmesan on top.

4. Bake until firm, about 30 minutes.

Yield: 4 servings

Tarragon Carrots and Chard

❈ ❈ ❈

Baby carrots and chard cook quickly in this tender vegetable dish. Don't overcook!

- 1 tablespoon butter
- 2 cups baby carrots, cut into sticks

- ¼ cup light cream
- 1 tablespoon minced fresh tarragon or 1½ teaspoons dried
- ¼ teaspoon ground rosemary
- 20 cups chard, deribbed and cut into thin strips
  salt and freshly ground black pepper

1. In a large sauté pan, melt the butter. Add the carrots, cream, tarragon, and rosemary. Cover and simmer for 4 minutes.

2. Stir in the chard; cover and cook for 3 to 4 minutes, or until the chard is wilted and the carrots are tender. Stir occasionally. Season to taste with salt and pepper. Serve hot.

Yield: 4–6 servings

ABOUT CHARD

Chard, often called "Swiss chard," is a member of the beet family, but it is grown for its greens rather than its root. Red or ruby chard has more of the characteristic beet flavor than white chard. Pretty rainbow chards in bright colors are also available. The ribbed stems of chard are usually cut away when cooking the greens, but they are delicious by themselves as a steamed vegetable.

Sesame Scallions

❈ ❈ ❈

Spring onions — leeks, chives, and scallions — are fun to plant in your garden, since they are among the first vegetables to show. You can almost watch them grow. Harvest them at any point, tiny or big; eat them raw or cooked; use them to scoop up dip or to garnish an entrée; or serve them as a side dish.

1 tablespoon vegetable oil
1 teaspoon toasted sesame oil
3 cups scallions, cut into 1-inch lengths
3 tablespoons soy sauce
1 tablespoon honey
3 tablespoons toasted sesame seeds (see note, below)

1. Heat vegetable and sesame oils in a skillet. Add scallions and sauté until lightly browned, about 3 minutes, stirring constantly.

2. Add the soy sauce, honey, and sesame seeds. Toss until well coated.

Yield: 4 servings

Note: To toast sesame seeds, in a small nonstick skillet, cook the seeds over medium heat, stirring frequently, until they are lightly browned and aromatic, about 1 to 2 minutes.

Scotch Scallion Scones

❈ ❈ ❈

These scones are made as they are in old-fashioned Scottish kitchens, cooked to golden perfection on a griddle. Another Scottish technique: Mix the batter very gently to ensure melt-in-your-mouth scones. Finally, don't cut them with a knife; pull them apart with your fingers to preserve the tender texture.

2¼ cups unbleached all-purpose flour
2 teaspoons baking powder
¼ teaspoon baking soda
½ teaspoon salt
½ cup (1 stick) butter, chilled and cut into bits
½ cup finely minced scallions with greens
½ cup buttermilk
2 eggs at room temperature, beaten
1 tablespoon honey

1. Sift together the flour, baking powder, soda, and salt in a large bowl. Using two knives or a pastry blender, cut in the butter until the mixture resembles small peas. Add the scallions and toss to mix.

2. Whisk together the buttermilk, eggs, and honey. Stir into the flour mixture with a fork just until the dry ingredients are moistened. Turn onto a floured surface.

3. Dust your hands with flour and gently press the dough together with your fingertips. Pat gently into a ½-inch circle. Using a floured knife, cut into wedges.

4. Preheat an ungreased griddle or skillet over medium heat. Reduce the heat to low. Place the wedges on the griddle. Cook for 10 to 12 minutes, or until the bottoms are golden and the scones begin to rise. Turn and brown on the other side. Cool slightly. Serve with plenty of butter.

Yield: 8 servings

VARIATION: For oven-baked scones, preheat the oven to 450°F. Proceed as directed for griddle scones. Before cooking, brush each wedge lightly with milk. Place wedges on a greased baking sheet. Bake for 12 to 15 minutes, or until raised and golden brown.

EDIBLE TIES

Give your vegetables a designer look! Blanch large chives or the green parts of scallions until just barely soft. Use them to tie asparagus, green beans, carrot sticks, or other long, thin vegetables into attractive little bundles.

SUMMER

S ummertime and the livin' is easy. It's time for outdoor eating and the peak of the produce: the corn, the green and wax beans, the fabulous tomatoes, the abundant zucchini. We use all of those great vegetables from the garden and the farm stands in our old favorite recipes, and we experiment with new cooking methods.

Corn in the Pot

❁ ❁ ❁

C orn that is cooked too long becomes tough. If corn is very young and tender, it does not even require any cooking time. Just drop the ears into boiling water, turn off the heat, and let sit for 3 to 5 minutes.

1 dozen ears of corn, husked and silk removed
butter (optional)
salt (optional)

1. In a stockpot that is large enough to hold all the ears easily, bring water to cover to a rolling boil.
2. Place the corn in the pot and cook for 3 to 5 minutes. Use tongs to remove the corn. Serve with butter and salt, if desired.
Yield: 12 servings

Note: If your corn was not picked that day, add a tablespoon of sugar to the pot. This will replace some of the sweetness.

Perfect Grilled Corn

❁ ❁ ❁

C orn on the grill keeps the steam (and you) out of the kitchen on hot summer evenings. You can husk the corn and wrap it in layers of foil, but it is preferable to leave the husks on. They provide a natural protection from scorching and impart a delicate, fresh flavor to the corn.

1 dozen ears of corn, in husks
butter
salt and freshly ground black pepper

1. Place the corn in a pan of cold water. Soak for 20 minutes. Trim the silks from the ends of the ears, but do not pull the husks back. Place the corn on the grill and cook for about 20 minutes, approximately 10 minutes per side.
2. Remove from the grill. Cool for a few minutes before shucking the ears. Serve with butter, salt, and pepper.
Yield: About 6 servings

Corn Fritters

❁ ❁ ❁

I n New England, our corn comes fairly late in the season, but it is well worth the wait. Sweet and golden, yellow and white, we eat corn in lots of ways, but these fritters are a favorite, particularly when they are drizzled with pure maple syrup.

3 eggs, separated
1⅔ cups cooked corn
¼ cup flour
½ teaspoon salt
¾ cup vegetable oil

1. Beat the egg yolks until creamy yellow. Add the corn, flour and salt.
2. Beat the egg whites until stiff. Lightly fold egg whites into egg yolk mixture.
3. In a large skillet, heat oil over medium heat until hot, but not smoking. Drop batter into hot oil by the tablespoonful. Cook on both sides until brown.
4. Drain on paper towels. Serve hot with maple syrup.
Yield: 4–5 servings

ABOUT CORN OFF THE COB

....

If you are cooking corn in a recipe, you will need to remove the kernels from the ears. I hold the cob upright in a bowl and run a sharp paring knife straight down the rows; the kernels fall into the bowl. Corn cut from the cob may be steamed, sautéed, or added to a recipe near the end of the cooking time. Five to six ears will produce about 3 cups of kernels.

Corn Pudding

✿ ✿ ✿

Fresh corn pudding makes a great side dish to a baked ham dinner. Soft and sweet, it can be spiced up by adding some chopped chili peppers, but my family likes it just like this.

  ½ cup all-purpose flour
  1 teaspoon salt
  ½ teaspoon dried oregano
  1 tablespoon sugar
     freshly ground black pepper
  3 cups fresh corn kernels
  ½ cup chopped onion
  ½ cup chopped red bell pepper
  5 eggs, beaten

1⅓ cups grated sharp Cheddar cheese
2½ cups light cream
  3 tablespoons butter, melted

1. Preheat oven to 350°F. In a small bowl, combine the flour, salt, oregano, sugar, and ground pepper. Blend well.

2. In a large bowl, combine the corn, onion, bell pepper, eggs, and Cheddar. Mix well. Stir in flour mixture, then cream and butter.

3. Pour into a large, buttered casserole. Place the casserole into a 9- by 13-inch pan that has at least 1 inch of hot water in it. Bake for 1 hour and 10 minutes, or until pudding is set.

Yield: 8 servings

Succotash

✿ ✿ ✿

Succotash is one of those classic dishes that tasted good long before it was proven to be nutritionally balanced. (Our ancestors had good instincts.) It is especially tasty with fresh corn and beans.

  1 cup fresh lima beans
  1 cup fresh corn kernels
     salt and freshly ground black pepper
  2 tablespoons butter (optional)

1. Blanch the lima beans and corn kernels in boiling water until tender, 5 to 10 minutes. Season to taste with salt and pepper. Stir in butter, if desired. Serve hot.

Yield: 4 servings

"CORNY" IDEAS

....

Herbs and spices that go well with corn are dill, mint, cilantro, basil, oregano, savory, marjoram, tarragon, chili powder, and curry powder.

- *Dress corn with a little bit of pesto for an unusual side dish.*
- *Add leftover corn kernels to your favorite quiches and frittatas.*
- *Mix corn with cubed tomatoes, black beans, and herb vinaigrette for a satisfying cold salad.*
- *Add up to 1½ cups of corn kernels to your favorite corn bread recipe.*
- *Use overripe corn in chowders.*

STUFFED CELERY STICKS

Crunchy and cold, celery can be stuffed with just about anything. Try some of these as hors d'oeuvres or lunchbox snacks.

- *Peanut butter, chunky or plain (add raisins for "ants on a log")*
- *Pimiento Cheese Spread (page 93)*
- *Chive cream cheese*
- *Cream cheese and olives*
- *Cream cheese and walnuts*
- *Tuna or egg salad*
- *Hummus (page 91)*

Cucumbers in Sour Cream

❈ ❈ ❈

Our cucumber patch went vertical a few years ago when John put up a trellis for the green beauties to climb. Now they are even easier to harvest. This fresh salad always reminds me of summer, even though I serve it throughout the year.

2–3 *medium cucumbers, peeled and thinly sliced*
2 *scallions, diced*
1 *cup sour cream*
2 *tablespoons cider vinegar*
1 *tablespoon sugar*
1 *teaspoon snipped fresh dill*
½ *teaspoon salt*
freshly ground black pepper

1. In a medium-sized bowl, combine the cucumbers and scallions.

2. In a small bowl, mix sour cream, vinegar, sugar, dill, salt, and pepper to taste until well blended. Toss over cucumbers and scallions; chill for at least 1 hour. Serve cold.

Yield: 6 servings

Steamed Baby Beets

❈ ❈ ❈

We grow several varieties of beets, including Detroit Dark Red and Golden Beets. We like to harvest them when they are tiny, no bigger than a golf ball. The smaller they are, the sweeter their taste, and they resemble little jewels after they're cooked.

1 *pound small fresh beets*
2 *tablespoons butter*
grated zest of 1 orange

1. Wash the beets. Leave the root on, and trim the stem so that 1 inch remains. Cut in half any beets that are larger than bite-size.

2. Place the beets in a saucepan, cover with water, and boil for about 15 min-utes, until tender. Drain and slip the skins off the beets with your fingers.

3. In a large saucepan, melt the butter; add the orange zest. Add beets. Cook and stir briefly until well coated. Serve warm.

Yield: 4 servings

Stir-Fried Celery and Carrot Strips

❈ ❈ ❈

Carrots and celery always seem to team up for munching raw; here's a novel way to serve them together hot.

2–3 *tablespoons vegetable oil*
5–6 *cups thinly sliced stalks of celery, cut crosswise or at an angle*
2–3 *carrots, cut into julienne strips*
¼ *cup chopped onion*
1 *tablespoon soy sauce or ½ teaspoon salt*
¼ *cup toasted sliced almonds*

1. In a large skillet, heat the oil. Add the celery, carrots, and onion.

2. Sauté until almost tender, about 6 minutes. Stir in the soy sauce and almonds.

3. Cook and stir until the celery is just tender crisp, about 2 minutes.

Yield: 4–6 servings

Carrots with Thyme Butter

❊ ❊ ❊

Quick, easy, fresh, and beautiful — a perfect and delicious side dish!

6 cups sliced carrots
2 cups water
1 teaspoon sugar
2 tablespoons butter
1 teaspoon chopped fresh
   thyme

1. In a large skillet, cook the carrots in the water until just tender. Drain.

2. Return the carrots to the skillet and sprinkle them with the sugar. Add butter and thyme. Cover and cook for 10 to 15 minutes longer, until the carrots are very tender and slightly browned and caramelized.

Yield: 6 servings

Radish Butter

❊ ❊ ❊

Radishes can be transformed into this delicious spread in less time than it takes to harvest them. Serve this piquant butter on pumpernickel or a similar dark bread for an intriguing appetizer that may just become a classic in your home, as it is in ours.

½ cup (1 stick) butter,
   softened
½ cup sliced radishes
1 teaspoon lemon juice

1. In a food processor, cream the butter. Add the radishes and lemon juice.

2. Using the pulsing action, process just enough to finely chop the radishes. Transfer the mixture to a bowl and serve.

Yield: ¾ cup

Tepee Bean Salad

❊ ❊ ❊

Daughter Jennifer loves to garden with her children. They plant beans on a tepee-shaped arrangement of poles, interlaced with twine. When the bean plants grow leaves, they make a shady hideout. The kids love to pick the beans and help make this salad.

1 pound green beans
1 red or white onion, thinly
   sliced
1 tablespoon olive oil
1 tablespoon red or white
   wine vinegar
1 teaspoon lemon juice
salt and freshly ground black
   pepper

1. Blanch the beans and drain. In a large bowl, mix the beans with onions; toss well with the oil, vinegar, and lemon juice. Add salt and pepper to taste.

2. Refrigerate salad until well chilled. Serve cold.

Yield: 4 servings

Green Beans with Red Pepper Confetti

❊ ❊ ❊

I steam my vegetables (page 197) to keep them crisp-tender and brightly colored. When these green beans are tossed with red pepper, garlic, and olive oil, no one can resist their fresh flavor, not even the grandkids.

1 pound green beans
1 red bell pepper, cored,
   seeded, and diced
1 clove of garlic, mashed
2 tablespoons olive oil
freshly ground black pepper

1. Steam beans for 3 to 4 minutes, until tender crisp. Drain and set aside.

2. In a skillet, sauté the bell pepper and garlic in the oil until soft and slightly browned. Add the beans and quickly toss together to heat, coating with the red pepper. Serve hot with pepper to taste.

Yield: 6 servings

Zucchini
with Mozzarella and Parmesan

❁ ❁ ❁

This is my favorite way to fix zucchini, and I always treat myself to extra helpings.

    3 slices bacon, cut into
       1-inch pieces
    1 large onion, chopped
    2 cloves of garlic, minced
  5–6 small zucchini, sliced
    4 plum tomatoes, diced
    2 teaspoons dried basil
    1 cup tomato sauce
    1 cup shredded mozzarella
   ⅓ cup grated Parmesan
       cheese

1. In a large skillet, cook bacon until fat is rendered. Add the onion and garlic; cook until soft.

2. Place a layer of zucchini slices in the pan, then a layer of tomatoes; repeat layering until vegetables are used up. Sprinkle with basil and simmer, covered, for 7 to 8 minutes on medium-high heat.

3. Turn the zucchini with a spatula so that the other side can begin to brown. Add the tomato sauce, then top with the mozzarella and Parmesan. Cover, turn heat to medium low, and simmer for 5 to 10 minutes, until cheese is melted and bubbly.

Yield: 6 servings

Sautéed Zucchini
with Garlic

❁ ❁ ❁

Here is a simple and delicious way to prepare zucchini. Garlic and basil give the mild squash just the right flair.

    1 pound small zucchini,
       well scrubbed and thinly
       sliced
   ⅓ cup olive oil
    2 teaspoons thinly sliced
       garlic
       salt and freshly ground black
       pepper
    2 teaspoons chopped fresh
       basil

1. In a large skillet, sauté the zucchini in the oil over medium heat for 5 minutes, stirring often. Add the garlic and salt and pepper to taste; cook for 5 minutes longer, stirring often.

2. Drain off excess oil. Stir in the basil.

Yield: 4 servings

Wax Beans
with Herbed Butter

❁ ❁ ❁

Golden yellow wax beans look beautiful and taste great with speckles of minced green herbs.

    1 pound fresh wax beans
    3 tablespoons butter
    1 teaspoon chopped fresh
       parsley
    1 teaspoon chopped fresh
       rosemary
   ½ teaspoon garlic salt
       freshly ground black pepper
    1 sprig of rosemary

1. Steam beans for 3 to 4 minutes, until tender crisp. Drain and set aside.

2. In the same saucepan, melt the butter. Add the parsley, rosemary, garlic salt, and pepper. Add the beans, stir to coat well. Serve hot with a fresh sprig of rosemary as garnish.

Yield: 6 servings

ABOUT STEAMING VEGGIES

Steaming is our favorite way to cook vegetables. It brings out the best flavor without making vegetables soggy or leaching out their precious vitamins. Fit a large pot with a colander or steamer basket. Bring 1 inch of water to a boil in the pot; place vegetables in the basket. Cover tightly and steam until vegetables are crisp-tender; this will take anywhere from 3 minutes for small vegetables, such as green beans or peas, to 6 minutes for larger, harder vegetables, such as carrots or cauliflower.

Summer Squash with Dilled Sour Cream

✺ ✺ ✺

Things that grow during the same season seem to naturally complement one another. The delicate flavor of summer squash goes so well with fresh dill. You can use other fresh herbs, but dill is my herb of choice.

2½   pounds small summer squash
 ½   cup sliced onion
 4   tablespoons (¼ cup) butter
1¼   teaspoons salt
 ⅛   teaspoon freshly ground black pepper
 1   tablespoon snipped fresh dill
 1   cup sour cream, at room temperature
sprigs of fresh dill
paprika

1. Cut the squash diagonally into slices about ½ inch thick. In a large skillet, sauté the onion in the butter until soft, but not browned, about 5 minutes. Add the squash, salt, pepper, and dill. Toss to combine.

2. Cover and cook over low heat for 12 to 15 minutes, stirring occasionally, until the squash is tender. Drain excess juice, if necessary.

3. Transfer to a serving dish and spoon the sour cream over the squash. Top with dill sprigs and paprika.

Yield: 6 servings

Crispy Fried Squash Blossoms

✺ ✺ ✺

Squash blossoms, often with tiny yellow or green squash attached, are frequently available in summer, either in markets or in your own garden. If you have the usual too-much-zucchini problem, eating the blossoms will certainly take care of it! Pumpkin blossoms can be used in the same manner.

15   squash blossoms
 ⅔   cup all-purpose flour
 ½   cup water
  vegetable oil for frying
  salt

1. Rinse the blossoms gently, dry well, and cut in half lengthwise. If tiny squashes are attached, cut them in half, too.

2. Stir the flour bit by bit into the water. In a skillet or wok, heat about ½ inch vegetable oil until very hot (about 375°F).

3. Coat a few blossoms at a time with batter. Cook in the oil, browning first one side, then the other, about 1 or 2 minutes per side.

4. Drain on paper towels and sprinkle with salt.

Yield: 6 appetizer-sized servings (30 blossoms)

Note: Fried squash blossoms reheat well in the oven.

ABOUT SUMMER SQUASH

．．．．．．．．．．．．．

Summer squashes — yellow, crookneck, pattypan, and zucchini — may be used interchangeably in most recipes. They all are best by far when picked young and tender. Older squash may need to be peeled and seeded. Figure on getting 4 cups of diced, sliced or julienned vegetable (or 3½ cups grated) out of each pound of squash.

Baked Eggplant Italiano

❈ ❈ ❈

Most eggplant Parmesan dishes require frying in a great deal of oil, but this broiling method is less greasy. I use smaller eggplants and slice them thinly, with the skin left on. The skin adds nice texture (and vitamins!) to the dish.

4–6 small eggplants
3 tablespoons olive oil
6 cloves of garlic, thinly sliced
1 cup fresh basil leaves
2 cups spicy tomato sauce
1 cup grated mozzarella
freshly ground black pepper
¼ cup grated Parmesan cheese

1. Preheat broiler. Slice eggplant thinly. Place on a baking sheet and brush both sides lightly with oil. Broil until light brown, turning once, about 7 minutes per side.

2. Preheat oven to 350°F. Coat a 9- by 13-inch pan with cooking spray. Alternate layers of eggplant, garlic, basil, several spoonfuls of tomato sauce, mozzarella, and pepper to taste. Repeat until all ingredients have been used. Top with the Parmesan cheese.

3. Bake for about 30 minutes, until bubbly and lightly browned.

Yield: 6 servings

Ratatouille

❈ ❈ ❈

Ratatouille hails from the south of France, where peppers, tomatoes, and eggplants abound. It is delicious hot or cold with some crusty peasant bread to dip into the juices.

12 ounces small eggplants, cut into ½-inch slices
12 ounces small zucchini, cut into ½-inch slices
salt
2 medium onions, sliced
½ cup olive oil
2 medium red or green bell peppers, stems and seeds removed, sliced
2–3 cloves of garlic, finely sliced
1 pound ripe tomatoes, peeled, seeds and excess liquid squeezed out, and roughly chopped
sprig of thyme
salt and freshly ground black pepper
1 tablespoon chopped parsley
10 torn basil leaves for garnish (optional)

1. Unless the eggplant and zucchini are very young and firm, salt them and leave them to stand for at least 30 minutes in a colander to drain the juices out. Rinse the slices, then gently pat them dry with paper towels.

2. Cook the onions in 2 tablespoons of the oil over medium heat for 5 minutes, until they begin to soften. Reduce heat; add peppers and garlic. Cook gently until the vegetables are just tender, about 15 minutes. Set aside.

3. Place 2 tablespoons of the oil in a saucepan. Over medium-high heat, add the tomatoes and quickly reduce them to a thick pulp (2 to 3 minutes). Add thyme and salt and pepper to taste; add tomato mixture to the onions and peppers. In a skillet, brown the zucchini slices over medium-high heat for 6 to 8 minutes in another 2 tablespoons of the oil; drain and set aside. Repeat browning process with the eggplant slices and the remaining oil; add the eggplant to the zucchini.

4. In a heatproof casserole, combine all the cooked vegetables and the parsley. Over very low heat, stir mixture gently and check the seasoning for taste. Serve warm or cold. Add basil garnish, if desired, just before serving.

Yield: 4 servings

Sautéed Sweet Peppers

❈ ❈ ❈

We grow lots of peppers each year and love the variety of colors and shapes. Last year we had a bumper crop of Italian Sweets, and this easy dish lets their sweet flavor shine through.

   1　pound long sweet peppers
   3　tablespoons olive oil
   3　tablespoons cider vinegar
1½　teaspoons sugar
   2　teaspoons capers

1. Cut peppers lengthwise and remove seeds. In a skillet, heat the oil and slowly fry peppers, covered, about 5 minutes. Turn frequently; do not overcook.

2. When the peppers are just soft, add the vinegar, sugar, and capers. Cook for 2 to 3 minutes, so that the flavors are well combined.

Yield: 4 servings

Stuffed Peppers

❈ ❈ ❈

A traditional meat and bread crumb stuffing fills these peppers, but this is a great recipe to experiment with. Try different kinds of bread crumbs, add favorite herbs, or use tomato juice instead of stock, until you find the flavor that tells your taste buds that the stuffing perfectly accents the sweetness of the peppers.

   6　green bell peppers
1¾　cups cooked finely ground
       beef, pork, or turkey
1¾　cups bread crumbs,
       moistened with beef or
       chicken stock
   ½　teaspoon salt
   ⅛　teaspoon freshly ground
       black pepper
   ½　onion, grated
   1　cup beef or chicken stock

1. Preheat oven to 350°F. Cut a slice from the stem end of each pepper. Remove the seeds and parboil the peppers for 5 minutes.

2. In a large bowl, mix the ground beef, bread crumbs, salt, pepper, and onion.

3. Stuff the peppers with the meat mixture and place in a baking pan. Add stock and bake for 30 minutes, basting frequently.

Yield: 6 servings

PEPPER PRIMER

....

Sweet bell peppers come in colors ranging from green to red, orange, yellow and black. Green peppers are less ripe and therefore sharper in flavor than their colorful cousins. Sweet peppers add color and crunch to salads and vegetable blends. To use sweet peppers raw, remove the stem, seed cluster, and loose seeds. For a rich, sweet flavor and soft texture, bake them in a very hot oven (about 475°F) for about 20 minutes, broil them, or roast them on a fork over a gas flame until the skin blisters and chars. Cool the peppers in a paper bag. Then rinse off the skin under cold tap water and pat dry.

Hot peppers (chilies) come in hundreds of varieties and degrees of "heat." They range from the medium-hot Anaheim and banana peppers to the fiery jalapeños and serranos. It is always wise to add peppers a little at a time until you discover how hot they are. To prepare chili peppers, cut off stalks, slit bodies, and remove all seeds. Take care to wear gloves or wash your hands after handling peppers, and don't let their oils get near your face or eyes.

AUTUMN

As the leaves begin to turn color and the days grow shorter, the lush summer crops give way to the sturdier, heavier fall harvest. The threat of frost looms large as the last of the tomatoes go into jars, and the only beans left on the vines are those left to dry for winter storage. During this season, we turn toward hearty potatoes and robust cabbages. The onions and their aromatic relatives, such as garlic, leeks, and shallots, are ready to store and use in warming soups and stews. The best pumpkins are set aside for jack-o'-lanterns, and the rest will be for table use in vegetable dishes and pies.

Baked Sweet Potato Sticks

❈ ❈ ❈

We love these savory sweet potato sticks. They take less time to bake than whole potatoes and have a wonderful sweet-tart coating.

    4 sweet potatoes
    4 tablespoons butter
 2½ teaspoons Dijon mustard
    1 teaspoon brown sugar

1. Preheat oven to 400°F.

2. Slice the potatoes into pieces the size and shape of large French fries. As you do so, drop the slices into cold water to prevent browning.

3. Melt the butter. Stir in the mustard and sugar until the mixture is smooth.

4. Drain the potatoes and pat them dry. Lay the potato sticks out on a baking sheet. Using a pastry brush, coat the sticks with the mustard-butter mixture. Be sure to cover all surfaces, or the potatoes will discolor.

5. Bake for 20 to 30 minutes, or until the potatoes are tender.

Yield: 6 servings

Sweet Potato and Carrot Casserole

❈ ❈ ❈

A visit to John's sister Helen always means the best in country cooking. John particularly looks forward to fall visits, because this beautiful casserole is likely to be on the table.

    4 large sweet potatoes,
        baked and peeled
    1 pound carrots, cooked

 ½ cup (1 stick) butter, melted
 ½ cup sour cream or plain
        yogurt, or ¼ cup of each
    1 tablespoon brown sugar
 ½ teaspoon ground nutmeg
        salt and freshly ground black
        pepper

1. Preheat oven to 350°F. Grease a 1½- to 2-quart casserole.

2. In a food processor fitted with a metal blade, or a food mill, purée the potatoes and carrots. Transfer mixture to a large bowl. Stir in the butter, sour cream, brown sugar, nutmeg, and salt and pepper to taste. Mix well.

3. Spread the mixture in the casserole; bake until heated through, about 25 minutes.

Yield: 8 servings

EASY "BAKED" POTATO

....

Scrub a white or sweet potato clean. Pierce several times with a fork, then place in a resealable plastic bag. Close the bag. Microwave on full power (High) for 7 minutes or until the potato is done. The potato will be moist and soft, with no overcooked ends.

Perfectly Baked Potatoes

A baked potato is a thing of glory. It is certainly worthwhile to buy baking potatoes, such as Idahos or russets, to ensure an ideal, fluffy consistency. Try to purchase potatoes of roughly uniform size, so that they can all come out of the oven at the same time without worry.

1 medium Idaho or russet potato per diner

1. Preheat oven to 400°F. Scrub the potato skins clean, prick them in several places with a fork, and insert a trussing needle, skewer, or baking nail lengthwise down the middle of each potato. If you prefer a soft skin to a crunchy one, oil or butter the skin before baking, but *do not* wrap them in foil. A medium-sized baking potato will be perfectly baked in 1 hour.

Yield: 1 potato per person

About Tater Toppers

Here's a baker's dozen of suggestions for topping the perfectly baked potato, starting with the classic.

- **Chili, grated Cheddar, and sour cream**
- **Herbed butter or cream cheese**
- **Mashed avocado and minced garlic**
- **Capers and bacon bits**
- **Yogurt spiced with cumin, ginger, or celery seed**
- **Sour cream and red caviar**
- **Chopped, cooked eggplant and pine nuts (browned in olive oil)**
- **Yogurt and a dab of anchovy paste**
- **Minced yellow and green bell peppers**
- **Chopped walnuts and sunflower seeds**
- **Chopped broccoli and grated cheese or cheese sauce**
- **Minced sausage — the spicier the better**
- **Crumbled blue cheese and minced parsley**

Note: If you are cooking potatoes along with other foods, plan on 1¼ hours' baking time at 350°F or 45 minutes at 450°F.

Mashed Potatoes

Great chefs debate the perfect way to make mashed potatoes. Some return them to the pot after draining and stir them over a hot burner for a few minutes to dry them out, a step that they believe makes mashed potatoes fluffier. Some prefer running cooked potatoes through a food mill instead of mashing them by hand. Most advise against mashing them in a food processor, because it makes them gooey. Many cooks whip potatoes with an electric mixer after mashing them to make them fluffier. I like to get out my old-fashioned potato masher, then get John to do the job for me. This recipe gives you a basic method to adapt to your liking.

2 large all-purpose or new potatoes, peeled and quartered
1 tablespoon cream or milk
2 teaspoons butter
salt and freshly ground black pepper

1. Bring a large pot of water to a boil. Add the potatoes and boil until soft, about 20 to 30 minutes. Drain thoroughly.

2. In a large mixing bowl, mash the potatoes with a potato masher or fork. Add the cream, butter, and salt and pepper to taste; continue mashing until the potatoes reach the desired consistency.

Yield: 4 servings

BROCCOLI BASICS

....

A pound of broccoli yields about 5 cups of florets and stems. Don't toss the stems; peel them if they are tough, steam, and season with salt, freshly ground black pepper, and lemon juice. Or slice or purée them for use in soup.

Broccoli and Blue Cheese Casserole

❈ ❈ ❈

Our broccoli plants produce well into the fall, and it is such a treat to eat broccoli fresh whenever we want it. The tender florets are delicious raw from the garden, but this rich and creamy recipe comes to our table often. Frozen broccoli can be substituted; you needn't cook it first, just be sure that it is thawed and drained.

- 2 tablespoons butter
- 2 tablespoons all-purpose flour
- ¼ teaspoon salt
- 3 ounces cream cheese, softened

- ¼ cup blue cheese, crumbled
- 1 cup milk
- 4 cups broccoli florets
- ⅓ cup Ritz cracker crumbs

1. Preheat oven to 350°F. In a saucepan, blend together the butter, flour, salt, cream cheese, and blue cheese. Add the milk all at once; cook until mixture comes to a boil. Stir in the broccoli to coat.

2. Pour the mixture into a 1½-quart casserole and top with the cracker crumbs. Bake for 30 minutes, until bubbly.

Yield: 6 servings

Cabbage in Sour Cream

❈ ❈ ❈

Sour cream and butter mellow the strong cabbage flavor. This dish often appeals even to those who don't think they fancy cabbage.

- 1 small cabbage (about 1½ pounds), shredded
- 3 tablespoons butter
- ½ cup sour cream
- 1 tablespoon lemon juice
- 2 teaspoons sugar
- 1 teaspoon caraway seeds
- salt and freshly ground black pepper

1. In a large saucepan, sauté the cabbage in the butter until tender but still crisp, 6 to 8 minutes.

2. In a large bowl, conbine the sour cream, lemon juice, sugar, caraway seeds, and salt and pepper to taste. Stir in the cabbage; toss to coat with the sour cream mixture. Serve.

Yield: 6–8 servings

Braised Leeks

❈ ❈ ❈

Leeks are an elegant relative of the onion. They make a delicious side dish to roasted meats, chicken, turkey, and broiled fish. Care must be taken to wash them well, but otherwise, they are easy to prepare.

- 4 medium leeks
- 1 cup chicken broth, beef broth, or water
- butter
- salt and freshly ground black pepper

1. To prepare the leeks for cooking, trim off the shaggy roots and remove damaged upper green leaves, leaving 2 to 2½ inches of tender greens. Slit the leeks open and wash them thoroughly under running water to remove grit and sand. Drain.

2. Place in a large skillet. Cover with chicken broth. Simmer for 12 to 15 minutes, or until tender crisp. Drain well. Add butter, salt, and pepper to taste. Serve immediately.

Yield: 4 servings

Sautéed Leeks

❁ ❁ ❁

The sauté process concentrates the leek flavor. The pale green and white rings look lovely as a side dish or topping.

4   medium leeks
1   tablespoon butter
1   tablespoon vegetable oil
salt and freshly ground black
    pepper

1. Trim the shaggy roots from the leeks and remove damaged upper green leaves, leaving 2 to 2½ inches of tender greens. Slit the leeks open and wash them thoroughly under running water to remove grit and sand. Drain. Slice into thin rings.

2. In a large skillet, melt butter and vegetable oil. Add leeks; sauté until tender crisp, 7 to 10 minutes. Season to taste with salt and pepper.

Yield: 4 servings

Baked Mushrooms

❁ ❁ ❁

My friend Judy Madden served this at one of her holiday gatherings. People lined up not only for her delicious buffet but also for the recipe!

1   pound fresh mushrooms
5⅓ tablespoons (⅓ cup)
    butter, melted
1   cup seasoned bread
    crumbs
¾   cup grated Parmesan
    cheese
3   cloves of garlic, minced
salt and freshly ground black
    pepper
1   can (15 ounces) plum
    tomatoes

1. Preheat oven to 350°F. Spread the mushrooms, cap side up, in a single layer in a 9- by 13-inch baking dish and drizzle with butter. Sprinkle bread crumbs, Parmesan, garlic, and salt and pepper to taste evenly over the mushrooms.

2. Break the tomatoes by hand over the casserole, allowing some juice to drizzle down; spread evenly. Discard any juice remaining in the can.

3. Bake, uncovered, for 20 to 30 minutes.

Yield: 8 servings

Swiss-Style Pumpkin

❁ ❁ ❁

Loren and Barbara Schnierer, friends of Storey author Gail Damerow, give this recipe to visitors to their Stonycreek Farm in Noblesville, Indiana. It's well worth passing on — use a small sugar pumpkin.

3   cups sliced raw pumpkin
5⅓ tablespoons butter
2   eggs, beaten
¼   cup milk
1   teaspoon salt
dash of cayenne pepper
¼   teaspoon dry mustard
½   cup shredded Swiss cheese
Parmesan cheese

1. In a large skillet, sauté the pumpkin in the butter until tender. Remove with a slotted spoon to a serving dish and keep warm.

2. In the remaining liquid, combine the eggs,

MUSHROOMS, WILD AND WONDERFUL

Wild mushrooms are becoming more prevalent in markets: large, meaty portobellas; richly flavorful shiitakes; plump little crimini mushrooms; pungent, clustered oyster mushrooms; and the queen of them all, the morel, with its filigreed cap and woodsy flavor. To develop a taste for the various flavors, cook the mushrooms in just a bit of butter or add a few of their cultivated cousins. Many types of mushroom are available dried, too. To use, cover them with boiling water and let them sit until replumped, about 10 minutes. Be sure to use the flavored steeping liquid, too.

milk, salt, cayenne, mustard, and Swiss. Heat until the cheese melts.

3. Pour the cheese mixture over the pumpkin. Top with Parmesan to taste.

Yield: 6 servings

IN A PUMPKIN SHELL

....

For a splendid natural soup tureen or vegetable serving bowl, remove the top of a pumpkin, scoop out strings and seeds, and bake just until heated through. Fill with hot soup or vegetables and take triumphantly to the table.

Garlic Purée

❂ ❂ ❂

This may seem like a lot of garlic, but it keeps for up to 2 months in the refrigerator. We like to have it on hand to add a quick touch of garlic to any vegetable dish, salad dressing, sauce, or stew.

12 *whole heads of garlic*
½ *teaspoon salt*
1½ *tablespoons olive oil*

1. Break the heads of garlic into individual cloves.

Place cloves of garlic in a small saucepan with enough water to amply cover. Add the salt.

2. Simmer over low heat for 3 minutes, or until extremely soft.

3. Drain. Run the garlic through a food mill or sieve. (You want to remove the skins, so don't use a food processor.)

4. Stir in 1 tablespoon of the oil. Transfer the mixture to a freshly washed screw-top jar. Drizzle the remaining ½ tablespoon of oil on top. Keep refrigerated.

Yield: About 1–1½ cups

Amber Onions

❂ ❂ ❂

The onions become a tawny amber color when baked in this piquant sauce. I often make a whole batch just for the two of

us; we reheat them to enjoy throughout the week.

6 *large yellow onions*
1 *tablespoon butter, melted*
2 *tablespoons tomato juice*
2 *tablespoons honey*
1 *teaspoon salt*
¼ *teaspoon paprika*

1. Preheat oven to 350°F. Peel onions and cut in half crosswise. Place in a buttered baking dish, cut side up.

2. In a small saucepan, mix butter, tomato juice, honey, salt, and paprika. Cook over medium heat until honey melts.

3. Pour mixture over the onions. Bake, covered, for 1 hour.

Yield: 6 servings

PUMPKIN PURÉE

....

Baked pumpkin makes the best purée — no excess moisture and a deep roasted flavor. Cut pumpkin in half and remove seeds and fibers. Brush the inside with butter and place face down on baking sheet, or wrap each piece in aluminum foil. Bake for 20 to 60 minutes at 350°F, until it is fork tender. Scoop the flesh from the rind and run through a strainer or food mill, or purée in a food processor. Try this with winter squash as well. Use the purée in recipes or as a side dish.

WINTER

While I enjoy serving the peas and beans that we froze from last summer's harvest, the true winter vegetables, for me, are the roots and the winter squashes. These days, a welcome variety of cooking greens are available in the market year-round, and I use the winter months to experiment with those that we don't grow in our own garden.

Baked Acorn Squash

⊗ ⊗ ⊗

We've found acorn squash easy to grow. We harvest them as late in the season as possible before the first frost and cure them in our warm, airy "harvest kitchen" for a week or so before storing in the cool, dry basement. Soft and sweet, baked acorn squash is wonderfully nutritious and pleases all sorts of palates.

2　medium acorn squash
½　cup (1 stick) butter
½　cup brown sugar, firmly packed
　ground cinnamon
　ground nutmeg

1. Preheat oven to 350°F. Carefully cut the squash in half, then in quarters, forming eight boat-shaped wedges. Scoop out the seeds.

2. Place the squash, cut side up, in a shallow 9- by 13-inch baking dish. In the center of each, place 1 tablespoon of butter, 1 tablespoon of brown sugar, a generous sprinkling of cinnamon, and a dash of nutmeg.

3. Add ½ inch of hot water to the baking dish, taking care not to get any in the squash cavity. Bake for about 1 hour, or until the squash is soft and nicely browned. Drizzle pan juice on top before serving.

Yield: 8 servings

ABOUT SQUASHED POTATOES

······················

We sometimes add a cup or so of mashed squash to a bowl of mashed potatoes. It makes the little ones eager to eat their vegetables; they enjoy both the taste and the silly name.

Fancy Mashed Hubbard Squash

⊗ ⊗ ⊗

This is a real "honey" of a dish — squash sweetened with mashed banana and baked with a swirly topping of honey meringue. It makes a novel buffet dish that is especially good for brunch.

1　medium Hubbard squash, or 4 cups home canned or frozen
1　very ripe banana
¼　cup honey
1　egg, separated
　salt
1　teaspoon honey, warmed

1. If using fresh squash, bake it until fork tender, about 1 hour at 350°F, with ¼ inch of water in the baking dish. Remove from the shell and mash well. Add the banana, ¼ cup of honey, egg yolk, and a pinch of salt. Beat until smooth.

2. Preheat oven to 350°F. Scoop the squash into a greased 3-quart ovenproof bowl (not a long casserole dish) until it almost reaches the top.

3. Beat the egg white with a pinch of salt until foamy. Gradually add the teaspoon of honey; beat until peaks form. With a spatula dipped into cold water, spread the meringue in peaks on top of the squash, bringing it all the way to the edges of the bowl.

4. Bake for about 25 minutes, or until the meringue browns.

Yield: 8 servings

Gratin of Kale

❊ ❊ ❊

Cooked greens are a mainstay of our winter fare. This gratin is a delicious way to transform a humble vegetable into a gourmet treat.

1 *large bunch kale (about 1 pound)*
salt
3 *cups water*
1 *large clove of garlic, chopped*
2 *tablespoons olive oil*
2 *tablespoons grated Parmesan cheese*
2 *tablespoons bread crumbs*
freshly ground black pepper

1. Rinse the kale in cold water to remove any sand. Trim off and discard the stems.

2. In a large saucepan, bring 1 to 2 cups of the water, lightly salted, to a boil. Add the kale, cover, and steam over medium-high to high heat for 5 to 7 minutes. Drain and cut into 2-inch pieces.

3. In a large skillet, sauté the garlic in the oil for 30 seconds. Add the kale and remaining cup of water. Cover. Cook over high heat, stirring often, for 10 minutes, or until the kale is tender. Add the Parmesan and the bread crumbs. Season lightly with salt and pepper. Serve immediately.

Yield: 4 servings

Sweet and Sour Bok Choy

❊ ❊ ❊

Bok choy, or Chinese cabbage, has a delightful crunch and a mild flavor that works well with pungent Asian-style sauces. Try it with a dish of rice and a platter of chicken wings for a novelty on a midwinter night.

1 *pound bok choy*
2 *tablespoons vegetable oil*
1 *teaspoon finely minced ginger root*
½ *cup water*
½ *teaspoon salt*
3 *tablespoons cider vinegar*
3 *tablespoons sugar or honey*

1. Cut the bok choy into 1-inch slices. (If you have baby bok choy, cut in half lengthwise.) In a wok or large skillet, heat the oil over medium-high heat. Add the bok choy and ginger and stir-fry for 1 minute.

2. Turn the heat down to medium, stir in the water and salt, cover, and cook for 3 minutes.

3. Add the vinegar and sugar. Stir over fairly high heat until the sauce has thickened.

Yield: 3–4 servings

Celeriac Salad

❊ ❊ ❊

This salad is a classic French first course known as *Céleri Rémoulade*. Its base is celeriac, also known as celery root or celery knob, an ugly, knobby brown vegetable that hides a delicacy with mild, celery taste and a firm texture.

½ *pound celeriac, peeled and cut into matchsticks*
½ *cup mayonnaise*
1 *tablespoon Dijon mustard*
lettuce leaves
chopped fresh herbs (parsley or dill, for instance)

1. Blanch the celeriac by plunging it into boiling water for 1 minute. Drain and cool.

2. In a medium bowl, combine the celeriac, mayonnaise, and mustard. Chill well.

3. Serve on lettuce leaves; top with fresh herbs.

Yield: 3–4 servings

Harvard Beets

❈ ❈ ❈

Harvard beets are an old-time New England favorite that have a sweet-and-sour tang. This variation, with additional spices and lemon peel, is so delicious that John jokingly calls it "Williams beets," in honor of his alma mater.

2½ teaspoons cornstarch
¼ cup water
¼ cup vinegar
½ cup honey
3–4 whole allspice berries
½ stick cinnamon
12 small beets, cooked, peeled, and sliced or cubed
   twist of lemon peel
1 tablespoon butter

1. In a medium-sized saucepan, combine the cornstarch and water; blend until smooth. Add the vinegar, honey, and spices. Boil for 5 minutes.

2. Let the sauce cool for at least 30 minutes. Before serving, add the beets, lemon, and butter. Heat the mixture to a boil.

Yield: 6 servings

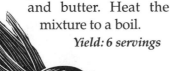

ABOUT ROASTED BEETS

....

A wonderful way to prepare beets is to roast them. Roasting intensifies their sweet flavor and lessens their tendency to bleed color. Scrub small or medium beets of fairly uniform size and wrap them in foil. Bake at 350°F until tender, about 1½ hours. Run the cooked beets under cold water; the skins should slip off easily. They taste particularly good in salads.

Sweet and Gooey Parsnips

❈ ❈ ❈

Years ago, at a church supper, Elizabeth Smith, proprietor of Caretaker Farm in the Berkshires, brought these delectable parsnips to share. Somehow, she had managed to transform this often forgotten vegetable into a simple and simply delicious side dish.

1 pound parsnips
2 tablespoons butter
¼ teaspoon ground nutmeg
   salt and freshly ground black pepper

1. Scrape or peel the parsnips, then cut them into sticks about the size of your little finger. Dry well with paper toweling.

2. In a heavy 10-inch skillet, melt the butter; then add the parsnips, shaking to coat. Sprinkle with nutmeg. Cover tightly and sauté on medium heat for about 5 to 10 minutes. The parsnips should be tender and gooey, and slightly caramelized. Add salt and pepper to taste.

Yield: 4 servings

Braised Turnips

❈ ❈ ❈

Braising involves cooking first in butter or fat, then slow-cooking in liquid. Braised turnips are tender but not mushy and become mellow with the flavor of the absorbed broth.

1 pound yellow turnips
1 tablespoon butter, softened
¾ cup low-sodium beef or chicken broth
   sugar
1 tablespoon lemon juice

1. Peel the turnips; cut into ½-inch slices.

2. In a large skillet, melt the butter. Cook the turnips over low heat until they have softened, about 10 minutes. Add the broth and sprinkle with sugar to taste.

3. Simmer until tender. Uncover and let sit for a few minutes, until sugar looks like a glaze. Sprinkle with lemon juice before serving.

Yield: 4 servings

Savory Dried Peas

❈ ❈ ❈

There is something homey and comfortable about a dish of peas and salt pork in the cold of winter. Sometimes we eat them with just a side of greens and a hot biscuit.

  4 *cups boiling water*
  2 *cups dried peas (black-eyed peas, cowpeas, or chickpeas)*
  1 *teaspoon salt*
  ¼ *teaspoon freshly ground black pepper*
  2 *ounces sliced salt pork*
  4 *small onions, peeled*

1. In a medium-sized bowl, pour the water over the peas. Soak for 3 to 4 hours. Drain.

2. Place the dried peas in a medium-sized saucepan. Add fresh water to cover, salt, pepper, pork, and onions.

3. Cover and cook over low heat until tender, about 1 hour.

Yield: 4–6 servings

Chestnut Potato Purée

❈ ❈ ❈

This creamy purée makes an excellent accompaniment to meat or poultry.

4–5 *medium potatoes*
  1 *pound chestnuts*
2–3 *cloves of garlic*
  3 *cups chicken broth*
  5 *tablespoons butter*
  ½ *cup milk*
  ½ *cup sour cream or yogurt*
  ⅛ *teaspoon ground nutmeg or mace*
4–5 *shallots*

1. Boil the potatoes until tender. Cool potatoes, peel them, and run them through a ricer or food mill.

2. Preheat oven to 425°F. Score the chestnuts and roast them on a baking sheet for about 10 minutes, or until the shells crack. Cool the chestnuts and remove the outer shells, then peel off the skins.

3. Peel and slice the garlic. Bring the broth to a boil in a saucepan; add the chestnuts and garlic, reduce heat, and simmer, covered, for 30 minutes, or until chestnuts are tender. Drain the chestnuts; discard the water and garlic. Put chestnuts through a sieve or purée them in a blender or food processor.

4. In a large saucepan, combine the potatoes, chestnuts, 4 tablespoons of the butter, milk, sour cream, and nutmeg.

5. In a separate small skillet, melt the remaining tablespoon of butter. Peel and finely chop the shallots; sauté them in the skillet over medium-low heat until they are soft but not browned, about 5 minutes. Stir the cooked shallots into the purée in the saucepan. Stir the purée over low heat, just until it is heated through. Serve warm.

Yield: 6–8 servings

ABOUT CHESTNUTS

··

To legions of Christmas carolers, the thing to do with chestnuts is roast them on an open fire. But there are many ways to enjoy this sweet, edible nut inside the hard, dark brown outer shell and bitter inner skin. Try boiling or puréeing, as in the Chestnut Potato Purée above, for a main course side dish. Or enjoy them with dessert, as in *marrons glacés*, chestnuts preserved in sweet syrup, an expensive but delicious treat.

FLAVORFUL FRUITS

When I think of fruit, fresh and juicy, I think of the eager, smiling faces of our grandchildren when they come to visit at our farm in the Adirondacks. Many summer mornings they are up early, wearing berry buckets around their necks, ready to pick their fill of sweet raspberries, strawberries, or blueberries to have on their cereal or pancakes. Several of these bushes came from our friend Lewis Hill's "Berry Hill" farm in the Northeast Kingdom of Vermont. Come fall, the kids climb the old apple tree near the garden and help shake the apples into bushel baskets for the sauce, pies, and muffins that they will help me make — and eat!

■ ■ ■ ■ ■ ■ ■ ■

Contributors to this chapter are Glenn Andrews; Liz Anton and Beth Dooley; Janet Ballantyne; Ruth Bass; Marjorie Page Blanchard; Andrea Chesman; Nancy Chioffi and Gretchen Mead; Carol Costenbader; Jennifer Storey Gillis; Ken Haedrich; Miriam Jacobs; Alexandra Nimetz, Jason Stanley, and Emeline Starr; Sara Pitzer; Edith Stovel; and Olwen Woodier.

| SPRING |
| SUMMER |
| AUTUMN |
| WINTER |

Applesauce Cake

❈ ❈ ❈

MomMom used to love to make fresh applesauce, and she used it in a lot of her recipes. This cake is terrific.

1 cup brown sugar, firmly packed
½ cup (1 stick) butter, softened
1 egg
1 cup unsweetened apple-sauce
1 teaspoon vanilla extract
1¾ cups all-purpose flour
1 teaspoon baking soda
1 teaspoon ground cinnamon
¼ teaspoon ground nutmeg
¾ cup raisins (optional)

Crumb Topping

6 tablespoons sugar
3 tablespoons butter
3 tablespoons all-purpose flour
3 teaspoons ground cinnamon

1. Preheat oven to 350°F. Combine the brown sugar, butter, and egg; stir in the applesauce and vanilla. Stir together the flour, soda, cinnamon, nutmeg, and raisins, if desired. Add to the sugar mixture and mix just until combined. Pour the batter into a greased 9- by 13-inch pan.

2. To make the topping, combine the sugar, butter, flour, and cinnamon. Sprinkle evenly over the cake batter.

3. Bake until a toothpick inserted in the center comes out clean, 45 minutes to 1 hour.

Yield: 12 servings

Applesauce Meat Loaf

❈ ❈ ❈

Meat loaf is one of those "hand-me-down" recipes that varies with each making, depending on what you have in the cupboard. My dad was the meat loaf maker in our house, and his trick was a cup of Rice Krispies or Wheaties. John's mom had her own twist for moistness: home-made applesauce. I put them together, added some "zing," and a family favorite was born!

2 pounds lean ground beef
1 cup applesauce
½ cup tomato salsa
½ cup grated Parmesan cheese
1 cup dry cereal, such as Rice Krispies or Wheaties
2 eggs
1 onion, finely chopped
¼ pound (about 6 slices) bacon, finely chopped
2 teaspoons dried basil
2 teaspoons dried oregano
2 teaspoons dried parsley
freshly ground black pepper

1. Preheat oven to 350°F. Mix the beef, applesauce, salsa, Parmesan, cereal, eggs, onion, bacon, basil, oregano, parsley, and pepper to taste until well combined.

2. Shape the mixture into a loaf; place in a lightly greased loaf pan. Bake for 1 hour.

Yield: 8 servings

Applesauce

❈ ❈ ❈

Daughter Jennifer loves to make applesauce for her brood. She recommends Golden Delicious or Winesap apples.

water
10–15 apples, peeled, cored, and quartered
ground cinnamon and sugar

1. Put about 1 inch of water in a saucepan; add the apples. Bring the water to a boil, then lower the heat and simmer the apples for about 30 minutes, until very mushy.

2. Drain the apples and place in a large bowl. Mash to desired consistency using a potato masher, or put through a food mill.

3. Sprinkle cinnamon and sugar on top. Enjoy warm or cold.

Yield: 5 cups

SPRING

Even though we can purchase fruit year-round at the market, the first fruits of the garden are welcome harbingers of the summer bounty to come. What a thrill to watch the strawberries blossom, turn to green-white berries, and finally ripen into sweet red glory. What a thrill to have the rhubarb pushing up from the earth, unfurling, and growing tall. And it seems part of Mother Nature's genius that these first-comers taste so perfect together!

Hot Rhubarb Pudding

❈ ❈ ❈

This baked pudding is a wonderful mixture of tart and sweet, and it is easier than pie to make!

    2   eggs
    1   cup sugar
    1   teaspoon vanilla extract
    ¼   cup unbleached all-
        purpose flour
    4   cups diced rhubarb
        whipped cream

1. Preheat oven to 350°F. Beat the eggs. Whisk together the eggs, sugar, vanilla, and flour. Stir in the rhubarb.

2. Grease a 1½-quart baking dish and pour in the rhubarb mixture. Bake for 40 minutes or until the pudding is firm. Serve warm with whipped cream.

Yield: 4 servings

Rhubarb Chutney

❈ ❈ ❈

If you don't give away all your chutney, you'll run out of it before you run out of ideas about how to use it. Warm it to pour over a pork roast or tenderloin, spoon it alongside omelettes or scrambled eggs, spread it on the bread for a turkey sandwich, or scoop it out of the jar with a cracker.

    4   pounds rhubarb, cut into
        small pieces
    1   pound pitted dates
    2   pounds brown sugar (5
        cups)
    1   tablespoon cinnamon
    1   tablespoon ground cloves
    2   cups cider vinegar

1. In a large saucepan, boil the rhubarb, dates, sugar, cinnamon, and cloves slowly

for 2 hours. Stir frequently. Add vinegar and boil 10 minutes longer. The chutney will keep well in the refrigerator, or you may can.

2. To process, pack the chutney into sterilized pint jars while hot, leaving ½ inch of headroom. Run a rubber spatula around the inside of the jar to release trapped air bubbles. Wipe the rims of the jars with a clean cloth. Place lids in position and tighten screw band.

3. Process in a boiling-water-bath canner (page 384) for 10 minutes.

Yield: 5 pints

A STRAWBERRY TOOL

....

A strawberry huller is like a miniature pair of tongs. It takes the leaf and the core out in one easy twist. If you want perfectly hulled berries, this little tool is a great help.

Strawberry-Rhubarb Pie

❈ ❈ ❈

My favorite version of this classic spring treat is fun to make. For ease, I toss it together with my hands.

2 cups rhubarb, cut into
    7-inch pieces
2 cups sliced strawberries
1½ cups sugar
⅓ cup all-purpose flour
½ teaspoon almond extract
    pinch of salt
    pastry for two 9-inch piecrusts
2 tablespoons butter, cut
    into pieces
    milk
    sugar

How Much Do I Need?

....

1 pint strawberries = 2½ cups sliced berries = 1⅔ cups purée.

---

1. Preheat oven to 400°F. Mix together gently the rhubarb, strawberries, sugar, flour, almond extract, and salt. Line a 9-inch pie pan with pastry; put fruit mixture into the pan. Dot with butter.

2. Cover with a pastry crust. Brush the crust with milk and sprinkle with sugar.

3. Bake for 40 to 50 minutes, until fruit is tender and the crust is lightly browned.

Yield: 6–8 servings

Strawberry Syllabub

❈ ❈ ❈

Syllabub is an old-fashioned dessert made of a frothy wine and cream sauce poured over fresh fruit or berries.

1 cup heavy cream
½ cup confectioners' sugar
2 egg whites or powdered
    egg white equivalent
2 tablespoons medium dry
    sherry
1 quart strawberries

1. In a large bowl, combine the cream and ¼ cup of the sugar; whip until stiff.

2. In another bowl, beat the egg whites with the remaining ¼ cup sugar until stiff.

3. Fold the egg whites into the cream mixture. Add sherry. Place the berries in a serving bowl and pour the sauce over them.

Yield: 4–6 servings

STRAWBERRY PURÉE

....

Fresh strawberry purée is one of the most delightful of dessert sauces. It is simple to make. Use the ripest berries you can find and either force them through a food mill or sieve or purée them in a blender or food processor. Sweeten to taste with honey or granulated sugar. Serve the purée over ice cream or custard; pass some along with a fruit salad or angel food cake. For a special occasion, pool some on dessert plates and top with a rich chocolate cake.

Frozen strawberries may also be puréed; thaw for about 15 minutes and purée in a food processor or blender. For a strawberry ice dessert, process just until the purée is coarse and icy and sweeten to taste. Process longer, and the purée will become smooth and creamy, rather like sherbet. This cold purée is good served on pancakes and French toast. If you use commercially frozen whole strawberries, a 1-pound package makes about 2 cups of frozen purée.

Strawberry Shortcake

❈ ❈ ❈

Strawberry shortcake is a June ritual in our family, more so since our son Matt bought a home with a strawberry patch. We insist on just-picked berries, fresh cream, and these authentic, not-too-sweet biscuits for the base. Mashing some of the berries with sugar brings out the best strawberry flavor; the whole berries look beautiful on top.

Biscuits

2   cups unbleached all-purpose flour
1   tablespoon baking powder
1   tablespoon sugar
½   teaspoon salt
4   tablespoons butter
2   eggs
⅓   cup light cream

Strawberry Filling

7½ cups sliced strawberries
½   cup sugar
1   cup whole strawberries

1. Preheat oven to 425°F. For the biscuits, sift together the flour, baking powder, sugar, and salt. Cut in the butter until the mixture resembles small peas. Make a well in the center.

2. Beat the eggs. Combine the eggs and cream and pour into the well in the flour mixture. Mix lightly, as you would for biscuits, just long enough to make the dough hold together.

3. On a lightly floured surface, pat the dough flat to about ½ inch thick. Use a biscuit cutter or large inverted glass to cut six individual cakes. (Gather up the scraps to form an extra cake for somebody who wants seconds.)

4. Place the cakes on a lightly greased baking sheet and bake 10 to 15 minutes, or until brown.

5. When the cakes are done, split them while they are hot, spread with butter, and fill and cover with strawberry filling.

6. For the filling, mash the sliced strawberries lightly with a fork as you stir in the sugar. Refrigerate for at least 1 hour to draw out the juice and dissolve the sugar. Wash, hull, and drain the whole strawberries. At serving time, stir the whole berries into the chilled, sugared berries and use the mixture between and on top of the shortcakes.

Yield: 6 servings

Note: This kind of shortcake is traditionally served with heavy cream passed in a pitcher to pour over each serving; but, by all means, whip it if you like!

SHORTCAKE FOR SUPPER

Surprise your family with a very special meal. My mother used to do this each summer. When the weather was stifling and our appetites were lacking, and it was too hot to do anything, she'd bake a large, family-sized shortbread for the six of us. Then she'd go out to the garden and pick several quarts of fresh strawberries, whip some real cream, and serve us the most outrageous strawberry shortcake for dinner. That's right, just strawberry shortcake and iced tea. Nothing else! We would eat and laugh and talk for a long time, and my mother would glow with pride, knowing that she had pleased and surprised us all.

SUMMER

Baskets of peaches and plums, fuzzy apricots, and blushing cherries — the summer orchard brings light, sweet pleasure to our table. Watermelons and berries add cool refreshment. We eat this plenty out of hand, tuck it into flaky tarts and golden cakes, and then try to capture its sunshine for the winter in preserves, jams, and freezer bags.

Baked Peaches
with Vanilla Ice Cream

✶ ✶ ✶

When peaches are ripe, this recipe is so easy and so good. The intense flavor of the hot peaches in contrast with the smooth coolness of the ice cream is heavenly!

4 ripe peaches
½ cup apple juice
2 tablespoons brown sugar
¼ teaspoon ground cloves
½ teaspoon vanilla extract
4 scoops nonfat vanilla ice cream

1. Preheat oven to 350°F. Slice the peaches in half and remove the pits.

2. Pour the apple juice into an ovenproof dish. Place the peaches, cut side up, side by side in the dish.

3. In a small bowl, combine the sugar, cloves, and vanilla. Spoon the sugar mixture into the cavities left by the pits. Cover the dish with aluminum foil and crimp the sides. Bake for 30 minutes.

4. Place two peach halves on a plate and top with a scoop of ice cream.

Yield: 4 servings

WHICH PEACH?

....

Freestone or clingstone? This is the primary distinction among peaches; it refers to the way the pit, or stone, comes out of the peach. In a freestone peach, the pit easily pulls away, leaving a clean cavity. The pit of a clingstone is firmly embedded in the peach flesh and usually must be cut away. While freestone peaches are easier to handle, some of the most flavorful peaches are old-fashioned clingstones. Whichever kind you choose, select tree-ripened fruit for true peach sweetness.

Apricot Salsa

✶ ✶ ✶

My Texas relatives chuckled at the idea of apricot salsa, but they stopped laughing as soon as they tasted it. I use it to baste chicken breasts as they broil, and then top them with more of it. It's tasty on grilled fish, as well.

1 pound fresh apricots
4 scallions, minced
1 bell pepper (preferably the orange-skinned variety), cored, seeded, and minced
2 tablespoons (or more) minced green chilies
1 tablespoon orange-flavored liqueur or 2 teaspoons grated orange zest

1. Peel the apricots by dipping them briefly into boiling water, then plunging them into cold water. The skins will come right off. Cut the fruit into small pieces, discarding the pits.

2. Combine all of the ingredients in a bowl and let sit, refrigerated and covered, for at least 1 hour.

Yield: About 2 cups

Note: When it's not apricot season, use ½ pound dried apricot halves. Plump them first: Simmer gently in water for 10 minutes, then drain.

Frozen Melon Sherbet

❈ ❈ ❈

Honeydew melon sherbet is refreshing and light, and it requires no added sugar. In fact, homemade sherbet made with any melon is a fine summer cooler.

    4 cups frozen melon
       chunks, 1–1½ inches in
       diameter
 ¼–¾ cups fruit juice or cider
       sweetener (optional)
    2 tablespoons liqueur
       (optional)

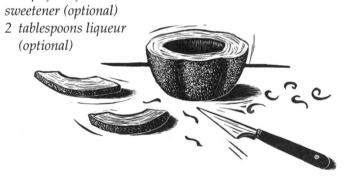

1. Drop the fruit, a little at a time, into a food processor with the motor running. Slowly pour in the juice, a little at a time. A sweetener is not necessary, but you can replace some of the liquid with honey, maple syrup, or sugar, if you like.

2. Process until smooth and thick. Stir in liqueur, if desired. Serve at once.

Yield: 4 servings

WATERMELON ICE POPS

••

One hundred percent natural goodness on a stick! This is a healthful frozen snack in Janet Ballantyne's cookbook that my grandchildren love; we grown-ups do, too, for that matter. Seed and peel the watermelon and purée it in a food processor or blender. Pour into plastic molds or paper cups and freeze for several hours. If you are using paper cups, wait until the mixture is partially frozen, then insert a wooden stick. Plastic molds are very convenient, and they catch some of the drips. This can be a messy treat, so it's best to serve it outdoors!

Batter-Crust Damson Plum Pie

❈ ❈ ❈

The sweet buttery crust is perfect with the tart fruit; if you can't find Damsons, other tart plums will do fine. When I serve it warm, I like to top it with vanilla ice cream for an "à la mode" appeal.

    1 pound Damson plums,
       halved and pitted (about
       2 cups)
    2 cups sugar
   ½ cup (1 stick) butter
    1 cup sifted self-rising flour
   ½ cup milk

1. Preheat oven to 350°F. Boil the plums with 1 cup of the sugar until sugar melts and plums are softened.

2. Melt the butter in a baking dish. Combine flour with the remaining cup of sugar and the milk; mix well. Pour batter into the baking dish.

3. Pour the hot fruit over batter and bake for 45 minutes or until browned on top.

Yield: 6 servings

Note: Damson plums are extremely tart; if you cannot find them, you may need to reduce the amount of sugar in this pie.

Plum Purée

❂ ❂ ❂

Plum purée can be made with almost any kind of plums; it's a great base for other sauces, both sweet and savory. Here is a basic recipe for the purée, followed by meat and dessert sauces using it.

1½ pound plums
1 tablespoon sugar

1. Cut the plums in half and remove the pits. Purée in a blender or food processor. Pour purée into a saucepan and add the sugar. Heat until sugar is dissolved. Freeze or process in a boiling-water-bath canner for 10 minutes (page 384).

Yield: 1½ cups purée

Nika's Plum Sauce

❂ ❂ ❂

This sauce is excellent for beef fondue or shish kabob, roast pork, or chicken.

1½ cups Plum Purée (see above)
4 large cloves of garlic, minced
    salt and freshly ground black pepper

1. Pour the purée into a saucepan and add the garlic and salt and pepper to taste.

Bring to a boil. Reduce the heat and simmer 5 minutes, stirring frequently. Serve at room temperature.

Yield: 1½ cups

Plum Dessert Sauce

❂ ❂ ❂

Wine and orange flavors add a little mystery to the plums in this fruit sauce.

2 tablespoons sugar
1½ cups Plum Purée (see above)
1 tablespoon cornstarch
¼ cup port wine
2 tablespoons grated orange zest

1. Stir the sugar into the purée. Heat, stirring constantly, over low heat until bubbling. Dissolve the cornstarch in wine and stir into the hot mixture. Cook, stirring constantly, until slightly thickened and smooth. Stir in the zest. Serve warm or cold over poached peaches or pears or hot winter puddings.

Yield: About 1½ cups

Berry Fool

❂ ❂ ❂

An old-fashioned delicious mixture of mashed cooked berries folded with whipped cream. This is so easy it's "foolproof."

4 cups strawberries, blackberries, or raspberries
1 cup sugar (depending on berries' sweetness)
¼ cup water
2 cups heavy cream

1. In a medium-sized saucepan, combine berries with sugar and water. Cook over low heat until tender, stirring frequently and pressing down with a fork to extract juices.

2. Purée the mixture in a food processor or blender. Strain to remove seeds, if desired. Chill the mixture.

3. Just prior to serving, whip cream until stiff peaks form. Fold into the berry mixture. Spoon into serving bowls or glasses. Garnish with additional berries.

Yield: 8 servings

SMOOTHIES

Smoothies are a great way to enjoy fruit in a healthful drink. Blend 1½ to 2 cups fresh fruit with 1 cup frozen yogurt and ½ cup juice, nectar, or milk. If you use frozen fruit, you can use plain yogurt. For a ready supply of frozen fruit, pop a few peeled ripe bananas into the freezer.
Try peaches, berries, mangoes, or melon, too.

Blackberry Pinwheel Cobbler

❈ ❈ ❈

Here's a cobbler with a twist; the fruit is rolled up into the dough, then the roll is sliced for a lovely swirled look.

½ cup (1 stick) butter
2 cups sugar
2 cups water
½ cup vegetable shortening
1½ cups self-rising flour
⅓ cup milk
3–4 cups fresh blackberries
1 teaspoon cinnamon

1. Preheat oven to 350°F. Place the butter in a 9- by 13-inch pan and melt in the oven. Set aside.

2. To make the sugar syrup, combine sugar and water in a saucepan and stir well. Cook over low heat until the sugar dissolves. Set aside.

3. Cut the shortening into flour until mixture resembles coarse meal. Add the milk and stir until ingredients are moistened.

4. Turn out on a floured surface and knead lightly four or five times. Roll dough into a 9- by 12-inch rectangle. Spread blackberries over the dough. Sprinkle with the cinnamon. Roll up jelly-roll fashion, beginning with the long side. Cut into twelve 1-inch slices and place, cut sides up, in the buttered baking pan. Pour syrup around slices. Bake for 55 to 60 minutes or until golden brown on top.

Yield: 10–12 servings

VARIATION: This cobbler can be baked in a microwave oven. Use appropriate bakeware and adjust the cooking time according to the size of the microwave oven — approximately 25 minutes in a small oven.

Blueberries Romanoff

❈ ❈ ❈

Storey author Ruth Bass came up with this variation on the classic strawberry dessert. We like to make it with strawberries in early summer and then her way at the end of the season.

2 pints fresh blueberries
1 cup confectioners' sugar
1 cup heavy cream
2 teaspoons minced fresh mint leaves
2 tablespoons orange-flavored liqueur

1. Gently rinse the blueberries with cold water. Drain. Place them in a medium-sized glass bowl, sprinkle with the sugar, and mix, taking care not to crush the berries. Refrigerate for 1 hour, stirring occasionally.

2. Whip the cream until stiff. While whipping, add the mint and the liqueur. Fold the cream mixture into the blueberries. Serve at once.

Yield: 6 servings

Sour Cherry Cake

❈ ❈ ❈

Make your pies and sour cherry preserves, but save some of your tart cherries for this wonderful cake.

½ cup (1 stick) butter
1 cup granulated sugar
2 eggs
1¼ cups flour
2 teaspoons baking powder
½ teaspoon salt
1 teaspoon ground cinnamon
½ teaspoon ground nutmeg
½ teaspoon baking soda
½ cup milk
2 cups sour cherries, pitted
confectioners' sugar

1. Preheat oven to 350°F. Grease a 9-inch square pan. Cream together the butter and sugar until light. Beat in the eggs, one at a time.

2. Combine the flour, baking powder, salt, cinnamon, nutmeg, and soda. Add alternately with the milk to the butter mixture. Stir until smooth and creamy.

3. Fold in the cherries. Pour batter into the pan. Bake 30 to 35 minutes, until a toothpick inserted in the center comes out clean. Cool completely; sprinkle with confectioners' sugar.

Yield: 9 servings

Cherry Clafouti

✖ ✖ ✖

Clafouti is a French country favorite, rather like a cross between a cake and a pudding and studded with fruit.

      3   cups sweet black cherries,
           pitted
      2   teaspoons lemon juice
      3   tablespoons cherry brandy
      5   tablespoons butter or
           margarine
      ½   cup plus 1 tablespoon
           granulated sugar
      1   teaspoon grated lemon zest
      ¼   teaspoon ground nutmeg
      2   eggs or egg substitute
      2   egg whites
      1   cup unbleached flour

1. Preheat oven to 375°F. Spray a 9- or 10- inch springform pan with vegetable cooking spray and dust with flour. Combine the cherries, lemon juice, and brandy in a medium-sized bowl and let stand for 30 minutes.

2. In a mixing bowl, cream the butter with ½ cup of the sugar, the lemon zest, and nutmeg. Beat in eggs and egg whites. Add the flour and mix well.

3. Spread the batter in the pan. Lift cherries from juice and spread over the batter; reserve juice.

4. In a small bowl, combine the remaining tablespoon sugar with reserved juice and dribble over all. Bake for 40 minutes. Let cool and serve.

Yield: 8 servings

Currant Jelly
(and Jam)

✖ ✖ ✖

When my friend's grandma had fresh currants, she put up currant jelly for glazing tarts and made "barleydoo" from the fruit pulp. We eat this pretty red preserve with cream cheese on plain crackers.

      3   quarts currants
      2   cups water
      3   cups sugar

1. Wash and stem the currants (stemming is unnecessary if you are making only jelly). Place the currants and water in a large saucepan; bring to a boil. Reduce heat and simmer 10 minutes. Place the cooked fruit in a jelly bag and allow juice to drip overnight. Reserve the pulp for making jam.

2. Measure out 4 cups of the juice and stir in the sugar. Heat to boiling. Continue cooking and stirring for 5 minutes, until mixture meets the jelly test (page 401). (Currants are high in natural pectin.) Skim, pour into jars, and seal. Process for 5 minutes in a boiling-water bath (page 384).

Yield: Four 8-ounce jars

Note: Bar-le-Duc (currant jam) may be made from the reserved pulp and any excess juice. For every cup of pulp, add ¾ cup sugar and cook (syrup will be thick) until desired consistency is reached.

Yield: 2 half-pints

AUTUMN

After the soft juiciness of summer fruits, the crisp bite of an apple has a welcome hardiness about it. The tawny pears and grapes are ready to harvest now, as are the smaller, sturdier plums. It's time for cider and pies, baked apples and sauces. And the cranberries arrive just in time for celebrating the harvest at Thanksgiving.

Fresh Cranberry Relish

❈ ❈ ❈

This cranberry sauce is what I think of as a modern classic. It can be made with seedless clementines or tangerines, too. If there's any left over, I eat it at breakfast on toast.

    2 cups cranberries, rinsed
       and seeded
    2 unpeeled oranges, cut in
       quarters and seeded
    1½ cups sugar

1. Place the cranberries, oranges, and sugar in a food processor; pulse until the cranberries are coarsely chopped. To store, cover and refrigerate.

Yield: 3 cups

Classic Cranberry Sauce

❈ ❈ ❈

We like trying out new cranberry sauces — with oranges or apricots, raisins, even onions — but we always make a batch of this classic, as well.

    2 packages (12 ounces each)
       cranberries, rinsed and
       sorted
    1 cup water
    2 cups sugar

1. In a medium saucepan, cook cranberries and water until they are soft and pop, about 8 to 10 minutes. Press through a sieve. Stir in the sugar, and boil for 3 minutes.

2. Pour into sterile jars, leaving ½ inch of headroom. Run a rubber spatula around the inside of the jar to release air bubbles. Wipe jars with a clean cloth; tighten screw bands. Process in a boiling-water bath (page 384) for 15 minutes.

Yield: 2 pints

SUGARED CRANBERRIES

These make a novel treat for holiday snacking and garnishes. Pick over and remove stems from one 12-ounce bag of cranberries. Beat 1 egg white until frothy; stir the cranberries gently into the egg white to coat. Put ⅔ cup sugar into another bowl; with a slotted spoon, transfer the coated berries to the sugar and toss to coat completely. Spread the sugared berries in a single layer in a shallow baking pan and put into a 150°F oven for about 12 minutes, until the sugar just begins to melt — don't let the berries pop or run juice. Remove from pan onto a large sheet of wax paper, separating berries. Sprinkle with 2 tablespoons sugar. Let berries air-dry overnight to harden the frosting, then store in an airtight container in the refrigerator.

Southwestern Cranberry Sauce

❈ ❈ ❈

We love visiting the Southwest, and this cranberry sauce brings back the strikingly fresh use of peppers and spices in that region. It's especially delicious when your bird has a corn bread stuffing.

1 package (12 ounces) fresh cranberries, rinsed and sorted
¾ cup sugar
1 medium jalapeño pepper, cored, seeded, and quartered (use rubber gloves)
1 scallion, coarsely chopped
3 teaspoons chopped fresh cilantro
¼ teaspoon ground cumin

1. Place all of the ingredients in a food processor; pulse the motor until cranberries are coarsely chopped.

2. Pour into three sterile 1-cup canning jars, leaving 1 inch of headroom.

3. Allow flavors to develop in the refrigerator overnight. The recipe will keep for 1 week in the refrigerator or 2 months in the freezer.

Yield: 3½ pints (twelve 2-ounce servings)

VARIATION: Add 1 or 2 teaspoons orange or lime zest for a citrus accent.

Granny Smith Apple Pie

❈ ❈ ❈

When Mother visits our Champlain Valley farm, the family asks, "Will you do an apple pie?" Beautiful to look at, Mother's apple pies seem to melt in your mouth. Piled high with tart, crisp apples — such as Granny Smith, a variety we get from the Gibbs Orchard just down the road — and with plenty of aromatic spices.

pastry for two 9-inch pie crusts
1 cup sugar
2 tablespoons all-purpose flour
1 teaspoon ground cinnamon
¼ teaspoon ground nutmeg
6 large, tart apples, cored, peeled, and sliced
2 tablespoons butter, melted
1 tablespoon lemon juice

1. Preheat oven to 450°F. Roll out half of the pastry and fit it into a 9-inch pie pan. In a small bowl, combine the sugar, flour, cinnamon, and nutmeg. Place the sliced apples in a large bowl; toss with the sugar mixture, coating each slice. Pile the apples high into the prepared piecrust.

2. Combine the butter and lemon juice; drizzle over the apples. Cover with top crust. Moisten the edges of the crust with water, then crimp to seal. Cut several openings in the top to allow steam to escape.

3. Bake for 10 minutes, then reduce the heat to 350°F and bake for an additional 45 minutes or until browned and bubbly. Serve warm.

Yield: 8 servings

Baked Apples

❈ ❈ ❈

Baked apples are a simple, traditional dessert, but John and I also like to have them for breakfast on a cold morning.

4 medium apples
6 tablespoons butter, cut into bits
2 tablespoons sugar
½ teaspoon ground cinnamon
¼ cup raisins or dried cranberries
½ cup cider or apple juice

1. Preheat oven to 350°F. Core apples and peel 1 inch down from the tops.

2. Cream together 2 tablespoons of the butter, the sugar, and cinnamon. Spoon one-quarter of the mixture into each apple. Divide the raisins and the remaining butter among the apples.

3. Place in a baking dish and add cider to cover the bottom. Bake for 45 minutes, basting occasionally.

Yield: 4 servings

Oniony Baked Apples

❈ ❈ ❈

This is an easy, savory side dish to accompany roasted turkey or chicken breast or a pork chop.

2   Granny Smith apples
¼   cup chopped onion
1   tablespoon pure maple syrup
⅛   teaspoon ground sage

1. Preheat oven to 450°F. Cut the apples in half and carefully remove the cores. In a small mixing bowl, combine the onions, syrup, and sage. Distribute this stuffing evenly over the four apple halves.

2. Add ¼ inch water to a baking dish; set a glass pie plate in the dish. Arrange the apples, stuffing side up, on the plate.

3. Bake for 30 minutes, or until the apples are soft when pierced.

Yield: 4 servings

Apple Snow

❈ ❈ ❈

Both the name and the creamy consistency made this dish a hit with our children. Powdered egg whites are available in the baking section of many supermarkets.

powdered egg white equivalent to 2 large eggs
2   tablespoons confectioners' sugar
½   cup heavy cream
2   cups applesauce
½   cup finely chopped blanched almonds or 2 tablespoons chopped crystallized ginger

1. Prepare the egg whites as package directs; beat until foamy. Add the confectioners' sugar; continue beating until the egg whites are stiff.

2. Pour the cream into a medium-sized bowl and beat until stiff. Gently stir in the applesauce.

APPLE VARIETIES AND THEIR BEST USES

Variety	Harvest/ Availability	Eating	Salad	Sauce	Baking Whole	Pie	Frozen
Baldwin	Nov./April	Good	Good	Good	Good	Good	Fair
Cortland	Sept./June	Good	Excellent	Good	Good	Good	Fair
Golden Delicious	Sept./June	Good	Excellent	Excellent	Good	Good	Good
Red Delicious	Sept./June	Good	Good	Poor	Poor	Poor	Poor
Jonagold	Oct./April	Excellent	Excellent	Good	Good	Good	Good
Jonathan	Sept./April	Excellent	Good	Good	Excellent	Excellent	Good
McIntosh	Sept./June	Good	Fair	Good	Poor	Fair	Poor
Melrose	Oct./April	Good	Good	Excellent	Excellent	Excellent	Excellent
Northern Spy	Oct./May	Good	Good	Good	Excellent	Excellent	Good
Rhode Island Greening	Oct./April	Poor	Fair	Good	Good	Good	Good
Granny Smith	Oct./June	Good	Good	Fair	Good	Good	Good
Winesap	Nov./July	Excellent	Excellent	Excellent	Good	Good	Good

3. Fold the egg whites, one-third at a time, into the sauce mixture.

4. Gently stir in the almonds. Chill at least 1 hour.

Yield: 4 servings

APPLE POMANDER

When apples are plentiful, my daughter Jennifer makes pomanders to keep closets and drawers smelling good. For one pomander, push the stem ends of whole cloves (about 1 ounce) into an apple to cover it completely. Combine 1 tablespoon cinnamon, 1 teaspoon nutmeg, 1 teaspoon allspice, and ⅛ teaspoon ginger in a small bowl. Roll the apple in the spice mixture. Leave the pomander in the bowl in a warm place for 2 to 3 weeks, rolling it occasionally in the spices to help the apple dry, harden, and shrink. Pierce the apple lengthwise with a skewer. Thread an 18-inch piece of ribbon (doubled) through the top of the pomander. Tie a knot and a bow at the bottom and make a loop for hanging at the top.

Rosemary Poached Pears

The delicacy of pears is enhanced by an almost candied taste and the fragrance of rosemary. The pears should be ripe but still firm, so that they will hold their shape in the cooking.

- 3 ripe pears
- zest of half a lemon
- ½ teaspoon finely chopped rosemary
- 1½ tablespoons sugar
- 1 tablespoon butter
- ½ cup dry white wine
- 3 tablespoons brandy

1. Preheat oven to 300°F. Cut the unpeeled pears lengthwise, removing the blossom and stem ends and scooping out the seeds with a melon baller. With foil, line a casserole that will hold the pears in a single layer.

2. Set the pears in the dish, skin side down. Sprinkle the lemon zest, then the rosemary and sugar, over the pears. Dot with butter. Pour the wine into the bottom of the casserole.

3. Bake until the pears are cooked but not soft, about 15 minutes, depending on the pears. Place the pears under the broiler until the sugar turns slightly brown. Spoon the brandy into the seed cavities, light with a match, and let burn for about 1 minute.

Yield: 6 servings

Ginger Pear Sauce

Ginger really adds sparkle to mellow autumn pears. This sauce is just right over gingerbread or ice cream.

- 2 pounds ripe pears
- ⅓ pound crystallized ginger, finely chopped
- 2 cups sugar
- grated rind and juice of 1 lemon

1. Cut pears in half and remove cores and stems. Peel. Put into a large saucepan with ginger, sugar, and lemon rind and juice. Cook uncovered over medium heat until soft, 30 to 45 minutes depending on how ripe the pears are. Run through a food mill or food processor until blended. Return to saucepan and cook until thickened.

Yield: About 2 pints

Concord Grape Pie

❁ ❁ ❁

I serve this unusual pie every September when Concord grapes are abundant. John's mom taught me her technique for slipping the skins off the grapes, which she called "spitting out the seeds" — that is exactly what it is like. While this may seem like a lot of work, it's well worth the effort. The season is short, so plan on making at least one pie for the freezer at the same time.

4½ cups Concord (blue) grapes
1 scant cup sugar
2 tablespoons lemon juice
1 teaspoon grated lemon zest
1 tablespoon grated orange zest
1 tablespoon quick-cooking tapioca
1 9-inch piecrust, unbaked
Cinnamon Crumb Topping (page 241)

1. Preheat oven to 425°F. Slip the skins from the grapes by pinching each one; set aside. Simmer the grape pulp for 15 minutes to loosen seeds. Remove the seeds by forcing the pulp through a sieve or food mill.

2. Combine the pulp, skins, sugar, lemon juice, lemon and orange zest, and tapioca. Let stand for about 20 minutes to thicken. Pour into the piecrust and top with Cinnamon Crumb Topping.

3. Bake for 12 minutes; reduce the oven temperature to 350°F and bake for 25 minutes longer.

Yield: 8 servings

Grape Conserve

❁ ❁ ❁

Though this fruit spread is wonderful slathered on toast, it's equally at home with chicken breasts or pork chops.

4 pounds Concord grapes
1 orange
4 cups sugar
⅓ teaspoon salt
1 cup chopped walnuts

1. Slip the skins from the grapes by pinching each one; set aside. Simmer the grape pulp for 15 minutes to loosen seeds. Remove the seeds by forcing the pulp through a sieve or food mill.

2. Remove seeds from the orange and chop, unpeeled.

3. Combine the grape pulp, sugar, salt, and orange. Stirring frequently, heat the mixture until it begins to thicken. Add the grape skins and cook 10 to 15 minutes longer until desired consistency is reached. Add the walnuts.

4. Pour the conserve into sterilized jars, seal, and process in a boiling-water bath for 5 minutes (page 384).

Yield: About eight 8-ounce jars

....

SIMPLY WONDERFUL

....

There's nothing simpler, nor better for dessert, than a bowl of halved green grapes moistened with sour cream and sprinkled with brown sugar. Good, indeed.

....

WINTER

Modern markets bring fresh excitement to the winter store of fruits. They supplement the preserves and jellies with an abundance of citrus choices and an increasing variety of tropical fruits. Now is the time to enjoy clementines and mangoes, pineapples and kiwis. Mango salsa livens a fish dinner, and baked bananas with maple syrup and rum warms a chilly night.

Lemon Mint Dressing for Fruit

❈ ❈ ❈

A fruit salad is festive on a buffet table at any time of the year. Choose fruits that are in season and nicely ripened. They should be carefully washed, peeled, and sliced, then placed in a handsome bowl.

- ½ cup sugar
- 1½ cups vegetable oil
  juice of 5 large lemons (about 1 cup)
- 1½ teaspoons salt
- 1 8-inch sprig of fresh mint leaves

1. Place the sugar, oil, lemon juice, salt, and mint in a blender. Blend until smooth.

2. Pour into a glass container, cover, and refrigerate at least 12 hours.

Yield: 3 cups

FRUIT BOWLS FOR SERVING

....

Halved pineapples and melons may be hollowed and filled with fruit salad. A watermelon half makes a pretty container for fruit salad for a crowd; cut the edge in decorative scallops or points. Sherbet or sorbet looks lovely in scooped-out orange or lemon shells, garnished with mint.

Zesty Grapefruit Salad

❈ ❈ ❈

Grapefruit isn't just for breakfast, and it sure can brighten up a winter dinner when added, along with almost any other fruit, to a fresh green salad and a favorite vinaigrette. It almost sparkles with flavor.

- 2 large grapefruit
- 1 cup strawberry slices or ½ cup blueberries, or both
- ⅓ cup olive oil

- 2 tablespoons balsamic vinegar
- 1 tablespoon chopped fresh chives
- 8 cups mesclun
- ½ cup blue cheese, crumbled

1. Cut the grapefruit in half and remove the sections, being careful to save any juice. Gently toss the berries with the grapefruit, then strain all juice into a separate small bowl.

2. To the juice, add the oil, vinegar, and chives. Beat well with a wire whisk.

3. Lightly toss the greens with some dressing and arrange on individual salad plates.

4. Arrange fruit on greens and dress with remaining dressing. Sprinkle with the blue cheese.

Yield: 4–5 servings

BROILED GRAPEFRUIT

....

For a perfect light dessert, special breakfast, or satisfying snack, halve grapefruits, cut between segments, and sprinkle with a little brown sugar, honey, or maple syrup. Set on a baking pan and broil until hot. For extra flavor, add a little rum before broiling.

Candied Orange Peel

❈ ❈ ❈

This is a simplified but superb candied orange peel. The only way you can improve it is to coat it with chocolate.

2   large navel oranges
½   cup sugar
¼   cup water
1   tablespoon light corn syrup
    extra sugar for rolling
    (optional)

1. Peel the oranges in long lengthwise strips. Simmer the orange peel in enough water to cover until it is tender. Save the pulp for another use.

2. Drain off the water and let the peel cool. Scrape away the white part. Cut the peel into strips about ¼ inch wide.

3. Put into a saucepan with the sugar, water, and corn syrup. Cook over low heat until the syrup is clear (230°F on a candy thermometer). Drain in a colander over a bowl. Save the syrup to add to cakes, cookies, or iced tea.

4. When cool, roll the strips in sugar if you're not planning to coat them with chocolate.

VARIATION: Chocolate-Coated Candied Orange Peel: Use candied orange peel (above) not rolled in extra sugar. Dip the entire piece of fruit into melted chocolate. Put on wax paper to set.

CITRUS POMANDER BALLS

....

For a delightful country room freshener, poke whole cloves into small oranges or lemons in pretty patterns or lines. Poking holes for the cloves with a skewer or needle makes your work go faster. Hang with ribbon or heap in a bowl. Kumquat pomanders are adorable and aromatic as Christmas tree ornaments.

....

Pineapple Upside-Down Cake

❈ ❈ ❈

Rich and old-fashioned, an upside-down cake is really fun to serve as well as eat. Be creative with the kind of fruit used, and for a real old-time feeling, bake it in an iron skillet.

¾   cup (1½ sticks) butter
    (¼ cup softened)
1   cup brown sugar, firmly packed
1   cup chopped nuts
    (I use pecans)
6–8   maraschino cherries, cut in half
1   can (8 ounces) sliced pineapple, drained
¾   cup granulated sugar
1   egg
½   cup milk
1   teaspoon vanilla extract
1½   cups all-purpose flour
1½   teaspoons baking powder
¼   teaspoon salt

1. Preheat oven to 350°F. Melt ½ cup of the butter in the bottom of a skillet or cake pan until bubbly but not browned. Remove from heat and stir in the brown sugar and nuts, spreading evenly. Arrange the cherries in a decorative pattern, then top with the pineapple slices.

2. Cream together the sugar, the softened butter, and the egg. Add the milk and vanilla. In a separate bowl, sift together the flour, baking powder, and salt. Combine the flour mixture with the sugar mixture, until well blended.

3. Pour batter over pineapple and bake until a toothpick inserted in the center of the cake comes out clean, about 35 minutes. Carefully turn the cooled cake upside down onto a serving plate. Serve with sweetened whipped cream.

Yield: 8 servings

Baked Bananas
in Maple Rum Sauce

❈ ❈ ❈

It's good to have a few dessert dishes like this in your repertoire — elegant, but ever so easy to make. If the bananas are large, three should be enough here. They can be served plain, but they are best served next to pound cake and topped with ice cream.

4   small to medium-sized
    bananas, peeled, halved
    lengthwise and then
    crosswise
2   tablespoons unsalted
    butter
⅓   cup pure maple syrup
¼   cup dark rum
1   tablespoon lemon juice
4   slices pound cake
    vanilla ice cream

1. Preheat oven to 375°F. Butter a large enameled skillet or baking dish and lay the bananas in it, flat side down. Set aside.

2. Melt the butter in a saucepan, then add the syrup. Bring to a boil, boil for 1 minute, then add the rum and lemon juice. As soon as the syrup returns to a boil, remove from the heat and pour over the bananas. Place in the oven and bake for 15 minutes, basting once or twice. While the bananas

bake, put a piece of pound cake on each dessert plate.

3. After 15 minutes, remove the bananas from the oven. Using a slotted spatula, transfer several banana slices next to each piece of pound cake. Put the skillet on the burner — or transfer the liquid to a saucepan if you have used a casserole — and quickly reduce the liquid to a thick syrup, over high heat. Spoon ice cream over the bananas and pound cake, then top each with plenty of hot sauce.

Yield: 4 servings

Kiwi Hazelnut
Meringue Cake

❈ ❈ ❈

A good choice for a party or shower, these airy layers of meringue filled with kiwifruit and cream topping make a dream of a dessert.

1   cup hazelnuts
3   egg whites
¾   cup granulated sugar

Filling

4–5 kiwifruit, peeled and
    thinly sliced
1   cup whipped topping
1   tablespoon confectioners'
    sugar
1   tablespoon orange liqueur

1. Preheat oven to 300°F. Toast the hazelnuts under the broiler or in a toaster oven for 3 to 4 minutes. Rub with a clean cloth to remove the skins. Discard the skins. Chop the nuts in a blender or food processor until very fine but not powdered. Set aside.

2. In a large bowl, beat the egg whites until stiff. Add half of the granulated sugar and beat until smooth. Carefully fold in the remaining sugar and reserved hazelnuts.

3. Cover a baking sheet with parchment paper or lightly greased aluminum foil and make three solid circles of meringue mixture, each about 5 inches in diameter. (One circle may have to be cooked on another sheet.)

4. Bake for 1 hour. Reduce the heat to 225°F and continue baking for 2 hours longer. Cook until dry and crisp. Layers may be stored in an airtight container.

5. To make the filling, cut kiwifruit in half. Blend together the whipped topping and confectioners' sugar. Gently fold in the liqueur.

6. Spread one-third of the whipped topping mixture on top of one circle of meringue and add a few slices of kiwifruit. Repeat the process two times, using all of the mixture and kiwifruit.

Yield: 8 servings

SWEETS AND TREATS

My family appreciates my enormous sweet tooth: We enjoy *something, neither fancy nor big, to provide a satisfying finale to the evening. Seasonal sweets are among the most special, because they celebrate a particular moment in time — when the peaches are ripe and just right for warm cobbler, or the maple syrup is fresh and perfect for a creamy maple pudding. But wonderful "anytime" sweet treats, like Chewy Chocolate Chip or Butterscotch Cookies or Oatmeal Crisps that we almost always have on hand, satisfy that craving as well. Indulging in these cookie-jar treats makes us feel a bit naughty. In truth, very little harm is done.*

Contributors to this chapter are Liz Anton and Beth Dooley, Joanne Barrett, Jane Cooper, Ken Haedrich, Gwen Steege, Edith Stovel and Pamela Wakefield, Maggie Stuckey, and Olwen Woodier.

CAKES
....
PIES & TARTS
....
BETTYS & BUCKLES
....
COOKIES
....
BAR COOKIES
....
CANDY
....
CHOCOLATE
....
CUSTARD & PUDDING

Sally's Best Chocolate Cake

⬖ ⬖ ⬖

My friend Sally Patterson has been making this cake, by request, for her daughter's birthday parties for years. You'll love it, too.

2 cups all-purpose flour
2 teaspoons baking powder
2 teaspoons baking soda
1 teaspoon salt
2 cups water
2 cups sugar
4 ounces unsweetened chocolate
6 tablespoons butter, cut into pieces
2 eggs, lightly beaten

1. Preheat oven to 350°F. Grease and flour two 9-inch round cake pans; line the bottoms with wax paper. Sift together the flour, baking powder, soda, and salt.

2. In a saucepan, combine the water and sugar. Bring to a boil over high heat; stir until sugar dissolves. Pour into a large bowl. Add the chocolate and butter and let sit until melted, stirring occasionally.

3. Gradually beat eggs into chocolate mixture with an electric mixer at medium speed. Add the dry ingredients all at once and beat until smooth.

The batter will be fairly thin. Divide the batter between the prepared pans and bake about 25 minutes, until a tester inserted into the centers comes out clean. Cool cakes in pans for 25 minutes, then turn out onto racks and cool completely.

Chocolate Frosting

Sinfully delicious, this is *the* frosting for Sally's cake.

1¼ cups heavy cream
1½ cups sugar
6 ounces unsweetened chocolate
¾ cup (1½ sticks) butter
2 teaspoons vanilla extract
⅛ teaspoon salt
ice

1. In a medium saucepan, bring the cream and sugar to a boil. Reduce heat to low; simmer, stirring occasionally, until slightly reduced, 5 to 6 minutes.

2. Pour the cream mixture into a medium bowl. Add the chocolate, butter, vanilla, and salt. Let the mixture stand, stirring it occasionally, until chocolate and butter are fully melted.

3. Fill a large bowl halfway with ice and water. Set the bowl with the chocolate mixture in the ice water and beat frosting at medium speed

until thick and shiny, about 5 minutes. Use immediately.

Cup Custard

⬖ ⬖ ⬖

Cup custard is my family's favorite pudding. This one is so good that, if there is any left over, we eat it for breakfast.

1 can (12 ounces) evaporated milk
4 eggs
½ cup sugar
1 teaspoon vanilla extract
½ teaspoon salt
⅛ teaspoon ground nutmeg

1. Preheat oven to 350°F; grease eight 6-ounce custard cups. Pour the milk into a 2-cup measuring cup, then finish filling it with water. Pour into a bowl and add 1 more cup water to make 3 cups liquid.

2. Beat the eggs, sugar, vanilla, salt, and nutmeg into the liquid. Fill the custard cups two-thirds full. Line a 9- by 13-inch baking pan with brown paper.

3. Put cups into the pan and fill the pan halfway with hot water. Sprinkle more nutmeg on top of each cup. Bake for 40 minutes, or until a knife comes out clean. Serve at room temperature.

Yield: 8 servings

CAKES

As a little girl, I'd visit my grandmother in Bells, Texas. She always seemed to have a cake in the oven, one cooling, or one freshly iced. In these busy days, cakes are more for special occasions, which is all the more reason to bake them from scratch for the purest taste and best texture.

Basic Yellow Cake

❈ ❈ ❈

Yellow cake is all-purpose, but it needn't be ordinary. When it's homemade, it is rich and moist; you and your family will certainly be able to tell the difference. This one is simple and tastes wonderful plain, but I like to dress it up with rich Chocolate Icing (page 231).

2 cups sugar
½ cup (1 stick) butter, softened
3 eggs
⅓ cup sour cream
1 teaspoon vanilla extract
2½ cups all-purpose flour
2 teaspoons baking powder
pinch of salt
1 cup milk

1. Preheat oven to 350°F; grease and flour a 9- by 13-inch or Bundt pan. In a large bowl, cream together the sugar and butter. Add the eggs and beat until light yellow. Add the sour cream and vanilla; mix well.

2. In a separate bowl, sift together the flour, baking powder, and salt. Add the flour mixture to the egg mixture, alternating with milk, until thoroughly combined.

3. Pour the batter into the prepared pan. Bake for 30 minutes (if you have used a 9- by 13-inch pan) to 50 minutes (if you have used a Bundt pan), or until a toothpick inserted in the cake comes out clean. Cool completely before icing.

Yield: 12 servings

CAKE-BAKING TIPS

Allow milk, butter, and eggs to reach room temperature before starting.

- Preheat! Be sure that your oven is at the correct temperature when your batter is ready. Follow instructions for mixing times — overbeating can toughen cakes.
- Vegetable shortening is better than butter for greasing your pans. If the cake is delicate, it's worth taking the time to line pans with wax paper or parchment, too.
- If you're making a chocolate cake, dust the pan with cocoa powder instead of flour.

- Unless otherwise specified, bake cakes on the middle rack of the oven for the most even rising.
- To give a nice finish to butter frostings, dip the knife or icing spatula in boiling water and smooth the icing surface.
- Cake flour is a finely milled flour made from soft wheat. It gives cakes a light, delicate texture. You can substitute ⅞ cup all-purpose flour sifted with 2 tablespoons cornstarch, for a similar texture. If you like an old-fashioned, nubby crumb, you'll find that all-purpose flour works beautifully in these recipes.

"Whomped-Up" Cake

❈ ❈ ❈

Because this spice cake goes together easily, in the pan, it's fun to make with kids. Thanks to my friend Nicki Gillis for sharing the recipe.

½ cup (1 stick) butter
2 cups all-purpose flour
1 cup granulated sugar
1 teaspoon baking soda
½ teaspoon baking powder
½ teaspoon ground cinnamon
½ teaspoon ground cloves
½ teaspoon ground nutmeg
½ teaspoon salt
2 cups applesauce
½ cup raisins
½ cup brown sugar, firmly packed

1. Preheat oven to 350°F. Melt the butter in a 9- by 13-inch pan in the oven.

2. Sift together the flour, sugar, soda, baking powder, cinnamon, cloves, nutmeg, and salt. Stir the flour mixture into the pan. Add the applesauce and raisins.

3. Stir the batter until all ingredients are well combined (the kids call this "whomping it up"). Sprinkle the top with the brown sugar. Bake for 30 minutes, or until a toothpick inserted in the center comes out clean.

Yield: 12 servings

CAKE MIX MAGIC

When you are busy and want the convenience of a boxed cake, you can still add a personal touch. Try using applesauce or pudding to replace part of the liquid; a cup of pumpkin purée in a packaged spice mix makes a lovely autumn cake. You can also add grated chocolate, ground nuts, mini chocolate chips, or a teaspoon of flavored extract, such as orange, peppermint, almond, or brandy.

Chocolate Icing

❈ ❈ ❈

When I was a child, my mom would spread this icing between two graham crackers to make me a "chocolate sandwich." Of course, it's great on cake too!

2 squares unsweetened chocolate
½ cup (1 stick) butter
3 tablespoons milk
2 cups confectioners' sugar
⅛ teaspoon salt
1 teaspoon vanilla extract

1. In a saucepan, combine the chocolate, butter, and milk. Cook, stirring, until the chocolate and butter are melted.

2. Remove from the heat and whisk in the sugar, salt, and vanilla.

3. Whisk until the icing is of spreading consistency; add more sugar, a tablespoon at a time, if it is too thin, or a few drops of milk if it's too thick.

Yield: 1¼ cups (enough for 12 cupcakes or one 9- by 13-inch cake)

Coconut-Pecan Icing

❈ ❈ ❈

When my Georgia relatives send me a package of pecans, I make a cake with this luscious praline-like topping.

1 cup evaporated milk
1 cup sugar
3 egg yolks
½ cup (1 stick) butter
1 teaspoon vanilla extract
1⅓ cups coconut
1 cup chopped pecans

1. In a saucepan, combine the milk, sugar, egg yolks, butter, and vanilla. Cook over medium heat, stirring constantly, until the mixture begins to thicken, about 12 minutes.

2. Add the coconut and pecans. Beat by hand until icing is cool and thick enough to spread.

Yield: 2⅔ cups

Mountainous Birthday Cake

❈ ❈ ❈

Edith Stovel (DeeDee to me) has been a friend and colleague for years. Crowned with glossy boiled icing, this was the birthday cake of her childhood. She says, "As one who usually loves a variety of textures, colors, and flavors, I can't explain my love of this sweet white cake. It's delicious and worthy of a special event! Decorate it with fresh edible flowers or a bunch of tall, slender, brightly colored tapers."

½   cup vegetable shortening
1½ cups sugar
4   egg yolks, well beaten (reserve egg whites for icing)
1   teaspoon vanilla extract
3   cups sifted cake flour
4   teaspoons baking powder
½   teaspoon salt
1¼ cups skim milk

1. Preheat oven to 375°F. Coat two 9-inch round cake pans with vegetable cooking spray. In a large bowl, beat the shortening and sugar until light and fluffy. Add the egg yolks and vanilla; continue beating until well mixed.

2. In a medium-sized bowl, sift together the flour, baking powder, and salt. Add the flour mixture to the egg mixture, alternating with the milk; stir between each addition. Stir until the batter is smooth.

3. Pour the batter into the prepared pans and bake for 30 to 35 minutes or until the cake is lightly golden, pulls away from the edges of the pans, and springs back in the center when lightly touched.

4. Cool in the pans on cooling racks for 10 minutes. Remove from the pans and cool completely.

Boiled Icing

This is a sweet, swirly icing that memories are made of. By the second day, if any cake is left, this icing develops a crunchy outer layer that shatters when cut.

2   cups sugar
¾   cup water
1   tablespoon light corn syrup
5   egg whites, gently warmed
2   tablespoons confectioners' sugar
1   teaspoon vanilla extract

1. In a large uncovered saucepan, boil the sugar, water, and corn syrup without stirring over medium heat. Cook until the syrup spins a thread (see note), beginning at 230°F, and then remove from heat.

2. While the syrup is cooking, beat the egg whites with an electric mixer until stiff peaks form; beat in the confectioners' sugar.

3. Slowly pour the boiling syrup over the egg whites, beating constantly. Add the vanilla. When the beaters leave tracks in the icing, it is stiff enough to spread.

4. Turn one layer of cake upside down onto a large plate. Cover with about one-third of the icing (the layer of icing should be ½ inch or more thick). Center the other cake on the iced layer; spread the top with a thick layer of icing. Ice the sides.

Yield: 10–12 servings

Note: **Egg Safety**: If you are concerned about using uncooked eggs, use the 7-minute method. Place all ingredients except vanilla in the top of a double boiler, over 1 inch of simmering water on medium heat. Beat constantly with an electric mixer for about 7 minutes, until the beaters leave a track. Add vanilla.

Sugar Syrup Threads: Stir the syrup with a wooden spoon; hold the spoon over the pan. If a coarse thread hangs down from the spoon, the syrup is at the crucial thread-spinning stage. Be careful not to burn the syrup.

Blueberry Sour Cream Cake

❂ ❂ ❂

Sue Pfeiffer (Sudie) was my best friend in Chatham, New Jersey, where I went to junior and senior high school. We shared a lot of laughter and tears over the years. I haven't seen her in 30 years, but we keep in touch at Christmas. I got this recipe from Sue's mother when I was 15, and I make it every July, when local blueberries are abundant.

    3   cups all-purpose flour
    ¾   teaspoon salt
    ½   teaspoon baking powder
    1½ cups sugar
    ¾   cup butter
    2   pints blueberries
    2   teaspoons ground cinnamon
    2   eggs
    1½ cups sour cream

1. Preheat oven to 400°F. Combine the flour, salt, baking powder, and ¼ cup of the sugar; mix well. Add the butter and blend in a food processor until well mixed and mealy.

2. Press the mixture firmly into a 9- by 13-inch pan, making sure it goes halfway up the sides. Spread the blueberries evenly over the crust.

3. Mix the remaining sugar and the cinnamon together; sprinkle over the blueberries.

4. Bake for 15 minutes.

5. While baking, mix together the eggs and sour cream, blending thoroughly.

6. Remove the cake from the oven. Pour the sour cream and egg mixture evenly over the top.

7. Reduce the oven temperature to 350°F; bake for 30 minutes longer, or until the cake is nicely browned on top. Cool and slice.

Yield: 12 servings

Cream-Cheese Chocolate-Chip Tube Cake

❂ ❂ ❂

Carole Stichweh, my pal for 40 years, is famous for her desserts, and this is one of her best. It is dense, moist, and delicious, even without icing.

    1   cup (2 sticks) butter, softened
    1   package (8 ounces) cream cheese, softened
    1½ cups sugar
    4   eggs
    2¼ cups unsifted all-purpose flour
    2   teaspoons baking powder
    ¼   teaspoon salt
    2   teaspoons vanilla extract
    12 ounces (2 cups) semi-sweet chocolate chips

1. Preheat oven to 300°F; grease a 10-inch tube pan. In a large mixing bowl, cream the butter and cheese. Gradually beat in the sugar until light and fluffy.

2. Add the eggs, one at a time, beating well after each addition.

3. In a separate bowl, mix together the flour, baking powder, and salt. Stir the flour mixture into the butter mixture. Stir in the vanilla and chocolate chips.

4. Pour the batter into the pan. Bake for 1 hour 10 minutes, or until the cake springs back when lightly touched with a finger. Cool the cake in the pan for 10 minutes, then turn onto a rack to cool.

Yield: 10–12 servings

- -

EASY LAYER-CAKE FILLINGS

- -

You can easily change the character of a cake with fillings that complement it or with icing flavors. Figure on about ⅓ to ½ cup of filling for a 9-inch cake. Try lemon or lime curd, jam, jelly, or marmalade. Or add chopped nuts, small candies, or glacéed fruits to your frosting. And don't forget whipped cream and fruit for a cake that will be eaten soon.

- -

Johnny Appleseed Cake

❁ ❁ ❁

We moved to Williamstown in the middle of daughter Jessica's second-grade year, and she had a pretty tough time getting used to her new school. She eventually overcame her sadness about the move, and the rest is history. Sometime during that year, she brought this recipe home from school thinking it was very special, and so it was.

1 cup chopped peeled tart apples, such as Granny Smith (about 2 apples)
¾ cup sugar
½ cup all-purpose flour
1 teaspoon baking powder
½ cup chopped nuts
1 egg, lightly beaten
1 tablespoon lemon juice
1 teaspoon vanilla extract
pinch of salt
ground cinnamon

1. Preheat oven to 350°F; butter an 8-inch pie pan. In a large bowl, combine the apples, sugar, flour, nuts, egg, lemon juice, vanilla, baking powder, and salt. Stir in cinnamon to taste. The batter will be very thick.

2. Spread the batter into the pie pan.

3. Bake for 25 minutes. Serve with whipped cream or ice cream.

Yield: 6–8 servings

Queen Elizabeth's Own Cake

❁ ❁ ❁

Years ago, Esther Greene's cake was one of the traditional bake sale items at our annual church fund-raiser. Her source was a secret, but she swore that it was authentically Queen Elizabeth's! Moist and delicious, it's fit for king and queen alike.

Cake

1 cup boiling water
1 cup chopped dates
1 level teaspoon baking soda
1 cup sugar
4 tablespoons butter, softened
1 egg, beaten
1 teaspoon vanilla extract
1½ cups sifted all-purpose flour
1 teaspoon baking powder
½ teaspoon salt
½ cup coconut or chopped pecans

1. Preheat oven to 350°F; grease a 9-inch square cake pan. In a large bowl, pour the water over the dates. Add the soda and let stand while the remaining ingredients are prepared.

2. Cream together the sugar and butter. Add the egg and vanilla; stir in the coconut, flour, baking powder, and salt. Pour into the date mixture and blend well.

3. Pour the batter into the cake pan. Bake for 35 minutes, or until a toothpick inserted in the center comes out clean. Cool the cake before icing.

Icing

5 tablespoons light brown sugar
5 tablespoons cream
2 tablespoons butter
½ cup coconut or chopped pecans

1. Combine all of the ingredients. Bring to a boil and cook, stirring, for 3 minutes. While the icing is still warm, spread it on the cooled cake. Sprinkle with coconut.

Yield: 9 servings

ANGEL FOOD CAKE

Angel food is a light, airy cake made with egg whites but no yolks. I find that angel food made from mix is very good, and so is store-bought. We enjoy it with fresh fruit and whipped cream or with coffee ice cream and Susan's Fudge Sauce (page 352).

Jelly-Roll Cake

❈ ❈ ❈

Our neighbors, Roger and Sally Holmes, had six kids, and their house was always filled with wonderful baking smells. Lori, the youngest, was very proud of her Jelly-Roll Cake, and she taught me the fine art of rolling it when she was still quite young. The trick is to use plenty of confectioners' sugar and a damp towel when you roll it up.

3 large eggs, separated
1 pinch cream of tartar
⅔ cup granulated sugar
¾ cup blanched powdered almonds
¾ cup sifted cake flour
⅛ cup orange juice, strained grated zest of 1 orange
¼ teaspoon almond extract
1½ tablespoons melted butter
¾ cup confectioners' sugar
¾ cup seedless raspberry or strawberry jam

1. Preheat oven to 375°F. Butter a 10- by 15- by 1-inch jelly-roll pan, then line it with wax paper and butter and flour the wax paper.

2. Beat the egg whites, cream of tartar, and 1 tablespoon of the granulated sugar until soft peaks form. Set aside.

3. In a separate bowl, beat the egg yolks and the remaining sugar. Add the almonds, flour, orange juice, zest, and almond extract; blend well. Fold in the egg white mixture with a rubber spatula. Fold in the butter.

4. Spread the batter in the prepared pan and bake on the middle rack of the oven for 10 minutes. The cake will feel spongy and pull away from the edges of the pan, but it will have only a faint color.

5. Sprinkle the top of the cake with confectioners' sugar. Cover it with wax paper, then with a slightly damp towel. Turn it upside down and leave for 20 minutes until cool. Remove from the pan while it is upside down; gently remove the wax paper and trim off the brown edges.

6. Spread the cake with the jam, then roll it up, starting from a long side, removing the sugared wax paper and towel as you go. Place on a serving platter and dust with additional confectioners' sugar. Slice.

Yield: 6–8 servings

STORING CAKES

....

Most cakes will last for up to 3 days if they are wrapped in plastic or kept in a cake tin or plastic cake holder. To keep a cut cake moist, put a slice of apple in your cake tin. If the cake contains custard or whipped cream, it must be refrigerated. If it has a soft icing, poke toothpicks into the frosting when covering, to keep the wrap from sticking.

You can freeze unfrosted cakes for up to 2 months. Make sure the cake has thoroughly cooled, then wrap it well in heavy foil and then plastic. Remove the plastic and open the foil when thawing. It is best to frost a cake after it comes out of the freezer, though some buttercream frostings freeze well. Cakes that are decorated with candies, colored icings, or gels should not be frozen, as the decorations tend to run when thawing.

Gingerbread

❈ ❈ ❈

Gingerbread has been a favorite since the Middle Ages. It is a moist, informal cake with a wonderful spice flavor. Dress it up with applesauce or Orange Honey Butter (page 285).

1 cup molasses
½ cup buttermilk
1 egg, slightly beaten
2 cups all-purpose flour
½ teaspoon salt
½ cup sugar
1 teaspoon ground allspice
1 teaspoon ground cinnamon
1 teaspoon ground ginger
1 teaspoon baking soda
½ cup (1 stick) butter, melted
1 cup heavy cream, whipped (optional)

1. Preheat oven to 350°F; grease a 9-inch square cake pan. In a small bowl, combine the molasses, buttermilk, and egg; stir to blend.

2. Sift the flour, salt, sugar, allspice, cinnamon, ginger, and soda into a large bowl. Add the molasses mixture and mix well. Add the butter; stir until just blended.

3. Pour the batter into the pan. Bake for 25 to 35 minutes, or until a tester inserted in the center comes out clean. Cool in the pan on a wire rack. Serve with whipped cream, if desired.

Yield: 6–8 servings

Michelle's Cheesecake

❈ ❈ ❈

Michelle Willmott is a busy mom, to say the least, but she is always such a gracious hostess, making everyone feel right at home. This is one of her favorite desserts — quick, easy, foolproof. One time she accidentally left it in the oven for twice as long, and I think it was just about twice as good!

3 packages (8 ounces each) cream cheese, softened
¾ cup sugar
3 eggs
1 teaspoon vanilla extract
1 9-inch graham cracker piecrust

1. Preheat oven to 450°F. Blend together cream cheese, sugar, eggs, and vanilla. Press the mixture into the piecrust.

2. Bake for 10 minutes. Reduce the heat to 350°F and bake for 35 minutes longer, or until the cheesecake is firm.

Yield: 8 servings

Pumpkin Orange Cheesecake

❈ ❈ ❈

You may have seen pumpkin cheesecake, but have you ever seen the pumpkin in the crust? Along with almonds, carrots, and orange rind, grated pumpkin makes a unique orange-colored shell for the creamy cheese mixture.

¾ cup slivered almonds
¾ cup grated carrot
5 eggs
1¼ cups sugar
3 cups grated pumpkin
6 tablespoons unbleached all-purpose flour
1 teaspoon grated orange zest
½ teaspoon minced ginger root
1 package (8 ounces) cream cheese, softened
1 cup sour cream
½ teaspoon salt

CHEESECAKE TIP

Cheesecake often cracks as it bakes. To help prevent this, you can do two things. Put a shallow pan of boiling water in the oven below the cheesecake to create an evenly moist environment, and, at the end of the baking time, turn off the oven and leave the cake in the oven with the door ajar, to let it cool very slowly. If the cake cracks anyway, don't worry! It will taste delicious all the same.

1. Preheat oven to 350°F and grease a 9-inch springform pan.

2. Set aside a teaspoon or two of almonds or carrot for the top of the cheesecake. Beat 3 of the eggs with ¾ cup of the sugar. Fold in the pumpkin, carrot, flour, orange zest, ginger root, and almonds. With a fork, spread this mixture in the prepared pan. Bake on a baking sheet for 40 minutes. The center will have a custardlike consistency.

3. In a food processor or mixing bowl, beat the cream cheese until smooth. Add the remaining ½ cup sugar, the remaining 2 eggs, the sour cream, and the salt.

4. Pour the cream cheese mixture into the baked pumpkin shell. Sprinkle the reserved almonds or carrots on top.

5. Bake for 45 minutes or until firm. Chill.

Yield: 8 servings

Citrus-Herb Cheesecake

❁ ❁ ❁

Lemon balm has a delightfully strong citrus flavor and is easy to grow, and calendula is a beautiful, edible marigold. This is one of my favorite herb-flavored desserts, and I warn you . . . it will disappear like magic!

½ cup (1 stick) plus 2 tablespoons butter
½ cup plus 2 tablespoons sugar
6 egg yolks
1½ packages (8 ounces each) cream cheese, softened
2 teaspoons chopped dried lemon balm, or
 4 teaspoons fresh
2 teaspoons grated lemon zest, fresh or dried
2 teaspoons grated orange zest, fresh or dried
2 teaspoons finely ground calendula petals (optional)
1 cup ground almonds
6 egg whites

1. Preheat oven to 325°F; grease a 10-inch tube pan.

2. In a medium-sized bowl, cream together the butter, sugar, egg yolks, and cream cheese. Add the lemon balm, lemon and orange zest, calendula petals, if desired, and almonds.

3. In a large mixing bowl, beat the egg whites until stiff. Fold the egg whites into the cream-cheese mixture.

4. Pour the mixture into the prepared pan. Bake for 55 minutes. Cool 10 minutes, then invert cake onto a serving plate.

Yield: 10–12 servings

ABOUT SPRINGFORM PANS

Springform pans have a circular bottom disk and straight metal sides that cinch around the bottom with a clip. They are ideal for making cheesecakes and other cakes that are fragile or can't be turned upside down. To remove a cake from a springform pan, run a knife carefully around the inside edges of the pan, unfasten the spring clip and lift off the sides. Do not attempt to remove the cake by pressing on the bottom disk. Leave the cake or tart right on the bottom disk; or, if you wish to remove it, slide a spatula underneath to loosen it, and gently slide the cake to a serving plate.

PIES & TARTS

Of all the reasons for taking to a life of crime, the only one that has ever been persuasive to me was the Knave of Heart's excuse. Those tarts that the Queen of Hearts made were just toooo tempting. A lovely sweet or savory filling encased in a flaky crust is certainly one of the nicest things that can come out of the oven.

Bulk Piecrust

⬡ ⬡ ⬡

When I make pies, I never make just one. Mother taught me that it's easier to make lots of pies and clean up once than to mess up the kitchen each time you want a pie. This is her recipe for a foolproof crust that rolls out easily and keeps well in the freezer.

> 5 *cups all-purpose flour*
> 2 *teaspoons salt*
> 2 *cups cold butter-flavored vegetable shortening*
> 1 *egg*
> ¾–1 *cup ice water*

1. Place the flour, salt, and shortening in the bowl of an electric mixer. Slowly mix until the batter is the consistency of coarse meal. In a 1-cup measuring cup, lightly beat the egg. Add enough ice water to make 1 cup and slowly add this mixture to the flour mixture. Blend a few seconds more.

2. Turn the dough out onto a floured surface and work with your hands until it just forms a ball. Wrap it in wax paper and place in the refrigerator for 20 to 30 minutes, so that it becomes firm.

3. Pinch off a ball of dough about the size of a baseball to make one 9-inch piecrust. Line the pan with crust and bake, or fill with fruit and then bake. The dough may be divided into individual balls, placed in plastic bags, sealed, and frozen for several months.

Yield: five 9-inch single crusts

Harvest Apple Pie

⬡ ⬡ ⬡

Apple pie, with its sweetly spiced fruit in a tender crust, is close to motherhood in the list of the best things in the world. Serve it with coffee, vanilla ice cream, a sliver of Cheddar, or all by its beloved self.

> *pastry for two 9- or 10-inch piecrusts (this page)*
> ¼ *cup melted apricot jam or marmalade*
> 5 *large apples (Ida Red, Jonathan, or Rome Beauty)*
> 2 *tablespoons lemon juice*
> ½ *cup brown sugar, firmly packed*
> 2 *tablespoons all-purpose flour*
> ½ *teaspoon ground cinnamon*

BASIC FRUIT PIE FILLING

....

A good rule of thumb for a 9-inch two-crust or lattice-top fruit pie is to use 5 cups fruit or berries, peeled and sliced; ¾ to 1 cup sugar; 3 to 4 tablespoons cornstarch or quick-cooking tapioca; 1 tablespoon lemon juice; 2 tablespoons butter, cut into small pieces. This formula may need small adjustments. If your fruit is very juicy, increase the thickener; if it is very tart, add more sugar. Add a pinch of salt or spices, if you like. Try using a combination of fruits for unique pies.

¼ teaspoon ground nutmeg
1 tablespoon unsalted butter
1½ teaspoons milk
1 teaspoon granulated sugar

1. Preheat oven to 400°F. Grease a 9- or 10-inch pie pan.

2. Roll out half of the pastry and fit it into the pie pan. Brush with the jam and refrigerate for 20 to 30 minutes or until ready to use.

3. Peel, core, and cut the apples into ¼-inch slices. Place in a bowl and toss with the lemon juice.

4. In a separate bowl, combine the brown sugar, flour, cinnamon, and nutmeg.

5. Layer half of the apple slices in the chilled crust and sprinkle with half of the sugar mixture. Repeat the layers until the ingredients are used up, ending with sugar mixture. Cut the butter into small pieces and scatter over the apples.

6. Roll out the top crust. Place over the filling and trim and flute the edges. Make three steam vents in the center.

7. Brush with milk and sprinkle with the granulated sugar.

8. Bake on the middle rack for 50 to 60 minutes. If the edges of the crust brown too quickly, cover with strips of foil. Cool at least 10 minutes before serving.

Yield: 8 servings

Maids of Honor

❈ ❈ ❈

These almond tarts were first baked at the court of Henry VIII and named for the queen's ladies-in-waiting. They are very sweet; you may want to serve them with a dollop of unsweetened whipped cream.

1 9-inch piecrust, unbaked
½ cup ground almonds
½ cup sugar
2 egg yolks
1 tablespoon grated lemon zest
1 tablespoon all-purpose flour
2 tablespoons light cream

1. Butter eight cups of a muffin pan. Sprinkle on flour; shake off excess. Roll out the piecrust and cut out circles about 1 inch wider than the muffin cups. Press the dough into the muffin cups, covering the bottoms and partway up the sides.

2. Preheat oven to 350°F. Beat together the almonds, sugar, egg yolks, zest, and flour. Slowly add the cream; beat until the mixture is smooth.

3. Add about 1 table-spoon of the filling to each cup (it should not reach the top). Bake for 15 to 20 minutes, until the filling is golden brown.

Yield: 8 tarts

A Lattice-Top Pie

To make a decorative lattice crust for your pie top, roll the crust into a circle about an inch larger than your pie pan. Cut it into ½-inch strips (a pastry wheel will give the strips a decorative edge). Arrange two dough strips to make a cross pattern over the pie. Place additional strips in each direction, folding every other strip back as an opposing strip is added. Continue until the pie is covered. Give the strips sheen by brushing them with a beaten egg before baking.

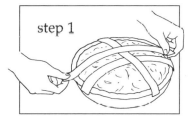

Arrange two dough strips in a cross pattern on top of the pie. Add additional strips in each direction.

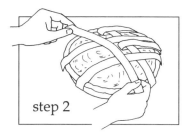

As you place the additional strips on the pie, fold every other strip back to make an alternate weave.

PERFECT PIECRUST

TEMPERATURE.
It is vital that the fat remain cold until the crust is put into the oven. This is why the liquid added in a piecrust recipe must be icy cold and why the dough is always chilled before it is rolled.

INGREDIENTS.
Flour. Unbleached white flour is best, but use all-purpose flour if you will be refrigerating the dough for any length of time; unbleached flour may turn grayish.
Fat. An ideal blend is 5 parts very cold butter to 1 part vegetable shortening. If you must substitute margarine, keep it extremely cold and work quickly.
Liquid. Use ice water (not just cold water).
Flavorings (all optional). Some cooks add salt to the crust or 1 tablespoon of sugar for fruit pies; grated citrus zest, cinnamon, or nutmeg may also be used.
Rolling. Use as little flour as possible to keep the pastry from sticking. Work the dough quickly and lightly; put pieces you aren't using back into the refrigerator immediately.

Mimi's Pecan Pie

❈ ❈ ❈

When I was growing up, we visited our Texas relatives every summer. I'll always remember the pecan trees, particularly in Auntie and Uncle Will's yard in Bonham. They were beautiful, with their huge climbing branches. Auntie (she answered only to Auntie and everyone called her that — just that) and Uncle Will always had burlap sacks of fresh pecans sitting on the porch next to the screen door. Grandpa would crack the shells while Mimi picked out the treasured nutmeats. Mimi's recipe for pecan pie is so easy, but so good. Jessica makes it each Thanksgiving, and she always calls Mimi for the recipe, just for the fun of it!

pastry for one 9-inch piecrust, baked
3 eggs, lightly beaten
1 cup sugar
2 tablespoons butter
1 cup corn syrup
1 teaspoon vanilla extract
1 tablespoon all-purpose flour
1 cup pecans

1. Preheat oven to 350°F. Fit the piecrust into a pie pan; make a decorative edge. In a large bowl, combine the eggs, sugar, butter, corn syrup, vanilla, flour, and pecans. Pour into the crust.

2. Bake for about 1 hour. Do not allow the top of the pie to become scorched. It's done when a toothpick inserted into the center comes out clean.

Yield: 8 servings

Grasshopper Pie

❈ ❈ ❈

This was one of Mom-Mom's favorite desserts to serve to company, because it was so pretty and delicious. I used to make it when John and I were newly married, but I somehow forgot about it for several years. Try it on your friends. They'll like it!

Crust

1½ cups crushed chocolate wafers
⅓ cup butter, melted

Filling

24 large marshmallows
½ cup milk
2 ounces green crème de menthe
1 ounce white crème de cacao
½ pint heavy cream

1. Combine the wafers and butter. Pat the mixture into an 8- or 9-inch pie pan. Chill.

2. In a medium saucepan, melt the marshmallows in the milk by warming very gently and stirring constantly. Remove from the heat.

3. Stir in the crème de menthe and crème de cacao. Allow to cool.

4. Beat the cream until soft peaks form; fold the whipped cream into the marshmallow mixture.

5. Pour the mixture into the crust and freeze. Serve frozen.

Yield: 8 servings

EASY CRUMBS

To make crumbs with no mess, place the cookies in a heavy resealable plastic bag and crush with a rolling pin.

Cookie Crumb Crust

❁ ❁ ❁

Y ou are probably familiar with graham cracker crumb crusts, which are used for many cheese pies and cheesecakes, but have you ever tried cookie crumbs?

1½ *cups crumbs of ginger-
     snaps, chocolate or vanilla
     wafers, chocolate sandwich
     cookies, zwieback, or
     shortbread*
4 *tablespoons butter, melted*
1 *tablespoon sugar or honey*

½ *cup chopped nuts and/or
   ½ teaspoon ground cinnamon (optional)*

1. Combine all ingredients. Using your fingers, press mixture firmly into a 9-inch pie pan or a springform pan. If you're using a filling that must be baked in the pie shell, your crust is ready to use now; simply chill the crust while you prepare the filling. If the filling doesn't require baking, put the crumb crust into a 350°F oven for 10 minutes. Cool thoroughly before adding the filling.

Yield: one 9-inch piecrust

Cinnamon Crumb Topping

❁ ❁ ❁

T his is great with Concord Grape Pie (page 224), as well as many other fruit pies.

6 *tablespoons sugar*
3 *tablespoons butter*
2 *tablespoons all-purpose
   flour*
3 *tablespoons quick-cooking
   oats*
2 *teaspoons ground cinnamon*
½ *teaspoon grated lemon
   zest (optional)*

1. Mix all ingredients with a fork until well blended and crumbly.

Yield: topping for 9-inch pie

PIE AIDS

- Rolling pins come in many materials, from brass to glass to marble to plastic. A hardwood or marble rolling pin has weight and balance that help you make smoother doughs with less effort. So-called American bakers' rolling pins have sturdy handles anchored with a steel rod running through the center of the pin and fitted with ball bearings. A French rolling pin does not have handles; some cooks like them because they get a better feel for the dough.

- While many of our great-grandmothers perfected cutting in butter or shortening with two knives, some cooks find the task easier with a pastry blender. That tool has about six parallel, U-shaped steel wires attached to a handle, usually wooden. Both methods — two knives or a pastry blender — assure that the cold fat gets mixed into the flour mixture without becoming warm.

Macon Ladies' Lemon Meringue Pie

❁ ❁ ❁

Years ago, the Methodist women of Macon, Georgia, gathered their favorite recipes for a fund-raiser, and this meringue pie was one of the stars. Tart and creamy, it's a blue-ribbon winner for sure!

Filling

1   cup sugar
2   tablespoons cornstarch
2   tablespoons all-purpose flour
¼   teaspoon salt
1½ cups hot water
2   egg yolks, lightly beaten
juice of 1 lemon
2   tablespoons grated lemon zest
1   9-inch piecrust, baked

Meringue

2   egg whites, at room temperature
¼   teaspoon cream of tartar
3   tablespoons sugar
¼   teaspoon vanilla extract

1. To make the filling, in a double boiler over simmering water, blend the sugar, cornstarch, and flour. Add the water and stir until smooth. Cook until thickened. Add the egg yolks one at a time, stirring constantly, then add the lemon juice and zest. Pour into the piecrust.

2. Preheat oven to 300°F. Beat the egg whites and cream of tartar for 1 minute at high speed. Add the sugar, 1 tablespoon at a time, and continue to beat until stiff peaks form and the sugar dissolves, about 2 minutes. Beat in the vanilla.

3. Using a spoon, spread meringue over the hot lemon filling. Cover the pie to the edges of the crust. Form little peaks with the spoon. Bake for 12 to 15 minutes, until lightly browned. Cool before serving.

Yield: 8 servings

Strawberry Chiffon Pie

❁ ❁ ❁

What is as light as a cloud, as pink as cotton candy, and full of fresh-fruit flavor? A strawberry chiffon pie — a great summer dessert.

1   envelope (1 scant tablespoon) unflavored gelatin
¼   cup cold water
3   egg yolks or egg substitute
¾   cup sugar
1   tablespoon lemon juice
1   cup crushed strawberries
3   egg whites
1   9-inch piecrust, baked
3–6 whole strawberries for garnish (optional)

1. Soften the gelatin in the cold water. In the top of a double boiler, beat together the egg yolks, ½ cup of the sugar, and the lemon juice. Bring water in the lower half of the double boiler to a boil and stir the egg mixture until it thickens. Add the gelatin and stir until it dissolves.

2. Remove from the heat and stir in the crushed strawberries. Chill for about 30 minutes, or until the mixture begins to set.

3. Beat the egg whites until they hold stiff peaks, then beat in the remaining ¼ cup sugar, a little at a time. Continue beating until the egg whites are stiff and glossy. Fold the egg whites into the strawberry mixture and pour into the prepared pie shell. Chill at least 3 hours before serving. Garnish with strawberries and low-calorie whipped topping, if desired.

Yield: 6–8 servings

BETTYS & BUCKLES

These old-fashioned fruit desserts never lose their appeal. Serve them with a drizzle of custard sauce (page 279) or some vanilla ice cream for a special treat.

Blueberry Buckle

❈ ❈ ❈

We stayed at Marilyn Robinson's bed-and-breakfast on the Maine coast several times when we visited our daughter Jessica at Bowdoin. It seemed that each time she would fix something more wonderful for breakfast. This was an old family favorite that her mother had made.

¾ cup sugar
4 tablespoons butter
1 egg, beaten
2 cups all-purpose flour
2 teaspoons baking powder
½ teaspoon salt
½ cup milk
2 cups blueberries

Topping

⅓ cup all-purpose flour
½ cup sugar
½ teaspoon ground cinnamon
4 tablespoons butter

1. Preheat oven to 375°F. Cream the sugar and butter together. Add the egg.
2. Stir in the flour, baking powder, and salt, alternating with the milk, but be sure to end with the flour mixture.
3. Fold in the blueberries.
4. In a separate bowl, combine all the topping ingredients; mix thoroughly with a fork until crumbly.
5. Pour the batter into an 8-inch square pan and sprinkle with the topping.
6. Bake for 45 to 50 minutes, until golden brown.

Yield: 6–8 servings

Olwen's Apple Brown Betty

❈ ❈ ❈

From apple aficionada Olwen Woodier, this homespun favorite is like a cross between apple pie and bread pudding; it offers the best of both.

¾ cup brown sugar, firmly packed
1 teaspoon ground cinnamon
½ teaspoon ground nutmeg
¼ teaspoon ground cloves
6 slices white, wheat, or raisin bread
½ cup (1 stick) unsalted butter
3 tablespoons lemon juice
4 large apples (Rome, Winesap, or Cortland)
¼ cup apple juice or cider

1. Preheat oven to 350°F. Grease a 2-quart baking dish.
2. In a large bowl, mix together the sugar, cinnamon, nutmeg, and cloves. Crumble in the slices of bread.
3. Melt the butter and add the lemon juice. Stir the butter mixture into the crumbled bread mixture.
4. Peel, core, and thinly slice the apples.
5. Cover the bottom of the baking dish with about one-third of the crumbs. Add half of the apples, half of the crumbs, the rest of the apples, and the remaining crumbs.
6. Pour the apple juice over the top. Cover with foil and bake for 30 minutes. Remove the cover and bake 20 minutes longer. Serve warm.

Yield: 8 servings

Peach Cobbler Ring

❊ ❊ ❊

In this novel cobbler, the filling is rolled right up into the biscuitlike dough. It makes a beautiful ring of fruit-spiraled slices.

Crust

- 2 cups all-purpose flour
- 4 teaspoons baking powder
- 1 tablespoon granulated sugar
- ½ teaspoon salt
- ½ cup vegetable shortening
- ⅔ cup milk

Filling

- 2 tablespoons butter, softened
- ¼ cup brown sugar
- 1 tablespoon all-purpose flour
- 1 teaspoon ground cinnamon
- 2 cups diced peeled peaches
  melted butter or milk

1. Preheat oven to 400°F. For the crust, sift together the flour, baking powder, sugar, and salt. Cut in the shortening until the mixture resembles coarse crumbs. Add the milk and stir to form a soft dough.

2. Turn out on a lightly floured surface and knead six to eight times. Roll into a 9- by 18-inch rectangle.

3. For the filling, spread the butter on the dough. Mix together the sugar, flour, and cinnamon; sprinkle on the dough. Cover with the peaches and roll up like a jelly roll.

4. Place the dough on an ungreased baking sheet and form into a circle. On top of the dough circle, make slits from the outside edge almost to the center every 2 inches. Turn each cut partly onto its side to show the filling. Brush lightly with butter or milk.

5. Bake for 25 to 30 minutes. Serve warm with milk or cream and peaches, if desired.

Yield: 8 servings

Rhubarb Crisp

❊ ❊ ❊

When the rhubarb starts to come through the earth, you know it's spring. This crisp is a perfect balance of tart and sweet, and it couldn't be simpler to make. My sister Margie sent the recipe to me from Colorado; she said that she often adds fresh strawberries, too.

Topping

- ½ cup (1 stick) butter
- ½ cup all-purpose flour
- ½ cup old-fashioned oats
- ½ cup brown sugar

Filling

- 4 cups chopped rhubarb
- 1 cup sugar
- 3 tablespoons all-purpose flour

1. Preheat oven to 350°F. Mix together all ingredients for the topping. Set aside.

2. Using your hands, toss the rhubarb, sugar, and flour together until well coated. Place in an 8-inch square pan and cover with the topping. Bake for 30 to 40 minutes, until browned and bubbly. It's great with vanilla ice cream.

Yield: 6–8 servings

OF BETTYS, CRISPS, AND FOOLS

I've always loved old-fashioned desserts and their comfy, homespun names.

BETTY. A baked pudding, layered with fruit, sugar, spices, and bread or bread crumbs.

BUCKLE. A fruit-filled coffee cake baked with a crumbly topping.

COBBLER. A deep-dish, baked fruit dessert with a thick biscuit-like crust.

CRISP. A layer of sweetened fruit or pie filling baked with a crisp crumbly topping of butter, sugar, flour, and sometimes nuts or oats. Sometimes called a "crunch."

FOOL. A dessert of fruit purée folded into whipped cream.

GRUNT OR SLUMP. A fruit dessert made by dropping biscuit dough onto bubbling, cooked fruit. The biscuit steams like dumplings, with the fruit peeking through.

COOKIES

When I think of cookies, I think of childhood: milk and cookies, the ideal after-school snack; the cookie jar, full and waiting for illicit raids; cookie cutters, helping Mimi bake. Perhaps nostalgia is what makes cookies so appealing to grown-ups, too. Maybe it's just that cookies are ideal for casual hospitality and taste so good!

Ginger Snaps

❋ ❋ ❋

PopPop Storey loved good cooking, so we weren't surprised when he married Marcella. She could cook! Their cookie jars were always filled with special treats when we visited. This favorite delighted my kids and filled the house with a warm, spicy aroma that was irresistible.

¾ cup (1½ sticks) butter
1 cup sugar
1 egg
¼ cup molasses
2 cups all-purpose flour
1½ teaspoons baking soda
¼ teaspoon ground cinnamon
¼ teaspoon ground cloves
¼ teaspoon ground ginger

1. Preheat oven to 375°F. Grease a baking sheet. Cream together the butter and sugar. Stir in the egg and molasses.

2. In a separate bowl, mix together the flour, soda, cinnamon, cloves, and ginger. Add gradually to the sugar mixture until well combined. Chill the dough for 1 hour or more.

3. Roll the dough into small balls, about 1 inch in diameter. Place on a baking sheet and flatten by using the bottom of a glass tumbler that has been buttered and dipped into sugar. Lightly sprinkle additional sugar on the flattened cookies before baking.

4. Bake about 10 minutes. Let stand 1 minute to let cookie firm up a bit before removing from baking sheet.

Yield: About 3 dozen

Gingerbread People

❋ ❋ ❋

We grew up calling these treats gingerbread men, but with boy- and girl-shaped cookie cutters, you can shape the cookies as you like. Our grandchildren love piping the names of their family members onto the cookies.

½ cup (1 stick) butter, softened
6 tablespoons honey
¼ cup blackstrap molasses
2 cups unbleached all-purpose flour
1½ teaspoons baking soda
1½ teaspoons ground cinnamon
1½ teaspoons ground ginger

1. Preheat oven to 375°F and grease two baking sheets. Combine the butter, honey, and molasses. Add the flour, soda, cinnamon, and ginger; stir until a dough is formed.

2. Divide the dough in half and knead each ball gently. The dough will be soft and buttery. Roll each ball to a thickness of ¼ inch on a lightly floured surface; cut the dough with cookie cutters.

3. Carefully transfer the cookies to the baking sheets; bake for 5 to 7 minutes, or until lightly browned. Watch that they do not burn.

Yield: 1 dozen

- - - - - - - - - - - -

APPLE SWEET

. . . .

Concentrated apple juice makes a terrific natural sweetener for drop or bar cookies, oatmeal, or muffins. You can use it in many recipes instead of sugar or honey.

- - - - - - - - - - - -

Butterscotch Cookies

❈ ❈ ❈

John really loves these soft, moist cookies that his mother made. They are best fresh from the oven, but if they are kept tightly sealed in a plastic container, they last well.

Cookie

½ cup (1 stick) butter
1½ cups brown sugar, firmly packed
2½ cups all-purpose flour
2 eggs
1 teaspoon vanilla extract
½ teaspoon salt
1 teaspoon baking soda
1 cup sour cream

Frosting

1½ cups confectioners' sugar
1 tablespoon butter, melted
2 tablespoons hot water
vanilla extract
dash of salt

1. Preheat oven to 325°F. Cream together the butter and sugar. Add the flour, eggs, and vanilla, mixing thoroughly.

2. Add the salt, soda, and sour cream.

3. Drop by spoonfuls onto a greased baking sheet. Bake for 15 minutes.

4. To make the frosting, mix together the confectioners' sugar, butter, and water until smooth. Add the vanilla and salt. If the mixture is too runny, add more sugar.

5. Frost cookies while they are still warm.

Yield: About 4 dozen

Peanut Butter Cookies

❈ ❈ ❈

Short and sweet (both the cookies and the recipe)!

1 cup peanut butter
1 cup sugar
1 egg

1. Preheat oven to 325°F. Mix all ingredients well and roll in small balls. Place on a cookie sheet and flatten with a fork, making a crisscross pattern on the top.

2. Bake for 10 minutes.

Yield: 3 dozen

Peanut Butter Blossoms

❈ ❈ ❈

If you take a classic peanut butter cookie and add a chocolate center, you've got pure heaven! For added crunch, use chunky-style peanut butter.

½ cup peanut butter
½ cup shortening
½ cup brown sugar, firmly packed
½ cup granulated sugar
1 egg
2 tablespoons milk
1 teaspoon vanilla extract
1¾ cups all-purpose flour
1 teaspoon baking soda
½ teaspoon salt
sugar for rolling
48 chocolate kiss candies

1. Preheat oven to 375°F. Cream together the peanut butter, shortening, brown sugar, and granulated sugar. Add the egg, milk, and vanilla; mix well.

2. In a separate bowl, sift together the flour, soda, and salt. Gradually combine the flour mixture and the peanut butter mixture.

3. Shape dough into 1-inch balls. Roll in sugar and place on an ungreased cookie sheet. Bake for 8 minutes. Remove from oven and place a chocolate kiss on top of each cookie, then press it down so that the cookie cracks around the edges. Return to the oven and bake for 2 to 5 minutes longer, until light brown.

Yield: About 4 dozen

Oatmeal Crisps

❈ ❈ ❈

We met Paul and Mary Sampson when we were young entrepreneurs. They lived in Charlotte, Vermont. Our kids adored these cookies, which Mary baked fresh, in an instant, just for us.

2 cups shortening
2 cups brown sugar, firmly packed
2 cups granulated sugar
4 eggs
2 teaspoons vanilla extract
2 teaspoons baking soda
1 teaspoon salt
6 cups old-fashioned oats
3 cups all-purpose flour
1 cup chopped nuts
6 ounces (1 cup) chocolate morsels (optional)

1. Mix together all of the ingredients. Put several large spoonfuls of dough onto a sheet of wax paper. Roll into a log, 2 inches in diameter; leave wax paper on. Chill at least overnight.

2. Preheat oven to 350°F. Slice and bake the dough on ungreased baking sheets for about 7 minutes, or until edges just begin to lightly brown. The dough keeps for weeks rolled up in the refrigerator, and it is easy to slice and bake at any time.

Yield: 6 dozen

Snickerdoodles

❂ ❂ ❂

We were so pleased when our son, Matthew, chose Jessica to be his bride. She's a very special young woman, but she also brought with her the coveted family Snickerdoodle recipe that we now call our own!

1 cup (2 sticks) butter, softened
2 cups sugar
2 eggs
2¾ cups all-purpose flour
2 teaspoons cream of tartar
1 teaspoon baking soda
½ teaspoon salt
1 teaspoon ground cinnamon

1. Preheat oven to 400°F. In a medium bowl, cream together the butter, 1½ cups of the sugar, and eggs. Add the flour, cream of tartar, soda, and salt, mixing thoroughly.

2. Combine the cinnamon and remaining ½ cup of sugar in a small bowl. Roll dough into 1-inch balls, then roll each in cinnamon-sugar mixture.

3. Place on an ungreased baking sheet. Bake for 8 to 10 minutes, or until barely golden.

Yield: 2½ dozen

Stained-Glass Heart Cookies

❂ ❂ ❂

Our daughter Jennifer is a first-class baker with lots of creative ideas. Her stained-glass heart cookies are almost too pretty to eat, though that never stopped anyone!

½ cup (1 stick) butter
½ cup sugar
1 egg
1¾ cups all-purpose flour
½ teaspoon baking powder
½ teaspoon salt
1 teaspoon vanilla extract
red raspberry jam

1. Cream together the butter and the sugar. Add the egg and beat until creamy. Add the flour, baking powder, salt, and vanilla; mix until the dough is smooth and stiff. Cover dough with plastic wrap and refrigerate for at least 2 hours.

2. Preheat oven to 375°F. Place a piece of aluminum foil on a baking sheet.

3. Take a piece of the dough and roll it out into a rope about ¼ inch thick. Form the rope of dough into a heart shape — small or large, as you like. Fill the inside of the heart with raspberry jam. Spread at least ⅛ inch thick. Repeat, using all the dough and filling.

4. Bake until the cookies are a light golden and the jam is bubbling, at least 10 minutes. The jam must bubble in order for it to harden as the cookies cool.

5. Place the baking sheet on a rack and allow the cookies to cool. Peel the aluminum foil off the back of each cookie.

Yield: 3–4 dozen, depending on size

Icebox Cookies

✵ ✵ ✵

When I was a child, there was always a roll or two of these cookies wrapped in wax paper in our refrigerator. Now, you can get them in the supermarket's dairy case, but I think that homemade is still the best. Add your own touch with raisins or chocolate chips.

2½ cups sugar
  2 cups vegetable shortening
  3 eggs
  1 teaspoon baking soda
  1 tablespoon molasses
  ½ teaspoon salt
  1 teaspoon vanilla extract
  1 cup chopped pecans or walnuts
5½ cups all-purpose flour, sifted

1. In a large bowl, cream together the sugar, shortening, and eggs. Dissolve the soda in the molasses; stir into the sugar mixture. Add the salt, vanilla, and pecans. Stir in the flour in several batches.

2. Place 1½ to 2 cups of dough on wax paper. Using the paper, firmly roll the dough into a log about 9 inches long and 1½ inches in diameter. Twist the wax paper at both ends to seal. Repeat until all of the dough is rolled. Store in plastic bags in the refrigerator overnight or until quite firm.

ICEBOX COOKIES

....

Icebox cookies are a wonderful convenience. Make the dough when you have time and keep it on hand for whenever you get the yen. The dough may be stored in the refrigerator but will keep better in the freezer; you don't even need to thaw it before cutting. The chilled dough should be rolled into cylinders in wax paper and then sealed in freezer bags or wrapped well in plastic. If you want to add an easy decorative edge to your cookies, roll the cylinders in chopped nuts, cookie crumbs, or colored sugar before wrapping.

3. When ready to bake, preheat oven to 400°F. Cut the dough into ¼-inch slices. Bake on ungreased baking sheets for 8 minutes, or until golden brown.

Yield: 8 dozen

Prizewinning Double Chocolate Chip Cookies

✵ ✵ ✵

In 1987, The Orchards, an inn in Williamstown, hosted a search for the perfect chocolate chip cookie. This rich, moist, double chocolate cookie was the grand prizewinning recipe of all 2,600 entries.

1¾ cups all-purpose flour
  ¼ teaspoon baking soda
  1 cup butter, softened
  1 cup granulated sugar
  ½ cup dark brown sugar, firmly packed
  1 teaspoon vanilla extract
  1 egg
  ⅓ cup unsweetened cocoa powder
  2 tablespoons milk
  1 cup chopped pecans or walnuts
  6 ounces (1 cup) semisweet chocolate chips

1. Preheat oven to 350°F. In a medium-sized bowl, combine the flour and soda. Set aside.

2. Using an electric mixer, cream the butter in a large bowl. Add the sugars and vanilla; beat until fluffy. Beat in the egg. At low speed, beat in the cocoa, then the milk. With a wooden spoon, mix in dry ingredients just until blended. Stir in the pecans and chocolate chips.

3. Drop the dough by rounded teaspoonfuls onto nonstick or foil-lined baking sheets. Bake for 12 to 13 minutes, until lightly browned. Cool slightly before removing from baking sheets.

Yield: 3 dozen

Note: This recipe was first published in *Winning at the Table* by the Junior League of Las Vegas.

Chewy Chocolate Chip Cookies

❈ ❈ ❈

Softer and chewier than most traditional chocolate chip cookies, these get their distinctive texture from using an electric beater. The recipe was submitted to the Orchards contest by Susan S. Grossman of Canton, Ohio.

3 *cups all-purpose flour*
1 *teaspoon baking soda*
1 *teaspoon salt*
1 *cup (2 sticks) butter, softened*
¾ *cup granulated sugar*
¾ *cup light brown sugar, firmly packed*
1 *teaspoon vanilla extract*
1 *teaspoon water*
2 *eggs*
18 *ounces (3 cups) semisweet chocolate chips*

1. Preheat oven to 350°F. Sift the flour before measuring, then resift with soda and salt. Set aside.

2. In a large bowl, combine the butter, sugars, vanilla, and water. Beat with an electric mixer about 2 minutes, until creamy. Add the eggs and beat until fluffy.

3. Gradually add the sifted ingredients. Beat with an electric mixer for about 2 minutes, until very well blended. Stir in the chocolate chips.

4. Drop by heaping teaspoonfuls onto a lightly greased baking sheet. Bake on the middle rack of the oven for 10 to 12 minutes. Do not overbake. Remove from oven when the cookies are lightly browned and slightly crisp on the bottom; they may seem slightly undercooked. Cool 1 minute on the baking sheet, then remove to paper towels to cool completely.

Yield: About 4 dozen

ADD-INS

Here are some fun things to add to your chocolate chip (or other drop) cookies:

- Candy-coated chocolate
- Chunks of chocolate bars
- Toffee crunch bits
- Nuts — peanuts, walnuts, hazelnuts, sliced almonds
- Dried fruit — cranberries, raisins, cherries, chopped apricots, candied pineapple
- Granola
- Crispy cereals
- Butterscotch, peanut butter, or mint chips

ABOUT BAKING CHOCOLATE CHIP COOKIES

Be sure not to overbake your chocolate chip cookies; most are best slightly underdone rather than overdone. When you take the cookies out of the oven, let them remain on the pans for a minute or two before removing. Allow your baking sheet to cool before doing another batch, or the cookies will melt and spread at the edges. To give frozen cookies a fresh-baked texture, pop them into the microwave at full power for 15 to 20 seconds.

BAR COOKIES

Bar cookies require less fuss than other cookies — everything goes into one pan, and they don't require much watching. They have almost universal appeal, with browned edges for those who like crunch and soft centers for those who like chewy cookies. In addition to the favorites here, try Jessica's wonderful brownies (page 315).

MAILING COOKIES

....

The only thing more fun than getting a care package of cookies is making one and sending it to someone you love. However, if you don't want the recipient to find a bunch of crumbs, choose your cookies wisely and pack them well. Sturdy snaps and crinkles, bars, and drop cookies are the best for mailing. Wrap them by twos in plastic wrap and snuggle them into a tin or sturdy box; fill all empty spaces with popcorn. If you are mailing soft and crisp cookies in the same package, pack them in resealable bags after wrapping, so that the moist cookies won't make the crisp ones go limp.

Lemon Squares

✖ ✖ ✖

The first time I ever had a lemon square was at John's house when I was still in high school. His mom made the best, and I could have eaten an entire batch myself.

Crust

¼ cup confectioners' sugar
⅛ teaspoon salt
1 cup all-purpose flour
½ cup (1 stick) butter

Filling

1 cup granulated sugar
½ teaspoon baking powder
⅛ teaspoon salt
2 eggs, beaten
2 tablespoons lemon juice
grated zest of 1 lemon

Topping

2 tablespoons lemon juice
¾ cup confectioners' sugar
1 tablespoon butter

1. Preheat oven to 350°F. Mix together the sugar, salt, and flour; cut in the butter. Pat the dough into an 8-inch square pan and bake for 15 minutes. Remove from the oven.

2. For the filling, beat together all the ingredients and spread on top of the crust. Return to the oven and bake for 25 minutes longer. Cool.

3. To make the topping, blend all the ingredients by using a small whisk. If necessary, add more sugar to make a good spreading consistency. Spread onto the filling and let set until top is hardened. Cut into 2-inch squares.

Yield: 16 squares

Top Hat Chocolate Chip Bars

✖ ✖ ✖

Hilda Garey of St. Albans, Vermont, entered this great bar cookie recipe in the Orchards cookie contest. It's topped with chocolate-flavored cream cheese, nuts, and chocolate chips.

2 cups all-purpose flour
1 teaspoon baking soda
1⅔ cups sugar
2 eggs
¾ cup water
⅓ cup vegetable oil
1 teaspoon vanilla extract
2 packages (8 ounces each) cream cheese, softened
¼ cup unsweetened cocoa powder
½ teaspoon salt

1   cup chopped nuts
12 ounces (2 cups) semisweet
    chocolate chips

1. Preheat oven to 350°F. Mix together the flour, baking soda, and 1 cup of the sugar. Add 1 of the eggs, the water, oil, and vanilla; stir until well blended.

2. Spread the batter onto a greased 10- by 15-inch jelly-roll pan. Bake for 15 minutes.

3. Meanwhile, combine the cream cheese, the remaining sugar, the cocoa, salt, and the remaining egg; cream well.

4. When the cookies have baked, remove from the oven and spread the cheese mixture over them while hot. Return the pan to the oven and bake for 15 minutes longer. Remove from the oven and, while still hot, sprinkle nuts and chocolate chips over all. Cut into squares.

5. You can make cookie "sandwiches" by placing two squares on top of each other, cheese sides facing, while they are still warm. Cool completely before storing in the refrigerator.

Yield: 2–3 dozen

CUTTING BAR COOKIES

Allow bar cookies to cool before cutting; using a sharp knife, cut smoothly through the cookies, wiping the knife after each cut. If you line the baking pan with foil, leaving an overhang at each end, you can lift the whole thing out of the pan for even easier cutting and trimming (not to mention easy cleanup). Cut bar cookies into squares, rectangles or diamonds. For diamond-shaped bars, cut straight lines lengthwise down the pan, then cut across them diagonally.

Butterscotch Brownies

❖ ❖ ❖

Despite their great gooey butterscotch taste, these cookies are more healthful than some desserts, because they include whole-wheat flour and wheat germ.

2   cups brown sugar, firmly
    packed
½   cup vegetable oil
2   eggs, beaten
1   teaspoon vanilla extract
⅔   cup whole-wheat flour
½   cup powdered milk
2   teaspoons baking powder
½   teaspoon salt
1   cup chopped walnuts
⅔   cup wheat germ

1. Preheat oven to 375°F; grease and flour an 8-inch square baking pan.

2. Combine the sugar, oil, and eggs; mix well. Add the vanilla. Sift the flour; stir into the sugar mixture. Stir in the milk, baking powder, and salt.

3. Dredge walnuts in flour (so they won't sink). Stir walnuts and wheat germ into the batter.

4. Spread the batter evenly in the pan; bake for 25 to 30 minutes, until the edges begin to brown. Cool for 5 minutes before cutting into squares.

Yield: 16 squares

ELEGANT AND EASY

For an easy, more elegant dessert, give brownies or bar cookies a topper. As soon as they come out of the oven, place thin chocolate mint candies all over the top. When these melt, drag a knife through the mints in a zigzag fashion.

CANDY

While it's fun to look at the big bins of bright-colored candies at the market or to eye the gorgeous packages in a chocolate shop, there isn't anything more delicious than candy made at home. This, I am convinced, is because making and sharing candy is so much fun for the participants. You take turns pulling the taffy or stirring the fudge or shelling the peanuts for brittle, and once it's ready, you laugh and tell jokes and nibble on the good old-fashioned sweets. Now, that's entertainment.

Vinegar Candy or Taffy

❋ ❋ ❋

This recipe dates back to pioneer days, when vanilla wasn't available for flavoring but vinegar was. It doesn't have a strong vinegar taste, only a pleasant sweet-and-sour effect. If you cook it only to the soft-crack stage (about 275°F), you can pull this candy like taffy.

　2　tablespoons butter
　2　cups sugar
　½　cup cider vinegar

1. Grease a large pan or baking sheet.

2. Melt the butter in a saucepan. Add the sugar and vinegar. Cook, stirring constantly, over medium heat, until the sugar has dissolved. Then turn the heat up a bit and boil gently, stirring, until the mixture reaches 300°F (the hot end of the hard-crack stage) on a candy thermometer, or until a small amount of mixture dropped into very cold water separates into threads that are hard and brittle. Watch carefully to prevent burning.

3. Pour into the greased pan. When the candy is cool, break into pieces. Wrap each piece of candy individually in wax paper or cellophane. Keep in an airtight tin.

Yield: About ¾ pound

Molasses Taffy

❋ ❋ ❋

Pulled into a light, chewy candy, this has a marvelous molasses flavor.

　2　cups unsulfured molasses
　1　cup sugar
　2　tablespoons butter
　2　tablespoons cider or white
　　　vinegar

1. Butter a platter or baking sheet. In a large saucepan, combine all the ingredients. Stirring constantly, bring to a boil and cook, without stirring, until the mixture reaches 250°F (the hard-ball stage) on a candy thermometer, or until a small amount of mixture dropped into very cold water forms a ball that is hard enough to hold its shape yet is pliable.

2. Pour onto the platter. Using a spatula, turn the edges toward the center to speed cooling. Pull (see "About Pulling Taffy," page 253).

Yield: About 1 pound

About Pulling Taffy

While taffy pulling is best known as an amusing group operation, it's perfectly possible to pull taffy all by yourself. Old-time kitchens often had "taffy hooks" permanently attached to a wall.

Before you begin, grease a pair of scissors and have on hand squares of wax paper for wrapping.

Let your cooked taffy sit just until it's barely cool enough to work with. (If it gets too cool, you can warm it in a 350°F oven for 3 to 4 minutes.)

1. Coat your hands well with cornstarch or butter. Form the candy into one or more balls. Now start pulling.

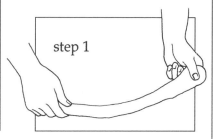

step 1

2. Working fast, pull a lump of candy between the fingertips of one hand and the other until it's about 15 inches long.

3. Now double it up and pull again. Continue pulling, as in step 1, until the candy is porous and hard to pull.

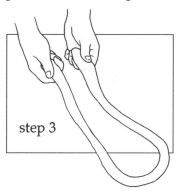

step 3

4. Stretch the candy into a rope about ¾ inch in diameter.

5. Cut with the greased scissors into 1-inch pieces. To prevent sticking, wrap each piece of candy individually in a square of wax paper; twist the ends to seal. Keep the wrapped taffies in a tightly closed tin.

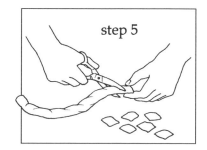

step 5

CANDY TEMPERATURES

Use a candy thermometer to test when your candy is ready. It should be immersed in the hot candy, but be sure it does not touch the bottom of the pan. To check the thermometer's accuracy, heat it in water; when the water boils, it should read 212°F.

Soft-ball stage	234–240°F
Firm-ball stage	244–250°F
Hard-ball stage	250–270°F
Soft-crack stage	275–290°F
Hard-crack stage	295–305°F

It's best to use a candy thermometer when making candy, but you can also determine at what stage candy is by dropping a small amount of sugar syrup into very cold water. Here's what it will do:

Soft-ball stage	Forms a soft ball that flattens of its own accord when removed
Firm-ball stage	Forms a firm but pliable ball
Hard-ball stage	Forms a rigid ball that is still somewhat pliable
Soft-crack stage	Separates into hard but pliable threads
Hard-crack stage	Separates into hard, brittle threads

Joe's Candy

My brother Joe was 19 years old and in the Army in Fort Benning, Georgia, when he sent this recipe to Mother. Every Sunday he had dinner with an old lady who had befriended him. This was his favorite specialty from her kitchen, even though he didn't like nuts.

1 cup (2 sticks) butter
1 package (7ounces) flaked coconut
1 pound dates, chopped
2 cups brown sugar, firmly packed
2 cups chopped nuts
4 cups Rice Krispies
confectioners' sugar

1. In a large saucepan, cook the butter, coconut, dates, and brown sugar over low heat for 6 minutes, stirring constantly. Remove from the heat and add the nuts and Rice Krispies.

2. Let cool slightly. Roll into balls the size of walnuts. Roll each ball in confectioners' sugar. Keep in an airtight container.

Yield: About 3 dozen

Peanut Brittle

Peanut brittle is as simple as can be — just caramelized sugar and nuts. Watch the sugar carefully so it doesn't burn. Brittle should be made only when the weather is dry.

1⅓ cups sugar
6½ ounces cocktail peanuts

1. Before you start, thoroughly butter a baking sheet.

2. In a skillet, cook the sugar over low heat until it has melted and turned light brown. Stir in the peanuts, then pour onto the baking sheet.

3. Immediately start to stretch the candy by pressing it out with the backs of two spoons. Don't touch it with your hands, as it will be very hot. Keep this up, working quickly, until the brittle is no more than one peanut deep.

4. When the candy is completely cool, break it into pieces. Keep in an airtight tin.

Yield: About 1 pound

BURNT-SUGAR BRITTLE

Some people know this treat as caramelized sugar candy. Make it exactly as you would Vinegar Candy, page 252, but cook until it reaches 325°F. (If you don't have a candy thermometer, this temperature is beyond the range of water tests. Go by color, then. It should be a strong brown.)

Mamie's Chocolate Fudge

Back when Dwight D. Eisenhower was in the White House, my mother (and much of America) was hooked on his wife, Mamie. Her fudge recipe fast became a holiday treat, and its popularity lasted long after the presidency changed hands.

4½ cups sugar
pinch of salt
2 tablespoons butter
1 can (12 ounces) evaporated milk
12 ounces (2 cups) semisweet chocolate chips
12 ounces German chocolate
2 cups marshmallow cream
2 cups chopped pecans

1. In a large saucepan, combine the sugar, salt, butter, and milk. Boil for 6 minutes.

2. In a large bowl, combine the chocolate chips, German chocolate, marshmallow cream, and pecans. Pour the hot milk mixture over the chocolate mixture; stir with a wooden spoon for at least 5 minutes, until the chocolate has melted and the fudge has begun to thicken.

3. Line a 9- by 13-inch pan with lightly buttered wax paper. Pour the fudge into the pan and let sit, covered, overnight, until fudge is firm enough to cut into small squares.

Yield: About 3 pounds

Penuche

❂ ❂ ❂

This creamy brown-sugar confection was a spring specialty in John's house. His mother made it around Easter; she wrapped pieces in cellophane and gave them as gifts to neighbors.

    3 cups brown sugar, firmly
       packed
    1 cup light cream or evapo-
       rated milk
    1½ tablespoons butter
    1½ teaspoons vanilla extract

1. In a large saucepan, combine the sugar and cream. Cook slowly over medium heat, stirring constantly, until the mixture reaches 234°F on a candy thermometer, or until a small amount of mixture dropped into very cold water forms a soft ball that flattens when removed from the water.

2. Remove from heat and add the butter, but do not stir. Cool to lukewarm. Add the vanilla.

CHOCOLATE GARNISHES

Heat squares of your favorite chocolate until most of it is melted; remove from the heat and stir gently until it is smooth. Pour the chocolate onto a baking sheet and allow to cool. Use small cookie cutters to cut out fancy shapes, or gently slide a spatula under the nearly cool chocolate and push it into curls. Or put melted chocolate into a resealable plastic bag, snip off a corner, and pipe lacy shapes or letters onto wax paper. Remove when cool.

3. Grease an 8-inch square pan. Beat the mixture until it is creamy and holds its shape. Pour into the pan and cool.

4. Cut into 1- or 2-inch squares.

Yield: 32 or 64 pieces

FUDGE FANCY

Two-Tone Confection: Make a batch of penuche and spread it out in a large pan. Then make a pan of fudge and spread it on top. When cool, cut it into a doubly good two-tone candy.

Rocky Road: Add nuts, mini-marshmallows, and chocolate bits or raisins to your cooling fudge.

Vanilla Caramels

❂ ❂ ❂

Caramels are adversely affected by even small amounts of moisture in the air, so wrap each little candy in plastic wrap or encase it in chocolate. This recipe makes a rather hard caramel that softens slightly later.

    2 cups sugar
    ½ cup corn syrup
    1½ cups heavy cream
    4 tablespoons butter
    1¼ teaspoons vanilla extract

1. Generously butter a marble slab or a baking pan. In a medium-sized saucepan, cook the sugar, corn syrup, cream, and butter over medium heat, stirring frequently, until the mixture reaches the firm-ball stage, 245°F on a candy thermometer, or until a small amount of mixture dropped into very cold water forms a firm ball that does not flatten when removed from water.

2. Remove from the heat and stir in the vanilla. Pour onto the marble slab or baking pan.

3. When the candy is thoroughly cooled, cut into small squares and wrap each candy in a piece of plastic wrap.

Yield: About ¾ pound

CHOCOLATE

Chocolate has to be one of the world's favorite treats. Lush, creamy, with that melting flavor . . . there really is nothing like it. My feeling about chocolate is that you should not indulge too often, but when you do, you should enjoy it extravagantly — in a rich cake, on luscious berries, or as melt-in-your-mouth truffles.

Chocolate Zucchini Bread

✖ ✖ ✖

Dee Saunders worked for us at Storey for about 6 years, and each summer she would bring in a few loaves of this bread. Chocolate and zucchini seem to contradict each other, but this is really delicious, even a little bit sinful!

1¾ cups sugar
3 eggs
1 cup vegetable oil
2 cups shredded zucchini
3 teaspoons vanilla extract
3 cups all-purpose flour
½ cup unsweetened cocoa powder
1¼ teaspoons salt
1 teaspoon baking soda
1 teaspoon ground cinnamon
¼ teaspoon baking powder
3 ounces (½ cup) chocolate chips
½ cup chopped nuts

1. Preheat oven to 350°F; lightly grease two loaf pans.

2. In a large bowl, combine the sugar, eggs, and oil until well blended. Stir in the zucchini and vanilla.

3. In another bowl, sift together the flour, cocoa powder, salt, soda, cinnamon, and baking powder.

4. Add the dry ingredients to the zucchini mixture; mix just until blended. Stir in the chocolate chips and nuts. Pour the batter into the prepared pans.

5. Bake for 1 hour or until a toothpick inserted in the centers comes out clean.

Yield: 2 loaves

SUBSTITUTING COCOA

....

**Cocoa powder can be substituted for baking chocolate by using the following proportions:
3 tablespoons cocoa plus 1 tablespoon butter, margarine, or shortening = 1 square of baking chocolate.**

Truffles

✖ ✖ ✖

The best tip for truffle makers is to hide truffles if you don't want them to disappear. These superchocolate morsels are impossible to resist.

12 ounces (2 cups) semisweet chocolate chips
6 tablespoons unsweetened cocoa powder
¼ cup heavy cream
1 teaspoon vanilla extract
6 tablespoons butter, softened

1. In a small saucepan, combine the chocolate chips, cocoa, and cream. Stir over very low heat until the chocolate has melted. Remove from heat and stir in the vanilla, then the butter.

2. Chill the mixture until firm enough to work with. Form into whatever size balls you wish.

3. Store truffles in an air-tight container for up to 3 weeks (refrigerate in hot weather). Truffles may also be frozen for up to 2 months.

Yield: About 2 dozen

Chocolate-Dipped Strawberries

❈ ❈ ❈

Chocolate-dipped strawberries are so much fun. Choose ripe, shapely berries and use them as elegant garnishes, simple desserts, and lovely hostess gifts.

½ pound white, dark, or milk chocolate
24 whole strawberries with stems

1. Line a baking sheet with wax paper.

2. Melt the chocolate in a double boiler over simmering water. Holding each strawberry by its stem, dip it into the chocolate and place on wax paper. Allow to dry in a cool spot.

3. If you like, you may drizzle white chocolate over chocolate-dipped strawberries and dark or milk chocolate over white chocolate–dipped strawberries.

Yield: 24 strawberries

A TRIO OF TRUFFLES

Basic truffles are terrific, but it's fun to experiment with variations.

- *Candy truffles started out as Cocoa-Coated Chocolate Truffles — the idea was to make them look like the freshly dug French fungi. To make these, roll balls of the truffle mixture or any of the variations below in cocoa, then put on wax paper to dry. Keep refrigerated or frozen until ready to serve.*

- *For grown-ups, try Liqueur Truffles. Follow the basic recipe for truffles, but eliminate the vanilla and add 1 tablespoon of Grand Marnier, amaretto, Kahlúa, or any other liqueur.*

- *Coffee lovers will enjoy Mocha Truffles. Follow the basic recipe for truffles, but add, along with the chocolate, 1 tablespoon of instant coffee granules (regular or decaffeinated). For a stronger coffee flavor, mix more instant coffee powder with the cocoa for rolling (ratio: three parts cocoa to one part coffee powder).*

Brandy Balls

❈ ❈ ❈

The holidays are a wonderful time for making, eating, and sharing sweet confections. My kids think that it wouldn't be Christmas without their favorites, and brandy balls are one of them.

2½ cups finely crushed vanilla wafers
1 cup confectioners' sugar, sifted
2 tablespoons unsweetened cocoa powder
½ cup finely chopped walnuts
¼ cup brandy
¼ cup light corn syrup
granulated or colored sugar

1. In a small bowl, combine the wafers, sugar, cocoa, and walnuts. Mix well.

2. Add the brandy and corn syrup. If necessary, add a teaspoon of water to form a claylike dough.

3. Form into ¾-inch balls. Roll each ball in granulated sugar. Store in an air-tight container.

Yield: About 3 dozen

CUSTARD & PUDDING

In my mother's kitchen, puddings were part of everyday cooking. They were plain or fancy, full of eggs and milk and flavorings; sometimes they contained bread or rice for body. I loved them all, from the lightest lemon sponge to substantial dark Indian pudding. Homemade puddings seem less common nowadays, but they deserve a revival — spooning into a fine pudding is one of the nicest treats there is.

Vanilla Pudding

⊠ ⊠ ⊠

This basic vanilla pudding is delicious as is, but we often dress it up with bananas and serve it at Sunday dinner (page 145).

2   cups milk
1   cup sugar
4   tablespoons all-purpose flour
2   eggs
½   teaspoon vanilla extract
    pinch of salt
    sweetened whipped cream

1. In a medium-sized saucepan, heat the milk.

2. In a medium-sized bowl, mix the sugar, flour, eggs, vanilla, and salt. Add to the hot milk and continue to cook over medium heat, stirring constantly, until the pudding thickens.

3. Serve warm or cold with whipped cream.

Yield: 6–8 servings

Cranberry Walnut Bread Pudding

⊠ ⊠ ⊠

The tartness of cranberries, the sweetness of orange juice, the softness of custard-soaked bread, and the richness of Cointreau combine in this treat to create comfort food for adult tastes.

2   cups cranberries
1 ¼   cups brown sugar, firmly packed
1   cup walnut pieces
2   tablespoons grated orange zest
1   tablespoon Cointreau
8   slices white bread, crusts removed
4   tablespoons butter, softened
1   cup milk
1   cup heavy cream
½   cup orange juice
3   eggs, lightly beaten
    sweetened whipped cream

1. In a food processor or blender, chop the cranberries.

2. Add ⅔ cup of the brown sugar, the walnuts, orange zest, and Cointreau; process until just combined. Spread the mixture in an 8-inch square baking pan.

3. Spread the bread with the butter. Arrange buttered side down in two layers over the sugar mixture.

4. In a small bowl, whisk together the milk, cream, orange juice, the remaining brown sugar, and eggs. Pour evenly over the cranberry mixture. Let the mixture stand, loosely covered, at room temperature at least 1 hour, or overnight in the refrigerator.

5. Preheat oven to 350°F. Put the baking pan into a larger pan. Add enough hot water to the larger pan to reach halfway up the sides of the 8-inch pan.

6. Bake for 30 minutes. Let the pudding cool in the water bath for 5 minutes. Serve the pudding warm with whipped cream.

Yield: 4–6 servings

Soul-Satisfying Rice Pudding

◙ ◙ ◙

MomMom's recipes were always scrumptious, and John loves her simple, wholesome desserts. He finds this recipe particularly satisfying on a chilly night.

1 quart milk
3 eggs
pinch of salt
½ cup sugar
1 teaspoon vanilla extract
¾ cup raisins
¾ cup cooked rice
¼ teaspoon ground nutmeg

1. Preheat oven to 350°F; grease a 2-quart casserole dish. In a large saucepan, bring the milk to a boil; remove from heat.

2. Beat the eggs well and add the salt. Add the sugar and vanilla to the eggs.

3. Add the egg mixture to the hot milk. Beat well.

4. Add the rice, raisins, and nutmeg.

5. Pour the mixture into the casserole dish. Put the casserole into a larger pan. Add enough hot water to the larger pan to reach halfway up the sides of the casserole.

6. Bake for 1 hour, until a knife inserted into the center comes out clean.

Yield: 6–8 servings

Indian Pudding

◙ ◙ ◙

There are hundreds of variations on this age-old recipe. Add raisins or chopped apple, if you like.

3 cups milk
⅓ cup unsulfured molasses
¼ cup cornmeal
¼ cup brown sugar, firmly packed
½ teaspoon ground cinnamon
½ teaspoon ground ginger
½ teaspoon ground nutmeg
3 eggs
2 tablespoons butter, softened

1. Preheat oven to 300°F and grease a 1½- to 2- quart baking dish.

2. In a large saucepan over low heat, cook 2 cups of the milk and the molasses to scalding (bubbles will form around pan sides).

3. Add the cornmeal, a little at a time, stirring constantly. Cook for 10 to 15 minutes, stirring occasionally, until the mixture thickens. Remove from heat; set aside.

4. In a small bowl, beat together the brown sugar, cinnamon, ginger, nutmeg, eggs, remaining 1 cup milk, and the butter. Stir this mixture into the hot cornmeal mixture, and beat together until thoroughly blended.

5. Pour into the prepared dish and bake for 1 hour 30 minutes. Serve warm.

Yield: 6 servings

ABOUT BAKING CUSTARD

....

Baking custards and custard-based puddings in a pan of hot water keeps the eggs from separating from the milk. Placing a piece of brown paper bag or a small towel in the bottom of the pan of hot water allows for more even cooking. To test custard for doneness, insert a clean knife into the center. If it comes out clean, the custard is done.

Creamy Maple Mocha Pudding

❊ ❊ ❊

The rich maple flavor of this pudding is intensified by the coffee and cocoa. It is lovely ladled into small glass dessert bowls or goblets and served with whipped cream.

> 3 tablespoons cornstarch
> 1 tablespoon powdered instant coffee or powdered instant espresso
> 1 teaspoon unsweetened cocoa powder
> pinch of salt
> 3 egg yolks
> 3 cups milk
> ½ cup pure maple syrup
> 1 tablespoon unsalted butter, cut into pieces
> 1 teaspoon vanilla extract

1. In a large, heavy-bottomed pot, combine the cornstarch, coffee, cocoa, and salt; whisk to mix. In a mixing bowl, whisk the egg yolks slightly, then add the milk and maple syrup. Stir into the pot.

2. Over medium-high heat, gradually bring the mixture to a boil, stirring gently but constantly with a rubber spatula. Be sure to scrape the sides as you stir. Boil for 1 minute, stirring constantly. Remove from heat and stir in the butter and vanilla.

3. Ladle into four or five individual serving bowls. To prevent a skin from forming, place a piece of wax paper, cut to size, on top of each. Cool, then chill for several hours before serving.

Yield: 4–5 servings

Easy Chocolate-Almond Pudding

❊ ❊ ❊

Making pudding is one of my earliest childhood memories. I remember standing on a stool next to my mother in our old Texas kitchen and handing her the ingredients, while she constantly stirred.

> 2 ounces (2 squares) unsweetened chocolate
> 2 cups milk
> 1 cup sugar
> 4 level tablespoons all-purpose flour
> 2 eggs
> ½ teaspoon almond extract or 1 teaspoon vanilla extract
> pinch of salt
> ½ cup sliced almonds
> sweetened whipped cream

1. In a medium-sized saucepan, melt the chocolate over low heat, stirring constantly once the melting begins. Add the milk and continue to heat, stirring well to blend.

2. In a bowl, whisk together the sugar, flour, eggs, almond extract, and salt. Add to the hot milk mixture. Continue to cook over medium heat, stirring constantly, until the pudding thickens.

3. Serve warm or cold in custard cups. Top each serving with a heaping tablespoon of sliced almonds and whipped cream.

Yield: 6 servings

Lemon Custard Sponge

❊ ❊ ❊

We love this "magic" pudding that bakes into a lemony custard on the bottom with its own crust on top. It's great served warm or cold, and it has a real lemony zing.

> 2 eggs, separated
> 1 cup milk
> 1 scant cup sugar
> ⅓ cup all-purpose flour
> pinch of salt
> juice and zest of 1 lemon

1. Preheat oven to 325°F. Grease six 6-ounce custard

cups. Beat the egg whites until stiff. In a separate bowl, beat the egg yolks.

2. In a small saucepan, heat the milk almost to a boil; do not scald it.

3. In a medium-sized bowl, mix the sugar, flour, and salt. Add to the beaten egg yolks. Add the warm milk and the lemon juice and zest.

4. Fold the mixture into the beaten egg whites. Fill the custard cups two-thirds full.

5. Line a 9- by 13-inch pan with a piece of a brown paper bag or a towel. Place the custard cups on the paper. Add enough hot water to the pan to reach halfway up the sides of the custard cups.

6. Bake for 45 minutes. A crust will form on top.

Yield: 6 servings

Zabaglione (Wine Custard)

❉ ❉ ❉

Zabaglione is a foamy, light-as-a-cloud, sweet egg pudding of Italian origin. It's a charming way to end dinner with special guests.

6 egg yolks
½ cup sugar
⅛ teaspoon salt
1 cup sweet wine, such as Marsala or another fruit-flavored wine

1. Beat the egg yolks with the sugar and salt until the mixture is thick and lemon colored.

2. Stir in the wine. Cook in a double boiler over simmering water, beating constantly with a rotary beater until the mixture foams and thickens. It will double or triple in volume.

3. Spoon the custard into sherbet glasses and chill at least 1 hour, or until serving time.

Yield: 8–10 servings

Rebeca's Delicious Flan

❉ ❉ ❉

In Mexico, where custard is called "flan," the process of baking in a water bath is known as *al baño Maria*. This recipe, passed from Rebeca Median Andrade of Guadalajara, Mexico, to Jane Cooper, and then to me, is simple but sensational.

6 eggs
2 cups milk
2 cans (14 ounces each) sweetened condensed milk

1. Preheat oven to 350°F; grease a 1½-quart custard dish or casserole. Combine the eggs, milk, and condensed milk; blend very well by hand or in a blender.

2. Pour into the custard dish. Put the dish in a larger pan. Add enough hot water to the larger pan to reach halfway up the sides of the dish.

3. Bake for 30 to 40 minutes, until a knife inserted in the center comes out clean.

Yield: 6 servings

VARIATION: For individual servings, bake in greased ramekins for 25 to 30 minutes.

- - - - - - - - - - - - -

CUSTARDS AND PUDDINGS

· · · · · · · · · · ·

What is the difference between a custard and a pudding? Custards are thickened with eggs; puddings are thickened primarily with some kind of starch, such as cornstarch, bread, rice, or cornmeal, though they may contain eggs as well.

- - - - - - - - - - - - -

SAUCES AND CONDIMENTS

A Frenchman once said, "A fine sauce will make even an elephant palatable." That may be true, but to me, a sauce or condiment should enhance and complement a dish, not disguise it. A truly great sauce or condiment is so delicious that it can be eaten by itself. I'm biased, but my Aunt Ina's Relish, for example, livens up any burger or sandwich, and it's terrific even on a plain saltine cracker. I've been known to sneak spoonfuls of Cranberry Salsa or Honey Mustard between meals, just to satisfy a craving.

■ ■ ■ ■ ■ ■ ■ ■ ■ ■

Contributors to this chapter are Glenn Andrews; Janet Ballantyne; Marjorie Page Blanchard; Betty Cavage; Janet Chadwick; Andrea Chesman; Nancy Chioffi and Gretchen Mead; Claire Hopley; Miriam Jacobs; Matt Kelly; Maggie Oster; Phyllis V. Shaudys; Edith Stovel; Maggie Stuckey; and Olwen Woodier.

CLASSIC SAUCES
....
GRAVIES
....
KETCHUP & MUSTARD
....
VINEGARS
....
BARBECUE SAUCES
....
MARINADES
....
DESSERT SAUCES
....
SALSAS
....
CHUTNEY & RELISH
....
FLAVORED BUTTERS

Aunt Ina's Relish

❈ ❈ ❈

Aunt Ina and Uncle Fred Anderson were not really related to us; they were very close friends of my mother's family. When Mother was in high school, she lived in Leonard, Texas, with the Andersons, so that she could go to school there. My dad courted her at their house and proposed to her on Uncle Fred's porch. He ran a country grocery store, and later they moved to Tyler, where I knew them. When I think of their home, I recall good smells coming out of Aunt Ina's kitchen and Uncle Fred bringing in the harvest.

- 2 large heads of cabbage, cored and quartered
- 12 large carrots
- 12 large onions, quartered
- 12 large red and green bell peppers, cored and seeded
- 12 large green tomatoes
- ½ cup plain salt (not iodized)
- 6 cups sugar
- 6 cups cider vinegar
- 1 tablespoon ground turmeric
- 1 tablespoon mustard seed
- 1 tablespoon celery seed

1. In a food processor, one at a time, finely chop the cabbage, carrots, onions, peppers, and tomatoes; mix thoroughly with the salt. Let stand for 2 hours.

2. Using your hands, squeeze all the juice out of the cabbage mixture; transfer the mixture to a large bowl.

3. In a large saucepan, combine the sugar, vinegar, turmeric, mustard seed, and celery seed. Simmer until the sugar is dissolved.

4. Add the vinegar mixture to the vegetables and mix thoroughly. Let stand for 20 minutes.

5. Pour into hot, sterilized jars and seal. This relish keeps well indefinitely in the refrigerator without processing. Or process it in a boiling-water-bath canner (page 384) for 5 minutes for pints, 10 minutes for quarts.

Yield: About 6 pints

Italian Tomato Sauce

❈ ❈ ❈

Tomatoes and seasonings cooked down to a thick, smooth sauce is an all-time favorite. It can be dressed up with sautéed vegetables or mushrooms, crumbled meat or sausage, meatballs, roasted garlic, or sun-dried tomatoes. It goes over pasta, chicken, or omelettes and makes a nice dip for savory appetizers.

- 2 tablespoons olive oil
- 1 cup diced onion
- 2 cloves of garlic, minced
- 1½ teaspoons minced fresh basil, or ½ teaspoon dried
- 1½ teaspoons minced fresh oregano, or ½ teaspoon dried
- 1½ teaspoons minced fresh thyme, or ½ teaspoon dried
- 1 bay leaf
- ¼ cup minced fresh parsley
- ¼ cup grated Parmesan cheese
- ½ cup dry red wine
- 1 teaspoon sugar or honey
- 4 cups thick tomato purée, preferably homemade
- salt and freshly ground black pepper

1. In a medium-sized saucepan, heat the oil and sauté the onion and garlic for about 5 minutes.

2. Add the basil, oregano, thyme, bay leaf, parsley, Parmesan, wine, sugar, tomato purée, and salt and pepper to taste. Cook for 30 minutes or more over low heat, stirring occasionally, until the sauce is the desired consistency.

Yield: 4–5 cups

CLASSIC SAUCES

A well-chosen sauce can make the ordinary extra-ordinary or tie together contrasting elements of a meal. Classic sauces are often rich, but that shouldn't stop you from using them. Just be sure to use top-quality ingredients so that they're worth the splurge, and then go easy on the serving; a little goes a long way.

SAUCY SUGGESTIONS

Use your imagination to create signature dishes, but if you need a starting point, consider these classic uses for sauces.

- Newburg on baked fish
- Horseradish or Béarnaise on slices of beef tenderloin
- Mornay or Hollandaise on broccoli or asparagus
- Mustard Sauce on baked ham or pork loin.

Béchamel Sauce

❁ ❁ ❁

A basic ingredient of many old-time recipes, this classic white sauce is quick and easy, and has endless uses and variations. It's important to remove any taste of raw flour. This is done by cooking the roux, or butter and flour mixture, before adding the liquid.

- 2 tablespoons butter
- 2 tablespoons all-purpose flour
- 1 cup milk
- ½ teaspoon salt or garlic salt
  freshly ground black pepper

1. In a small heavy saucepan, melt the butter over medium heat; whisk in the flour. Cook, whisking constantly, for 3 to 4 minutes. The mixture will be golden and bubbly.

2. Add the milk all at once; continue cooking, whisking constantly, until mixture comes to a boil and is smooth and thick. Remove from heat; add salt and pepper to taste.

Yield: 1 cup

VARIATIONS:

Chicken- or Fish-Flavored Sauce: Replace half the milk with chicken broth or fish stock or clam broth.

Herbed White Sauce: Add 1 teaspoon dried herbs with the salt and pepper.

Cheese Sauce: Add ½ cup grated Cheddar or Parmesan with the salt and pepper.

Newburg Sauce: Beat in 2 egg yolks, 2 tablespoons sherry, and 1 teaspoon dry mustard.

Horseradish Sauce: Add 3 tablespoons prepared horse-radish, 2 tablespoons heavy cream, 1 teaspoon sugar, 1 teaspoon mustard, and 1 teaspoon vinegar.

Mornay Sauce: Add 1 egg yolk and 4 tablespoons grated cheese.

Sauce Supreme: Replace ¼ cup milk with white wine and add 1 teaspoon brandy.

Hollandaise Sauce

❁ ❁ ❁

Hollandaise sauce is considered tricky because it has a tendency to curdle. If you make it in the blender, as I describe below, your chances of this happening are greatly reduced, and the flavor remains superb.

    3 egg yolks
    2 tablespoons lemon juice
    ¼ teaspoon salt
       pinch of white pepper
    ½ cup (1 stick) butter, melted

1. Prepare this sauce just before you are ready to serve a meal. Combine the egg yolks, lemon juice, salt, and pepper in a blender. Blend until smooth.

2. With the blender running, pour in the hot melted butter in a thin, steady stream. Serve immediately.

3. If you must reheat the sauce (not advised), do so in a double boiler, gently. If the sauce begins to separate, beat in 1 tablespoon of boiling water and whisk as rapidly as possible.
    Yield: 1 cup

VARIATIONS:
Orange Hollandaise Sauce: Substitute 1 tablespoon of orange juice for 1 tablespoon of the lemon juice. Add 1 teaspoon grated orange zest to the egg yolk mixture.
Mustard Hollandaise Sauce: Add 1 teaspoon ground mustard and 2 teaspoons Dijon mustard to the egg yolk mixture.

Cheese Sauce

⊠ ⊠ ⊠

Cheese sauce is a wonderful way to dress up vegetables. When we're home alone, we sometimes make a simple supper of a baked potato that is split open, filled with broccoli, and topped with this sauce.

    4 tablespoons butter
    4 tablespoons unbleached all-purpose flour
    1½ cups milk
    1½ cups grated Cheddar or Swiss cheese
       dash of hot sauce
       dash of Worcestershire sauce
    ½ teaspoon Dijon mustard
       salt and freshly ground black pepper

1. In a saucepan, melt the butter and stir in the flour. Add the milk a little at a time, stirring well after each addition to prevent lumps.

2. Add the Cheddar, hot sauce, Worcestershire, and mustard; heat to melt the cheese. Season to taste with salt and pepper. Serve with 6 to 8 cups of cooked vegetables.
    Yield: 3 cups

SIMPLE COCKTAIL AND TARTAR SAUCE

....

Making homemade cocktail and tartar sauce is so easy, and the results so superior to store-bought products, that I easily forgo the convenience of prepared sauces.

For cocktail sauce, which we love on cold shrimp and other seafood, simply stir together 1 cup ketchup, 1 tablespoon freshly squeezed lemon juice, 1 tablespoon prepared horseradish, and a dash of Worcestershire sauce. Add more or less horseradish to suit your taste.

Chill at least 1 hour before serving to allow flavors to blend.

I prepare my tartar sauce with Aunt Ina's Relish (page 263), but any good-quality sweet relish will do. Mix ¼ cup sweet relish with 1 cup mayonnaise, blend well, and chill. This tastes great on Fried Ice Fish (page 348) and other fried seafood.

Béarnaise Sauce

❀ ❀ ❀

Delicately flavored with shallots, this French sauce is named after Béarn, the beautiful region in the Pyrenees, where it originated. It's great on broiled red meats or beef tenderloin and complements fish and eggs.

2 tablespoons minced shallots
2 teaspoons minced fresh chervil
2 teaspoons minced fresh tarragon
¼ cup dry white wine
2 tablespoons tarragon vinegar
¼ teaspoon white pepper
dash of cayenne pepper
3 egg yolks, beaten
2 tablespoons lemon juice
¾ cup (1½ sticks) butter, melted
salt and freshly ground black pepper
2 tablespoons chopped fresh parsley

1. In a small, heavy saucepan, combine the shallots, chervil, tarragon, wine, vinegar, pepper, and cayenne. Bring to a boil and simmer until reduced by half. Remove from heat and cool.

2. In the top of a double boiler over barely simmering

A SHORT COURSE IN SAUCES

....

Sauces have come a long way since the days of the Romans when the sauces did not necessarily relate to the food they accompanied and the flavors were so strong that they turned birds into fish and meat into birds.

One of the earliest of these sauces was *garum,* an extract of juices from fish of the mackerel family with honey, vinegar, fish livers, and anchovy purée.

Today, besides loving many of the classic sauces from French cookery, we enjoy sauces made of puréed fruits and vegetables.

A perfect sauce adds zest, flavor, or piquancy. It should enhance the flavor of a dish, whether as an essential part of it or an accompaniment. At the same time, it should be tasty on its own. And it should never cover or smother the flavor of the food it accompanies.

---

water, whisk together the egg yolks and lemon juice. Add the shallot mixture and beat briskly with a whisk or portable electric mixer until thickened. Remove from the heat and add the butter in a thin stream, beating constantly. Season with salt and pepper to taste and serve garnished with the parsley.

Yield: 1 cup

Mustard Sauce

❀ ❀ ❀

This is one of MomMom's Pennsylvania Dutch recipes that she shared only with family. It keeps a long time in the refrigerator and is wonderful on ham or smoked turkey. MomMom always used a

---

double boiler, but if you stir the sauce constantly, taking care not to let it burn, you can do it in a saucepan over moderate heat.

1 cup brown sugar, firmly packed
½ cup cider vinegar
½ cup water
⅓ cup dry mustard
2 eggs
1 tablespoon all-purpose flour

1. In the top of a double boiler, whisk together all the ingredients. Cook the mixture over simmering water, stirring constantly, until thick, about 5 minutes. Serve warm or cold. This sauce keeps well in the refrigerator.

Yield: 2 cups

Cumberland Sauce

❈ ❈ ❈

This recipe comes from Betty Cavage, who was born in a town formerly called Cumberland on the border of Scotland and England. A generations-old recipe with a rich, red color and superb flavor, it combines elegantly with ham, poultry, venison, or roast beef. Cumberland sauce is traditionally served cold, but if you prefer, spoon it straight from the saucepan.

juice and zest of 2 oranges
juice and zest of 2 lemons
1 cup port wine
1 small shallot, peeled and diced finely
1 cup red currant jelly
½ teaspoon dry mustard
¼ teaspoon ground ginger
dash Worcestershire sauce

1. Make sure that none of the bitter white pith is removed with the orange and lemon zest. Cut the zest into matchstick strips.

2. Place the zest in a small saucepan with the wine and shallot. Simmer for 5 minutes. Cool and set aside.

3. Combine the orange and lemon juice with the wine mixture.

4. Stir in the jelly, mustard, ginger, and Worcestershire sauce. Bring to a boil. Cook, stirring constantly, over low heat for 15 minutes.

5. Remove from heat and cool. Refrigerate until the sauce thickens.

Yield: 2½ cups

Soubise Sauce

❈ ❈ ❈

A rich, white onion sauce with a multitude of uses. It has an affinity for eggs, fish, poultry, and vegetables.

3 tablespoons butter
2 cups chopped onion
¼ cup unbleached all-purpose flour
¼ teaspoon ground fresh nutmeg
dash freshly ground black pepper
1½ cups chicken stock
½ cup heavy cream
chopped fresh parsley

1. In a large, heavy skillet, melt the butter. Stir in the onion and cook over low heat until tender. Do not brown.

2. Let the mixture cool slightly, then spoon it into a blender or food processor. Whirl until puréed.

3. Put the onion mixture into a heavy saucepan; stir in the flour, nutmeg, and pepper. Cook over medium heat, stirring constantly, for several minutes. Gradually add the chicken stock. Cook and stir until bubbly and thick.

4. Add the cream and heat through. Serve immediately. Garnish with parsley.

Yield: 2½ cups

Rémoulade Sauce

❈ ❈ ❈

A dressier alternative to tartar sauce on shellfish, this classic French sauce also complements salads, julienned celery root, or turnips.

1 cup mayonnaise
1 tablespoon drained, finely chopped pickle
1 tablespoon drained capers
1 teaspoon Dijon mustard
1 teaspoon minced fresh parsley
1 teaspoon chopped fresh chervil
½ teaspoon anchovy paste (optional)

1. Combine all ingredients; serve immediately or chill until ready to use.

Yield: 1¼ cups

GRAVIES

For some people, meat without gravy is unthinkable. We don't have it for everyday meals, but for holidays and entertaining, gravy is a must. It makes use of the caramelized essences of the meat and the vegetables cooked along with it. The roasting pan is deglazed using water or wine to pick up all the nuggets of flavor. Then the mixture is thickened with just enough flour to give it body and smoothness.

Never-Fail Pan Gravy

❖ ❖ ❖

The most frequent problem that inexperienced cooks have in making gravy is determining how much water to add to the pan juices. It's pretty safe to start with 1 cup for a small roast (3 to 4 pounds) and 2 cups for a large roast (10 pounds). Use broth if you have it — it will stretch the gravy considerably. Always use cold water or cold broth. Use chicken broth to extend juices from poultry, pork, and veal; for beef and older veal, use beef broth.

pan drippings
salt and freshly ground black pepper
water
beef or chicken broth
all-purpose flour

1. Bring the pan drippings to a boil, stirring and scraping to loosen the small bits of browned meat from the bottom of the pan.

2. Season lightly with salt and pepper and taste the juices. If they taste very rich, add more water or broth, a little at a time, tasting as you go along.

3. When you feel that you have stretched the pan drippings as much as you can while retaining good flavor, remove the pan from the heat and pour the drippings into a blender container. Do not fill the blender more than half full.

4. Let the drippings stand for 1 or 2 minutes to allow the fat to rise to the surface. If there is too much fat (more than 2 tablespoons per cup of drippings), skim the excess fat from the juices.

5. Add 1½ to 2 tablespoons flour (1½ for thin gravy, 2 for thick) to the blender for each cup of juice. Blend until smooth.

GRAVY TECHNIQUES

If you don't have a blender, use my jar method for foolproof gravy. I like to shake up the flour and water in a jar until they are thoroughly blended, then add the mixture to the pan juices. Other cooks stir the flour into the pan drippings, as is done when making a roux, before adding any additional liquid.

Kitchen stores sell gravy separators that are helpful for skimming off excess fat from the pan juices. Some cooks simply float a paper towel over the juices to absorb extra fat before making the gravy right in the roasting pan.

With a pot roast, you can make gravy without flour by using the vegetables cooked with the meat as a thickener. Use the blender or food processor to purée the cooked vegetables and cooking liquid.

If you are not yet comfortable making pan gravy, try all of these methods to determine which works best for you.

6. Return the drippings to the pan. Cook over medium heat, stirring constantly, until the gravy has thickened. Continue to heat for 2 minutes to cook the flour. Adjust seasonings to taste.

Red Wine Gravy

❈ ❈ ❈

I usually make this gravy to serve with Christmas Crown Roast Pork (page 338), but it's also great with a beef roast.

¼ cup pan drippings from roast pork or beef
½ cup dry red wine
1 tablespoon butter
1½ cups water
4 tablespoons all-purpose flour
½ teaspoon garlic salt
½ teaspoon dried rosemary
  freshly ground black pepper

1. Scrape the crusty drippings from the roasting pan and place in a skillet. Add the wine. Cook over medium heat, whisking constantly, until liquid is slightly reduced and bubbling. Add butter; stir well. Remove from heat.

2. Put the water into a pint jar (with a tight lid); add flour. Shake vigorously until the flour and water are blended. Pour flour mixture into the skillet and return to heat. Continue to cook, whisking constantly, until the gravy begins to thicken. Add garlic salt, rosemary, and pepper to taste. Reduce heat to low and simmer for 5 minutes.

Yield: 2 cups

....

FREEZING TIP

....

Soup stocks and gravies can be frozen in ice cube trays so that you can thaw small portions as needed. After the stock or gravy is frozen solid, remove the cubes from the trays and place them in resealable plastic freezer bags or freezer containers. Be sure to label and date them. Freeze for up to 6 months; thaw in the refrigerator, or add directly to cooking liquid.

....

Onion & Mushroom Gravy

❈ ❈ ❈

Succulent pan drippings lend a rich flavor and color to this thick, delicious gravy bubbling with golden onions and tender mushrooms.

pan drippings
1 *tablespoon butter*
1 *tablespoon vegetable oil*
2 *medium onions, sliced*
¼ *pound chopped mushrooms*
¼ *cup unbleached all-purpose flour*
2 *cups water or beef or chicken stock*
¼ *teaspoon freshly ground black pepper*
salt to taste
2 *tablespoons chopped fresh parsley*

1. Drain and degrease the drippings from the roasting pan. Measure out ¼ cup; discard remainder.

2. In a heavy saucepan, melt the butter with the oil. Cook the onions until tender and golden, about 10 minutes. Add the mushrooms. Cook until the liquid evaporates.

3. Blend in the flour. Add the reserved drippings. Cook and stir until light brown.

4. Add the water and stir until thickened. Simmer for 5 minutes. Season with the pepper and salt to taste. Serve hot, garnished with parsley.

Yield: 2½–3 cups

KETCHUP & MUSTARD

If the first thing that comes to mind when you think of ketchup and mustard is red and yellow plastic squeeze bottles, making your own homemade condiments will be a delightful adventure. These recipes are not difficult, but some require a lengthy cooking time. Why not make a day of it? This is a nice project to do with a friend; you can visit while you take turns chopping, stirring, and bottling.

Homemade Ketchup

✖ ✖ ✖

This recipe eliminates a lot of stirring, because much of the cooking is done in the oven.

- 12 *ounces thick tomato paste*
- 3 *green bell peppers*
- 5 *large onions*
- 2 *cups cider vinegar*
- 8 *quarts tomato purée (approximately 24 pounds tomatoes)*
- 1 *cup light corn syrup*
- 1 *cup sugar*
- 1 *teaspoon freshly ground black pepper*
- 2 *tablespoons salt*
- 2 *teaspoons ground allspice*

1. Preheat oven to 200°F. Using a blender, purée the tomato paste, peppers, and onions with about ½ cup of the vinegar. In a large roaster, mix this purée with the tomato purée, the remaining vinegar, the corn syrup, sugar, pepper, salt, and allspice. Stir well. Bring to a boil on top of the stove. Remove from heat.

2. Bake, uncovered, for 10 hours. Do not stir.

3. One hour before the cooking time is up, fill a canner with hot tap water. Preheat water and jars in canner and prepare lids.

4. When the cooking time is up, ladle the hot ketchup into the hot pint jars. Leave ½ inch of headroom. Run a rubber spatula around the insides of the jars to release air bubbles. Wipe the jar rims with a clean cloth. Place lids in position and tighten screw bands.

5. Process in a boiling-water bath for 15 minutes.
Yield: 12 pints

Cranberry Ketchup

✖ ✖ ✖

Cranberries make a dark, rich red ketchup with a tangy fruit flavor. It is sensational on turkey sandwiches and makes a good glaze for baked ham slices.

- 2 *cups chopped onions*
- 4 *cups water*
- 4 *strips (1 by 3 inches) orange zest*
- 8 *cups cranberries (fresh or frozen)*
- 1 *cup white wine vinegar or rice vinegar*
- 1 *cup brown sugar, firmly packed*
- 1 *cup honey*

KETCHUP WITHOUT STIRRING

Spaghetti sauce and ketchup can be reduced on top of the stove by cooking for 3 hours, but you must stir often to avoid boiling over or sticking. Sauces cooked in the oven take longer to reduce, as much as 10 hours, but they do not need to be stirred. They will not boil over, nor will they stick to the pot. To hurry the process toward the end, you can quickly reduce the sauce by cooking it for a short time on top of the stove.

1½ teaspoons plain salt (not iodized)

1 cinnamon stick (3 inches), broken

1 teaspoon whole allspice berries

1 teaspoon whole cloves

3 slices (the size of a quarter) fresh ginger root

1. In a large, heavy, nonreactive pan, combine the onion, water, and zest. Cover and bring to a boil over medium-high heat. Reduce the heat to low and simmer until the onion is softened, about 10 minutes.

2. Add the cranberries and bring the mixture to a boil. Stirring frequently, simmer until the berries are very soft, about 15 minutes.

3. Purée half of the mixture at a time in a blender, food processor, or food mill. Rinse the pan and return the purée to it; add the vinegar, sugar, honey, and salt.

4. Place the cinnamon, allspice, cloves, and ginger in a small muslin spice bag or a square of muslin and tie tightly. Add to the cranberry mixture. Over medium heat, bring to a boil, stirring frequently. Reduce heat to low and cook until very thick, about 30 minutes.

5. Remove the spice bag. Ladle ketchup into six sterilized half-pint jars. Run a rubber spatula around the insides of the jars to release air bubbles. Wipe the jar rims with a clean cloth. Place the lids in position; tighten screw bands.

6. Process in a boiling-water bath for 15 minutes.

Yield: 6 half-pints

Ballpark Mustard

❈ ❈ ❈

Some like it yellow — the little ones especially. This is the mustard for hot dogs and other sausages; it can also be used in potato salads. Turmeric gives it that bright color and a spicy flavor, too.

2 tablespoons dry mustard

1 tablespoon ground turmeric

¼ teaspoon salt

1 teaspoon sugar

water or mixture of water and distilled white vinegar

1. In a small bowl, combine the mustard, turmeric, salt, and sugar. Gradually add water, stirring to make a smooth paste of the desired consistency.

Yield: ¼ cup

Note: Quantities may be doubled or tripled.

KETCHUPS

·················

Our basic tomato ketchup, so necessary for French fries, hamburgers, and hot dogs, is most closely identified with Asian origins, though similar spicy condiments have been around at least since Roman times. *Ketsiap* in China, *kechap* in Malaysia, and *ketjap* in Indonesia are basically brined fish condiments. Seventeenth-century British sailors took these home, where they came to be made of everything from green walnuts to mushrooms. North American colonists made them primarily with tomatoes, though other fruits were also used. Today, ketchups are cooked sauces, used as a condiment, that are made with fruits or vegetables, vinegar, sugar, and spices.

Homemade Mustard

❂ ❂ ❂

Making mustard is fun. Buy mustard seed in bulk from a health food store and you are on your way. If you don't care to use wine, you can substitute water, vegetable broth, or cider.

- 2 ounces (½ cup plus 2 tablespoons) mustard seed
- 1 cup white wine
- ½ cup vinegar (wine, cider, malt, or white)
- ½ cup water
- 2 tablespoons honey
- ½ teaspoon pickling salt
- ½ teaspoon ground allspice

1. Place the mustard seed in a small bowl; cover with the wine, vinegar, and water, and soak overnight. Pour the seeds and liquid into a blender or food processor. Add the honey, salt, and all-spice. Blend until the mixture is thick and smooth. If the mustard is too thick, add more vinegar, water, or wine, 1 tablespoon at a time.

2. Give the mixture a final pulse in the blender and pour into small sterilized jars with airtight screw-top lids. Store in the refrigerator.

Yield: 1½ pints

VARIATIONS: During blending, add 1 tablespoon (or more or less to taste) of your favorite dried herbs, such as tarragon, lemon thyme, or oregano, or add ¼ to ½ cup drained green peppercorns or ½ cup fresh basil. In addition, you can use molasses instead of honey.

CANNON-BULLET COOKING

Mustard seeds should be "bruis'd with a polished Cannon-Bullet, in a large wooden Bowl-Dish," at least according to John Evelyn, author of Acteria: A Discourse on Sallets, *which was published in 1699. If your country store does not sell polished cannon bullets, just grind your mustard seeds with an electric coffee or spice grinder or with a mortar and pestle.*

STORING HOMEMADE MUSTARDS

....

If you like to make larger batches of mustard to give to friends, remember that you can keep mustard 3 to 4 weeks in the refrigerator, though it loses its potency the longer you keep it.

Honey Mustard

❂ ❂ ❂

This mustard is a good spread for sandwiches made with boiled ham or other cold cuts. We also like it with cheese and apple slices on plain crackers.

- 4 tablespoons dry mustard
- 2 tablespoons water
- 1 teaspoon vinegar
- 1 tablespoon vegetable oil
- 2 tablespoons honey

1. In a small bowl, mix the mustard to a stiff paste with the water and vinegar. Stir in the oil until the mixture is smooth, then stir in the honey.

2. Pour into a sterilized jar. Refrigerate, tightly covered.

Yield: ⅓ cup

VINEGARS

Making flavored vinegars, whether spiced, herbal, or fruited, takes little effort and yields impressive results. Infused vinegars add nuances of flavor to your cooking, look great in pretty bottles, and make wonderful culinary gifts.

MAKING FLAVORED VINEGARS

....

Many flavored vinegars can be made right in the bottles in which you will store them or give them away — as long as you have enough time at your disposal to allow the flavor to gradually build during the steeping process. Simply insert the flavoring ingredients into the bottle, add the vinegar — and wait for about a week.

If, however, you suddenly decide in mid-December that you want to give your friends some marvelous herb or spice vinegar for the holidays, you can speed up the process. To do this, first bruise your seasoning ingredients: Crush them with a garlic press, pepper mill, or mortar and pestle. (In the case of fresh herbs, just crumple them a bit.) Place them in a jar with a cover (a mayonnaise jar works well), heat the vinegar to the boiling point, and add it to the jar. Put the lid on and store at room temperature.

Start tasting the vinegar in a day or two. When the flavor is just right, strain out the flavoring ingredients. If the vinegar is cloudy, run it through coffee filters until it's clear. Put some of the seasoning ingredients, this time left whole, into gift bottles, and pour in the vinegar.

Fruit vinegars, such as raspberry, are best made by cooking the main ingredients briefly in the vinegar, then steeping. No matter which method you use, there's very little effort involved and the rewards are tremendous.

All vinegars will keep indefinitely. If you plan to keep them for a long time, though, it's wise to sterilize the vinegar you use as a base.

Base Vinegars

Your choice of vinegar will affect the flavor and color of the final product. Red wine vinegar adds to the color of raspberry vinegar; white wine vinegar shows off herbs, thyme, lemon peel, and spices, and so forth. Distilled white vinegar is fine for such unsubtle uses as hot pepper or pungent garlic vinegars. Experiment according to your own inclinations and preferences.

MAKING VINEGAR

....

To start your flavored vinegars from scratch, you can make the vinegar itself. This requires a large container, a "mother," and liquid to process. The mother is a cloudy or filmy substance that is present in vinegars that have not been sterilized. You can buy a vinegar kit from specialty culinary stores or look for a cloudy deposit or a light film on the top of the vinegar that you have. Add leftover wine or cider to the mother and set aside at room temperature. It takes about 2 weeks for the mother to make vinegar of whatever you've added.

The following vinegars are available in most grocery stores. You don't need to use the most expensive brands; your infusions will make them special enough to please the most epicurean taste.

RED WINE VINEGAR: Attractive to the eye; mildly gutsy.

WHITE WINE VINEGAR: Off-white; delicate in taste.

JAPANESE OR CHINESE RICE VINEGAR (white or red): Very subtle, delicate flavor; be aware that the "seasoned" variety contains sugar.

DISTILLED WHITE VINEGAR: Colorless; very acidic.

APPLE CIDER VINEGAR: Light brown; strong flavor of apples.

Raspberry Vinegar

❈ ❈ ❈

Many people consider raspberry the best of all flavored vinegars. Don't omit the sugar or honey; this vinegar needs a touch of sweetening to bring out its full flavor.

2–2½ cups fresh red raspberries, lightly mashed (frozen raspberries can be used, but if they're presweetened, don't add the sugar or honey)
2 cups red wine vinegar
2 tablespoons sugar or honey

1. Combine all ingredients in the top of a nonreactive double boiler. Place over boiling water, reduce the heat, and cook over barely simmering water, uncovered, for 10 minutes.

2. Pour into a large screw-top jar. Store for 3 weeks, then strain to separate the vinegar from the berries, pressing gently on the berries to extract the juice. If your vinegar is cloudy, pour it through a coffee filter. Pour into bottles, adding a few fresh berries.

Yield: About 2 cups

Note: Paul Corcellet, maker of one of the finest commercial raspberry vinegars, also markets an excellent raspberry syrup that you can find in many gourmet stores. A little of it added to some red wine vinegar will give you an instant raspberry vinegar that may not be exactly like fresh-made, but is still very good.

VARIATIONS:
BLUEBERRY VINEGAR: This ultra-chic and ultragood fruit vinegar is made in exactly the same way as the raspberry vinegar. Use your choice of red or white wine vinegar. The red will give a darker color, but it will have a purplish tinge. For an appealing presentation, bottle the finished vinegar with a few large fresh blueberries and a small cinnamon stick.

PEACH, APRICOT, OR NECTARINE VINEGAR: Follow the procedure for raspberry vinegar, but use white wine vinegar as the base. Peel apricots, peaches, or nectarines before using by dipping them briefly into boiling water, then removing the skin with your fingers. If the fruits are big, cut them into chunks.

USING FRUIT VINEGAR

....

Can you imagine peach vinegar sprinkled on a fruit salad, raspberry vinegar mixed with mayonnaise and used in a chicken salad, and perfect leaves of butterhead lettuce sprinkled with a few edible flowers and dressed in blueberry vinaigrette? Fruit vinegars add a special touch to light marinades and dressings; blend them with mild oils so that their delicate flavors won't be overwhelmed.

Basil and Other Single-Herb Vinegars

❂ ❂ ❂

Follow this basic pattern for any fresh herb vinegar. Dill and chervil make nice alternatives, and tarragon makes one of the best vinegars. Chives make a subtle vinegar; be sure to use a lot of them in the bottles. For small-leaved herbs, such as thyme, use an extra sprig or two.

4 large sprigs of fresh basil
2 cups white wine vinegar

1. Place the basil sprigs into a pint bottle (or divide between two smaller bottles) and pour in the vinegar. Seal.
2. Store for 2 to 3 weeks before using.
Yield: 2 cups

Bouquet Garni Vinegar

❂ ❂ ❂

This vinegar takes on the flavors of a classic French herbal combination. It is ideal in marinades for beef and for dressing roasted vegetables.

1 cup sprigs of parsley
½ cup bay leaves
½ cup sprigs of rosemary
½ cup sprigs of thyme
1 quart white wine vinegar

WHAT GOES WITH WHAT?

As a rule, stronger flavors go with strong vinegars and subtler flavors with more delicate vinegars. When you anticipate lovely color from your herbs or petals, a white wine vinegar would usually be the best choice. Here are some great combinations.

RED WINE VINEGAR
• Rosemary, savory, sage, basil, bay, and garlic
• Sage, parsley, and shallots
• Raspberries and thyme
• Red bell pepper, hot red peppers, garlic, rosemary, and tarragon

WHITE WINE VINEGAR
• Dill, basil, tarragon, and lemon balm

• Savory, tarragon, chervil, basil, and chives
• Blackberries and lavender flowers
• Green onions, green peppercorns, thyme, marjoram, and a bay leaf

APPLE CIDER VINEGAR
• Horseradish, shallot, and hot red pepper
• Dill, mustard seeds, lemon balm, and garlic

SHERRY VINEGAR
• Parsley, thyme, rosemary, and bay leaf
• Apricots and allspice berries

CHAMPAGNE VINEGAR
• Pears and hyssop
• Rose flowers and lemon balm

1. Using a wooden spoon, pack the parsley, bay leaf, rosemary, and thyme into a glass jar. Cover with the vinegar, seal with plastic wrap, and screw on the lid. Allow to steep for 4 to 6 weeks.
Yield: 4½ cups

Mixed Herb Vinegar

❂ ❂ ❂

Here is an all-natural instant salad dressing. Just whisk it with olive oil, and you're ready to toss.

¾ cup chopped fresh basil
¾ cup chopped fresh marjoram
½ cup chopped fresh rosemary
½ cup chopped fresh savory
½ cup chopped fresh thyme
1 quart white wine vinegar

1. Using a wooden spoon, pack basil, marjoram, rosemary, savory, and thyme into a glass jar. Cover with vinegar, seal with plastic wrap, and screw on lid. Allow to steep for 4 to 6 weeks.
Yield: 4¼ cups

BARBECUE SAUCES

You can't grow up in Texas and not love barbecue. Of course, all of us have a special sauce that we insist is the "only" way to go. While I'm partial to my brother's recipe, I love trying new flavors and trading secrets with my friends. Plan on about 1 cup of barbecue sauce for 6 chicken legs or pork chops or 8 to 10 country-style ribs.

Brother Joe's Texas Barbecue Sauce

❁ ❁ ❁

Along with the rest of us, brother Joe was born in Texas. There's nothing Joe likes more than barbecued chicken, and he has spent a lifetime in search of the perfect barbecue sauce. At least once a week he fires up his smoker, makes a batch of Texas Barbecue Sauce, and cooks enough chicken breasts to feed an army. His sauce is equally great on ribs, pork, and beef.

    1   medium onion, chopped
    ½   cup diced celery
    2   tablespoons butter
    1   tablespoon cider vinegar
    2   tablespoons brown sugar
    2   tablespoons lemon juice
    2   cups ketchup
    3   tablespoons Worcestershire sauce
    1   teaspoon dry mustard
    ½   cup water
    ½   teaspoon salt

1. In a skillet, brown the onion and celery in the butter. Add the vinegar, sugar, lemon juice, ketchup, Worcestershire sauce, mustard, water, and salt; simmer on low for 10 to 15 minutes.

Yield: About 3½ cups

BASTING & MARINATING SAFETY TIPS

....

The U.S. Department of Agriculture recommends that food always be marinated in the refrigerator and advises that marinades are for imparting flavor, not destroying bacteria. Bacteria grow rapidly at room temperature and can be transferred to other foods or surfaces. Don't reuse the marinade used on raw meat, poultry, or seafood unless it's boiled first to destroy any bacteria.

Beer & Mustard Barbecue Sauce

❁ ❁ ❁

This is a simple sauce. Since it has little sugar, it isn't quick to burn. When we use it for pork, we add a little more brown sugar, because we like it a tad sweeter.

    2   tablespoons dry mustard
    1   tablespoon brown sugar
    1   cup beer
    1   cup tomato purée or sauce
  4–5   drops Tabasco sauce

1. In a large bowl, combine the mustard and brown sugar. Pour in the beer; stir to mix. Stir in the tomato purée and add the Tabasco sauce. Use as a marinade and brush-on sauce for barbecued chicken and pork.

Yield: 1 cup

Bourbon Barbecue Sauce

❁ ❁ ❁

There are as many barbecue sauces as there are outdoor chefs. Try this one. It's fabulous, indoors or out, for basting and spicing foods and licking off fingers.

1 tablespoon butter
1 tablespoon olive oil
2 cups finely chopped onion
2 cloves of garlic, crushed
½ cup molasses
1 cup ketchup
¼ cup red wine vinegar
1 teaspoon dry mustard
¼ teaspoon freshly ground
   black pepper
2 tablespoons lemon juice
½ teaspoon grated lemon
   zest
1 tablespoon soy sauce
1 tablespoon Hungarian
   paprika
⅓ cup bourbon whiskey

1. In a large, heavy saucepan, melt the butter with the oil. Sauté the onions until tender.

2. Add the garlic and cook 2 minutes longer.

3. Combine the molasses, ketchup, vinegar, mustard, pepper, lemon juice, zest, soy sauce, paprika, and bourbon. Stir into the onion mixture.

4. Bring to a boil, reduce heat, and simmer for 30 minutes, stirring occasionally. Cool and refrigerate in a covered container.

Yield: 2½ cups

Ginger Sauce for Ribs

❈ ❈ ❈

Ooh, are ribs cooked in this spicy sauce something else! The wonderful contrasts of tomato and lemon, honey and coriander are all brought together by the "secret" ingredient — fresh ginger.

1 cup ketchup
3 tablespoons lemon juice
2 tablespoons honey
2 tablespoons Worcester-
   shire sauce
4 teaspoons butter
1 teaspoon ground
   coriander
1 teaspoon finely chopped
   fresh ginger root
1 clove of garlic, finely
   chopped

1. Combine all of the ingredients in a saucepan. Bring to a boil and stir to mix thoroughly (the combination of ginger and vinegar will tickle your nose.) Brush the sauce onto steamed ribs and grill for 10 minutes per side.

Yield: About 2 cups

ABOUT RIBS

....

Spareribs come from the underbelly or side of the pig. Although they have the least meat per bone, spareribs are a favorite among barbecue fans. Pork back ribs, cut from the blade and center section of the pork loin, contain rib bones and the finger meat between the ribs. Country-style ribs are the meatiest variety of pork ribs, and need to be eaten with a knife and fork.

For spareribs and back ribs, allow 1 to 1½ servings per pound, as they have a lot of bone. Plan on about two servings per pound for country-style ribs.

If you cook ribs directly on the grill, they require almost constant attention; they must be basted with oil and turned frequently as they cook for about 45 minutes. Barbecue sauce should be added in the last 10 minutes of cooking.

Steaming ribs before grilling makes them moist and tender and cuts the grilling time. Steam for about 50 minutes in a wok or steamer, then baste them with sauce and grill, covered, for about 10 minutes a side. For smokier meat, sprinkle some sawdust onto the flame before you put the meat onto the grill.

MARINADES

Marinades add flavor nuances to foods, in addition to tenderizing them and adding protective moisture. They are especially useful for foods that will be in contact with high heat, such as those cooked on the grill or under the broiler.

Zesty Beer Marinade

❈ ❈ ❈

When grilling season comes along, we often turn to this piquant marinade. It works its magic equally well on beef, pork, and chicken.

1 cup (8 ounces) flat beer (a light beer is not recommended)
½ cup vegetable oil
2 tablespoons soy sauce
1 tablespoon honey
1 teaspoon dry mustard
½ teaspoon ground ginger
2 cloves of garlic, minced
dash of hot sauce (optional)

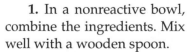

1. In a nonreactive bowl, combine the ingredients. Mix well with a wooden spoon.
Yield: 1½ cups

Soy Ginger Marinade

❈ ❈ ❈

This recipe is one that just showed up from somewhere, but Matthew loves it. It makes a piece of flank steak taste like heaven, and it is good on tuna steaks, too. Use low-sodium soy sauce for a more healthful mix.

½ cup vegetable oil
¼ cup soy sauce
3 heavy dashes of toasted sesame oil
3 tablespoons honey
2 tablespoons vinegar
1½ teaspoons ground ginger
1–1½ teaspoons minced garlic

1. In a large bowl, combine all of the ingredients and beat thoroughly.
Yield: 1 cup

Note: To use, make holes in steak using the tines of a fork. Pour on marinade and refrigerate for at least 2 hours, or overnight, if possible. Turn the meat regularly. Grill over charcoals.

Sesame Lime Marinade

❈ ❈ ❈

The bright Asian flavors of this marinade taste especially great on grilled chicken or fish.

1 cup tamari or soy sauce
½ cup lime juice
½ cup sesame oil
¼ cup mirin (sweet cooking sake)
4 large cloves of garlic, minced
3 tablespoons crushed red pepper flakes
2 tablespoons grated ginger root

1. Combine all ingredients in a small bowl.
Yield: About 2 cups

Note: To use, pour over chicken or fish and marinate, covered, in the refrigerator for 30 minutes.

FROM THE ITALIAN

The English words "marinade" and "marinate" come from the Italian word *marinato*. A marinade is a savory acidic sauce in which a food is soaked to enrich its flavor or to tenderize it. To marinate is to steep food in a marinade.

DESSERT SAUCES

It may seem like gilding the lily to add a sweet sauce to an already sweet dessert, but sometimes a dollop of whipped cream or a pool of light custard is just the touch needed to finish off a dessert in style. For other sweet sauce ideas, look for fruit purées (chapter 10) and classic sundae sauces (page 352).

English Custard Sauce

❈ ❈ ❈

Dinner in England is followed by "pudding," the name given to any sweet dessert. Pies and baked puddings are often accompanied by a sweet, light custard such as this one. You can also serve this sauce with baked apples and any crisp or cobbler.

  ⅓ cup sugar
  2 tablespoons cornstarch
  3 egg yolks
  2 cups milk or light cream
  1 tablespoon vanilla extract

1. In the top of a double boiler, combine the sugar and cornstarch. Whisk in the egg yolks until smooth.

2. In a medium-sized saucepan, heat the milk. When

PERFECT WHIPPED CREAM

Who doesn't love a cloud of fresh whipped cream? It is so easy to make that I can't imagine why so many people opt for the kind in an aerosol can. For a perfect whipped cream to dollop on desserts, chill the cream, beaters, whisk, and bowl for at least 15 minutes. Add 1 tablespoon sugar (or to taste) and ½ teaspoon vanilla extract to 1 cup cream. Beat with an electric mixer until soft peaks form (the cream will flop over slightly when the beaters are lifted straight up). Finish the beating with a whisk, or watch carefully and beat on low until the cream just begins to stand up when the beaters are lifted. Do not overbeat. The cream should be about double in volume, yielding about 2 cups. Use whipped cream as soon as possible.

To make chocolate whipped cream, add 2 tablespoons cocoa powder and increase the sugar to 3 tablespoons. Let the cream chill for 45 minutes to 1 hour before whipping; this will allow the cocoa powder to dissolve into the cream.

---

it reaches a boil, pour half over the egg mixture, stirring constantly. Add the rest of the milk and the vanilla.

3. Place the top of the double boiler over simmering water (it must not touch the water). Stirring constantly, cook for 2 minutes or until the mixture thickens and is smooth.

4. Remove from heat and pour into a small jug. Serve immediately or cover with wax paper to prevent a skin from forming.

Yield: 2 cups

VARIATION: For a richer custard, whip ½ cup heavy cream until it is thick but not stiff and fold into the custard. Chill, if desired.

SALSAS

Salsa *simply means "sauce" in Spanish. It is traditionally made with red or green tomatoes, peppers, onion, and cilantro (fresh coriander) and is used as a dip for tortillas or as a sauce. With the ever-increasing popularity of southwestern cuisine, many flavorful variations have appeared. Salsas are wonderful with grilled chicken and fish, as well as with beans and rice and tortilla chips.*

Classic Red Restaurant Salsa

❂ ❂ ❂

This salsa is close to the salsa you'll most often find on the table, along with chips, when you sit down in a Mexican restaurant. Try it with a basket of blue, white, and yellow corn chips for added interest.

1 pound Roma or plum tomatoes, seeded and minced
3 tablespoons tomato paste
1 serrano or jalapeño
   pepper, seeded and minced
¼ cup minced cilantro
¼ cup minced onion
½ teaspoon minced garlic

1. Combine all ingredients in a small bowl and let sit, covered, at room temperature for 30 minutes before using. Or chop all of the ingredients roughly and then run them in a food processor, leaving quite a bit of texture. Again, let the salsa sit before serving.

Yield: About 1¼ cups

Black Bean Salsa

❂ ❂ ❂

The combination of black beans and oranges has been popular in Brazil for years, but turning it into a sprightly salsa is a recent innovation. You could also stir a little of this salsa into chicken broth to make a delicious "instant" soup.

½ cup minced onion
2 tablespoons olive oil
1 teaspoon ground cumin
   juice of ½ lime
¼ cup orange juice
   sections from 1 navel orange,
   cut in half
½ cup black beans, soaked,
   cooked, and drained (or
   use a 1-pound can of black
   beans, well rinsed)
¼ cup chopped fresh cilantro
   or parsley

1. Cook the onion in the olive oil until limp. Add the cumin and cook for 2 or 3 minutes longer.

2. Add the lime and orange juices, the orange, beans, and cilantro and mix well. Keep covered and chilled until needed.

Yield: About 2½ cups

Tomatillo Salsa

❂ ❂ ❂

Tomatillos look like small green tomatoes wrapped in a papery husk. If you can't find them, green tomatoes work well, too, especially if you add a little more lemon juice. This is a very mild salsa: Roasted poblano peppers are not very hot, and the tomatillos are pleasantly tart. If you want it zippier, add hot sauce, chili pepper, or pinches of cayenne.

1 poblano pepper
8 medium tomatillos
1 cup chopped red onion
¼ teaspoon vegetable broth
   mix
¼ cup water
⅛ teaspoon lemon juice
3 tablespoons minced fresh
   cilantro

1. Preheat broiler. Have a brown paper bag ready.

2. Place the pepper 6 inches under the broiler and char it without burning. After about 6 minutes, use wooden spoons to rotate the pepper, taking great care not to pierce it. Continue to turn and blacken all sides. When all sides are done, immediately place the pepper in the brown bag and let it cool for 10 minutes. The steam released in the bag will help loosen the skin.

3. Remove the pepper from the bag and slip off the skin. Cut off the stem, remove the seeds, and chop.

4. Husk and quarter the tomatillos. In a medium-sized saucepan, combine the tomatillos, pepper, onion, broth mix, water, and lemon juice. Bring the mixture to a boil; reduce the heat and simmer for 15 minutes.

5. When the mixture has cooled, blend in the cilantro. Serve at room temperature or chill and serve cold.

Yield: About 1 cup

Pineapple Salsa

❂ ❂ ❂

Refreshing pineapple salsa lends a tropical flair to broiled chicken or grilled fish.

1 cup finely chopped pineapple (if you're using canned pineapple, don't use the crushed variety)

2 tablespoons finely minced onion

3 tablespoons fresh cilantro or mint

1 serrano chili, seeded and finely minced

1. In a small bowl, combine all ingredients. Refrigerate for at least 30 minutes.

Yield: About 1⅓ cups

Tomato-Mango Salsa

❂ ❂ ❂

Tomatoes and mangoes combine for a wonderful, mellow salsa that is terrific over flounder, turbot, or sole. This makes a classy company dish that is prepared in very short order.

½ mango, peeled and chopped

1½ medium tomatoes, seeded and chopped

½ onion, diced

1 teaspoon chopped fresh parsley

1 teaspoon lemon juice freshly ground black pepper

1. In a medium bowl, mix the mango, tomatoes, onion, parsley, lemon juice, and pepper to taste. Cover and refrigerate until chilled.

Yield: 2 cups

Note: To use with fish, place four 6-ounce fillets of turbot, flounder, or sole fillets

CREATIVE USES FOR SALSA

....

- Serve with eggs for a perked-up brunch.

- Use in hero sandwiches and wraps for a light, spicy alternative to mayonnaise.

- Mix a drained, rinsed can of black beans and a drained can of corn; add salsa to taste for dressing. This makes a super last-minute lunch or supper.

- Serve over fish or chicken breasts, or mix with a little mayonnaise for a snappy tartar sauce.

in a microwave-safe dish. Cover and microwave on high for 2 minutes, then check. The fish should be cooked through and have a flaky texture. (Depending on the size of the fillets, you may need to microwave them for another minute or two.) Arrange the fillets on plates. Ladle some of the chilled salsa on top of each fillet and serve immediately.

CHUTNEY & RELISH

In olden times, when there was little or no refrigeration, chutneys and relishes were one way of preserving garden produce for winter days when fresh tastes (and vitamins) were scarce. That they are still enjoyed today shows the ingenuity of our ancestors in assembling appetizing combinations of fruits, vegetables, and spices and in borrowing cooking traditions from other cultures. These condiments are a boon in livening up quickly prepared food in busy modern households.

STORAGE GUIDELINES

....

If chutneys and relishes are to be stored in the pantry, they must be processed in a water bath. Because of their sugar and vinegar content, they'll also keep well in the refrigerator, without processing, for 4 to 6 weeks.

Pear Ginger Chutney

❁ ❁ ❁

Of all the chutneys, pear is my favorite; the fruit mellows the spicy sauce so perfectly. I like to add it to chicken salad, and I have been known to plunk a spoonful on top of a bagel and cream cheese.

    10 cups (5 pounds) peeled,
        sliced, firm, ripe pears
    ½   cup finely chopped
        green bell peppers
    1½ cups seedless raisins
    4   cups sugar
    1   cup chopped crystallized
        ginger
    3   cups cider vinegar
    ½   teaspoon salt
    ½   teaspoon whole allspice
        berries
    ½   teaspoon whole cloves
    3   cinnamon sticks (2 inches
        long)

1. Place the pears, peppers, raisins, sugar, ginger, vinegar, and salt in a saucepan.

2. Tie allspice and cloves in a cheesecloth bag and add to the pan, along with the cinnamon.

3. Cook slowly until pears are tender and mixture is thick, about 1 hour. Remove spices.

4. Ladle into hot, sterilized jars, leaving ½ inch of headroom. Run a rubber spatula around the insides of the jars to release air bubbles. Wipe the jar rims with a clean cloth. Place lids in position and tighten screw bands.

5. Process in a boiling-water-bath canner (page 384) for 10 minutes.

Yield: About 10 half-pints

Fruit & Tomato Chutney

❁ ❁ ❁

Robustly fruity and with a nice, tawny color, this is a chutney John likes with pork chops or grilled swordfish.

    4   pounds red tomatoes,
        peeled, cored, and chopped
    5   large tart green apples,
        peeled, cored, and
        chopped
    1   large onion, diced
    2   cloves of garlic, minced
    1½ cups raisins

1 cup diced dried apricots
1 cup cider vinegar
⅓ cup finely diced crystallized ginger
2 teaspoons salt
1 teaspoon ground cinnamon
dash of cayenne pepper

1. In a stainless steel or enameled pot, combine all ingredients. Cook, uncovered, on medium heat for 1 hour 30 minutes, or until very thick, stirring occasionally.

2. Fill hot, sterilized half-pint jars, leaving ½ inch of headroom. Run a rubber spatula around the insides of the jars to release air bubbles. Wipe the jar rims with a clean cloth. Place lids in position and tighten screw bands.

3. Process in a boiling-water-bath canner (page 384) for 10 minutes.

Yield: 11 half-pint jars

Corn Relish

❉ ❉ ❉

My grandmother always had this wonderful relish on her table for holidays and dinner with company. She'd put it in her best cut-glass dish, which showed off its bright colors and made the whole table festive.

8 cups raw corn kernels, cut from the cob
3 cups chopped onions

3 cups cider vinegar
¾ cup brown sugar, firmly packed
½ cup white corn syrup
½ cup chopped green bell pepper
½ cup chopped red bell pepper
7 teaspoons pickling salt
1 tablespoon dry mustard

1. In a large saucepan, mix all ingredients thoroughly.

2. Cover and boil for 15 minutes, stirring often.

3. Pour into clean, hot pint jars, leaving ½ inch of headroom.

4. Process in a boiling-water-bath canner (page 384) for 15 minutes.

Yield: 4–5 pints

Pepper Relish

❉ ❉ ❉

Whether on a simple hot dog or a grilled pork tenderloin steak, this puts the green bottled relish served at cookouts to shame.

12 onions
12 green bell peppers
12 red bell peppers
2 quarts boiling water
2 cups sugar
2 cups white vinegar
3 teaspoons pickling salt

1. Chop the onions and peppers. Cover with the

water. Let stand for 5 minutes and drain.

2. Combine the sugar, vinegar, and salt. Add the vegetables and boil for 5 minutes.

3. Pour into hot, sterilized jars, leaving ½ inch of headroom. Seal. Process in a boiling-water-bath canner (page 384) for 5 minutes.

Yield: 6 pints

CONDIMENT PARADE

- CHUTNEY. Consisting of fruit, vinegar, sugar, and spices, chutneys can be smooth to chunky in texture and mild to fiery in spiciness. The name comes from the East Indian word *chatni*. In India, sweet chutneys are often paired with curry dishes.

- RELISH. A mixture of chopped vegetables, often pickles or peppers, vinegar, and spices.

- VINEGAR. An essential ingredient in many sauces and condiments, vinegar relies on bacteria to convert fermented liquids, such as wine or cider, into weak acetic acid. The term stems from the French *vin aigre*, or "sour wine."

FLAVORED BUTTERS

Lift everyday foods out of the ordinary by dressing them up with delectable buttery spreads. Since a little goes a long way, a flavored butter is often a healthier choice than a quantity of rich sauce. The seasoning possibilities are almost limitless.

CLARIFYING BUTTER

....

Clarified butter, also called drawn butter or ghee, is simply butter from which the milky solids have been removed. This has several advantages: It is pure golden butter, without sediment, to serve with lobster, artichokes, and other dipped foods; it cooks longer and hotter than plain butter without scorching, separating, or becoming bitter; and it keeps longer without becoming rancid.

To clarify butter, melt as much butter as you want over low heat. Allow the solids to settle to the bottom, then carefully pour or skim off the clear butterfat from the top. Store in the refrigerator for up to 6 weeks if you are not going to use it immediately.

Shallot or Chive Butter

❈ ❈ ❈

Butter is the perfect complement to these aristocrats of the onion family. Serve shallot or chive butter on hot steaks, chops, fish, or vegetables. It's also great on sandwiches and baked potatoes.

- 4 small shallots (if making shallot butter)
- 2 tablespoons finely snipped fresh chives (if making chive butter)
- ½ cup (1 stick) unsalted butter, softened
- salt
- freshly ground black pepper

1. For shallot butter, crush the shallots in a garlic press. Mix with the butter. Cream well and season to taste with salt and pepper.

2. For chive butter, cream the chives with the butter. Season to taste with salt and pepper.

3. Cover and chill butter until flavors blend, at least 4 hours.

Yield: ½ cup each flavor

Garlic-Butter Garlic Bread

❈ ❈ ❈

Garlic bread of this sort is strictly an American invention, regardless of the fact that it's served in thousands of Italian restaurants in this country. And we love it! There are many milder versions of garlic bread, including those made with garlic powder and commercial garlic salt. This is not one of those.

- 1 loaf French or Italian bread
- 2 tablespoons butter, softened
- 2 tablespoons olive oil
- 1 tablespoon minced garlic
- ⅓ cup minced fresh herbs (optional)

1. Preheat broiler.

2. Cut the loaf of bread lengthwise, as though you were making a sub or hero sandwich.

3. Combine the butter, oil, garlic, and herbs, if desired, in a small bowl. Spread onto the inside of the bread (both top and bottom portions). Place, opened sides up, on a flat baking sheet.

4. Broil briefly, just until brown at the edges. (You don't want to burn the garlic.)

5. To serve, put the halves back together into a loaf shape, then cut into slices as wide or narrow as you wish.

Yield: 1 loaf

Winter or Summer Herbed Butter Blend

❀ ❀ ❀

These are basic guidelines for tasty butters; feel free to try other herbs that you have on hand. Serve herb butters in little ramekins, or spoon them onto wax paper, roll up gently, and refrigerate. When they are firm, roll them again until uniformly round. Then you can cut them into pretty round pats.

Winter Blend

- 3 cloves of garlic, minced
- 3 teaspoons dried oregano
- 2 teaspoons dried marjoram
- 1 teaspoon dried thyme
- ½ teaspoon freshly ground black pepper
- 1 cup (2 sticks) unsalted butter, softened

Summer Blend

- 2–3 tablespoons dried dillweed
- 1 tablespoon chopped fresh parsley
- 2 cloves of garlic, minced
- 2 teaspoons chopped fresh lemon verbena, or 3 drops lemon oil
- ½–¾ teaspoon freshly ground black pepper
- 1 cup (2 sticks) unsalted butter, softened
- salt
- dry mustard

1. For each blend, mix all the herbs and pepper thoroughly. Add the herb mixture to the butter; blend well. For the summer blend, add salt and mustard to taste.

2. Cover and chill butters until flavors blend, at least 4 hours.

Yield: 1 cup each flavor

Note: Herb butters may be frozen for up to 3 months.

Honey-Orange Butter

❀ ❀ ❀

My grandchildren love to have afternoon tea with me when they visit. I give them chamomile, mint, or cambric tea and fresh scones with this simple butter topping.

- 2 tablespoons orange juice concentrate
- 2 tablespoons honey
- ½ cup (1 stick) butter, softened

1. Stir the orange juice concentrate and honey into the butter; mix thoroughly. Make 1 day ahead, to let flavors blend.

Yield: ½ cup

· · · · · · · · · · · · · · · · · · · ·

BROWNED BUTTER FOR VEGETABLES

· · · · · · · · · · · ·

Browned butter has a wonderfully nutty flavor. It is not hard to make, but you must use clarified butter, or it will burn easily. Place ¼ cup clarified butter in a saucepan and cook over low heat until lightly browned; add a teaspoon of lemon juice, if desired.

· · · · · · · · · · · · · · · · · · · ·

BEVERAGES

I was once told at a local restaurant that "iced tea isn't in season"! My Southern roots tell me that iced tea is a year-round beverage that goes with anything, anytime. Today, wonderful variations are available, Iced Chai and Apple Mint Iced Tea among them. But I do understand why many beverages have a seasonal appeal. A cup of steaming Hot Mulled Cider in late November is a great warmer. In February, a mug of homemade Hot Chocolate helps us cozy up with a good book in front of the fire. And a tall, frosty glass of Old-Fashioned Homemade Lemonade quenches a summer thirst. Many beverages also have event appeal: mint juleps and the Kentucky Derby, a Chocolate Soda and a big date, Wassail and Christmas caroling. So, cheers — whatever the season!

■ ■ ■ ■ ■ ■ ■

Contributors to this chapter are Glenn Andrews, Stephen Cresswell, Jennifer Storey Gillis, Miriam Jacobs, Elizabeth Knight, Maggie Oster, Nancy Ralston and Marynor Jordan, Bertha Reppert, Diana Rosen, Marian Sebastiano, Phyllis V. Shaudys, Edith Stovel and Pamela Wakefield, Maggie Stuckey, and Pattie Vargas and Rich Gulling.

ADES & QUENCHERS
....
TEA
....
COFFEE
....
CHOCOLATE DRINKS
....
SPICED DRINKS

········· MARTHA'S FAVORITES ·········

Old-Fashioned Homemade Lemonade

❈ ❈ ❈

In the heat of the summer, ice-cold lemonade is the quintessential drink, and fresh-squeezed is the best kind. Loaded with vitamin C, it cools you quickly while giving you a fast pick-me-up. I keep a jar of sugar syrup in the refrigerator at all times, so that we can make a pitcher of lemonade on short notice.

Lemon Zest Sugar Syrup

2 *cups water*
4 *cups sugar*
strips of zest from 3 lemons

Lemonade

1 *cup lemon juice (about 4 lemons)*
pinch of salt
½ *cup Lemon Zest Sugar Syrup*
4 *cups ice water*
fresh springs of mint

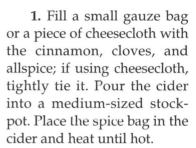

1. For the syrup, bring the water and sugar to a boil in a medium-sized saucepan. Cook for 5 minutes, until the sugar is dissolved. Add the lemon zest. Allow the mixture to cool to lukewarm; pour into a glass jar and store in the refrigerator.

2. For the lemonade, combine the lemon juice, salt, syrup, and ice water in a tall pitcher. Stir well and pour into tall, ice-filled glasses. Garnish with fresh sprigs of mint.

Yield: Lemon Zest Sugar Syrup, 4 batches of lemonade; 1 batch of lemonade, six 8-ounce servings

Hot Mulled Cider

❈ ❈ ❈

Mulled cider is to winter-time what lemonade is to summer. It warms the body and the spirit when it's cold outside.

2 *cinnamon sticks*
12 *whole cloves*
1 *teaspoon allspice berries*
1 *gallon cider*
2 *cups bourbon whiskey (optional)*

1. Fill a small gauze bag or a piece of cheesecloth with the cinnamon, cloves, and allspice; if using cheesecloth, tightly tie it. Pour the cider into a medium-sized stock-pot. Place the spice bag in the cider and heat until hot.

2. Simmer for 30 minutes, so that the spices can permeate the cider. Add the bourbon before serving, if desired. Serve piping hot.

Yield: 12–14 servings

Cranberry Fizz

❈ ❈ ❈

This is a popular punch for any special occasion. It's simply fruit juice jazzed up with a little bit of bubble and an optional splash of vodka.

1 *quart cranberry juice*
1 *quart orange juice*
1 *quart club soda*
1½ *cups vodka, (optional)*
fresh fruit or ice ring

1. Combine juices, soda, and vodka, if desired, in a punch bowl. Add fruit for garnish.

Yield: 16 servings

VARIATION: Use pineapple juice or grapefruit juice instead of cranberry.

ADES & QUENCHERS

Picture a long, cold drink in an iced glass, and you have the image of summer refreshment. At your next gathering, put away the bottled soft drinks and see if everyone isn't delighted by these old-fashioned homemade beverages.

Rhubarb Punch

✠ ✠ ✠

We make this punch in the late spring and early summer, when rhubarb is abundant. If you choose bright red stalks, the punch will have a lovely pink tinge.

    4 cups chopped rhubarb
    4 cups water
    1 cup sugar
       sliced lemons

1. In a medium-sized saucepan, combine the rhubarb and water. Cook for 10 minutes, until rhubarb is tender. Let the mixture cool. Strain and add the sugar. Serve with lemon slices.

Yield: 6–8 servings

Raspberry Shrub

✠ ✠ ✠

On a nineteenth-century farm, cool places for food storage were at a premium. Recipes such as this one produced a concentrate that would occupy little room in the springhouse but made quite a bit of drink when mixed with water. The addition of vinegar helped prevent spoilage and gave the drink a pleasant nip.

    2 cups raspberries (fresh or
       frozen)
    ½ cup white wine vinegar
    2 cups sugar

1. Place the raspberries in a small saucepan. Cover with the vinegar and mash with a potato masher. Begin heating on low heat; add the sugar gradually until all of it is dissolved. Bring to a boil and remove from heat.

2. Strain into another vessel; allow the mixture to drip so as to extract as much liquid as possible. Cool slightly, but pour into a bottle just before it becomes luke-warm. Refrigerate.

3. To make one drink, stir ¼ cup of shrub into a glass of water. Add ice.

Yield: 12–14 servings

Molasses Switchel

✠ ✠ ✠

Switchel was like a pioneer version of Gatorade; it was used as a thirst-quencher during haying. It replaced body fluid after exertion and acted as a digestive aid. Try it after a back-yard baseball game.

    3–4 quarts water
      ½ cup apple cider vinegar
    1½ cups sugar
      ⅓ cup light molasses
      2 ounces freshly grated
         ginger root

ICE IS NICE

To make an ice ring, pour a small amount of water in a ring mold and add fruit slices, berries, mint leaves, or edible flowers. Freeze, then add water and fruit to fill the mold. Freeze solid. Remove the ring from the mold and use it to chill and adorn a punch bowl. You can also add fruit to ice-cube trays to make attractive individual cubes. If you want ice that won't dilute your drinks, freeze ginger ale, white grape juice, or another clear juice.

1. In a large saucepan, combine 1 quart of the water, the vinegar, sugar, molasses, and ginger root. Simmer, uncovered, for about 5 minutes. Remove from heat, cover; cool for about 30 minutes.

2. Pour slowly into a glass jug containing 2½ quarts of water. Top off with enough water to make 1 gallon. Chill immediately.

Yield: Eleven 12-ounce servings

Passion Punch

❂ ❂ ❂

It's not just the bright red color that gives this punch its name; it's that in my family, kids and adults alike have a passion for it!

1 gallon apple juice
1 gallon unsweetened cranberry juice
6 ounces apple juice concentrate, thawed
1 liter sparkling mineral water
ice cubes

1. Combine all ingredients in a punch bowl.

Yield: 20 servings

Herb and Fruit Juice Combinations

❂ ❂ ❂

Appetizing and healthful, fruit juices are refreshing on their own, but with the addition of herbs, they provide even more pleasure and nutrition.

Apple juice or scented geranium infusion/scented geranium
Cider or apple juice/sage
Cranberry juice/savory
Grapefruit juice/marjoram
Lemonade/lemon verbena
Mint infusion or apple juice/mint
Orange juice or sherry/rosemary
Parsley infusion or dry white wine/parsley
Purple grape juice/thyme
Red grape juice/lemon balm
Tomato or vegetable juice/basil or lovage
White grape juice/lemon thyme
White wine or tarragon infusion/tarragon (add vinegar instead of all or part of the lemon juice)
White wine/sweet woodruff (this is the famous May Wine taste)

1. For each 1 cup of juice, add 1 teaspoon of fresh herbs. Allow herbs to steep in the juice for 30 minutes before serving.

DRINKING WORDS

....

ADE. A drink made by combining water, sugar, and citrus juice.

COOLER. An iced drink, usually with an alcoholic beverage as a base.

GROG. A hot drink made with rum, sugar or honey, and boiling water. Usually garnished with a slice of lemon and a few whole cloves.

PUNCH. Traditionally, a concoction of hard liquor, wine or beer, and nonalcoholic beverages. Many punches today are nonalcoholic. The word comes from the Hindi word *pãc*, or five, for five ingredients.

SHRUB. Fruit juice, sugar, and vinegar combinations, shrubs are served over ice, with or without soda water. Colonial-day shrubs usually had brandy or rum in them.

TODDY. Usually hot, toddies are made with brandy or rum, whiskey, very hot water, sugar, spices, and lemon.

Basic Wine Cooler

❁ ❁ ❁

A wine cooler is a delicious way to have your wine and drink it, too. You can sip this all afternoon for refreshment without taking in too much alcohol. It is especially attractive and tasty with white or golden-colored wines.

½ glass wine, such as Peach
    Wine (page 442)
¼ glass lemonade
¼ glass Sprite or other
    lemon-lime soda

1. Chill all ingredients; combine in a glass. Add ice, if desired.

Yield: 1 serving

. . . .

MIMOSAS

. . . .

Mimosas add a little elegance to a brunch or afternoon party. Serve them in flutes or other stemmed glasses. Fill ⅔ of the glass with chilled orange juice. Top off with chilled champagne and stir.

. . . .

Whiskey Sour Punch

❁ ❁ ❁

John's sister Judy passed on this fun punch recipe. She serves this when small crowds gather at her California home.

Stretch it with more club soda or lemonade.

1 can (12 ounces) frozen
    lemonade concentrate
1 can (6 ounces) frozen
    limeade concentrate
1 quart club soda, chilled
1 bottle (750 ml) whiskey

1. In a large pitcher or punch bowl, combine all ingredients. Serve over ice.

Yield: About twelve 6-ounce servings

A Proper Kentucky Derby Mint Julep

❁ ❁ ❁

Kentuckians — and the honorary ones who go for the Derby or celebrate this great horse race elsewhere — care deeply about their mint juleps. Silver cups are traditional for serving juleps, but glasses are just fine, too.

½ tablespoon sugar
1 tablespoon minced fresh
    mint leaves
1 tablespoon water
crushed ice — lots of it
1½ ounces Kentucky bourbon
1 large sprig of fresh mint
1 straw, cut in half

1. In a small bowl, combine the sugar and mint leaves. Using the back of a wooden spoon or a muddler,

mash the sugar and mint until a paste is formed. Add the water and stir for 1 or 2 minutes.

2. Fill a julep cup or glass halfway with crushed ice. Pour in the bourbon and the mint mixture, then fill the rest of the glass with more crushed ice. Insert the sprig of mint into the glass, along with the straws.

3. Put onto a tray, then place in your refrigerator or freezer for 1 hour to frost the glasses.

Yield: 1 serving. To make more, multiply the ingredients by the number of servings.

Note: A muddler, usually made of lignum vitae wood, is a rod with a flattened end designed to mash or crush ingredients, usually mint for juleps. Good hardware stores often stock muddlers.

. . . .

EASY GARNISHES

. . . .

Spear melon cubes, cherries, and pineapple chunks on thin drinking straws.

• Add an old-fashioned candy stick to each drink for a sweet swizzle.

• Put your glasses in the freezer until they become frosty, then dip their rims in salt or colored sugar.

. . . .

TEA

There are teas for all occasions: for morning, afternoon, and bedtime, teas to soothe, and teas to stimulate. In recent years, our appreciation of tea has expanded to include herbal tisanes (some of which are centuries old) and a wide array of green teas, barks, and spices. Taking a break for tea or making a pot to share with a companion is somehow very relaxing.

About Tea

All the world's tea, more than 3000 varieties, comes from just one plant: *Camellia sinensis*, an evergreen bush native to China. Tea varies in flavor according to soil, altitude, and climate. The delicate first leaves and bud are prized over the more mature leaves. Processing further distinguishes teas: Green tea is merely steamed, rolled, and dried; black tea is fermented; and oolong is semifermented, a compromise between green and black. Teas are often blended with other teas or combined with fruit, flowers, and spices.

Popular Varieties of Tea

Ceylon Black (Sri Lanka). A crisp, clean, refreshing tea that is excellent with foods, sweet, and savory. It adds brightness to blends.

Darjeeling. The champagne of teas, darjeeling comes from India and is fragrant in the cup. It's available in green and oolong varieties.

Earl Grey. A blend of Chinese or Indian black teas and oil of bergamot, a Mediterranean, pear-shaped citrus fruit.

English Breakfast. A combination of Keemun for fragrance, Ceylon for brightness, and Assam for heartiness.

Lapsang Souchong. A Chinese tea that is strong and smoky because it is dried over wood. Enjoy plain or with lemon.

Sencha. This excellent green tea from Japan is lightly steamed and refreshing, perfect as a "guest tea" or with meals.

Ti Kwan Yin. From China and Taiwan, *ti kwan yin* is an oolong with an exquisite fragrance and full-mouth taste that defies description.

HOW TO MAKE A PERFECT POT OF TEA

Start with cold water, and bring to a boil. Meanwhile, prewarm your teapot by filling it with hot water from the tap. As soon as the water boils, empty the teapot and measure in your tea; use approximately 1 teaspoon for each cup of tea. (Why do you think it's called a teaspoon?) Tradition demands that you take the teapot to the kettle and pour in the boiling water.

Let steep for 3 to 5 minutes. The exact timing depends on your taste preferences and on the tea you start with: Large leaves take longer to brew. Pour through a strainer into teacups.

Using a tea ball to hold the loose tea makes things much simpler; you won't have to strain the tea into the cups, and you can remove it so that the tea doesn't get too strong.

Set to a Tea

Tea may be served from a dining table, coffee table, sideboard, cart, or tray. Cloth napkins are a must. Various serving pieces of different heights, shapes, and materials will add visual interest to your table. Don't fret if you don't have a matched tea set; a mix of patterns and materials will create a unique and stylish setting. Below are the essentials for a seated afternoon tea.

Centerpiece. Keep fresh flowers or plants small and below eye level. Do not light candles unless it is dark enough that you need them.

Cozy. This colorful padded or quilted device covers your teapot to keep the contents warm.

Creamer or pitcher. Used for serving milk, this piece usually matches the sugar bowl.

Lemon plate and fork. Any small plate may be used. Place a two-pronged fork atop thinly sliced lemon.

Pedestal cake stand. Line the surface with a pretty napkin or doily.

Sandwich plate. This rectangular or square plate may also be used for sweets.

Strainer and stand. Use these to remove loose tea and to prevent drips from staining the tablecloth.

Sugar bowl. Remove the lid and place a spoon, tongs, or sugar shell in the bowl. If you are serving honey, use a small pitcher.

Teacups, saucers, and plates. Pieces need not match as long as they complement one another and share common colors.

Teapot. Silver is the queen of teapot materials, but a ceramic, pottery, or bone china pot holds heat better. Use a pot that is large enough to pour each guest one cup of tea, but not too heavy to lift easily. Keep a second, smaller pot filled with hot water on hand for diluting strong tea.

Tiered server. Stack, from the top down, with scones, sandwiches, and pastries.

Tray. Choose one to reflect the formal or informal nature of your party. The tray should be big enough to hold inedible necessities.

Waste bowl. Use any small, wide-mouthed bowl in which the cold tea dregs may be placed.

Three Ways to Make Iced Tea

Brewed Tea. Make tea approximately double strength and steep only 5 minutes. Pour into a pitcher over an equal amount of ice. (If you are using a glass pitcher, let the tea cool before pouring it in.) If you sweeten the tea while it is hot, you'll need only half as much sugar.

Refrigerator Tea. Follow the procedure for sun tea, except let the mixture brew in the refrigerator overnight. This method has two advantages: When it's done, it's already cold, and no matter how long it sits, it doesn't get cloudy.

Sun Tea. In a glass jar or pitcher, place 1 teaspoon of

PORTABLE "TEA SPOT"

Consider creating a portable "tea spot," such as a good-sized basket, wicker hamper, or hat box, and keeping it in a closet. Or take it with you wherever you go. It can hold a Thermos for boiling water, a box of tea, a teapot and cups, a spoon, and a ceramic bowl to keep spent leaves. That's all you really need.

Can't drink tea without milk and sugar? Keep jars or restaurant-style packages of sugar and creamer in the tea spot. If you have the room, you can even store a bottle of springwater and an electric tea-kettle. Now you have no excuses to go without your tea and, more important, your tea break.

loose tea or 1 tea bag per pint of tap water (with sugar, if you wish). Cover and set in the sun for 1 hour or so. Timing is not critical — because the water doesn't boil, the tea will not get bitter.

Apple-Mint Iced Tea

❈ ❈ ❈

The combination of mint and apples makes a pleasant change from regular iced tea, and it is ideal for children.

- 2 *cups apple juice*
- 1 *cup water*
- 1 *cup chopped fresh mint leaves*
- 6 *teaspoons loose black or herbal tea, or 6–8 tea bags*
- *fresh mint leaves for garnish*

1. In a medium-sized saucepan, mix the apple juice, water, and mint leaves. Bring to a boil.

2. Add tea; steep 5 minutes. Strain and chill. Serve over ice with fresh mint leaves.

Yield: 6 servings

Lemon Blend Tea

❈ ❈ ❈

Lemon-flavored herbs intensify the citrus flavor of this lemonade-based iced tea.

- ½ *cup fresh lemon balm leaves*
- ½ *cup fresh lemon verbena leaves*
- 1 *tablespoon dried grated lemon zest*
- 2 *quarts boiling water*
- 1 *cup lemonade*
- *lemon thyme (optional)*
- *calendula petals (optional)*

1. Mix the lemon balm and lemon verbena leaves; stir in lemon zest.

2. Put the mixture into a teapot or heatproof container and pour boiling water over it. Let steep for about 20 minutes. Strain and cool.

3. Just before serving, stir in the lemonade. Serve over ice; garnish each glass with lemon thyme and/or calendula, if desired.

Yield: 2 quarts

Note: If you use dried herb leaves, use only ¼ cup of each.

Dude's Spiced Tea

❈ ❈ ❈

Dude and Iley Smith were our wonderful neighbors in Dallas when I was a child. I remember sipping a mug of this spiced tea, which was always in Dude's cupboard, with her son Mike on rainy days.

- 2 *cups orange-flavored Tang*
- 2 *cups sugar*
- 1½ *cups instant tea*
- ½ *cup Wyler's powdered lemonade mix*
- 1 *teaspoon ground cinnamon*
- 1 *teaspoon ground cloves*

1. Mix all ingredients and store in an airtight container. To use, mix 1½ to 2 tablespoons in a mug of hot water.

Yield: 6 cups mix; about 48–60 servings

HERBS THAT HEAL

Many people find medicinal value in certain herbs, and tea brewed from them is healing as well as soothing. Favorite teas for colds and sore throats are horehound, mint, lemon balm, and sage. For nausea or cramps, try peppermint. For digestive calm, use anise, fennel, or lemon verbena.

Lavender Mint Tea

❊ ❊ ❊

Lavender adds a pleasant but not too flowery contrast to the sweetness of mint.

1   teaspoon fresh lavender
    flowers or ½ teaspoon
    dried lavender flowers
1½–2 tablespoons fresh mint
    leaves or 2 teaspoons
    dried mint
1   cup boiling water

1. In a teapot, combine the lavender flowers and mint. Pour boiling water over mixture; steep 5 minutes.

Yield: 1 cup

VARIATION: For more interesting blends, add rosemary, lemon balm or lemon verbena, and rose geranium.

Peppermint Punch

❊ ❊ ❊

Tea punches are economical, low in sugar, and high in fruity flavor.

6   bags peppermint tea
    (about 4 tablespoons loose
    tea)
2   quarts water
1   tablespoon honey
1   quart cranberry juice
    cocktail
juice of 1 lime
sprigs of fresh mint

1. Place the tea bags in a heavy glass pitcher with a silver spoon in it. Bring the water to a boil; immediately pour water and honey into the pitcher. Let steep for 30 minutes.

2. Remove the tea bags. Add the cranberry and lime juices; chill. Serve in tall glasses over ice, garnished with a sprig of mint.

*Yield: 3 quarts; 10–12
servings*

Patriot's Punch

❊ ❊ ❊

During the U.S. Bicentennial celebration, our friend Bertha Reppert concocted this superb herbal iced tea to commemorate the Boston Tea Party. She suggests dividing it into two punch bowls and adding dry white wine to one bowl.

FAVORITE HERBS & FLOWERS FOR TEA

Chamomile	Small, daisylike blossoms; calming
Hibiscus	Ruby red blossom; rich in vitamin C
Jasmine	White flowers, intensely perfumed
Lavender	Tiny aromatic blossom; usually combined with other herbs or teas
Lemon balm	A cousin of mint with a strong citrus nose
Lemon verbena	Lance-shaped leaves with the strongest lemon scent of any herb
Mints	Flavors include peppermint spearmint, and fruit-scented apple, orange, and pineapple mints
Raspberry Leaves	Earthy, rather like green tea
Sage	Gray-green leaves with a distinctive aroma; warming

5   tablespoons dried whole
      peppermint
3   tablespoons dried whole
      sage
2   tablespoons dried whole
      rosemary
3   gallons water
1   sugar (or to taste)
1   can (6 ounces) frozen
      lemonade concentrate
4   tablespoons instant tea
      lemon slices, whole cloves,
      and rosemary for garnish

1. In a nonreactive, heat-proof large bowl or a saucepan, combine the peppermint, sage, and rosemary. Bring 1 quart of the water to a boil; pour over the herb mixture and steep for 10 to 15 minutes.

2. Strain into a large bowl, pitcher, or saucepan. Add the remaining 11 quarts of water, the sugar, lemonade concentrate, and instant tea. Stir well until sugar is dissolved. Chill at least 4 hours.

3. Serve over ice, garnished with lemon slices studded with sprigs of rosemary and lemon slices studded with whole cloves.

Yield: 6 quarts;
48 servings

SWEETENERS FOR TEA

White sugar is not the only sweetener for tea. Large-crystalled Demerara sugar adds a hint of molasses flavor. Honey is especially good with herbal teas. Cinnamon and mint provide natural sweetness as well as spice. Fruit juice concentrates and syrups add flavor, and in Russia, they use jam or preserves.

Hibiscus Tea

❁ ❁ ❁

A dramatic-looking red tea, this is very fresh and tart.

1   teaspoon dried hibiscus
      flowers
1   cup boiling water
      honey

1. Place the hibiscus flowers in a warm teapot. Pour the water over the flowers; let steep for 1 minute.

2. Pour the tea through a sieve into a cup. Sweeten with honey to taste; serve immediately.

Yield: 1 serving

Note: Dried hibiscus flowers are sold in herb shops and many health food stores.

Iced Hibiscus Tea

❁ ❁ ❁

For a spectacular look, float a fresh hibiscus flower atop this cool, refreshing tea.

1½ teaspoons dried hibiscus
      flowers
1   cup boiling water
      honey
1   slice lemon

1. Place the dried hibiscus flowers in a warm teapot. Pour the water over the flowers; let steep for 1 minute.

2. Pour the tea through a sieve. Sweeten with honey to taste. Chill the tea until cold.

3. When the tea is cold, strain it again and pour it over ice cubes. Add a lemon slice; serve immediately.

Yield: 1 serving

COFFEE

Coffee starts the day, lifts the mood, fuels conversation, and provides quick hospitality. The smell of a pot brewing on the stove or campfire signals welcome and respite. The slight bitterness of coffee makes it a perfect companion to sweet snacks and desserts. For the ideal coffee experience, buy whole beans and grind them yourself.

Coffee Beans

Ever since the Arabs started cultivating coffee in the fifteenth century, its popularity has steadily increased. There are two main kinds of beans: delicately flavored *arabica* and sturdier, less subtle *robusta*. They are often blended for balanced flavor or economic reasons. Beans differ in taste in part according to where they are grown — there are clear, light javas, such as Sumatra; rich, dark Kenya beans; the legendary mellow Hawaiian kona beans; and the distinctively smooth Central and South American beans, especially those from Costa Rica, Guatemala, and Colombia. However, the roasting procedure makes the biggest differences in taste. Light roasting produces the mildest drink; a medium roast produces moderate-bodied "American" coffee; and dark roasts, in which the beans become almost black, produce the characteristic coffee and espresso served in European cafés.

Brewing Coffee

There are hundreds of kinds of pots and machines for brewing coffee. Whatever brewing system you prefer, the following tips will ensure the best cup of coffee:

• Always start with a clean pot; a buildup of coffee oils can impart bitterness.
• Use fresh-roasted coffee that, ideally, has been stored for no more than 2 weeks.
• Store coffee in an airtight container at room temperature; do not refrigerate or freeze, as moisture will deteriorate the flavor.
• Use the right grind for your type of pot; it affects the amount of flavor that will be extracted.
• If you are making coffee manually, bring the water to a boil, then wait a minute before pouring through the grounds.
• Never reuse your grounds; only the undesirable bitterness will be left.

Brewing Methods

No matter the brewing method, the ratio of coffee to water is usually 2 tablespoons coffee to 6 ounces water. Adjust the amounts to suit your taste for weaker or stronger coffee.

Of the most popular methods for brewing coffee — percolation, drip, and plunger — drip and plunger are preferred. Percolators boil the coffee, which extracts bitterness and sourness from the grounds.

Filter cones use a manual drip process: Hot water is poured through ground coffee measured into a filter that is set into a cone to drip into a glass or thermal pot. Electric drip coffeepots use the same principle, but they pour water over the coffee electrically from a water reservoir. For best coffee quality, don't leave the pot on the warmer for more than 15 minutes; transfer it to a thermal warmer that has been preheated with hot water.

Coffee connoisseurs recommend use of gold-washed metal filters in both manual and drip coffeemakers, because paper filters can affect the texture of coffee. If you use paper filters, store them away from strong spices or other substances, because paper absorbs odors that can affect the taste of your coffee.

Plunger pots brew coffee that is thicker in texture and especially enhance the flavors of dark-roasted coffees. For this method, coarsely ground coffee and hot water are allowed to steep in a glass pot, which is also called a French press pot. Then a metal screen attached to a plunger is pushed down slowly to force the coffee grounds to the bottom of the pot. Coffee cools quickly when brewed by this method, so it's best to wrap the pot in a cozy or towel while the coffee steeps and transfer it to a preheated thermal warmer immediately after brewing.

Café Brûlot

❈ ❈ ❈

In New Orleans, this sweet, spiced dessert coffee is flamed with brandy. This is a tamer version, but with all the classic spice flavors. Offer brandy along with it, if you wish.

6 cups strong coffee, just out of the coffeemaker
5 tablespoons sugar
4 teaspoons grated lemon zest
2 sticks cinnamon
1 teaspoon whole allspice

1. In a large saucepan, mix all ingredients. Cook over *very* low heat for about 10 minutes. Strain into coffee cups and serve.

Yield: 6 cups

Mocha Java

❈ ❈ ❈

When we were working in France, our hotel brought pots of coffee and hot chocolate to our room with our morning croissants. Pouring the two hot drinks together is simply heaven. We like to add a sprinkling of cinnamon as well.

3 cups cocoa or Hot Chocolate (page 298)
3 cups freshly brewed coffee
½ teaspoon ground cinnamon
milk
sugar

1. Mix together the cocoa, coffee, and cinnamon. Add milk and sugar to taste.

Yield: 6 servings

Coffee Whizzer

❈ ❈ ❈

This is a fun variation on iced coffee, because the milk actually whips, forming a nice layer at the top of the glass not unlike whipped cream, but with less fat content.

1 pint cold coffee (brew, then chill)
½ cup cold milk
2 teaspoons sugar

1. Put the coffee, milk, and sugar into the blender and mix on the "whip" speed for about 45 seconds. Pour quickly into clear glasses. This may be made with regular or decaffeinated coffee, as desired.

Yield: 2 servings

COFFEE EMBELLISHMENTS

Milk and cream are the simplest additions to coffee. A twist of lemon peel is traditional with espresso. Whipped cream and a whiff of cocoa powder or grated chocolate is a Viennese tradition. Whiskey, brandy, or liqueurs add a sophisticated touch. Many flavored coffees are available, and some stores sell special syrups to add to coffee.

CHOCOLATE DRINKS

The Mayans of Central America used to grind cacao beans, mix them with water, and flavor them with hot peppers, honey, and spices. Centuries later, we still love chocolate drinks, but we usually omit the peppers! Few things compare to a mug of chocolate or cocoa after a day of sledding or ice-skating.

HOT CHOCOLATE AND COCOA

....

Many people use the terms "hot chocolate" and "cocoa" interchangeably. However, properly speaking, cocoa is made with cocoa powder and hot chocolate is made with melted chocolate.

Hot Chocolate

⊠ ⊠ ⊠

For those who prefer melted chocolate to cocoa powder in their beverage, there are many opinions about the type of chocolate to use and whether Hot Chocolate should be prepared with milk, half-and-half, or even heavy cream. I find that too rich. This version is just right.

- 1 cup whole milk
- 2 ounces semisweet or bittersweet chocolate
- 1 teaspoon vanilla extract, Chambord, or Grand Marnier
- whipped cream or marshmallow cream (optional)

1. In a double boiler over simmering water, heat the milk and chocolate until chocolate is melted and well incorporated; do not boil.

2. Remove from heat; stir in vanilla. Pour into a mug and top with whipped cream, if desired.

Yield: 1 large or 2 small servings. To make more, multiply all of the ingredients by the number of people you plan to serve.

Cocoa Mix

⊠ ⊠ ⊠

Ryan Corey has been son Matthew's best friend since the seventh grade. This is a recipe that his mom made regularly for the kids; Matt enjoyed it so much that he got the recipe for us.

- 8 cups nonfat dry milk
- 7 ounces dry nondairy creamer
- 1 pound Nestlé Quik
- 1 pound confectioners' sugar

1. Mix all the ingredients and store in an airtight container.

2. For one mug of cocoa, pour 1 cup hot water over ¼ cup mix.

Yield: About 16 cups mix; 64 servings

....

GREAT GIFTS

....

Cocoa Mix, Hot Mocha Mix, and Dude's Spiced Tea make great gifts. Write directions for using on a handwritten or decorative label. Fill jars with the mix, attach the labels, and package with a fun spoon and some mugs.

....

Hot Mocha Mix

✹ ✹ ✹

Just add boiling water to this easy mix and you have a warm drink for a cold winter day. Add a touch of whiskey for a delicious after-dinner dessert drink.

1   cup unsweetened cocoa
    powder
2   cups sugar
2   cups nonfat dry milk
2   cups dry nondairy
    creamer
½   cup instant coffee
    granules
1   vanilla bean, cut into
    quarters

1. Combine the cocoa, sugar, dry milk, creamer, and coffee granules. Mix well.

2. Pack into four pint jars and place a piece of vanilla bean in each jar. Seal, label, and store in the refrigerator for at least 1 week before using, so that the flavor from the vanilla bean is absorbed.

3. To serve, put 1 tablespoon of mix into a mug and add 6 ounces of boiling water. Stir. Top with marshmallow or sweetened whipped cream.

Yield: 7½ cups mix;
120 servings

DUTCH-PROCESS COCOA

··

Dutch-process cocoa is treated with an alkaline solution that removes some of the acidity, leaving the chocolate darker and smoother. It is usually more expensive, but the fine, mellow flavor makes it worth the price. If you need to use regular, nonalkalized unsweetened cocoa powder, adding ½ teaspoon baking soda to the dry ingredients in the recipe will neutralize the acid taste.

Chocolate Soda

✹ ✹ ✹

Old-fashioned soda fountains, which sadly are few and far between these days, often served this treat, usually prepared by a teenage "soda jerk" trying to impress his customers. A sip of this one brings back memories!

1   tablespoon sugar
2   teaspoons unsweetened
    cocoa powder
2   tablespoons milk
8–12 ounces seltzer water or
    club soda

1. In a tall glass, combine the sugar and cocoa. Add the milk and stir until well blended.

2. Slowly pour in the seltzer, pausing to allow some bubbles to disappear to prevent overflowing the glass. Serve immediately with a long-handled spoon and a straw.

Yield: 1 serving

VARIATION: To make a chocolate ice cream soda, fill the glass only two-thirds full and gently add a scoop of ice cream.

• For a Minty Chocolate Soda, add ⅛ teaspoon peppermint extract.

• To make a fruit-flavored chocolate soda, replace the seltzer with Cherry Coke.

• For a creamier treat, replace the milk with cream or half-and-half.

SPICED DRINKS

Marco Polo made his fortune bringing exotic Asian spices back to European markets, and no wonder. Can you imagine how empty our cupboards would be without cinnamon, cloves, nutmeg, and allspice? These and other wonderful spices have culinary uses that range from preserving to making flavored beverages, such as the classics described below.

Wassail

❈ ❈ ❈

Derived from old English words meaning "be well," "Wassail" is usually made with dark ale. It was traditionally served to revelers at Yuletide. This is a less potent but equally delicious version, and it's great to serve to carolers. You can substitute other juices or combinations of juices, such as pineapple, orange, or peach.

  4 *quarts water*
 20 *tea bags or ½ cup black*
     tea leaves
  1 *cup sugar*
  4 *sticks cinnamon*
  1 *gallon apple juice or cider*
  1 *quart cranberry juice*
  ½ *cup lemon juice*

1. Boil the water. In a large bowl or pitcher, mix tea, sugar, and cinnamon. Pour the water over the tea mixture; steep for 5 minutes. Strain the and add fruit juices. Chill and serve in a punch bowl, or serve hot in a coffee urn or Crock-Pot.

Yield: 36 (4-ounce) servings

Orange Froth

❈ ❈ ❈

Reminiscent of the drinks we used to see at the stands in shopping malls, this is a healthful way to get a dose of vitamin C into kids. Add a ripe banana and it has a bit more substance as well.

  2 *cups orange juice*
  ½ *cup milk*
  1 *tablespoon vanilla extract*
  1 *tablespoon sugar*
  ⅛ *teaspoon cream of tartar*
  6 *ice cubes*

1. In a blender, mix the orange juice, milk, vanilla, sugar, cream of tartar, and ice cubes. Blend on high for about 1 minute, or until drink is frothy and ice is well crushed. Serve immediately in tall glasses.

Yield: 3½ cups or 3 tall servings

Blackberry Sangria

❈ ❈ ❈

You've never had sangria like this! Our guests love it at holiday get-togethers — and any holiday will do. It really sparkles when served with a make-it-yourself assortment of Mexican foods.

  1 *gallon port-style blackberry wine or 2 quarts white wine, 1 quart port, and 1 quart blackberry wine*
  1 *quart orange juice*
  1 *cup lemon juice*
  ½ *cup brandy*
  ½ *cup sugar*
  1 *quart seltzer water*
  2 *oranges, thinly sliced*
  1 *lemon, thinly sliced*

1. In a large bowl or pitcher, mix the wine, juices, brandy, and sugar; you can add more or less sugar to taste. Chill. When you're ready to serve, pour into a punch bowl, add the seltzer, and garnish with the orange and lemon.

Yield: About 1¾ gallons, or 35 (6-ounce) servings

Diana's Favorite Chai

❈ ❈ ❈

Tea expert Diana Rosen finds experimenting with quantities and varieties of spices to be quite intriguing (and delicious). This is her favorite mixture, and we love it, too.

1½ cups water
8 green cardamom pods
6 whole black peppercorns
2 slices ginger root, peeled
1 stick cinnamon, 2 inches long
2 whole cloves
⅔ cup whole milk
4 teaspoons sugar
3 teaspoons loose black Assam tea

1. Put the water, cardamon, peppercorns, ginger, cinnamon, and cloves into a saucepan and bring to a boil.

2. Reduce the heat to low and let simmer for about 6 minutes.

3. Add the milk and sugar and heat to almost boiling.

4. Add the tea and turn off the heat. Allow the brew to infuse the tea for 3 minutes.

5. Warm two teacups by filling them with hot water. Strain the chai brew and serve.

Yield: 2 servings

Mocha Chai

❈ ❈ ❈

Who doesn't like chocolate? This chai latté is chocoholic heaven.

2 tablespoons loose black Assam tea
1½ cups boiling water
½ cup whole milk or ¼ cup unsweetened condensed milk
½ teaspoon ground cinnamon
¼ teaspoon ground cloves
1 tablespoon unsweetened cocoa powder
whipped cream (optional)
cocoa powder for dusting (optional)

1. Steep the tea in the water for about 5 minutes. Add the milk, cinnamon, cloves, and cocoa; simmer over low heat for 2 or 3 minutes.

2. Warm two mugs by filling them with hot water. Pour in the Mocha Chai, add a dollop of whipped cream and a dusting of cocoa, if desired. Serve immediately.

Yield: 2 servings

Iced Chai

❈ ❈ ❈

Any of your favorite chai recipes can be iced. For best results, the tea should be brewed slightly stronger than usual, so that the ice will not dilute the taste.

1 cup prepared chai
ice cubes

1. Allow the brewed tea to cool slightly, then pour over ice. For a slushy consistency, pour the chai and ice cubes into a blender and blend for about 30 seconds or as desired. Serve in a chilled tumbler or, for a slush, in a chilled parfait glass.

Yield: 1 serving

WHAT IS CHAI?

....

In India, where people speak many languages, the generic word for tea is *chai*. It derives from the Chinese word for tea, *cha*, which the British turned into "tay" and eventually, "tea." Today, the Japanese and the Chinese say *"cha"* for tea, and Indians still say *"chai."*

When we talk about chai, we usually mean masala chai — a mixture of Indian spices, blended with milk and sugar, that is heated and drunk alone or in combination with black tea. Whatever it's called, it is a calming, nourishing drink that is utterly delicious.

HERBS AND SPICES

Herbs and spices are perhaps the most important staples in my kitchen. I have one pantry drawer filled with bottles, shakers, and cans, and a second containing bags of herbs and spices. Some I've bought at the markets, but I have grown, harvested, and dried many of them myself. With a wide selection of herbs and spices at my elbow, I can turn an ordinary dish into a star. Rub a blend of herbs and spices into pork chops or steaks before grilling — there's no wrong combination. Change an herb or a spice in an old favorite recipe, and it becomes a new favorite. Add dillweed to plain tuna salad, dried basil to scrambled eggs, or grated nutmeg to white sauce, and — presto! — smiles will appear.

■ ■ ■ ■ ■ ■ ■ ■ ■

Contributors to this chapter are Glenn Andrews, Gail Damerow, Sheryl L. Felty, Maggie Oster, Phyllis V. Shaudys, and Adriana and Rochelle Zabarkes.

USING HERBS
....
SPICES, BLENDS, RUBS & MIXTURES

Chicken with Tarragon Sauce

✿ ✿ ✿

Chicken is one of my favorite things to cook, since it can be prepared in a thousand different ways. The aroma of cooking with fresh tarragon is wonderful, and the flavor in this recipe is remarkable.

4   large boneless, skinless
     chicken breast halves
salt and freshly ground black
     pepper
2   tablespoons olive oil
2   tablespoons dry white
     wine
1   tablespoon butter
1   tablespoon all-purpose
     flour
1¼ cups milk
2–3 tablespoons chopped fresh
     tarragon
2   sprigs of fresh tarragon

1. Wash the chicken breasts and pat dry. Dust with salt and pepper.

2. In a heavy medium-sized skillet, heat the oil. Sauté the chicken breasts until browned on both sides. Add the wine, shake the pan, cover, and simmer for 10 minutes, or until breasts are fully cooked. Transfer the chicken to a warm plate; cover loosely with foil.

3. Combine the butter and flour in the same skillet, scraping pan and blending well. Add milk and simmer, whisking constantly, until thickened. Add the tarragon and juice from the chicken on the plate. Cook for 1 minute longer.

4. To serve, spoon sauce over chicken. Garnish with sprigs of fresh tarragon.

Yield: 4 servings

Natural Mint Jelly

✿ ✿ ✿

The "natural" in the name of this jelly refers to the fact that it's made without artificial coloring. Natural mint jelly is golden tan in color and fabulous in taste. If you wish, you can add green food coloring, but try to have the courage not to! The whole mint leaves in each jar add a touch of green and tell the world what sort of jelly it is. (Before starting this recipe, see page 400 for information on making jams and jellies.)

2   cups fresh mint, stems
     and all (try to use the
     younger sprigs)
1⅔ cups water
⅓   cup cider vinegar
3½ cups sugar
½   bottle liquid pectin
8–12 large fresh mint leaves

1. In a small saucepan, gently simmer the 2 cups mint in 1 cup of the water for 10 minutes to make an infusion. Strain through cheese-cloth or a jelly bag into a fresh saucepan; add the remaining ⅔ cup water, vinegar, and sugar.

2. Stir over medium-high heat until the sugar has dissolved and the mixture comes to a boil; immediately add the pectin. Bring to a boil and remove from heat.

3. Put two or three mint leaves in each of four sterilized jelly glasses. Pour in the jelly and seal. Process in a boiling-water bath canner (page 384) for 5 minutes.

Yield: Four 8-ounce jars

CINNAMON TOAST

My mother sometimes called this "floppy toast," because it stays soft on one side. It's the real McCoy, no matter what you call it. The key is to put the sugar and cinnamon on separately, not mixed together, then broil the bread until it is bubbly and brown.

Spread each slice of bread with butter, coat with 1 teaspoon sugar, and top with a generous sprinkling of cinnamon. Broil until the bread is toasted around the edges and the sugar has begun to melt and brown.

USING HERBS

Herbs are prized for the flavor they impart to food. *They are delightful to grow and use fresh, but dried herbs also work well and are often more practical. Experiment with different combinations to take food from bland to glorious. And don't forget to use fresh herbs as decoration and garnish.*

Herbes de Provence

❈ ❈ ❈

This is a blend of summer herbs from the south of France. Use in soups, stews, and chicken dishes; with tomatoes and sauces; or in anything even remotely Mediterranean.

2 teaspoons dried thyme
1 teaspoon dried basil
1 teaspoon dried marjoram
1 teaspoon dried rosemary
1 teaspoon dried savory

½ teaspoon ground fennel
½ teaspoon dried lavender flowers

1. Combine all ingredients; store in an airtight container.

Yield: About ¼ cup

Bouquet Garni

❈ ❈ ❈

This traditional French herbal mixture will enhance any soup or stew. Tie sprigs of fresh herbs together in little "bouquets," or use dried herbs and make up pouches to pop into the pot.

1 tablespoon fresh parsley
1 teaspoon fresh marjoram
1 teaspoon fresh summer savory
1 teaspoon fresh thyme
1 bay leaf

1. Cut a 4-inch square of cheesecloth and lay it flat. Pile herbs into the middle. Gather up the corners of the cheesecloth and tie with a length of string. Store in a closed container until ready to use.

Yield: 1 bouquet

VARIATION: You can vary the recipe by adding rosemary, basil, celery seed, or tarragon.

ABOUT HERBS

....

Dried herbs are more potent than fresh — 1 teaspoon dried equals 1 tablespoon fresh.

To store fresh herbs, wrap them in barely damp paper towels, place inside resealable plastic bags, and keep refrigerated.

Add most herbs about 30 minutes before the end of cooking time; simmer slowly to release flavor and retain volatile oils.

The chopped leaves of fresh herbs may be frozen with water in ice cube trays, then stored in labeled airtight freezer bags. Use to quickly add herbal flavor to soups or stews.

Use herbs in moderation. Some may be overpowering if too much is used.

HERBS AND THEIR USES

KEY — stems, leaves, seeds, flowers, bulbs

Herb	Annual/ Perennial	Part to Harvest	Sweet	Savory	Tea	Classic Uses/Recipes
Anise	A	stems, leaves, seeds	✓			pastry, cookies/Rolled Sugar Cookies (p. 327)
Basil	A	stems, leaves		✓		pesto, tomatoes/Pesto (p. 306)
Bay leaf	P	leaves		✓		stocks, stews, marinades/Brown Stock (p. 74)
Caraway	A	seeds	✓	✓		breads, cheese, cabbage/Cabbage in Sour Cream (p. 203)
Chamomile	A/P	flowers			✓	calming tea
Chervil	A	stems, leaves		✓		eggs, salads/Basic Herb Vinegar Salad Dressing (p.142)
Chives	P	stems		✓		salads, soups, cheese/Basic Herbed Omelette (p. 52)
Coriander	A	seeds, leaves		✓		curries, salsas, salads/Crab Boil (p. 309)
Dill	A	leaves, flowers, seeds		✓		pickles, salads, soups/Dilly Beans (p. 409)
Fennel	A/P	seeds, leaves, stems		✓	✓	fish, stews, tea
Garlic	P	bulb		✓		sauces, soups, shrimp/Shrimp Scampi (p. 160)
Horehound	P	leaves, stems	✓		✓	horehound candy, tea
Lavender	P	flowers	✓	✓	✓	Provençal, teas/Herbes de Provence (p. 304)
Lemon balm	P	stems, leaves	✓	✓	✓	salad dressing, fish/Banana Lemon Bread (p. 114)
Lemon verbena	P	leaves	✓	✓	✓	sauces, tea, desserts/Lemon Blend Tea (p. 293)
Lovage	P	leaves, stems	✓	✓	✓	soups, fish/Vegetable Stock (p. 76)
Marjoram	A/P	leaves, stems		✓		meat, stocks, salads/Greek Omelette (p. 53)
Mint	P	leaves, stems	✓	✓	✓	jelly, drinks, peas, sweets/Natural Mint Jelly (p. 303)
Oregano	P	leaves, stems		✓		pasta, sauces, stews/Italian Tomato Sauce (p. 263)
Parsley	P	leaves, stems		✓		salad, soup, sauce, garnish/Tabbouleh (p. 133)
Rosemary	P	leaves, stems		✓	✓	lamb, eggs, game, stuffing/Herb Bread Blend (p. 306)
Saffron	P	stigma/styles		✓		sauces, breads, fish, rice/Paella (p. 172)
Sage	P	leaves		✓		poultry, stuffing, cheese/Farmhouse Stuffing (p. 336)
Savory	A/P	stems, leaves		✓		beans, meats/Basic Sausage (p. 421)
Shallots	P	bulb		✓		sauces, soups/Shallot Butter (p. 284)
Sorrel	P	leaves		✓		soups, sauces/Spinach Soufflé (p. 191)
Tarragon	P	leaves, stems		✓		eggs, sauces, chicken/Béarnaise Sauce (p. 266)
Thyme	P	leaves, stems		✓		fish, meat, soup/Manhattan Clam Chowder (p. 84)

Salt-Free Herbal Blend

❈ ❈ ❈

If you are trying to reduce your salt intake, or if you just want a novel seasoning blend, try this balanced mixture of herbs as a shake-on seasoning. It's also delicious in soups and stews and on eggs, beans, and meats.

    3 tablespoons dried basil
    2 tablespoons celery seed
    2 tablespoons dried savory
1½ tablespoons dried sage
    1 teaspoon powdered kelp
    1 tablespoon dried marjoram
    1 tablespoon dried thyme

1. Powder the herbs in a spice grinder or blender. Blend well and transfer to a shaker.

Yield: About ¾ cup

BARBECUE BRUSH

Phyllis Shaudys suggests a barbecuing technique I love using: basting your food with a fragrant brush made of sage, rosemary, parsley, and thyme sprigs tied together. For easy reach, tie the brush onto the handle of a wooden spoon.

Herb Bread Blend

❈ ❈ ❈

The Herb Society of Palm Beach County, Florida, offers this good mixture to liven up bread. Knead some into your dough or brush flattened dough with butter, sprinkle with the herb mixture, and roll up into a spiral.

    4 tablespoons dried rosemary
    4 tablespoons dried sage
    4 teaspoons dried chives
    4 teaspoons dried Italian
       (flat-leaf) parsley

1. Combine all ingredients and mix well. Store in an airtight container away from heat and light.

2. To use this blend, add some to butter and spread on French bread (may be grilled). For herb bread, add 3½ tablespoons of blend to a standard bread recipe. Add to soda bread, bread stuffings, scones, biscuits, cheese twists, and focaccia.

Yield: ⅔ cup

VARIATION: Add freshly grated Parmesan, Cheddar, or Gruyère cheese to blend before combining with bread dough. In season, try making this blend with fresh herbs, increasing quantities by one-third to one-half.

SPICED-UP SPICES

Roasting spices intensifies their flavors. Roast whole spices in a hot, dry saucepan, shaking frequently, for 2 to 3 minutes. Then grind them in a coffee grinder or use a mortar and pestle.

Ground spices can be roasted in as little as 30 seconds — don't let them burn!

Pesto

❈ ❈ ❈

Pesto is an Italian basil sauce that is fabulous on pasta, hot or cold. It also enlivens grilled fish, steamed vegetables, crostini, or omelettes. Experiment with substituting parsley or other herbs for some of the basil, and use pecans or walnuts in place of the pine nuts.

    2 cups fresh basil leaves
       pinch of salt
    1 or 2 cloves of garlic
    ½ cup grated Parmesan or
       Romano cheese
    ½ cup extra virgin olive oil
¼–½ cup pine nuts

1. Using a food processor, preferably with a plastic blade, combine the basil leaves, salt, and 1 or 2 peeled and crushed cloves of garlic until a coarse paste is formed. Add the grated Parmesan and process to blend. With the processor running, slowly add the oil in a thin stream. Add the pine nuts and process until almost smooth.

2. Use immediately or store in the refrigerator with a ½-inch coating of olive oil on top. To freeze pesto, prepare without the cheese and cover with ½ inch of olive oil; add the cheese after thawing. To make it easy to use small amounts of pesto, freeze it in ice cube trays; when frozen, transfer the cubes to plastic freezer bags for storage.

3. To use refrigerated pesto, pour off oil, remove the amount needed, and recover with fresh oil.

Yield: About 2 cups

Note: For a lower-calorie version, substitute low-fat vegetable stock or broth for half of the oil. For even fewer calories, use nonfat Parmesan or eliminate the cheese altogether. To include fresh parsley, substitute 1 cup of it for 1 cup of the basil.

EDIBLE FLOWERS

Many flowers not only are lovely to look at but also add delicate texture or taste to foods. Use them as garnish, or to decorate a cake. Some of our favorites are borage, calendula, chive blossoms, clove pinks, elderflowers, lavender, mint, nasturtium, rose petals, and violets. Larger flowers, such as daylilies and squash blossoms, may be stuffed or fried. For culinary purposes, be sure to use organically grown flowers that are free from pesticides.

Rosemary Black Olive Pesto

❈ ❈ ❈

This pesto variation from Good Thyme Farm of Bethlehem, Connecticut, proves you can have pesto even when you don't have basil.

  1 cup fresh parsley leaves
  ⅓ cup fresh rosemary leaves
2–3 cloves garlic
  ½ cup walnuts
  ½ cup pitted black olives
  ½ cup olive oil
  ½ cup grated Parmesan cheese

1. Place the rosemary, parsley, garlic, walnuts, and olives in a food processor. Slowly add the oil and process to a chunky paste (do not overprocess). Add more oil, if needed. Fold in cheese.

2. Store for up to 1 week in the refrigerator. To freeze pesto, prepare without the cheese and cover with ½ inch of olive oil; add the cheese after thawing.

Yield: About 2½ cups

Note: Pesto is excellent with lamb, either spread on cooked meat or mixed with drippings for a great sauce. It goes well with other red meats and mushrooms.

ABOUT MINCING HERBS

Herb-mincing gadgets are available in kitchen shops. They are helpful for cutting large amounts of herbs, but kitchen shears are great for snipping a few fresh herbs into small pieces.

SPICES, BLENDS, RUBS & MIXTURES

In ancient times, the spice trade sparked adventure, caused wars, and generated fortunes. Today we may take exotic spices somewhat for granted, but we can't imagine living without them. Cinnamon, pepper, vanilla, and ginger are kitchen essentials, and our use of such spices continues to expand as we adopt recipes from around the world.

It's fun to get out a spice grinder, coffee grinder, or mortar and pestle to blend your own special seasoning mixtures. You'll be delighted by the difference fresh-ground spices can make. Store blends in airtight jars, out of direct sunlight.

Pickling Spice

❊ ❊ ❊

You can alter the ingredients in this basic mix according to the type of food being pickled. Cinnamon and cloves should predominate in fruit pickles, while mustard seeds, celery seeds, and turmeric should be well in evidence in savory pickling mixes.

1 tablespoon whole allspice berries
1 tablespoon dill seeds
1 tablespoon yellow mustard seeds
1 tablespoon freshly grated nutmeg
1 tablespoon black peppercorns
1 tablespoon hot red pepper flakes
1 cinnamon stick, broken into pieces
2 bay leaves, crumbled
2 teaspoons ground ginger
1 teaspoon cloves
1 teaspoon coriander seeds
1 teaspoon fennel seeds

1. Tie all the ingredients into a piece of cheesecloth. Place in brine (page 407); remove when pickling is finished.

Yield: 1 bunch

Basic Curry Powder

❊ ❊ ❊

A homemade curry blend tastes much better than the generic supermarket variety, and dry-roasting the spices makes the kitchen smell delightfully exotic. Add a pinch to chicken salad, lentil soups, carrots, or rice, or mix with yogurt and serve as a dip.

6 dried red chili peppers, seeded
2 tablespoons coriander seed
2 teaspoons cumin seed
1 teaspoon fenugreek seed
1 teaspoon black peppercorns
½ teaspoon cardamom seed
½ teaspoon fennel seed
½ teaspoon mustard seed
1 piece cinnamon stick (1 inch), broken up
1 tablespoon ground turmeric
½ teaspoon ground cloves
½ teaspoon ground ginger

1. In a small saucepan, combine the chilies, coriander, cumin, fenugreek, peppercorns, cardamom, fennel, mustard, and cinnamon. Dry-roast over low heat, stirring constantly, until the spices darken slightly and are aromatic. Allow to cool.

2. Place the mixture in a spice grinder or food processor. Add the turmeric, cloves, and ginger. Grind to a powder.

Yield: About ⅓ cup

Crab Boil

❂ ❂ ❂

An aromatic blend for boiling or poaching seafood, this is a specialty of the Chesapeake Bay area, where crabs and shellfish abound.

1 teaspoon whole allspice berries
1 teaspoon cloves
1 teaspoon coriander seeds
1 teaspoon dill seeds
1 teaspoon mustard seed
1 teaspoon black peppercorns
1 teaspoon crushed red pepper
1 teaspoon salt
1 teaspoon dried thyme
3 bay leaves
½ teaspoon celery seed

1. Tie all ingredients into a piece of cheesecloth. Add to the water for boiling seafood. Remove and discard when cooking is finished.

Yield: 1 use

Barbecue Rub

❂ ❂ ❂

This spicy rub flavors beef, pork, or chicken without adding sugar or fat.

½ cup ground sweet paprika or Aleppo pepper
2 tablespoons chili powder
2 tablespoons ground cumin
2 tablespoons freshly cracked black pepper
2 tablespoons brown sugar
1 tablespoon ground cayenne pepper
1 tablespoon garlic powder
1 tablespoon salt
1 teaspoon five-spice powder

Combine all ingredients and mix well.

Yield: About 1 cup

Jamaican Blend

❂ ❂ ❂

Reliance on fine spices to flavor food is as Jamaican as rum and reggae music. This recipe was created by the Mari-Hann Herb Company. Use the blend dry or as the base for a spicy rub.

6 tablespoons ground allspice
3 teaspoons freshly ground black pepper
1½ teaspoons ground cinnamon
1½ teaspoons ground nutmeg
1½ teaspoons salt (optional)

Mix spices thoroughly.
Yield: About ½ cup

VARIATION: Grated lemon zest (½ teaspoon) adds a nice flavor.

Note: To make a Jamaican Rub, combine 2 tablespoons of Jamaican Blend with 1 jalapeño pepper, cored, seeded and chopped, 1 tablespoon freshly grated ginger root, 2 cloves of garlic (crushed), and 2 tablespoons vegetable oil. Mix all ingredients well and rub onto fish, beef, lamb, or pork; grill. The amount of jalapeño pepper may be increased or decreased according to taste.

MIXING SPICY CONCOCTIONS

For some tasks, an old-fashioned, person-powered mortar and pestle is superior even to a food processor. Crushing such spices as fennel seeds or peppercorns in a machine works well only with large quantities. You will also have more control over the texture of a mixture if you crush it by hand.

The mortar is the vessel in which you place the material; the pestle does the pounding or rubbing. Choose a ceramic or marble mortar and pestle, because unlike wooden sets, they don't absorb food odors and they are easier to clean.

Meat and Poultry Seasoning

※ ※ ※

Use this specialty of The Secret Garden Herb Shoppe as a dry rub, or add a pinch to your marinades and sauces.

- 2 *tablespoons dried marjoram*
- 2 *tablespoons sage*
- 1 *tablespoon dried basil*
- 1 *tablespoon dried oregano*
- 1 *tablespoon dried rosemary*
- 1 *tablespoon dried savory*
- 1 *tablespoon dried thyme*
- 1½ *teaspoons dried tarragon*
- 6–8 *whole bay leaves or 1 teaspoon dried bay leaf*

1. Mix all ingredients and store in an airtight glass container. Sprinkle onto meat or poultry along with onion and garlic powder before roasting or broiling.

Yield: About ½ cup

Note: If using whole bay leaves, be sure to discard the bay leaf pieces before eating.

Garlic Salt

※ ※ ※

To make garlic salt, use the freshest garlic you can find and good coarse salt, such as sea salt or kosher salt. Use this blend for making garlic bread and for seasoning dressings, sauces, and soups.

Pumpkin Pie Spice

※ ※ ※

You can buy pumpkin pie spice at the grocery store, but it's easy to create your own unique blend, adjusting the amounts of each spice until the flavor tickles your taste buds. Here, to get you started, are three popular formulas.

	Version 1	Version 2	Version 3
Cinnamon	¼ cup	¼ cup	¼ cup
Ginger	4 teaspoons	1 tablespoon	2 tablespoons
Nutmeg	2 teaspoons	1 tablespoon	1 tablespoon
Cloves	none	1 tablespoon	1 tablespoon

1. Mix spices well. Store in an airtight container. Use about 2 teaspoons spice mix for a 9-inch pie.

Yield: about ⅓ cup

- 6 *large cloves of garlic (but not elephant garlic)*
- 1 *cup coarse salt*

1. Preheat oven to 200°F. Leave a thin layer of skin on the cloves of garlic; it adds flavor. In the bowl of a food processor, process the garlic and salt for about 30 seconds, or until the salt starts to turn to powder and the garlic has just about disappeared.

2. Spread the mixture in a large, flat baking dish and bake for about 2 hours, or until completely dry.

3. Break the salt cake into small pieces and place them in the bowl of a food processor. Process until all lumps are gone and the salt is smooth. Store in a tightly closed glass jar.

Yield: About ¾ cup

Sweet Spice Blend

※ ※ ※

Anywhere that you want a fragrant whiff of spice — in fruit salads, baked goods, or pies — use this sweet blend from Woodland Herbs.

- 2 *tablespoons ground cinnamon*
- 1 *tablespoon ground cloves*
- 1 *tablespoon ground ginger*
- 1 *tablespoon ground nutmeg*
- 1 *tablespoon powdered orange peel*

1. Mix ingredients thoroughly.

Yield: About ⅓ cup

Note: Stir this blend into yogurt, fruit, or oatmeal, or add 2 to 3 tablespoons to cake or quick-bread batters.

SPICES AND THEIR USES

Spice	Whole / Ground	Part to Harvest	Uses Sweet	Savory	Classic Uses/Recipes
Allspice	G	berry	✓	✓	pickling, desserts, meats/Hot Mulled Cider (p. 287)
Cardamom	G	seeds from pods	✓	✓	baking, curries, drinks/Diana's Favorite Chai (p. 301)
Celery seed	W	seed	✓		dressings, vegetables/Mimi's Picnic Potato Salad (p. 315)
Chili pepper	W/G	pod	✓		chili, stews, sauces, rubs/Knock-Your-Socks-Off Chili (p. 86)
Cinnamon	W/G	bark	✓	✓	baking, beverages, lamb/Cinnamon Crumb Topping (p. 241)
Cloves	W/G	bud	✓	✓	baking, ham, preserving/Baked Ham (p. 149)
Cumin	W/G	seed	✓		curries, salsas, rubs/Spicy Lentils (p. 175)
Fenugreek	G	seed	✓		curries, gumbo, stews/Basic Curry Powder (p. 308)
Ginger	W/G	root	✓	✓	baking, meals, marinades/Gingerbread (p. 236)
Juniper	W/G	berry	✓	✓	marinades, cabbage, game/Root Beer (p. 450)
Mace	G	nutmeg covering	✓	✓	baking, chicken, stews/Traditional Pumpkin Pie (p. 337)
Mustard	W/G	seed	✓		condiments, dressings /Mustard Sauce (p. 266)
Nutmeg	G	seed	✓	✓	baking, sauces, spinach/Eggnog (p. 339)
Paprika	G	pod	✓		chicken, seafood, garnish/Hungarian Goulash (p. 179)
Pepper	G/cracked	seed	✓		Just about everything!
Poppy	W/G	seed	✓	✓	baking, breads, dressings/Arkansas Pound Cake (p. 324)
Sesame	W/paste	seed	✓	✓	baking, stir-fry, noodles/Hummus (p. 91)
Turmeric	G	root	✓		curries, soups, sauces/Pickling Spice (p. 308)
Vanilla	W/G/extract	pod	✓		desserts, sugar, beverages/Vanilla Pudding (p. 258)

VANILLA SUGAR

In an airtight container, bury 1 vanilla bean in ½ pound of sugar. Let stand for at least 1 week, shaking or stirring occasionally. The resulting sugar will add a delightful vanilla aroma to baked goods or desserts. The vanilla bean may be reused.

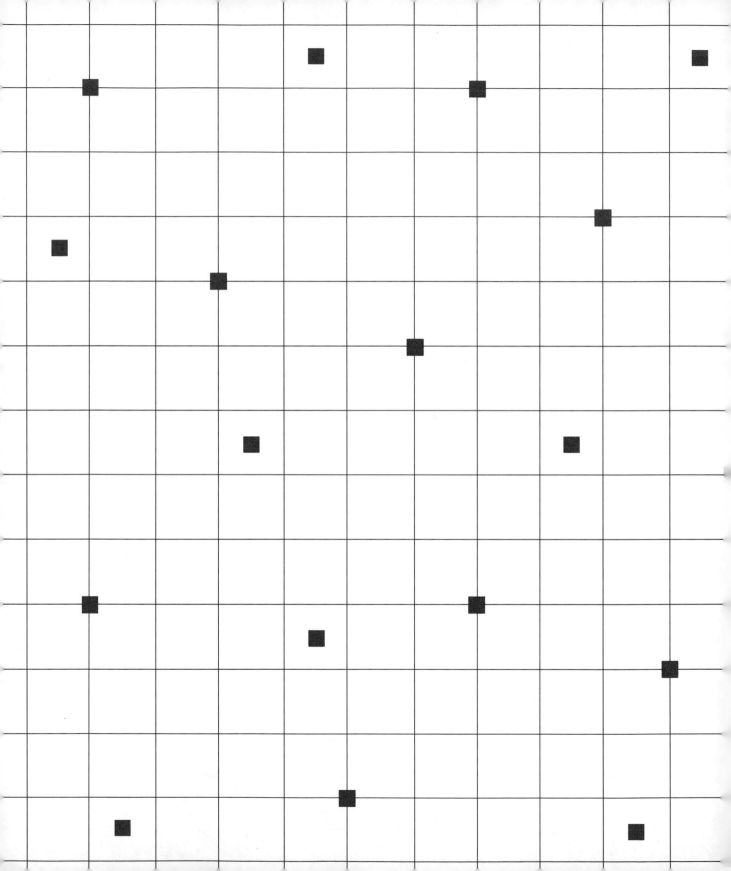

PART THREE

COUNTRY

OCCASIONS

COUNTRY CARRYOUTS

Potluck suppers are great fun, and almost everybody I know enjoys sharing special recipes with a crowd. We often have potluck lunches at our small publishing company, and the food is always terrific. One of my favorite contributions is Mimi's picnic Potato Salad, unique because of the secret ingredient — sweet pickle relish. Another favorite carryout dish is Stuffed Acorn Squash. That recipe contains vegetables and meat all in one; just add a salad and a loaf of bread, and it makes the perfect meal to take the new neighbors as a welcome gift or to a brand-new mom who has little time and even less energy to cook for her family.

■ ■ ■ ■ ■ ■

Contributors to this chapter are Ruth Bass, Jane Cooper, Ken Haedrich, Geri Harrington, Ellen Foscue Johnson, Gwen Steege, Edith Stovel, and Maggie Stuckey.

PICNICS
....
BY THE CAMPFIRE
....
POTLUCKS & COVERED DISH SUPPERS
....
BAKE SALE BEST-SELLERS
....
FOOD FOR FRIENDS

Mimi's Picnic Potato Salad

❖ ❖ ❖

Once again, my mother's is the best! She makes it fresh the day it is to be eaten, then serves it at room temperature, as its flavor is better when it isn't cold.

2–3 *pounds white potatoes, peeled and cubed*
¾ *cup chopped celery*
¾ *cup chopped onion*
3 *hard-cooked eggs, chopped (optional)*
1 *cup mayonnaise*
½ *cup sweet pickle relish*
2 *tablespoons yellow mustard*
3 *tablespoons sugar*
2 *teaspoons salt*
freshly ground black pepper
1 *teaspoon celery seed*
⅓ *cup cider vinegar*

1. Boil the potatoes until just tender, about 8 minutes. Drain and set aside to cool.

2. When cool, add the celery, onion, and eggs. In a separate bowl, mix the mayonnaise, relish, mustard, sugar, salt, pepper to taste, celery seed, and vinegar.

3. Toss the mayonnaise mixture with the potato mixture until well blended. Adjust the seasonings, if necessary.

Yield: 8–10 servings

Jessica's Brownies

❖ ❖ ❖

Daughter Jessica was always bringing recipes home from her friends' houses when she was young. Somehow, she must have thought their moms were better cooks and that I needed all the help I could get. In this case, I'm glad she did. These brownies are great!

¾ *cup all-purpose flour*
¼ *teaspoon baking soda*
¼ *teaspoon salt*
¾ *cup sugar*
5⅓ *tablespoons butter*
2 *tablespoons water*
12 *ounces (2 cups) semisweet chocolate chips*
1 *teaspoon vanilla extract*
2 *eggs*
½ *cup chopped pecans*

1. Preheat oven to 325°F; grease a 9-inch square baking pan. In a small bowl, combine flour, soda, and salt; set aside.

2. In a medium saucepan, combine sugar, butter, and water. Bring just to a boil. Remove from heat. Add 1 cup of the chocolate chips and the vanilla. Stir until chocolate melts and mixture is smooth.

3. Add eggs, one at a time, to the chocolate mixture; mix well. Gradually blend in flour mixture. Stir in remaining 1 cup chocolate chips and the pecans.

4. Spread in the prepared pan. Bake for 30 to 35 minutes. Cool completely before cutting into 2¼-inch squares.

Yield: 16 brownies

French Dressing for a Crowd

❖ ❖ ❖

Church suppers or potluck dinners always produce the most creative dishes, and a cold, fresh, crispy salad tossed with this tasty dressing is a real crowd pleaser.

1 *can (10¾ ounces) condensed tomato soup*
1 *cup vegetable oil*
1 *cup vinegar*
1 *onion, finely minced*
½ *cup sugar*
3 *teaspoons salt*
1 *teaspoon paprika*
1 *clove of garlic, finely minced*
½ *teaspoon dry mustard*

1. Place all ingredients in a quart jar and shake until well blended.

2. Chill for at least 1 hour to allow flavors to blend. Store in the refrigerator.

Yield: About 1 quart

PICNICS

A picnic evokes leisure time, relaxation, and enjoyment of the outdoors. Whether in your backyard, in the course of a berry-picking adventure, on the beach, or at an outdoor cultural event, picnic entertaining allows you to enjoy the occasion, because you prepare everything ahead. Some of the best picnics are the least planned ones and may even involve store-bought food. Fried chicken dinners from famous chains or a sandwich from a favorite deli tastes great in the right setting with the right company.

ELEGANT PICNIC

Mediterranean Chicken
Salad (page 141)

....

Cheese Bread (page 109)

....

Fresh peaches and Maids
of Honor (page 239)

....

Sun tea or chilled
white wine

....

Candlesticks, candles,
china, and pretty linens

Safe Picnicking

Make sure your picnics are memorable only for the fun and the great food. To avoid foodborne illness, the U.S. Department of Agriculture's Food Safety and Inspection Service offers two basic rules, whether at home or in the great outdoors: Keep hot foods hot and cold foods cold, and keep everything clean.

Most bacteria do not grow rapidly at temperatures below 40°F or above 140°F. The temperature range in between is known as the "danger zone." Bacteria multiply rapidly at these temperatures and can reach dangerous levels within 2 hours.

If you are traveling with cold foods, take a cooler with a cold source. If you are cooking, use a hot campfire or portable stove. It is difficult to keep foods hot without a heat source when traveling, so it's best to cook foods before leaving home, cool them, and transport them cold.

When transporting raw meat or poultry, double wrap or place the packages in plastic bags to prevent juices from the raw product from dripping onto other foods. Always wash your hands before and after handling food, and don't use the same platter and utensils for raw and cooked meat and poultry. Soap and water are essential to cleanliness, so if you are going somewhere that will not have running water, take it with you. Even disposable wipes will do.

"TAKE THREE CORKSCREWS"

....

Your great-great-grandparents seeking advice about picnic planning may have referred to **Mrs. Beeton's Book of Household Management,** *in which she lists "things not to be forgotten at a picnic." Our idea of essentials is somewhat different from Mrs. Beeton's in 1859: "a stick of horseradish, a bottle of mint-sauce well corked, a bottle of salad dressing, a bottle of vinegar, made mustard, pepper, salt, good oil, and pounded sugar. If it can be managed, take a little ice. It is scarcely necessary to say that plates, tumblers, wine-glasses, knives, forks, and spoons, must not be forgotten; as also teacups and saucers, 3 or 4 teapots, some lump sugar, and milk, if this last-named article cannot be obtained in the neighborhood. Take 3 corkscrews."*

To keep foods cold, several types of coolers will do the job. Foam chests are lightweight, low cost, and have good "cold retention" power. But they are fragile and may not last through numerous outings. Plastic, fiberglass, or steel coolers are more durable and can take a lot of outdoor wear. They also have excellent "cold retention" power, but, once filled, larger models may weigh 30 or 40 pounds.

You'll also need a cold source. A block of ice keeps longer than ice cubes. Before leaving home, freeze clean, empty milk cartons filled with water to make blocks of ice, or use frozen gel-packs. Fill the cooler with *cold* or *frozen* foods. Pack foods in reverse order. The first foods packed should be the last foods used. (There is one exception: Pack raw meat or poultry below ready-to-eat foods to prevent raw meat or poultry juices from dripping onto the other foods.) Take foods in the smallest quantity needed (e.g., a small jar of mayonnaise). Put the ice chest in the air-conditioned passenger section of the car, not in the trunk.

When your picnic is over, discard all perishable foods if there is no longer ice in the cooler or if the gel-pack is no longer frozen.

Picnic Essentials

Besides carefully chosen and prepared food, a picnic includes plates, flatware, colorful napkins, tablecloths, and cups. Matches are essential. Special touches are fresh flowers, mints, and candles. Don't forget the corkscrew.

A ground cloth, blanket, old quilt, or folding chairs are nice. Add a garbage bag and paper towels, and cleanup will be easy.

To avoid forgetting an essential item, a checklist is helpful; a prepacked picnic basket is even better, because you can be spontaneous and just grab your basket and go.

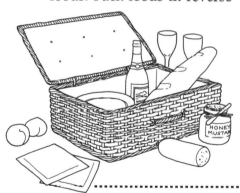

❧

SUMMER BEACH PICNIC

....

Savory Vegetable Turnovers
(page 94)

....

Grilled Tuna with Lime
(page 159)

....

Garden Fresh Tomatoes with Basil and Balsamic Vinegar
(page 187)

....

Macaroni Salad (page 134)

....

Fresh strawberries and whipped cream

....

Cream Cheese Chocolate-Chip Tube Cake
(page 233)

....

cold beer, sparkling water, or chilled white wine

....

For this picnic, you will also want to take a cutting board, sharp knife, picnic platter for tuna, serving dish for tomatoes, charcoal and starter, hibachi, and matches.

❧

PICNICS WITH A MISSION

Like me, the country cooks I know just love using the freshest possible ingredients. We also love making food gathering part of a celebration. If you're lucky enough to have berry bushes or apple trees in your backyard, host a picking picnic at home. If not, invite friends to join you at your favorite pick-your-own farm. Reward your helpers with a country picnic. Make your bounty part of your menu: strawberry shortcake for dessert or apples and cheese for lunch.

BY THE CAMPFIRE

Nothing ever tastes quite as good as food eaten at a campsite. Whether it is the appetizing smell of the wood smoke and fresh air, the hiking or other outdoor activities before eating, or just the back-to-nature approach to cooking, we always find hearty appetites around the campfire. Though we've done our share of short-cut camp cookery — pork and beans, tinned hash, oatmeal — we love to cook really good soups and stews, too. This goulash is a great example of gourmet camp fare, and the skillet corn bread is a perfect accompaniment. So what's for dessert? S'mores, of course! And who could refuse hot, buttery, and sweet Apple Slaps for breakfast?

Great Goulash

◆ ◆ ◆

In a heavy Dutch oven or cast-iron kettle, this stew can simmer on your campfire until you're ready to eat it. Just heed *The Century Cook Book's* 1894 admonition that "a stew boiled is a stew spoiled" and move the pot around so it doesn't get too hot.

- 2   tablespoons oil
- 2   medium onions, finely chopped
- 2   cloves of garlic, minced
- 3   tablespoons sweet Hungarian paprika
- 2   pounds stewing meat, cut into 1½-inch cubes
- ½   teaspoon caraway seeds
- 4   cups chicken or beef stock
- ½   teaspoon salt
- 4   peppercorns
- 2   medium potatoes, cut into 1-inch cubes
- 1½ cups tomatoes, peeled and finely chopped
- 2   green bell peppers, finely chopped
- 1   pound mushrooms, cleaned and halved
- ½   teaspoon dried marjoram

1. In a Dutch oven, heat the oil until a light haze forms over it. Move the pot to a moderate heat and add the onions and garlic. Cook until the onions are lightly browned. Remove from heat.

2. Stir in the paprika. Add the meat, caraway seeds, stock, salt, and peppercorns. Bring liquid to a simmer, cover, and cook over low heat until the beef is almost tender.

3. Add the potatoes, tomatoes, peppers, mushrooms, and marjoram. Simmer for 30 to 40 minutes longer, or until the vegetables and meat are tender. Skim off any fat. Serve as is or with a dollop of sour cream.

Yield: 4–6 servings

Flipped Skillet Corn Bread

◆ ◆ ◆

Mimi says that this recipe is "in her head." This means that she has made it so many times over the years that she wouldn't use a written recipe even if she had one. Now she usually bakes hers in the oven, but cooking it on the stovetop or over a campfire, then flipping it, gives it a wonderfully crispy crust.

2   cups cornmeal
1   cup flour
1   tablespoon sugar
1   tablespoon baking powder
1½   cups buttermilk
½   teaspoon baking soda
4   tablespoons butter or
      bacon fat, melted

1. In a large mixing bowl, whisk together the cornmeal, flour, sugar, and baking powder. In a measuring cup, mix the buttermilk and soda; pour into the cornmeal mixture; stir until blended. Add the butter and stir.

2. Grease an iron skillet with butter or cooking spray, then heat on the burner until hot but not burning. Reduce heat to low and pour in the batter, cover, and cook for 10 to 15 minutes, making sure not to burn it. When the batter looks browned around the edges, firm, and doesn't jiggle in the center, remove it from the heat and lift it with a wide spatula onto a plate. Turn the skillet upside down onto the corn bread and flip it back into the pan. Continue to cook on low for 5 minutes longer, or until bottom is well browned.

VARIATION: You can bake the corn bread in a preheated 400°F oven for about 20 minutes, until brown.

Yield: 8 servings

Campfire S'mores

❖ ❖ ❖

Ghost stories around the campfire are often preceded by debates over the best techniques for toasting the marshmallow and ensuring that the chocolate will melt for this campfire classic. For peanut butter lovers, spread a little peanut butter onto the graham cracker before assembling this snack.

1   milk chocolate candy bar
2   graham crackers
2   marshmallows

1. Place half of the chocolate bar on half of a graham cracker. Toast the marshmallows and place on top of the chocolate. Top with another graham cracker half and gently press together.

Yield: 1 serving

Apple Slaps

❖ ❖ ❖

On their own or as part of a hearty camp breakfast of coffe, juice, hash, eggs, and home fries, these fritterlike treats sneak in nutritious wheat germ.

⅓   cup flour
¼   cup wheat germ
1   teaspoon baking soda
½   teaspoon ground cinnamon
½   teaspoon salt
½   cup milk
1   egg, beaten
1½   tablespoons vegetable oil
      butter
3   large apples, cored and
      sliced
      confectioners' sugar
      (optional)
      maple syrup (optional)

1. In a mixing bowl, combine flour, wheat germ, soda, cinnamon, and salt. Stir in the milk, egg, and oil just until dry ingredients are moistened.

2. Grease a hot skillet well with butter. Dip the apple slices into the batter, turning to coat. Fry the coated apples in the butter until golden brown, about 2 minutes. Turn and brown the other side, about 2 minutes longer.

3. If desired, dust the slaps with confectioners' sugar just before serving or serve with maple syrup.

Yield: 4 servings

◇◇◇

POTLUCK & COVERED DISH SUPPERS

One of the nicest ways of sharing food is the traditional potluck or covered dish supper. It makes planning so much easier when the hosts don't know how many guests to expect. If each family brings a generous dish, no matter how many people show up, there should always be enough to go around. Then, too, there is the fun of getting to sample so many new dishes.

Sweet-Sour Meatballs

◇ ◇ ◇

These should be served with hot, cooked rice; make the rice along with the rest of the recipe.

- 1 pound ground beef
- 1 cup bread crumbs
  salt and freshly ground black pepper
- ½ cup hot water
- 1 bouillon cube
- 1 cup pineapple chunks
- ¼ cup brown sugar, firmly packed
- 3 tablespoons cornstarch
- ½ cup water
- ¼ cup cider vinegar
- 1 teaspoon soy sauce
- 1 can (5 ounces) water chestnuts, drained and thinly sliced
- 1 green bell pepper, cut into strips

1. Mix the beef and bread crumbs with salt and pepper to taste, and form into medium-sized meatballs. Sauté until well browned on all sides. Drain fat. Add the hot water and bouillon cube. Cover and simmer for 30 minutes.

2. Drain the pineapple, reserving syrup. In a medium-sized saucepan, combine the sugar and cornstarch. Blend in the pineapple syrup, ½ cup water, vinegar, and soy sauce. Cook and stir over low heat until mixture thickens.

3. Gradually stir in the meatballs with their pan gravy, the water chestnuts, bell pepper, and pineapple. Heat to boiling. Serve over hot rice.

Yield: 4 servings

A Megabatch of Pancakes

◇ ◇ ◇

For a community pancake event — a staple of country living — this large-quantity recipe for cornmeal pancakes can't be beat. Ken Haedrich got this recipe from his friend Margaret Fox, chef/owner of the now-famous Café Beaujolais, in Mendocino, California. Ken reports that Margaret's great breakfasts draw large, hungry crowds.

- 7½ cups unbleached all-purpose flour
- 6 cups cornmeal
- 1 cup plus 2 tablespoons granulated sugar
- 2 tablespoons baking powder
- 1 tablespoon baking soda
- 1 tablespoon salt
- 1½ dozen eggs, separated
- 12 cups buttermilk
- ¾ cup (1½ sticks) butter, melted

1. Sift together the flour, cornmeal, sugar, baking powder, soda, and salt and set aside.

2. Mix together the egg yolks, buttermilk, and butter

and add to the dry ingredients, stirring just until combined.

3. Beat the egg whites until stiff (but not dry) and fold in gently. Cook on a hot griddle.

Yield: 75 pancakes

Note: Margaret says this recipe can be doubled without any significant adjustments.

Take-Along Green Beans

❖ ❖ ❖

This tried-and-true casserole is easy and delicious, and families all over America have a version of their own. We like it best with fresh green beans, but frozen will do when beans aren't in peak season. A great addition to any picnic or buffet, just double or triple the recipe to feed a crowd.

1 *pound green beans, parboiled and cut into bite-size lengths*
½ *pound white mushrooms, sliced*
1 *cup chopped onion*
1 *can (10¾ ounces) cream of mushroom soup*
1 *cup mayonnaise*
1 *can (2.8 ounces) fried onions*

1. Preheat oven to 350°F. Combine the beans, mushrooms, chopped onion, soup, and mayonnaise in a large bowl. Toss to mix well.

2. Lightly grease a 2-quart casserole. Fill it with the vegetable mix, top with the fried onions, and bake for 35 to 40 minutes, until beans are tender.

Yield: 6 servings

Applejack-Spiked Baked Apples

❖ ❖ ❖

Baked apples bathed in applejack, maple, butter, and vanilla will draw raves from your potluck-party guests. They are delicious lukewarm, at room temperature, or even cold, and they travel well.

¼ *cup finely chopped dates*
¼ *cup finely chopped walnuts or pecans*
3 *tablespoons unsalted butter, softened*
4 *large baking apples*
⅓ *cup pure maple syrup*
¼ *cup water*
⅓ *cup applejack*
1 *teaspoon vanilla extract*
¼ *teaspoon ground cinnamon*

1. Preheat oven to 375°F. Combine the dates and walnuts in a small bowl. Rub about ½ tablespoon of the butter into the date-nut mixture, so it all holds together. Set aside.

2. Core the apples, a little on the wide side, then peel the upper third of each one; this will help prevent them from bursting. Trim the very bottom of each apple, so they sit flat in the pan. Carefully stuff the reserved date-nut mixture into the apples. The filling should come a little below the top of the apple, so there's some space left to hold the basting juice. Place the apples in a large pie pan.

3. Bring the maple syrup, water, and remaining 2½ tablespoons butter to a boil in a saucepan. Boil briefly, remove from the heat, then stir in the applejack, vanilla, and cinnamon. Pour this over the apples, and bake for about 50 minutes, basting every 10 minutes. Remove from the oven and cool, periodically basting with the pan juices.

Yield: 4 servings

POTLUCK POINTERS

I love hosting potluck parties, because they allow people to showcase their favorite recipes. If you don't want to have to remember to take your dish home, prepare the food in a disposable foil pan and leave it behind. Or buy a new casserole dish or plastic container and leave it behind as your gift to the hostess.

BAKE SALE BEST-SELLERS

Bake sales must be one of the most popular ways to raise money for good causes, from soccer teams to school field trips to grange events and scholarships for promising youngsters. People always ask for the recipes for items I've taken, so I've learned to take copies along.

Nicki's Taffy-Apple Bread

❖ ❖ ❖

If you want to take an unusual treat to a bake sale, this is the one. It has always been a big hit for us, and it is usually the first item to disappear from the table.

25–30 caramels (most of a
          14-ounce bag)
      3 cups all-purpose flour
      1 cup butter, softened
      4 cups confectioners'
          sugar
      1 tablespoon vanilla
          extract
      6 eggs
      2 teaspoons
          ground
           cinnamon
      1 teaspoon
          ground allspice

3–4 cups peeled and chopped
      Granny Smith apples
      (about 3–4 medium apples)

1. Preheat oven to 350°F. Grease and flour two 9- by 5-inch loaf pans. Unwrap caramels; using scissors, cut each into eight pieces. Toss with 1 tablespoon of the flour in a small bowl to prevent them from sticking together. Set aside.

2. In a large bowl, use an electric mixer to beat the butter, sugar, and vanilla until fluffy. Add the eggs, mixing well. In another bowl, combine the remaining flour, cinnamon, and allspice. Add the flour mixture to the butter mixture; blend well.

3. Using a wooden spoon, stir in the apples and caramel pieces. Divide between the prepared loaf pans. Bake for 1 hour 10 minutes to 1 hour 20 minutes, or until a toothpick inserted into the centers comes out clean. Cool completely, on a wire rack, then remove from pans.

Yield: 2 loaves

MomMom's Wheaties Cookies

❖ ❖ ❖

When I donate these to a bake sale, someone always comments on being glad to find something wholesome and simple among the rich goodies.

      1 cup brown sugar, firmly
          packed
      1 cup granulated sugar
      1 cup butter, softened
   2½ cups flour
      2 cups coconut
      2 cups Wheaties cereal
      2 eggs
   1½ teaspoons baking powder
      1 teaspoon baking soda
      ½ teaspoon vanilla
          dash of salt

1. Preheat oven to 400°F. Combine the sugars and butter until well blended. Add the flour, coconut, Wheaties, eggs, baking powder, soda, vanilla, and salt.

2. Shape dough into balls about 1 inch in diameter. Bake on ungreased baking sheets, 2 inches apart, for 12 minutes, or until edges are lightly browned.

Yield: 4 dozen

Double Peanut Butter Chocolate Chip Cookies

❖ ❖ ❖

Triple-power nuttiness with peanut butter, peanut butter chips, and pecans all in one chocolate chip cookie makes these a big hit at bake sales, or in your cookie jar.

- 2 cups sifted all-purpose flour
- 2 teaspoons baking soda
- ½ cup butter, softened
- 1 cup brown sugar, firmly packed
- 1 cup granulated sugar
- 2 eggs
- 1 teaspoon vanilla extract
- 1 cup chunky peanut butter
- ½ cup chopped pecans
- 6 ounces (1 cup) semisweet chocolate chips
- 6 ounces (1 cup) peanut butter chips

1. Preheat oven to 350°F. Sift together the flour and soda; set aside.

2. With an electric mixer, cream together the butter and the sugars. Beat in the eggs and vanilla. Add the peanut butter and beat until well mixed.

3. Stir in the sifted ingredients. Add the pecans, chocolate chips, and peanut butter chips.

4. Drop by teaspoonfuls onto greased baking sheets. Bake for about 12 minutes, or until cookies are lightly browned.

Yield: 4½ dozen

Coconut Blender Pie

❖ ❖ ❖

People who don't have the time or inclination to bake just love getting a whole pie from a bake sale. This one is truly tempting.

- ⅓ cup honey
- 4 eggs
- 1 cup milk
- ½ teaspoon salt
- ½ cup butter, softened
- ½ cup all-purpose flour
- 1 cup shredded coconut
- 1 teaspoon vanilla extract
- 1 9-inch piecrust, unbaked

1. Preheat oven to 350°F. Put the honey, eggs, milk, salt, butter, flour, coconut, and vanilla into a blender and blend for 2 minutes.

2. Pour into piecrust and bake for 30 to 40 minutes, or until a table knife inserted in the center comes out clean.

Yield: 6 servings

BAKE SALE STARS

To raise more money for your favorite cause, package bake sale items uniquely and attractively. Tie brightly colored ribbons (in school colors if it's a school fund-raiser) around the ends of packages of cookies and attach construction-paper tags with the name of the goodies clearly printed on them. Display the treats at different heights so people can see all the choices. Cookie packages in wicker baskets lined with pretty napkins are quite tempting; individually wrapped brownies stacked in a pyramid on a cake pedestal are harder to walk by.

FOOD FOR FRIENDS

Country folks are among the most thoughtful and generous around, and they frequently show their caring with gifts from their kitchens and gardens. Friends experiencing busy times, whether happy or sad, greatly appreciate them.

Arkansas Pound Cake

❖ ❖ ❖

If you like a moist, dense cake, this is for you. John's sister Helen gave me this recipe when we first moved to the country. It's so good you can serve it plain or with some fresh fruit and a dusting of powdered sugar.

- 2 cups sugar
- 1 cup (2 sticks) butter, softened
- 2 teaspoons vanilla extract
- ½ teaspoon almond extract
- ⅛ teaspoon salt
- 5 eggs
- 2 cups sifted cake flour

1. Preheat oven to 350°F; grease and flour a tube or Bundt pan.

2. With an electric mixer, beat the sugar and butter until light and fluffy. Add the vanilla, almond extract, and salt. Add the eggs, one at a time, beating well after each addition. Add the flour, ¼ cup at a time; beat well after each addition.

3. Pour batter into the prepared pan; batter will be stiff. Bake on lowest rack in the oven for 20 minutes. Reduce heat to 325°F and bake for 40 minutes longer, or until a toothpick inserted in the cake comes out clean.

4. Cool completely in the pan before turning onto a serving platter.

Yield: 12 servings

VARIATION: Use lemon extract instead of almond and add ⅓ cup poppy seeds.

Stuffed Acorn Squash

❖ ❖ ❖

Hearty and flavorful, this is an entire meal. In fact, you can prepare it in advance through step 2, then deliver it to a new neighbor or mom with instructions to finish baking. Add a fresh green salad and a loaf of bread and you've provided dinner.

- 3 acorn squash, cut in half and seeded
- 5 tablespoons butter, melted salt and freshly ground black pepper
- ¾ pound ground beef
- ¼ pound bulk sausage
- ½ cup chopped celery
- ½ cup chopped onion
- ½ cup chopped mushrooms
- 2 tablespoons dry red wine
- 1 cup sour cream
- ½ cup seasoned bread crumbs

1. Preheat oven to 400°F. Cut squash in half and scoop out seeds. Brush insides with 3 tablespoons of the butter, then season with salt and pepper to taste. Bake, cut side down, in a shallow baking dish for 40 minutes.

2. In a large skillet, brown the beef and sausage, then add the celery, onion, and mushrooms. Cook until the celery is tender. Add the wine and stir, then add the sour cream; mix well. Remove from heat. In a small bowl, combine the bread crumbs

and the remaining 2 tablespoons butter. Spoon the meat mixture into cooked squash halves; sprinkle the top with the bread-crumb mixture.

3. Bake, uncovered, for 20 minutes, or until squash is very tender.

Yield: 6 servings

Maple Buttermilk Muffins

❖ ❖ ❖

Rich and crunchy, these satisfying muffins are great with any meal, so bake a batch to take with you the next time you are an overnight guest.

1¾ cups unbleached
      all-purpose flour
1½ teaspoons baking powder
 1 teaspoon baking soda
 ½ teaspoon ground cinnamon
 ½ teaspoon salt
 2 eggs
 ⅓ cup buttermilk or sour
      milk
 4 tablespoons unsalted
      butter, melted
 ⅓ cup pure maple syrup
 ¾ cup chopped pecans or
      walnuts

1. Preheat oven to 400°F; grease 12 to 14 muffin cups. Sift together the flour, baking powder, soda, cinnamon, and salt.

2. In another bowl, beat the eggs until light in color and slightly thickened. Add the buttermilk, butter, and maple syrup; beat to mix. Stir in the pecans. Add the flour mixture. Blend with a rubber spatula or wooden spoon, stopping before flour is absorbed. Batter will be rough and lumpy.

3. Spoon batter into muffin cups, filling each about two-thirds full. Bake for 15 to 20 minutes, or until a toothpick inserted in centers comes out clean.

Yield: 12–14 muffins

Cock-a-Leekie Soup

❖ ❖ ❖

A country soup from Scotland that dates back to the sixteenth century, this soup is comfort food. Deliver it to your friends with a basket of corn bread, so they can make a whole meal of it.

2½ pounds boneless, skinless
      chicken breast halves
 3 cups water

 1 stalk of celery, diced
 2 carrots, diced
 ½ cup barley
 1 cup chicken broth
 2 bay leaves
 2 teaspoons minced fresh
      rosemary
 1 teaspoon salt
 ½ teaspoon freshly ground
      black pepper
 ¾ pound leeks, white and
      green parts, sliced (about
      1½ cups)

1. In a large saucepan, combine the chicken breasts, water, celery, carrots, barley, chicken broth, bay leaves, rosemary, salt, and pepper. Heat to a boil. Reduce heat, cover, and simmer for about 30 minutes.

2. Add the leeks, heat to a boil, reduce the heat again, and simmer until the chicken is tender.

3. Remove the chicken and let cool. When it is cool enough to handle, cut into bite-size pieces.

4. Skim any fat from the broth and remove the bay leaves. Put the chicken pieces back into the broth and reheat for about 5 minutes.

Yield: 6 servings

COUNTRY HOLIDAYS

Holidays are about reconnecting with family and friends and passing along cherished traditions. In fact, this book grew out of efforts to collect family recipes to hand down to Jennifer, Jessica, and Matthew, now that they have started homes of their own. Our family works hard to gather on each major holiday. Not surprisingly, the kitchen is the center of our activities. Whether preparing a traditional pumpkin pie, decorating a gingerbread house, or creating brandy balls for a holiday cookie swap, we all work at the large kitchen counter, adding our own talents to the task at hand and creating lasting memories in the process.

■ ■ ■ ■ ■ ■ ■ ■ ■ ■

Contributors to this chapter are Glenn Andrews, Betty Cavage, Stephen Cresswell, Gail Damerow, Jennifer Storey Gillis, Rhonda Massingham Hart, Charles G. Reavis, Pattie Vargas and Rich Gulling, and Olwen Woodier.

HOLIDAY FAVORITES
....
A SPRING
CELEBRATION
....
FOURTH OF JULY
....
HALLOWEEN
....
THANKSGIVING
....
CHRISTMAS
....
NEW YEAR'S

Rolled Sugar Cookies

❖ ❖ ❖

Nothing is quite as much fun as making sugar cookies with the kids. Two of my grand-sons, Matthew and Tommy, seem to be the most interested in this process at the moment. They mix, help roll out, and cut the dough, then decorate the cookies with great creativity.

¾	cup sugar
½	cup vegetable shortening
1	egg
½	teaspoon vanilla extract
1	teaspoon grated orange zest
2	cups all purpose flour
¼	teaspoon salt
½	teaspoon baking powder
½	teaspoon baking soda
2–3	tablespoons milk

1. Preheat oven to 375°F. In a large bowl, beat the sugar and shortening until fluffy and well blended. Add the egg and beat well. Add the vanilla and orange zest.

2. In a separate bowl, sift together the flour, salt, baking powder, and soda. Add dry ingredients to the sugar mixture, alternating with milk. Mix until dough is slightly dry and easily gathered into a ball. Wrap dough in plastic; chill for 1 to 2 hours.

3. On a lightly floured surface, roll dough to a ⅛-inch thickness. Cut with lightly floured cookie cutters. Transfer to ungreased cookie sheets.

4. Bake for 7 to 10 minutes. Transfer to wire racks; cool completely before decorating.

Yield: 1–2 dozen, depending on size

Licorice Flavor: For sophisti-cated flavor in a sugar cookie, omit orange zest and add 1 teaspoon ground anise seed to the dough.

COOKIE DECORATING IDEAS

Remember that some of the pret-tiest cookies are the simplest: drop cookies with a drizzle of white glaze and pieces of red or green cherry, heart-shaped cut-outs with a cinnamon candy pressed into the center, or Christ-mas stars outlined in blue with a silver dragée at each point.

- **Create your own patterns on cardboard and cut around them with a sharp knife. A template of a child's hand is a great place to start!**
- **Use several different-sized cutters of the same shape, or use a tiny cutter to make a cut-away shape in a larger cookie.**
- **Outline cookies in piping or cover entirely with frosting.**
- **Use candied fruits and peels, silver dragées, colored sugars, and miniature candies to add highlights.**
- **Dip the ends or edges of the cookies in melted chocolate and dredge in chopped nuts or nonpareils.**

PRETTY PRESENTATIONS

- **Make cookie ornaments: Poke a hole in each cookie before baking. After baking, decorate and thread with narrow satin ribbon after decorating and hang on a Christmas tree, a budding branch, or a twiggy wreath.**
- **Pack Christmas cookies in colorful tins, or present them on deco-rated plates covered with tinted plastic wrap. Make a cone out of a large paper-lace doily to hold valentine cookies. Tuck Easter cook-ies into a basket with Easter grass. A simple white box with a bow of satin ribbon makes a lovely presentation for any season.**
- **Present your cookies on different types of dishes — a silver platter or a pedestal cake plate for decorated cookies, a lined basket or even a china tureen for drop cookies or bars.**

HOLIDAY FAVORITES

On holidays, many of us serve foods that our parents, grandparents, or great-grandparents enjoyed in the countries they called home before coming to America. These favorite foods are traditions to cherish.

Irish Soda Bread

❖ ❖ ❖

When St. Patrick's Day comes, we're all a little Irish. This delicious fruit-studded bread is good on the 364 other days of the year, too. And it is one of the easiest breads you'll ever make — no blarney!

4   cups all-purpose flour
1   tablespoon salt
¾   teaspoon baking powder
1   teaspoon baking soda
½   cup raisins or dried currants (optional)
1½–2 cups buttermilk (or use regular milk combined with 2 teaspoons white or cider vinegar)

1. Preheat oven to 375°F. Butter a baking sheet or cake pan.

2. In a large bowl, mix together the flour, salt, baking powder, and soda, then stir in the raisins, if desired. Add enough buttermilk to make a soft, kneadable dough.

3. Turn out the dough onto a floured surface and knead it briefly. Shape it into a round loaf and place it on the baking sheet. Cut a cross in the top of the loaf with a single-edged razor blade or a very sharp floured knife.

4. Bake for 35 to 40 minutes. Remove from oven and cool on a rack.

Yield: 1 loaf

Potato Pancakes (Latkes)

❖ ❖ ❖

This recipe is adapted from a 30-year-old Jewish cookbook by Betty Braun. Our neighbor Susan Gold passed it on to me. Latkes are usually served at Hanukkah, but we find that they make a splendid short-order supper anytime. When I have fresh herbs on hand, I mince some and add a tablespoon or so.

5   Idaho baking potatoes, grated and drained
2   medium onions, grated and drained
3   eggs, beaten
½–1 tablespoon salt
1   tablespoon all-purpose flour or matzo meal
pinch of baking powder
vegetable shortening or oil for frying
applesauce or sour cream

1. In a large bowl, combine the potatoes and onions. Drain the potato-onion mixture thoroughly in a colander. Return the mixture to the bowl. Stir in the eggs, salt, flour, and baking powder. Add more flour if the mixture seems too watery.

2. Line a platter with paper towels. In a large, heavy skillet, heat ½ inch of shortening over medium-high heat until very hot. Drop the pancake mixture by tablespoonfuls into the hot shortening. Fry until brown on the bottom, 3 to 5 minutes; turn and brown the other side, another 3 to 5 minutes. Drain the pancakes on the lined platter. Serve with applesauce or sour cream.

Yield: 6–8 servings

Note: Grate the potatoes and onions separately in a food processor, then together to make them finer; just don't overgrind them.

A SPRING CELEBRATION

*W*hether you are celebrating Easter, Passover, or just the return of light and balmy days, spring is a grand time for feasting. The lambs are young, the garden is getting going again, and the spirit of joyous beginnings is in the air. With luck, you'll even be able to cook or eat part of your feast outdoors.

Minted Butterfly of Lamb

◇ ◇ ◇

*W*hen I want to serve something extra special but easy, I ask the butcher to "butterfly" a leg of lamb. Seasoned with this delicious marinade, then cooked on the grill, it is a treat for family and guests alike.

1 leg of lamb, butterflied (4 to
   5 pounds)
¾ cup (1½ sticks) butter,
   melted
¾ cup gin
¾ cup lemon juice
¾ cup Worcestershire sauce
1 jar (8 ounces) mint jelly
   (page 303)

1. Place the lamb in a non-reactive dish or large resealable plastic bag. Combine the butter, gin, lemon juice, and Worcestershire sauce; pour over the lamb

and marinate, with the dish covered or the bag tightly closed, for several hours. Turn the lamb every half hour.

2. During the last half hour of marinating, prepare a grill for high heat. Drain the meat, reserving the marinade. Grill the lamb about 4 inches over the hot coals for about 20 minutes per side. Check for doneness after 30 minutes. Lamb is cooked medium when the internal temperature is 160°F on an instant-read thermometer.

3. In a small saucepan, cook the marinade over medium heat until it comes to a low boil. Add mint jelly and

SPRING DINNER

Spring Onion Soup (page 79)

Minted Butterfly of Lamb
(this page)

Marinated asparagus

Boiled new potatoes with
olive oil and rosemary

Mother's Sunday Dinner Rolls
(page 118)

Rhubarb Crisp (page 244)

simmer for 5 to 8 minutes, until the jelly is melted and the sauce begins to thicken.

4. Cut the lamb into thin slices. Serve with mint sauce.

Yield: 8–10 servings

Butterflying a Leg of Lamb

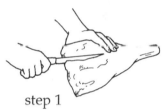

step 1

With a sharp boning knife and the lamb fat side down, cut through the meat to expose the main leg bone.

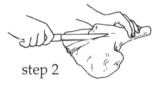

step 2

When you reach the knee joint, turn the leg slightly and cut around the knee joint, then down to the second leg bone. Remove bone.

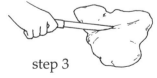

step 3

To even the thickness of the meat, cut thick muscles horizontally and open the meat like a book to make it flatter. Trim excess fat.

FOURTH OF JULY

Bring out the flags, the mosquito repellent, the bathing suits, and the basting brush. Cover the picnic table with a red-and-white-checked cloth, add a jar of daisies and bachelor's buttons, and get the gang together for a barbecue. Keep it as casual as can be, and when the last crumb of cake disappears, pile into the car and go watch some fireworks.

COOKOUT MENU

Assorted pickles
and veggie sticks

....

Salsa Ranchero (page 90)
with assorted chips

....

East Coast Barbecued
Chicken (this page)

....

Confetti Cole Slaw
(page 126)

....

Mimi's Picnic Potato Salad
(page 315)

....

Corn in the Pot (page 193)

....

Flag Cake (page 331) or
Strawberry Shortcake (page
214) (with blueberries, too)

East Coast Barbecued Chicken

If you have eaten barbecued chicken at an outdoor event in the Northeast, such as a community supper or a fire-fighters' field day, it was probably basted in this sauce. This basic chicken baste is simple to prepare, and the flavor it gives to chicken cannot be topped.

2 cups cider vinegar
1 egg
2 teaspoons salt

1 tablespoon ground poultry
   seasoning
1 tablespoon freshly ground
   black pepper
1 cup vegetable oil
   (preferably corn)
2 broiler or fryer chickens
   (2½–3 pounds each),
   cut into serving pieces,
   halved or quartered

1. Prepare the grill for medium heat.

WHY USE HARDWOODS FOR GRILLING?

....

Gas and charcoal grills are quite popular because they make it easy to cook outdoors over fire. But using hardwoods gives grilled foods wonderful natural flavor.

One of the great things about barbecuing is the light, smoky taste that permeates the food. If you use soft woods, such as pine, the smoke will be strongly resinous. Scrap wood may be pressure-treated, which means it could be infusing a breath of arsenic among its chemical perfumes. Charcoal often has petroleum distillates to make it "self-igniting." Hardwoods give off pleasing, natural aromas, and once started, a hardwood fire is long-burning, and a pleasure to maintain.

2. Mix the vinegar, egg, salt, poultry seasoning, and pepper in a bowl. Add the oil in a slow stream, stirring constantly, until it is incorporated into the mixture.

3. Wash the chicken and pat dry with paper towels.

4. Cook the chicken slowly, turning and basting often with the sauce, until the meat is tender and the juices run clear when meat is pierced with a fork, about 15 minutes per side. Total cooking time will vary depending on the size of the pieces being cooked.

Yield: 8 servings

Note: If you are using a hardwood fire, grill this chicken over hickory, oak, or maple or add soaked chips to a charcoal fire.

Flag Cake

❖ ❖ ❖

Children and grown-ups alike are delighted by this fanciful cake's patriotic stripes. And it is a wonderful way to make the most of the summer berry crop. Take a picture of the cake before your guests dig in — once they start, this flag won't wave for long.

1   9- by 13-inch yellow or
      white cake
2   *cups white icing*

PATRIOTIC PINWHEELS

The kids will enjoy making and displaying these patriotic pinwheels. For each pinwheel, you will need a 6-inch square piece of red, white, or blue construction paper; a red, white or blue pencil with eraser; and a thumbtack.

1. *Draw two diagonal lines connecting the opposite corners of the paper; the lines should form a large X that crosses in the center of the square.*

2. *From each corner, cut along the lines of the X to about ½ inch from the center of the square; you should have four connected triangles.*

step 2

3. *Dab the left corner of the top triangle with glue, bend it to the center of the square, and press until the glue holds; repeat with remaining triangles.*

4. *Lift the pinwheel up and position the center of the back against the eraser of the pencil. Press the thumbtack through the front center of the pinwheel into the eraser.*

step 3

1   *pint blueberries*
1   *pint strawberries, sliced*

1. Make sure that the cake has cooled completely. Ice the top and sides of the cake; smooth with a knife dipped in very hot water to make the surface as even as possible.

2. Arrange the blueberries in short rows to create a field of "stars" in the top left corner. Place the strawberries, overlapping slightly, to make "stripes" across the rest of the cake.

3. If desired, pipe additional white icing between strawberry stripes, using a pastry bag fitted with a large star tip or a tube of decorating icing.

Yield: 12 servings

◇◇

HALLOWEEN

Is there a child who doesn't love dressing up and going out in the night, yelling "Boo" and being rewarded with candy? In my mother's day, it was called "going out for cold pieces"; now it's called trick-or-treating, but it is just as much fun. This tradition, combined with carving pumpkins, making Apple Cider Doughnuts, and hanging spooky decorations, makes Halloween one of our favorite holidays.

Apple Cider Doughnuts

◆ ◆ ◆

Served with hot or cold cider, these doughnuts — glazed, dusted with cinnamon sugar, or left plain — are the stuff of autumn memories.

2½ cups all-purpose flour
1½ teaspoons baking powder
1 teaspoon baking soda
½ teaspoon ground cinnamon
½ cup sugar
3 tablespoons unsalted butter, softened
1 egg
¼ cup milk
¼ cup apple cider or juice
1 tablespoon vanilla extract
1 medium apple (McIntosh, Jonagold, or Golden Delicious)
2–4 cups vegetable oil for deep frying

1. In a large bowl, combine the flour, baking powder, soda, and cinnamon. Make a well in the center.

2. In a small bowl, cream together the sugar and butter. Beat in the egg.

3. Add the milk, apple cider, and vanilla. Beat all together. Pour into the center of the dry ingredients and stir until smooth.

4. Peel, core, and finely chop the apple and stir into the batter.

5. Cover and chill the dough for 1 hour.

6. Place half of the dough on a floured surface, knead lightly, and roll out to approximately ⅜ inch thick. Cut with a floured 2½-inch doughnut cutter.

7. In a wok or skillet, heat the oil to 375°F on a

GOOD 'N' GHOULISH

....

Everybody becomes a kid at Halloween. At least I hope they do! Halloween provides lots of opportunity for funny getups, great goodies, and creepy decor. A glowing jack-o'-lantern (or several) is essential, of course. Here are some other ideas to get you in the spirit:

- Stuff old clothing with straw or fallen leaves; make heads of pumpkins, stuffed cloth, or old masks. Leave them lurking about the yard or on the porch.
- Replace some lightbulbs with black and orange lights.
- Play creepy music.
- Decorate your buffet table with a few crawly spiders or rubber rats or bats. Serve black and orange foods — carrot sticks and olives, black bean chili with taco chips, salad of sliced oranges or orange gelatin, and spooky cupcakes for dessert.

- To make spooky cupcakes, frost them with chocolate icing. Cut one end off long rounded cookies, such as Milano cookies, to resemble gravestones. With decorator icing or a pastry tube, pipe "RIP" on each cookie piece, and stand it up on the iced cupcake. (Or frost the cookies with thin white icing and pipe on ghostly faces.)
- For another look, frost cupcakes in orange icing. Make spiders on the top using large and small black gumdrops and black licorice legs.

deep-fat thermometer. Fry the dough for 1 to 2 minutes on each side until golden brown. Do not overcrowd. Drain on absorbent paper and dust or glaze while warm.

8. To dust the doughnuts, sift 1 cup confectioners' sugar with 1 tablespoon ground cinnamon; sprinkle over the doughnuts. To make a glaze, stir 2 tablespoons apple juice into the sugar and cinnamon mixture; brush over the doughnuts.

Yield: 20 doughnuts

Toasted or Fried Pumpkin Seeds

❖ ❖ ❖

Nutritious pumpkin seeds are a good addition to salads, breads, or muffins, or just as a snack.

> 2 cups pumpkin seeds
> 1 tablespoon cooking oil
> salt

1. Wash the pumpkin seeds and dry thoroughly for a day or so on a paper towel.

2. To toast the seeds, preheat the oven to 350°F. Place the seeds in a medium-sized bowl and toss with oil to coat. Spread them in a single layer on a baking sheet. Bake them for 30 to 40 minutes or until the seeds are crisp and lightly browned. Stir every 10 or 15 minutes. (To fry the seeds, pour oil into a skillet. Add the seeds and cook over medium-high heat, stirring constantly, until they begin to swell and pop a bit.)

3. Sprinkle the pumpkin seeds with salt while they are still hot.

Yield: 2 cups

Chocolate Candied Apples

❖ ❖ ❖

Candied apples are great fun at Halloween. These are easier to make and to eat than the ones dipped in rock-hard red glaze. Children can make a project of them with a little bit of supervision.

> 8 medium apples
> 1 pound chocolate, or carob, chips
> 8 wooden craft sticks

1. Cover a cookie sheet with wax paper and place next to the stove. Wash, dry, and remove the stems from the apples; insert a stick firmly into each apple.

2. Melt the chocolate chips in the top of a double boiler; one at a time, dip each apple into the pot, swirling until well coated. Stand apples on wax paper to cool and dry.

Yield: 8 servings

Variation: Caramel apples: Replace chocolate with 28 ounces of caramels (two 14-ounce bags). Place coated apples in the refrigerator for about 20 minutes to set the caramel.

DIPPITY-DOO DAHS

Make your candied apples even more of a treat by dipping them, as soon as they are coated, in one or more of the following:

- *chopped peanuts or walnuts*
- *colored sprinkles (orange and chocolate are good for Halloween)*
- *crushed gingersnaps*
- *crisp cereal*
- *toffee bits*
- *coconut*

Or use various larger candies, raisins, nuts, etc., to make witchy faces on the apples.

PUMPKIN CARVING

For carving, select a pumpkin that's big enough for the design you have in mind. But remember that a really big pumpkin can take hours, or days, to carve. An even, symmetrical pumpkin will make a pleasant face, but an irregular shape enhances the eerie look of a witch or ghost face. A good carving pumpkin has a flat bottom, so that your creation will stay put and won't roll.

Check your designated pumpkin carefully to make sure it's not bruised. Carefully brush off dried dirt and other debris; if necessary, wash the pumpkin and dry it well.

Cutting the Lid

1. Cut a hole in the pumpkin either at the top or at the bottom. Traditionally, a lid is cut at the top, around the pumpkin's stem. But since the stem end tends to be thick and tough, some carvers prefer to cut a hole at the bottom. Having the opening at the bottom lets you easily set your carved pumpkin over a candle or lightbulb. However, this technique works best only with smaller pumpkins; it can weaken a larger fruit.

2. When carving a lid, instead of trying to cut a circle around the stem, carve five straight sides to form a penta-

gon. Make the lid at least 4 inches in diameter for a small pumpkin, 8 inches for a big one.

step 2

THE JACK-O'-LANTERN

The jack-o'-lantern has its origins in an Irish folk tale. It seems a fellow named Jack was barred from heaven because he was stingy, and he was barred from hell because he was so mischievous that he had once played a trick on the Devil himself. Jack was instead condemned to walk the earth until Judgment Day, carrying a lantern to light his way.

Jack's lantern, lit with an ember from Satan's supply, was originally made not from a pumpkin but from a turnip. Pumpkins and turnips both being storable staples, and pumpkins being much easier to carve, it doesn't take much imagination to see how easily the turnip carving of old Ireland evolved into the pumpkin-carving tradition of the United States.

Angle the sides of the lid inward so that it won't fall into the pumpkin after the edges have dried out in a few days. Cut away the fibrous pulp clinging to the bottom of the lid.

Tools

You can use the tools normally found in any kitchen or handyman's shop to carve, or you can use tools designed especially for carving pumpkins. The back-and-forth motion of a saw or serrated knife lets you more easily and safely penetrate the shell. Always supervise children, even if they are using the safest carving tools.

Creating a Design

You can find terrific patterns in a pumpkin-carving pattern book, adapt patterns from a coloring book, or design your own patterns.

3. If you're artistic, draw your pattern directly on the pumpkin shell with a pencil, china marker (grease pencil), or felt-tip pen; or scratch it on with a nail or the tip of a knife. Most of us have to work out a design on paper first.

When you're satisfied with your pattern, tape it to your pumpkin so your design won't get shifted before it's all transferred. Transfer the design by poking a pushpin or nail along the lines at ¼-inch intervals. Use the pushpin to mark an X in the center of each area you plan to cut away. If you have trouble seeing the dots, connect them with a pencil or the tip of a paring knife, or run a dark felt-tip pen over the dots to bring them out, then use a paper towel to rub off excess ink between dots.

To carve your design, just follow the dots. First, though, you'll need to hollow out your pumpkin.

Cleaning Out the Pumpkin

Cleaning out a pumpkin is a messy job, best done outdoors or with lots of newspapers to catch the goop.

4. Remove the lid you cut previously, reach in, and pull out as many of the seeds and stringy fibers as you can. Then use an ice cream scoop, strong soupspoon, or pumpkin scooper to scrape the inside wall down to hard flesh.

Carving

5. With your pumpkin hollowed out, you're ready to start carving your design. Use a sharp knife or a carving saw to cut along the dotted lines. Cut straight in at a 90-degree angle to the shell,

so that the cutout pieces can easily be popped out with gentle finger pressure. To make a clean corner, cut from one direction to the corner, then start from the other direction and again work toward the corner. Check the job as you go to make sure that all your cuts are straight through the shell. A jagged cut will let through light, which may spoil your design. A potato peeler works well for cleaning out circles and curves.

Because large cutout areas tend to weaken the shell and make it more difficult to work, begin by carving out smaller features, such as the eyes, then move on to larger ones, such as the mouth.

If your design breaks despite your best efforts, repair the broken piece with sturdy wooden toothpicks.

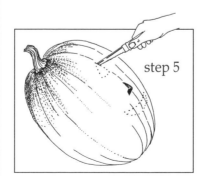
step 5

Shading and Sculpting

6. Shading, alone or in combination with carving, will give your design a three-dimensional look. Shading involves using the tip of the knife to cut through the shell but not through the flesh. This is useful for creating hair, facial wrinkles, and other thin lines.

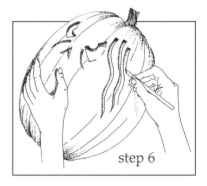
step 6

Final Touches

A carved pumpkin usually lasts no more than five days. For best results, carve it the day before you put it on display. To keep your creation from drying out, cover it with a damp towel when it's not on display. If the weather is especially warm and your pumpkin is small enough to fit into the refrigerator, put plastic wrap over the carved design, tilt the lid to let air inside, and store the pumpkin in the refrigerator until you're ready to display it.

THANKSGIVING

Thanksgiving started as a harvest celebration, in which the Pilgrims gave thanks for the abundance that would see them through the coming winter. Even though supermarkets have made our modern food supplies more reliable, the custom of gathering to offer thanks for our many blessings remains. Traditional Thanksgiving foods remind us of how our forebears worked, hunted, shared, and survived.

Roast Turkey
with Farmhouse Stuffing

Turkey always says Thanksgiving, and for such an important holiday I like to make the stuffing extra special. This one, with dried cherries, sausage, and walnuts, is so delicious that you can serve it as a meal by itself, which has been known to happen more than once during our Thanksgiving weekends.

Stuffing

- 1 pound turkey sausage
- ½ cup (1 stick) butter
- 1 cup chopped celery
- 1 cup chopped onion
- 1 teaspoon dried sage
- 1 teaspoon dried thyme
- 1 package (14 ounces) herbed stuffing mix
- 2 cups turkey or chicken broth
- 1 cup dried cherries or cranberries
- 1 cup chopped walnuts
- salt and freshly ground black pepper

Turkey

- 1 roasting turkey, 12–15 pounds, fresh or completely thawed
- salt
- 4 tablespoons butter, melted

1. To make the stuffing, crumble the sausage into a large skillet; cook until browned. Remove from skillet and drain well.

2. In the same skillet, melt the butter. Sauté the celery and onion until the onion is translucent. Add the sage and thyme; mix well. Remove from heat.

3. In a large mixing bowl, combine the onion mixture, stuffing mix, broth, cherries, and walnuts; toss together lightly. Season with salt and pepper to taste. Set aside.

4. Preheat oven to 325°F. Place the oven rack in the lowest position.

5. Rinse the turkey inside and out and dry it with a cloth. Rub the cavity with a little salt and set the turkey in a roasting pan. Loosely pack the body and neck cavities with stuffing. Tuck the legs under with the metal cleat or truss and tie the legs down. Brush the entire outside of the turkey with melted butter.

6. Roast the turkey, basting every 30 minutes with additional melted butter or pan drippings, until an instant-read thermometer inserted into the thickest part of the thigh registers 180°F; the stuffing temperature should be 165°F. If the turkey is done but the stuffing is not, remove the bird from the oven. Spoon out the stuffing and transfer it to a buttered baking dish to finish cooking while the turkey rests. Cooking time for a stuffed turkey is about 12 to 15 minutes per pound; for an unstuffed turkey, 10 to 12 minutes per pound. Transfer the cooked turkey to a platter; allow it to rest for 20 minutes before slicing.

7. In the meantime, skim off and discard any excess fat from the pan juices and add water or broth to the pan to make gravy (page 268).

Yield: 12 servings

Candied Sweet Potatoes

❖ ❖ ❖

Many of us remember this old-fashioned way of serving sweet potatoes, particularly at Thanksgiving. Mother still serves hers this way each year, much to the family's delight.

- 4 medium sweet potatoes, peeled and cut into 1-inch slices
- ½ teaspoon salt
- 4 tablespoons butter
- 1 cup sugar
- ½ cup chopped pecans
- ½ teaspoon ground cinnamon
- ¼ teaspoon ground cloves
- ¼ teaspoon ground nutmeg
- ¼ cup pure maple syrup
- 4–5 cups (from a 10½-ounce package) mini marshmallows

1. Preheat oven to 375°F. Butter a 9- by 13-inch baking dish.

2. In a medium-size saucepan, cover the potatoes with water; add the salt. Boil the potatoes until tender. Drain.

3. Combine the potatoes, butter, sugar, pecans, cinnamon, cloves, nutmeg, and maple syrup. Mix well, but leave a few chunks of whole potato. Pour into the baking dish and bake until browned, about 30 minutes.

4. Remove from the oven and top with mini marshmallows. Continue to bake until marshmallows are lightly browned and melted; do not allow to burn.

Yield: 6–8 servings

FESTIVE FLOWERS

Put cranberries into the water in a clear vase before putting flowers in — it instantly creates a festive holiday feeling.

Traditional Pumpkin Pie

❖ ❖ ❖

Pumpkin maven Gail Damerow has this to say: "Of all the pumpkin pies I've tasted over the years, this one is my absolute favorite. Sometimes I make pumpkin pudding by baking the filling in individual custard cups. Whether I make pudding or pie, I heap each serving with whipped cream, vanilla ice cream, or rum raisin ice cream."

- 2 eggs
- ¾ cup brown sugar, firmly packed
- 5 ounces evaporated milk
- 1½ teaspoons ground cinnamon
- ½ teaspoon salt
- ½ teaspoon ground ginger
- ¼ teaspoon ground nutmeg or mace
- 2 tablespoons boiling water
- 1½ cups baked pumpkin
- ¼ cup half-and-half
- 1 9-inch piecrust, unbaked

1. Preheat oven to 425°F.

2. In a medium-sized bowl, beat the eggs. Add the sugar, milk, cinnamon, salt, ginger, nutmeg, and water.

3. Place pumpkin and half-and-half in a large bowl. Add the egg mixture; blend well.

4. Pour mixture into the pastry shell or six greased custard cups or ramekins. Bake for 15 minutes, then lower the heat to 300°F. and bake for 25 minutes longer, or until the filling completely coagulates except for a small circle at the center.

Yield: one 9-inch pie

Note: If you make your own Pumpkin Pie Spice (page 310), use 2 to 2½ teaspoons of the spice mix instead of the cinnamon, salt, ginger, and nutmeg in this recipe.

CHRISTMAS

Deck the halls and bring out the figgy pudding. Christmas lights up the dark of the year with parties, presents, and all sorts of rich goodies to eat. Family comes from afar to be together; the cracking of nuts, stringing of popcorn, and toasting with eggnog and wassail punctuate the laughter, talk, good times. And the little ones love to set out milk and cookies for Santa.

CHRISTMAS DINNER

....

Shrimp cocktail

....

Crown Roast of Pork
(this page)

....

Roasted apples and onions

....

Scalloped Potatoes
(page 171) or herbed
mashed potatoes

....

Green beans with almonds

....

Mimi's Pecan Pie (page
240) or Queen Elizabeth's
Own Cake (page 234)

....

Brandy Balls (page 257)

....

Assorted cookies

Crown Roast of Pork
with Apple-Rye Stuffing

❖ ❖ ❖

On Christmas Day, our house brims over with family, friends, children, and magical gifts. We enjoy sitting down to a big dinner together, spending thoughtful time with those we love. Dinner needs to be simple to prepare but most festive. I believe that a crown roast of pork fits these criteria perfectly. The butcher does most of the work in preparing it, and I make the stuffing in advance. The presentation is sensational, the taste is fabulous, and the fuss is minimal.

Roast

1 crown roast of pork
   (8–10 pounds)
3 cloves of garlic, sliced
1 6-inch sprig of fresh
   rosemary
   salt and freshly ground black
   pepper

Stuffing

½ cup (1 stick) butter,
   melted

1 large sweet onion
3 Granny Smith apples,
   sliced
5–6 cups cubed rye bread
2 teaspoons chopped fresh
   rosemary
2 teaspoons dried sage
1 cup apple cider
1½ cup chopped pecans
½ cup golden raisins

1. Preheat oven to 450°F. Using the tip of a sharp knife, make small cuts in the sides of the roast and insert garlic slices. Rub the roast all over with the rosemary sprig, then salt and pepper it to taste. Cover the bones with foil or protective papers.

2. Place the pork on a rack in a large roasting pan and put it into the oven. Immediately reduce the oven temperature to 350°F. Roast until an instant-read thermometer inserted into the thickest part of the meat registers 160°F, about 20 minutes per pound.

3. In the meantime, melt butter in a large skillet. Sauté onion and apples together until soft but not browned. In a large bowl, combine the onion-apple mixture, bread, rosemary, sage, cider, pecans, and raisins, tossing lightly.

4. To stuff the roast, remove the pork from the

oven about 1 hour before it is fully cooked. Spoon the stuffing into the center of the crown; return the roast to the oven to finish cooking. Serve with Red Wine Gravy (page 269).

Yield: 10–12 servings

Simple Eggnog

❖ ❖ ❖

In this recipe, vanilla extract replaces the traditional rum; we make it this way so that the grandchildren can partake. But we offer a nip of rum or brandy to those who like it, and we always grate fresh nutmeg on top. The use of milk instead of cream makes a more healthful eggnog that we enjoy even more than the richer concoctions. Use leftover eggnog instead of milk in French toast for your holiday breakfast.

2 *eggs*
2 *cups whole milk*
2 *teaspoons vanilla extract*
4 *tablespoons sugar*
dash of salt
freshly grated nutmeg

1. In a medium-sized saucepan, combine the eggs, milk, vanilla, sugar, and salt. Cook, whisking or stirring often, over very low heat, until slightly thickened (be sure to stop before the eggnog turns to pudding). Top with grated nutmeg. Serve warm or chilled.

Yield: 2 servings

Note: The traditional method of making eggnog is to whip all ingredients together, without cooking, and top with grated nutmeg. I have modified this approach, however, given the dangers of infection with salmonella from uncooked eggs.

COOKIE SWAP

∙∙∙∙∙∙∙∙∙∙∙∙∙∙∙∙∙∙∙∙∙∙∙∙

Have a cookie swap before the Christmas holiday season. Everyone brings four or five dozen of one type of cookie to the party and goes home with the same number of cookies, but in a wide variety. Ask each guest to bring note cards with the recipe written on them to distribute with the cookies. This saves all of you time and provides you with new recipe ideas.

SIMPLICITY VERSUS ENJOYMENT

∙∙∙∙∙∙∙∙∙∙∙∙∙∙∙∙∙∙∙∙∙∙

Every year at the holidays, I make more than 20 dozen sticky buns (page 101) as gifts to my family and friends for their Christmas-morning breakfasts. This longtime family tradition, started by my mother-in-law more than 50 years ago, is far from simple.

At this busy time of year, I could much more easily buy something to give that would be lovely and enjoyed by all, but here's the thing: I really enjoy making the sticky buns. I enjoy the preparation of the dough, the kneading and pounding, the smell of the house as they bake, the wrapping with tissue and ribbon, and even the Christmas Eve delivering. In this case, simplicity isn't the issue; it is the pleasure I get from making and giving my sticky buns. Sometimes that's simply most important.

One year there was a storm, and we were having a difficult time delivering the sticky buns. We decided to get up early Christmas morning and complete the job then. At 11 P.M. on Christmas Eve, a longtime recipient phoned us, saying, "Martha, if it would help, I'll come over with my plow and pick 'em up!"

∙∙

Gingerbread House

❖ ❖ ❖

This is a wonderful project to make with or for children. They love to help add the decorations and to fantasize about living in such a fairytale abode. The house makes a fabulous centerpiece or decoration for a holiday party, too.

1 cup (2 sticks) butter or vegetable shortening
1 cup brown sugar, firmly packed
1 cup molasses
5 cups flour (all-purpose, bleached or unbleached)
2 teaspoons baking soda
1½ teaspoons ground cinnamon
½ teaspoon ground cloves
½ teaspoon salt
⅓–½ cup water

1. In a large mixing bowl, beat the butter until softened. Add the sugar and beat until fluffy, at least 3 minutes. Add the molasses and beat well. In a separate bowl, combine the flour, baking soda, cinnamon, cloves, and salt. Alternately add the flour mixture and the water to the batter a little at a time, mixing in each addition thoroughly. Use only enough water to hold the dough together; you will have to use your hands to work in the last additions.

2. Divide dough into thirds and shape into balls. Cover with plastic wrap and chill for several hours, preferably overnight. The dough must be sufficiently chilled before rolling to prevent stickiness.

3. Preheat oven to 375°F. On a piece of aluminum foil, roll out one ball to approximately ³⁄₁₆-inch thick. To prevent pulling, lightly flour the foil, your hands, and the rolling pin before rolling, or roll dough between the sheet of foil on the bottom and a sheet of wax paper on top.

4. Position pattern templates (page 343) on top of the dough at least 1 inch apart to allow for a little spreading of dough during baking. Carefully cut out the pieces by using a pastry wheel or paring knife. Gingerly lift the scraps away from the cutout shapes, and return them to the refrigerator.

5. Carefully slide the foil with the cutouts on it onto a baking sheet. Bake for 9 to 11 minutes, until just firm but not browned. In ovens that do not produce even heat, bake one sheet at a time, centered in the oven. Once all of the dough has been used, form the scraps into another ball and roll out again. Avoid rolling the dough out more than twice if you plan to eat your gingerbread; the extra handling makes it tough.

6. When the pieces have finished baking, remove from the oven and allow to cool slightly on the baking sheets. As soon as the pieces come out of the oven, check the edges to be sure that the sides are square with those of the template. Lay the corresponding templates over each piece and, if necessary, trim with a sharp knife, so that the pieces will fit together. The dough will have spread somewhat, but the basic shape should be the same. The dough hardens as it cools, making it more difficult to trim later.

7. Transfer the pieces to racks; cool completely. If you can't start construction right away, slide the fully cooled pieces onto foil-covered cardboard or back onto the baking sheets, wrap with foil or plastic wrap, and store flat.

Royal Icing

powdered egg whites equiva-
lent to 3 eggs
1½ pounds confectioners'
sugar
food coloring (if desired)

1. Prepare the egg whites as package directs and beat until frothy. Gradually beat in sugar until icing reaches the desired consistency. The more you whip the icing, the fluffier it will get. Icing that is less fluffy is best for piping out details, such as siding, roof, and window designs; fluffier icing makes good glue for holding the pieces of the house together. Add food coloring a few drops at a time, or smudge a little at a time if using the paste type, and mix thoroughly. Immediately wrap and refrigerate leftovers.

Note: Powdered egg whites are used to avoid the possibility of salmonella infection from uncooked eggs.

GINGERBREAD HOUSE DECORATING INGREDIENTS

- *Bread sticks — rafters, beams, pillars, logs*
- *Candy canes — pillars, support beams, fence posts, light posts*
- *Cereal — colored O's for Christmas chain garland, tiles, and small wheels; flat types for shingles*
- *Chocolate bars — door, shutters, shingles*
- *Cinnamon candies — red roofing tiles, paving stones, flowers*
- *Coated candies — tree decorations, Christmas lights*
- *Confectioners' sugar — light dusting of snow, frost*
- *Crystallized flowers — frosted garden flowers, rare jewels, lady's corsage*
- *Foil-wrapped chocolate kiss — church bell, roof decoration*
- *Frosting — mortar, snow, flowers, siding, hair, ribbons, bows*

- *Fruit leather — window shades, fabric*
- *Gum candies — slice into shingles, shape into flowers*
- *Gumdrops — bushes, flowers, ornaments*
- *Hard candies — melted for stained glass windows, mirrors, reflecting pools; crushed for colored gravel, beads, gems*
- *Ice cream cones — trees, tower turrets, hats, hoop skirts*
- *Icing — garlands, flowers, snow, bows, siding*
- *Licorice — railings, edgings, exposed beams, fireplace bricks*
- *Licorice ropes — rope, edging, window pane dividers, harness*
- *Lollipops — road signs, people, trees, bushes*
- *Marshmallows — snowballs for snow forts, snowmen*
- *Marzipan or fondant — anything you can shape it into*

- *Nuts — stones; slivered almonds for shingles*
- *Pretzel sticks — logs, winter trees, firewood*
- *Pretzels — fancy ironwork fences, bed headboards, scrollwork*
- *Rock candy — rocks, stepping stones, stone walls*
- *Round crackers or cookies — wagon wheels, doors, tabletops*
- *Shredded wheat cereal — roof thatching, hay, hair*
- *Silver dragées — doorknobs, ornaments, jewelry (not edible)*
- *Sprinkles — flowers, Christmas lights, ornaments*
- *Wafer cookies, crackers, or candies — roof shingles, siding*

Putting It All Together

1. Build a firm foundation. You will need a sturdy base to act as a steady anchor, to define the limits of your display, and to make moving and storing easier. Cut plywood or heavy cardboard to the size and shape desired. Cover with wax paper or aluminum foil taped in place on the bottom. Frost the entire base, or only where the walls of the house will contact it.

2. Ice first. Except for the roof of the house, most decorative icing should be applied before putting the house together. It is easier to create straight lines (such as for clapboards or bricks) and to pipe fancier icing on gingerbread that is lying flat than on an assembled house. So ice first, and allow plenty of time (several hours or overnight) for the icing to dry before piecing your house together.

Tint icing to any color you desire. Use a metal spatula or butter knife to spread the icing as evenly as possible over the surface of each piece. Pipe on contrasting icing for trim and other effects. Cake-decorating tips, even in the most inexperienced hands, can turn plain into fancy. Edge doorways and windows with a fancy tip to create the look of exotic molding.

3. Put up walls. Start with the biggest walls of the house. Pipe a generous line of icing along the meeting edges of two walls and press together. Ice the bottom edges of the walls before setting them in place to help secure them to the foundation. Position side walls between the front and back pieces to make the front of the house more attractive. Place canned goods on either side of the walls to hold them in place while the icing dries.

Run icing along the meeting edges of the next two pieces, press them together, and settle into position, making sure that all iced edges fit squarely together. Again, use cans for support.

As you press the iced edges together, icing will ooze from the seams. Before the icing dries, run a metal spatula or butter knife along the seams to tidy up. Later, you can pipe an even line or a decorative edging along the seams to hide any unevenness where the walls meet.

4. Build bay windows, chimneys, dormers, and towers. As the major walls of your gingerbread house dry, the smaller structures can be pieced together. When the icing holding them together is dry enough that they can safely be handled, join these structures to the house. Apply icing to all edges that will touch and gently ease them into place, holding for a moment or two. Support with cans as needed. Chimneys and dormers will be added once the roof is in place.

5. Ice again. After the walls are thoroughly dry — from 1 or 2 hours to overnight — pipe a line of icing along the seams from the inside. This extra bit of glue helps make the house more solid. Let it dry again.

6. Add the roof. Ice along the top edges of the walls and edges where the roof pieces will meet. Set one side of the roof in place, then the other. Carefully adjust the two pieces until they meet at the top. Press firmly so that the icing is smushed together;

- -

GINGERBREAD HOUSE–MAKING PARTY

· ·

Host a gingerbread house–making party. If you don't want to bake your own gingerbread walls and roofs, use graham crackers, icing, and small milk cartons to construct mini houses, then decorate with a variety of candies. Serve simple hors d'oeuvres, hot mulled cider, and eggnog.

- -

smooth icing along roof peak. Add dormers and chimneys.

Be sure to allow the icing plenty of time to dry before adding snow, shingles, reindeer, and so on. To secure shingles or roof ornaments, first frost the roof with snow, then gently press the objects into place. If laying shingles made of slivered almonds, cereal, or fondant, apply a strip of icing a little wider than a row of shingles to the bottom of the roofline. Press the shingles into place. Then frost the next row up, press the next row of shingles into place so that they overlap the first row a little bit, and continue on to the top of the roof. If the shingles don't match up perfectly at the peak of the roof, cut smaller shingles or camouflage the peak under a blanket of snow.

7. Finishing touches. From whimsy to realism, the finishing touches are what make your gingerbread house spring to life. Icing details, landscaping, figurines, snow, and roof decorations are the last features to add to your edible art.

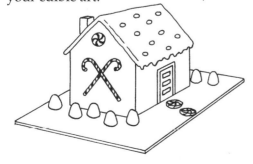

GINGERBREAD TEMPLATES

Use these gingerbread patterns, or create your own, to make templates for cutting out the pieces of your gingerbread building. Enlarge them on graph paper or by using the zoom feature of a copy machine. An 8- to 12-inch square gingerbread house is a good size.

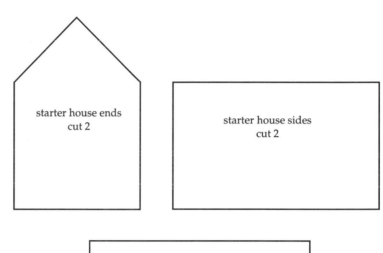

starter house ends
cut 2

starter house sides
cut 2

starter house roof
cut 2

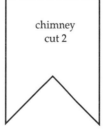

chimney
cut 2

chimney
cut 2

NEW YEAR'S

These days, our New Year's celebrations turn away from crowded champagne-and-noisemaker galas and lean toward an evening of charades and firelight, followed by a day of friends' dropping over to watch a televised football game indoors and have a snowball fight outside. The food is casual but plentiful, and beans and greens make it wholesome enough not to challenge any freshly minted resolutions.

NEW YEAR'S DAY

....

Crudités with Ginger Dip
(page 91)

....

Hoppin' John
(page 345)

....

Collard Greens
(page 345)

....

Waldorf Salad
(page 123)

....

Sweet Potato Muffins
(page 121)

....

Jessica's Brownies
(page 315) or
Grasshopper Pie (page 240)

Champagne Lime Punch

❖ ❖ ❖

John's mother gave me this recipe nearly 30 years ago. It has helped ring in a millennium (and century), and many a new year. It has pleasant tropical zing, and the bubbly adds just the right lift.

1 bottle (8–12 ounces) lime juice
1 can (46 ounces) pineapple juice
1 fifth of rum
3 small cans frozen limeade, defrosted
1 lime, thinly sliced
1 bottle champagne, chilled

1. Combine lime juice and pineapple juice and freeze in an ice ring.

2. In a tall container, combine rum, limeade, and lime slices. Chill for several hours.

3. When it is time to serve, place the ice ring in a large punch bowl and add the chilled rum mixture. Slowly add chilled champagne, stir and serve.

Yield: About 25 (5-ounce) servings

CHAMPAGNE CHIC

....

My theory is that it is better to have a little bit of the best champagne that you can afford than a lot of something lesser. Though champagne is often served in wide-mouthed glasses, it bubbles best and longest in tall flutes, preferably with hollow stems. Even if you do not have fine crystal, you can dress up your glasses in a number of ways:

• Tie bows of gold lamé or wired French ribbon to the stems of the glasses

• Slit a perfect strawberry and stand it on the side of the glass

• Run a piece of orange peel around the rim of each glass and dip the rims in superfine sugar to frost very lightly

• Pass champagne on a silver tray, decorated with a single perfect rose or gardenia

• Sprinkle serving tray with sequins or metallic confetti

• Serve by candlelight to the one you love; it will need no embellishment at all!

NEW YEAR'S EVE PUNCH

We usually spend New Year's Eve at the farm with our family, grandkids and all. We make a block of ice from lemonade by filling a small bowl with lemonade and orange and lemon slices and freezing it. For punch for about 15 revelers, mix ½ cup lemon juice, 1 cup cranberry juice, 1 cup orange juice, 1 cup strong tea, and ¼ cup superfine sugar in a large punch bowl; stir until sugar dissolves. Add one bottle (750 ml) of white rum, 12 whole cloves, and the lemonade ice ring, and enjoy. We make it without rum for the kids and serve theirs in pretty glasses over orange sherbet.

Collard Greens

❖ ❖ ❖

A staple in many southern homes, collard greens may be an acquired taste. My brother Joe cooks up a "mess of greens" (and you do need a lot!) regularly. Mother says, "First you wash, wash, wash, then you boil, boil, boil with a bit of salt pork, but it won't smell terribly good while you're cooking them!" I like to sauté them quickly with bacon and onion, much like spinach. You can decide for yourself which way is more delicious.

12 cups fresh collard greens, washed and rinsed thoroughly
4 slices bacon, cut into 1-inch pieces
1 tablespoon olive oil
1 medium onion, chopped
½ teaspoon salt
2 tablespoons garlic-flavored cider, or red wine vinegar
freshly ground black pepper

1. Lay the washed greens flat and cut the tough stems from the leafy greens. Chop leaves.

2. In a large skillet, fry the bacon until it is almost crisp and the fat is rendered. Add the oil and onion; sauté until onions are translucent. Add greens, tossing them to coat with the onion and bacon. Cover and cook for about 5 minutes. Greens will be limp but still a lovely shade of green. Season with the salt and vinegar and pepper to taste.

Yield: 3–4 servings

Hoppin' John

❖ ❖ ❖

B rought to the New World centuries ago by African slaves, this delicious combination of black-eyed peas and ham is traditionally eaten on New Year's Day to ensure good luck throughout the year. But don't wait until January 1 to try it!

2 cups (1 pound) dried black-eyed peas
6 cups water
1 meaty ham bone
2 cups chopped onion
1 cup chopped celery, including tops
1 bay leaf
1 clove of garlic, minced
¼ teaspoon freshly ground black pepper
¼ teaspoon crushed red pepper flakes
2 tablespoons chopped fresh parsley
1 cup uncooked wild or long grain rice

1. Combine the peas with the water in a large soup kettle. Boil for 2 minutes. Remove from the heat and let stand for 1 hour. Add the ham bone, onion, celery, bay leaf, garlic, black and red peppers, and parsley. Cover and simmer for 45 minutes.

2. Stir in the rice. Cover tightly and simmer until peas and rice are tender, about 45 minutes. Remove the ham bone. Dice the remaining ham and return to the pan. Discard the bone. Remove and discard the bay leaf. Reheat and serve immediately with a cruet of vinegar for sprinkling.

Yield: 6–8 servings

ENTERTAINING

We really enjoy entertaining, and we do so almost every week — sometimes even more often! It gives us a chance to pick up where we left off with old friends and to meet new ones. Because our home is very informal (the front door opens into the kitchen), comfortable, casual entertaining tends to follow suit. Whether our guests are business associates, friends, or family, whether they are our grown children or our grandchildren, everyone participates in the preparation and the cleanup of the meal. When people work together at the large kitchen counter, conversations happen easily, and the labor of preparation seems to vanish with so many helping hands. We keep entertaining fun, and we keep it simple.

Contributors to this chapter are Nancy C. Ralston and Marynor Jordan, Charles Reavis, and Maggie Stuckey.

CASUAL GATHERINGS
....
COMPANY'S COMING
....
ICE CREAM SOCIAL
....
COUNTRY TEA PARTY
....
BARN RAISING

A Simple Plan

Some people are born list-makers, and others find it to be just one more burden. However you organize yourself, though, be sure that you have a plan to help you get your entertaining under way. Whether it's a shopping list or a full-blown battle plan for the event, just having something in writing will help you get started, stay focused, and keep calm — key ingredients in simplifying your entertaining style.

Some people feel better when they can keep tight control of an event. Knowing exactly what they will be serving, which utensils will be used, and where on the buffet everything will go helps them feel relaxed. But if you are in the other camp and are willing to accept help from your friends in creating an unstructured evening, you may be surprised at how easy it can be to throw a party.

I once went to a caroling party at a good friend's house. Dinner was potluck, and when I asked what I could bring to be helpful, the host said, "I know I'm serving a ham, but whatever you want to bring would be great. Just make sure it feeds a lot of people." No guidance, no "Dessert would be great" or

"Make yours an appetizer." And when we arrived at the buffet table, there was a beautiful assortment of dishes, no two alike, not too many salads and no desserts. It was simply perfect, and it started with her simple plan of no plan at all. Our host enjoyed herself at least as much as anyone else at the party.

The keys to a stress-free event are simple — plan ahead and do as much ahead as possible. While this advice may sound obvious, you may not follow it unless you remind yourself.

Make a list. If you make a list, organized by task, of what needs to be done, you won't be overwhelmed. For example, if your errands will take you all over town, jot them down in logical order, so that you don't waste time backtracking.

Ongoing tasks. Clean and organize your refrigerator and freezer regularly. If you know what's in there, you won't be surprised to find an empty bottle of ketchup, and you won't be squeezing a second bag of carrots into the freezer.

Inspired Events

You'll never be at a loss for a great party if you make collecting ideas an ongoing process.

Food and entertaining ideas can come from anywhere, anytime. Keep your eyes and ears open. Jot down the idea you heard on the radio on your way to work or from a colleague during lunch.

Use magazines you subscribe to as sources of information. Before you recycle them, tear them apart. Keep a file, envelope, or drawer for clipped recipes that made your mouth water, menus that sound

intriguing, party ideas you'd like to try, and decorating tips that will impress your guests.

When a party or menu is a big success, make a record of it in a notebook or an electronic file on the computer so that you can plan an encore — to more rave reviews, of course.

CASUAL GATHERINGS

Some of the best and most memorable entertaining I've done has been very informal. My best advice for keeping it easy so that you can focus on your guests is to do as much ahead as possible. For example, Marinated Brussels Sprouts and Crabbies can be made ahead and are almost ready to use from the refrigerator and freezer. Pour the Brussels sprouts into a pretty serving dish while the Crabbies bake, and hors d'oeuvres will be ready in no time.

AROUND THE KITCHEN TABLE

Marinated Brussels Sprouts

❖ ❖ ❖

Brussels sprouts are rarely anyone's favorite. Serve these, though, and you'll be surprised at just who not only eats but enjoys them.

10 ounces frozen Brussels
     sprouts
½   cup vegetable oil
½   cup tarragon vinegar
2–3 scallions, chopped
2–3 tablespoons chopped fresh
     parsley
1   tablespoon sugar
1   clove of garlic, finely
     minced
1   teaspoon salt
Tabasco sauce

1. Prepare the Brussels sprouts as the package directs, cooking only 5 minutes. Rinse them under cold water to stop cooking; drain and set aside.

2. In a large bowl, combine the oil, vinegar, scallions, parsley, sugar, garlic, salt, and Tabasco to taste. Add Brussels sprouts, tossing to coat. Marinate, covered, overnight in the refrigerator.

Yield: 6–8 appetizer servings

FRIED ICE FISH

Each winter, we look forward to the bounty that the ice fishermen reap from frozen Lake Champlain. If the fishermen haven't delivered their buckets full of shining smelt to Ernie's Market in time for dinner, we drive down to the boat launch, blink our car lights, and wait for a delivery fresh from the fishing shanties. Fried smelts served with fresh coleslaw and oven-fried potatoes is a meal worth waiting for.

We serve 6 to 12 fish per person, depending on the size of the fish (and the person!). Wash and clean the fish, leaving them whole. Coat each fish with a mixture of flour and cornmeal seasoned with salt and pepper to taste. After coating the fish, quickly fry them in a combination of butter and olive oil (about ½ cup each) until browned on both sides, no more than 5 minutes. Drain on paper towels, and serve with lots of lemon wedges.

And don't forget to make a toast to the good health of the fishermen.

Crabbies

❖ ❖ ❖

When it comes to making hors d'oeuvres, Marcella (John's father's wife) is a pro. She always presents a great array of nibbles with cocktails, and she considers Crabbies a personal specialty. Not only are they delicious, they're quite convenient; you can make them ahead, freeze between layers of plastic wrap, and bake them when you need them.

1 can (6½ ounces) crab-
    meat, drained and rinsed
1 jar (5 ounces) Old English
    sharp process cheese
    spread
½ cup (1 stick) butter
1½ teaspoons mayonnaise
½ teaspoon dry mustard
    dash of Worcestershire sauce
    dash of garlic salt
8 English muffins

1. In a medium-sized bowl, combine the crabmeat, cheese spread, butter, mayonnaise, mustard, Worcestershire sauce, and garlic salt.

2. Split the English muffins. Spread the crab mixture evenly on the 16 halves.

3. Line a baking sheet with plastic wrap or wax paper. Freeze the muffins on the sheet until firm, at least 1 hour. Transfer the Crabbies to a freezer container or resealable plastic freezer bag, placing a sheet of plastic wrap between each one.

4. To serve, preheat the broiler. Cut as many Crabbies as desired into six wedges each. Broil until bubbly and browned, about 3 to 5 minutes.

Yield: 48 wedges

VARIATION: For extra flavor, add a dash of Tabasco sauce and replace the garlic salt with cayenne pepper.

PERSONALIZED PLACE MATS

To give young children an important role in the party preparations and keep them occupied while you cook, ask them to draw place mats for each family member and guest. If you buy a roll of white paper or newsprint from a school- or office-supply store, they can color a whole tablecloth.

BACKYARD BARBECUE

Blackberry Sangria
(page 300) or
Lemon Coolers (page 427)

Apple-Mint Iced Tea
(page 293)

Decibel Dip (page 73)
with potato chips

Fresh vegetable sticks

East Coast Barbecued
Chicken (page 330)
or hamburgers
and hotdogs

Cucumbers in
Sour Cream (page 195)

Perfect Grilled Corn
(page 193)

Baked Sweet Potato
Sticks (page 201)

Blueberry Sour Cream
Cake (page 233)

◇◆◇

COMPANY'S COMING

For a festive occasion, or just to make your friends feel special, have a dining-room-table dinner (even if you don't have a dining room). Set the table with a linen tablecloth and napkins, spring for fresh flowers, and make it all glow by candlelight.

COMPANY'S COMING

Sage Cheese Spread
(page 92)

....

Assorted olives

....

Fresh Steamed Vegetable
Platter (this page)

....

Cajun-Style Grilled
Swordfish (this page)

....

Spinach, Fennel, Apple,
and Walnut Salad
(page 125)

....

Zucchini Parmesan
Jalapeño Flat Bread
(page 115)

....

Dry white wine

....

Michelle's Cheesecake
(page 236) with
fresh strawberries

Cajun-Style Grilled Swordfish

◆ ◆ ◆

Simply adorned, with perhaps just salt, pepper, and lemon juice, grilled swordfish is tasty and easy to serve to guests. But with just a little more effort, you can add the zest of Cajun flavors to your menu.

- 4 swordfish steaks (about 10 ounces each)
- 2 tablespoons peanut oil
- 1 teaspoon freshly ground black pepper
- 1 teaspoon cayenne pepper
- 1 teaspoon celery salt
- 1 teaspoon garlic powder
- 1 teaspoon grated lemon zest
- 1 teaspoon onion powder
- 1 teaspoon paprika

1. Prepare a medium-hot grill.

2. Brush the steaks with the oil.

3. In a small bowl, combine the pepper, cayenne, celery salt, garlic powder, lemon zest, onion powder, and paprika; mix well.

4. Coat the steaks evenly on all sides with the spice mixture.

5. Grill the steaks for about 5 minutes on one side; turn carefully and grill 5 minutes longer or until done.

Yield: 4 servings

Note: Grilling fish exactly 10 minutes per inch of thickness most often yields perfect results.

Fresh Steamed Vegetable Platter

◆ ◆ ◆

I love to make this beautiful dish, particularly in the summer, when the vegetables are fresh from our garden. I often serve it as a meal by itself, though my favorite menu also includes a crusty semolina bread and fresh broiled salmon. The quantities and types of vegetables vary according to how many people I am serving and what vegetables are in season. A general rule is about ¼ to ⅓ pound of vegetables per person, depending on what else you're serving; plan on more if the platter is for your main course.

Dressing

1 small onion, finely
    chopped
¾ cup olive oil
⅓ cup lemon juice
½ teaspoon salt
2 tablespoons chopped fresh
    parsley
2 tablespoons chopped fresh
    rosemary
freshly ground black pepper

Vegetables

small new potatoes
2 tablespoons olive oil
Italian green peppers
red bell peppers
cauliflower florets
broccoli florets
snap peas
carrots, cut 2 inches long
lemon wedges
fresh sprigs of parsley
fresh sprigs of rosemary

1. To make the dressing, in a small bowl whisk together the onion, oil, lemon juice, salt, parsley, rosemary, and pepper to taste. Set aside.

2. Boil the potatoes until just tender. Drain, then run them under cool water to stop cooking. Toss with 1 tablespoon of the oil. Set aside.

3. Slice the peppers into long strips, remove seeds, and place under the broiler, skin side up, until lightly charred.

SENSATIONAL CENTERPIECES

Although fresh flowers — in a low arrangement so as not to impede conversation — make a lovely centerpiece, be creative. Here are some ideas to get you started:

- *A bowl of fresh fruit or vegetables.*
- *Small pots of fresh herbs.*
- *An arrangement of home-canned, multi-colored fruits and vegetables. Give a jar to each guest to take home.*
- *In the fall, an arrangement of autumn-colored leaves.*
- *For a family reunion, several photographs in small frames of the kids when they were young. (Their kids will get a kick out of seeing Mom and Dad as children.)*
- *A cluster of pillar candles of different heights, on their own or surrounded by flowers.*
- *Small bouquets at each place setting instead of one large centerpiece. You don't even need vases; teacups or jelly glasses will do.*

Remove from broiler and toss with the remaining tablespoon of oil. Set aside.

4. Steam the cauliflower until just tender, about 3 to 5 minutes. Add the broccoli and snap peas for the last 2 minutes of cooking. Cook the carrots separately until tender, 5 to 7 minutes. All the vegetables should be tender yet crisp and brightly colored. Drain and rinse with cool water.

5. In a large bowl, use your hands to toss all vegetables together with the dressing. Arrange on a large platter; garnish with lemon wedges, parsley, and sprigs of rosemary.

Yield: Enough dressing for 3 pounds of vegetables

VARIATION: Make the dressing with balsamic vinegar in place of 3 tablespoons of the lemon juice.

ICE CREAM SOCIAL

We all scream for ice cream!" is a rallying cry for a party. Whether you invite everyone over to take turns cranking as you make your own ice cream or purchase your favorite flavors from a local dairy or supermarket, a make-your-own sundae party is fun. Set the table with an assortment of sauces and toppings, put out the ice cream, and sit back and have fun.

Butterscotch Sauce

This simple recipe is the perfect topper for vanilla ice cream—especially homemade.

- ½ cup dark corn syrup
- ½ cup light cream or evaporated milk
- ½ cup sugar
- 3 tablespoons butter

1. In a small saucepan, combine all ingredients. Cook over medium heat, stirring occasionally, until thickened, about 5 minutes. Serve immediately, or store, tightly covered, in the refrigerator for up to 2 months.

Yield: About 1½ cups

Susan's Fudge Sauce

Sue Pfeiffer's fudge sauce is the best I've ever had, and I'm awfully glad that she shared the recipe with me when we were kids. It's easy and foolproof, it keeps well, and it reheats nicely in the microwave.

- 4 tablespoons butter
- 2 squares unsweetened chocolate
- 1½ cups sugar
- ⅛ teaspoon salt
- 1 cup minus 1 tablespoon evaporated milk
- 1 teaspoon vanilla extract

1. In a medium saucepan, cook the butter and chocolate together over medium heat, stirring constantly so that it doesn't burn. Add the sugar and salt; remove from heat. Gradually stir in milk. Return to heat and cook a few minutes longer, stirring constantly, until sauce begins to thicken. Stir in vanilla.

2. Serve immediately, or store, tightly covered, in the refrigerator for up to 2 months.

Yield: About 1½ cups

White Oaks Farm Maple-Walnut Sauce

This treat is especially wonderful on homemade vanilla ice cream. We first tried it when our friend Meredith Maker gave us a jar for Christmas one year.

- 1 cup pure maple syrup
- 2 cups light corn syrup
- 1 cup water
- 1 cup sugar
- 3 cups broken walnut pieces

1. In a large saucepan, combine the maple syrup, corn syrup, water, and sugar. Bring to a boil, stirring constantly to prevent sticking. Reduce heat and simmer, stirring occasionally, until thickened, about 30 minutes.

2. Add nuts. Cook 5 minutes longer.

3. Refrigerate for up to 2 months. For longer storage, ladle the hot syrup into hot, sterile jars, leaving ¼ inch of headroom. Run a rubber spatula around the inside of the jars to release trapped air bubbles. Wipe the rims of the jars with a clean cloth. Place lids in position and tighten screw bands. Process for 10 minutes in a boiling-water-bath canner (page 384).

Variation: Substitute pecans or toasted almonds for the walnuts.

Yield: 1 gallon (about eight half-pint jars)

Baked Alaska

A very special ice cream treat, indeed, is this classic dessert, filled with ice cream and covered with a snowy coating of meringue. Because the meringue acts as insulation, the dessert can be baked without melting the ice cream. It always makes a dramatic and somewhat mystifying presentation, and though it requires last-minute assembly, the cake and ice cream can be prepared in advance. Then it's just a matter of slathering on the meringue and popping it into the oven for a few minutes.

  2 *quarts ice cream*
  1 *9-inch round cake layer, cooled*
  6 *egg whites*
  ½ *teaspoon cream of tartar*
  ¾ *cup sugar*
  ½ *teaspoon vanilla extract*

1. Pack ice cream firmly into a round 8-inch bowl lined with plastic wrap. Freeze for several hours or overnight at the coldest setting of your freezer.

2. Just before serving time, place the cake layer on an unglazed wooden board; then place the board on a baking sheet. Using a serrated knife, trim top of cake so that it is flat. Preheat oven to 500°F.

3. Using an electric mixer, beat the egg whites with the cream of tartar until thick but not quite stiff. Gradually beat in the sugar, a tablespoon at a time; add vanilla and continue beating until meringue is glossy and stands in stiff peaks.

4. Working quickly, unmold the ice cream and

ICE CREAM TOPPERS

....

- Fresh fruit with honey
- Chopped almonds, pecans, and walnuts
- Crushed cookies
- Broken bits of toffee candy bars
- Glorious Granola (page 46)
- Perfect Whipped Cream (page 279)
- Chocolate or sprinkles
- Chocolate, butterscotch, and peanut butter chips

---

remove the plastic wrap. Center the mound of ice cream on the cake layer. It should come to within ½ inch of the edges of the cake. Using a rubber spatula, cover the ice cream and cake thickly with the meringue, swirling meringue into attractive peaks. The meringue should come all the way down the sides of the cake, covering it completely.

5. Place the dessert in the upper third of the oven for 3 to 5 minutes, or until the meringue is lightly browned. Watch carefully. Remove dessert from the oven directly to a serving platter, and serve immediately.

Note: Any kind of cake or even a brownie may be used as the base; sponge cake is especially good. For an extra-fancy look, use two kinds of ice cream, packed in layers.

Yield: 12 servings

COUNTRY TEA PARTY

Many of the English settlers in Colonial America brought with them the tradition of afternoon tea. Tea parties have had somewhat of a revival in the United States; some fine hotels and country inns offer proper tea to their guests. But a tea party served in ceramic is as much fun as one that features silver trays and china teacups.

AFTERNOON TEA

Assorted teas

Fresh lemon slices

Milk

Sugar cubes

Tea sandwiches

Maids of Honor (page 239)

Ginger Scones (page 117)

Orange Marmalade
(page 406)

Rum Cookies

◇ ◇ ◇

Made with rum, these make tasty treats for an afternoon tea celebration, a special occasion, or a holiday.

- 2 cups confectioners' sugar, sifted
- 2 cups graham cracker crumbs
- 2 cups chopped pecans
- 4 tablespoons unsweetened cocoa powder
- ½ cup rum or fruit juice
- 3 tablespoons light corn syrup
- granulated sugar

1. Combine the confectioners' sugar, graham cracker crumbs, pecans, and cocoa in a large bowl. Stir in rum and corn syrup; mix well.

2. Roll into 1-inch balls, then roll each ball in the granulated sugar. Store in an airtight container.

Yield: 3 dozen

VARIATIONS: Use colored granulated sugar for special occasions, such as red and green for a Christmastime tea party. Change the flavor by using gingersnaps instead of graham cracker crumbs.

ABOUT TEA SANDWICHES

To make tea sandwiches, use white or whole-wheat bread from which the crusts have been trimmed. Closed sandwiches, cut into small pieces or fingers, are easier to eat than open-faced ones. Here are some ideas for fillings:

Egg salad

Deviled ham

Chicken Tarragon. Whip butter with chopped fresh or dried tarragon and a splash of lemon juice. Spread thickly on bread; top with thin slices of chicken breast and crumbled bacon.

Ham and Apricot. Mix three parts cream cheese with one part apricot preserves; blend well. Top with sliced ham.

Cheese-Nut. Make a cheese spread of grated Cheddar and mayonnaise in approximately equal parts; mix in chopped pecans.

Cheese-Orange. Mix three parts cream cheese with one part orange marmalade; blend well.

BARN RAISING

*F*ew people these days have need for an old-fashioned barn raising, but the custom shouldn't be forgotten. The help and camaraderie of friends make any large task easier, especially when the promise of a good meal afterward awaits. A do-ahead meal is in order for these kinds of occasions.

Worker Bees

All-day affairs. We all have big jobs that need to get done, such as painting the garage, assembling a swing set, or planting the cooperative garden. Invite your close friends over for the day to help you out. Don't forget to include the kids; someone can entertain them while the grown-ups work.

After the work is finished, serve some fun food and plan a workday at another house the following month. It's an inexpensive and sociable way to finish big jobs quickly. Many hands truly do make light work.

Cross-It-Off-the-To-Do-List Party. Host a get-together to which all the guests bring a small project that has been hanging over their heads. Some things are easier and a lot more fun to do with company present — arranging photo albums, ironing, garden planning, knitting, mending. This kind of gathering is especially good for mothers of young children, who never seem to have time to sit down, chat, and accomplish something.

Hominy Cheese Soufflé

◇ ◇ ◇

*A*s easy as it is delicious, this cheesy soufflé will satisfy a hungry gang. Use your favorite cheese, or combination of cheeses, and choose different herbs for variety. Don't worry: This dish is not as delicate as the word "soufflé" suggests.

- 2 *cups boiling water*
- ½ *cup hominy grits*
- 1 *teaspoon salt*
- ¾ *cup grated sharp Cheddar cheese*
- 1 *cup milk*
- 3 *eggs, beaten*
- 3 *tablespoons chopped fresh chives*

1. In a medium saucepan, cook the water, grits, and ½ teaspoon of the salt for 25 minutes. Remove from heat, add the cheese and let cool for 10 minutes.

2. Preheat oven to 350°F and butter a 2-quart casserole.

3. Add milk, eggs, chives, and remaining ½ teaspoon salt to the grits. Whisk until all ingredients are well blended.

4. Pour into the casserole, then place casserole in a larger pan. Pour boiling water into the larger pan until it reaches halfway up the sides of the dish. Bake for 40 minutes.

Yield: 6 servings

WORKER BEE DINNER

....

Pimiento Cheese Spread
(page 93)

....

Assorted crackers

....

Chicken and Mushroom
Bake (page 178)

....

Hominy Cheese Soufflé
(this page)

....

Green Beans with Red
Pepper Confetti (page 196)

....

Cider Salad Mold
(page 138)

....

Top Hat Chocolate Chip
Bars (page 250)

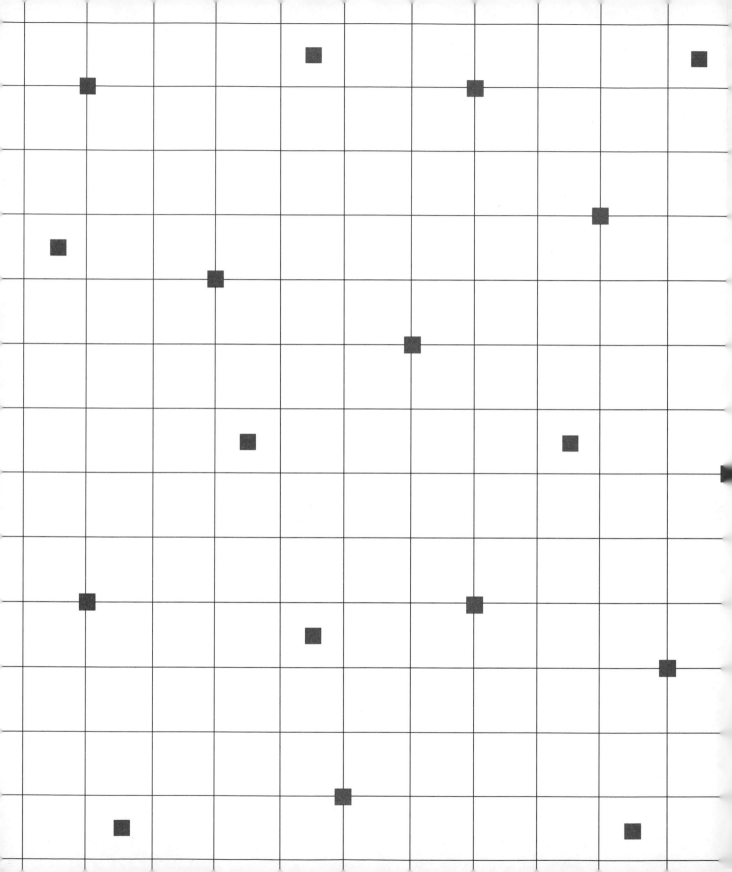

PART FOUR

ARTS OF THE COUNTRY KITCHEN

FROM THE MILK PAIL

My Aunt Ina and Uncle Fred lived off a small farm, and an even smaller grocery store, in Tyler, Texas. Ina's old-fashioned kitchen was the center of family activity and the source of memorable aromas. To me, summer meant Texan relatives and Aunt Ina's prized recipe, home-made peach ice cream. Peaches were picked from her orchard, cream came from her brown cow, and eggs were gathered warm from the coop, ensuring a heavenly delight. We all took turns on the crank, and it was nearly impossible to wait for the ice cream to "ripen" under the old Army blanket that kept it cold as it hardened under a shade tree. Milk, whether starring in Aunt Ina's ice cream; in one of the favorite beverages at the beginning of this chapter; in cheese, yogurt, or butter; or by the glass, is a country favorite.

■ ■ ■ ■ ■ ■ ■ ■

Contributors to this chapter are Glenn Andrews, Joanne Barrett, Ricki Carroll and Robert Carroll, Ken Haedrich, Geri Harrington, Phyllis Hobson, Maggie Oster, Phyllis V. Shaudys, and Olwen Woodier.

MAKING ICE CREAM, SHERBET & FROZEN YOGURT

CHEESEMAKING

MAKING YOGURT

BUTTER

················· MARTHA'S FAVORITES ·················

Hot Cocoa with Peppermint Stirrers

❀ ❀ ❀

When the snow is falling and the kids and grand-kids have just come in from sledding or skating on the pond, nothing warms them up faster than a cup of hot cocoa. Made from cocoa powder and whole milk, it's rich and satis-fying, and the added fun of peppermint sticks to stir with makes it seem like a party.

- ½ cup sugar
- ⅓ cup hot water
- ¼ cup unsweetened cocoa powder
- 4 cups whole milk
- 1 teaspoon vanilla extract
- 6 peppermint-stick candies

1. In a medium sauce-pan, combine the sugar, water, and cocoa. Bring to a boil and cook, stirring, for 2 minutes.

2. Add the milk, and reheat, being careful not to boil. Stir in the vanilla. Pour into mugs, and serve with peppermint-stick stirrers.

Yield: 6 servings

Variation: Replace the pep-permint-stick candies with cinnamon sticks.

Maple Yogurt Smoothie

❀ ❀ ❀

The maple flavor is a won-derful taste treat in this cal-cium-rich drink!

- 1 cup plain yogurt
- ½ cup milk
- ⅓ cup maple syrup
- 1 ripe banana, peeled
- pinch of cinnamon
- several ice cubes

1. Combine the yogurt, milk, maple syrup, banana, and cinnamon in a blender.

2. Wrap the ice cubes in a tea towel and shatter them with a hammer. Add them to

SUGAR EQUIVALENTS

····························

When making ice cream, 1 cup white sugar is equal to each of the following:
- ½ cup honey
- ½ cup molasses
- ⅔ cup maple syrup
- ⅓ cup crystalline fructose
- 1½ cups maltose
- ½ cup sorghum
- 1 cup brown sugar, lightly packed

the blender and process until smooth; it's fine if shards of ice remain after blending. Serve immediately.

Yield: 2 servings

Variation: If you use a frozen banana to thicken the smoothie, you can omit the ice cubes.

Milk Shake

❀ ❀ ❀

In many parts of New England, this is called a "frappé." Delicious by any name.

- 1 cup fresh fruit (straw-berries, sliced peaches, or blueberries)
- 3 tablespoons honey
- 2 cups milk
- ½ pint vanilla ice cream

1. In a blender, stir together the fruit and honey; add milk. Whirl to blend, then add the ice cream and blend again. Serve in cold glasses.

Yield: 2 servings

MAKING ICE CREAM, SHERBET & FROZEN YOGURT

The words "ice cream social" take on a new meaning when you feature ice cream making as part of a gathering at your home. Whether your guests are taking turns cranking the churn on a hand-powered ice cream freezer or just monitoring the salt level in an electric freezer, they'll enjoy dessert even more for having been part of its creation.

ICE CREAM LINGO

DASHER. The paddle inside the inner container of an ice cream maker that agitates the freezing mixture and makes the ice cream smooth and creamy.

RIPEN. To hold the ice cream mixture frozen for a few hours after its initial freezing. Ripening ice cream improves the flavor.

MAKING ICE CREAM AT HOME

Homemade ice cream first became a staple of country living in 1846, when a woman named Nancy Johnson invented an ice cream churn, complete with dasher, hand crank, two tubs, and space for ice and salt. By 1851, ice cream was produced commercially. With the widespread use of refrigeration, electricity, supermarkets, and convenience foods in the twentieth century, homemade ice cream became a delicacy

ICE CREAM–MAKING EQUIPMENT

- **Ice cream freezer.** For home use, these come in sizes ranging from 1 quart to 2 gallons. Most are relatively inexpensive but very functional. Some freezers come equipped with an ice cream churn.
- **Old-fashioned ice cream churn.** Churns are available as hand-cranked models or electrically powered units.
- **In-freezer ice cream churn.** Such churns include a 1-quart unit with a dasher, metal can, plastic tub, and electrical assembly that uses the frigid air of a deep freezer or refrigerator freezer rather than ice and salt to freeze the mixture inside. Churning is usually completed in 1½ hours.
- **Self-contained ice cream churn.** These models come in sizes slightly more and slightly less than 1 quart. Using their own freon freezing unit and powered electrically, they can make ice cream in 20 minutes. Although expensive, their ease of operation, speed, and lack of mess make them appealing.
- **Measuring spoons and measuring cups**
- **Blender, food processor, or food mill**
- **Fine strainer**
- **Bowls** (glass, ceramic, or stainless steel)
- **Whisk**
- **Electric mixer or rotary beater**
- **Shallow pans,** such as 8-inch round or square cake pans
- **Freezer storage containers**

for special occasions, because we came to accept commercially made ice creams and other frozen desserts as good.

Over time, what was once a simple mixture of milk, sweetener, flavoring, and possibly eggs became a frozen chemical soup of more than 60 additives with almost 50 percent more air than in homemade ice cream.

For many, making ice cream at home has a great deal of mystique. Recipe books warn that the proportion of salt and ice has to be just right for the mixture to freeze correctly. Use too much sugar and the mixture won't freeze; too little, and it will freeze as hard as a brick. Many writers encourage the use of perfectly good ingredients such as gelatin and flour, but somehow these seem alien to such a simple delight.

Maggie Oster was one of those people who feared making ice cream at home. She says she became converted when she made a mixture of fresh strawberries and honey, mashed them together, cooked it briefly, and stirred in some half-and-half. Then she put it into the deep freezer. Just like that — no magic incantations. Later that day, she sampled the concoction. The result was sensational. Yes, there were ice crystals and the texture was less than creamy, but the flavor! Like nothing that ever came off a food technologist's shelf. A whole new world opened up for Maggie, who has since become such an expert that she wrote a booklet about making ice cream.

Simply put, making ice cream and other frozen desserts yourself makes good sense and is a lot of fun. The flavors you can create are limitless, and the ingredients are readily available. Your ice cream will cost less than the premium brands and will be vastly superior to the cheaper brands. Most important, you can control what goes into your ice cream, making it as sinfully rich or as austerely slimming as you want, with no unnecessary ingredients.

For the best smooth texture and a minimum of ice crystals, ice cream needs to be constantly agitated throughout the freezing process; this is easily achieved with a modern ice cream maker with a freezer unit or with an old-fashioned ice cream maker, ice, and rock salt. Ice cream made with this process is called "churned" ice cream, because the dasher in the machine constantly churns the mixture to aerate it and scrapes the freezer container's sides, breaking up any ice clusters that have formed.

We call ice cream made without benefit of a machine "still-frozen" ice cream.

ICE CREAM INGREDIENTS

- **Dairy products.** *Heavy cream, light cream, half-and-half, whole milk, low-fat milk, buttermilk, evaporated milk, sour cream, soy milk*
- **Sweeteners.** *Granulated white sugar, brown sugar, honey, unsulfured molasses, maple syrup, light corn syrup, dark corn syrup, fructose, maltose, sorghum*
- **Flavorings.** *Vanilla extract, chocolate, carob, fruits, nuts, coffee, liqueurs*

Basic Procedure for Churned Ice Cream

Be sure to follow the manufacturer's directions for your particular equipment.

1. Prepare ice cream or other frozen dessert mixture, pour into a bowl, cover, and refrigerate for several hours.

2. Wash the dasher, lid, and can of your ice cream churn, then rinse and dry. Refrigerate to chill.

3. Pour the chilled mixture into the chilled can, making sure it is no more than two-thirds full, to allow for expansion. Put on the lid.

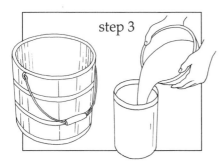

step 3

4. Put the can into the freezer tub and attach the crank-and-gear assembly.

5. Fill the tub one-third full of ice. Sprinkle an even layer of salt, about ⅛-inch deep, on the top. Continue adding layers of ice and salt until the tub is filled to the top of the can.

6. If using ice cubes, add 1 cup of cold water to the ice and salt mixture to help the ice melt and settle. If using crushed ice, let the ice-packed tub sit for 5 minutes before beginning to churn. While churning, add more ice and salt in the same proportions, so the ice remains up to the top of the can.

step 6

7. For hand-cranked churns, crank slowly at first — slightly less than one revolution per second. When the mixture begins to pull, churn as quickly and steadily as possible for 5 minutes. Finally, churn at a slightly slower pace for a few minutes longer, or until the mixture is reasonably hard.

8. For electrically powered churns, fill the can with the mix and plug in the unit. Allow it to churn until it stops (15 to 20 minutes). Restart if necessary by turning the can with your hands.

9. When the ice cream is ready, remove the crank-and-gear assembly. Wipe all ice and salt from the top, so that none can fall into the cream when you uncover it. Remove the lid and lift out the beater. The ice cream should be the texture of mush.

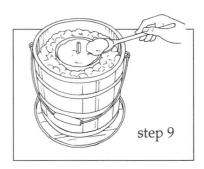

step 9

10. Scrape the cream from the beater. Add chopped nuts and fruit or sauce for ripple, if desired. Pack down the cream with a spoon. Cover with several layers of wax paper and replace the lid, putting a cork in the cover hole.

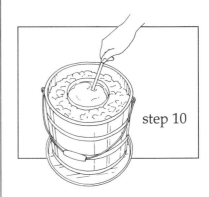

step 10

11. Eat the ice cream in its soft state, or ripen and harden the ice cream by placing it in a deep freezer or refrigerator freezer, or repack it in the tub with layers of ice and salt until the can and lid are covered. Use more salt than you previously used, making each layer about ¼-inch deep. Cover the freezer with a blanket and set in a cool place until ready to serve, about 1 hour.

step 11

THE SCOOP ON SCOOPING

Our favorite kind of scoop is the solid aluminum, rounded type without a lever. Running the scoop along in smooth, long lines helps get perfect scoops. Don't wet the scoop: The water will freeze to a thin layer of ice and add ice crystals to your otherwise perfectly textured ice cream.

Basic Procedure for Still-Frozen Ice Cream

1. Prepare the ice cream mixture as directed and pour into a shallow tray, such as a cake pan.

2. Place the tray in the freezer compartment of the refrigerator at the coldest setting or in a deep freezer for 30 minutes to 1 hour, until the mixture is mushy.

3. Scrape the mixture into a chilled bowl and beat it with a rotary beater or electric mixer as rapidly as possible, until the mixture is smooth.

4. Return the mixture to the tray and the freezer. When almost frozen solid, beat again. Add chopped nuts and fruits or ripple sauce, if desired.

5. Return to the tray and cover the mixture with plastic wrap to prevent ice crystal formation. Place in the freezer until solid.

6. Serve immediately or pack into airtight containers for storing in the freezer. Press a piece of plastic wrap to the surface to prevent ice crystal formation.

BUTTERFAT CONTENT

Whipping or heavy cream has 36 percent butterfat and produces the richest ice cream, but with the most calories. Most kinds available in grocery stores are ultrapasteurized and contain emulsifiers and stabilizers.

Light or coffee cream contains 20 percent butterfat and makes relatively rich ice cream.

Half-and-half is a mixture of milk and cream with 12 percent butterfat; it makes a satisfactory ice cream with a hint of richness.

Whole milk has 3½ percent butterfat. It's the basic ingredient in most ice creams and sherbets.

Low-fat milks —2 percent butterfat, 99 percent fat-free and skim (less than ½ percent butterfat) — are useful when you want to limit calories, but you will get a coarser texture in the ice cream.

Basic Vanilla Ice Cream

❧ ❧ ❧

There's nothing like rich, high-butterfat ice cream, but in this basic recipe, Maggie Oster gives the option of making the ice cream lower in calories.

1 *quart heavy or light cream or half-and-half or 2 cups each heavy and light cream*
1 *cup sugar or ½ cup honey*
1 *tablespoon pure vanilla extract*

1. The ingredients can be mixed and used as is, or the cream can be scalded. Scalding concentrates the milk solids and improves the flavor. To scald, slowly heat cream in a saucepan until just below the boiling point. Small bubbles will begin to appear around the edges. Stir for several minutes, then remove from the heat.

2. Stir in the sugar. Pour into a bowl, cover, and chill. When completely cooled, add the vanilla.

3. When the mixture is thoroughly chilled, follow directions for either churned or still-frozen ice cream.

Yield: 1 quart

VANILLA VARIATIONS

....

Once you've mastered basic vanilla ice cream, the variations are limited only by your ingredients. Here's a sampling:

BANANA ICE CREAM. Use the basic recipe, but add 1 tablespoon lemon juice and 1½ cups mashed banana to the cream mixture just before freezing.

BUTTER PECAN ICE CREAM. Use the basic recipe, but add to the mushy ice cream ⅔ cup chopped pecans that have been sautéed in 3 tablespoons butter until lightly browned.

CHOCOLATE CHIP ICE CREAM. Use the basic recipe, but add 1 cup finely chopped chocolate chips to cream mixture just before freezing.

CHOCOLATE ICE CREAM. Use the basic recipe, but melt 2 to 6 (1-ounce) squares of bitter or semisweet chocolate in a small pan over low heat and add to the scalded milk. Increase the sugar to taste, usually doubling the standard quantity.

COFFEE ICE CREAM. Use the basic recipe, but dissolve 3 tablespoons instant coffee, espresso, or grain beverage in 4 tablespoons hot water or ¾ cup brewed coffee. Add to the cream mixture just before freezing.

FRUIT ICE CREAM. Use the basic recipe, but before freezing add 1½ cups fruit purée stirred with 2 teaspoons fresh lemon juice and 2 tablespoons sugar or 1 tablespoon honey. Use fresh or unsweetened frozen fruit. If you use pineapple, use canned, not fresh. Strain fruits with seeds, such as raspberries and blackberries, after puréeing.

ICE MILK. Use the basic recipe, but substitute whole, low-fat, or skim milk for the cream.

ICE SOY MILK. Use the basic recipe, but substitute soy milk for the cream, without scalding. Combine soy milk, sweetener, flavoring, and ¼ cup vegetable oil and whirl in a blender.

MINT ICE CREAM. Use the basic recipe, but reduce vanilla extract to 1 teaspoon and add 2 teaspoons peppermint extract to the chilled cream mixture.

PISTACHIO ICE CREAM. Use the basic recipe, but add 1 teaspoon almond extract with the vanilla. Add 1 cup finely chopped pistachio nuts when the ice cream is mushy. If desired, add green food coloring with the extracts.

SUPER-CREAMY VANILLA ICE CREAM. Use the basic vanilla recipe, but soften 1½ teaspoons unflavored gelatin in ¼ cup water and add with the sugar to the scalded milk. Continue cooking over low heat until the gelatin is dissolved. Or substitute 1½ tablespoons agar.

Aunt Ina's Peach Ice Cream

❧ ❧ ❧

Simply the best! Be sure the peaches are perfectly ripe and drip-down-your-chin juicy.

3 cups milk
2 cups sugar
6 eggs, lightly beaten
2 cups heavy cream
2 cups peaches, pitted, peeled, and mashed
1 tablespoon vanilla extract

1. Combine the milk, sugar, and eggs in the top of a double boiler. Cook the mixture, set over barely simmering water, stirring constantly, until it coats the spoon. Set the top of the double boiler into a pan of cold water and let the mixture cool, stirring often.

2. Stir in cream, peaches, and vanilla until well blended. Pour mixture into ice cream maker.

3. Churn until crank is too hard to turn. Carefully remove the dasher, tightly re-cover, and allow to ripen under more ice and salt, and covered with a blanket or newspapers.

Yield: Almost 1 gallon

JUST LIKE GRANDMA

Your grandparents (or possibly great-grandparents) may have made ice cream in an old utensil called a fireless cooker. This is a heavily insulated contrivance that was used as a slow cooker in the 1920s by heating a flat stone and the kettle of food on the kitchen stove. Then both were placed down in an insulated well to continue cooking by their heat. To make ice cream, the cooker well can be lined with the salt and ice mixture and the kettle filled with ice cream mixture. The inner container should be turned occasionally, and it makes for a smoother product if the ice cream is stirred with a spoon at least once during the freezing process.

Frozen Custard

❧ ❧ ❧

Storey author Phyllis Hobson describes frozen custard as a "rich, creamy frozen dessert." This recipe produces a custard that is richer than the commercial variety.

1 cup sugar
2 tablespoons cornstarch
½ teaspoon salt
1 quart milk
4 egg yolks
3 cups heavy cream
2 tablespoons pure vanilla extract

1. Combine ¾ cup of the sugar, the cornstarch, and salt in a medium-sized saucepan. Gradually add the milk and cook over hot water for 5 to 10 minutes, or until mixture comes to a boil. Stir constantly during this time.

2. Slightly beat the egg yolks with the remaining ¼ cup sugar. Add a small amount of hot mixture and stir well. Pour the egg yolk mixture into the cooked milk mixture and continue cooking, stirring constantly, 3 minutes longer.

3. Cool. Add cream and vanilla and freeze.

Yield: About 2 quarts

EGG CAUTION

The U.S. Department of Agriculture strongly recommends that you do not use raw eggs, raw egg yolks, or raw egg whites in making ice cream, in order to avoid salmonella poisoning. Use eggs only when they can be cooked. Cook all custard mixtures to a temperature of 160°F to kill any possible bacteria.

Sherbets and Ices

The differences between sherbets, sorbets, and ices are ambiguous and open to much culinary debate. They are as variable as the cook and the country of origin.

Basically, sherbets consist of fruit purée or juice, sweetener, and water or milk. They may be churned or still-frozen. Gelatin can be used to make a product that is smoother, but sherbets are supposed to be somewhat coarse in texture, so it really isn't necessary. Using a sugar syrup, honey, or other syrup form of sweetener is recommended for texture.

However sherbets are made, the result is an intensely flavored, refreshing treat. They are particularly delightful as a light dessert during summer's hot days — or any time you're counting calories.

Water ices are simple, easy-to-make desserts made by freezing sweetened, diluted fruit juice. Ices made using the still-frozen method should be stirred at least once or twice during the freezing process.

Fruit Sherbet

🌸 🌸 🌸

Cool off a warm summer evening with a refreshing sherbet made from the bounty of your backyard, orchard, or local farm stand.

- ½ cup simple syrup or ¼ cup honey
- 2 cups fruit purée or juice
- 2 cups milk (whole, 2 percent, low-fat, skim, buttermilk, or reconstituted dry)
- 2 tablespoons lemon juice

1. To make simple syrup, combine ⅓ cup sugar and ⅓ cup water in a small saucepan and cook over medium heat until the sugar is dissolved. Remove from the heat just before the syrup comes to a boil. When the mixture is cool, cover and chill.

2. Combine the syrup with the fruit purée, milk, and lemon juice. Use the purée or juice of such fruits as lemon, lime, orange, grapefruit, grape, apricot, plum, apple, pear, peach, strawberry, blackberry, raspberry, or melon. Strain out the seeds of such fruits as blackberry and raspberry. To make a creamier sherbet, substitute half-and-half, light cream, or heavy cream for the milk. The combined mixture of ingredients may appear curdled, but it won't affect the final product.

3. Chill thoroughly, then follow the basic procedure for churned or still-frozen ice cream.

Yield: 1½ quarts

Mint Sorbet

🌸 🌸 🌸

Sorbet may seem only to be a fancy French word for sherbet, but a distinguishing feature of sorbet is that it is not made with milk. Herbal sorbets are very refreshing for a light starter, a palate cleanser between courses, or a lovely, light treat anytime.

- 3 cups water
- 2 cups sugar
- 1 large bunch fresh mint, coarsely chopped (about 1 cup)
- 3 tablespoons fresh lemon juice
- 1–2 tablespoons green crème de menthe (optional) sprigs of mint for garnish (optional)

1. To make simple syrup, put 2 cups of the water into a saucepan. Add the sugar and boil, stirring, until the sugar has dissolved. Set aside to cool.

2. Bring the remaining cup of water to a boil in another pan. Add the mint and the lemon juice and remove from heat. When cool, strain into the pan containing the simple syrup. Add the crème de menthe, if you are using it; it will emphasize the mint flavor and give the sorbet a pretty green tint.

3. Chill the infusion mixture thoroughly; then freeze in an ice cream maker, according to the manufacturer's directions.

4. Serve the sorbet, garnished with fresh mint sprigs, if desired.

Yield: 1½ pints

Lemon Ice

❧ ❧ ❧

It's tart and sweet — like lemonade in a spoon. Scoop it into pretty glasses and garnish it with lemon verbena or mint leaves.

 4 *cups water*
 2 *cups sugar*
 1 *cup lemon juice*

1. Heat water and sugar until sugar is dissolved. Chill. Add lemon juice and freeze in an ice cream maker.

Yield: 1½ quarts

VARIATION: Replace the lemon juice with lime juice or make grapefruit ice using 3 cups grapefruit juice and 1½ cups each sugar and water.

Cider Ice

❧ ❧ ❧

Cider ice is a perfect palate refresher for a special autumn dinner. Add a pinch of minced sage or rosemary to give it an herbal flair.

 1½ *cups water*
 1½ *cups sugar*
  4 *cups apple cider*
  ¼ *cup lemon juice*

1. Heat water to boiling, add sugar, and stir to dissolve. Cool. Add cider and juice. Freeze in an ice cream maker.

Yield: 2 quarts

Frozen Yogurt

Yogurt's unique taste has made it a favorite frozen dessert. Homemade frozen yogurt is a delicious yet economical treat.

Basic Vanilla Frozen Yogurt

❧ ❧ ❧

This recipe will yield either vanilla or fruit-flavored frozen yogurt.

  4 *cups plain yogurt*
 ½–¼ *cup honey or other sweetener*

 1 *tablespoon vanilla extract*

1. Combine the yogurt, honey, and vanilla in a blender or beat with a mixer to a light, smooth texture.

2. Follow the procedure for either churned or still-frozen ice cream.

Yield: 1½ quarts

VARIATIONS: Smoother Frozen Yogurt. Soften 1½ teaspoons unflavored gelatin or 1½ tablespoons agar in ¼ cup cold water. Cook over low heat until completely dissolved. Add to the Basic Vanilla Yogurt recipe.

Fruit-Flavored Frozen Yogurt. Using the Basic Vanilla Frozen Yogurt recipe, omit the vanilla and add 2 cups puréed unsweetened fresh, frozen, or canned fruit or juice.

CHEESEMAKING

Few families, even those with several milk drinkers, can keep up with the output of a good cow, and most goats will average a gallon of milk a day during the summer months. The best solution to a surplus of milk is cheese — the most delicious, nutritious method of preserving milk yet devised. If you don't have a family cow — or took yours to college to pay for your room and board, as my dad did — you can still make cheese.

Even if you do not have a cow or goat of your own, you can probably find fresh raw milk, free from chemicals, from a farm or a dairy. You can often buy milk at a lower price during the summer.

Not only is homemade cheese cheaper than supermarket cheese, it is also better tasting and better for you, because it contains no preservatives. If you are a vegetarian, you can make your own cheese with an all-vegetable rennet. Making cheese is a simple procedure that is easily adapted to the kitchen. Few ingredients are needed, and most of the necessary equipment is already on hand.

The instructions for making cheese sound complicated, but the process is really much simpler than baking a

CHEESEMAKING TERMS

....

CLABBER. To curdle or sour; or milk that has curdled

CULTURE. The live bacteria used to develop or sour milk for sour cream and yogurt

CURD. The white, solid portion of milk

RENNET. A product, usually made from the stomach linings of animals, that causes milk to curdle quickly

WHEY. The clear, watery, liquid component of milk

ITEMS FOR MAKING CHEESE

....

- **CHEESE FORM.** Buy one or make your own from a 2-pound coffee can by punching nail holes in the bottom of the can. Punch the holes from the inside out. The cheese form is lined with cheesecloth and filled with the wet curd before pressing.
- **FOLLOWER.** A follower is a circle of ½-inch plywood cut to a diameter slightly smaller than that of the coffee can. The follower forces the wet curd down in the cheese form.
- **CHEESE PRESS.** You can buy a press or make one in an afternoon out of scrap wood and a broomstick. The cheese form is set on the press, the fol-

lower is set in place, and the top board of the press is weighted down with one or two bricks. This exerts slow pressure on the cheese.
- **CONTAINERS.** For a container, I set a 24-quart hot-water canner inside a 36-quart canner, double-boiler style. The smaller canner holds 4 or more gallons of milk.
- **OTHER ITEMS.** You'll also need a strainer, a thermometer, a long-handled spoon, a large knife, two pieces of cheesecloth (1 square yard each), six to eight bricks, and 1 pound of U.S. Department of Agriculture–approved cheese coating.

cake. For each cheese recipe, review the basic cheesemaking directions first, then read the specific recipe. With only a little practice, you can become an expert at making cheese.

As you gain confidence, you will learn the variables of cheesemaking — the degree of ripening of the milk and its effect on flavor, the length of time the curd is heated and how that affects the texture, the amount of salt, the number of bricks used in pressing and the effect on moisture content, and how long the cheese is cured for sharpness of taste. The more you learn about it, the more fascinating cheesemaking will become.

The Three Basic Kinds of Cheese

Hard cheese is the curd of milk (the white, solid portion) separated from the whey (the watery, clear liquid). Once separated, the curd is pressed into a solid cake and aged for flavor. Most hard cheeses are better flavored if they are aged. The longer the aging period, the sharper the flavor. The heavier the pressing weight, the harder the texture. Hard cheese is best when made with whole milk.

Soft cheese is made the same way as hard cheese, but it is pressed just briefly. It is not coated, and it is aged a short time or not at all. Most soft cheeses can be eaten immediately and are best when eaten within a few weeks. Soft cheese can be made with whole or skim milk.

Cottage cheese is a soft cheese prepared from a high-moisture curd that is not allowed to cure. Commercially, it is usually made of skim milk, but it can also be made of whole milk.

YOGURT HERB CHEESE

Drain 3 cups of very fresh yogurt for 6 to 8 hours, or overnight, in the refrigerator. Scrape into a bowl and add 2 cloves of crushed garlic, ½ teaspoon of crushed pepper (about 20 turns on the pepper mill), 1 teaspoon each of crushed dried herbs — thyme, basil, and oregano — and ¼ cup of chopped chives or parsley. If this seems a little too tart for your taste, whip ½ cup of heavy cream to a thick, but not fluffy, consistency, and beat it into the yogurt cheese. Refrigerate so that the flavors can blend.

INGREDIENTS FOR CHEESEMAKING

- *Milk. Raw whole milk from goats or cows makes the richest cheese, but partially skimmed milk can also be used.*
- *Starter. Starter is necessary for good cheese flavor. You can buy buttermilk, yogurt, or a commercial powdered cheese starter, or you can make a tart homemade starter by holding 2 cups of fresh raw milk at room temperature for 12 to 24 hours, until it curdles. If you can't get raw milk, buy starter-culture kits (in freeze-dried packets) from cheese supply catalogs.*
- *Flake salt. Flake salt is absorbed faster than ordinary table salt.*

Making Hard Cheese

❧ ❧ ❧

Here are general directions for making hard cheeses. You will find many variations in specific recipes, particularly for processing temperatures and pressing times.

2–3 gallons milk
  2 cups cheese starter
  ½ teaspoon liquid rennet or
     1 tablet rennet dissolved
     in ½ cup cool water
1–2 tablespoons flake salt
  ½ pound U.S.D.A.-approved
     cheese coating

1. **Ripen the milk.** Warm the milk to 86°F and add starter. Stir thoroughly for 2 minutes. Cover and let sit in a warm place overnight. In the morning, taste the milk. If it has a slightly acidic taste, it is ready for the next step. If you are not using rennet, skip the next step and let the milk sit 18 to 24 hours longer, until the curd has formed and the whey is separating.

2. **Add the rennet.** With milk at room temperature, add rennet; stir for 2 minutes to mix in the rennet thoroughly. Cover the container and let it remain undisturbed until the milk has coagulated, 30 to 45 minutes.

3. **Cut the curd.** When the curd is firm and a small amount of whey appears on the surface, it is ready to cut. With a clean knife, slice the curd into ½-inch cubes. Stir the curd carefully with a wooden spoon; cut any cubes that do not conform to size.

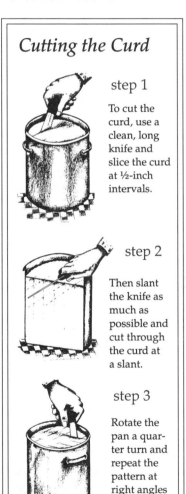

Cutting the Curd

step 1
To cut the curd, use a clean, long knife and slice the curd at ½-inch intervals.

step 2
Then slant the knife as much as possible and cut through the curd at a slant.

step 3
Rotate the pan a quarter turn and repeat the pattern at right angles to the first cut.

Continue cutting ½-inch pieces, and then stir the curd carefully.

4. **Heat the curd.** Place a small container into a larger one filled with warm water, double-boiler style. Heat the curds and whey slowly at the rate of 2°F every 5 minutes. Heat to a temperature of 100°F over 30 to 40 minutes, then hold this temperature until the curd has developed the desired firmness. Keep stirring gently to prevent the cubes of curd from sticking together and forming lumps. Test the curd for firmness by squeezing a small handful gently, then releasing it quickly. If it shows little tendency to stick together, it is ready. When the curd is firm, remove the container.

5. **Remove the whey.** Pour the curds and whey into a large container lined with cheesecloth. Lift the cheesecloth with the curd inside and let it drain in a colander or large strainer. Reserve the whey for optional use. When most of the whey has drained off, remove the curd from the cheesecloth, put it into a container, and tilt it several times to remove whey. Stir the curd or work it with your hands to keep the curds separated. When it has cooled to 90°F and has a rubbery texture, it is ready to be salted.

6. **Salt the curd.** Sprinkle the flake salt over the curd

and mix well. Once the salt has dissolved and the curd has cooled to 85°F, spoon the curd into a cheese form whose sides and bottom have been lined with cheesecloth.

7. **Press the curd.** Place a circle of cheesecloth on top of the curd. Insert the wooden follower and put the cheese form into the cheese press. Start with a weight of three or four bricks for 10 minutes, remove the follower, and drain off any whey that has collected. Replace the follower and add a brick at a time until you have six to eight bricks. After an hour under this much pressure, the cheese should be ready to dress.

8. **Dress the cheese.** Remove the weights and the follower and turn the cheese form upside down so the cheese will drop out. Remove the cheesecloth from the cheese and dip the cheese into warm water to remove fat from surface. Smooth over any small holes with your fingers to make an even surface. Wipe dry.

Cut a piece of cheesecloth 2 inches wider than the cheese is thick and long enough to wrap around it with a slight overlap. Roll the cheese tightly, using two round circles of cheesecloth to cover the ends. Replace the cheese in the cheese form, insert the follower, and press with six to eight bricks for 18 to 24 hours longer.

9. **Dry the cheese.** Remove the cheese, take off the cheesecloth, and wipe the cheese with a clean, dry cloth. Check for any openings or cracks. Wash the cheese in hot water or whey for a firm rind. Seal holes by dipping the cheese into warm water and smoothing with your fingers or a table knife. Put the cheese on a shelf in a cool, dry place. Turn and wipe it daily until the surface feels dry and the rind has started to form. This takes 3 to 5 days.

10. **Coat the cheese.** Follow the package directions on the U.S.D.A.-approved coating; the coatings are available from catalogs offering cheesemaking supplies.

11. **Cure the cheese.** Put the cheese back onto the shelf to cure. Turn it daily. Wash and sun the shelf once a week. After about 6 weeks of curing at a temperature between 40 and 60°F, the cheese will have a firm body and a mild flavor. Cheese with a sharp flavor requires at least 3 to 5 months of curing. How long to cure depends on individual taste.

Cheddar Cheese

With a little effort in the spring, you can have perfectly ripened Cheddar in time for your fall apple pies.

To make Cheddar cheese, follow the basic directions for hard cheese through **step 5,** removing the whey. Then place the cubes of heated curd in a colander and heat to 100°F. This can be done in a double-boiler arrangement or in the oven. After 20 to 30 minutes, the curd will form a solid mass. It should then be sliced into 1-inch strips, which must be turned with a wooden spoon every 15 minutes for even drying. Bake or cook these strips at 100°F for 1

WHAT TO DO WITH THE WHEY?

Phyllis Hobson writes in Making Cheese, Butter & Yogurt *that she thinks whey has "an undesirable yeasty flavor." She reports that, while some people use it in soups and stews and as a milk substitute in baking, she prefers to feed it to pets. But Ricki and Robert Carroll, authors of* Cheesemaking Made Easy, *think whey is particularly delicious if used in baking breads. They also recommend it as a "refreshing summertime drink if served with ice and crushed mint leaves."*

hour. Remove from heat and continue with the basic directions, beginning at **step 6.** Cure the cheese for 6 months.

FLAVORED CHEDDARS

You can use 1 to 3 tablespoons of fresh chopped or dried sage, ½ to 2 tablespoons of caraway seeds, or ½ to 4 tablespoons of chopped jalapeño peppers to flavor 2 pounds of cheese. The amount depends on the degree of flavor you want in the final cheese. Place the desired seasoning in ½

....

WELSH RABBIT

....

Welsh rabbit or rarebit is a simple way to make a supper of your homemade cheese. A country cousin to cheese fondue, it is made of cheese melted with milk or beer and seasonings and served over toasted bread. To make it, simply melt 1 tablespoon butter in a pan. Add 1 tablespoon flour; mix well. Add ½ cup milk or beer; cook until thick. Add 1 handful of grated cheese—Cheddar or any leftover cooking cheese you have. Stir until melted and blended. Add a little dry mustard. Serve over toast. Just enough for 1 person.

....

cup water and boil for 15 minutes, adding water as needed, so that it does not all boil away. Strain the flavored water into the milk to be used for cheesemaking. Follow directions for Cheddar cheese. Add the sage, seeds, or peppers during the salting process.

Colby Cheese

Colby is similar to Cheddar but is softer and milder, and it's ready to eat without a long curing time.

To make a small Colby cheese, add 3 tablespoons of starter to 1 gallon of lukewarm milk. Let it stand overnight to clabber, then proceed with the basic directions for hard cheese through **step 4,** heating the curd.

When the curd is heated to the point where it no longer shows a tendency to stick together, remove the container from the heat and let it stand 1 hour; stir every 5 minutes.

Now continue with **step 5,** removing the whey. After pressing the curd for 18 hours, the cheese can be dried for a day or so and used as a soft cheese spread or ripened for 30 days.

Mozzarella Cheese

Mozzarella is a delicate, semihard Italian cheese that is used fresh.

To make it, follow the basic directions up to **step 3.** Instead of cutting the curd with a knife, break it up with your hands. Heat the curd to as hot as your hands can stand. Then stir and crumble it until the curds are firm enough to squeak when you chew a small piece.

Proceed with the basic directions at **step 5,** removing and reserving the whey, and continue to **step 9.** At this point, remove the pressed cheese from the cheese form and discard the cheesecloth wrapping. Set the cheese in the whey, which has been heated to 180°F. Cover the container and let the cheese stand until cool.

Remove the cheese from the whey and let drain for 24 hours. The cheese is now ready to eat or to use in recipes.

Longhorn Cheese

The kids love a simple lunch of toasted cheese sandwiches and apple slices, and longhorn — named after the longhorn cow — is the cheese of choice.

Add 2 cups of starter to 1½ gallons of warm raw milk. Cover and set in a warm place for 12 to 24 hours or until thick and clabbered. Follow **steps 4, 5,** and **7** of the basic directions, omitting **step 6.** Remove the cheese from the press and add 4 tablespoons of butter and 1 teaspoon of baking soda. Chop until the curd is quite fine and the butter and soda are thoroughly mixed in.

Press the mixture into a bowl or crock and let it stand in a warm place for 2½ hours. Then put the curds into a double boiler with ⅔ cup of thick sour cream and 1¼ teaspoons of salt and heat slowly. As the mixture begins to heat, stir until all ingredients melt into a mass. Then pour it into a well-greased bowl and allow it to cool. It is ready to eat as soon as it is cold, but it can be cured for 2 to 3 months.

Romano Cheese

Romano is a hard, granular Italian cheese often used for grating. In this recipe, skim milk can be used

Follow the basic directions to **step 4,** heating the curd. At this point, heat the cut curd slowly to 118°F and hold it at that temperature, stirring occasionally until the curd is quite firm (you can tell by touch or by tasting.) Then proceed with the basic directions to **step 7,** pressing the curd. Follow the directions, pressing the cheese for 18 hours. Then remove the cheese from the form and immerse the cheese in salt brine (¼ cup salt dissolved in 1 quart warm water). Let it stand 2 to 3 hours. During the first stages of the curing process, salt is rubbed onto the surface. For a real Italian Romano appearance, color the coating black and rub the surface of the cheese with olive oil at the end of the curing period. Romano is cured for 5 to 8 months for slicing and 1 to 2 years for grating.

MAKE YOUR OWN CHEESE PRESS

To make a cheese press, you'll need scrap wood and a wooden broomstick. Take a 36-inch piece of ¾-inch plywood or a 36- by 12-inch board and cut the wood to make two pieces about 11½ by 18 inches each. Drill a hole about 1 inch in diameter in the center of one of the boards. Whey will drain through this hole.

Drill two holes in the other board, each 1 inch in diameter, 2 inches from each end of the board. The holes should be just big enough so the broomstick moves through them easily.

Cut the broomstick into three lengths: two pieces 18 inches long and one piece 15 inches long. Nail each 18-inch piece 2 inches from the ends of the bottom board, matching the holes in the top board. Nail the other length to the center of the top board, and nail your round cheese follower to the broomstick at the other end. Nail two blocks of wood to the bottom or set the press on two bricks or blocks so you can slide a container under the drainage hole to catch the whey.

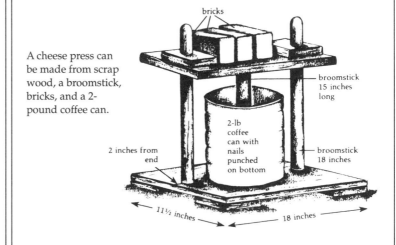

A cheese press can be made from scrap wood, a broomstick, bricks, and a 2-pound coffee can.

bricks

broomstick 15 inches long

2-lb coffee can with nails punched on bottom

broomstick 18 inches

2 inches from end

11½ inches

18 inches

Making Soft Cheese

🌿 🌿 🌿

The simplest soft cheese is fresh curds. Phyllis Hobson reminds us that Grandmother made it by setting fresh warm milk in the sun until the curds separated from the whey. The most familiar soft cheese is cream cheese, which is made by draining curds for a few minutes in a cloth bag. If you gather from this that making soft cheese is not nearly as complicated as making hard cheese, you are right. Here are some of the simplest recipes.

Cream Cheese

The classic spread for date nut bread, cream cheese is wonderful on its own or in any number of recipes.

Add 1 cup starter to 2 cups warm cream and let it set for 24 hours. Add to 2 quarts warm cream and let it clabber for another 24 hours. Warm over hot water for 30 minutes, then pour into a cloth bag to drain. Let it set 1 hour. Salt to taste and wrap in wax paper. It is now ready to use. Refrigerate to store.

Another method of making cream cheese is to add 1 tablespoon salt to 1 quart thick sour cream. Place in a drain bag and hang in a cool place for 3 days.

Neufchâtel Cheese

The original French cheese, Neufchâtel, is from the town of that name in the Normandy region of France. Because it's made from milk, it's lighter than cream cheese.

To make it at home, cool 1 gallon of freshly drawn milk or heat refrigerated milk to 75°F. Add ⅓ cup of sour milk or starter. Stir for 1 minute, then add half of a rennet tablet dissolved in ¼ cup cool water. Stir for 1 minute longer. Let it set undisturbed in a warm place (about 75°F) for 18 hours.

At the end of that time, dip off the whey on the surface of the curd. Then put the curd into a cheesecloth bag and hang it in a cool place to drain. When the curd appears dry, place it in a bowl and add salt to taste. Mix in the salt thoroughly.

Ladle the salted curd into a cheesecloth-lined cheese

ROLLING CHEESE

....

Soft cheeses may be rolled in finely chopped herbs, cracked peppercorns, chopped nuts, or toasted sunflower or sesame seeds. Wrap in plastic wrap after rolling, and use within a day or two.

....

form, press it smooth with a spoon, and top with a layer of cheesecloth. Insert the wooden follower and apply pressure (six bricks). The length of time required to press the cheese into a cake suitable for slicing varies according to the temperature, the amount of moisture, and the weight applied, but it is usually from 45 minutes to 1 hour 30 minutes. When the cheese is firm enough to cut, it is ready to eat. It is best fresh but will keep a week or more in the refrigerator.

GARLIC-HERB CHEESE

....

Make a sensational spiced cheese for bagels, sandwiches, and hors d'oeuvres. Into 8 ounces of fresh cream cheese, mash 3 cloves of garlic; 1 tablespoon each dried basil, chives, caraway seeds, and dillweed; 2 teaspoons dried parsley; and freshly ground black pepper to taste. If you use minced fresh herbs, triple the quantities.

Soft Goat Cheese

This is a delicious, soft goat's milk cheese. The milk is ripened for a lengthy period with goat cheese starter culture. A very small amount of rennet is also added to the milk. After 18 hours, the milk coagulates. It is placed in small goat cheese molds to drain and in 2 days small and delicious 1½- to 2-ounce cheeses are ready for eating. These are firm yet spreadable cheeses that will keep under refrigeration for up to 2 weeks.

½ gallon whole goat's milk
1 ounce mesophilic goat cheese starter culture
4 tablespoons cool water liquid rennet

1. **Ripening and renneting.** Warm goat's milk to 72°F. Stir in 1 ounce of mesophilic goat cheese starter culture. Place the water in a measuring cup. Add 1 drop of rennet and stir. Add 1 tablespoon of this diluted rennet to the milk. Stir thoroughly. Cover and allow the milk to set at 72°F for 18 hours, until it coagulates.

2. **Molding and draining.** Scoop the curd into individual goat cheese molds. These molds are made of food-grade plastic and measure 3¼ inches in height. When the molds are full, they should be placed to drain in a convenient spot at 72°F.

3. **Day 3:** After 2 days of draining, the cheese will have sunk to about 1 inch in height and will maintain a firm shape. The cheese can now be eaten fresh or can be wrapped in cellophane (better) or plastic wrap and stored for up to 2 weeks in the refrigerator. If desired, the cheese may be lightly salted on its surface, immediately after being taken from the mold.

Yield: Almost 1 pound

VARIATIONS: For herbed soft goat cheese, follow the directions for making soft goat cheese. When you scoop the curd into the cheese molds, sprinkle in layers of herbs. Chopped garlic, onion, and paprika make a tasty combination. Dill seeds, caraway seeds, or freshly ground black pepper can be added separately or in various combinations to spice up this cheese.

Marinated Goat Cheese: Place garlic cloves, fresh herbs, or softened sun-dried tomatoes in the bottom of an 8-ounce jar. Drizzle with 1½ teaspoons olive oil. Place 1 slice of goat cheese atop herbs or tomatoes. Drizzle with more oil. Repeat layering to fill jar completely. Seal tightly. Refrigerate for up to 1 week.

Sour Milk Cottage Cheese

This soft, fresh-cooked curd cheese is usually eaten within a week after it's prepared.

Pour 2 quarts of sour milk into a double boiler. Heat over warm water until a soft curd is formed. Pour into a drain bag and let drain. After 3 to 4 hours, remove cheese from bag, break into pieces, and moisten with cream. Season with salt and pepper.

Drain the whey from soft cheese by hanging the curds in a cloth bag.

MAKING YOGURT

Making yogurt is essentially the same as making cheese starter. The milk is warmed to 100 to 110°F, the culture is added, and the mixture is kept at the desired temperature for several hours. At about 100°F, you can make yogurt in 5 to 6 hours, but you can leave it 10 to 12 hours if you like a tarter flavor.

It is important to keep the mixture at the proper temperature for the necessary length of time to let the culture develop. If you have a yogurt maker, simply follow the manufacturer's directions. If you don't, use one of the ingenious methods described by Phyllis Hobson.

Basic Yogurt Recipe

❧ ❧ ❧

Homemade yogurt has a delicate, creamy body that is hard to find in the multitude of supermarket concoctions, full of additives and flavorings. Making it at home is a simple matter of adding culture to milk and keeping it warm for several hours.

- 1 quart whole milk
- ⅓ cup instant nonfat dry milk (optional. It produces a thicker texture and increases the protein content by 2 grams per cup.)
- 1 rounded tablespoon plain yogurt or recommended quantity of powdered culture

Flavored Yogurt

It's fun to enhance yogurt with different flavorings, preserves, and sweeteners. Treat your family to nutritious flavored yogurts for snacks and dessert.

Scald 1 quart of milk and stir in ¼ to ⅓ cup of sugar, honey, maple syrup, chocolate syrup, malt, molasses, or artificial sweetener. If other flavors are desired, after dissolving the sugar or honey, stir in 1 tablespoon of extract, such as vanilla, lemon, almond, or peppermint, or instant coffee. Another time, try adding 1 teaspoon of ground spices, such as cinnamon, nutmeg, mace, ginger, or your own special combination. Add the instant

---

EQUIPMENT FOR MAKING YOGURT

....

Not much is required for making yogurt. You can buy yogurt-making machines that will keep your yogurt at the steady warm temperature that is best for incubating. But you can easily improvise. Here is what you will need:

- Candy thermometer (or yogurt spoon thermometer supplied with yogurt makers)
- 1½- to 2-quart saucepan
- Measuring spoons
- Large jug or bowl for mixing
- Wire whisk
- Various containers with lids: glass or porcelain jars; stainless steel, enamel, or porcelain bowls

- Unless your equipment is sterilized, some undesirable bacteria may be present, which can destroy your yogurt culture. I usually run my utensils through a dishwasher cycle (if they are clean, the rinse cycle is adequate) just before I begin to heat my milk. That way, the utensils are prewarmed, and I know that my equipment is absolutely clean. An alternative is to immerse the utensils in a pot of boiling water for 1 minute. Various-sized canning jars with screw-on or snap-on lids make excellent yogurt containers.

nonfat dry milk, cool the mixture to 110°F, and stir in the culture. Pour into warm containers, cover, and incubate. For jam, preserve and peanut butter flavors, put 1 tablespoon of the flavoring into the bottom of 1-cup containers and pour the warm milk–yogurt mixture over. Cover and incubate as usual. If fresh, canned, or dried fruit is desired, it is best to make such additions to the yogurt after it has incubated. The acid content of some fruits can curdle the milk–yogurt mixture and prevent proper fermentation. Whenever you are flavoring yogurt, always remember to leave 1 cup plain, so that you will have fresh starter for the next batch.

Making Yogurt Without a Yogurt Maker

Here are Phyllis Hobson's techniques for making yogurt if you do not have an appliance designed for it.

With a thermos. Almost fill a thermos bottle (preferably widemouthed) with milk heated to 100°F. Add 2 tablespoons of plain yogurt and mix thoroughly. Put the lid on and wrap the thermos in two or three terry towels. Set it in a warm, draft-free place overnight.

In an oven. Pour 1 quart of milk into a casserole dish and add 3 tablespoons of plain yogurt. Stir well and cover the casserole. Place in a warm (100°F) oven with the heat off. Let it sit overnight.

On a heating pad. Mix 1 quart of milk and 3 tablespoons of plain yogurt. Set an electric heating pad at medium temperature and place in the bottom of a cardboard box with a lid. (A large shoebox works well.) Fill small plastic containers with the milk-yogurt mixture; put on the lids. Wrap a heating pad around the containers, then cover with towels to fill the box. Put the lid onto the box and let sit, undisturbed, for 5 to 6 hours.

In the sun. Pour 1 quart warmed milk into a glass-lidded bowl or casserole. Add 3 tablespoons plain yogurt and cover with the glass lid or a clear glass pie pan. Place in the sun on a warm (not too hot) summer day and let sit 4 to 5 hours. Watch it to make sure it is not shaded as the sun moves.

On the back of a woodstove. Many grandmothers made clabber by setting a bowl of freshly drawn milk on the back of the stove after supper. Make yogurt this way by adding 1 cup starter to 2 quarts milk and let it sit, loosely covered with a dish towel, on the back of the cooling wood range overnight.

In a Crock-Pot. Preheat a Crock-Pot on low for about 15 minutes, until it feels very warm to the fingertips. Put covered containers of yogurt mixture into the Crock-Pot, cover it, and turn off the heat. At 35- to 45-minute intervals, heat the Crock-Pot on low for 10 to 15 minutes.

WHAT WENT WRONG?

....

Problem:	Cause(s):
Yogurt won't thicken.	• Starter was inactive. • Not enough starter was used. • Incubating temperature was too hot or too cold. • Milk was too hot or too cool when starter was added. • Culture was stirred or moved while incubating. • Utensils were not clean.
Yogurt is too thin.	• Starter is too old.
Whey separates from yogurt.	• Yogurt incubated too long. • Culture was stirred or moved while incubating.
Yogurt is too tart.	• Yogurt incubated too long.

BUTTER

Butter can be made from sweet or sour cream. Sweet cream butter is sometimes preferred for its mellow, bland flavor. Sour cream butter has a richer taste. Sweet cream butter takes longer to churn than sour-cream butter. If the cream is very fresh, it may take several hours to become butter. Sour cream churns into butter in 30 to 35 minutes. Both sweet and sour cream churn more quickly if they have been aged 2 to 3 days in the refrigerator.

Sweet-Cream Butter

❧ ❧ ❧

If you make butter weekly from cream accumulated during the week, it will give the cream time to ripen a little, which improves the taste and makes it easier to whip. Or leave the cream a day or so at room temperature, until it begins to clabber. One quart of well-separated heavy cream makes about 1 pound of butter and ½ quart of buttermilk.

1. Pour the cold, heavy cream into a chilled mixing bowl. Turn the mixer slowly up to high speed and let the cream go through the stages of whipped cream, stiff whipped cream, and, finally, two separate products—butter and buttermilk. As the butter begins to separate from the buttermilk, turn the speed to low. To make butter in a food processor, chill the processor bowl and metal blade in the freezer for 15 minutes. Process, scraping down the sides of the bowl at least once, for about 4 minutes, until the solids separate from the liquids.

2. When the separation has taken place, pour off the buttermilk and save it for making biscuits or pancakes.

3. Knead the soft butter with a wet wooden spoon or a rubber scraper to force out

BUTTER IN A JAR

······················

A very simple way to make butter at home — using just a canning jar and a marble. Pour 1 pint of well-chilled heavy cream into a clean quart-sized or larger canning jar. Add a glass marble and close the jar. Shake the jar vigorously until cream begins to thicken, then more gently until suddenly you have a lump of butter in the jar. Grandchildren Tommy and Miranda enjoy helping with the shaking. (The shaking process will take about 30 to 40 minutes; you can do it while you listen to music, or pass the jar around while you chat with friends!) Reserve the buttermilk for another purpose; rinse the butter, kneading gently with a rubber spatula, in several changes of cold water. Knead in a pinch of salt, if you like.

the milk, pouring the milk off as you knead. When it seems that all of the milk is out, refill the bowl with ice water and continue kneading to wash out any remaining milk. Any milk left in with the butter will cause the butter to spoil. Pour off the water again and repeat the process until the water is clear.

4. You now have sweet butter. If you want it salted, mix in a teaspoon of flake salt. If you want it bright yellow instead of white, add butter coloring.

Sour-Cream Butter

❧ ❧ ❧

Sour-cream butter was probably invented by lucky accident when lack of refrigeration made it difficult to keep milk fresh. Souring the cream first yields a butter that churns more rapidly and has a distinctive, rich flavor.

1. Ripen cream by adding ¼ cup of starter (see box on page 369) to each quart of heavy cream. Let it set at room temperature for 24 hours, stirring occasionally.

Chill the ripened cream for 2 to 3 hours before churning.

2. Pour the cream into a wooden barrel or glass-jar churn. If desired, add butter coloring at this point. Keep the cream and the churn cool and turn the mechanism with a moderately fast, uniform motion. About 30 minutes of churning will usually produce butter; but the age of the cream, the temperature, and whether the cream is from a morning or night milking will affect the length of time required.

3. When the butter forms grainy lumps, draw off the buttermilk and add very cold water. Churn slowly for 1 minute, then draw off the water.

4. Move the butter to a wooden bowl and sprinkle it with 2 tablespoons of flake salt for each pound of butter. Let stand for a few minutes, then press with a wooden paddle to work out any remaining buttermilk or water and to mix in the salt. Taste. If the butter is too salty, wash with cold water. If it's not salty enough, add a bit more salt. Keep the butter cold while you're working.

BUTTER GARNISHES

••••••••••

In olden times, many dairies had fancy butter molds or stamps to embellish their butter for market.

You can dress up your own butter by rolling it into little balls, and then in chopped herbs, cutting it into long curls with a vegetable peeler, or using a pastry bag to pipe softened butter into simple roses.

Press softened butter into small molds and freeze, then remove by dipping the molds quickly into lukewarm water and using the tip of a knife to ease the butter out. Serve decorative butters on a chilled dish.

Or roll softened butter between sheets of plastic wrap, chill slightly, then cut butter shapes with cookie cutters. Freeze cutouts until firm.

Make whipped butter by using an electric mixer to beat softened butter until it's light and fluffy.

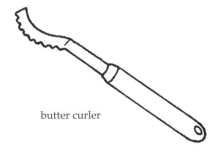

butter curler

PRESERVING THE HARVEST

To me, the jewel-like jars of home-preserved jams, jellies, pickles, relishes, sauces, and ketchup that line the shelves of my kitchen pantry are a source of great pride. I also dry herbs, onions, peppers, tomatoes, and apples. These provisions ensure that I always have a great gift for spur-of-the-moment events and that my family eats tasty, high-quality foods throughout the winter. They make wonderful additions to soups and stews, and they retain their homegrown fresh flavor. I learned most of the preserving techniques in this chapter from my mother, who, at 87, still "puts up" far more than she will ever consume. We're all proud to see the results of our annual gardening season, ready and waiting for winter consumption.

CANNING

DRYING

FREEZING

JAMS & JELLIES

PICKLES

Contributors to this chapter are Glenn Andrews,
Janet B. Chadwick, Andrea Chesman, Nancy Chioffi
and Gretchen Mead, Carol W. Costenbader,
Mary Anna Dusablon, Phyllis Hobson, Imogene McTague,
Sara Pitzer, and Olwen Woodier.

Bread & Butter Wedding Pickles

❧ ❧ ❧

When our older daughter, Jennifer, got married, my mom and dad came up to Williamstown from Georgia. Mother wanted to bring something special from her kitchen that she could share with the entire wedding crowd. She found a way to carry a 2-gallon jar of her famous Bread & Butter Pickles on her flight. We placed a little bowl of pickles on each table at the reception, following Mother's philosophy that "if there's enough for one, there's enough for all."

    5 medium cucumbers
    3 medium onions, peeled
    ¼ cup salt
    1 cup sugar
    1 cup vinegar
    1 cup water
    ½ teaspoon mustard seed
    ½ teaspoon ginger
    ½ teaspoon celery seed
    ¼ teaspoon turmeric

1. Wash and thinly slice the cucumbers and onions. Place in a large ceramic or other nonreactive bowl. Add salt and let stand for 2 hours.

2. Drain and rinse the cucumbers and onions in cold water three times.

3. In a large saucepan, combine the sugar, vinegar, water, mustard seed, ginger, celery seed, and turmeric. Bring to a boil. Add the cucumbers and onions; return to a gentle boil. Simmer until cucumbers are tender and transparent.

4. Pack into sterilized jars while hot. Run a rubber spatula around the insides of the jars to release trapped air bubbles. Wipe the rims of the jars with a clean cloth. Place lids in position and tighten the screwbands.

5. Process in a boiling-water-bath canner (page 384) for 10 minutes for pints.

Yield: 6 pints

Canned Tomatoes

❧ ❧ ❧

Canned tomatoes are like canned sunshine. When you open them in the middle of the winter, it'll take you right back to August in the garden.

    12 medium tomatoes (about
         3 pounds)
     1 teaspoon salt (optional)
     ½ teaspoon citric acid or 2
         tablespoons lemon juice

1. Wash and sort tomatoes by size. They should be relatively uniform in size so they fit evenly in jars. Dip into boiling water for 30 seconds. Set in a bowl of cold water for 1 minute.

2. Pull off skins. Cut off stems, blemishes, and green spots. Cut into large sections.

3. Pack tomatoes tightly into a 1-quart jar, pushing down so that the tomatoes are covered by their own juice; leave ½ inch of headroom. Add salt, if desired, and citric acid. Run a rubber spatula around the insides of the jars to release trapped air bubbles. Wipe the rims of the jar with a clean cloth. Place lid in position and tighten screwband.

4. Process in a boiling-water-bath canner (page 384) for 40 minutes for pints, 45 minutes for quarts.

Yield: 1 quart

CANNING

Whether you are canning for practical reasons, such as to provide food for the winter, or just for fun, you can't beat the satisfaction you'll get from seeing row upon row of glass jars lined up on your pantry shelves or serving food that you put up yourself. To get started, you'll need some basic equipment and information about two methods of home canning: boiling-water-bath canning and pressure canning.

Getting Started with Canning

Before you begin, gather all the utensils, ingredients, and information you need. Set aside plenty of time, so that you don't have to cut corners on processing times. Clear a large surface, and make sure that all of your equipment is clean. For either method of canning, you will need the following:

- **Jars.** Jars are a canner's stock-in-trade. Most recipes call for pint or quart jars. Jars come in widemouthed and regular varieties. Widemouthed jars are easier to fill but cost slightly more than regular jars. Check all jars carefully for cracks and flaws.
- **Lids.** The lids for standard, modern canning jars have two parts: a screwband and a one-use "replacement" lid. Screwbands can be stored in a dry place and used again next year. Don't reuse the lids, however; the rubber inside is good for only one sealing. To clean and use the lids, follow the directions that come with them.
- **Jar lifter.** A jar lifter is used to remove hot jars from a pressure canner.
- **Hot pads.**
- **Canning funnel.**
- **Knives, cutting boards, kettle,** and **colander.**
- **Magnetic lid lifter.** Used to remove lids from boiling water.
- **Labels.**

For boiling-water-bath canning, you'll need a **deep kettle** with a **lid** and a **rack**. Keep a **teapot** handy for adding hot water, if necessary.

For pressure canning, you'll need a **pressure canner** and **rack**.

CANNING SAFETY

Never taste even a tiny bit of canned food that you suspect may be spoiled. Before using home-canned food, examine the jars carefully for signs of spoilage, such as:

- Mold on the jar
- Leakage of food from the jar during storage
- Lid with mold inside
- Food that has completely and very darkly discolored
- Food that looks shriveled, spongy, slimy, or cloudy
- Liquid in the jar that is not stable and seems to bubble
- Contents that "shoot out" when the lid is opened
- Food that has an off odor

Dispose of suspect food, so that it will not be consumed by people or animals.

Preparing Food and Jars for Canning

1. Wash the food to be canned. If necessary, cut it into uniform pieces. For raw-pack processing, set prepared food aside. For hot-pack processing, place food in a large saucepan, cover with water, and bring to a boil. Simmer 2 to 5 minutes

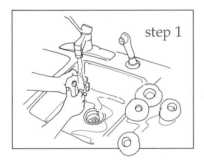

step 1

2. Sterilize clean jars by filling them with hot (not boiling) water and lowering them onto a rack in a water-filled pot. Make sure that there is at least 1 inch of water above the rims of the jars. Bring water to a boil and boil for 10 minutes. Keep jars hot. Alternatively, wash in a dishwasher.

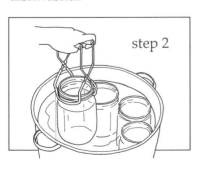

step 2

3. Remove a jar from the water, empty it, and fill it immediately with food. If you are using the raw-pack method, pack the jar tightly. If you are using the hot-pack method, fill it loosely.

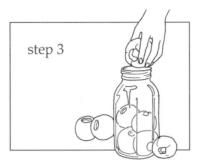

step 3

4. Add very hot water, syrup, or juice, according to the recipe, until it covers the food. Allow the appropriate amount of headroom.

step 4

5. Remove air bubbles by inserting a nonmetallic utensil, such as a rubber spatula, into the food at the edge of the jar and gently pressing against the food as you run the utensil around the jar.

step 5

6. Wipe the rim of the jar thoroughly with a clean towel to allow a good seal.

step 6

7. Apply the lid and secure it with the screwband.

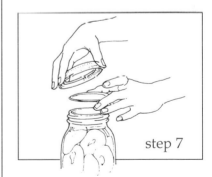

step 7

8. Repeat steps 3 through 7 until all jars are filled. Reserve the water used to sterilize jars for the canning process. Finish by using the boiling-water-bath or pressure canning method.

Boiling-Water-Bath Canning

A boiling-water bath is the cheapest and easiest method of preserving foods with a high acid content. These include fruits, pickles, and low-acid vegetables to which vinegar has been added.

1. Place a jar rack in a large kettle and add enough water to cover the jars, once they are added. Bring water to a boil; reduce to a simmer. Use a jar lifter to lower packed and prepared room-temperature jars into simmering water. Cold jars should be put into water that is warm, not simmering; they will crack if exposed to a sudden change in temperature. To ensure good heat circulation, make sure that the jars are not touching one another or the sides of the pot.

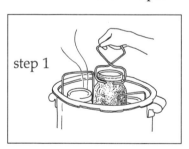

step 1

2. Make sure that the water covers the jars by 2 or 3 inches. Put on the kettle lid and bring the water to a rolling boil; once the water is boiling (not before), start keeping track of the processing time.

HOW TO TEST A SEAL

Often you'll hear a "plink" as the jars are cooling; this indicates that the lids have been pulled down to form a vacuum seal. To check for a proper seal, wait until processed jars of canned goods have cooled, then use your thumbs to press down hard on the center of each lid. If the lid does not move downward or give, your jar is well sealed and ready for storage. If the seal hasn't taken, reprocess the jars (see below), or refrigerate them and consume the contents within a few days.

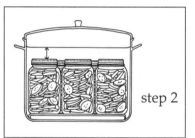

step 2

3. When the recommended time is up, remove the kettle from the heat and take out the jars by using a jar lifter. Be careful not to knock the jars together; they will shatter easily when hot. Do not cover the cooling jars unless there is a draft.

step 3

4. Let jars sit undisturbed until thoroughly cooled, then test the seal. If it isn't tight (see above), you can add a new lid and screwband and reprocess within 24 hours of the original processing. If the seal is good, remove the screwbands from the jars. Wipe the jars dry and label them with the name of the product, its origin, and the date.

5. Store the jars in a cool, dry, dark place for no more than 1 year. The U.S. Department of Agriculture recommends storing canned goods between 50° and 70°F.

CANNING WITH HONEY

Honey is more healthful than sugar, but it should be used in moderation when substituted for sugar in canning recipes. For satisfactory results, use mild-flavored clover or orange blossom honey in half the quantity of sugar called for in a recipe. Buckwheat honeys are typically stronger and will overpower the subtle flavors of fruits in preserves. Old-fashioned recipes, some of which have been in use since the eighteenth century (when honey was more available than sugar), call for all honey and no sugar.

Honey in any form should never be given to babies younger than 1 year of age. Children that young are apparently susceptible to a particular botulism organism that occurs in honey even when cooked.

HIGH-ACID FOODS FOR BOILING-WATER-BATH CANNING

Produce	Pack	Headroom (Inches at Sea Level)	Processing Time (Minutes at Sea Level)	
			Pints	Quarts
Apple	hot	½	20	20
Apricot, peaches	raw	½	25	30
	hot	½	20	25
Blackberries, blueberries, raspberries	raw	½	15	20
	hot	½	15	15
Cherries	raw	½	25	25
	hot	½	15	20
Citrus fruit (grapefruit, oranges, tangerines)	hot	½	10	10
Currants and grapes	raw	½	15	20
	hot	½	10	10
Peaches	raw	½	25	30
	hot	½	20	25
Pears	raw	½	25	30
	hot	½	20	25
Plums	raw	½	20	25
	hot	½	20	25
Purées (high-acid fruit)	hot	¼	20	20
Rhubarb	hot	½	15	15
Tomatoes (juice)	hot	½	40	45
Tomatoes (juice and flesh)	hot	½	40	45
Tomatoes (crushed, no liquid added)	hot	½	40	45
Tomatoes (sauce)	hot	¼	40	45
Tomatoes (halved or whole, in juice)	raw or hot	½	85	85
Tomatoes (halved or whole, no liquid)	raw	½	85	85

Pressure Canning

All vegetables except tomatoes (which are actually fruit), sauerkraut, and pickles are low in acid content and must *always* be processed in a pressure canner. Other canning methods are not safe, and because it takes only one spoonful from one jar of poisoned food to cause serious illness or death, a pressure canner may be the most important investment you make.

All pressure canners work according to the same principle. The pan has a tight-sealing lid with a regulator. A small amount of water (usually 1 to 3 inches) heated in the canner is converted to steam, which builds pressure and reaches temperatures higher than the boiling

pressure canner

release valve, left,
and pressure gauge

point of water. At 10 to 15 pounds of pressure, the temperature inside the canner is 240° to 250°F. Safety features maintain pressure at reasonable levels and release pressure if it becomes too high.

There are two types of pressure canners: those with a dial gauge that shows the pressure, and those with a weighted control that makes a noise when the required pressure is reached. Before using any pressure canner, ensure that all of its parts are in good working order and read the manufacturer's directions, including temperatures necessary at different altitudes.

1. After packing canning jars and fitting them with lids and screwbands, put a rack into the canner and add 2 to 3 inches of water. Place the jars on the rack. If you prefer, you may fill the rack before placing it in the canner. Place the lid on the canner and fasten it securely.

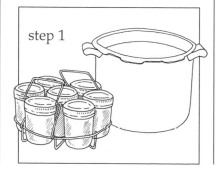

step 1

2. Open the petcock (the valve on the lid of the canner) or remove the weight. Heat on high until steam flows out.

step 2

3. Continue to heat on high for 10 minutes before closing the petcock or placing the weight on the vent port. During the next 3 to 5 minutes, pressure will build.

4. When the dial gauge shows the recommended amount of pressure, or when the petcock begins jiggling or rocking, set the timer for the processing time specified in your recipe. At high altitudes, increase the pressure ½ pound for each 1,000 feet above sea level.

5. Maintain a temperature at, or a little bit above, the specified gauge pressure. Weighted gauges will jiggle 2 or 3 times per minute or rock slowly, depending on the brand. Avoid large variations in temperature, which may cause liquid to be

forced from jars, jeopardizing the seal.

6. When the processing time is up, turn off the heat, remove the canner from the heat (if possible), and let it depressurize. Do not use cold water to speed depressurization, and avoid opening the vent port. Let the canner sit undisturbed for 30 minutes if it is loaded with pint jars or 45 minutes for quart jars. Some models cool more quickly and have vent locks that indicate when pressure is normal; consult the manufacturer's directions for your model.

7. When pressure has returned to normal, remove the weight or open the petcock. Let the canner sit for 2 minutes longer before unfastening and removing the lid. Keep your face away from the canner to avoid burns from escaping steam.

8. Using a jar lifter, remove the jars and place them on a folded towel, allowing at least 1 inch of air to circulate between them.

9. Let cool. Store in a cool, dry, dark place.

Canning Applesauce

❧ ❧ ❧

Even though it takes a while to make applesauce, the finished product is so superior to store-bought that you may find it well worth the time. You can sweeten it or not, add spices or — in short, make it exactly to your liking. Leaving on the peels adds flavor, color, and more nutrients and saves lots of time.

3 pounds apples
sugar (optional)

1. Wash, core, and quarter apples; do not peel. Place in heavy-bottomed kettle with 2 inches of water. Cover and cook until soft, stirring occasionally to prevent scorching, about 30 minutes.

2. In the meantime, preheat water in canner and tea kettle. Prepare jars and lids.

3. Run softened apples through a hand-cranked strainer or food mill. Add sugar to taste, if desired. Return apples to kettle and reheat to boiling.

4. Pack hot applesauce into a hot, clean jar, leaving ½ inch of headroom. Run a rubber spatula around the inside of the jar to release air bubbles. Wipe the rim of the jar with a clean cloth. Place lid in position and tighten screwband.

5. Process in a boiling-water-bath canner (page 384) for 20 minutes for both pints and quarts.

Yield: 1 quart

APPLESAUCE IDEAS

We make lots of applesauce, so I like to gussy it up now and then so no one gets tired of it.

- *Mix it with whole-berry cranberry sauce*

- *Serve it hot with maple syrup*

- *Add apricot or seedless raspberry jam*

- *Bake it with a streusel topping*

- *Mix it with swirls of yogurt (my grandchildren call this a "cloud")*

- *Add a dash of hot sauce for a snappy side dish with meat or chicken*

Apple Slices

❀ ❀ ❀

Canned apple slices are great to use in pies, crêpes, and baked desserts. They are also delicious in fruit salads. However, peeling apples for canning is a chore. When I am working with large quantities of apples, I slice some and make applesauce with the rest.

1 gallon plus 2 cups cold water
1 cup extra-fine granulated
  sugar
2 tablespoons lemon juice
3 medium apples

1. In a medium saucepan, slowly bring 2 cups of the water and the sugar to a boil, stirring to dissolve the sugar. Boil for 5 minutes; remove from heat.

2. In a large bowl, combine the remaining 1 gallon water and the lemon juice. Peel, core, and slice the apples approximately ¼ inch thick. Drop immediately into the bowl.

3. Drain and pack into quart jars, without crushing the slices. Leave ½ inch of headroom.

4. Return the syrup to a rolling boil. Pour over the packed slices; leave ½ inch of headroom. Run a rubber spatula around the insides of the jars to release air bubbles. Wipe the rims of the jars with a clean, damp cloth. Place lids in position and tighten screwbands.

5. Process in a boiling-water-bath canner (page 384) for 20 minutes.

6. Remove jars. Adjust the screwbands to tighten the seals. Leave the jars undisturbed for 12 hours to cool. Store in a cool, dry place.

Yield: 1 quart

Green Tomato Mincemeat

❀ ❀ ❀

In the old days, mincemeat recipes actually contained minced spiced meat. It is still sometimes made with suet. This recipe contains no meat, but it has the dark, spicy sweetness that mincemeat lovers prize. It's a great way to use tomatoes at the end of the season, when frost is threatening.

2½ quarts apples (about 4
     pounds)
  2 quarts green tomatoes
     (about 5 pounds)
  1 orange
  1 tablespoon salt
  1 pound seeded raisins
3½ cups brown sugar
  ½ cup vinegar
  2 teaspoons ground cinnamon
  1 teaspoon ground cloves
  1 teaspoon ground nutmeg
  ½ teaspoon ground ginger

1. Wash and drain the apples, tomatoes, and orange, for both pints and quarts. Run tomatoes through a meat grinder, sprinkle with salt, and let stand for 1 hour. Drain and cover with boiling water for 5 minutes. Drain again.

2. Grate rind and chop pulp of orange. Core, pare, and chop apples.

3. In a large stockpot, mix all ingredients; boil slowly until tender, about 30 minutes. Pour into hot, clean pint jars, allowing ½ inch of headroom.

4. Run a rubber spatula around the inside of the jar to release air bubbles. Wipe the rims of the jars with a clean cloth. Place lids in position and tighten screwbands.

5. Process in a boiling-water-bath canner (page 384) for 25 minutes.

Yield: 6 pints

Note: Mincemeat is excellent in pies and cookies, used in place of applesauce or as a filling.

FLAVORED TOMATOES

Basil and garlic add marvelous flavor to tomatoes. If you like, tuck a couple of clean basil leaves and a clove of garlic into the jars when you're canning tomatoes.

TIMETABLE FOR PRESSURE-CANNING VEGETABLES*

VEGETABLE	METHOD	HEADROOM (INCHES)	MINUTES TO PRECOOK	MINUTES TO PROCESS	
				Pints	Quarts
Asparagus	raw pack	½	—	30	40
	hot pack	½	2–3	30	40
Beans, fresh lima	hot pack	1	bring to boil	40	50
Beans, snap	raw pack	½	—	20	25
	hot pack	½	5	20	25
Beets	hot pack only	½	15	30	35
Broccoli, Brussels sprouts, celery, cauliflower, parsnips	hot pack only	1	3	30	35
Cabbage	hot pack only	1	3	45	55
Carrots	raw pack	1	—	25	30
Corn, cream style	hot pack only	1	bring to boil	85	pints only
Corn, whole kernel	raw pack	1	—	55	pints only
	hot pack	1	bring to boil	55	pints only
Eggplant	hot pack only	1	5	30	40
Mushrooms	hot pack only	½	boil 5 minutes	45	pints only
Okra	hot pack only	½	1	25	40
Peas, field	raw pack	1½ (pints)	—	35	40
	hot pack	2 (quarts)	bring to boil	35	40
Peas, fresh green	raw pack	1	40	40	pints only
	hot pack	1	bring to boil	40	40
Peppers	hot pack only	1	3	35	½ pints/pints only
Potatoes, white (whole)	hot pack only	½	10	35	40
Potatoes, cubed	hot pack only	½	2	35	40
Soybeans	hot pack only	1	bring to boil	55	65
Spinach and other greens	hot pack only	½	steam 10 minutes	70	90
Squash, summer	hot pack only	½	bring to boil	30	40
Sweet potatoes	dry pack	1	20–30	65	90
	hot pack	1	20	65	90

*Process at 10 pounds of pressure.

Tomato Sauce

❧ ❧ ❧

With this sauce on your shelf, you can prepare homemade dinners in minutes. Add sautéed meat if you wish, or serve over summer squash topped with cheese. It's also great over baked chicken.

30 pounds (½ bushel) ripe tomatoes
2 tablespoons olive oil
1 pound mushrooms, sliced
2 medium onions, chopped (about 1 cup)
2 stalks of celery, chopped
4 cloves of garlic, minced
½ cup brown sugar, firmly packed
2 tablespoons dried basil
2 tablespoons dried oregano
2 tablespoons dried parsley flakes
2 bay leaves

1. Peel, core, and quarter tomatoes. In a heavy nonreactive 16-quart saucepan, bring the tomatoes to a boil, stirring often, and pressing lightly to release juices. Reduce heat and simmer, uncovered, for 20 minutes, stirring often. Run tomatoes through a food mill; return to saucepan.

2. Heat the oil in a heavy skillet. Add the mushrooms, onions, celery, and garlic. Sauté, stirring often, until all of the vegetables are soft, about 8 to 10 minutes.

3. Add the mushroom mixture to the tomatoes, along with the brown sugar, basil, oregano, parsley, and bay leaves. Simmer uncovered until sauce is thick, about 4 to 6 hours. Stir often and take care not to burn the sauce. You may simplify this process by placing the pot uncovered on the bottom rack of a 350°F oven for several hours. Remove and stir every 30 minutes to prevent sticking.

4. Remove the bay leaves. Pour into hot, sterile jars, leaving 1 inch of headroom. Run a rubber spatula around the insides of the jars to release air bubbles. Wipe the rims of the jars with a clean cloth. Place lids in position and tighten screwbands.

5. In a pressure canner following manufacturer's instructions, process at 10 pounds pressure for 30 minutes for pints, 35 minutes for quarts.

Yield: 10 pints or 5 quarts

Canned Winter Squash & Pumpkin

❧ ❧ ❧

Winter squash and pumpkins must be fully cooked before they can be frozen or canned. For preserving, you should cut squash and pumpkins into cubes (see note at right). Pumpkins and squash should have a hard rind and stringless, mature pulp that is of ideal quality for cooking fresh from the garden. Smaller pumpkins will give you better results.

1 small winter squash or pumpkin
½–1 teaspoon salt

1. Remove seeds and fibers; peel. Cut into 1-inch cubes. Place in a large saucepan, cover with water, and bring to a boil. Remove cubes from water, reserving cooking water.

2. Fill hot, sterile jars with hot cubes, leaving ½ inch of headroom; add ½ teaspoon of salt to pints, 1 teaspoon of salt to quarts. Bring cooking water to a boil.

3. Add cooking water to jars, leaving ½ inch of headroom. Run a rubber spatula around the insides of the jars to release air bubbles. Wipe the rims of the jars with a clean cloth. Place lids in position and tighten screwbands.

4. Process in a pressure canner at 10 pounds (240°F) for 55 minutes for pints, 90 minutes for quarts.

Yield: 1 quart for each 1½ to 3 pounds of squash or pumpkin

Note: CAUTION. The U.S. Department of Agriculture considers it *unsafe* to can mashed or puréed winter squash or pumpkins.

Sauerkraut

❧ ❧ ❧

Many krauting recipes call for vast amounts of cabbage; I prefer to make a smaller amount and ferment it in individual jars. We enjoy it with corned beef or pork chops and on grilled sausages or hot dogs.

2½ Percent Brine

2   tablespoons salt
1   quart water

Kraut

10   pounds firm cabbage,
       at room temperature
6   tablespoons salt

1. To make the brine, dissolve the salt in the water. Set aside.

2. To make the kraut, trim off the outer leaves of the cabbages and wash the heads. Cut into quarters; remove the cores. Shred cabbage very thin.

3. In a large saucepan, mix the shredded cabbage with the salt. Let sit for 15 or 20 minutes. The salt will reduce the bulk of the cabbage and make it easier to pack.

4. Pack tightly into hot, sterile jars. Insert two or three wooden sticks, cut slightly longer than the width of the jar mouth, into the jar; catch the ends up under the shoulders of the jars. This will hold the kraut under the juice it will produce.

5. If the cabbage does not produce sufficient brine in 24 hours, add brine to cover. Cover tops of jars with two layers of sterile cheesecloth, then place lids on jars loosely so that gas formed during fermentation can escape. Place the jars on trays or newspapers to catch the juice that oozes out with the gas.

After 1 or 2 weeks, the level of the kraut may sink enough to make it necessary to combine the kraut from several jars — about 1 quart of kraut will be needed to supplement the contents of 4 other quarts. Do not add fresh vegetables to a batch of already-started sauerkraut or other salted vegetables.

If scum forms in these small containers, remove it with a spoon. If the level of the brine is so low that it is difficult to reach the scum, add more brine. The scum will rise to the surface of the brine, where it can be reached more easily.

7. After about 2 to 6 weeks, the fermentation process will cease. The kraut should have a pleasantly acid taste and should be a slightly translucent pale gold-white color. At this point, kraut packed in large containers can be transferred to smaller canning jars. Run a rubber spatula around the insides of the jars to release air bubbles. Wipe the rims of the jars with a clean cloth. Place lids in position and tighten screwbands.

8. Process in a boiling-water-bath canner (page 384) for 15 minutes for pints, 20 minutes for quarts, to be processed for storage; or it can be stored for several months in the original container in a cold (38°F) place. For storage, add brine to cover the surface of the kraut, if necessary, re-cover with fresh cheesecloth, and cover with a tight-fitting lid.

*Yield: About 5 quarts
or 10 pints*

VARIATIONS: For a change of pace, sauerkraut can be made more interesting by adding herbs (caraway or dill) or cloves of garlic to small batches of the cabbage before fermenting. Remove the garlic before cooking or serving the finished kraut. A few sliced carrots, whole green tomatoes, or pieces of cauliflower or broccoli can be scattered in the cabbage to ferment with it.

DRYING

Drying foods is an excellent alternative for people who have limited time and limited space for storing frozen or canned foods. Almost any food can be dried, but the most popular are fruits, herbs, and a few vegetables, including mushrooms.

Preparing Foods for Drying

Drying foods does not stop the enzymatic action that causes them to mature and decay; it only slows it down. Some foods keep well without pretreatment, but others deteriorate in color, flavor, texture, and nutrients in the months after drying unless they are pretreated.

Blanching or dipping. For more information about blanching, see the section on preparing vegetables for freezing (page 399). Dipping can be accomplished by using various preparations.

Salt water dip. Dissolve 6 tablespoons flaked pickling salt in 1 gallon lukewarm water. To keep fruit from darkening, slice or chop it directly into the water. Soak for no more than 5 minutes, or the fruit will absorb too much water and acquire a salty taste.

Drain before loading onto drying trays. This method is not recommended for persons on a low-sodium diet.

Ascorbic acid dip. Ascorbic acid is a form of vitamin C. Dissolve 2 tablespoons ascorbic acid crystals or 2 tablespoons ascorbic acid powder in 1 quart lukewarm water. Slice or chop fruits directly into the solution. When 1 to 2 cups of fruit accumulate, stir and remove the fruit with a slotted spoon. Drain well before drying.

Fruit juice dip. Dip sliced peaches, apples, or bananas into 1 quart undiluted pineapple juice or 1 quart lukewarm water into which ¼ cup of lemon juice has been stirred. Soak for 5 to 10 minutes. Drain well before drying.

commercial dehydrator

Drying Food in a Dehydrator

You will get the most consistent results if you use a dehydrator. Dehydrator drying is easy and convenient; you can leave a dehydrator operating overnight or while you're at work. If a load is almost dry at bedtime, reduce the heat to 105° to 110°F and go to bed. By morning, the food will be ready to store.

1. Clean a work surface. Assemble knives, peelers, a cutting board, measuring cups and spoons, a bowl (if pretreating), a colander, and a heavy towel. Dehydrators come with their own drying trays.

2. Select young, fresh vegetables and fruits that are table-ready or slightly immature. Wash; drain on towels.

3. Preheat dehydrator or oven to the desired temperature. Recommended temperatures are 115°F for uncooked fruits, 120°F for vegetables and some cooked fruits, and 110°F for leafy herbs.

4. Prepare food according to recommendations above.

5. Spread food evenly over trays in thin layers. Different foods can be dried at the same time, but very moist foods should not be dried with almost-dry foods, nor should you combine foods with strong odors or flavors.

6. Dry according to times specified for each food. Rotate the trays front to back, side to side, and top to bottom at least once. When you rotate the trays, also stir or turn the food.

7. Package dried foods in airtight bottles, jars, or plastic bags. Store in a cool, dark place.

Drying Food in a Conventional Oven

Drying food in an oven has the advantage of controlled, even temperatures but the disadvantage of poor air circulation. Prepare foods and use recommended temperatures as you would if you were using a dehydrator (page 392).

1. Set the thermometer on the top shelf of the oven and begin preheating.

2. When placing food in the oven, leave 1 inch of space on each side, 3 inches on top and bottom, and 2½ inches between trays. In addition, leave the door ajar a few inches and place an electric fan in front of the door to blow away moist air.

3. Stir or turn the food occasionally and rotate the trays front to back, side to side, and top to bottom every 2 to 3 hours.

LET THE SUN DO YOUR DRYING!

Sun-drying is the least expensive and simplest method of preserving foods. But drying outdoors is unpredictable, unless the temperatures are over 100°F and humidity is low.

Begin by pretreating and preparing your foods. Your drying trays can be cookie sheets or homemade wooden trays, but those made of fiberglass or stainless steel screening work best. Do not use galvanized screening, which contaminates food. You'll also need cheesecloth to protect food from insects and birds.

1. Spread foods sparsely but evenly over your drying trays in thin layers. Cover with cheesecloth.

2. Place the trays in a well-ventilated spot in full sun. Turn or stir the food every few hours, and take the trays inside at night.

3. Before storing, place foods in an oven set at 125°F for 30 minutes to kill insect eggs that may have been deposited on them, or place the foods in a freezer for a day or two.

ABOUT DRYING HERBS

The simplest method of drying herbs is air-drying. Herbs should be harvested when their oils are at their peak level, right before flowering or going to seed. Harvest in midmorning, after the dew has evaporated but before the hottest sun. Rinse quickly, if necessary, and shake dry. (If you spray them with the hose the night before picking, they will not need to be washed.) Cut within 6 to 8 inches of the base of the plant. Tie herbs tightly together in small bunches by using twine or a rubber band. Hang bunches, leaves downward, in an airy, warm, dry place, out of direct light. If desired, complete the drying on a tray in a warm oven (115°–120°F). When thoroughly dry, store in containers kept out of direct sunlight.

DRYING TIMES

Produce	Hours in Dehydrator
FRUITS	
Apples	6–8
Apricots	8–12
Bananas	6–8
Berries	12–24
Cherries	12–24
Figs	36–48
Grapes	24–4
Peaches	10–12
Pears	12–18
Persimmons	18–24
Pineapple	24–36
Plums	36–48
Rhubarb	8–12
Strawberries	8–12
VEGETABLES	
Asparagus	8–10
Beans	48
Beets	4–8
Broccoli	8–10
Brussels sprouts	8–10
Cabbage	12–15
Carrots	12–18
Cauliflower	8–12
Celery	12–18
Corn	8–12
Cucumbers	8–10
Eggplant	3–4
Green beans	12–14
Kohlrabi	18–24
Mushrooms	8–12
Okra	8–12
Onions	12–24
Parsnips	8–12
Peas	12–18
Peppers	8–12
Potatoes	18–24
Pumpkin	12–18
Sprouts	8–12
Squash (summer)	6–8
Squash (winter)	12–18
Sweet potatoes	12–18
Tomatoes	6–8
Turnips	12–18

Making Fruit Leather

❧ ❧ ❧

Fruit leather is a nutritious snack to keep on hand for lunchboxes or times when you crave something sweet.

Any fruit (or vegetable) or combination of fruits can be made into leathers. Leathers are an excellent way to use slightly overripe fruits, which have more flavor than just ripe fruit. They are generally made from purées of raw or cooked fruit. Two cups of purée should fill a standard 10- by 15-inch cookie sheet.

1. Strain cooked or ripened raw fruit through a food mill, or liquefy it in a blender until smooth. If necessary, add juice or water to make the mixture thin enough to pour.

2. Line a drying tray with plastic wrap, or use the fruit leather sheet that came with your dehydrator. Spread the purée ⅛-inch thick on the drying tray.

3. To dry in a dehydrator, set the tray in the dehydrator at 120°F for 6 to 8 hours, or until the leather can be pulled easily from the plastic. Invert, pull leather off the plastic, and continue drying for 4 to 6 hours longer. To dry in a conventional oven, put the tray in at 120°F for 6 to 8 hours, or until the leather can be pulled easily from the plastic. Invert, pull off the plastic, and continue drying for 6 to 8 hours longer. To dry in the sun, set the tray outdoors for 1 day, or until the leather can be pulled easily from the plastic. Invert, pull off the plastic, and dry for 1 more day.

4. To store, roll the leather in wax paper or plastic wrap, close and twist the ends, and keep in the refrigerator for up to 6 weeks.

Drying Citrus Peels

❧ ❧ ❧

Dried peels may be used as a substitute for fresh lemon or orange juice in many cookie or cake recipes. They add an interesting touch when sprinkled over fruit salads and whipped cream toppings. One-half teaspoon dried lemon peel replaces 1 tablespoon lemon juice in most recipes.

1. Wash lemon or orange peel in hot water; cut into ½-inch strips.

Scrape and discard the white membrane from the inside of peel. Cut peel into small pieces. No pretreatment is necessary.

2. *Dehydrator:* Spread small pieces of peel onto trays. Dry at 115°F for 6 to 8 hours until crisp, stirring occasionally. Grate by processing in a blender or food mill. Store in small bottles.

Oven: Spread small pieces of peel onto trays. Dry at 115°F, stirring occasionally, until peel is crisp, about 8 to 12 hours. Grate by processing in blender or food mill. Store in small bottles.

Sun: Spread small pieces of peel onto trays. Dry in full sun in a well-ventilated place, stirring occasionally. They should be crisp after 1 day of good drying weather. Grate by processing in a blender or food mill. Store in small bottles.

Oven-Dried Tomatoes

❧ ❧ ❧

We often can't wait until the tomatoes are completely dry to use them. We eat some when they are reduced to about half volume — at this stage, the tomato taste is concentrated and the texture is still moist but slightly chewy. We use them in vegetable or pasta salads, on sandwiches, in sauces, and as an accompaniment to meat.

1. Wash tomatoes, cut out cores, and slice ⅛-inch thick.

2. *Dehydrator:* Dry at 120°F for 8 to 10 hours. Turn slices and dry for 6 to 8 hours longer, until crisp.

Oven: Dry at 120°F for 18 to 24 hours, until crisp; turn slices and rotate trays once or twice during this time.

Sun: Dry for 1 to 2 days, until brittle. Take the trays in at night.

3. Cool and package in airtight containers.

Making a Chile Ristra

❧ ❧ ❧

Early fall is a good time to make a pepper ristra — one of those beautiful, fat clusters of dried hot peppers you see hanging everywhere in New Mexico.

4 pounds Anaheim or New Mexico chilies, fully red
cotton string
heavy twine or picture wire

1. Working with three peppers at a time, use the cotton string to tie them together at their stems. Knot the string tightly and well, but don't cut it off. Instead, attach a group of three peppers to it every 3 or 4 inches. Make two strings, using up the peppers.

2. Attach the twine or wire to something from which it can hang — a doorknob, for instance. Make a braid, using wire or twine as the third strand. Push the peppers around until the cluster looks pleasing. Secure the bottom with a knot.

3. Dry the ristra by hanging it in direct sunlight in a spot with good air circulation. Turn it from time to time, and be sure to bring it inside in damp or freezing weather.

ABOUT DRIED BEANS

··

The simplest way to dry beans is to leave them on the vine until the hulls have dried and begun to open, then shell out the beans. However, this method invites insect problems, and you may lose as many beans as you save. A better method is to pull up the plants and allow them to dry in an airy place. Once the hulls are brittle, you can shell out the beans easily. Put the shelled beans in a warm oven for about 1 hour to kill any insects or larvae.

Drying Mushrooms

❋ ❋ ❋

Dried mushrooms are useful to have on hand for soups and sauces. Reconstitute them by covering them with boiling water and letting them soak for about 10 minutes. Be sure to use the soaking liquid in your cooking.

1. Wipe or wash mushrooms briefly in cold water, without soaking or peeling. Trim ⅛ inch off stem end. Thinly slice or finely chop.

2. *Dehydrator:* Dry at 120°F for 8 to 12 hours, stirring occasionally and rotating trays once or twice.

Oven: Dry at 120°F for 12 to 18 hours, stirring occasionally and rotating trays once or twice.

Sun: Dry for 1 to 2 days; take trays inside at night.

Whatever method is used, well-dried mushrooms should be tough and leathery, with no sign of moisture in the center.

3. Cool and package in airtight containers.

Note: When using dried mushrooms, substitute ¼ cup dry for 1 cup cooked.

Garlic Braid

❋ ❋ ❋

Braiding garlic heads is probably the best way to preserve them so that the garlic can be used for months after harvest. Air circulating around the hanging braid helps keep the garlic fresh. Garlic braids make sensational presents — as long as you're sure the recipient is a garlic lover!

12–15 heads of fresh garlic, with leaves still attached
light wire (optional)
twine or raffia

1. Start making the braids as soon as you pull the heads of garlic from the ground, so that the stems will still be pliable. Do not rinse the heads; simply brush away any soil.

2. Clear a flat surface. Start with three heads of garlic. Braid their leaves together, then weave in other heads (like French-braiding hair). If you plan to give the braid away, or if you care a

step 2

lot about the looks of the braid, weave the heads so closely together that the leaves don't show. Otherwise, a little space between the heads will make it easier to remove them one at a time as needed. You may find it reassuring to work in some light wire to reinforce the braids.

3. When you've used as many heads as you want, braid the last of the leaves and tie off with twine, forming a loop for hanging. Wrap the twine several times around the braid for extra support.

4. Hang the finished braids where air will circulate freely around them.

Variation: If you grow shallots, you can braid them the same way; use about 25 shallots per braid.

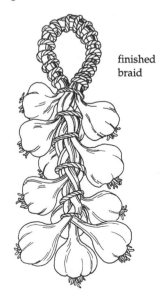

finished braid

FREEZING

Freezing is an easy storage method that can be used for almost any fruit or vegetable. Frozen foods remain quite nutritious; the only vitamins that are significantly diminished are vitamins E and B_6. The texture remains as close to fresh as possible, and, except for blanching in some cases, the foods need little preparation.

HOW TO FREEZE

- Select only prime-quality produce.
- Process vegetables as soon as you get them and work quickly to get them into the freezer.
- Freeze fruit only when the flavor has completely matured.
- Work with sanitary conditions and equipment.
- Wash or scrub food thoroughly. Peel and slice as needed. Blanch vegetables in boiling water or hot steam and cool them quickly in ice water. Drain well or pat dry.
- Sort for uniform size (or cut).
- Package promptly, expelling as much air as possible from the container. Allow headroom; foods expand during freezing.
- Label and freeze as quickly as possible.

PACKING AND LABELING TIPS

Whatever packaging method you choose for freezing foods, it should keep out air and moisture. Use rigid containers, jars, plastic boxes, wax-coated cardboard boxes, or heavy, sealable plastic bags. Leave some headroom for expansion in the freezer; if you are using jars, be sure to leave at least ½ inch headroom.

To speed thawing, place in cold water; never use hot water.

To make bags of food easy to stack, pack them in square boxes just until frozen. Remove bags, label, and reuse the boxes.

Use an indelible marker to label each container with the name of the food and the date of preparation. If you plan to reuse containers, you may want to make labels by using freezer tape or masking tape.

Sugar Syrups for Freezing Fruit

The day before you freeze fruit, make a syrup by using one of these recipes.

Thin Syrup
- 4 *cups water*
- 2 *cups sugar*

Medium Syrup
- 4 *cups water*
- 3 *cups sugar*

In a large saucepan, combine the water and sugar. Bring mixture to a boil to dissolve the sugar. Chill.

Yield: 5 cups of thin syrup or 5½ cups of medium syrup

Freezing Fruits

Fruits are the ultimate food for freezing. They do not need blanching; they retain most of their nutrients; and the color, texture, and flavor of frozen fruits are superior to canned versions. They do, however, suffer some softening in the freezing process.

Pretreat the fruit. To prevent darkening, dip cut-up apples, apricots, peaches, and nectarines in ascorbic acid, citric acid, or lemon juice before freezing. This may change the flavor of the fruit, but it's sometimes for the better. Steam blanching for 3 to 5 minutes eliminates the darkening without altering taste.

Dry pack. The dry-pack method involves freezing fruit without adding liquids or other ingredients. Wash the fruit and dry it on clean towels. Handle fruit carefully to avoid bruising it.

Spread clean, dry fruit in single layers on baking sheets and place in the freezer. When the fruit is solid, pack it loosely in clean containers. Allow ½ inch of headroom.

Wet pack. The wet-pack method involves adding a liquid — sugar syrup, juice, or water — to the fruit before freezing.

To pack fruit, add ⅓ to ½ cup of cold sugar syrup, juice, or water to 1-pint containers packed with prepared fruit.

Mix gently, label, and freeze. Allow ½ inch of headroom for pints and 1 inch for quarts.

Sugar pack. Sprinkle sugar to taste over fresh fruit. Mix the fruit and sugar carefully, or mash the mixture slightly to draw the juices from the fruit. Stir to dissolve all sugar. Pack the sweetened fruit into clean containers, label, and freeze. Allow ½ inch of headroom for pints and 1 inch for quarts.

FREEZING FRUITS

Fruit	Preparation
Apples	wash; peel, core, and slice; pretreat to prevent darkening or use wet pack
Apricots	dip into boiling water 15 to 30 seconds, then into cold water; slip off skins, halve, remove pit; wet pack
Bananas	peel, cut into chunks; mash when thawed for banana bread; pretreat to prevent darkening
Blueberries, elderberries, huckleberries	wash, dry; pack loosely in cartons; or mash, purée or wet pack
Cherries (sour and sweet)	wash; halve and pit; dry pack with nondarkening agent
Cranberries	wash, dry pack; or crush fruit, simmer 1 cup water with 1 pint fruit until skins burst, then wet pack
Grapes (seedless)	wash; remove stem; dry pack
Kiwifruit	peel and slice; wet pack only
Melons	cube, slice, or ball melon flesh; dry pack
Nectarines	wash; peel and pit; slice or halve; pretreat or wet pack with nondarkening agent
Peaches	wash; peel and pit; slice or halve; pretreat or wet pack with nondarkening agent
Pineapple	peel, core, slice, or cube; wet pack
Plums	wash; halve and pit; pretreat or wet pack with nondarkening agent
Raspberries	gently wash and pick over, dry pack; or wet pack with very light syrup
Rhubarb	wash; cut into small pieces and remove tough stalks; blanch 1½ minutes in steam or boiling water, then dry pack; or wet pack in syrup without blanching
Strawberries	gently wash; slice, halve, or freeze whole for dry pack; or wet pack in light syrup

Blanching Vegetables

Vegetables that are blanched and then frozen turn out better than those that are frozen raw.

If you live 5,000 feet or more above sea level, heat 1 minute longer than the time given for both steam and boil blanching.

Steam blanching. This method produces the best taste after freezing and provides the most protection against vitamin loss. You can use a special steamer pot or insert a steamer basket into a pot with a lid. Bring 4 to 5 inches of water to a boil under the steamer basket. Place the vegetables in the basket in a thin layer. Begin timing when you put the lid on the steamer (see chart, at right).

Boil blanching. This is an easy method, but the outcome is not as good as with steam blanching, because the high temperature and immersion in water tend to diminish flavor and nutrient content. Bring 4 quarts of water to a rapid boil. Add 1 pound of clean, pared vegetables. Let the water return to a boil and begin timing.

The final step. Regardless of which blanching method you use, stop the cooking by plunging the vegetables into ice-cold water.

BLANCHING AND FREEZING VEGETABLES

·····················

With the exception of pumpkin, which stores for only 2 to 3 months, these vegetables will keep for 1 year at 0°F if properly prepared and packaged.

VEGETABLE	PREPARATION	BLANCH TIME IN MINUTES BOIL	STEAM
Artichokes	cut off tops and thorns, trim stems, wash	8	8–10
Asparagus	cut into even-sized pieces, wash	4	3
Beans (green)	wash; cut into desired length, remove stem end	3	4
Beans (lima)	wash, blanch, shell	2	4
Beans (yellow)	wash; cut into desired lengths, remove stem end	3	4
Broccoli/Brussels sprouts	wash; trim into uniform sizes; check for worms; soak in cold salt water 10 to 15 minutes	2–4	3–6
Cabbage	wash, shred, or wedge	1½–2	2–3
Cauliflower	wash, cut into florets, check for worms, soak in cold salt water 10 to 15 minutes	3	5
Corn	husk, remove silk, wash; blanch 3 ears per batch, cool, cut corn from cob	4	6
Eggplant	wash; peel, slice, or cube; blanch using 1 tablespoon lemon juice to 1 quart water	4	6
Okra	wash; remove stem, slice if desired	2–3	5
Peas (green)	shell but do not wash	2	3
Peas (snow or sugar)	wash	2	3
Peppers (sweet)	wash and halve; remove seeds; blanching is not crucial but makes them easier to pack	2	2
Pumpkins and winter squash	wash; cut into uniform pieces; bake in 350°F oven until soft; remove skins	– not recommended –	
Summer squash	wash; shred, slice, or cube	2–3	2–3
Zucchini	wash; shred, slice, or cube	2–3	2–3

JAMS & JELLIES

In my great-grandmother's day, jams and jellies were an important source of winter vitamins. Nowadays, we enjoy them just for their delicious taste. From a simple grape jelly to go with peanut butter to a luscious preserve to pair with scones at tea, these concentrated fruit mixtures add a touch of sweetness to any day.

Making Homemade Jelly

Boiling-water-bath canning — the method used to preserve fruits and other high-acid foods — is the method used to process jams, jellies, conserves, and other fruit spreads (page 384). The main components of jam or jelly are fruit, sugar, and pectin. Some low-acid fruits may also require added fruit acid. Using some under-ripe fruit will increase the natural pectin, helping the product jell.

1. **Extract the juice.** Wash fruit and cut up into a kettle. If you're using berries, mash the 1½ inches at the bottom. Add a small amount of water to prevent scorching, if the fruit lacks juice; apples and plums always require added water. Start cooking over low heat; gradually increase heat as juice builds up. Cook until fruit is soft, about 3 minutes for berries and 15 to 25 minutes for harder fruit.

2. **Strain juice.** You can make a jelly bag by tying four layers of cheesecloth together at the corners. Dampen the jelly bag and suspend it over a bowl. Pour cooked fruit into the damp jelly bag in a bowl; let juice drip into bowl. Avoid

GETTING STARTED WITH JAMS AND JELLIES

If you've done some canning, you should already have most of the equipment you'll need for jams and jellies. However, a few items are needed especially for making fruit spreads. Here is a list of useful equipment.

- Large stainless steel or enamel pot (not aluminum or iron)
- Jars and lids designed for canning
- Cooling rack
- Measuring cups and spoons
- Jelly bag, or cheesecloth and kitchen twine
- Potato ricer or other masher
- Long-handled wooden spoon
- Pierced long-handled metal spoon
- Clean cloth or tea towel
- Candy thermometer
- Colander
- Soft vegetable brush
- Knife
- Timer
- Spatula
- Ladle
- Widemouthed funnel
- Jar lifter
- Boiling-water-bath canner

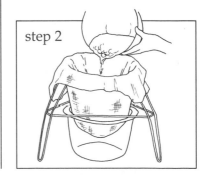

step 2

pressing or squeezing the bag, as this will cloud the juice and the jelly.

3. Test for pectin. Put 1 tablespoon of juice into a glass. Add 1 tablespoon rubbing alcohol and shake gently. Do not taste the mixture. If the pectin content is high, one transparent glob should form. In this case, use equal amounts of juice and sugar in making jelly. If two or three globs form, the pectin content is lower; use ⅔ to ¾ cup of sugar to 1 cup juice. If very small globs form, use ½ cup sugar to 1 cup juice. The pectin level can be increased by adding tart apple juice to the juice you've prepared.

High-pectin fruits, such as underripe apples, are often used in combination with low-pectin fruits to make jellies. Other recipes call for the addition of commercial pectin. Liquid pectin is added *after* sugar is added to the juice and the mixture is brought to a boil. Powdered pectin is added to the unheated, unsweetened juice.

4. Cook to jelly stage. Measure juice into a kettle. Simmer 5 minutes in the open kettle. Skim off the froth, then add sugar. Boil rapidly.

5. Test for jelly stage. The jelling point is 220°F, when the jelly comes off a cool saucer or spoon in a sheet. Begin testing 10 minutes after boiling starts. When ready, remove from heat and skim off any foam.

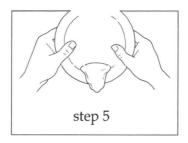

step 5

6. Seal the jars. Ladle or pour the hot jelly into hot, sterilized jars, leaving ¼ inch of headroom. Run a rubber spatula around the inside of the jar to release air bubbles. Wipe the rim of the jar with a clean cloth. Place lid in position and tighten screwband. Wipe jar rims with a clean, damp cloth to remove any jelly that could spoil the seal. Take lids from hot water and place them on jars. Screw the bands on tightly.

7. Immerse in bath. After the jars are closed, immerse them in a boiling-water-bath canner (page 384) for 10 minutes. Be sure the water level is at least 2 inches above the tops of the jars. After processing for 10 minutes, remove the jars and place them on a rack to cool. Check seals; label the jars and store them in a cool, dry place.

JAM, JELLY OR . . .

What's the difference? Although people use the word "preserves" to refer to all forms of sweetened jarred fruit, there are many different varieties.

BUTTER. Fruit pulp that has been cooked with sugar, and sometimes spices, until thick.

CHUTNEY. A condiment of fruits and spices cooked with sugar and vinegar.

CONSERVE. A spread usually consisting of mixed fruits and citrus with raisins and nuts.

CURD. Smooth fruit spread with egg and/or butter added, often made from citrus fruit.

JAM. A jelled spread made from ground or crushed fruit cooked with sugar.

JELLY. A clear spread made with strained fruit juices or other flavored juices and jelled just enough to be firm.

MARMALADE. A clear jelly with pieces of citrus peel or other fruit suspended in it.

PECTIN. A jelling agent found naturally in all fruits. Fruit that is underripe contains much more pectin than ripened fruit. You can buy pectin in either powdered or liquid form in most supermarkets.

PRESERVES. A spread containing whole or large pieces of fruit in lightly jelled syrup.

Basic Strawberry Jam

❧ ❧ ❧

Strawberries and sugar, plain and simple. This basic jam is beloved by all, especially when it's made from hand-picked, sun-sweetened berries.

2 *quarts crushed straw-*
   berries
6 *cups sugar*

1. Preheat the canner, sterilize the jars, and prepare the lids.

2. Wash the berries carefully.

3. Combine the berries and sugar in a tall, heavy, nonreactive saucepan.

4. Bring slowly to a boil, stirring occasionally, until sugar dissolves. Boil rapidly until thick, about 40 minutes. As the mixture begins to thicken, stir frequently to prevent scorching.

5. Test for doneness — 220°F on a thermometer, or when the jam sheets off a cool saucer or spoon (page 401).

6. Remove from heat and skim off any foam that formed during boiling.

7. Pour into the sterilized jars, leaving ¼ inch of headroom. Run a rubber spatula around the insides of the jars to release air bubbles. Wipe the rims of the jars with a clean, damp cloth. Place lids in position and tighten screwbands.

8. Process in a boiling-water-bath canner (page 384) for 5 minutes once the water has returned to a boil.

9. Use a jar lifter to carefully remove the jars from the canner.

10. Cool sealed jars. Check seals. Remove screwbands. Label and store.

Yield: 7 to 8 half-pint jars

MAKE YOUR OWN PECTIN

....

You can use apples to make your own fruit pectin for use in jam made from strawberries, peaches, and other low-pectin fruits. Choose hard, tart, ripe apples. Weigh, wash, and cut fine, leaving stems and cores in. Add 1 pint water and 1 tablespoon lemon juice for each pound of apples. Cover and boil rapidly for 30 minutes, stirring occasionally to prevent scorching. Press through a jelly bag or damp cheesecloth, then strain through several layers of cheesecloth without squeezing. Heat liquid back to the boiling point, seal in canning jars, and process in a boiling-water-bath canner (page 384) for 10 minutes. To use, mix the pectin and the juice of a low-pectin fruit in equal amounts.

Old-Fashioned Peach Preserves

❧ ❧ ❧

This recipe is one of our all-time favorites, maybe because it is so hard to get real peach flavor in any season but summer. You can omit the almond extract, but I think it accentuates the peach flavor.

½ *teaspoon ascorbic acid*
   (crystals, powder, or
   crushed tablets)
1 *quart water*
3½ *pounds (about 7 large)*
   peaches, peeled, pitted,
   and chopped
5 *cups sugar*
¼ *cup lemon juice*
¾ *teaspoon almond extract*

1. In a large nonreactive bowl, prepare an acid bath by adding the ascorbic acid to the water.

2. Dip the peaches in the acid bath; drain well. Combine the fruit, sugar, and lemon juice in a heavy 6- to 8-quart saucepan. Cook over medium heat, stirring to dissolve sugar. Bring to a boil.

3. Boil slowly, stirring constantly, until mixture thickens and fruit is translucent and reaches 220°F on a cooking thermometer.

4. Stir in the almond extract.

5. Remove from heat and skim off any foam with a

metal spoon. Ladle into sterile jars, allowing ¼ inch of headroom. Run a rubber spatula around the insides of the jars to release air bubbles. Wipe the rims of the jars with a clean, damp cloth. Place lids in position and tighten screwbands.

6. Process in a boiling-water-bath canner (page 384) for 10 minutes.

Yield: 7 pints

Solar-Cooked Jams

❧ ❧ ❧

You can cook cherry, strawberry, and raspberry jams in the sun. The process requires full sun and patience, however, and the preserves should be made in small batches. Get children to help you; they are fascinated by the process.

3   *pounds strawberries, raspberries, or cherries*
3   *pounds sugar*
¾   *cups water*

1. Wash and hull the berries; pit cherries. In a large saucepan, layer the fruit and sugar and let sit for 20 to 30 minutes; add the water. Heat and stir until sugar is dissolved. Pour mixture in batches, about ½ inch deep, onto shallow baking dishes or platters. Cover with glass, plastic wrap, or cheesecloth to deter curious and voracious insects.

2. Jelling time depends on the weather; it may take several days for the mixture to jell to the thickness desired. The platters should be brought inside when the late-afternoon sun loses its potency. If you weary of this adventure, finish cooking on the stove.

Yield: 5 pints

Summer Squash Conserve

❧ ❧ ❧

We make this pretty conserve when yellow squash are abundant. It makes a delicious novelty to serve with lamb, chicken, or pork. It's good on toast, too.

2   *pounds small, tender yellow squash, peeled and sliced*
5   *cups sugar*
1   *can (13½ ounces) crushed pineapple in its own juice, drained*
juice of 2 lemons
2   *tablespoons chopped crystallized ginger*
1   *teaspoon grated lemon zest*
1   *package (1¾ ounces) powdered pectin*

1. Combine the squash, sugar, pineapple, lemon juice, ginger, and lemon zest in a heavy saucepan. Bring to a simmer, reduce heat, and cook uncovered for about 15 minutes, stirring frequently.

2. Remove from heat. Add the pectin, stirring well. Bring the mixture to a boil and boil for exactly 1 minute. Remove from heat.

3. Pour the hot mixture into clean jars, leaving ¼ inch of headroom. Run a rubber spatula around the insides of the jars to release air bubbles. Wipe the rims of the jars with a clean cloth. Place lids in position and tighten screwbands.

4. Process 10 minutes in a boiling-water-bath canner (page 384).

Yield: 5 pints

Grape Jelly

❊ ❊ ❊

If you think your days of peanut butter and grape jelly are over when your last child leaves for college, think again. Just wait till the grandchildren start showing up!

3½ pounds grapes
½ cup water
3 cups sugar

1. Wash the grapes and remove the stems. Crush the grapes and combine with water in a nonreactive, heavy-bottomed saucepan. Bring to a boil, then reduce the heat and simmer for 10 minutes.

2. Pour into a damp jelly bag or colander lined with a double thickness of damp cheesecloth and allow the juice to filter out.

3. Allow the juice to sit overnight, so that any sediment can settle to the bottom. Do not squeeze fruit pulp, as the resulting juice will not be clear.

4. When you are ready to make the jelly, preheat the canner, sterilize the jars, and prepare the lids.

5. Combine 4 cups of grape juice with the sugar in a deep-sided, heavy-bottomed saucepan. Stir to dissolve the sugar.

6. Bring rapidly to a boil. Continue boiling until jelly reaches 230°F on a jelly thermometer or sheets off a cool saucer or spoon (see page 401).

7. Remove from heat and skim off any foam that formed during boiling.

8. Pour into the sterilized jars, leaving ¼ inch of headroom. Wipe the rims of the jars with a clean, damp cloth. Place lids in position and tighten screwbands.

9. Process in a boiling-water-bath canner (page 384).

10. Cool sealed jars. Check seals. Remove screwbands. Label. Store.

Yield: 3–4 half-pint jars

Apple Jelly

❊ ❊ ❊

Amber-colored apple jelly is both simple and elegant. It is especially good on hot, buttered biscuits or scones. Making it is a wonderful warm-up project after a chilly morning picking apples. Add ¼ cup minced fresh herb to the cooked jelly if you want to make it fancier.

4 pounds firm, tart apples
4 cups water
3 cups sugar

1. Wash the apples. Remove and discard stems and blossom ends. Cut into small chunks and place in a large saucepan; add water. Bring to a boil; reduce heat and simmer 25 minutes.

2. Place the fruit and juice in a suspended cheesecloth jelly bag. Allow juice to drip overnight.

3. In the morning, measure 4 cups of juice into a kettle; add the sugar. Cook over medium heat, stirring constantly, until sugar dissolves. Bring to a boil and cook rapidly until the jelly test is met. Skim off foam.

4. Ladle into sterile jars, leaving ¼ inch headroom. Run a rubber spatula around the insides of the jars to release trapped air bubbles. Wipe the rims of the jars with a clean cloth. Place lids in position and tighten screwbands.

GIFTS OF PRESERVES

When giving preserves as a gift, it is nice to dress the jars up a bit. Top jam jars with circles of pretty gingham or calico, secured with a rubber band. Cover the rubber band with satin ribbon, raffia, or kitchen twine. Attach a gift label with an anecdote, recipe, or idea for use. For an interesting label, photocopy a nice woodcut of the fruit or vegetable in your preserve and color it with marking pens. A basket lined with a linen towel makes perfect packaging.

5. Process in a boiling-water-bath canner (page 384) for 5 minutes.

Yield: 4–5 half-pint jars

Hot Pepper Jelly

❧ ❧ ❧

Good crackers topped with a sliver of sharp Cheddar cheese or cream cheese and a swipe of hot pepper jelly make a zippy appetizer. Or use it to spice up any meat or poultry. Use all green peppers or all red ones, so that the jelly will have a pretty, soft color.

¾ cup bell peppers, chopped
   and seeded
¼ cup jalapeños, or other
   small hot peppers, seeded
   and chopped
6 cups sugar
2½ cups cider vinegar
2 3-ounce pouches liquid
   pectin
a few drops red or green food
   coloring (optional)

1. Whirl the bell peppers and jalapeños in a blender or food processor until finely ground. In a large nonreactive saucepan, combine peppers, sugar, and vinegar. Bring to a full boil over high heat, stirring constantly; reduce heat and simmer for 10 minutes.

2. Strain; return the liquid to the saucepan. Add about 2 tablespoons of the pepper mixture from the strainer. Return to a boil. Add the pectin and, if you are using it, the food coloring. Return to a boil once more and boil for 1 minute.

3. Ladle into freshly sterilized jelly glasses with two-part canning lids, leaving ¼ inch of headroom. Run a rubber spatula around the insides of the jars to release air bubbles. Wipe the rims of the jars with a clean cloth. Place lids in position and tighten screwbands.

4. Process in a boiling-water-bath (page 384) for 10 minutes.

Yield: About six 8-ounce jars

Tomato Marmalade

❧ ❧ ❧

If tomato marmalade sounds strange, remember that tomatoes are actually in the fruit family. When combined with citrus, they make a remarkable marmalade.

1 medium orange
1 lemon
5 pounds tomatoes, peeled,
   cored, and chopped
   (about 8 cups)
3 cups sugar
¼ cup cider vinegar
1½ teaspoons ground allspice
1½ teaspoons ground
   cinnamon
½ teaspoon ground cloves

1. Peel the orange and lemon in strips. Carefully remove the membrane; discard membrane but reserve peel. Chop the fruit and cut the peel into thin slivers

2. In a heavy nonreactive 8-quart saucepan, combine the citrus fruit, peel, and tomatoes.

3. Add the sugar, vinegar, and spices. Bring to a boil over high heat. Reduce heat and simmer, uncovered, 1 hour or more, until mixture is reduced to about 4 cups. Stir frequently and be careful not to let burn.

4. Ladle into sterilized jars, leaving ¼ inch of headroom. Run a rubber spatula around the insides of the jars to release trapped air bubbles. Wipe the rims of the jars with a clean cloth. Place lids in position and tighten screwbands.

5. Process in a boiling-water-bath canner (page 384) for 5 minutes.

Yield: 4½ pints

Orange Marmalade

※ ※ ※

My favorite way to eat this traditional marmalade is slathered on a fresh, hot scone.

6 large oranges
2 medium lemons
6 cups water
about 6 cups sugar

1. Wash the fruit. Using a sharp knife, remove the peel from the oranges and thinly slice. Chop the orange pulp. You should have 4 cups of thinly sliced peel and 4 cups of orange pulp. Thinly slice the lemon. You should have 1 cup of slices.

2. Combine the fruit and the water in a tall, heavy-bottomed saucepan. Heat to simmer and simmer for 5 minutes. Cover and let stand for 12 to 18 hours.

3. Return the mixture to the stove and cook over medium heat until the peel is tender, about 1 hour.

4. Preheat the canner, sterilize jars, and prepare lids.

5. Measure fruit and liquid. For each 1 cup of fruit mixture, add 1 cup of sugar. Bring slowly to a boil, then cook rapidly until marmalade reaches 220°F or passes the jelly test (page 401), about 25 minutes.

6. Pour hot marmalade into sterilized jars, leaving ¼ inch of headroom. Run a rubber spatula around the insides of the jars to release air bubbles. Wipe the rims of the jars with a clean cloth. Place lids in position and tighten screwbands.

7. Process in a boiling-water-bath canner (page 384) for 5 minutes.

Yield: About 7 half-pint jars

Apple Butter

※ ※ ※

We like to serve apple butter with pancakes or rolled into crêpes. It is dark, spicy, wonderfully smooth. The only trick to making it is to keep a close eye on it, stirring often, so that it won't scorch.

6 pounds apples (24–30 medium apples)
2 quarts water
1 quart sweet cider
3 cups sugar
ground cinnamon
ground cloves

1. Wash the apples and cut into small pieces, leaving the skins and cores. In a large, heavy saucepan, boil water and apples until they are soft (about 30 minutes). Run them through a food mill or press through a sieve.

2. In a large saucepan, boil the cider down to half its volume. Add the hot apple pulp, sugar, and spices to taste. Cook to spreadable consistency, stirring often to prevent scorching.

3. Ladle into hot, sterilized canning jars, leaving ¼ inch of headroom. Place lids in position, and tighten screwbands. Process in a boiling-water-bath canner (page 384) for 5 minutes.

Yield: 5–6 pints

Pumpkin Butter

※ ※ ※

You've tried pumpkin pies, purée, soup, and seeds. Here is one more great way of preparing the pumpkins from your patch. You can also use canned pumpkin.

4 cups cooked pumpkin pulp
4 cups brown sugar
juice of 2 lemons
zest of 2 lemons, grated
½ teaspoon cinnamon
½ teaspoon grated ginger root

1. In a double boiler, combine all ingredients. Cook over simmering water for 45 to 60 minutes, watching carefully and stirring frequently, until thick.

Yield: About 3 pints

Note: Do not can or store this recipe in sealed containers. May be refrigerated for up to 3 months.

PICKLES

Pickling lets you preserve low-acid vegetables by using a boiling-water-bath canner rather than a pressure canner. The added salt and vinegar in the brine keep the veggies from spoiling. Pickles add a delicious pucker to salads, dressings, sandwiches, and burgers.

Brined Dill Pickles

❧ ❧ ❧

These are the old-fashioned brined pickles that you used to find in a big barrel at every country general store. These pickles need to sit in the crock for 3 weeks, so plan ahead. However, maintaining the pickles will take only a few minutes each day and they're worth it.

- 20 pounds (about ½ bushel) pickling cucumbers, 3–6 inches long, scrubbed
- ¾ cup mixed pickling spice
- 2½ gallons water
- 2½ cups cider vinegar
- 1¾ cups salt
- 10 cloves of garlic
- 3 large bunches fresh dillweed

1. In a 5-gallon crock, layer half of the cucumbers, spice, and dill; layer again to within 3 to 4 inches of the top of the crock.

2. In a large bowl, mix the water, vinegar, and salt. Pour over the cucumbers. Insert a ceramic plate that fits inside the crock and weight down cucumbers.

3. Make certain that the cucumbers are completely submerged in the brine. Cover crock loosely with a clean towel.

4. Keep pickles at room temperature (80°–85°F).

5. In about 3 days, begin skimming off the foam. Do not stir pickles. Keep them completely covered with brine throughout this process; add brine, if necessary.

6. Check cucumbers daily, removing scum and foam. In 3 weeks, the cucumbers should be an olive green color. Any white spots inside the cucumbers will disappear when processed.

7. Pour the cucumbers into 10 sterile 1-quart jars. Add 1 clove of garlic to each jar and divide the dill sprigs evenly among the jars.

8. Strain the brine through a coffee filter. Pour into the jars, leaving ½ inch of headroom. Run a rubber spatula around the insides of the jars to release air bubbles. Wipe the rims of the jars with a clean cloth. Place lids in position and tighten screwbands.

9. Process in a boiling-water-bath canner (page 384) for 15 minutes.

Yield: 10 quarts (160 two-ounce servings)

Note: Start timing the canning process as soon as jars are put into boiling water instead of waiting for the water to boil again. This will ensure a crisp, processed pickle without actually cooking the cucumbers.

PICKLING TIPS

Use a widemouthed funnel and wooden spoon to pack vegetables neatly and firmly into jars. Run a chopstick or spatula between the food and the side of the jar to remove bubbles. Add more brine, if necessary to achieve the correct amount of headroom. Yields are approximate, so have an extra jar or two ready.

Freezer Dills

❧ ❧ ❧

Here's a newfangled way to make delicious, crisp, pickles. The taste, however, is old-fashioned good.

6 *cups thinly sliced cucumbers*
1 *large onion, sliced thinly*
3 *tablespoons pickling salt*
1 *cup sugar*
1 *cup white vinegar*
2 *cloves of garlic, minced*
3 *tablespoons dill seed*
½ *teaspoon crushed red pepper*

1. In a large bowl, combine the cucumbers and onion. Sprinkle 2 tablespoons of the salt over the vegetables; let stand for 2 hours. Rinse under cold running water; drain well.

2. In a large glass bowl, combine the sugar, vinegar, garlic, dill seed, and red pepper. Stir well to dissolve the sugar. Add drained cucumbers and onions. Mix well.

3. Pack into freezer bags or containers and freeze. Defrost in the refrigerator for 8 hours before serving.

Yield: 3 pints

GETTING STARTED WITH PICKLES AND RELISHES

- **PANS, BOWLS, AND UTENSILS.** Always use stainless steel, glass, or ceramic equipment. The salts and acids in pickles react with metals to produce an off flavor.

- **CANNER.** The U.S. Department of Agriculture recommends processing pickles in a boiling-water-bath canner.

- **FOOD PROCESSOR.** This is a great time-saver that gives uniform results to cut pickles, thus improving their texture.

- **CANNING JARS WITH TWO-PIECE LIDS.** Old-fashioned bail-wire jars can also be used if you store the pickles in the refrigerator. Beware of scratches and chips in the lid or rim of a jar, as they may prevent a perfect seal.

- **GLASS, PLASTIC, OR CERAMIC CROCKS.** These are useful for slow-brined pickles.

Mixed Pickles

❧ ❧ ❧

A dish of these mixed pickles was always on the Thanksgiving table (and usually during the rest of the year) at my grandmother's house. The mixture of vegetables varied according to what she had on hand, but they always looked and tasted great together.

3 *cups cauliflower*
4 *quarts sliced cucumbers*
1 *quart sliced onions*
1 *green pepper, sliced*
3 *cloves of garlic*
⅓ *cup pickling salt*
   ice cubes
5 *cups sugar*
2 *tablespoons mustard seeds*
½ *tablespoon celery seeds*
1 *quart white vinegar*

1. In a large bowl, break up the cauliflower. Add cucumbers, onion, pepper, garlic, and salt. Cover with ice cubes, mix, and let stand for 3 hours. Drain well and transfer to a large saucepan.

2. In a small bowl, combine the sugar, mustard seeds, celery seeds, and vinegar; pour over the vegetables in the saucepan and bring to a boil.

3. Pour into eight clean, hot 1-pint jars, allowing ½ inch of headroom. Run a rubber spatula around the insides of the jars to release air bubbles. Wipe the rims of the jars with a clean cloth. Place lids in position and tighten screwbands.

4. Process in a boiling-water-bath canner (page 384) for 15 minutes.

Yield: 8 pints

Dilly Beans

❈ ❈ ❈

The fresher the green beans, the crisper the pickles. We grow several varieties of green beans each summer, but we think that Blue Lake make the most delicious dilly beans — they are long, firm, and snap back when you bite into them.

Beans

4 *pounds green beans*
8–10 *cloves of garlic*
8–10 *small hot peppers*

Brine

2 *quarts water*
1 *quart vinegar*
½ *cup salt*
1 *bunch fresh dill*

1. Wash the beans; leave whole. Stand them up straight in eight to ten sterilized 1-pint jars. Add 1 clove of garlic and 1 hot pepper to each jar.

2. In a large nonreactive saucepan, combine the water, vinegar, salt, and dill. Boil for 5 minutes. Pour hot brine over beans in jars.

3. Run a rubber spatula around the insides of the jars to release trapped air bubbles. Wipe the rims of the jars with a clean cloth. Place lids in position and tighten screwbands.

4. Process in a boiling-water-bath canner (page 384) for 10 minutes. Store in a cool, dark place. Beans will be ready to use in 4 to 6 weeks.

Yield: 8–10 pints

Watermelon Rind Pickles

❈ ❈ ❈

Thrifty pioneer homemakers couldn't let something like watermelon rind go to waste, so they created this spicy pickle. They probably never had a shortage of volunteers to eat the pink fruit for the purpose!

1 *large watermelon*
2 *quarts water*
½ *cup canning salt*
3 *cups white or brown sugar*
2 *cups vinegar*
4 *lemons, thinly sliced*
5 *sticks cinnamon*
2 *tablespoons whole allspice berries*
7 *teaspoons whole cloves*

1. Remove skin and pink from watermelon rind. Cut rind into 1-inch cubes or chunks, for a yield of about 8 cups.

2. In a crock, combine water and salt. Add rind; soak overnight. Drain; rinse in fresh water. Drain again. In a large pan, cover rind with water and then simmer until tender; drain.

3. In a large saucepan, combine the sugar, vinegar, and lemons. Tie cinnamon, allspice, and cloves in a cheesecloth bag; add to vinegar mixture. Simmer 5 minutes. Add rind and cook until clear.

4. Pack rind into hot, sterilized 1-pint jars. Pour in syrup, leaving ½ inch of headroom. Run a rubber spatula around the insides of the jars to release air bubbles. Wipe the rims of the jars with a clean cloth. Place lids in position and tighten screwbands. Process in a boiling-water-bath canner (page 384) for 10 minutes.

Yield: 3 pints

Cucumber-Onion Mustard Pickles

❧ ❧ ❧

Mustard pickles add a gorgeous yellow glow to your pickle shelf. Their flavor is pungent and sensational with ham and other favorite picnic foods.

    6 pounds cucumbers
    1 pound onions
    ½ cup pickling salt
 1 ¼ cups brown sugar
    2 tablespoons cornstarch
    1 teaspoon turmeric
    1 teaspoon ground ginger
    1 teaspoon crushed red
       pepper
    3 cups cider vinegar
    1 cup water
    ¼ cup Dijon mustard

1. Thinly slice the cucumbers. Peel and thinly slice the onions. In a large bowl, combine the cucumbers and onions; sprinkle with the salt. Let stand for 3 hours. Drain.

2. In a large saucepan, combine the sugar, cornstarch, turmeric, ginger, and red pepper. Stir in the vinegar, water, and mustard. Cover and bring to a boil. Add the cucumbers and onions.

3. Pack into clean, hot pint jars, leaving ½ inch of headroom. Run a rubber spatula around the insides of the jars to release air bubbles. Wipe the rims of the jars with a clean cloth. Place lids in position and tighten screwbands.

4. Process in a boiling-water-bath canner (page 384) for 15 minutes.

Yield: 8 pints

PICKLING TIP

Cucumbers come in two types: pickling and slicing. Pickling cucumbers are thin-skinned and small. They may be warty. Small slicing cucumbers are acceptable for sliced pickles such as bread-and-butters, and they work in relishes. However, they rarely make good dills.

Pickled Beets

❧ ❧ ❧

Pickled beets are wonderful as a side dish or in a salad. Roasting them before you can them deepens the flavor and helps seal in the color so it won't leach out as much in the brine.

 10–12 pounds beets
     1 quart cider vinegar
     1 cup water
    ⅔ cup sugar
     2 tablespoons
        pickling salt

1. Completely cut the tops and roots off the beets. Scrub beets thoroughly.

2. Place the beets on a rack in a large roaster. Cover and bake at 400°F until just tender, about 1 hour for medium-sized beets.

3. Meanwhile, preheat the water and jars in the canner. Prepare lids.

4. In a saucepan, mix the vinegar, water, sugar, and salt. Bring to a boil. Reduce heat, cover, and hold at a low simmer.

5. When the beets are tender, fill the roaster with cold water. Slip the skins off the beets. Pack the beets in hot, clean 1-pint jars; the beets can be whole or cut up. Add hot brine to cover. Leave ½ inch of headroom.

6. Run a rubber spatula around the insides of the jars to release air bubbles. Wipe the rims of the jars with a clean cloth. Place lids in position and tighten screwbands. Process in a boiling-water-bath canner (page 384) for 10 minutes.

Yield: About 10 pints

Green Tomato Pickles

❧ ❧ ❧

Frost comes too soon for most home gardeners, and the age-old question of what to do with the green tomatoes always comes up. When they'd had their fill of Fried Green Tomatoes (page 187), these tiny pickles were my mom and dad's solution.

Brine

- 6 cups water
- 6 cups cider vinegar
- 1 cup salt

Pickles

- 16–18 small green tomatoes (cherry tomatoes work well) per quart jar
- 6 cloves of garlic
- 6 stalks of celery
- 6 green bell peppers, quartered
- 6 stems fresh dill, with seed head

1. In a large saucepan, boil the water, vinegar, and salt until salt is dissolved, about 5 minutes. Set aside.

2. Wash the tomatoes and cut off stems and blemishes. Pack whole in sterilized quart jars.

3. To each jar, add 1 clove of garlic, 1 stalk of celery, 4 bell pepper quarters, and 1 stem of dill. Repeat until six jars are prepared in this manner. Pour equal amounts of hot brine into jars.

4. Run a rubber spatula around the inside of the jar to release trapped air bubbles. Wipe the rim of the jar with a clean cloth. Place lid in position and tighten screwband.

5. Process in a boiling-water-bath canner (page 384) for 30 minutes. Store in a cool, dark place. Pickles will be ready to use in 4 to 6 weeks.

Yield: 6 quarts

Pennsylvania Chow-Chow

❧ ❧ ❧

It's said that Chinese railroad workers brought this colorful relish to America. In any case, it became an American classic. Serve it with an Asian-inspired meal.

- ½ cup pickling salt
- 5 quarts finely chopped green tomatoes
- 3 quarts finely chopped onion
- 3 cups finely chopped bell peppers
- 5⅓ cups cider vinegar
- 2 cups sugar
- 2 cups honey
- ½ cup cornstarch
- 1 teaspoon dry mustard
- 1 teaspoon turmeric
- 1 teaspoon curry powder

1. In a large crock, sprinkle the salt over the chopped vegetables; mix well. Cover loosely with a towel and allow to sit overnight.

2. The next day, drain the vegetables. Place them in a large stainless steel pot; add 5 cups of the vinegar, the sugar, and the honey. Cook for 1 hour over medium heat, stirring occasionally.

3. In a small bowl, make a paste with the cornstarch, mustard, turmeric, curry powder, and the remaining ⅓ cup vinegar. Pour into the vegetable mixture. Cook on low heat for 15 minutes. The mixture will become quite thick.

4. Ladle the mixture into hot, sterilized pint jars, leaving ½ inch of headroom. Run a rubber spatula around the insides of the jars to release air bubbles. Wipe the rims of the jars with a clean cloth. Place lids in position and tighten screwbands.

5. Process in a boiling-water-bath canner (page 384) for 5 minutes.

Yield: 10–11 pints

ALL ABOUT
MEAT, POULTRY, FISH, AND SAUSAGE

I have an early memory of my Texas grandmother, Addie, chasing chickens around the farmyard, catching one, and deftly wringing its neck. Even if you never put that fresh a chicken on your table, clean a fish, or butcher a pig, knowing a bit about how it's done will help you select and serve the best meats and fish for your family's table. And learning about the country arts of curing meat or fish and making it into tasty sausage will make you a better consumer as well as cook.

■ ■ ■ ■ ■ ■ ■
Contributors to this chapter are Gail Damerow, Wilbur F. Eastman, Jr., Phyllis Hobson, Kelly Klober, and Charles G. Reavis.

BEEF & PORK
....
POULTRY
....
FISH
....
GAME MEAT
....
CURING MEAT
....
MAKING SAUSAGE

BEEF & PORK

The Primary Cuts of Beef

The following lists show the uses of the primary cuts of beef. Do not be misled into thinking that there aren't other uses for some of the primary cuts; these are simply the ones that are more or less standard.

FROM THE FOREQUARTERS

Chuck	pot roasts
	some steaks
	corned beef
	short ribs
	stew meat
	ground meat
Foreshank	stew meat
	soup bone
	ground meat
Prime ribs	standing rib roasts
	rib steaks
Plate	short ribs
	corned beef
	stew meat
	ground meat
Brisket	corned beef
Neck	ground meat
	bone for soup

FROM THE HINDQUARTERS

Short loin and loin end	steaks: club, porterhouse, T-bone, tenderloin, and sirloin
	roasts: trimmings for ground meat or for braising
Flank	ground meat or flank steak
Rump	boneless roasts (remove bone, roll, and tie)
	corned beef
Round	steaks; however, the last 6 inches are good for stew and ground meat
	roasts
	dried beef
Hind shank	boiled or ground meat
	bone for soup

PRIMARY CUTS OF BEEF

1. neck		7. round	
2. chuck		8. hock	
3. prime ribs		9. flank	
4. short loin		10. plate	
5. loin end		11. brisket	
6. rump		12. foreshank	

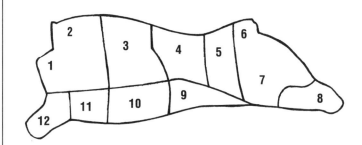

WHERE'S THE BEEF?

....

Look for information on buying and storing meat, fish, and poultry in chapter 3, In the Pantry (pages 22 to 41). Recipes for specific meat and fish dishes may be found in Entrées, Country Carryouts, Country Holidays, and Great Starts: Breakfasts.

The Primary Cuts of Lamb

The customary uses of these primary cuts are as follows:

Legs	roasts
Shoulders	roasts
	chops
	trimmings for stewing meat
Ribs	chops
	roasts
Loin	chops
	roasts
Breasts	roasts
	stew
	ground meat
	spareribs
Neck	stew
	ground meat
Shanks	stew
	ground meat

PRIMARY CUTS OF LAMB

1. leg
2. loin
3. rack/ribs
4. breast
5. shoulder
6. neck

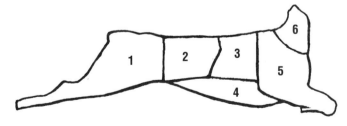

The Primary Cuts of Pork

The customary uses of these primary cuts are as follows:

Legs	(comparable to the round in beef)
Boneless leg	ham
Loin	ham steaks
	blade chops
	loin chops
	butterfly chops
	country-style ribs (page 276)
	back ribs
	Canadian-style bacon
	roasts
	tenderloin
Side pork	bacon
Spareribs	ribs
	salt pork
Shoulder	Boston roasts
	pork cubes
	shoulder roll
	pork steaks
Picnic shoulder	roasts
	steaks
	ground pork
	sausage

PRIMARY CUTS OF PORK

1. leg
2. loin
3. side pork
4. spareribs
5. Boston shoulder
6. picnic shoulder
7. jowl

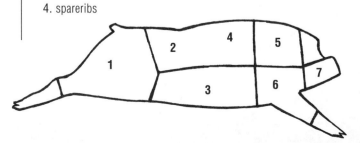

POULTRY

How to Cut Up a Chicken

To cut up a chicken, use a sharp, heavy knife and follow these steps:

1. Cut skin between thighs and body.

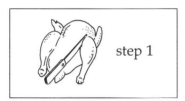
step 1

2. Grasp one leg in each hand, lift the bird, and bend the legs back until the hip joints pop free.

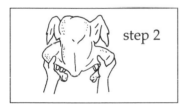
step 2

3. Cut the leg away by slicing from the back to the front at the hip, as close as possible to the backbones.

step 3

4. If you wish, separate the thigh from the drumstick by cutting through the joint between them. You can find the joint by flexing the leg and thigh to locate the bending point.

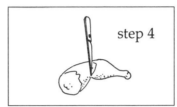
step 4

5. On the same side, remove the wing by cutting along the joint inside the "wing pit," over the joint and down around it. Turn the bird over and remove the other leg and wing. To create mini drumsticks (drumettes), separate the upper, meatier portion of each wing from the lower two bony sections.

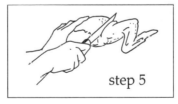
step 5

6. To divide the body, stand the bird on its neck and cut from the tail toward the neck, along the end of the ribs on one side. Cut along the other side to free the back. Bend the back until it snaps in half; cut along the line of least resistance to separate the ribs from the lower back.

step 6

7. Place breast on the cutting board, skin side down, and cut through the white cartilage at the V of the neck.

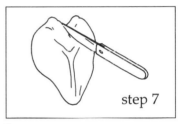
step 7

8. Grasp the breast firmly in both hands and bend each side back, pushing with your fingers to snap the breastbone. Cut the breast in half lengthwise along the bone.

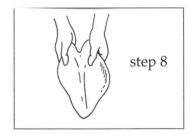
step 8

For boned breasts, place the breast skin side up on a cutting board. Insert the knife along one side of the bone and cut the meat away from the bone. Repeat for the other side.

FISH

How to Clean a Fish

Preparing fish for cooking is an easy matter with a little know-how and a good knife.

1. Most fish must be scaled before cleaning. To make this job easier, first soak the fish for a few minutes in cold water. Holding the fish down firmly, scrape with a dull knife or a spoon from the tail to the head. Be sure to remove all the scales near the base of the fins and head. It is a good idea to do this outdoors or on a large piece of paper, as scales have a tendency to fly.

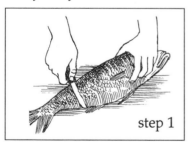

step 1

2. To clean a fish, use a sharp knife to slit the belly from vent to gills.

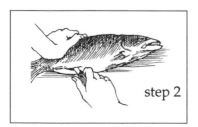

step 2

3. Remove the entrails and discard them.

step 3

4. Cut around and remove fins, and cut off the head. Rinse quickly in cold water and wipe dry. Do not soak in water after cleaning.

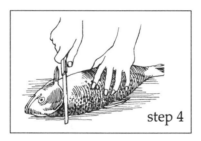

step 4

5. Small fish usually are cooked whole with the tail on, but larger fish may be cut crosswise into steaks or lengthwise into fillets, cutting from the head to the tail.

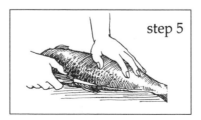

step 5

6. To cut a boneless fillet, use a sharp knife to cut the meat away from the backbone from the tail to the head. Cut the piece loose and lift the entire side of the fish in one piece. Turn the fish over and repeat the process on the other side. You will have two boneless fillets per fish. The remainder of the fish may be discarded or used for soup.

step 6

RUSTIC SCALER

My grandfather loved to fish, and we'd clean dozens at a time from his catch. He'd nail two metal bottle caps side by side, with the edges facing out, onto a stick of wood. This simple tool would scale the fish in a jiffy.

GAME MEAT

The meat of every species has its own distinct characteristics. Most people would be hard put to describe what chicken tastes like, or what the taste difference is between a freshly caught brook trout and one that has languished 3 months in a freezer; however, we know the difference when we taste it. That's the problem one runs into when trying to describe what rabbit or elk or pheasant taste like to someone who has never eaten them.

The following chart is a rough guide to what you can expect when you taste more common game species.

GAME	CHARACTERISTICS
Bear	Lean, dark meat
Bison	Very similar to beef, but somewhat leaner
Boar	Very much like pork, but with a richer flavor
Dove	Similar to the dark meat of chicken; tender and rich in flavor
Duck	Dark, tender meat; very rich in flavor
Elk	Dark meat similar to beef
Goose	Dark, meat; very flavorful
Moose	Similar to beef, but darker and richer in flavor
Opossum	Similar to pork, but with a distinctive gamy flavor
Rabbit (cottontail)	Similar to chicken; light meat
Squirrel	Pink, sweet meat
Venison (whitetail deer)	Similar to beef, but with more flavor
Wild turkey	Lean, dark meat; very rich in flavor
Woodchuck	Rich, red flesh; distinctive gamy flavor

TENDERIZING GAME

....

Meat from mature game and tougher cuts from young animals can be fried if they are first tenderized. There are several ways to tenderize meat.

USE A COMMERCIAL TENDERIZER. Commercial tenderizers, made from a natural enzyme, will soften the tough muscle tissue in a few minutes. Follow the package directions.

MARINATE. Place meat slices in a shallow bowl or baking dish and pour over it your favorite marinade. Refrigerate for 24 hours, turning it several times.

PRESSURE-COOK. Stew or braise at 15 pounds of pressure for 15 to 20 minutes, following the manufacturer's directions.

BREAK DOWN THE FIBER. Tenderize by pounding with a meat mallet, chopping, or grinding the meat.

CURING MEATS

The curing process not only lengthens the storage life of meats but also adds its own distinctive flavor. Although hams and bacon are the cuts traditionally cured, any meat can be cured with delicious results. Pork chops and spareribs are good when cured, and almost any beef cut can be cured for dried beef or corned beef. Cured chickens or turkeys are also tasty.

To obtain a good cure, you must provide cool temperatures and the right amount of salt. It is also important that the process be timed correctly. To ensure the safety of home-cured foods, follow U.S. Department of Agriculture (U.S.D.A.) guidelines.

Cool temperatures. The meat must be kept cold throughout the curing process. If you cannot trust the weather to stay below 40°F, it is possible to cure small batches of meat in the refrigerator in a covered bowl or plastic bag. Sometimes cold-storage space can be rented at a local butchering plant.

Salt. Sugar gives the cured meat its flavor, but the salt keeps it from spoiling. Use fine granulated table salt, not iodized.

Water. It is best to boil the water used for curing meat, because the bacteria in tap water can taint the mixture. After boiling, be sure that the water is thoroughly chilled before being used to make brine.

Time. Timing is important in curing. If you allow too much time, the meat will be hard and salty; too little, and it will spoil. Meat should remain in the brine or dry-cure for 1 to 3 days per pound, depending on the size of the cut and the amount of cure desired. Consult the U.S.D.A. guidelines for recommended processing time.

After curing, the meat should hang in a cool place for 1 to 3 weeks to age and to let the salt spread evenly through the meat.

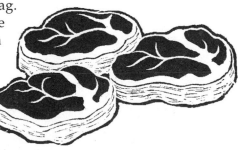

Basic Brine Cure

❧ ❧ ❧

This basic brine recipe is recommended by the U.S.D.A.

  12 pounds salt
   3 pounds white or brown
      sugar
   6 gallons water
100 pounds chilled meat

1. In a stockpot, dissolve the salt and sugar in the water. Bring to a boil. Stir well and chill thoroughly.

2. When meat and brine are well chilled, pack meat into a clean stone crock or wooden barrel. Pack meat tightly and weight it down, so that it will not float in brine.

3. Pour the cold brine over the meat until all meat is immersed.

4. Keep container in a cool place (below 40°F) for 7 days.

5. After 7 days, pour the brine into a pan. Remove the meat and repack it, repositioning the pieces for an even cure.

6. Pour the brine back over the meat. Keep in a cool place until curing is complete according to U.S.D.A. guidelines.

7. After curing, hang the meat in a cold place for 1 to 3 weeks. It can then be smoked or used as is.

How to Build a Smokehouse

Smoking meats brings forth tantalizing flavors, it drives out moisture from the meat, and gives the meat a pleasing color. The amount of smoking, the kinds of chips used for fuel, and the type of cure that preceded smoking (such as sugar, honey, or maple) determine the particular flavors.

The fire pit. Set the fire pit in a hole 2 to 2½ feet deep. The pit itself can be an old kettle, a nonflammable box, or any other type of enclosure in which a fire may be built. A simple hole works well if it is lined with rocks. The pit must have a top, even if it's only a board set across it to act as a damper. A metal cover is ideal.

The smoke chamber. The smoke chamber should be large enough to accommodate the amount of meat being processed. You can use an old but clean metal drum, a wooden box made of long-seasoned hardwood, or a metal cabinet. Some people use old refrigerators. Wash the unit with a mild detergent, then rinse it with pure water and let it air-dry until ready for use.

The smoke chamber must have a top that can be opened and closed to act as a damper for the draft. It can be improvised from boards, the top of a metal drum, a piece of sheet metal, or other household items. You'll also need provisions for suspending meat. Branches or dowels can be suspended across the top of the chamber to act as crosspieces. Use twine, wire, or S-hooks to suspend the meat from the crosspieces.

The base of the smoke chamber should ideally be slightly uphill from the top of the fire pit and about 10 feet away. This facilitates draft from the fire pit to the smoke chamber and makes construction of the smoke tunnel a simpler matter.

The smoke tunnel. In the side of the fire pit, make a hole about 6 inches in diameter about 1 foot from the top. Make a similar hole in the bottom of the smoke chamber. You'll then connect the two by way of the tunnel, using an elbow section of stovepipe.

The smoke tunnel will be entirely underground. This will keep the smoke at the proper cool temperatures. To create it, dig a trench between the fire pit and the smoke chamber. Connect by using elbow stovepipe connections. Cover the trench with a board, then cover the board with dirt to ground level.

The fire. You want a low, steady fire that produces smoke. Some people prefer to start it with a charcoal base and add wood to it; others use an electric hotplate and put wood chips into a pan on the plate to smolder.

The fuel. Use the kind of wood that appeals most to your tastes — experiment and have fun. However, use only hardwood — maple, birch, apple, hickory, chestnut, or ash. Dried corncobs have been used successfully for years, especially in New England.

Cut your fuel into small bits, shavings, or sawdust. If the fuel burns too fast, dampen it with water, or use green twigs or green leaves from hardwood trees to smolder and generate smoke.

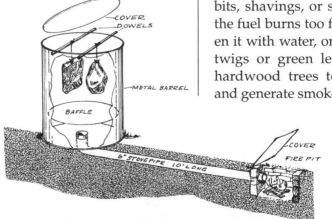

homemade smokehouse

Smoking Fish

Fish may be prepared for smoking either as drawn fish or as fillets. Large fish are often cut into steaks. Splitting the fish along the back but not cutting the belly portion makes it simple to spread it open to hang in the smoke chamber.

Use only freshly caught fish that have been kept clean and cold; don't use fish with damaged flesh. When brining and smoking fish, you'll have the best results if you confine your activities to one kind of fish at a time and if your fish are nearly all the same size.

Brining. Prepared fish should be submerged in brine for 12 hours and kept at a temperature of 38° to 40°F. The brine solution should be made of 1½ cups of salt for each gallon of water; this amount will cure about 4 pounds of fish. Flavorings such as black pepper or garlic may be added to the brine.

After brining, the fish should be removed and drained, then rinsed to remove all accumulated salt. So that air can circulate all around them, it is best to dry the fish on S-hooks laced through the gill or under the collarbone, or to lay them skin side down onto a piece of greased wire mesh. Fillets with the skin removed may be spread over three-sided wooden rods or nailed to dowels.

Drying. Proper drying is the most important step in preparing fish for smoking. A thin, glossy sheen will develop on fish that is dried properly; this skinlike film is known as the pellicle. It may take up to 3 hours of drying for this to appear. A good pellicle acts as a smooth and attractive surface for the smoke, and it will help retain and seal in the juices during the smoking process. Fish must always be dried in the shade; a cool breeze or fan will help. Direct sun will cause spoilage.

Once the pellicle is formed, the fish is ready for the smoke chamber. Inside the chamber, the fish should be hung on dowels or S hooks by the collarbone, split and hung on rods, or placed on wire mesh racks. If wire racks are used, they should first be coated with cooking oil, so that the fish will not stick during the smoking process.

Hot Smoking. Hot-smoke fish you plan to use within a couple of weeks. For this process, smoke the fish at no more than 90°F for 2 hours, then increase the temperature to 150°F for 4 to 8 hours, depending on the thickness of the fish. Store the hot-smoked fish in the refrigerator for up to a few days or in the freezer for longer.

Cold Smoking. Cold-smoke fish you want to store for several months. Keep the temperature of the smoker between 80° and 90°F and smoke the fish for a minimum of 5 days; larger fish will require an additional week of smoking. Cold-smoked fish may be kept, refrigerated, for several months.

Because fish spoils rapidly, the smoking process should be continued without interruption once it has begun. You should be prepared to smoke day and night until the fish is smoked to your liking.

When smoking is completed and the fish is completely cooled, it should be removed and packaged for storage.

MAKING SAUSAGE

The smell of sausage sizzling on your grill is enough to whet even the mildest appetites, but, somehow, when the sausage is fresh and homemade, it's even more enticing. And making sausage is easy.

Basic Sausage

❧ ❧ ❧

These country-style sausage links are a good place to start in sausage-making. Once you have mastered this basic technique, you will be able to try the variations that follow and create your own recipes.

4   *feet small (1½-inch diameter) hog or sheep casings*
    white vinegar
2½ *pounds lean pork butt, cut into 1 inch cubes and chilled*
½   *pound pork fat, cut into 1-inch cubes and chilled*
1½ *teaspoons dried sage*
1½ *teaspoons coarse salt*
¾   *teaspoon finely ground white or black pepper*
¾   *teaspoon sugar*
½   *teaspoon crushed red pepper*
½   *teaspoon dried thyme*
¼   *teaspoon dried summer savory*

1. Preparing the casing. Rinse the casing under cool running water to remove any salt clinging to it. Place in a bowl of cool water; soak for 30 minutes. While you're waiting for the casing to soak, begin preparing the meat (step 2).

After soaking, rinse the casing under cool running water. Slip one end of the casing over the faucet nozzle. Hold the casing firmly on the nozzle, and then turn on the cold water, gently at first, and then more forcefully. This procedure will flush out any salt in the casing and pinpoint any breaks. Should you find a break, simply snip out a small section of the casing.

Place the casing in a bowl of water and add a splash of vinegar — 1 tablespoon of vinegar per cup of water is sufficient. The vinegar will soften the casing and make it more transparent, which in turn will make your sausage more pleasing to the eye. Leave the casing in the vinegar solution until you are ready to use it. Rinse well and drain before stuffing.

ABOUT SAUSAGE SAFETY

When making sausage, you must be responsible for providing food that is safe to eat.

Here are some rules to follow:

1. Use hot water and dish detergent to scrub all surfaces that will be in contact with the meat. In particular, clean your cutting board very well. Rinse everything thoroughly. When you are finished, wash and sanitize the cutting board (use a mixture of 1 teaspoon chlorine bleach and 1 quart of water as a sanitizing solution).

2. Assemble your utensils and equipment: grinder, sausage funnel, knives, mixing spoons, and a large pan for mixing.

3. Pour boiling water over the grinder and the utensils that will come into contact with the meat. Allow everything to cool completely before proceeding, so as not to raise the temperature of the meat and thus encourage the growth of bacteria.

4. Take off any rings you are wearing and wash your hands carefully. Wash them again if you are called away from your work, such as for a phone call.

2. Preparing the meat. Trim the fat from the chilled pork butt and reserve. Chop pork butt into 1-inch cubes. Refrigerate the meat cubes and reserved fat for 30 minutes to firm them up before grinding.

If you are using a food processor, process the meat and fat to a very fine dice and mix in the seasonings after the entire batches of meat and fat have been processed.

If you are using a hand grinder, run the meat through the fine disk (¼ inch or smaller) twice. Mix in the sage, salt, white pepper, sugar, red pepper, thyme and savory with your hands between the first and second grindings.

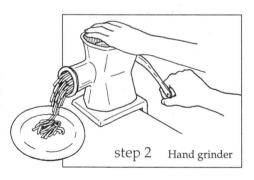

step 2   Hand grinder

If you are using an electric grinder with a sausage-stuffing attachment, sprinkle the seasonings over the meat and fat and mix with your hands before grinding, because the grinding and stuffing will be one continuous operation.

3. Stuffing the sausage. Slide a piece of prepared casing over the sausage funnel or over the attachment of the electric grinder. Push it along until the entire piece of casing is on the funnel and the end of the casing is even with the funnel opening.

If you are using an electric stuffer, turn it on and feed the seasoned cubes of meat into the hopper. When the ground meat mixture is flush with the opening of the tube, turn off the grinder. Pull about 2 inches of casing off the tube and tie it into a knot; this will prevent air bubbles from getting into the sausage.

If you are using a sausage funnel, push the ground meat mixture through with your fingers until it reaches the lip of the opening. Tie off the casing.

- -

SAUSAGE-MAKING EQUIPMENT

With one or two exceptions, you probably already have the equipment in your kitchen that you will need to make sausage. Here's a list of the basic tools.

- GRINDER. An old-fashioned cast-iron hand grinder like the one in your grandmother's kitchen is still available and is still a bargain, even at today's inflated prices.

- POWER GRINDER. If you don't want to grind meat by hand, purchase an electric food grinder with at least two cutting disks.

- SAUSAGE FUNNEL. If your grinder doesn't have a sausage-stuffing attachment or if you use a food processor to grind your meat, you will need a sausage funnel to stuff the meat into casings.

- KNIVES. The knife is the most important tool you'll use to make sausage, because so much of the job involves cutting, boning, and trimming the meat. A boning knife aids the cook in removing as much meat as possible from the bone. For slicing, use a 8- to 10-inch chef's knife.

- BUTCHER'S STEEL. This steel or ceramic rod with a handle is used to finely hone a knife blade.

Continue stuffing the casing until all the meat has been used. Feed small amounts of meat through the funnel at a time, packing the casing firmly but not to the bursting point. If the casings are packed too firmly, you will be unable to twist off the links without rupturing the casing. Try to maintain an even thickness throughout the length of the casing. Try to avoid trapping air in the casing. When all the meat has been used, remove any leftover casing from the funnel.

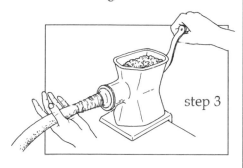

4. Forming the links. Beginning at the tied end of the stuffed casing, grasp about 3 inches of sausage and give it two or three twists in the same direction to form a link. Continue twisting off

links until the entire length of casing is done. With a very sharp knife, cut the links apart and cut off any empty casing at the end. The casing will fit the mixture like a glove, and the mixture won't squeeze out. Cooking will firm up the links, so that the meat will not pour out even though the ends of the links are open.

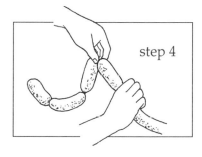

step 4

5. Aging. Sausage tastes better if it ages, because the herbs and spices can penetrate the meat more completely. Arrange the links in a single layer on a platter and refrigerate them for at least a couple of hours.

6. Cooking. Fresh sausage should be cooked slowly and

thoroughly, because it contains raw pork. See Cooking Fresh Sausage, below.

7. Storing. If you are not going to eat the sausage within 2 days, wrap the links or patties individually in plastic wrap, pack them into a plastic freezer bag, and freeze. Frozen sausages will retain their flavor for about 3 months. Thaw them completely in the refrigerator before cooking.

Yield: About 3 pounds

COOKING FRESH SAUSAGE

....

The best way to cook fresh sausage is in a covered, cold skillet with about ½ inch of water. Bring to a boil, then reduce to a simmer; cook until juices run clear. Then drain and fry or grill over medium-high heat, turning frequently, until it's well browned. This technique keeps the casing from bursting. Sausage patties should be cooked over medium-low heat until the juices run clear. Turn the patties once during the cooking time.

MISSING LINKS

You don't have to stuff sausage into links; you can use it as bulk sausage and crumble it or shape it into patties for cooking. Stack patties between squares of wax paper and seal in heavy plastic bags for freezing.

Sicilian-Style Hot or Sweet Sausage

❧ ❧ ❧

This recipe provides enough that you can please everybody by making hot and sweet sausages at the same time. Just add crushed red pepper to only half of the sausage mixture.

Version 1

    5   feet medium (2-inch-
        diameter) hog casings
  4½   pounds lean pork butt,
        cubed
    ½   pound pork fat, cubed
    1   tablespoon fennel seed
    1   tablespoon freshly coarse-
        ground black pepper
  2½   teaspoons salt, or to taste
        crushed red pepper: ½ tea-
        spoon for sweet sausage,
        to taste for hot sausage

Version 2

    ingredients for Version 1
    2   cloves of garlic, finely
        minced
    1   teaspoon anise seed

1. Prepare the casings (page 421).
2. Using the coarse disk of a food grinder, grind the meat and fat together.
3. Mix the fennel seed, black pepper, salt, and red pepper together with the meat and fat.
4. Stuff the mixture into the casings. Twist off into 3- or 4-inch links.
5. Refrigerate and use within 3 days, or freeze.

Yield: 5 pounds

Chorizo

❧ ❧ ❧

In Spain and Mexico, spicy chorizo is used alone or to add flavor to many dishes. Smoked or fresh pork can be used. The wine and brandy in the mixture give extra savor to the meat and help extract the flavor of the herbs and spices.

    5   feet medium (2-inch diam-
        eter) hog casings
  3½   pounds lean pork butt,
        cubed
    ½   pound pork fat, cubed
    ¼   cup dry red wine
    2   tablespoons brandy
    4   cloves of garlic, finely
        chopped
    1   tablespoon red wine vine-
        gar
    2   teaspoons freshly coarse-
        ground black pepper
    2   teaspoons salt, or to taste
    1   teaspoon fennel seed
    1   teaspoon crushed red
        pepper

1. Prepare the casings (page 421).
2. Using the coarse disk of a food grinder, grind the meat and fat together.
3. Mix the wine, brandy, garlic, vinegar, black pepper, salt, fennel seed, and red pepper together with the meat.
4. Place the mixture in a large covered pan. Let sit in the refrigerator for 3 or 4 hours, so that the wine and brandy have time to extract the flavor from the herbs and spices and the meat can absorb some of the liquid.
5. Stuff the mixture into the casings. Twist off into 3- or 4-inch links.
6. Refrigerate and use within 3 days, or freeze.

Yield: 4 pounds

Country Chicken Sausage

❧ ❧ ❧

Chicken makes a light sausage that is very low in fat. Be sure that the chicken is well chilled to begin with, and work quickly, so that it will not get warm during processing.

This recipe calls for a traditional "country sausage" combination of ginger, sage, thyme, and savory.

2 feet small (1½-inch-diameter) hog or sheep casings
2 pounds chicken meat
1 teaspoon freshly ground black pepper
1 teaspoon salt, or to taste
½ teaspoon ground ginger
½ teaspoon ground sage
½ teaspoon summer savory
½ teaspoon ground thyme
½ teaspoon cayenne pepper (optional)

1. Prepare the casings (page 421).

2. Using the fine disk of a food grinder, grind the chicken.

3. Mix the pepper, salt, ginger, sage, savory, thyme, and cayenne, if desired, with the chicken.

4. Using the fine disk of a food grinder, grind the mixture.

5. Stuff the mixture into the casings. Twist off into 2- to 3-inch links.

Yield: 2 pounds

Old Bay Sausage

❧ ❧ ❧

If you love the taste of sausage but are trying to maintain a light, low-fat diet,

this recipe may be the answer. The flavor of the fish is neutral; the seasonings are essentially what you taste. Try it even if your family isn't fond of fish, because unless you tell them what they are eating, they probably won't guess.

4 feet small (1½-inch-diameter) hog casings
2 pounds whitefish fillet, thawed if frozen
1 egg, beaten
1 teaspoon lemon juice
1 teaspoon sweet paprika
½ teaspoon celery salt
¼ teaspoon ground bay leaf
¼ teaspoon cardamom
¼ teaspoon ground cloves
¼ teaspoon ground ginger
¼ teaspoon mace
¼ teaspoon crushed mustard seed
¼ teaspoon finely ground black pepper

1. Prepare the casings (page 421).

2. Cut the fish into 2-inch cubes. Process in a food processor until the fish is just broken, about three pulses.

3. Add the egg, lemon juice, paprika, celery salt, bay leaf, cardamom, cloves, ginger, mace, mustard seed, and pepper. Process just until well blended.

4. Stuff the mixture into casings. Twist off into 3- to 4-inch links.

Yield: 2 pounds

Bratwurst

❧ ❧ ❧

In German, *Wurst* means sausage, and the Germans have created many varieties of sausage. This one resembles plump hot dogs.

3 feet small (1½-inch-diameter) hog casings
1½ pounds lean pork butt, cubed
1 pound veal, cubed
½ pound pork fat, cubed
1 teaspoon freshly ground white pepper
1 teaspoon salt
½ teaspoon crushed caraway seeds
½ teaspoon dried marjoram,
¼ teaspoon ground allspice

1. Prepare the casings (page 421).

2. Grind the pork, veal, and pork fat separately through the fine blade of the grinder.

3. Mix the ground meats and grind again.

4. Add the pepper, salt, caraway, marjoram, and allspice; mix thoroughly.

5. Stuff the mixture into the casings and twist off into 4- or 5-inch lengths.

6. Refrigerate for up to 2 days. The bratwurst can be panfried or grilled over charcoal.

Yield: 3 pounds

BARREL, BOTTLE, AND JUG

Sooner or later, a home brewer emerges in the family. In our case, son Matt and son-in-law Blair got the itch, and then the gear. Blair generally has a keg of a special recipe, such as ginger or pumpkin beer, brewing in the basement. Last year, he actually put a tap into the door of an old refrigerator so that cold beer would always be available; in addition, frosty mugs are always in the freezer. But beer isn't the only beverage that's fun and easy to brew at home. There's root beer, sarsaparilla, and more. We make our own cider with apples from our trees and wine from grapes, herbs, fruits, and even flowers. Although the quality of these homemade beverages can be unpredictable, they're always fun to make and share.

■ ■ ■ ■ ■ ■ ■ ■

Contributors to this chapter are Robert Cluett, Jeff Cox, Stephen Cresswell, Gail Damerow, Joe Fisher and Dennis Fisher, Karl F. Lutzen and Mark Stevens, Dave Miller, Annie Proulx, Tess and Mark Szamatulski, and Pattie Vargas and Rich Gulling, and Jim Wearne.

BREWING BEER
AT HOME

·············

COUNTRY WINES

·············

CORDIALS

·············

CIDERMAKING

·············

HOMEMADE ROOT
BEER & SODA

Lemon Cooler

❧ ❧ ❧

This recipe works with almost any wine, and each choice is an adventure, so experiment freely! Use a white wine for regular lemonade, a red or rosé for pink lemonade.

juice of ½ lemon
sugar to taste
4 ounces dry or sweet wine —
    white, red, or rosé
seltzer
lemon slice or raspberries
    (optional)

1. Mix the lemon juice, sugar, and wine in a collins glass with cracked ice. Stir until the sugar is dissolved. Fill the glass with seltzer.

2. Garnish the glass with a lemon slice and raspberries, if desired.

Yield: 1 serving

Blackberry Liqueur

❧ ❧ ❧

In the nineteenth century, ladies often kept a bottle of this cordial in the cupboard for "medicinal purposes" or for reviving themselves after exertion or fainting spells. These days, we prepare it for the frank enjoyment of its deep, fruity flavor.

1½ cups sugar
1 cup water
1½ teaspoons concentrated
    blackberry extract
1½ cups 100-proof vodka

1. Make a simple syrup by bringing the sugar and water to a boil over medium-high heat, stirring constantly to prevent scorching. When clear, remove from heat and let stand until just warm. Pour into a clean 1-quart jar with tight-fitting lid. Add the flavoring and vodka; cover and shake well. The cordial may be served immediately, but it's better if it is allowed to age for 1 month.

Yield: Approximately 1 fifth
(25 ounces)

USING FRUIT LIQUEUR

. . . .

Fruit liqueurs are not just for sipping. A dash of one of these richly flavored concoctions can add a grace note to many a delicious dish.
• **Drizzle over ice cream,** sorbet, or fruit salad.
• **Add to sparkling wine or water** for a fresh, fizzy cooler.
• **Use with melted butter** to baste chicken breasts.
• **Fold a splash into a bowl** of freshly whipped cream, for a delicate taste and tint.

ROOT BEER FLOAT

We often had brown cows when I was growing up — root beer floats, that is. My mom would serve them as a summertime treat, sometimes as dessert after a dinner of hamburgers on the grill. The sight and sound of the foamy explosion of the root beer when you pour it over vanilla ice cream are as much a part of the enjoyment of drinking a brown cow as the cool, creamy taste of ice cream mingled with root beer.

The glass or mug needs to be frosty cold, as does the root beer. Purists use only vanilla ice cream, but try it with chocolate for an even richer treat. If you don't brew your own root beer, try using A&W brand (if you're of a certain age, it may remind you of pulling up at the old A&W drive-in restaurants) or Hires, which is the brand Mother used.

The recipe? Simple. Put 3 scoops of vanilla ice cream in a tall glass. Slowly pour ice-cold root beer over the ice cream. Serve with a long-handled iced-tea spoon and a straw.

BREWING BEER AT HOME

Brewing is an ancient skill; it has been refined with modern equipment and standardized ingredients, but basically it hasn't changed much in centuries. The steps, briefly, are sanitizing equipment, chilling water, steeping malt in water, adding flavoring, cooling, adding yeast, fermenting, bottling, and aging (if you can stand the wait). If you follow these steps as directed, you'll soon be enjoying your own special brew. In future batches, you can experiment with other kinds of malt concentrates, different varieties of hops, different yeasts, other varieties of crystal malt, and variations on the techniques. Experimentation is one of the things that make brewing so much fun. Keep a brewing notebook so you will have a record of what you love and what you'd rather not repeat. Most home brewers like to vary the recipe with the seasons: amber autumn ale, strong Christmas ale, golden spring lager, light summer lager.

BREWING EQUIPMENT

The basic equipment you need to get started with home brewing will last through many batches of beer; with care and proper cleaning, very little will ever have to be replaced. Round up all equipment, supplies, and ingredients before starting. Once the process gets rolling, it can't be put on hold while a missing item is located.

KITCHEN EQUIPMENT
- **Stockpot.** 12 to 20 quarts; not aluminum; stainless steel recommended.
- **Spoon.** The handle should be at least 1 foot long.
- **Funnel.**
- **Measuring equipment.** A 1-cup measure and standard measuring spoons.
- **Mason jar.** 1 quart.
- **Saucepan.** Small.

These items will be found at a brewing equipment supplier.

- **Primary fermenter.** A bucket made of special food-grade plastic; the snap-on lid has a hole in the top to fit the fermentation lock.
- **Fermentation lock.** A plastic device that lets carbon dioxide out but does not let air in. You will need two, one with a rubber stopper that will fit the mouth of the carboy.
- **Carboy.** A 5-gallon bottle with a narrow neck.
- **Siphoning tube.** Thin, clear plastic hose, about 6 feet long.
- **Grain bag.** A heat-resistant mesh bag, used to add malt flavorings to the wort. Smaller bags are used for adding hops.
- **Hydrometer.** A graduated glass instrument that measures the specific gravity of the wort.
- **Beer bottles.** Two cases' worth (48 or more). New or used, but whole, without chipped rims, and clean. Be sure that they do not take twist-off caps; twist-offs will not work properly with the caps and capper you will use.
- **Bottling bucket.** A large bucket with a spigot built in.
- **Bottle filler wand.** A rigid plastic tube that attaches to the siphoning tube.
- **Crown bottle caps.** Get at least 50; they must be new.
- **Capper.** Bench style or handheld; the bench style provides better leverage.
- **Brushes.** One basic bottle brush for bottles, one long-handled brush for the carboy.
- **Powdered chlorine concentrate.** Used to sanitize all items that come into contact with the wort. Or use household bleach in a solution of 2 tablespoons bleach to 1 gallon of cold water.
- **Optional items.** Labels, a brass bottle washer, a carboy handle .

Basic Homebrew

❧ ❧ ❧

Learning a basic recipe is a must and this one is intended to produce a Continental-style lager that will please most palates.

> 5 gallons brewing water, 4 gallons chilled, 1 gallon at room temperature
> 2 cans (3.3 to 4 pounds each) unhopped amber malt concentrate
> ½ cup corn sugar
> 1 packet lager yeast
> ½–1 pound crystal malt
> 1½–3 ounces hops pellets

Preparation

Thorough preparation is essential to the success of any homebrewing effort — it cannot be overstressed. Preparation includes cleaning and sanitizing all equipment and procuring all necessary supplies before beginning. **It is best to use baking soda and warm water for cleaning brewmaking equipment, as soap leaves a residue that can harm the beer.** *Be sure to allocate sufficient time for each step.*

The items you will use immediately are:

- *Ingredients*
- *Stockpot*
- *Long-handled spoon*

BASIC BREWING INGREDIENTS

....

- **Water.** *5 gallons. Bottled springwater or tap water that is preboiled may be used. Boil 6 gallons of tap water uncovered for 15 to 20 minutes. Cover and let cool. Siphon the water into sanitized containers. For most types of beer, a pH of 5.0 to 5.5 is best; adding gypsum or Burton Water Salts will lower the pH of brewing water. Burton Water Salts also treats water with minerals for optimal beermaking.*

- **Malt concentrate.** *6 to 8 pounds of malt concentrate, a molasseslike syrup made from malted barley sugar. Available in amber, dark, and light.*

- **Hops.** *1½ to 3 ounces of hops pellets, depending on desired bitterness. Hops is an herb that flavors the beer.*

- **Yeast.** *Brewer's yeast, available in dry and liquid form, usually comes in amounts that are right for one batch.*

- **Crystal malt.** *Toasted, malted barley for adding mellow flavor.*

- **Corn sugar.** *A small amount of corn sugar to add at bottling time to produce carbonation.*

- *Grain bag*
- *Mason jar*
- *Primary fermenter with fermentation lock*
- *Aluminum foil*

Other items, such as the bottles and the carboy, should be washed and stored in a clean area. Now you're ready to begin.

1. Prepare chlorine sanitizing solution according to package instructions, or use homemade solution. *Plastic items should be dipped into the solution but should not be allowed to soak; they may pick up and transmit an unpleasant chlorine taste. ALL items should be rinsed three times in very hot tap water after being sanitized.*

2. Wash the stockpot and the spoon. These need not be sanitized, because they will be in contact only with the boiling wort.

3. Wash and sanitize the Mason jar and a piece of aluminum foil large enough to cover the mouth of the jar. Rinse, then let the jar drain by placing it upside down on clean paper towels.

4. Wash and sanitize the primary fermenter, its lid, and the fermentation lock.

Steeping & Primary Fermentation

It is a good idea to read and understand all these steps before you begin to work. They will take you from preparation of the yeast through the start of the fermentation process.

1. Have the 4 gallons of chilled brewing water ready. Pour the remaining gallon into the stockpot.

2. Prepare the yeast. In a small saucepan, measure 2¼ cups of the brewing water. Heat it to steaming. Add 1 tablespoon of the malt concentrate and 1 level tablespoon of the corn sugar; stir until dissolved. Increase heat and simmer for 10 minutes. Let cool until lukewarm.

3. Pour the mixture into the sanitized Mason jar. Add the yeast; gently swirl the jar to mix. Cover the jar with aluminum foil; set aside.

4. Heat the gallon of water in the stockpot until it is

steaming but not quite boiling. Meanwhile, pour the crystal malt into the grain bag; tie off to prevent spillage and lower the bag into the stockpot. The crystal malt will begin to flavor the water and prepare the grain for cooking. Remove the stockpot from the heat; remove grain bag and set it in a clean container.

step 4

5. Add the remaining malt concentrate to the hot water. Stir until it is dissolved.

6. Return the stockpot to high heat; heat the mixture until it is almost boiling. Return the grain bag to the hot mixture. Stir frequently but gently.

7. Vigorously pour the 4 gallons of chilled brewing water into the primary fermenter. (Vigorous pouring will aerate the water.) Cover the fermenter.

8. When the mixture in the stockpot is heated almost to boiling, remove from heat and transfer the grain bag to the primary fermenter.

9. Stir the grain bag and the water briefly; replace the cover. Add the hops pellets to the hot mixture in the stockpot; stir. Return the pot to high heat; stir frequently.

READ THIS PARAGRAPH CAREFULLY.

Now that all the ingredients have been added to the stockpot and the grain bag has been removed, you will bring the mixture to a boil. As the mixture approaches boiling, a froth will form on the surface. When it reaches the boiling point, it will vigorously foam to as much as twice its normal volume. This is the reason for using such a large pot for what seems to be such a relatively small amount of liquid. An overflow of hot foam can scald you badly on contact; at best, it will make a sweet foamy mess all over your stove.

After foam-up occurs, the froth will die down of its own accord and the liquid will maintain a rolling boil. Stir occasionally during this time. Let it boil about 20 minutes from foam-up.

10. After 20 minutes of boiling, remove the pot from heat. Let the mixture cool in the pot until the outside of the pot feels cool. You can hasten this step by placing the pot in a sink full of cold water, being careful not to let any of the sink water get into

the pot. As the mixture is cooling, remove the grain bag from the fermenter and discard the grain. Clean the grain bag immediately in warm water; it can be reused almost indefinitely.

11. When the outside of the pot feels cool, dry the outside and pour the mixture into the water in the fermenter. The mixture should not be stone-cold, but if it is too warm, the heat will kill the yeast preparation. Stir the contents (now called the wort) of the fermenter to mix well.

12. By this time, the yeast preparation in the Mason jar should be actively working. Swirl the jar gently and carefully pour the preparation into the wort. Cover the fermenter. Put the fermentation lock in place, following directions for its proper use.

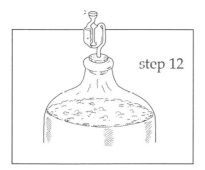

step 12

13. Place the fermenter in a location that maintains a fairly constant temperature of about 65° to 70°F. When yeast becomes active, move fermenter to a cooler (45° to 50°F) location. *Note:* When making ale, do not move the fermenter to a cooler location.

14. The time that the wort will spend in the fermenter in its primary fermentation will depend largely on ambient temperature and on such conditions as initial water temperature and the type of yeast used. After as little as 2 days or as many as 7, the foam head on top of the wort will collapse and the top of the wort will be visible. (Resist the temptation to lift the lid and examine the wort too often. Any opening of the lid invites the invasion of unwanted microorganisms that can spoil the beer. The bubbling of outgoing carbon dioxide through the fermentation lock will let you know that things are progressing well.) When the bubbling slows to 1 bubble every 90 seconds, it is time to siphon the wort into the glass carboy.

Secondary Fermentation

The second fermentation will take longer than the first and will complete the principal production of alcohol in the wort. It will also contribute much of the flavor and character to the beer. The steps to accomplish the second fermentation are very simple, but you must follow them carefully so as not to spoil the wort.

1. Wash the carboy thoroughly, sanitize it with chlorine solution, and rinse it thoroughly with hot water three times. Wash, sanitize, and rinse the carboy's fermentation lock, rubber stopper and siphoning tube.

2. Use the siphoning tube to transfer the wort between fermenters. To do this, set the primary fermenter on a surface above the carboy.

AIR IS THE ENEMY

Remember that in brewing, air is the enemy. Once the wort is in the fermenter, a delicate process is taking place. Living yeast is consuming sugar and producing alcohol and carbon dioxide. The environment in the fermenter is the perfect place for this to happen. It is vital to keep aeration of the fermenting wort to a minimum. Whenever you move, siphon, skim, stir, or otherwise disturb the process (as you sometimes must), take care to cause the least possible agitation. Fermenting beer is a living thing — nurture it.

3. Start the siphon: Sanitize the tube; fill it completely with water, using your thumbs to seal the ends of the tube. While holding your thumb over one end of the tube, place the other end into the fermenter. Let the water flow into the catch container. When beer starts to flow out of the tube, stop the end again, using your thumb.

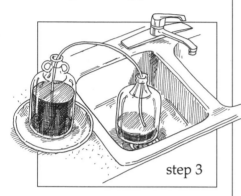

step 3

4. Insert the tube into the carboy, with the end of the tube at the bottom of the carboy. Release your thumb and let the flow resume.

5. It will take several minutes for the wort to flow from the fermenter into the carboy. During this time, hold the tube in the fermenter as steadily as possible to prevent bubbles or agitation. Channeling the wort against the side of the carboy helps.

6. When you begin to hear sucking noises from the inflow of the tube, stop the siphon and remove the siphon hose.

7. If necessary, add brewing water to the carboy until the top of the wort is about 1 inch below the lip of the carboy. Insert the rubber stopper (which should not touch the wort) and fermentation lock into the top of the carboy right away.

8. Place the carboy in a location with a steady temperature of 40° to 50°F and minimal light exposure. (You can cover it with a lightproof cover, such as a coat or black plastic bag.)

9. Leave the carboy undisturbed and listen for the bubbles through the fermentation lock. These will occur less frequently than during the primary fermentation, but they will come.

10. Thoroughly wash the siphon hose and the fermenter. These need not be sanitized at this time, but they must be kept clean. They will be used again before you are done.

11. The secondary fermentation will take anywhere from 2 to 6 weeks. It is complete when bubbles have just about stopped rising to the top of the wort and a ⅛-inch-wide ring of bubbles has formed at the surface.

12. You should wait at least 1 week after secondary fermentation is done to let the sediment settle, and you may wait an additional week to suit your convenience.

13. During this waiting period, make sure that all of your bottling supplies and equipment are ready. It's best to thoroughly wash the bottles well in advance, so that they are ready to be sanitized and rinsed right before they are needed for bottling.

WHERE DO I GET THAT?

....

Equipment and ingredients for beermaking are often available in home wine and beer supply stores; check your local Yellow Pages under "Brewing Supplies" or "Winemaking Supplies."

You may also obtain information about brewing and supplies from the Home Wine and Beer Trade Association, P.O. Box 1373, Valrico, FL 33595; www.hwbta.org.

Many homebrewers learn more about making beer by joining homebrew clubs. Ask about clubs when you visit a local supplier, or contact the American Homebrewers Association, P.O. Box 1679, Boulder, CO 80306; www.hwbta.org.

Bottling & Storage

We won't kid you — bottling your beer is tedious. Enlist a friend to help and to keep you company. **Be sure to read this section through entirely before starting any of the following procedures.** *We suggest practicing the bottling procedure with water in the fermenter before you actually attempt to bottle beer. It can be a bit tricky, and it is better to learn on water than to waste beer.*

1. If you haven't already, thoroughly wash the bottles and make sure that the other supplies and ingredients are ready. Have corn sugar at hand, the primary fermenter clean, the bottle caps ready,

TOO MANY BUBBLES?

Excessive carbonation occurs for many reasons: The fermentation temperature may have been too low, there may not have been enough fermentation time, or there may have been too much corn sugar in the bottling process, for example. Most of the time, the worst that happens is that the beer has too much foam, and you'll have to wait a little longer than usual for the foam to die down in the glass before you drink. The beer isn't ruined.

and the siphon tube and filler wand clean. Make sure that the bottle capper has been adjusted to the proper setting, so that the caps crimp properly onto the bottles; practice on some empties.

2. Sanitize and rinse three times with hot tap water everything that will come into contact with the beer: the primary fermenter, the siphon hose, the stainless steel spoon, the bottle caps, and the bottles.

3. In a small saucepan, heat 1 cup of water. When it is steaming, dissolve ½ cup of corn sugar in it; bring the mixture to a boil, stirring frequently. Remove from heat, cover the pan, and let cool.

4. Siphon the beer out of the carboy into the bottling bucket, leaving the sediment behind. Try to aerate the beer as little as possible.

5. Gently pour the cool sugar solution into the beer in the fermenter. Slowly and without agitation, stir to mix thoroughly.

6. Place the bottling bucket on a surface above the one on which the bottles will rest as they fill. Some spillage is inevitable, so choose your location carefully. Clean the area very thoroughly.

7. **Think through steps 8 through 11 and plan how to most efficiently and quickly accomplish them in your work area.**

8. Sanitize the bottling bucket spigot. Attach the tube to the spigot; attach the filler wand to the other end of the tube.

9. Open the spigot to start the beer flowing.

10. Position a bottle and place the filler wand down to the bottom of the bottle. Press the wand gently against the bottom of the bottle and let beer flow in until it reaches the mouth of the bottle. Lift up the wand to stop the flow of beer. As you remove the wand from the bottle, the level of the beer in the bottle will drop down to the appropriate height.

11. Place a bottle cap over the mouth of the bottle and position it in the capper. Press down on the handle of the capper until the cap is firmly sealed on the bottle. Set the full bottle aside.

12. Repeat steps 10 and 11 with the remaining bottles.

13. Thoroughly wash all of the equipment you have used and store it in a clean, dry place. You will get years of use out of most of the gear if it is properly maintained.

14. Once the beer is bottled, it should be stored for 6 weeks before tasting. You may want to label and date the beer. Wipe dry the full bottles; place them upright into the case crates. Put the crates in a cool, dark place.

15. During storage, the little remaining yeast is processing the corn sugar that you added at bottling and producing a little more alcohol and carbon dioxide. This carbonates the beer so that it will foam when you open it.

After 6 weeks, the beer is ready to taste. It will improve even more over time, but it is ready for a first taste now.

Yield: About 48 bottles

Pale Horse Pale Ale

❧ ❧ ❧

Pale ale is an amber- to copper-colored bitter, malty beer of medium body and alcoholic strength.

  5 *gallons brewing water (1½ gallons chilled)*
3.3 *pounds Black Rock East India Pale Ale kit*
3.3 *pounds Northwest Gold malt extract syrup*
  ½ *ounce East Kent Goldings hop plug*
  ½ *ounce Fuggles hop plug (for aroma)*
1½ *gallons chilled water*
  1 *packet Whitbread ale yeast*
  ⅔ *cup corn sugar*

1. In a stockpot, bring 1½ gallons of the water to a boil. Remove from heat, add the Black Rock and Northwest Gold extracts, and return to a boil. Boil 60 minutes.

2. Add the East Kent Goldings hop plug; and boil 15 minutes. Remove from heat; add the Fuggles hop plug. Steep for 5 minutes.

3. Strain hot wort into a fermenter containing the chilled water. Rinse hops with ½ gallon boiled water. Top off up to 5 gallons.

4. Add yeast to wort when cool.

5. Ferment at ale temperatures (60°–70°F). Bottle when fermentation ceases (7 to 10 days), using corn sugar for priming. Ale should be ready to drink in 2 weeks.

Yield: 5 gallons

Brown Ale

❧ ❧ ❧

This mellow dark ale, developed by Steve Hodos of Rochester, New York, won a medal in the Brown Ale category at the 1989 Upstate New York Homebrewers Association Members Only Mini-Contest.

5½ *gallons brewing water*
 20 *ounces Russian malt beverage concentrate (contains rye and barley malt, rye flour, and clear water)*

SERVING BEER

Do not chill your beer too much. If you intend your beer to resemble bottled beer of a German or other European sort, naturally you will refrigerate it. Just don't make it icy cold, or you won't taste it properly.

If you have an English ale flavor in mind, you may not want to refrigerate it at all. If you can store your ale at cellar *temperature, about 55 to 60°F, you will find that the lack of chill enhances the ale taste.*

Use a large, uncolored beer glass or mug. Tilt the glass slightly and pour the beer gently down the side. Pour in one smooth, continuous motion without stopping. Continue to pour until you see sediment approach the mouth of the bottle. At that point, stop pouring.

If you are tasting a 6-week-old beer for the first time, the richer, fuller complexities of the hops will not yet have matured. After the first bottle, put the rest away for a couple of months. You'll be pleased at how much it improves.

3 pounds Laaglander light dry malt extract

1½ ounces Northern Brewer hops pellets

1 packet Red Star dry ale yeast

5¼ ounces cane sugar

1. In a stockpot, bring the water, malt concentrate, and dry malt extract to a boil. Boil for 4 minutes.

2. Add the hops. Boil for 70 minutes longer. Remove from heat and allow to cool.

3. Transfer the mixture to the primary fermenter, and top off up to 5½ gallons. Pitch yeast.

4. When primary fermentation subsides, rack to a secondary fermenter. Add ¾ ounce of the cane sugar.

5. When fermentation is complete, prime with the remaining cane sugar. Bottle.

Yield: 5½ gallons

Rogue Torpedo Common Beer

❧ ❧ ❧

California Common is a great American beer, and this is a variation of it. One of the joys of home beermaking is thinking up fanciful names for your own brews. Rogue Torpedo is the creation of brewmaster brothers Joe and Dennis Fisher.

5 gallons water (1½ gallons chilled)

½ pound Vienna malt, crushed

6.6 pounds Northwest Gold malt extract syrup

2 ounces Northern Brewer hops pellets

2 ½-ounce Cascade hop plugs

1 packet Yeastlab L35 California Lager yeast

½ ounce Willamette dry hops

¾ cup corn sugar

1. In a stockpot, heat 1½ gallons of the water to 150°F. Put the grains into a grain bag; immerse in the hot water. Steep for 15 minutes in water between 150 and 170°F. Remove the grains and rinse the brew pot with ½ gallon of the water, boiled.

2. Add the malt extract and hops pellets. Boil 45 minutes. Add one of the hop plugs; boil 15 minutes longer. Remove from heat and add the other hop plug. Steep for 5 minutes.

3. Strain hot wort into fermenter containing the chilled water. Rinse hops with boiled water. Top off up to 5 gallons.

4. Pitch the yeast when cool.

5. Ferment at ale temperatures (60 to 70°.). When fermentation dies down, add the dry hops. Bottle when fermentation stops (2 to 3) weeks, using corn sugar for

priming. Age 4 to 6 weeks at cellar temperature (55°F) before drinking.

Yield: 5 gallons

Note: If you have not purchased the grains precrushed, use an electric grain mill or put them into a resealable plastic bag and crush them with a rolling pin or a can.

BREW TALK

....

PITCH. Add yeast to the wort to begin the fermentation process.

PRIME. The process of adding sugar or malt extract to beer at bottling to induce carbonation.

RACK. The process of siphoning unfinished homebrew from the primary fermentation vessel to the secondary fermentation vessel or bottling bucket.

WORT. Brewing liquid, steeped with malt and flavorings, before fermentation; pronounced "wert."

Skinny Puppy Pumpkin Ale

❦ ❦ ❦

The recipe for this robust beer was created by David Ruggiero, owner of a home-brew supply shop in Newton, Massachusetts. David got interested in brewing with pumpkins after reading about the use of native ingredients in the beers of old New England. "It should be obvious," says David, "that you are drinking a liquid, alcoholic pumpkin pie." If you don't agree, reduce the amount of spices or leave them out.

7 pounds amber malt extract
2 gallons boiling water
1 ounce bittering hops (Cascade, Mt. Hood, or Willamette)
½ teaspoon Irish moss
4 pounds pumpkin, cut into 1-inch cubes
1 teaspoon cinnamon
½ teaspoon ginger
¼ teaspoon nutmeg
7 grams ale yeast (Munton & Fison or Edme)
1 cup water
¾ cup corn sugar

1. In a stockpot, dissolve the malt extract in the boiling water. Stir until it returns to a boil. Place the hops in a grain bag.

2. Add the hops to the wort in the stockpot; boil for 60 minutes. After 40 minutes, add the Irish moss. After 55 minutes, add the pumpkin and spices.

3. Combine the yeast and 1 cup of water. Set aside.

4. Transfer the pumpkin and wort to a fermenter. Remove the grain bag. Fill the fermenter to 5 gallons with boiled, cooled water.

5. When the temperature falls below 75°F, stir in the dissolved yeast. Starting gravity (as determined by a hydrometer; page 428) is 1.045 to 1.048.

6. When fermentation stops, rack the beer into a carboy, straining out the pumpkin and taking care not to stir up the sediment.

7. Rack the beer into clean bottles when the gravity reaches 1.015 to 1.012.

8. To each bottle, add 1 teaspoon of corn sugar for priming. Age 4 to 6 weeks at cellar temperature (55°F) before drinking.

Yield: 5 gallons

Just-Like-Bass Ale

❦ ❦ ❦

This recipe yields a copycat version of beloved British Bass Ale. It is copper-colored with a creamy, off-white head. The splendid hop and malt aroma leads into a smooth, well-balanced flavor. Malt is on the palate followed by a dry hop aftertaste.

14 ounces British crystal malt
  about 7 gallons brewing water
6 pounds Munton & Fison light dry malt extract
1¾ ounces Northdown hops at 9% alpha acid
1 teaspoon Burton water salts
¼ ounce Challenger hops
1 teaspoon Irish moss
¾ ounce Northdown hops
  Wyeast's 1098 British ale yeast
¾ cup corn sugar

1. Crush the British crystal malt and heat ½ gallon of the water to 150°F. Steep the crushed malt in the water for 20 minutes.

2. Strain the grain water into the brew pot. Rinse the grains with another ½ gallon of the water, heated to 150°F. Top the brew pot with enough water to make 1½ gallons total volume. Bring the mixture to a boil. Remove from heat and add the dry malt extract, 1 ounce of the Northdown hops, and the water salts.

3. Add water until total volume in the brew pot is 2½ gallons. Boil for 45 minutes. Add Challenger hops and Irish moss.

4. Boil for 5 minutes. Add another ½ ounce of the Northdown hops.

5. Boil for 9 minutes. Add remaining ¼ ounce of the Northdown hops.

6. Boil for 1 minute. Remove pot from heat; allow to cool for 15 minutes. Strain the cooled wort into the primary fermenter. Add cold water to top off to 5 gallons. When the wort temperature is less than 80°F, pitch the yeast.

7. Transfer the wort to a fermenter for 4 to 5 days or until fermentation slows.

8. Siphon into the secondary fermenter. When second fermentation is complete, add the corn sugar to bottles for priming; bottle.

Yield: 5 gallons

Two-Pints-off-the-Port-Bow Porter

❦ ❦ ❦

Porter is a medium-bodied, moderately hopped dark ale of medium alcoholic strength.

5–5½   *gallons chilled brewing water*
4   *pounds Telford's Porter Kit*
3   *pounds Northwest Gold extract syrup*
1   *ounce Willamette hop plugs*
1   *packet Whitbread Ale yeast*
½   *cup corn sugar*

1. Bring 1½ gallons of the water to a boil. Remove from heat, add porter kit and extract syrup and return to a boil. Boil for 60 minutes.

2. Add the hop plugs and boil for 5 minutes.

3. Strain the hot wort into a fermenter containing 1½ gallons of the water. Rinse the hops with ½ gallon water. Top off up to 5 gallons.

4. Pitch yeast when cool. Starting gravity (as determined by a hydrometer; page 428) is 1.044 to 1.052.

5. Ferment at ale temperatures (65° to 70°F. Bottle when fermentation ceases, in 7 to 10 days, using the corn sugar for priming. The beer should be ready to drink in 2 weeks.

Yield: 5 gallons

COUNTRY WINES

Country wines are those made with homegrown ingredients; they may not have the balance and complexity of wines from the great châteaus, but they can be surprisingly good and are delightful to use for drinking and cooking. You can make wine from many easy-to-find fruits and plants, peaches, grapes, herbs, and even dandelions.

Country wines come from diverse traditions. Recipes accompanied immigrants from many different countries. Other recipes were developed by pioneers who made wine by following the most basic principles: Mix fruit juices, sugar, and yeast; allow the mixture to ferment away from air; wait patiently. In a few months, a new wine would be ready for tasting.

WINEMAKING INGREDIENTS

• **Yeast.** Bread yeast should not be used for winemaking; commercial wine yeasts yield superior results and are inexpensive. Wine yeasts come in several specific varieties for different kinds of wines; they give you a firmer sediment than does bread yeast, which makes racking easier and more efficient.

• **Yeast nutrient.** A natural "vitamin pill" helps the yeast develop efficiently. Especially useful for honey-based wines.

• **Pectic enzyme.** With honey wines and wines made from certain high-pectin fruits, clarity can be a problem even after diligent racking. Cloudiness probably results from too much pectin — the same substance that turns fruit juice into jelly. Adding pectic enzyme to these wines solves the problem; it digests the pectin that keeps the wine from clearing.

• **Acid blend.** A commercial formula that provides nutrients essential for fermentation as well as the acid component that gives wines their character. Some older recipes use citrus fruit or juice for this purpose.

• **Campden tablets.** Tablets that release sulfur dioxide gas when dissolved. They are used to sanitize the winemaking equipment and to ensure that wild yeasts and bacteria that would interfere with the wine yeast are not present.

• **Tannin.** A component of the skins and stems of some fruits — especially red fruits, such as grapes, plums, apples, and elderberries — tannins give wine a certain zip by creating a hint of dryness in the mouth when you drink it. Equally important, tannins improve a wine's keeping qualities. Old-time winemakers used raisins or a tablespoon of strong tea.

WINEMAKING EQUIPMENT

The following tools are the basics of the winemaker's kit. The plastic fermentation vessel isn't essential, but it is our favorite modern convenience. It comes with its own fermentation lock, which makes the airtight secondary fermentation easier. Many other gadgets, from hydrometers (to measure the alcohol content of the wine) to corkers, are widely available in specialty stores and catalogs. They are not necessary but are fun to acquire if you are going to make more than a few trial batches.

- **2-gallon plastic bucket.** Even if you are making only 1 gallon of wine, you need a container large enough to allow room for active fermentation.
- Plastic cover for bucket.
- **Siphon tube.** About 4 to 6 feet of narrow clear-plastic tubing.

- **1-gallon glass jugs or plastic fermentation vessels.**
- **Fermentation lock.**
- **Wine bottles.** New or used.
- **Corks.** Must be purchased new each time.
- **Mallet.** For pounding corks.
- **Strainer.**

  Cleanliness in every aspect of the winemaking process is extremely important. Equipment must be sanitized. Bacteria that cause spoilage or turns wine to vinegar always lurk in the background. Sanitizing every piece of equipment greatly improves the taste and keeping quality of wine. You can also use a bleach solution (see Basic Homebrew, step 1, page 429) to sanitize equipment (which then must be rinsed well in hot water three times) or Campden tablets (see page 438).

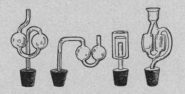

A collapsible plastic fermentation vessel (*left*) and fermentation locks top the list of useful winemaking equipment.

Basic Steps in Winemaking

Winemaking is an adventure to be enjoyed from the first crushing of the fruit to the last sip of your homemade vintage. Use fresh fruit and flavoring; read all the basic steps of the recipe before you begin.

Primary Fermentation

During the primary fermentation, the basic ingredients — fruit, juice, sweetener, yeast — are combined into must. The must sits and ferments vigorously as the yeast takes on oxygen and reproduces.

2–4 pounds fruit
   1 cup sugar
   1 gallon boiled water
      citric acid or acid blend
        (if specified in recipe)
   1 Campden tablet, crushed
   1 teaspoon yeast or yeast
      starter culture

Yeast Starter Culture (optional)

1½ cups tepid fruit juice
      (orange juice or juice from
      the fruit in the wine recipe)
   1 package (5–7 grams) wine
      yeast
   1 teaspoon yeast nutrient

1. Sanitize all equipment. Rinse thoroughly with hot tap water. You will need:

- 2–3-gallon plastic container (for primary fermenter)
- Plastic cover with fermentation lock
- Strainer (if specified in recipe)
- Siphon tube
- 1-gallon glass container

2. Crush the fruit; placing fruit in a straining bag makes the later removal of the pulp much easier. Place in a 2-gallon container.

3. Add sugar, water and acid, according to recipe directions.

4. Add the Campden tablet; let sit for 24 hours to work and dissipate before adding yeast.

5. Make yeast starter culture (optional). This helps the yeast develop more rapidly and efficiently (just as with breadmaking). In a small, sanitized container, combine the fruit juice, wine yeast, and yeast nutrient; cover and shake vigorously. Let stand at room temperature for 1 to 3 hours, until it gets bubbly.

6. Add yeast or yeast starter culture to the must. Cover; attach the fermentation lock.

7. Allow must to ferment according to time in recipe, usually 3 to 5 days; it should work actively and may develop a "cap" or layer of solids floating on top.

8. Punch a hole in the cap if recipe calls for it, taking care not to push the solids back down into the liquids.

9. Strain, if directed in recipe. Most wines do not need to be strained; the racking process usually separates the wine from its cap and lees (sediment).

10. Insert the siphon tube to 1 inch above sediment. Rack (siphon) wine into the clean gallon jar.

11. Discard lees and cap that are left behind in the fermentation vessel.

Secondary Fermentation

By the secondary fermentation, the liquid is now called wine; it is racked into a clean vessel and sealed with a fermentation lock. It will now sit again to ferment until clear, while the yeast converts the sugars to alcohol and carbon dioxide. For some wines, the racking and air-locked fermentation process needs to be repeated a third time.

1. Sanitize all equipment. Rinse thoroughly with hot tap water. You will need:

- 1-gallon plastic or glass container (for secondary fermenter)
- Fermentation lock
- Siphon tube

2. Fill the container almost to the rim. Attach fermentation lock to the spout of the plastic container or rubber stopper; this will allow carbon dioxide to escape without letting air in.

3. Let the wine sit to work until clear, anywhere from 2 weeks to several months. This fermentation will not be nearly as vigorous as the first one.

4. Rack again into a clean container, if necessary, for further clarification.

BIGGER BATCHES

If you increase the ingredients in your wine recipe to make a larger amount of wine — say, 5 gallons instead of 1 — you do not have to add additional starter culture. The yeast in your wine is alive and growing, and it will continue to grow in the must until it has converted the sugar to the maximum concentration of alcohol that a given yeast will tolerate. Once the alcohol content reaches that point, fermentation will stop and whatever sugar remains in the solution gives the wine its sweetness. Dry wines have little sugar remaining in them; sweet ones have more.

Bottling

You could store your wine in a jug, but regular wine bottles are much nicer and keep the wine better for longer.

1. Gather equipment and sanitizing materials:

- wine bottles
- siphon tube
- corks
- mallet, or corker (alternatively, country wines can be capped as described for home-brewing, page 433)

Sanitize wine bottles and the siphon tube. Rinse three times in hot tap water.

2. Using the siphon tube, rack wine into bottles.

3. Insert corks one-quarter of the way into bottles. Allow to sit for 1 or 2 weeks. If the corks pop, the wine may not be completely fermented, and it may need to go back into an airlocked container for another period of fermentation.

4. If the corks have not popped after the first 2 weeks, cover them with thick cardboard to prevent chipping the bottles, and use a mallet to tap them firmly into the bottles.

5. Cellar in a cool, dark place, usually at least 6 months, before sampling. Wine is best stored on its side, with the neck of the bottle slightly lower than the bottom; this keeps the cork moist and swollen, so that it prevents air from entering the bottle. Be sure to label each bottle before you store it.

high shoulders

sloping shoulders

German and Alsatian

Bordeaux

Burgundy

When selecting wine bottles, look for high-quality dark-green bottles. Thick glass and deep indentation denote quality.

OPTIMUM SERVING TEMPERATURES

TYPE OF WINE	TEMPERATURE
Robust red wines	60–65°F
Light red wines	55–60°F
Robust white wines	55–60°F
Light white wines	50–55°F

WINE WORDS

BODY. The texture and fullness of a wine, the way it feels in your mouth.

BOUQUET. The rich, complex smell that develops in wines as they age.

CAP. The somewhat firm layer of grapes or other solids that rise to the surface during the first fermentation.

CELLAR. To store wine while it ages, usually in a cool, dark place.

LEES. The sediment of solids and yeast cells in the fermentation vessel.

MEAD. Any wine whose primary fermenting sugar is honey.

MELOMEL. A wine sweetened with honey but flavored with fruit.

MUST. The first stage of wine, when there are large particles of fruit and yeast in the mixture.

NOSE. The aroma or bouquet of wine when it is swirled in a wineglass.

RACKING. The use of a siphon to transfer wine from a fermentation vessel to a clean container, leaving solids and sediments behind.

OLD-TIMER METHODS

A crock made airtight by a plate, a handful of dried beans to hold it down, and Great-Grandpa was in the winemaking business. He probably nicked a little of Great-Grandma's bread yeast to get the fermentation process started, then waited patiently for nature to take its course. If his wine was cloudy after repeated siphoning and straining over several months' time, he added a dried eggshell or two to clear the mixture. He siphoned the liquid into jugs or bottles a few days later, driving the cork home with a block of wood and a hammer.

Peach Wine

The peachy flavor of this wine makes it lovely for sipping or for making coolers. Use very ripe fruit; greener fruits have more pectin, making the wine harder to clear.

3–3½ pounds ripe peaches (about 10 peaches)
2 quarts water, boiled and cooled
3 pounds sugar
1 teaspoon acid blend
½ teaspoon tannin or 1 tablespoon strong tea
1 Campden tablet (optional)
1 package (5–7 grams) wine yeast
1 teaspoon yeast nutrient
1½ cups tepid orange juice
1–2 teaspoons pectic enzyme

1. Wash the peaches and slice them into a 2-gallon plastic container; toss in the pits too. Add the cooled water, in which you've dissolved 1½ pounds of the sugar, the acid blend, tannin, and Campden tablet, if desired. Wait 24 hours before proceeding.

2. Make a yeast starter culture by combining the wine yeast and yeast nutrient with the orange juice. Cover, shake vigorously, and let stand until bubbly, about 1 to 3 hours. Add to the must.

3. Add the pectic enzyme; ferment for 3 days.

4. Rack or strain the wine into another container. Discard the solids.

5. Boil the remaining sugar in water to cover; let cool and add it to the other ingredients with enough water to make 1 gallon. Ferment for 10 days, or until the energetic bubbling slows down. Rack the wine into a 1-gallon, airlocked fermentation vessel; ferment to completion.

6. Bottle, cork, and cellar your wine. Wait at least 3 months before serving.

Yield: 1 gallon

Grape Melomel

Known as "pyment," this fine country wine was popular in ancient Egypt, where wild grapes and honey abounded.

3 pounds light honey
3 pounds Concord grapes
1 Campden tablet (optional)
1 packet (5–7 grams) champagne yeast
1 teaspoon yeast nutrient
1½ cups tepid orange juice
1 teaspoon pectic enzyme

1. Remove impurities from the honey by boiling 1 part honey with 2 parts water in a large, nonreactive pot and skimming off the foam. Cool.

2. In a 2-gallon plastic container, crush the grapes.

3. Add the honey-and-water mixture. Add water to top off to 1 gallon, if necessary. Add a Campden tablet, if desired. Let the mixture stand for 24 hours, well covered, stirring two or three times in an up-and-down motion to introduce oxygen into the mixture.

4. Make a yeast starter culture by combining the

champagne yeast and yeast nutrient with the orange juice. Cover, shake vigorously, and let stand until bubbly, 1 to 3 hours. Add to the must. Add the pectic enzyme.

5. Ferment for 5 days and strain out the solids. Transfer the liquid to an airlocked vessel.

6. Rack after 2 weeks. When all fermentation has ceased, bottle, cork, and cellar the wine. Wait 6 months or more before opening.

Yield: About 1 gallon

Herb or Dried-Flower-Petal Wine

❧ ❧ ❧

Many delicious wines are made from herbs or flower petals. When using fresh herbs or petals, increase the amount to 1 to 4 pints, depending on your taste and how strongly flavored the herb or flower is.

2 *ounces dried herbs or flower petals*
1 *quart water*
1 *pound minced sultanas or other light raisins, or juice of 3½–4 pounds grapes*
1 *teaspoon citric acid or 2 teaspoons acid blend*

1 *teaspoon tannin*
1 *Campden tablet (optional)*
1 *package (5–7 grams) wine yeast*
1 *teaspoon yeast nutrient*
1½ *cups tepid orange juice*
2¼ *pounds sugar for dry wines, 2 ¾ for sweet*

1. Place the herbs in an enamel or glass saucepan with the water. Bring the mixture to a boil; simmer for 20 minutes.

2. Transfer to a 2-gallon plastic container. Add the raisins, citric acid, and tannin. Allow the mixture to cool; add a Campden tablet, if desired, and let the mixture sit, covered, for 24 hours.

3. Make a yeast starter culture by combining the wine yeast and yeast nutrient with the orange juice. Cover, shake vigorously, and let stand until bubbly (1 to 3 hours); add to the must.

4. Loosely cover the pulp and allow it to ferment for 3 days. Rack the liquid into a 1-gallon fermentation vessel that can be fitted with an airlock. Add the desired amount of sugar and water to make 1 gallon. Fit the airlock and let the wine ferment to completion, about 3 to 4 weeks.

5. Bottle, cork, and cellar the wine.

Yield: 1 gallon

Note: Whenever you use flowers in wine or cooking, make sure they come from edible plants. The oleander bloom is toxic, as are the flowers of lily of the valley. **If you aren't sure that it's edible, don't use it.**

·············

FLAVORINGS FOR HERB OR FLOWER WINE

·············

To get you started, here are some ingredients that may be used in the Herb or Dried-Flower-Petal Wine recipe on this page:

- white herbal wines
- agrimony
- bramble tips
- burnet
- coltsfoot
- coltsfoot flowers
- cowslip flowers
- dandelion
- elderflowers
- elecampane root
- lemon balm
- rosemary
- rose petals
- rhubarb

Easy-to-Make Mead

❧ ❧ ❧

This traditional recipe is simple, but the results are tasty.

1 gallon water
4 cups honey
3 nutmegs, chopped
1 packet champagne yeast

1. In a stockpot, boil water, honey, and nutmeg for 30 minutes, or until the white foam rises no more. Skim off foam as the mixture boils. Cool for 24 hours.

2. Strain hot wort into a 1-gallon fermenter. Cover and allow to cool to 75°F.

3. Add the yeast and ferment at ale temperature (60° to 70°F), until fermentation slows.

4. Rack into 1-gallon glass jugs, and age 6 months before bottling.

Yield: About 4 quarts

Elderflower Champagne

❧ ❧ ❧

Despite being called champagne, this recipe is for a soft drink. Children will enjoy

ABOUT MEAD

....

I like to think of mead as wine from a meadow. Indeed, both words derive from a Greek word for honey. In ancient times, long before refined sugars were available, honey was the primary sweetener for fermented beverages.

Honey wines are usually full-bodied and delicious, but it is necessary to boost the nutrients in the honey in order to ensure proper fermentation. Meads are often flavored with spices or fruits to counterbalance the sweetness of the honey, and citrus fruits or a commercial acid blend are usually added for tartness.

helping gather the flowers, brew the beverage, and drink the finished product. Put elderflower champagne on your calendar for June, in most areas, when hillsides light up with the flowers of elder shrubs.

3–4 quarts water
1 ounce ginger root, grated
1 quart elderflower heads
juice of 1 lemon
2 teaspoons white wine vinegar
scant 2 cups sugar
⅛ teaspoon granulated ale yeast
¼ cup lukewarm water

1. In a large pot, heat the water and ginger; simmer, uncovered, for 20 minutes. Remove from heat. Cool for 10 minutes.

2. Add the flowers, lemon juice, and vinegar. Cover and let sit for 12 hours.

3. Heat slightly to lukewarm only; add the sugar. Stir until sugar dissolves. Remove from heat and cover.

4. Pour yeast into a teacup with the lukewarm water; allow to rehydrate for about 5 minutes. Add yeast mixture to the pot of lukewarm liquid.

5. Strain into a 1-gallon glass jug. Pour into clean bottles and cap.

6. Check the carbonation after 48 hours; refrigerate when carbonation is sufficient (the beverage should be pleasantly bubbly, but should not gush out when opened).

Yield: Eleven 12-ounce bottles

CORDIALS

When we have dinner guests, we love the greetings, the cocktail hour, and the good food and table conversation, but perhaps the nicest part of the evening is retiring to comfy places in the living room with a decanter of homemade cordial and tiny crystal glasses. Liqueurs are easy to concoct, and they make splendid gifts.

Strawberry Liqueur

❧ ❧ ❧

This vivid cordial has a bright red color and the splendid taste of fresh strawberries. The citrus additions bring out the best of the berry flavor.

- 3 cups fresh strawberries, ripe and unblemished
- 1½ cups sugar
- 2 cups 100-proof vodka
- 1 cup water
- 1 teaspoon fresh-squeezed lemon juice
- 1 teaspoon orange zest
- ½ teaspoon lemon zest

1. Wash and stem the strawberries. In a bowl, crush the strawberries and sugar together. Let stand for about 1 hour.

2. Transfer mixture to a clean 2-quart container. Add the vodka, water, lemon juice, orange zest, and lemon zest. Cover and let stand in a cool, dark place for 2 days, shaking several times each day.

3. Press the mixture through a fine-mesh sieve; discard solids.

4. Transfer liqueur to a clean container. Cover and let stand for 1 week.

5. Rack or filter into a decorative bottle with a tight-fitting lid. Age for at least 1 month before serving.

Yield: Approximately 1 quart

Almond Liqueur

❧ ❧ ❧

Almonds impart a delicate, nutty taste to this liqueur. The glycerin, if you decide to use it, adds a slightly fuller body or "mouth feel" to the drink.

- 1 pound shelled almonds
- 1 cup 100-proof vodka
- 1 cup brandy
- 1 cup sugar
- ½ cup water
- 2 teaspoons pure vanilla extract
- 1 teaspoon glycerin (optional)
- caramel coloring (optional)

1. Using a food processor, coarsely chop almonds. Transfer to a clean 1-quart container; add the vodka and brandy. Cover and let stand in a cool, dark place for 1 month, shaking or stirring every couple of days. Use a coarse sieve or colander to strain out solids. Strain again, using a fine mesh strainer.

2. Transfer the liqueur to a clean jar. Cover and let stand for 2 days longer. Rack into a clean jar.

3. Make a simple syrup. In a medium-sized saucepan, bring sugar and water to a boil over medium-high heat, stirring constantly to prevent scorching. When the mixture is clear, remove from heat; let stand until just warm.

4. Add the syrup, vanilla, and glycerin, if desired, to the liqueur. Add caramel coloring, if desired, drop by drop, stirring after each addition, until desired color is achieved. This cordial may be served immediately, but it's better if it's aged for 1 to 2 months in a covered jar.

Yield: Approximately 1 quart

AGING CONTAINERS

- Widemouthed glass jars with lids (1- or 2-quart size)
- Wine or liquor bottles with tight-fitting lids
- Assorted decanters, cruets, and decorative bottles with lids or new corks

---

Cream Base

❧ ❧ ❧

Cream-based cordials are rich and luxurious. Use this base recipe as the springboard for creating your own recipes with liqueurs and flavoring agents, or try it in the Brandy Orange Cream below.

Simple Syrup

½ cup sugar
½ cup water

1. In a small saucepan, combine the sugar and water. Bring the mixture to a boil over medium-high heat, stirring constantly, until the sugar dissolves. Boil the mixture just until clear. Remove from heat.

1 teaspoon potassium sorbate (optional; see note)
1 cup Simple Syrup
1 can (14 ounces) sweetened condensed milk
1 can (12 ounces) evaporated milk
1 cup whipping cream

1. If you are using potassium sorbate, dissolve in heated Simple Syrup.

2. In a sterile 2-quart container, mix all ingredients together.

Yield: Approximately 1 quart

Note: Potassium sorbate will help stabilize the liqueur by keeping the cream from separating. It is available where winemaking supplies are sold or through mail-order catalogs.

Brandy Orange Cream

❧ ❧ ❧

A little like a sophisticated eggnog, this cordial will be a hit at your holiday party.

½ cup sugar
½ cup water
1 cup brandy
½ teaspoon pure vanilla extract
¼ teaspoon orange flavoring oil

2½ cups Cream Base
¼ teaspoon ground cinnamon
¼ teaspoon ground cloves

1. Make a simple syrup by bringing the sugar and water to a boil over medium-high heat, stirring constantly to prevent scorching. When clear, remove from heat and let stand until just warm.

2. Combine the syrup, brandy, and flavorings in a sterile 1-quart container. Add Cream Base, cinnamon, and cloves. Cover and shake until thoroughly mixed. Refrigerate immediately and age for 1 week before serving. Store for up to 1 month.

Yield: About 1 quart

LIQUEUR OR CORDIAL?

....

In Europe, alcoholic beverages with a high sugar content and flavoring agents consisting of herbs, nuts, fruits, spices, and creams are called liqueurs. In the United States, these beverages are usually called cordials.

The legal definition of a cordial varies somewhat according to location. In New York and New Jersey, for example, a cordial is defined as an alcoholic beverage containing at least 2.5 percent sugar.

CIDERMAKING

The heady fragrance of fresh sweet cider running from the press evokes mellow apples, fallen leaves, and the brisk country air cleared by early-morning frost. Make your cider outside, preferably on a cool, breezy day. Pour the washed apples into the hopper and grind them, cores, skin, and all. Catch the fresh cider in a clean container and you're on your way to a taste treat of your own making.

Making Apple Cider

Apple cider is the fresh, untreated juice of pressed, ground apples. To prevent contamination or spoilage, all materials and equipment used must be sanitized.

1. Apple harvest and "sweating." Harvest or buy mature, ripe, sound apples. Store the apples in a clean, odor-free area for a few days to several weeks, "sweating" them until they yield slightly to the pressure of a firm squeeze. Keep different varieties of apples separate if you want to make a balanced blend after pressing.

2. Selecting apples for blending. You can make a good blended cider from the following amounts of fruit in each category (see chart below):

• Neutral or low-acid base: 40 to 60 percent of the total apples. The bland, sweet juice will blend happily with sharper and more aromatic apples.
• Medium- to high-acid base: Tart apples can make up 10 to 20 percent of the total.
• Aromatic: 10 to 20 percent of fragrant apples will give your cider bouquet.
• Astringent (tannin): 5 to 20 percent of the total juice. Go easy with tannin; too much will sour your cider.

The chart will help you blend cider with your local apple varieties.

3. Milling or grinding. Just before grinding, wash the apples in a large tub of clear, cool water. Squirt a garden hose directly on them; use a high-pressure setting. Place the washed apples into the hopper of a grinder and reduce them to a fine, mushy pomace. If this is your first cidermaking experience, keep the apple varieties, the pomace, and the juice separate and blend to taste later. Press the pomace immediately.

COMMON APPLE VARIETIES FOR CIDERMAKING

....

HIGH-ACID APPLES
 Gravenstein
 Jonathan
 Northern Spy
 Pippin
 Rhode Island Greening
MEDIUM-ACID APPLES
 Baldwin
 Cortland
 Empire
 IdaRed
 McIntosh
 Winesap

LOW-ACID APPLES
 Delicious
 Golden Delicious
 Rome Beauty
AROMATIC APPLES
 Delicious
 Golden Delicious
 McIntosh
 Pippin
 Russet
ASTRINGENT (TANNIN) APPLES
 Crabapple
 Most wild apples

4. Pressing. Using a single-tub screw press or ratchet press, place the nylon press bag in the tub and fill it with apple pomace. Do not use galvanized or metal scoops, which react with the acid in the pomace. Tie or fold the bag closed. Slowly apply increasing pressure to the pulp. As the juice flows out, tighten the screw or pump the ratchet to bring the pressure up again.

step 4

Dump the washed apples into the hopper and grind them, cores, skin, and all.

Catch the fresh cider in a clean stainless steel, plastic, or unchipped enamel container. Do not allow the cider to come into contact with other metals. If you are planning to blend the juices from different varieties, keep the pressed-out juices separate.

5. Blending the juices. Take quart samples of each kind of juice. Use a measuring cup to figure exact amounts, and try to achieve a good balance of flavors. Taste-test for tannin (acid) content first. Add small amounts of high-tannin cider to the neutral or low-acid cider base until the level of astringency pleases you. Add aromatic juice, then cautiously blend in the high-acid juice until the cider is lively, fragrant, and well balanced. Repeat, using the same proportions to blend in greater quantities.

6. Filtering. To create faintly hazy, natural sweet cider, pass the juice through a light layer of cheesecloth or nylon mesh. This will remove impurities and flecks of pomace.

7. Storage. Refrigerate cider in clean glass or plastic jugs or in waxed cardboard containers. It will stay fresh-tasting for 2 to 4 weeks. After refrigeration, the preferred method of preserving cider is freezing. Allow 2 inches of headroom in containers for expansion during freezing. Defrost the cider for a day in the refrigerator before drinking it.

GETTING STARTED WITH APPLE CIDER

- GRINDER. Usually an oak frame set with stainless steel or aluminum cutters or rollers, with a hopper on top that can accommodate up to a bushel of fruit. Grinders are usually hand-powered.
- CIDER PRESS. A single-tub, hand-operated screw press or ratchet system.
- PRESSING BAGS AND CLOTHS. Most are made of nylon.
- FILTER CLOTH. A layer of cheesecloth or nylon filter cloth.
- PRIMARY CONTAINER. A bucket, bowl, or vat made of stainless steel, polyethylene plastic, glass, or unchipped enamel.
- PLASTIC SIPHON TUBING (OPTIONAL). A 4-foot section of ¼-inch plastic tubing will help you fill cider jugs and bottles.
- STORAGE CONTAINERS. Clean plastic or glass jugs with screw tops.

HOMEMADE ROOT BEER & SODA

An integral notion in American farming was pride in self-sufficiency, which extended to making and bottling refreshing beverages for year-round use. In addition to wine and beer, farm families brewed nonalcoholic drinks flavored with the roots, bark, sap, and leaves of wild plants.

Old-Fashioned Root Beer

The steps in making root beer were identical to those used in making beer, except that the bottling took place just after the yeast was added and the fermentation was stopped after a day or two by cooling the bottles. These root beers were not nonalcoholic, but the alcohol content was very low.

Bottling Soft Drinks

Bottle capper and bottle caps. Cappers range from inexpensive models to sturdy table models made of plastic or steel. Caps are sold by the gross and are inexpensive.

Unthreaded glass bottles. Eleven 12-ounce bottles will allow you to bottle 1 gallon of beverage. Use strong, heavy bottles. Another option is eight 16-ounce bail-top beer bottles, which do not need caps. Bail-top bottles require reusable rubber gaskets.

For bottling instructions, please see the instructions for bottling beer, page 433; omit steps 3 through 5.

Let the bottles sit to ferment at a room temperature of 62 to 77°F. Check the bottles after 48 hours and 72 hours. During this period, the yeast is consuming some of the sugar, and natural carbonation results. If the room is hot, check after 36 hours. After carbonation is complete, store bottles under refrigeration.

Use a "test bottle" to check carbonation. When the carbonation level is right (the beverage should be pleasantly bubbly, but should not gush out when opened), put all bottles into the refrigerator immediately. For better flavor, wait a couple of days before drinking. The flavor improves because the yeast settles out, allowing your flavoring agents to shine through.

SASSAFRAS ROOT CAUTION

....

Sassafras root has been used by American herbalists for many years. However, the U.S. Food and Drug Administration does not allow sassafras root to appear in processed food products such as bottled root beer for the retail market because of a finding that laboratory rats fed very large quantities of safrole (the active ingredient in sassafras) were more likely to develop cancer than rats in a control group.

Sassafras may, however, be sold as a raw food product, and herb suppliers usually have little bags of sassafras root bark for sale for teas. Herbalists point out that humans, unlike the laboratory rats, don't eat massive quantities of pure safrole.

If you prefer to avoid consumption of a beverage made from sassafras root, use bottled root beer extract.

Homemade Root Beer Extract

❧ ❧ ❧

This recipe makes 8 gallons of root beer in extract form. You can then prepare 1-gallon batches as you need them by adding water and yeast to the extract and bottling the mixture. Making an extract more concentrated than the one described below would be possible and would save space on your pantry shelf. Be well aware, however, of the dangers of scorching a highly concentrated sugary mixture. After trying this recipe, you may want to experiment with making extracts for other beverages.

For this recipe, you will need eight 1-quart canning jars with bands and lids. Clean and sanitize the canning jars, bands, and lids, and ensure that the rims of the jars are free from chips and cracks. You will also need a water-bath canner that will hold eight 1-quart jars. If all goes well and the dome lids seal properly, this extract can be stored almost indefinitely at room temperature.

1½ cups raisins, coarsely chopped
3 cups boiling water
2 gallons water
1½ ounces dried sassafras root bark (see box, page 449)
7½ pounds (15 cups) sugar

1. Put raisins into a large pan. Pour the 3 cups boiling water over them and cover, allowing the raisins to steep.

2. Meanwhile, place the 2 gallons water in a stockpot over medium heat; add sassafras root bark. As the water heats, stir in the sugar slowly. Simmer, uncovered, for about 40 minutes.

3. Remove from heat and strain raisin water into the bark mixture. Allow to sit, covered, for 30 minutes. You needn't worry about wild yeast infections; the canner will destroy any unwanted microbes.

4. Pour the extract into the canning jars. Using a clean cloth, wipe off any spills on the rims. Put bands and lids in place and process in a water-bath canner (page 384) for 15 minutes.

Yield: 8 quarts of extract (makes 8 gallons of root beer)

Root Beer

❧ ❧ ❧

Updated from a 1912 recipe from the Fleischmann Yeast Company, this recipe's pungent, spicy sweetness is refreshing.

2 ounces sassafras root (see box, page 449)
1 ounce dandelion root
2 ounces juniper berries, crushed
2 ounces wintergreen bark
1 ounce hops or ginger root
2 gallons boiling water
5 pounds sugar
2 gallons water
1 cake compressed yeast
¼ cup cool water

1. Wash sassafras and dandelion roots well in cold water. Place in a large stockpot. Add juniper berries, wintergreen bark, and hops. Pour the boiling water over root mixture; boil slowly for 20 minutes. Strain through a flannel bag.

2. Add the sugar and the remaining 2 gallons water. Let stand until lukewarm.

3. Dissolve the yeast in the ¼ cup water. Add to root mixture. Stir well. Let settle; strain again and bottle.

4. Cork tightly. Keep in a warm room for 5 to 6 hours, then store in a cool place. Put on ice as required for use.

Yield: About 4½ gallons

Sarsaparilla Soda

❧ ❧ ❧

Traditionally, sarsaparilla soda is made with sassafras root as well as sarsaparilla root. This raises the question of the best ratio of the two roots. Some believe that sarsaparilla is not flavorful enough on its own to make an excellent soft drink, but sassafras easily overpowers. Specifying the exact amount of each root is difficult, because strength and aroma vary from plant to plant. Start with the proportions suggested below and let your eyes, nose, and taste buds adjust from there.

4　quarts water
9　tablespoons chopped dried
　　sarsaparilla root (less if
　　your supply is pungent)
5　tablespoons (or more)
　　chopped dried sassafras
　　root (see box, page 449)
¼　cup raisins, coarsely
　　chopped
1¾　cups sugar
¼　cup lukewarm water
⅛　teaspoon granulated ale
　　yeast

1. In a large saucepan, heat 2 quarts of the water to a simmer. As the water heats, add the roots, raisins, and sugar. Simmer, uncovered, for about 25 minutes. The color of the liquid should be a very deep red, and the mixture should be quite aromatic. If the color is weak or the aroma is not very strong, add more sassafras and/or sarsaparilla.

2. Remove from heat, cover, and let cool. Pour 1 quart of the remaining water into a jug.

3. After the sarsaparilla mixture has cooled 30 minutes, pour it slowly into the jug, straining as you pour. Add as much of the remaining quart of water as needed to bring the liquid nearly to lukewarm temperature. Discard the roots and raisins.

4. Cap the jug and shake vigorously.

5. Put the lukewarm water into a teacup; add the yeast. Meanwhile, top off the jug, leaving about 2 inches of headroom, aiming for an overall lukewarm temperature. (If the liquid is hotter than lukewarm, allow it to cool with the cap on.) The liquid must be lukewarm when the yeast is added to avoid killing the yeast.

6. Add the yeast water to the jug; shake vigorously. Bottle and let sit at room temperature.

7. Check the carbonation after 48 hours and again after 72 hours (sooner if the air temperature is especially warm). When the carbonation is right (the beverage should be pleasantly bubbly but should not gush out when opened), refrigerate.

Yield: Eleven 12-ounce bottles

ABOUT SARSAPARILLA

....

For many of us, our introduction to the word "sarsaparilla" came from watching cowboy movies and seeing the hero walk into the saloon and ask for a tall "sa's'parilla." We didn't know what it was that our hero wanted, but we knew that he didn't drink beer or whiskey!

In the eastern United States, sarsaparilla sodas were always less common than drinks made from the more readily available sassafras, birch, and spruce trees. Arizona and New Mexico were closer to sources of sarsaparilla root (in Central America) than to plant products from the East Coast. Like sassafras, sarsaparilla was considered to be a general tonic, invigorating at once all the body's systems. Herbalists also prescribe sarsaparilla infusion for colds, fever, rheumatism, and gout and to aid in digestion.

FROM FIELD AND FOREST

Our love affair with country things really began when our children were young and we found ourselves in rural Connecticut surrounded by a 25-acre nature preserve. We enjoyed exploring the outdoors, and we decided to strive toward greater self-sufficiency. Our three children were willing students as we worked together to make maple syrup without burning the pot, cut honeycomb without getting too much all over the kitchen, and pick rose hips without getting pricked by the thorns. We gathered dandelions to add to our summer salads and tiny wild strawberries to pop into our mouths. We learned a lot, laughed a lot, and, most important, experienced the joy of instilling a love of country living in the next generation.

▪ ▪ ▪ ▪ ▪ ▪ ▪ ▪ ▪ ▪

Contributors to this chapter are Glenn Andrews, Joanne Barrett, Marjorie Page Blanchard, Charlene Braida, Kathleen Brown, Phyllis Hobson, Miriam Jacobs, Imogene McTague, and Noel Perrin.

MAKING MAPLE
SYRUP
....
MAKING HONEY
....
FROM THE WILD

MAKING MAPLE SYRUP

It is nearing the end of winter. After being cooped up by the woodstove all winter long, it is delightful to rouse yourself and bundle out into the maple grove to set the taps for the first flow of sap. Later, the smell of wood smoke mingled with the sweet boiling sap will fill you with happy expectation of pouring your own dark golden syrup over fresh hotcakes or fritters. After the last of the syrup is bottled, the maple grove will continue to give pleasure with leafy summer shade followed by a dazzle of orange foliage. Your homemade syrup will continue to bring the joy of natural sweetness to your table and those of your lucky friends.

The basic process of making maple syrup is extremely simple. All you do is boil maple sap down — way down. It takes about 9 gallons of sap to make 1 pint of syrup. If you intend to sell the syrup you make, there are some further steps, such as filtering it and grading it, but these are not necessary for making a delicious product for home use.

The equipment for making syrup can be as simple as two or three spouts, some large tin cans, and a kettle. Or it can be as complicated as a full-scale sugarhouse with evaporator, finishing rig, and holding tank. We'll take you through the steps to make only a couple of quarts of syrup; for this, you'll have to invest very little in equipment.

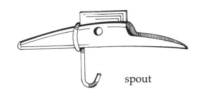

spout

Maple Trees

First of all, your part of the country has to have sunny days and freezing nights in early spring, or your maples won't yield any sap to mention. Where is the climate right? In virtually all of New England, in most of New York State, in western Pennsylvania, in a broad sweep of the Midwest, especially Ohio, Indiana, Michigan, and Wisconsin, and in parts of Canada.

MAPLE SYRUP SUPPLIES

- *Spouts. You'll need one to five spouts, which are usually available in hardware stores in sugaring country. They come in four or five varieties; I favor spouts that come with precast hooks, like those made by Warner and Soule, but any of the metal spouts on the market will work just fine.*

- *Drill. A hand drill with a ⁷⁄₁₆-inch bit is best, though you could probably get away with a ³⁄₈- or ½-inch bit.*

- *Containers. Sap buckets; plastic gallon jugs, such as those that cider and milk come in; or even coffee cans, though you would have to empty them rather often. A large plastic pail for gathering the sap is also helpful.*

- *Heat. Boiling the sap down requires plenty of heat for a long period of time. The simplest way is to put it into an ordinary cooking pot on the kitchen stove or woodstove, but the sticky steam may be a problem in the house. Most people prefer to do their boiling in the yard, on an outdoor fireplace.*

Next, you must be able to recognize a sugar maple. Most people who grew up in the city or suburbs cannot. (Our maple syrup expert, Noel Perrin, admits that years ago, he paid a neighbor's teenage son three dollars to walk through his newly bought woods with him, pointing out the sugar maples while he marked them with red paint.)

In the winter and spring, however, it can sometimes be hard to tell, so if you're going to tap maples in a woodlot, identify them the fall before you plan to start.

To help you identify sugar maples, you'll need to recognize two other maples. The Norway maple is usually planted in yards as an ornamental tree. It has the same classic maple leaf as a sugar maple — the leaf that is on the Canadian flag. But the leaf of the Norway is about twice as wide as a sugar maple leaf, and much larger altogether. And the bark has a fine, diamond-shaped pattern that sugar maples lack.

The other common variety is the red maple, also called swamp maple. In the fall, it's easy to tell one from a

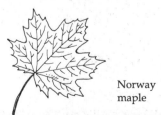

Norway maple

red maple

sugar maple: It is among the first of all trees to turn color, and it turns bright scarlet. A sugar maple will turn pink to yellow to orange several weeks later. Also, red maples have small saw-toothed leaves, while the edges of a sugar-maple leaf are smoothly curved.

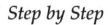

sugar maple

Step by Step

1. Tapping. The right day to start is a sunny one on which the temperature is at least 40°F after a freezing night. Depending on where you live, such days will begin to occur anywhere from late February to late March. If you tap too early, your spouts will dry up before the season is over. The tree usually closes off the flow of sap in 4 to 6 weeks. This becomes a problem if you tapped on a freak early warm day that is then followed by a couple of weeks of cold weather, during which no sap runs. On the other hand, if

you tap too late, you miss the early runs. A good rule of thumb is to tap about 1 month before the last snow usually goes. If your snow is usually all gone by April 10, you should tap around March 10.

You'll need one to five spouts, a drill, and a hammer. In each tree, drill a hole about 2½ inches deep and about 2 feet above the ground. Gently drive the spout in with the hammer — if it's a hookless spout, remember to put a hook on, facing outward, before you do. Use several light strokes to tap the spout in. If you drive it in too hard, you will split the bark, and a good deal of sap will leak out through the split and be lost. But if you drive it in too lightly, it may pull out under the weight of a full container.

drilling holes for the taps

If you're using tin cans to collect the sap, make a hole near the rim and hang one on the hook. If you're using gallon plastic jugs, hang it by a hole in the handle, because it is the strongest part of the jug.

If you get the jugs up by 10 o'clock or so, they should be full by suppertime. In fact, if it is a really good day, you may have to empty them twice. About then you'll wish you had a gathering pail — a cheap plastic bucket will work nicely.

collecting sap in a plastic jug

2. **Start boiling.** As soon as you've gathered, you can start boiling. A pot that will hold at least 2 gallons is best. Just pour the sap in and leave it to simmer all night. At this stage, no special precautions are necessary.

In the morning, if you're lucky, the volume will be down about half, and by afternoon it will be down to about a quarter. At this point, you will need to decide whether to keep adding fresh sap or to finish off each batch separately. Since 2 gallons of sap make less than 1 cup of maple syrup, it's a good idea to add fresh sap to make at least 1 pint at a time.

Once the sap has boiled down to about one-tenth of its original volume, you should start watching it carefully. Skim off the thick white foam from the top and discard it. The syrup may boil up abruptly if the heat is too high. Adding a single drop of cream will send it right back down and enable you to keep it boiling.

If you have a candy thermometer, use it to test whether the syrup is done. It should read 7 degrees above the boiling point of water — 219°F. Or dip an ordinary spatula into the boiling sap and hold it vertically over the pot. If the syrup is ready, a thin "apron" of maple will appear at the bottom of the spatula. If the sap is still too thin, it will simply drip back into the pot.

3. **Filtering.** All right, it aproned. You have syrup. Since this is for home use, you can immediately store it in a clean glass jar with an airtight lid. The next day, however, there will be unattractive sediment at the bottom of the jar. The old-timers just poured off the clear syrup from above it, but you may prefer to filter it. Commercial sugarers use a special felted-wool filter, but you can simply pour it through a paper coffee filter, or even a funnel lined with paper toweling.

Repeat these steps until the season ends or you get tired, whichever comes first. Small-scale sugaring is so slow a process that people often do tire of it while the sap is still running. In that case, simply pull out the spouts and stop.

4. **End of season.** But suppose you don't get tired. How will you know when to stop? Over several weeks, your cans or jugs fill more and more slowly. One afternoon, you'll go out to gather and find that they contain either nothing or just a little bit of pale yellow, or maybe bright yellow, sap. The tree is now ready to bud, and the sap is worthless for making syrup. Throw it out and call the season over.

If you kept going all season, you should have about 1 quart of syrup per tap.

GRADING SYRUP

....

Maple syrup is graded by its color, which is an accurate indicator of its flavor. A commercial grading set, consisting of little bottles of colored syrup for matching, can be purchased if you want to test your own.

Fancy — pale golden, delicately flavored

Grade A — light amber, rich but mild in flavor

Grade B — medium amber, robust flavor

Grade C —dark amber, strong in flavor

MAKING HONEY

We have friends who keep bees, and they find that the rewards are many: You have all the honey you need for cooking and table; you have a supply for wonderful gifts; your garden will be pollinated by your own bees, and will grow better for it; and you may eventually earn money for your honey. Best of all, you have a fascinating hobby.

What You Need to Get Started

Location. The location of your hives should be selected with care. Check your zoning laws to be sure that beekeeping is permitted. Choose a quiet, sunny, secluded spot. Bees follow a landing and takeoff pattern in front of the hive — be sure that their flight path doesn't cross a sidewalk, road, or walkway. If your hive will not be near a natural source of water, provide one.

Time. Beekeeping demands little time and fits in well with other weekend chores.

Timing. In northern states, it is important to get your bees early in the season. They must have time to build their combs and raise new bees, so that the hive population will be large at the time of the main honey flow. Arrange to have your bees delivered about when fruit trees bloom in your area.

Knowledge. A little bit of knowledge will get you started, and you'll know it all. Begin by following a good manual; from there, you can explore the subject in as much depth as you want.

Bees. Bees can be obtained in many ways. You can buy them from mail-order beekeepers. You may be able to purchase an established hive of bees from a nearby beekeeper. Or you might have a nearby beekeeper place a swarm of bees in a hive for you. If you buy an established hive of bees, ask for a certificate of inspection signed by the state apiary inspector stating that the hive is free from disease.

The most popular bees to start with are *Italian* bees. They are industrious, and a good queen will quickly build up a strong hive. Start with a 3-pound package of bees (about 10,000 bees).

Equipment. Bee equipment firms sell beginner's kits. If you buy one, make certain that you get all of the items in the equipment box before you begin setup.

drone bee

queen bee

worker bee

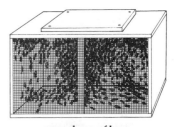

a package of bees

BEEKEEPING EQUIPMENT

Your basic start-up needs are listed below. The cost may vary, depending on your regional supplier.

- *A standard ten-frame hive with bottom board, entrance block, outside cover, inside cover, frames, and foundation.*

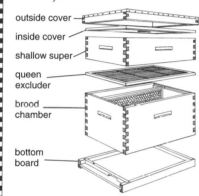

outside cover
inside cover
shallow super
queen excluder
brood chamber
bottom board

- *A 3-pound package of bees, with queen*
- *A bee veil to protect your face*
- *Gloves*
- *A bee smoker*
- *A hive tool for prying the hive and frames apart*
- *A feeder to feed the bees sugar syrup until they can support themselves with nectar*
- *A bee brush*
- *A beginner's book on beekeeping*

Step by Step

Keeping bees is not complicated, but upkeep is essential, and a manual on beekeeping will be a necessary companion to teach you the tricks as you go along. Here is a rundown of the basic steps that a novice beekeeper will need to learn.

1. Installing bees in the hive. A few general hints: Don't rush. Work calmly (it's so easy to tell someone else that). Install the bees in the evening. And remember that they aren't inclined to sting you after they are fed. This is the basic installation procedure:

Get your package of bees. As soon as you get your bees, feed them. They'll need to subsist on sugar water until they start producing honey. Install them as soon as possible; hold them no more than 2 or 3 days.

Prepare the hive. Before you get your bees, the hive should be assembled, painted, and in its permanent location. Remove five frames to make an open chamber. Fill the entrance feeder with syrup.

Get yourself ready. Light the smoker. Don your bee attire and net. Have a hive tool and bee brush handy.

Open the shipping cage. Pry off the cover of the cage with your hive tool. Remove the queen cage. Replace the cover.

Look at the queen cage. Get a good look at the queen, so you'll learn to recognize her. Place the queen in the hive.

Put the bees in the hive. Carefully replace the five frames. Working gently, so that you don't pinch the bees, replace cover.

Confine the bees to the hive. Plug the hive with the entrance feeder and a handful of grass. Check several days later. Replenish the syrup, if necessary.

After about a week. Using a little smoke, remove covers and check the queen.

2. **Maintaining the hive.** The hive should be maintained about once a week throughout the spring and summer to prevent feeding problems or preparations for swarming. The best time to work on the hive is on a sunny day. Here's what it takes:

Put on your protective clothing.

Light your smoker.

Open the hive. Pry it open, using the smoker to subdue the bees.

Check frames. Look for cell building and honey production.

Keep feeding. Replenish sugar syrup until bees have a large store of honey.

Check on queen. Look for eggs and larvae to be sure that the queen is producing.

Add to the hive. When the hive becomes full of honey and bees, add extra "stories," called "supers," to the hive.

Watch for swarming. Check the bottom edges of the hive for large queen cells, which may indicate that the hive intends to swarm.

There are several things you can do to reduce the chance of swarming: Provide room by adding supers before they are needed; requeen every year; and replace honeycombs in the brood chamber with empty cells for egg laying.

3. **Harvesting the honey.** The flowers have bloomed and fed the bees. The bees have painstakingly collected and stored the honey. You've placed super on super on super, and they are all filled. What next? It's time to enjoy the fruits of your bees' labors.

The honey in the frames is ready to be taken when the bees have capped it with a layer of wax. It has a finished, packaged look, and none of the honey will leak out.

Removing the super. You will take honey from the super on the top of the hive. Fit a bee escape into the inner cover and wait 24 hours, so that most of the bees will have time to find their way down into the hive. Take the super off the hive. Brush off any lingering bees near the hive entrance. Take the super inside to work on it.

Taking the comb honey. You're now ready to package your honey in one of its most delicious and natural states. You will need:

- a wire cake rack, 12 by 18 inches
- a baking pan, 12 by 18 inches or larger
- containers for the honey
- a knife for cutting the comb
- a spatula to move the chunks to the containers

Using the knife, cut the comb from the frame and place this large chunk on the rack. Cut smaller chunks to

---

HOW BEES MAKE HONEY AND WAX

....

The nectar that bees collect is generally one-half to three-fourths water. The bees evaporate most of the water from it by adding enzymes to it. These enzymes change the nectar into honey. The bees seal the honey into cells of the honeycomb.

Beeswax begins as a liquid exuded from the worker bee's abdomen. As it hardens into tiny wax scales, the worker bees use it to build honeycomb.

Beekeepers often provide their bees with honeycomb foundations made of sheets of beeswax. They fit into hive frames and become the base of the honeycomb. These foundations enable bees to speed up comb construction and provide a pattern for straight and easy-to-remove comb.

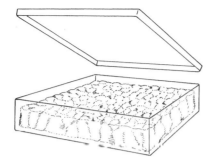

Cut comb honey can be conveniently packed in square plastic boxes, available from bee equipment suppliers.

fit your containers. Separate the chunks and let the honey drain from the sides. Then place them in the containers and seal.

Another method of packing cut comb honey is to cut the chunks and place them in widemouthed glass jars. Heat some honey to 150°F, let it cool, and fill the jar with it. This type of pack is commonly called chunk honey. The honey in these jars tends to crystallize quickly, even though you have heated it to prevent this.

Sharing with the bees. Remember that you should always leave enough honey in the hive to allow the bees to winter over comfortably. Requirements vary throughout the country, so precise amounts are difficult to state. Consult with a practiced beekeeper in your area if you aren't sure how much the bees will need.

THE FLAVORS OF HONEY

There are as many flavors of honey as there are flowers. In early summer, honey comes from wild berries and locust trees. The main honey flow in the northern part of the United States occurs during July, when beekeeper Joanne Barrett harvests a delicious light honey made from the blossoms of clover, alfalfa, and wildflowers. As the season progresses, honey made from the later flowers, goldenrod and aster, is darker in color and has a more pronounced flavor. Honey can be as dark as molasses, to which those who know buckwheat honey can attest. Its dark color and distinctive flavor cannot be mistaken. If one type of flower predominates in an area, the honey will have its flavor. You have probably seen orange blossom, tupelo, or sourwood honey for sale.

GETTING STUNG!

Here's the big question: Will I get stung? Yes.

You almost certainly will get stung from time to time, but after a while you'll begin to tolerate it pretty easily. Many stings can be avoided. Here are some tips:

- Work with the bees in good weather, when they are out of the hive and gathering nectar.
- Wear protective gear and light-colored clothing. Bees tend to crawl into dark places, so have tight wristbands on your sleeves and tuck the bottom of your trousers into your socks.
- Use a smoker when working with bees. Watch the reaction of the bees to the smoke. You will soon learn the minimum amount that can be used to achieve results.
- When you get stung, remove the stinger quickly by scraping it with the hive tool or your fingernail. Don't try to pull it out with your fingers. This will only force more venom into your body.
- Finally, make certain you are not allergic to bee stings. Most beekeepers eventually develop an immunity to stings. If you become allergic to bee stings and the effects of the sting grow worse each time, consult an allergy specialist. Such an allergy can become deadly.

FROM THE WILD

I find it thrilling to forage in the wild for food. It makes me feel hardy and linked to my forebears and my roots. For many people, foraging is limited to the occasional jaunt of berry picking. While this is a lovely thing to do, the wild offers many other natural foods that make delicious eating. Besides, searching for food provides a grand excuse to go for a ramble.

Dandelion Salad

❧ ❧ ❧

The dandelion in this salad is complemented by hard-cooked eggs, which add gentle flavor and texture, and a garlicky dressing that stands up to the strongly flavored greens.

½ pound dandelion leaves
2 hard-cooked eggs, sliced
5 tablespoons vegetable oil
1½ teaspoons vinegar
1 clove of garlic, finely chopped
½ teaspoon salt
⅛ teaspoon freshly ground black pepper

1. Clean the dandelion by removing the roots and shaking out all the sand. Discard brown or unsightly leaves. Cut remaining leaves into 3-inch segments. Rinse thoroughly in cold water four or five times; take care to wash away all sand. Drain first in a colander, then on paper towels. When the greens are dry, transfer them to a large bowl.

2. In a small bowl, combine eggs, oil, vinegar, garlic, salt, and pepper. Pour over greens; the volume of the greens will be reduced by about half after the liquid ingredients are added. Wait 5 to 10 minutes before serving, so that the flavors have a chance to mingle.

Yield: 2 servings

Flower Fritters

❧ ❧ ❧

Although daylilies aren't strictly wild plants, so many have escaped from gardens that they abound in fields and on roadsides, so they are fun to forage. Basil flower stalks, small clusters of sage leaves, and nasturtium blossoms may also be prepared this way.

⅔ cup flour
½ teaspoon salt, or more
½ teaspoon garlic powder
¼ teaspoon freshly ground black pepper
   pinch cayenne pepper (optional)
1 egg yolk
⅓–½ cup beer or nonalcoholic beer
   vegetable oil, for frying
12 daylily pods

ABOUT DANDELION GREENS

....

Dandelion greens are a welcome spring tonic and a delightfully fresh way to perk up early spring salads. Many early spring greens have a somewhat bitter taste — nature seems to know what our bodies need after their long winter's nap.

Pick dandelion greens as early as possible, before the flowers bloom. Pick them in a wild field that has not had any lawn or pesticide treatments. If you are introducing your family to wild greens, start slowly; add just a few leaves to a lettuce salad.

1. Line a plate with several paper towels. In a small bowl, combine the flour, salt to taste, garlic powder, black pepper, and cayenne, if desired. Add the egg yolk; mix until well blended.

2. Add beer, a little at a time, whisking constantly, until the mixture is the consistency of thick pancake batter.

3. Heat about 2 inches of oil in a deep skillet. Drop a little batter into the oil; when the batter starts to brown, reduce the heat to medium. Pick up a daylily by the stalk and swish it in the batter to coat the whole flower except the part you are holding.

4. Place the batter-covered stalks in the hot oil, a few at a time. Fry until brown on both sides, turning once (carefully, to avoid spattering the hot oil).

5. Transfer the fritters to the paper-towel-lined plate; serve immediately.

Yield: 12 fritters

Crystallized Violets

❧ ❧ ❧

Delicate violets make a lovely garnish for cakes and other desserts. You can purchase them at gourmet confectionery shops, but it's easy to make your own.

FIDDLEHEADS

....

If you know where to find them, fiddleheads are best picked fresh. Increasingly, though, they are available in specialty markets and at farm stands. Looking like fuzzy green spirals, they are the tightly furled fronds of the ostrich fern. They have a flavor somewhat reminiscent of asparagus, to which they are related.

Preparing fiddleheads takes a little care. They must be washed in at least three changes of water; swish the fiddleheads in the water, ruffling the curled fern with your fingers to release as much of the fuzzy brown coating as possible. It will come off in small particles, and be skimmed off the water and discarded. Blanch the cleaned fiddleheads for about 1 minute in boiling water; immediately refresh them under cool water, then drain thoroughly.

Blanched fiddleheads are delicious when sautéed with butter and garlic, cooked in an omelette, or added to pasta or soup. They may also be served with a light cream or cheese sauce.

10–20 violet flowers
powdered egg white
equivalent to half
of 1 egg white
superfine sugar

1. Gently wash the violet flowers. Dry on paper towels.

2. Prepare the egg white as package directs for beaten egg whites.

3. Using a fine brush, coat each flower with the egg white. Dust with sugar. Snip off the stems. Set aside in a warm place (but not in direct sunlight) until dry, usually about 24 hours.

4. Store the violets in a sealed jar between layers of paper. Keep the jar in a cool, dark location.

VIOLET SYRUP

....

My grandchildren love to sit on the lawn in early spring and help me pick violet blossoms to make this delicate, old-fashioned syrup. We love its perfumey fragrance when it's spooned over vanilla ice cream or added to plain tea or soda water.

Fill a glass jar with violet blossoms; cover with boiling water. Put on the lid; let steep for 24 hours. The next day, strain out the blossoms and measure the liquid. To each cup of liquid, add 1½ tablespoons of lemon juice and 2 cups of sugar. Bring to a boil, stirring, until sugar is dissolved. Bottle in a sterilized jar. How much does it make? Depends on how many flowers you pick!

Rose Hip Jam

❧ ❧ ❧

When we go to Cape Cod during Indian summer, we pick a large sack of rose hips from the wild beach roses. Back home, we make them into this jam that brings back memories of the shore.

4 cups rose hip pulp
5 cups sugar
1 tablespoon lemon juice

1. For the pulp, collect ripe rose hips, preferably just after the first frost. Wash and stem the hips. In a medium-sized saucepan, cover rose hips with water; simmer until soft, about 15 minutes. Run pulp through a food mill or sieve.

2. Combine pulp, sugar, and lemon juice. Bring to a boil; reduce heat. Simmer until it passes the jelly test (page 401). Ladle into hot jars.

3. Adjust lids and process in a boiling-water-bath canner (page 384) for 5 minutes.

Yield: 2–3 pints

ABOUT ROSE HIPS

....

In late fall, after the leaves have dropped, snip the partially dried orange-red rose hips from your rosebushes. Trim off and discard both ends; cut the remainder into thin slices. Dry the slices according to your favorite method.

DEHYDRATOR: Spread slices thinly over trays and dry at 110°F, stirring occasionally. Dry for 12 to 18 hours, or until crisp and hard.

OUTDOORS: Spread slices over trays in a thin layer and allow to dry in a well-ventilated, shady area for 2 or 3 days, until crisp and hard. Take trays inside at night.

OVEN OR HOMEMADE DRYER: Spread slices thinly over trays. Dry at 110°F, stirring occasionally, until crisp, about 18 to 24 hours.

Rose hips are a good winter source of vitamin C. Rose hip tea benefits from the addition of other herbs, such as lemon balm or mint. To make rose hip tea, cover ⅓ cup dried rose hips with 1 quart cold water. Cover and slowly bring to a boil. Simmer over low heat for 15 minutes. Strain liquid, mashing the hips with a fork to extract all the vitamin-rich juice. Drink hot or cold with a spoonful of lemon juice and honey or sugar.

Beach Plum Jelly

❧ ❧ ❧

Beach plums grow wild along the cooler areas of the Atlantic coast. Their cherry-sized fruit starts out green, turns red, and then ripens into a lovely purple-blue. They make a distinctive jelly.

2 quarts beach plums
water to cover
about 4 cups sugar

1. Wash plums and remove stems. Place in a large nonreactive pot with just enough water to cover. Cook, mashing with a potato masher, until very tender, about 15 minutes.

2. Strain liquid from mashed plums through a jelly bag. It should amount to 3 or 4 cups.

3. Return juice to pan and add 1 cup of sugar per cup of juice. Bring juice to a boil; simmer until it passes the jelly test (page 401), about 25 minutes. Ladle into sterilized jars. Adjust lids and process in a boiling-water-bath canner (page 384) for 5 minutes.

Yield: 3–4 cups

Note: Use ripe plums for the most part, but use some underripe ones as well to increase the pectin content.

If you want to make this into jam, remove pits from the plums after cooking. Measure juice and pulp together, and add an equal amount of sugar.

Gentled Nettles

❧ ❧ ❧

Nettles, which are esteemed for their healthful properties, have been eaten for centuries. Samuel Pepys had a recipe for a nettle pudding in his diary. This is a simpler preparation, moistened with a little cream, that makes a delightful side dish. Just be sure to handle the nettles with care until they are cooked!

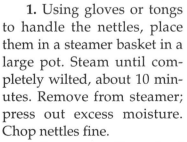

1½ pounds net-
      tles, washed
½   cup cream
⅛   teaspoon
      ground nutmeg
      salt and freshly
      ground black
      pepper

1. Using gloves or tongs to handle the nettles, place them in a steamer basket in a large pot. Steam until completely wilted, about 10 minutes. Remove from steamer; press out excess moisture. Chop nettles fine.

2. In a medium-sized skillet, cook nettles, cream, and nutmeg over medium heat until cream thickens and reduces, about 3 to 5 minutes. Season with salt and pepper to taste. Serve hot.

Yield: 4–6 servings

VARIATION: If you don't have enough nettles, make the dish with part spinach.

ABOUT NETTLES

· · · · · · · · · · · · · ·

If you've ever come into contact with stinging nettles, you will undoubtedly recall with dread the swift, nasty rash that they caused when they touched the skin. However, you might be very pleasantly surprised by how mellow and delicious nettles are when they are cooked. They completely lose their characteristic prickle and taste like a mild, tender spinach.

Wearing long sleeves and rubber kitchen or gardening gloves, pick whole nettles when they are very young, or pick just the small-leaved tops of more mature plants. Using tongs, swish the nettles in a bowl of cool water, and then drop them directly into the pot. Do *not* touch the nettles or try to chop them or work with them until they are cooked.

Creamed Morels

❧ ❧ ❧

Creamed morels call for candlelight, champagne, and a big budget — unless you find your own. But first you should find an expert in foraging for mushrooms: There are too many toxic varieties of wild mushrooms to take any chances with mistaken identity.

1 pound fresh morels,
    cleaned and trimmed
2 tablespoons butter
1 tablespoon olive oil
1 tablespoon flour
1 cup heavy cream
1 tablespoon Madeira
4 slices toast

1. Sauté the morels in the butter and oil over medium-low heat for 10 minutes, or until they are lightly browned.

2. Mix in the flour and stir for about 2 minutes, until it is well incorporated; add the cream and Madeira.

3. Cover and simmer over very low heat for 10 minutes. Serve on toast.

Yield: 4 servings

Gifts from Your Country Kitchen

I truly believe in the old saying that "the gift is in the giving," and to me, a gift that I have made myself is most special. Something given from my kitchen is also a gift to myself, because it provides me an opportunity to slow down a bit and take time to do what I so love. During the summer, I make extra jars of apple butter or blueberry jam to have on hand for hostess gifts throughout the year. At Christmastime, my favorite gifts are Sticky Buns (page 101), and even though it's the busiest of times, they are made and given with love. It's important to me that my gift conveys how I feel about the recipient, and gifts from my kitchen are my favorite way to show I care.

Contributors to this chapter are Joanne Barrett, Janet B. Chadwick, Maggie Oster, Annie Proulx, Nancy C. Ralston and Marynor Jordan, and Phyllis V. Shaudys.

SWEETS FOR
THE SWEET
......
FROM HEARTH
& HOME
......
PERFECT
PACKAGES

Herb and Flower Heart Wreath

❧ ❧ ❧

The instructions for this old-fashioned botanical wreath come from Cheryl Willson, a friend of Phyllis Shaudys. Like me, Phyllis loves to exchange recipes and craft techniques with her friends. This delicate wreath is simply made of artemisia wrapped on wire and decorated. If you want to invest in special wreath frames and a glue gun, craft stores supply them; they can be handy for making more elaborate wreaths.

wire, both heavy (14 gauge)
    and fine (26- or 30-gauge)
white florist tape
Silver King artemisia or
    wormwood, 1 large bunch
small dried flowers or seed
    heads, such as yarrow,
    ammobium, globe ama-
    ranth, rose hips, dried
    roses, strawflowers, or
    statice
narrow picot ribbon in the
    color of your choice, about
    1½ yards
tacky glue, or glue gun

1. Bend a piece of heavy wire, about 24 inches long, into a heart shape. Make a hanger by fastening a piece of fine wire at the top of the heart, making a little bridge across the cleft. This wire will later be concealed by flowers.

2. Wrap the heart in white florist tape to make it less slippery.

3. Attach overlapping clumps of artemisia or wormwood to the wire base by wrapping it spirally with fine wire.

4. Attach dried flowers, beginning at the center top and working down both sides. Add increasingly bushy pieces as you work down the sides to make the heart fuller at the bottom.

5. Wrap the heart with the picot ribbon. End with a bow at the base. On larger heart wreaths, let the long ends of the ribbons hang free. Tuck in sprigs of artemisia to fill in any sparse spots.

6. Using tacky glue, add more dried flowers and seed heads for color and accent. Using tiny ones at the top and larger ones toward the base works well; use more flowers at the bottom. Tacky glue or a glue gun makes this step easy.

Note: This design makes charming smaller (5- or 8-inch) wreaths for wedding or shower decorations, centerpieces, or candle rings. If you use dried flowers with candles, protect the flowers from flame with hurricane lamps, or do not light the candles.

VARIATIONS: For very small wreaths, you can use dried baby's breath instead of artemesia for the base. Though slower in the making, the resulting wreaths are delicate and pretty. You can also weave eucalyptus around your wire frame. Treated eucalyptus comes in several colors and makes a wreath both decorative and aromatic.

SWEETS FOR THE SWEET

Nothing makes a country cook prouder than presenting friends with gifts from his or her kitchen. These foods always seem to taste better than anything store-bought. Since almost everybody has a bit of a sweet tooth, sweet confections make welcome gifts. Take a sophisticated rum cake to a dinner party, or make a batch of Popcorn Balls or Pumpkin Pie–Spiced Nuts for your favorite nieces and nephews. Keep a few jars of chutney or cider jelly on hand for gifts for everyone from your next-door neighbor to your kids' favorite teacher. When you make the butter-crunch candy, be sure to set aside a wee stash to share with your best guy during a late-night movie!

Crunchy Topping

❧ ❧ ❧

This recipe makes enough topping for four yummy fruit crisps or cakes. It can be stored in the freezer in batches, ready for use at any time. Tuck a jar of it into a basket of apples or pears and add a gift tag with the simple instructions for baking a crisp. Better still, make the crisp with your friend while you visit!

    4   cups old-fashioned oats
    1   cup granola
    2   cups chopped walnuts or
        pecans
    2   cups brown sugar, firmly
        packed
    ½   cup all-purpose flour
    2   tablespoons ground
        cinnamon
    1   teaspoon ground nutmeg
    1½ cups (3 sticks) softened
        butter

1. In a large bowl, blend all ingredients until crumbly. Store in four resealable plastic bags in your freezer until ready to use.

2. Sprinkle the topping onto fruit crisp baked in an 8-inch square pan, onto applesauce cake, or muffins.

Yield: 4 crisps or cakes

Meet-Your-Maker Apricot-Date Chutney

❧ ❧ ❧

My longtime colleague Meredith Maker has given us this to-die-for chutney at Christmas for some years now. She was kind enough to part with the recipe so that I could share it with you.

    2   pounds dried apricots
    2½   cups pitted dates, chopped
    3   cups brown sugar, firmly
         packed
    3   cups golden raisins
    2   cups white wine vinegar
    2   cups water
    1   tablespoon mustard seed
    1   tablespoon salt
    2   teaspoons ground ginger
    1   teaspoon ground coriander
    ½   teaspoon ground nutmeg

1. Soak the apricots in enough water to cover for 30 minutes. Drain and put into a large saucepan. Add the dates, brown sugar, raisins, vinegar, water, mustard seed, salt, ginger, coriander, and nutmeg.

2. Simmer on low heat until thickened, stirring frequently to prevent sticking, 45 minutes to 1 hour.

3. Ladle hot chutney into sterilized ½-pint jars, leaving ¼ inch of headroom. Run a rubber spatula around the insides of the jars to release trapped air bubbles. Wipe the rims of the jars with a clean cloth. Place lids in position and tighten the screwbands. Process for 10 minutes in a boiling-water-bath canner (page 384).

Yield: About twelve ½-pint jars

Boiled Cider Jelly

❧ ❧ ❧

Cider carried one step further into concentrated jelly, this is a great favorite in Vermont. As a real novelty gift, I take cider jelly, Vermont cheese, and country-store common crackers to my relatives in Georgia and Texas. They enjoy the taste of New England and we all enjoy this jelly with fowl.

2 gallons fresh-pressed cider

1. Put the cider into a stainless steel or enamel pan and boil the liquid down rapidly until the jelly sheets. (page 401) The proper jelling point is reached when about seven volumes of fresh cider have been reduced to about one volume of jelly.

2. When the jelly sheets, (page 401) strain it quickly through cheesecloth into hot, sterilized jelly jars. Run a rubber spatula around the insides of the jars to release trapped air bubbles. Wipe the rims of the jars with a clean cloth. Place lids in position and tighten screwbands. Refrigerate or process in a boiling-water-bath canner (page 384) for 5 minutes.

Yield: About four ½-pint jars

Zucchini Walnut Spread

❧ ❧ ❧

Taking surplus zucchini as a gift has become the subject of much country humor. The laughter will turn to appreciative smiles, however, if you take it already prepared in this nutty cheese spread. An assortment of crackers, fruits, or vegetable sticks and strips are an ideal accompaniment for this "instant appetizer."

1   cup grated zucchini
⅛   teaspoon salt
1   cup grated sharp Cheddar cheese
¾   cup regular or low-calorie mayonnaise
½   cup chopped walnuts or pecans
1   teaspoon lemon juice

1. Place the zucchini in a colander or sieve, and sprinkle with the salt. Allow to drain for about 20 minutes. Using a spoon or your hands, press out as much liquid as you can from the zucchini.

2. In a small mixing bowl, combine well the zucchini, Cheddar, mayonnaise, walnuts, and lemon juice. Refrigerate for 2 or 3 hours. Pack into a simple crock or ramekin for gift-giving.

Yield: 2 cups

VARIATION: Add a few drops of Tabasco or hot pepper sauce for a nippier spread, or add a couple of teaspoons of sherry for a mellow, touch.

FROM-THE-HEART GIFT TAGS

Write out a recipe or suggestions for using your kitchen gift on card stock or heavy paper. Make a pretty gift card to tuck it into. Decorate cards with:

- *Drawings*
- *Photocopies of attractive woodcuts*
- *Glued-on dried flowers or herbs*
- *Cutouts from seed packets or catalogs*

Tie the card to your basket or bottle with ribbon, raffia, or rustic twine.

Apple Butterscotch Cake

❧ ❧ ❧

This terrific fall cake freezes well and makes a great housewarming gift. My friend Nicki Gillis gave me the cake and the recipe when our grandson, Henry, was born, and it has been a hit ever since.

2   cups all-purpose flour
1   teaspoon baking soda
2   teaspoons baking powder
1   teaspoon ground cinnamon
1   teaspoon salt
2   cups sugar
1   cup vegetable oil
2   eggs
2   teaspoons vanilla extract
1   cup chopped nuts
3   cups apples, peeled and chopped
11 ounces (2 cups) butterscotch chips

1. Preheat oven to 350°F. Grease and flour a 9- by 13-inch pan.

2. In a medium-sized bowl, sift together the flour, baking soda, baking powder, cinnamon, and salt.

3. In a large bowl, mix sugar, oil, eggs, and vanilla until well blended. Beat the dry ingredients into the wet, just until blended; stir in nuts and apples.

4. Sprinkle butterscotch chips on top of the batter. Bake for 1 hour to 1 hour 15 minutes, until a toothpick inserted in the center comes out clean. Cool 10 minutes in the pan; invert onto a rack to finish cooling.

Yield: 12 servings

Grennon Family Butter Crunch

❧ ❧ ❧

Maribeth Casey, a longtime family friend of Storey staff members, has been making this delicious candy for Christmas gifts since she was a child. She learned the technique from her mother, Betty Grennon. Now Maribeth makes the candy with her own children. Over the years, she has shared the tradition with several other Storey staffers. We certainly look forward to receiving our share each year.

1   pound whole almonds, finely chopped
24   ounces milk chocolate, broken into bits
3   cups sugar
1½   cups water
1   pound butter (do not substitute margarine), cut into cubes
1   teaspoon vanilla extract

1. Oil an 18- by 36-inch marble surface. Measure out 1 cup of chopped almonds; set aside. Line several baking sheets with wax paper.

2. Melt the chocolate, stirring constantly. Use a double boiler set over simmering water, or heat in a microwave oven on 100 percent power for about 2 minutes, stirring at 20-second intervals.

3. In a large, heavy saucepan, bring the sugar and water to a boil over high heat; cook, without stirring, until mixture reaches 310°F on a candy thermometer, about 20 minutes. Stirring constantly, add the butter a chunk or two at a time (it works best to have a helper to add the butter while you stir). Do not let the temperature of the mixture go below 290°F or above 300°F.

4. When all of the butter is incorporated, remove the pan from heat; stir in vanilla and the reserved 1 cup of almonds.

5. Working quickly, pour the mixture onto the oiled surface in a series of S patterns, using a long metal spatula or wooden spoon to spread the mixture out as evenly as you can (if possible, have your butter helper spread while you pour). Spread the mixture as thinly as possible.

6. Spread about half of the chocolate in a thin layer over the top of the candy. Sprinkle the surface with half of the almonds.

7. While the candy is still warm, cut it into thirds. Carefully flip each piece over; repeat the spreading and sprinkling processes with the remaining chocolate and almonds.

8. Transfer the candy to the prepared baking sheets and place in a cool spot to harden.

9. Break candy into pieces and store in airtight containers.

Yield: About 4 pounds

Note: If you don't have a marble surface or marble cutting board, the candy can be poured onto chilled, greased baking sheets.

VARIATION: Substitute dark chocolate for half of the milk chocolate.

Popcorn Balls

❀ ❀ ❀

These honey-molasses popcorn balls are not difficult to prepare, but I find it better to make them *for* children than *with* them. You will need a candy thermometer for this recipe, and you need to work quickly to make the balls before the syrup cools.

  8 cups popped popcorn (⅓
      cup before popping)
  ½ cup light molasses
  ½ cup honey
  ¾ cup (1½ sticks) butter
pinch of salt (optional)

1. Pop the popcorn; put into a large bowl.

2. In a small saucepan, cook molasses and honey until the thermometer reads 270°F (the hard-crack stage). Stir in the butter and the salt, if desired.

3. Slowly add the mixture to the popcorn, stirring with a wooden spoon until all the popcorn is coated. Butter your hands lightly and shape the popcorn into balls. Set the balls on wax paper and let them harden. To store them, wrap each ball in wax paper.

Yield: About 16 balls

VARIATION: For zesty popcorn balls, add ½ teaspoon Worcestershire sauce and cayenne pepper to taste with the salt.

CINDERELLA GRAHAMS

Plain graham crackers are transformed in minutes into glamorous cookies, fit to take to any fete. Preheat oven to 375°F. Lay 12 graham crackers on a jelly-roll pan. In a medium-sized saucepan, melt together ⅔ cup each butter (not margarine) and firmly packed brown sugar, stirring until sugar melts. Stir in 1 teaspoon cinnamon, and pour the mixture over the graham crackers, smoothing evenly. Sprinkle 1 cup of sliced almonds over the top. Bake for 10 to 12 minutes. Allow to cool completely before cutting into bars.

FROM HEARTH & HOME

Savory treats are always much appreciated. Almost any food, pickle, or preserve makes a suitable gift given the right occasion. Homemade mixes are thoughtful, and this bread mix will be sure to please seasoned cook and beginner alike. Spreadable cheeses, with flavors fresh from the garden, make for instant enjoyment.

Homemade Bread Mix

❧ ❧ ❧

Everybody loves a gift of homemade bread. This large recipe allows you to bake in bulk or to give some as a bread mix to friends who enjoy baking but never seem to find the time. Premeasure the mix into bags and attach a tag with easy instructions for mixing and baking (this page)

14 cups unbleached all-purpose white flour
2 tablespoons salt
1 cup sugar
1 cup vegetable shortening
4 cups stone-ground whole-wheat flour

1. Mix 3½ cups of the all-purpose flour, 1½ teaspoons of the salt, ¼ cup of the sugar, and ¼ cup of the shortening in a food processor bowl fitted with a steel chopping blade. Process until the dough is the consistency of cornmeal. Empty the mix into a very large bowl.

2. Repeat three times until all of the all-purpose flour is used up.

3. Add the remaining flour to the contents of the bowl. Mix thoroughly with a wire whisk to incorporate all the ingredients evenly.

4. Store in a large covered container at room temperature.

Yield: 6 loaves

Homemade Bread

❧ ❧ ❧

Get a jump-start on kneading by mixing dough in the food processor. You need a 9- by 5- inch bread pan for this recipe.

3⅓ cups Homemade Bread Mix (this page), stirred well before measuring (unless premeasured)
1 package quick-rising active dry yeast
¾–1 cup hot tap water (120–130°F)

1. Measure the well-stirred bread mix into a food processor bowl fitted with a steel chopping blade. Add the yeast.

2. With the processor running, slowly pour in ¾ cup of the hot tap water. The dough should form a ball that leaves the sides of the bowl. If it does not, add more water, a little at a time. The dough should feel sticky and try to stick to the sides of the bowl, but it should not actually stick. Let the ball of dough revolve around the bowl 45 times.

3. Turn the dough out onto a clean countertop. (If the dough sticks to the countertop, it's too wet; add more mix, 1 tablespoon at a time.) Knead the dough 20 times.

4. Form the dough into a ball. Spray a 9- by 5- by 3-inch bread pan with vegetable oil; insert dough. Turn once to coat the dough with the vegetable oil. Cover with oiled wax paper and a light towel. Place in a warm spot, free from drafts, and let rise for 10 minutes.

5. Punch down the dough. Turn it out onto a clean countertop and knead it 10 times.

6. Shape the dough into a loaf; return it to the pan. Cover again using the same wax paper. Let the dough rise again until it is slightly more than double, about 1 hour. It should come to just a little over the top of the bread pan.

7. Place the bread in a cold oven and set the oven temperature at 375°F. Bake for 30 to 35 minutes, or until the bread sounds hollow when tapped and is very brown.

8. Remove the bread from the oven and brush the top with melted butter, if desired.

9. Remove from the pan and cool on a wire rack.

Yield: 1 large loaf

Pumpkin Pie-Spiced Nuts

❧ ❧ ❧

Besides gift-giving, these nuts created by Judy Kehs of Cricket Hill Herb Farm in Rowley, Massachusetts, are always gobbled up at a party.

8 ounces dry-roasted peanuts
½ cup pecan halves
½ cup walnut halves
2 eggs, lightly beaten
2 teaspoons water
¾ cup sugar
1 tablespoon Pumpkin Pie Spice (page 310)
¾ teaspoon salt

1. Preheat oven to 300°F; lightly grease a baking sheet.

2. In a medium-sized bowl, combine the nuts. Mix together the eggs and water; toss with the nut mixture.

3. Combine the sugar, Pumpkin Pie Spice, and salt; toss with the nuts until they are well coated. Spread nuts in a single layer on the baking sheet.

4. Bake for 20 to 25 minutes. Break up any large clusters and allow to cool.

Yield: 4½ cups

Boursin with Fresh Herbs

❧ ❧ ❧

Phyllis Shaudys included this recipe from Lucinda Hutson's *Herb Garden Cookbook* in Storey's *Herbal Treasures,* and I'm so glad she did. We love making this for ourselves and for friends: It's less expensive than store-bought, and tastes better. For gifts, pack it into pretty 1-cup ramekins, or line ramekins with plastic wrap, fill them with the cheese, and chill overnight; unmold cheese and wrap in plastic wrap or foil. A baguette or a package of water biscuits makes a nice accompaniment.

1 pound farmer cheese, or ½ pound cottage cheese and ½ pound ricotta cheese
8 ounces cream cheese, softened
½ cup (1 stick) butter, softened
4 large cloves of garlic, minced
2 medium shallots, minced
½ cup finely minced fresh parsley, tightly packed
½ cup chopped fresh thyme (preferably part lemon thyme)
⅓ cup minced chives
1 teaspoon freshly ground black pepper
¼ teaspoon cayenne pepper salt (optional)

1. In a medium-sized bowl, blend the cheeses and butter. Add the garlic, shallots, parsley, thyme, chives, pepper, cayenne, and salt, if desired. Mix thoroughly and store in a crock or ramekins in the refrigerator.

Yield: About 4 cups

DANISH VARIATION: Replace thyme with ⅔ cup chopped fresh dill.

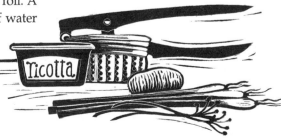

PERFECT PACKAGES

Just as "location, location, location" is the standard for real estate, "presentation, presentation, presentation" is the standard for fabulous gifts. A lovely basket, a special jar, a snippet of gold ribbon, or a cluster of lavender spikes or cinnamon sticks tucked into the bow transform an ordinary item into something thoughtful and pleasing that will show the recipient how much you care.

General Presentation Tips

Packaging. Boxes, baskets, cartons, tins, and sacks can all be used (or reused) for gifts. If you are reusing them, make sure they are scrupulously clean. You can spray or paint your containers, as well as add stencils, glitter, or glued-on fabric or lace. An attractive serving dish, teacup, baking pan, or platter makes special packaging that lives on as a gift after the food is long gone. Be on the lookout for attractive bottles and glasses that can be sanitized and reused for dressings, sauces, and syrups.

Padding. When you need to protect a fragile item, toss out the foam peanuts and get creative. We've used popped corn, puffed cereal, jelly beans, or real peanuts (in the shell) for edible packaging. Easter grass, straw, pine needles, or cedar chips are different and fun. Terrycloth, sponges, hot pads, and tea towels can also be used.

Wrapping. Some surprising things can be used to wrap presents. Try construction paper, collages cut from magazines, wallpaper samples, paper-lace doilies, foil, assorted tissue papers, and all sorts of paper sacks. For small gifts, a pretty handkerchief or napkin makes a soft wrapper. I like to wrap gifts in plain white butcher wrap or recycled brown bags, then let the children loose with rubber or potato stamps and markers for one-of-a-kind designs.

Tying. Tie up your packages in style. Make use of paper and cloth ribbon. Create a tailored look by tying the ends of ribbon and securing them to the package with a pretty decal or sticker. Raffia, twine, and yarn make rustic-looking ties, while foil, wired French silk ribbon, or shiny Mylar lends a little glitz. Narrow-topped bottles may be tied with a circlet of chive or grass stems.

Add-ons. Fresh or dried flowers, herbs, cinnamon sticks, candles, pinecones, wooden spoons, and specialty kitchen gadgets make great little extras on a package. And, of course, don't forget the finishing touch: personalized gift tags (page 467).

Packing Special Items

Bread. Wrap bread in plastic. Line a rectangular

GIFTS GALORE

While the gifts in this chapter are some of our favorites to give (or to receive), throughout this book you'll find recipes that are lovely for giving, such as homemade cheeses, syrup, and honey; pickles and preserves; fudge, truffles, cookies (in fact, almost all baked goods); jars of soup or chili; liqueurs; and scented vinegars and condiments. A gift of even the simplest food can be a boon for the busy family. No matter how much one loves to cook, not having to is a welcome break. But whenever you are making food for gifts, be sure to keep some for your own family to enjoy!

basket with a new kitchen towel. Set the bread in the basket and fold the towel over it. Tie colorful ribbon both ways around the basket, and top with a bow or a small sheaf of gold-sprayed or plain wheat or barley stalks.

Jams, jellies, or pickles. Decorate jars with bright fabric "caps" tied with ribbon. Set two jars snugly side by side in a napkin-lined basket, with another folded napkin between them. Use a frill of ribbon to tie a small pickle fork or jelly spoon to the handle of the basket.

Herbs or flowers. For a sweet little gift, make a small flower arrangement in a teacup, or buy a small herb pot and package it in a mug. Place the cup or mug on a sheet of cellophane and pull it up around the top of the cup. Tie so that the flower or herb is uncovered but surrounded by a frill of cellophane.

Cookies. Arrange attractively on a serving platter with a few seasonal candies added for color. Or tuck cookies into a nice pail, tin, or apothecary jar.

Cakes. For bases, use cardboard rounds from a baking supply store or a pizzeria, or cut them out of cardboard sheeting. Cover with foil, craft foam sheets, wrapping paper, and then plastic wrap, or use fabric and then clear Contact paper. For fancy cakes, glue lace around the edges of the cardboard. Deliver the cake under a protective dome, in a plastic cake carrier, or wrapped in plastic. A few toothpicks stuck into the top and sides will help keep the plastic from sticking to the frosting.

Bottled gifts. Sprigs of rosemary or other herbs look great on a bottle of dressing or condiment. A pound of coffee beans or a couple of tiny glasses make a nice addition to a gift of liqueur.

Casseroles. Entrée items may be packaged in reusable plastic containers or in serving dishes. Be sure to add reheating instructions, if necessary. By all means, let your friends know at the time you give the gift whether you expect them to return the dish.

Candy. Small wrapped candies look pretty in a mug or a snifter, or in special gold-flecked cellophane bags that can be obtained in party-goods stores. Use tiny fluted paper cups to hold truffles or large candies. When making fudge, line tin or cardboard gift boxes with wax paper or foil; spray with vegetable cooking spray. Let the fudge cool slightly and pour it directly into its box. When cool, score with a knife.

Potpourri. Sachets of potpourri can be made by cutting a circle of tulle and a layer of lace. Set the tulle on the lace, put potpourri in the center, and gather with a rubber band and then a bow. A small basket, bowl, or jar also makes a fine container for potpourri. Set a few perfect dried flowers or leaves on top of the potpourri as a finishing touch.

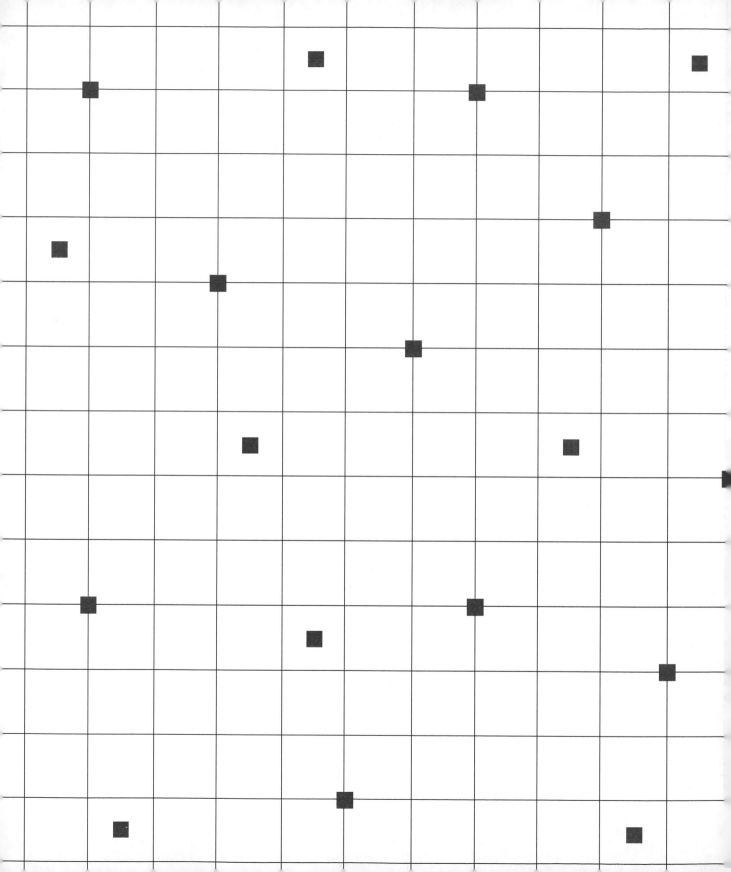

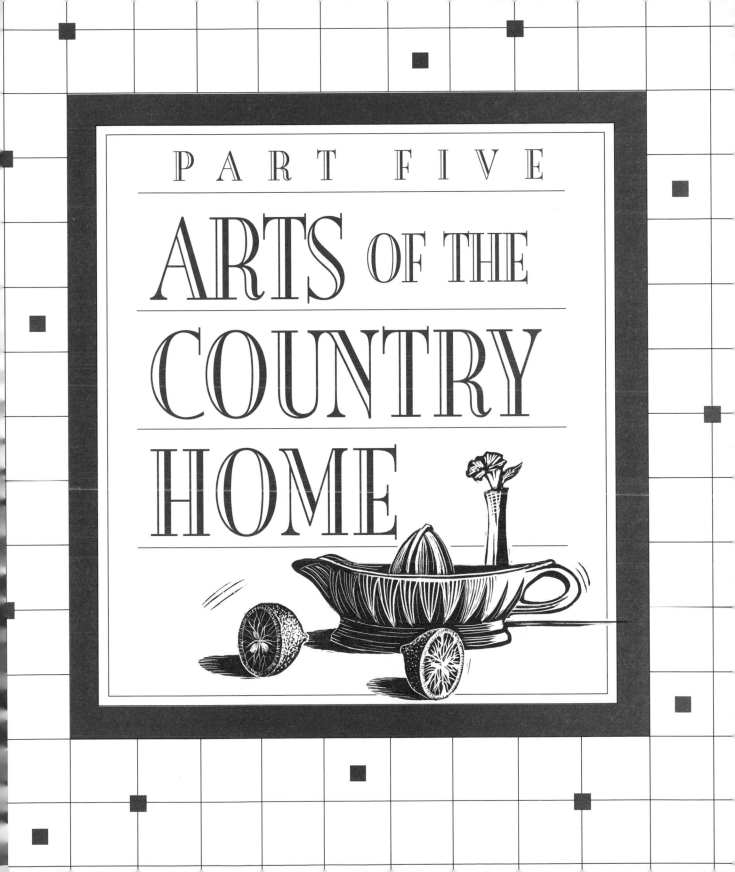

PART FIVE

ARTS OF THE COUNTRY HOME

HOME SWEET HOME

Isn't it remarkable how certain aromas can transport you instantly to a different place and time, evoking wonderful memories in the process? Every time I wash my cast-iron skillet with hot water and soap, I think of my Aunt Ina's Texas kitchen when I was a small child. She'd add a few drops of lemon oil to her dishwater to cut the grease. The smell of lavender wafting through an open window in summer reminds me of my longtime neighbor in New Jersey, Mrs. Blakey, who kept lavender wands in her closets and used a few drops of lavender oil on her dust cloth to freshen the entire house. Here are some ideas for cleaning and freshening your own home; they are as simple as they are inexpensive.

Contributors to this chapter are Patti Barrett,
Karyn Siegel-Maier, and Stephanie Tourles.

FRESH
FORMULAS
....
PAMPER
YOUR FAMILY

MARTHA'S FAVORITES

Top Brass Cleaner

❀ ❀ ❀

Sometimes the difference between plain and pizzazz is just a little shine. This cleaner will quickly and easily bring out the luster of anything brass around your home. With just a little elbow grease, it leaves candlesticks, pots, and doorknobs gleaming.

½ cup ammonia
½ cup Tide laundry detergent powder
1 quart hot water
steel wool pads

1. In a resealable plastic container, combine ammonia, laundry detergent, and water. Use steel wool pads to apply mixture to surface to be cleaned. Rub gently in a circular pattern. Rinse surface with clean water; dry well.

Yield: 1¼ quarts

Milk Bath

❀ ❀ ❀

This swirl of milk plus gentle oil will leave your skin with a moisturized glow when you step from the bath.

½ cup powdered whole milk
1 tablespoon apricot kernel, castor, jojoba, grapeseed, or first-quality vegetable oil
8 drops essential oil of chamomile, jasmine, lavender, rosemary, or marjoram

1. Pour powdered milk and oil together directly under running bathwater. Add essential oil immediately before stepping into the tub. Swish water with hands to mix. Relax!

Yield: 1 treatment

FRAGRANT IDEAS

Bowls or baskets of potpourri are lovely for scenting a room, but there are other simple ways to add a note of fragrance to your home. Below are a few of our favorites.

- Hang dried herbs or herbal sachets in closets and storage rooms to deter insects. Some good choices are mint, rosemary, lavender, sage, lemongrass, and citronella.

- Place a few drops of essential oil on the outside of the filter bag of your vacuum cleaner.

- If you have a fireplace, place two or three drops of essential oil of choice on the wood before lighting.

- Add a few drops of a citrus essential oil to your humidifier. Do not do this if you have asthma, however.

- Add one or two drops of essential oil to a ring that is made to fit a standard lightbulb. The heat of the bulb will release the fragrance when the lamp is in use. Do not allow the essential oil to come into direct contact with the bulb; it can cause the bulb to explode and possibly result in a fire.

- Do not use oils directly on drapes or other fabrics; they can leave spots and stains.

FRESH FORMULAS

If you have become accustomed to the odors of commercial cleansers, bleaches, and artificial perfumes, the natural scents of plant oils and essences will be a refreshing surprise. They smell cleaner, with hints of uplifting fragrance — lavender, citrus, pine, rosemary — that will remind you of sunshine in a garden. The best part: They also do the job!

Citrus-Sweet Dishwashing Blend

❊ ❊ ❊

A fruit-scented blend may not have you actually looking forward to washing dishes, but it will make this daily chore more agreeable.

    liquid castile soap
15 drops lemon or
    lemongrass
    essential oil
 6 drops lavender
    essential oil
 5 drops bergamot
    essential oil

1. Fill a clean 22-ounce plastic squirt bottle with castile soap (dilute according to directions if using concen-

trate). Add the essential oils. Shake the bottle before each use. Add 1 to 2 tablespoons of the liquid to dishwater; wash dishes as usual.
Yield: 22 ounces

Herbal-Clean Dishwashing Blend

❊ ❊ ❊

This soap is like aromatherapy in a dishpan! Lavender is the classic "washing" herb.

    liquid castile soap
10 drops lavender
    essential oil
 8 drops rose-
    mary
    essential oil
 4 drops eucalyptus
    essential oil

1. Fill a clean 22-ounce plastic squirt bottle with castile soap (dilute according to directions if using concentrate). Add the essential oils. Shake the bottle before each use. Add 1 to 2 tablespoons of the liquid to dishwater; wash dishes as usual.
Yield: 22 ounces

Kitchen-Fresh Cleaner

❊ ❊ ❊

Give your kitchen a wholesome and natural cleansing with this formula. It is gentle but effective on cabinets and counters; it even wipes away the greasy film that builds up on the surfaces of appliances.

 2 cups water
¼ cup oil-based soap
    (Murphy's is good)
10 drops rosemary, lavender,
    or citrus essential oil

1. In a large plastic spray bottle, combine all ingredients. Shake well before each use. Spray generously on the surface and wipe with a damp cloth or sponge. Wipe dry with a cloth or towel.
Yield: 2½ cups

VARIATION: For use on wooden cabinets, make a blend with a subtle woodsy scent. Replace the rosemary, lavender, or citrus oil with 15 to 20 drops of cedar or patchouli essential oil.

NOT JUST A PRETTY SCENT!

Essential oils give the cleaning products on page 478 a very appealing fragrance, but that's not all they do. Citrus oils are natural degreasers. Many herbs have antibacterial, antiviral, and/or antifungal properties; some even have all three.

- *Antibacterial. Bay leaf, citronella, ginger, lemongrass, orange, pine, spearmint, wintergreen*

- *Antiviral. Cinnamon, clove*

- *Antifungal. Sage, patchouli, savory*

- *All three. Eucalyptus, lavender, lemon, sandalwood, tea tree, thyme.*

Kitchen Tips and Stain Removal Tricks

Some of these tips and tricks have been passed down through generations of homemakers. Why? Because they really work!

KITCHEN TIPS

To rid the cutting board of garlic or onion smell, cut a lime or lemon in half and rub the surface with the cut side of the fruit. Or make a paste with baking soda and water and apply generously. Rinse off.

If you break an egg on the floor, sprinkle it heavily with salt; after 5 to 15 minutes, sweep the dried egg into the dustpan.

Remove paint spots from glass with hot vinegar.

To remove streaks on stainless steel, rub with baby oil.

Wash your sponge in the dishwasher. The hot water will make it look better and will kill the bacteria that grow in a moist environment.

Remove food easily by sprinkling the broiler pan, while hot, with dry laundry detergent. Cover with a damp paper towel and let the burned food set until loosened, 10 to 30 minutes. The food will come off easily.

Loosen grime on the can opener by brushing with an old toothbrush.

Clean the outside of cast-iron pans with a commercial oven cleaner. Let set for 2 hours; remove the accumulated black stains with vinegar. After cleaning the pan, warm it and wipe around the inside with wax paper to prevent rusting. Or rub a little oil on the inside of the pan to keep it seasoned.

To clean copper pots, fill a spray bottle with vinegar and add 3 tablespoons salt. Spray solution liberally on the pot; let set for a while, then rub clean. A combination of toothpaste and Worcestershire sauce, or ketchup, can also be used to polish copper pots. Rub these substances on the copper, wipe off and tarnish will disappear.

Get rid of bad kitchen odors by grinding a lemon half or orange rinds in the garbage disposal.

Brush salad oil on the grater before using for a fast cleanup. Use a toothbrush to brush lemon rind, cheese, onion, or whatever out of the grater before washing. In addition, before you grate lemon or orange peel, wrap your grater with plastic wrap; when you're done, just lift the wrap and the fine peel will lift off, too.

Scour out coffee and tea stains from plastic cups and dishes with baking soda.

To clean a thermos bottle, fill it with warm water and a few tablespoons of baking soda, then rinse. To maximize your chances of removing a stain, be sure to get to it as soon as possible.

To remove wax coated on candleholders, place the holders in the freezer for an hour or so. The wax will peel right off.

If your drinking glasses stick together, fill the top glass with cold water and set the bottom one in hot water to separate them.

STAIN REMOVAL TRICKS

Alcoholic beverages. Rinse in clear, warm water until the stain is gone, then wash as usual. Nonwashable fabrics can be rinsed with clear warm water and dried well.

Blood. Cover the stain with meat tenderizer. Apply warm water to make a paste and wait 20 minutes; sponge with cool water or soak in a presoak product. Use diluted chlorine bleach, if needed.

Chocolate. Sponge stain with cold water; do not use hot water. Add 2 tablespoons borax to 2 cups warm water and sponge the stain with the solution. Rinse well and wash as usual.

Coffee. Sponge fresh stains with borax solution (see "Chocolate"). Rinse and wash as usual. Sponge old stains with cold water, then rub well with glycerin. Let sit for 30 minutes, then rinse with warm water.

Egg. Soak fabric in a warm paste of biodegradable laundry detergent and water. Wash.

Grass stains. Wash in hot suds, or sponge with denatured alcohol before washing.

Ink. Saturate with hair spray and rub with a clean cloth; the ink should disappear. Repeat if stain stays. For polyester fabrics, rub with alcohol.

Mildew. Wash new stains in hot, soapy water as soon as possible. For bad stains on whites, soak in a solution of one part chlorine bleach to eight parts cold water for 10 minutes. Wring out the water and place the stained item in a weak solution of cold water and white vinegar to neutralize the bleaching action. Rinse well and wash.

Milk. Rinse in cool water, then wash with cold liquid-detergent suds.

Perspiration. Remove stains in any of these ways: Sponge with a weak solution of white vinegar and water; sponge with lemon juice; dissolve two aspirins in water and soak the article; or soak the article in a mild solution of liquid detergent.

Red wine. Sprinkle spill immediately with lots of salt. Dunk article into cold water and rub the stain out before washing.

❀❀❀

PAMPER YOUR FAMILY

These gentle natural grooming products are good for your body and for your spirit. Mixing your own potions offers the luxury of the spa with a large dash of old-fashioned and customized TLC.

Herbal Bath Salts

❀ ❀ ❀

Sink into a skin-softening tub and bathe away your calluses and your cares. This blend is good for all skin types and is especially soothing to itchy skin and rashes.

½ cup baking soda
½ cup sea salt
15 drops essential oil of clary sage, marjoram, lavender, or sandalwood

1. Mix the soda and salt; pour the mixture directly under running bathwater. Add the essential oil immediately before stepping into the tub. Swish water with your hands to mix.

Yield: 1 treatment

Hand and Nail Butter

❀ ❀ ❀

Prevent dry, chapped hands and cuticles with this special butter. Pack it in a pretty little jar for your own use or for a thoughtful gift.

2 tablespoons beeswax
2 tablespoons cocoa butter
4 tablespoons grapeseed or jojoba oil
1 tablespoon anhydrous lanolin
20 drops essential oil of rose, carrot seed, rosemary, geranium, or sandalwood (optional)

1. In a small saucepan or double boiler, warm the beeswax, cocoa butter, grapeseed oil, and lanolin until wax is melted. Remove from heat and stir occasionally until almost cool. Add essential oil, if desired, stir again, and store.

To use: Use approximately 1 teaspoon per application as a hand cream or nail and cuticle treatment. Use on hands and feet as an overnight intensive treatment; wear gloves or socks. Use within 3 to 4 months. Requires no refrigeration.

Nail and cuticle treatment: Soak clean hands in a bowl of warm water for 2 minutes. Pat dry. Apply a dab of "butter" onto the base of each nail and massage in. Using a small piece of cotton flannel, gently push cuticles back and lightly buff nails with the cloth. Leaves fingertips soft and smooth.

Naturally shiny nail treatment: Apply the "butter" as for the nail and cuticle treatment above, but use a nail buffer to gently polish nails to a soft sheen. Don't rub so hard that your nails burn. Use once a week.

Yield: Approximately 27 treatments

Note: This recipe may harden in cold weather but will soften on contact with your skin.

CRAFTS FROM YOUR COUNTRY HOME

My home is always a hub of activity, whether we're cooking, eating, relaxing, or crafting. When my 5-year-old grandsons Matthew and Tommy visit, we gather natural materials from around the farm, spread them out at the kitchen counter, and make treats for family and friends. Last summer, we wound the wild vines that had taken over the arborvitae into wreaths for the boys' moms. Last fall, we cooked special suet treats for the birds that winter over, and we stitched dream pillows filled with fresh and dried rosemary that they "monogrammed" with markers for their teachers. My grandkids' creativity and energy are boundless, and they love making something out of nothing.

Contributors to this chapter are Gayle O'Donnell, Betty Oppenheimer, Althea L. Sexton, and Judy Tuttle.

DECORATIVE
DESIGNS
....
NATURAL
CREATIONS
....
GOOD SCENTS

Bouquet Garni Wreath

❀ ❀ ❀

A culinary herb wreath in the kitchen offers stimulation for the senses! It looks great, smells wonderful, and provides freshly dried herbs for all of your culinary creations. Fresh herbs tucked into a raffia braid will dry in place, and they can be replenished, so your wreath will last for years as a kitchen staple.

Materials

> thick hank of raffia, about 2 inches in diameter, plus several spare strands
> one 9-inch wreath frame
> fresh sage, thyme, oregano, tarragon, or other culinary herbs
> dried chili peppers, for color (optional)
> gift card or label (optional)

Equipment

> yarn needle
> scissors

1. Tie one end of the raffia hank firmly with a spare length of raffia.

2. Divide the hank into three sections. Braid it, working it into a curve to match the wire wreath.

3. Tie off the other end.

4. Working with the frame side up, sew the braid to the frame, using the needle threaded with the spare length of raffia. Keep the stitches hidden on the back of the wreath, and bend the braid so that it lies flat.

5. When the frame is completely covered, lay the end of the braid over the start and bind tightly with raffia, giving the illusion of a bow. Trim the ends so that they are even.

6. Tie the herbs into small bundles and tuck them into the braid, distributing them evenly around the wreath. The bundles can be of single herbs or a combination of bouquet garni herbs, which can then be used to season a classic dish. Insert chili peppers, if desired.

7. For hanging the wreath, make a raffia loop and connect it to the braid and/or wire frame at the top.

8. If you are giving the wreath to someone who is unfamiliar with whole-leaf herbs, make a card or label that identifies what is in the wreath, and what each herb looks like.

VARIATION: Straw Wreath Using a premade straw wreath, attach the herb bundles directly into the straw, or loosely wire them around the wreath using green florist's wire. If you arrange the bundles so that they are all inserted with the leaves facing upward, you will always be able to pull up to remove a bundle of herbs and push down to insert a new one.

DECORATIVE DESIGNS

It's so satisfying to decorate your home with items that you have crafted yourself. Whether a simple candleholder, hot pads stenciled with a pineapple (the symbol of hospitality), or a recyclable bag for groceries or many other uses, these projects provide simple pleasure, both in the making and in the using.

Stenciled and Quilted Hot Pad

❀ ❀ ❀

A hot pad makes a fine project for a beginner at stenciling; it is easy enough that even an older child can do it, with a little guidance in cutting and sewing.

Materials

½ yard of unpatterned 36- or 45-inch-wide cotton fabric
¼ yard 36-inch-wide quilt batting (100 percent cotton is preferable for heat resistance)
thread to match fabric
2 9- by 12-inch stencil sheets
fabric paint (2 colors)
scrap paper
contrasting single-fold bias tape, matched to one of the paint colors

Equipment

cutting tool
stencil brush
paint tray
straight pins
quilting hoop
compass and pencil

1. Cut the fabric into eight 9-inch squares; you will need two squares per pad. Cut the batting into four squares that are ¼ inch smaller all around than the cloth squares; use one square per hot pad. Use the template (p. 485) to cut two stencils, one for each color.

2. Make a mark at the center of each hot pad. Using the registration marks as guides, center the stencil on the fabric. Stencil the leaves onto each of the hot pads.

To stencil, stir or shake the paint, if necessary, and dribble a small amount onto a paint tray or a piece of glass or plastic. Using a circular motion, rub the stencil brush in the paint until a little bit has been taken up.

On a piece of scrap paper, scrub the paint out of the brush until only a faint shade shows. For best results, stenciling must be done with a very dry brush. Holding the brush upright, apply the paint through the stencil by using a circular scrubbing motion, as though you were scribbling on a piece of paper. It is usually best to work from the edge of the stencil toward the center of the area being printed. When you have scrubbed over all of the open areas of your design, remove the stencil and observe how much paint has been applied.

Before printing the next stencil, you may need to add more paint to the brush. Again, don't take up too much, and always wipe the brush on scrap paper before applying your design. If your print smears or runs in any way, you have probably used too much paint.

3. Align the pineapple center cut-out on the pad; stencil. To change colors, clean your brush well and allow it to dry completely before attempting to print with the next color. Using wet brushes will probably result in blurring. It helps to have several brushes on hand.

4. To set the design, follow the directions included with your paint.

5. To quilt the pad, place the stenciled square face down on a table. On top of it, place the batting and then an unstenciled fabric square for backing. Using straight pins, pin the pieces in place. Place the pad in a quilting hoop. To avoid ending up with a knot on the back of the hot pad, bring a needle and knotted thread up to the front from the batting layer. Taking ⅛-inch stitches, stitch just outside the pineapple. Stitch around the design through all the layers of material; pull the stitches tight as you work. When you need to tie off the thread, fold the backing aside so you can tie off in the batting layer. Quilt all four hot pads.

6. With a compass, mark a very light circle around the outside of each pineapple; quilt around the circles.

7. Finish the edges by covering them with bias tape, following the directions on the package. Make hanging loops by using short lengths of tape.

Votive Candleholder

❀ ❀ ❀

Turn a simple tin can into a pretty votive candleholder by using our bird template or a favorite design of your own. The candlelight sparkles through the pattern of holes. Place several votives together and surround with greenery for a charming holiday centerpiece.

Materials

design template
1 8-ounce tin can
floral clay
1 votive candle
holly

Equipment

washable marker
nail punch
glue

1. Trace the desired pattern and cut it out. If you have a larger can, enlarge your pattern by photocopying or by applying a grid.

2. Using a washable marker, trace the outline of the pattern onto the side of the can.

3. Fill the can with water and freeze. The ice will support the can while you punch your design.

4. Using the nail punch, make the holes for the design. Allow ice to melt.

5. Press a small wad of floral clay into the bottom of the candleholder. Firmly

push a votive candle into the clay.

6. Glue a few sprigs of holly on for decoration. You can change the look by painting the can to match your decor.

DECORATIVE DESIGN TEMPLATES

....

Use these patterns to make templates for these craft projects. Enlarge them on graph paper or by using the zoom feature of a copy machine. When the patterns are the desired size, trace and cut them.

registration marks

1 square = 1 inch

pineapple stencil

template for candleholder pattern

Grocery Bag

❀ ❀ ❀

A basic rectangular tote bag, this project features a double-reinforced bottom. The reinforcement piece has triangular extensions that mimic the triangular folds of a real paper grocery sack. The bag also has a strap webbing handle that extends all the way around the bottom of the bag, allowing you to carry extra-heavy groceries without tearing the seams. Make this tote out of a heavier fabric, such as canvas, heavy twill, or pack cloth. A vinyl laminate is also a good choice for the bottom reinforcement, since it is water repellent.

1½ yards fabric, 60 inches wide (2 yards, if narrower)
2½ yards cotton or nylon strap webbing, 1 inch wide
2 yards double-fold bias binding, ½ inch wide
sewing thread

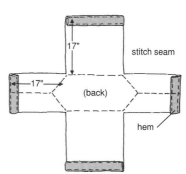

Cutting Layout

1. Following the measures and layout shown, draw the pieces on the fabric and cut out.

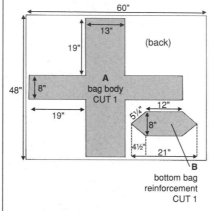

Reinforcing the Bottom

2. Turn under and press ½ inch on all sides of the bottom reinforcement piece. Pin the wrong side of the bottom reinforcement to the right side of the bag body, so that it fits just inside the seam allowances of the bag body. Stitch ⅛ inch from the edge all the way around the reinforcement piece.

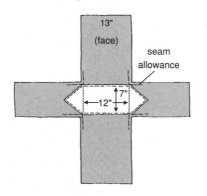

Hemming the Top Edges

3. Turn under 1 inch twice on all of the hemlines of the bag body (the four cross ends). Measure each side of the cross shape to be sure they are all 17 inches. Stitch all four hems ⅛ inch in from the inner turned edge, and again at ⅛ inch in from the outer edge. With chalk, mark a straight line from both triangle points of the bottom reinforcement piece out to the center of the narrower bag sides. Stitch along these lines through the hems. This stitch line will help the bag fold just like a grocery bag.

Attaching the Strap Webbing

4. With chalk, mark lines 2 inches in from the edges of the wider bag sides, turning the full length (across the bottom reinforcement). Starting at the center of the cross (the bottom of the bag), pin the strap webbing to these lines, so that its outer edge runs along the chalk lines. When you reach the hems, make 12-inch loops for the handles, being sure not to twist the webbing. Once you return to the starting point, turn under 1 inch of webbing and pin it over the raw edge.

5. Stitch ⅛ inch in from both edges of the webbing. Make box stitches where the ends of the webbing meet and at the four points where the straps meet the hems.

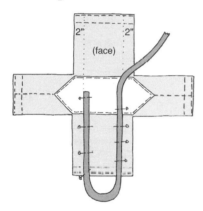

Stitching and Binding the Side Seams

6. Pin together adjacent sides of the cross, right sides together, to form four side seams. Using a ½-inch seam allowance, sew all four seams so that the top hems meet at the top of the bag, and the bottom corners meet at the finished edges of the bottom reinforcement. Trim the seam allowances to ¼ inch.

7. Cut four 18-inch pieces of bias binding. On one end of each piece, with right sides together, stitch across the

binding ¼ inch in from the end. Turn the press right side out. Place one of these finished binding ends around the top edge of one of the four side seam allowances, and stitch the rest of the binding close to the edge, over the seam allowance.

Before reaching the bottom corner, turn under the binding edge and backstitch it in place. Repeat for the three other side seams.

8. Decorate the bag with painted motifs, embroidery, or different trims and bric-a-brac, as desired.

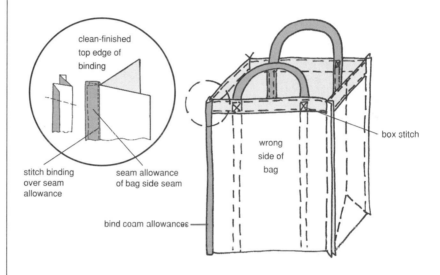

clean-finished top edge of binding

stitch binding over seam allowance

seam allowance of bag side seam

bind coam allowances

box stitch

wrong side of bag

DOUBLE-FOLD BIAS BINDING

Both edges of double-fold bias binding are folded under, and then the bias tape is folded a second time. To apply, place the off-center fold over the edge of the fabric with the slightly wider side of the bias tape placed against the back of the fabric. Then topstitch close to the edges of the bias tape through all layers with the fabric face up. Placing the slightly wider side of the bias tape in back ensures that you will catch it in the stitch line. Some people find it helpful to use a zipper foot when topstitching the binding, to hold it in place. If you don't want a topstitched look, you can apply double-fold bias tape using any of the three methods described for attaching single-fold binding.

NATURAL CREATIONS

Give a rustic look to your creations by making simple but elegant crafts made with natural "finds." Grapevine wreaths are charmingly simple but may be adorned with bows or ornaments. Pinecones lend themselves to many uses, including cute little bird feeders to brighten winter for our feathered friends.

Feed-the-Birds Ornaments

❋ ❋ ❋

My grandchildren love to make these bird-feeding ornaments with me. I love to watch them learn about nature as they supply the needs of our feathered friends. When melting suet, use a very low flame; it can ignite if it gets too hot. Allow it to cool slightly before handling.

Materials

¾–1 cup suet per medium to
   large cone
   pinecones
   florist wire, 18 gauge
¾–1 cup birdseed per medium
   to large cone:
   clean cotton rags, torn into
   1-inch strips

Equipment

cupcake pan with paper
   liners

1. In a saucepan, melt half of the suet. Pour into paper-lined cupcake pan, filling cups three-quarters of the way.

2. Let suet cool slightly, about 20 minutes. Press the wide end of a pinecone into each suet cup. Let cool completely.

3. Remove pinecones from the pan. They should have a base of suet attached. Peel off the paper cups and discard.

4. Wrap florist wire around the top of each pinecone and form a loop for hanging.

5. Melt the remaining suet just until soft; dip pinecones into it. You may need to let cool and dip again to get a good coverage. Sprinkle birdseed onto the cooling suet.

6. Tie the cotton rags into a bow at the top of each pinecone.

7. Hang outside for the birds to enjoy.

VARIATIONS: Add raisins or dried currants to melted suet before pouring into cupcake pan. You can also press raisins or dried currants into the pinecones before dipping them into melted suet.

Tear rag strips into 3-inch lengths. Fold in half and dip folds into melted suet, then press into pinecones. This will provide nesting materials for birds.

Cut oranges, grapefruit, or coconuts in half. Scoop out the fruit. Pour melted suet into the empty fruit cups. Use florist wire to hang these suet holders from tree branches for a colorful wintertime treat.

Round and Full Grapevine Wreath

❋ ❋ ❋

A grapevine wreath has a warm rustic look on its own, but it also makes an excellent base for all kinds of craft projects. You can add natural finds, such as rose hips, pinecones, seed pods, wheat or grasses, shells, or dried flowers. Or you can make more elaborate wreaths using materials from your local craft shop — ribbons, silk flowers, miniature birds or bird nests, dried fruit slices, and the like.

Materials

medium-weight branched
   vines, 6 feet or more in
   length
a few long single vines

Equipment

clippers

1. Select two or three vines, line up the butt ends together, and hold them all in one bundle. Bring the ends around to form a circle and make a simple overhand knot. Check your measurement. Pull the knot tighter if you want a smaller wreath; let it out a little if it is not big enough.

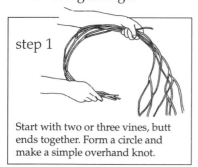

Start with two or three vines, butt ends together. Form a circle and make a simple overhand knot.

2. Coil the remaining vines around the circle that you just made, grasping the vine circle in one hand as you coil with the other. (Think of the way you would coil up a length of hose or rope.) Tuck the ends of the vines into the circle. For more fullness, add another few vines. Insert the thicker ends into the circle and coil these vines around in the same manner as before, tucking in the ends.

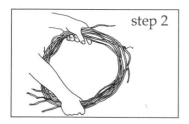

step 2

3. Select a long single length of vine. This piece will be wrapped in and out around the circle, holding the vines and any loose ends together. Tuck the thicker end of this vine into a snug spot on the circle. Grasp the other end and begin to thread it in and out, all around the circle of vines. Go around the wreath as many times as you can with that piece. When it runs out, tuck the end into a snug spot on the wreath.

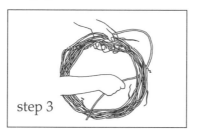

step 3

No one can tell you when your wreath is done; it's all up to you. A wreath is finished when its appearance is pleasing to you. Give it a final trim, as much or as little as you like.

A second method to achieve a full wreath is by piling up single rings or circles of vine. This is a method to use when the vines are not long enough to coil or when you accumulate a lot of short, leftover pieces. As long as the vine is long enough to make a knot, you can make a single ring, and a pile of rings will make a wreath.

For a 12-inch-diameter wreath, make several circles 10 to 12 inches across. Staggering the knot areas, pile the circles up until the wreath appears to be the thickness you want. Then continue as in step 3 by selecting a long single vine to wrap around all of the rings. Simply insert the end into the pile of rings you are holding and thread this piece in and out, going completely around a few times until all rings and ends are secured.

VARIATIONS: Vary the tension of the wrapping vine in step 2. By wrapping it loosely, your wreath will look lighter and fuller. By pulling it tighter, the wreath will be more compact.

Vary the thickness or appearance of the wrapping vine. A thicker vine wrapped around a circle of many thin vines will emphasize the pattern of the wrap. A stripped green vine, a shaggy brown vine, or a silver-gray vine can also be wrapped around the vine circle to emphasize different colors and textures.

GOOD SCENTS

Appeal to several senses at once with these lovely projects that smell as good as they look. They add gentle natural fragrance all over the house. Imagine a jar of roses on the dressing table, a basket of spicy potpourri in the den, or sweet sachets in your bureau drawer, your linen closet, and tucked in among the pillows of the guest-room bed.

Small Rose Jar

❀ ❀ ❀

This is potpourri at its simple best. Orrisroot is the rhizome or rootstock of a fragrant European iris. It adds little fragrance on its own, but it absorbs and holds other fragrances, making potpourri last longer. It is available ground or chopped; either variety works well in potpourri, but the ground root may leave a slightly chalky residue.

    2   cups dried rose petals and
        leaves
    ½   teaspoon allspice
    ½   teaspoon cinnamon
    ½   teaspoon cloves
    1½ teaspoons orrisroot
    6   drops rose oil

1. In a quart jar, combine the rose petals, allspice, cinnamon, and cloves. Add orris-root and drop the oil onto it. Shake well. Age for 3 weeks, shaking daily. This light rose fragrance keeps well.

Sachets

❀ ❀ ❀

Once you begin to create sachets, you'll probably find them irresistible. You'll need to purchase a few ingredients, such as the fixative and the oils, but the rest can be grown in your garden. The sachet bags can be made from scrap material and kept ready to use whenever the spirit moves you to make a batch of potpourri.

Materials

    6- by 6-inch piece of tightly
        woven fabric (cotton or
        silk is classic)
    sewing thread
    ribbon
    rubber band (optional)

1. Turn under (toward wrong side) and press ½ inch, then 1 inch of fabric on one edge, and stitch ⅛ inch in from the bottom of the hem (or ⅞ inch down from top edge of hem).

2. With right sides facing, fold the bag in half and stitch ½ inch from the edge on the two raw edges.

3. Clip the raw-edged corner and turn the bag right side out. Press seams.

Filling the Sachets

4. If your fabric is not tightly woven, make inner bags, using a double layer of cheesecloth, but make the bags 2 by 2½ inches.

5. Fill the sachet bags (or inner bags) about two-thirds full with sachet mix, about 3 tablespoons.

6. Tie a ribbon around the bag, around the seam line from the hem. If the ribbon is not secure enough, fasten the bag closed with a rubber band first, then hide the rubber band with the ribbon.

Sachet Filling

Keep this filling in a glass jar with an airtight lid and age it for several weeks before using. This allows the oils and fixative to blend, and all the scents to meld. The recipe makes a large batch — enough to fill several dozen sachets. You can store any extra filling in the jar for later use.

Forever Lavender Sachet

16 ounces lavender flowers
8 ounces dried orange peel
4 ounces gum benzoin
2 ounces sweet woodruff
½ ounce oakmoss
½ ounce thyme
  several handfuls of other herbs and flowers (such as peppermint, violets, rose geranium petals)
¼ ounce cloves and anise, combined

1. Combine all of the ingredients and shake occasionally during aging.

Apple Spice Potpourri

❀ ❀ ❀

Bright rose hips give a pretty red color to this spicy potpourri, which smells heavenly as soon as it is blended, yet improves with age. This is a "from-scratch" recipe, with instructions for drying your own apple slices; save time by purchasing dried slices and adding the nutmeg along with the rose hips and allspice oil.

2 teaspoons grated nutmeg
1 large apple, quartered, cored, and thinly sliced
1 cup 1-inch cinnamon sticks
7 drops cinnamon oil
½ cup red rose hips
12 drops allspice apple-spice oil

1. Sprinkle 1 teaspoon of the grated nutmeg onto a metal pie pan. Lay the apple slices onto the prepared pie pan; sprinkle with remaining nutmeg and dry until leathery. Any source of low, dry heat will do: the top of a radiator, or a gas or electric oven that has been preheated to 150°F, then had the heat turned off. In about 2 days, the slices will be dry and you can proceed.

2. Put the cinnamon sticks into a quart jar; drop 7 drops of cinnamon oil onto it. Allow to rest for a day.

3. Add the rose hips to the jar. Drop in the apple-spice oil; shake well. Add the apple slices and shake well.

Pinecone Fire Starters

❀ ❀ ❀

Used as kindling over newspaper in the fireplace or woodstove — or to start the campfire in the woods — these fragrant fire starters are made from recycled materials. Pair them with a decoupaged matchbox filled with long wooden matches and present them as a housewarming gift for friends who have their first fireplace.

Materials

sawdust or dried herbs (rosemary or lavender works well)
cardboard egg carton
pinecones
paraffin, old candle ends, or candle wax with 135°–145°F melting point
ribbon (optional)

Equipment

kraft paper or sheets of unprinted scrap paper
double boiler
mixing bowl or coffee can
knife or scissors

1. Cover your work area with kraft or other unprinted paper.

2. Put some sawdust or dried herbs into each compartment of the egg carton and work a pinecone firmly into the sawdust.

3. Melt the paraffin in the top of a double boiler. Use a bowl that you intend for wax and craft projects, now and forever, or set a coffee can on a metal trivet in a large pot of water for a makeshift double boiler.

4. Pour paraffin over each pinecone in the egg carton, coating thoroughly. As it cools, if the wax level drops, add more melted paraffin.

5. When the paraffin has cooled, cut the egg carton into individual fire starters. Tie a ribbon around each pinecone, if desired.

YOUR KITCHEN GARDEN

Our garden, visible from several rooms in the house, is a happy place. It's near the old apple tree, which the grandkids love to climb, and my clothesline, where I hang linens to dry in the sun. Everyone enjoys spending time in the garden, whether planting tiny onion sets or spring peas, digging for potatoes as if they were buried treasure, or weeding wide rows of beets. We love to harvest fresh lettuce and spinach for our dinner salads or watch Sara and Miranda pull long, golden carrots from the earth. Each summer, our grandchildren have a "Who can find the biggest onion?" contest — the winner keeps the prize onion. Our garden changes with the seasons, filling our days with pleasurable work and our table with the freshest foods.

■ ■ ■ ■ ■ ■ ■

Contributors to this chapter are Patti Barrett, Sheryl L. Felty, and Edward C. Smith.

HOW DOES YOUR GARDEN GROW?
....
VEGETABLES IN CONTAINERS
....
GROW HERBS FOR THE KITCHEN

A word about W-O-R-D

Our good friend Ed Smith, a champion Vermont gardener, has developed a gardening concept that he calls *W-O-R-D*. His labors are streamlined with this system and his results are very impressive

Wide planting rows. Most gardens have almost as much walking space as they have room for growing vegetables. Wide rows maximize vegetable space and minimize wasted space.

Organic methods. Using organic compost and mulches to improve and protect your soil will provide the best balance of soil nutrients. You will have the satisfaction of a vibrant, vigorous garden, the most healthful, natural foods, and an earth-friendly environment.

Raised beds. Raised beds are not just easier on your back. They also inhibit weed growth and provide a place that will never be compacted by being walked on. Raised beds may be freeform, made by heaping up the topsoil from neighboring walkways, or enclosed in wooden supports.

Deep soil. Depth is more important than the width of the beds. Raised beds provide for an extra-deep layer of prepared topsoil, so that roots have plenty of room to dig down and spread out. Your plants will be healthier and far more drought-resistant.

ABOUT SOIL-SAMPLING SAVVY

Soil test kits measure chemical reactions, which is one reason they are so reliable. Just as with any other scientific research, however, the accuracy of the test depends on the quality of the soil sample you collect and prepare. This is true whether you do your own soil tests or have them done by a laboratory.

- Follow the test lab or test kit manufacturer's instructions carefully.
- Take samples before working the soil.
- Home tests involve mixing water with soil samples. It's best to use distilled water; it is pH neutral and does not contain dissolved minerals that might affect test results.
- Use a clean trowel and wear clean latex gloves to avoid contaminating the samples.
- You'll get more accurate results, particularly on nitrogen tests, if the soil is warm and neither very dry nor very wet.
- Don't take samples from areas that you know to be atypical, such as the spot where you piled the manure before you spread it onto other parts of the garden or a depression where runoff collects.
- Don't take samples within 2 weeks of adding fertilizers.
- Be sure to take samples of your results, including the date, weather conditions, and location of soil samples, along with the readings.
- If you need assistance testing your soil, contact your state's Cooperative Extension Service or a private lab.

The test determines the soil pH (degree of acidity or alkalinity). A pH of 7.0 is neutral; below 7.0 is acidic, and above is alkaline. Ideal pH values for vegetables range from 5.0 to 7.5; while most herbs prefer a pH in the range of 6.0 to 7.5. If your soil's pH is too acidic, you need to "sweeten" it with lime or wood ash. Adding 5 pounds of lime to each 10- by 10-foot area will raise the pH one point. Add the lime the fall before planting, so that it has sufficient time to work into the soil.

In addition to acidity or alkalinity, a soil test will tell you which nutrients your soil has and which ones it lacks. The major nutrients that a plant needs for growth are nitrogen, phosphorus, and potassium. These are the main ingredients of most chemical fertilizers.

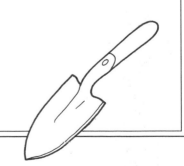

HOW DOES YOUR GARDEN GROW?

The styles and goals of gardening are as individual as the people who create them. Some are content with a few containers of tomatoes and herbs on the deck; others aim to feed a family throughout the year. Diverse theories on how to get the most from your efforts in the garden also abound. We concentrate on showing you how to create a small but productive garden that will yield plenty of vegetables for summer use but leave enough for preserving as well.

Make Your Beds!

The most important work you do in your garden happens before you plant a single seed. Choosing a site and preparing garden beds well is half the battle. Here is what you need to keep in mind when planning a vegetable garden site. You may want to have several sites; they do not all have to be contiguous.

Sunshine, sunshine, sunshine. Most vegetables need at least 6 hours of direct sunlight to thrive. Morning sun is particularly helpful, because it dries dew, thereby inhibiting molds and diseases.

Air flow. Good air circulation without high winds is necessary. If the area is exposed, a fence or hedge may help provide wind protection. Cold air moves downhill and collects in valleys or where dense growth blocks its movement; frost will be less of a problem in gardens planted on slopes, where cold air can move past rather than settling in.

Drainage. Plants love water, but they don't like standing in it. Beware of locating your garden in a place that is slow to dry or where puddles often form.

Preparing the beds. How wide? How wide a bed you make depends on how wide a bed you can comfortably tend. You need to be able to reach easily into the center of the bed to weed, cultivate, prune, and harvest. You should not ever have to walk on the soil of your bed.

How deep? Digging or raising your beds so that the plants have at least 18 inches of prepared soil to root in almost guarantees that your plants will thrive.

How long? The length of your garden depends on how much space you have. A bed that is about 15 feet long is good, but a 3- by 6-foot bed will produce a surprising amount. Remember, no rule says that beds must be rectangular; as long as they are deep enough and easy to reach across, they can be almost any shape — wedges, circles, or octagons, for example. All add interest to a landscape.

Garden Care

Soil. Test your soil at least once a year (page 493) and plan your fertilizing needs based on the test results.

Seeds and seedlings. Seed catalogs offer a wealth of planting information, especially if you choose a supplier who shares your regional growing conditions. For the best chance of success, follow directions for planting depth, planting time, and thinning. Avoid the temptation to plant seeds too close together. Seedlings that have to compete will not be as strong, and crowded plants are harder to thin.

You can also start seedlings indoors or buy packs of ready-to-plant seedlings from your local nursery. Be sure to water newly transplanted seedlings frequently for the first few days; cover them with a shade cloth or inverted planter to protect from glaring sun or high wind.

Crop rotation. Crop rotation simply means that you don't grow the same plants or plant families in the same place two (or more) seasons in a row. Crop rotation discourages transmission of diseases and insects and minimizes the depletion of soil nutrients.

Mulch. Organic mulches keep soil warm, retain moisture, and hinder weed growth. Organic mulches include straw, hay (but only hay that has not gone to seed), grass clippings, and pine bark. Plastic mulches make effective weed fighters

Water. All plants need water to grow. A good rule of thumb is that plants should have at least 1 inch of water per week, either from rain or from supplemental watering. The best time to water is the late afternoon; the water won't evaporate in the heat of the day, nor will it keep the foliage damp all night.

Garden notebook. A garden notebook is a big help in planning and storing hard-earned garden lore from year to year. Keep track of frost dates, seed varieties, soil additives, crop rotation, and other information.

DIG IT!

Here's what you'll need to dig your garden.

- HOE. A long-handled instrument with a flat blade for cutting off and pulling away weeds.

- CULTIVATOR. A three-pronged device with a long or short handle; used to loosen and aerate soil around plants.

- SPADE. A shovel-like tool with a flat, rectangular blade for cutting neat edges on a bed or for cutting sod.

- SHOVEL. The convex shape of a shovel makes it a good tool for lifting and moving soil.

- STEEL RAKE. Steel rakes are useful for moving soil within beds and for combing beds for weeds.

- FORK. Useful for deep tilling of the soil, a well-made garden fork has strong, thick tines that won't bend if they encounter a rock.

- TROWEL. A small digging tool; the best ones are made of stainless steel and have a sturdy wooden handle.

- WEEDER. Also called a Cape Cod or farmer's weeder, this is a handheld tool with a small blade for weeding in small spaces.

When buying tools, look for forged steel, good balance, and a comfortable grip. Cheap tools almost always end up costing more than expensive ones in the long run.

hoe

shovel

fork

weeder

handheld fork

Plan for a Small Garden

Whether your garden is large or small, a plan is important to its success. With a plan for succession planting, a raised bed only 3 by 6 feet can provide a steady supply of vegetables from spring through late fall. Not only that, but the herbs and flowers look great!

You can adapt the plans shown here to grow the vegetables that you and your family like most. Instead of celery, perhaps you'd like more herbs, such as oregano and dill. Herbs make great fillers in a small garden like this; you could even plant them instead of flowers. In summer, plant New Zealand spinach or eggplant instead of some (or all) of the peppers. Be sure to plant tomatoes, or any other tall-growing crop, on the north side of the garden, so that they don't cast shade onto the other plants.

You can either stake the tomatoes or use a trellis. It's especially easy to install trellises in a raised bed: Simply fasten the posts to the inner sides of the wooden bed with a metal strap. Remember to prune your tomatoes when they reach the top of their support, so that they don't slouch over the other plants.

MID-MAY GARDEN

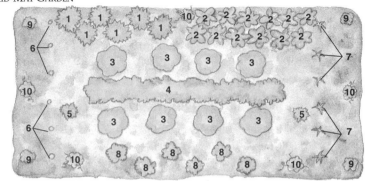

MID-JULY GARDEN

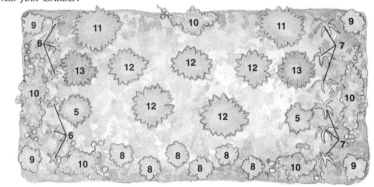

EARLY-SEPTEMBER GARDEN

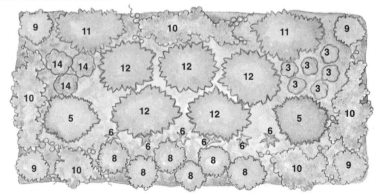

KEY TO PLANTS

1. Spinach	6. Garlic	11. Tomato
2. Beet	7. Leek	12. Pepper
3. Lettuce	8. Parsley	13. Basil
4. Radish	9. Marigold	14. Kale
5. Celery	10. Nasturtium	

VEGETABLES IN CONTAINERS

If you don't have the space for a vegetable garden, you can grow vegetables in containers. Container gardening has some advantages: The plants are portable, they can be turned to face the sun, and they can even be brought inside if a sudden storm threatens.

Choosing Vegetables

You can grow almost anything in containers, but stay away from large plants, such as sweet corn; the yield won't be great and the space required is considerable.

It's better to choose vegetables with relatively small root systems, such as peppers, tomatoes, lettuce, onions, carrots, and eggplant. Fast-growing vegetables, such as lettuce, Swiss chard, and New Zealand spinach, are made for container gardening. Fruiting vegetables — tomatoes, peppers, eggplant, and summer squash — that produce over a long period are good choices, too. Compact-vined muskmelons also grow well in containers.

Read seed catalogs carefully for information on which varieties grow well in containers.

Planting in Pots

Container-grown vegetables are subject to the same problems as all container-grown plants — they dry out quickly and need frequent feeding. But growing vegetables is worth the extra effort.

To grow vegetables, the containers need to be larger than those used for ornamental plants — from 3 to 30 gallons. In smaller containers, the plant will dry out too quickly and there won't be enough room for root development.

Think about your needs before choosing or building your containers. You may need a series of boxes if you are going to grow a variety of crops. Boxes that are 8 inches deep and 2 by 3 feet are good for such vegetables as beets, carrots, zucchini, and onions.

For vegetables that will grow up a trellis, try a narrower box: one that is 8 inches deep but 1 foot by 4 feet. For crops that grow singly — tomatoes, peppers, and eggplant — use pots that hold 4 to 5 gallons of soil.

Remember that pot-grown vegetables need high-quality soil. Be sure to add a slow-release fertilizer to the mix.

It is easy to transplant seedlings to containers. Leave 1 to 2 inches of headroom so you can water heavily without washing soil out of the top of the container. Gently pack the soil around the roots of the young plants, and set them back at least 2 inches from the edge of the container to keep the roots from drying out.

Planting Mixes

The planting mixture is the most important factor in container gardening. You will need a good mixture that is able to hold nutrients and water even through hot, dry weather. Ordinary garden soil is usually too heavy for container gardening, and it may contain insects and disease. It also tends to dry out quickly.

The planting mix needs to have a pH of 5 or 6 to 7.0.

Some gardeners prefer not to use garden soil in their mixes; they choose soilless mixes, which are free from disease organisms and weed seeds.

Soilless mixes, which are available from garden centers and mail-order and Internet seed companies, are also lightweight, which is a plus when you have to lug the pots from one spot to another.

GROW HERBS
FOR THE KITCHEN

One of the easiest ways to add flavor, without calories, to your cooking is to use fresh or dried herbs. I grow my own herbs near the back door in a small garden that I find satisfying on several counts. From the kitchen window, the herb garden looks beautiful in bloom, and dozens of distinctive aromas waft in on gentle breezes. The proximity also lets me be instantly creative in combining fresh herbs in my cooking. I love to pluck garlic, rosemary, and thyme from the garden and rub them immediately onto a chicken. I fill the cavity with fresh herb sprigs and lemon wedges, and roast the bird with new potatoes. The house fills quickly with wonderful smells, and a dinner that is simple yet fit for company cooks up easily.

Growing Herbs in an Outdoor Garden

Herbs will flourish in most types of good garden soil, especially a fertile, well-drained, sandy loam. Because most herbs are native to the poorer, rocky soils of the Mediterranean, they make a fine showing under less than optimum conditions. However, if you are considering a long-term perennial bed, it is advisable to make your soil the best possible.

Most soils benefit from the addition of organic matter, such as compost, chopped leaves, or peat moss. Organic matter improves the texture of soil.

Most herbs require well-drained soil (the exception being some types of mint). Well-drained means that water seeps down into the soil at a fairly constant rate, so that it never pools on the soil surface, resulting in soggy roots for the herbs. Do not plant in poorly drained areas unless you plan to build raised beds.

All soils should be tested (page 493) before you start growing. The test results will help you decide the amount and type of any fertilizer needed. Many herbs require only small amounts of fertilizer and are sensitive to overfeeding.

The best time to fertilize herbs is in the early spring, just as they are planted or when they start to put on new growth. I prefer to use organic fertilizers, such as compost, alfalfa meal, bonemeal, blood meal, or cottonseed meal. Well-rotted or dehydrated manure can also be used. If the plants look as if they could use a lift later in the season — indicated by yellowing foliage and sparse growth — give them a shot of a liquid fertilizer, such as fish emulsion or seaweed, mixed with water.

You can use a complete chemical fertilizer such as 5–10–10, if you wish. Add a couple of tablespoons around each perennial shrub in the early spring. Mix it into the soil and water well to send the nutrients down to the roots.

Most perennial herb gardens benefit from a layer of mulch. Spread on the soil surface, mulch maintains even soil temperatures and moisture content. It also discourages weed growth, primarily because it blocks out light, which prevents weed seeds from germinating. Mulching the herb garden cuts out a large percentage of the time you would spend watering or weeding.

Organic mulches decompose and add fiber and nutrients to the soil.

Growing Herbs Indoors

Choose herbs that you often use in cooking or those that are hard to find in stores. Compact, low-growing herbs, such as thyme, marjoram, savory, parsley, sage, basil, or chives, are easy to grow indoors — you certainly would not want a 6-foot-high angelica plant on your windowsill! Help your herbs stay bushy by pinching off the terminal ends of the shoots.

Pots made of porous materials are desirable, because they allow excess water to seep through. Clay pots are therefore preferable to plastic ones. Whatever type of container you choose, *a drainage hole is a must.*

Use a suitable growing mixture. A sterilized potting soil mix is the best bet. Bags of soil mixtures are available in most gardening stores.

Place a small piece of broken pottery or a few pebbles in the bottom of the container to keep the soil from spilling out of the drainage hole. Fill the container about halfway with soil mix. Place the herb cutting or transplant in the pot and gently pack soil around it, leaving 1 inch of headroom. Water well.

Herbs are sun lovers. They should receive at least 5 to 6 hours of direct sunlight each day. Grow lights can be used if sufficient natural light is lacking; a combination of warm and cool white fluorescent tubes is recommended. The lights should be placed about 6 inches from the tops of the plants and should shine 8 to 10 hours a day, if they are the only light source.

Herbs prefer daytime temperatures of 65 to 70°F and nighttime temperatures about 10 degrees cooler.

Moreover, herbs tend to prefer some moisture in the air. Most houses tend to be dry in the winter; the more humidity you can put into the air, the better.

Let your plants dry out between waterings. Too much water has probably killed more container-grown herbs than too little. Feel the soil and be sure that it is dry about an inch down. Water thoroughly, so that it flows out of the drainage hole. Plants are like people — they prefer a warm bath to a cold shower!

Potted herbs thrive on small, regular doses of water-soluble fertilizer. Treat them with a *dilute* solution of liquid seaweed or fish emulsion once a week, but halve the recommended dose.

HERB HAPPY

Herb-gardening maven Sheryl Felty offers her choices for 15 satisfying, easy-to-grow herbs for the kitchen garden:

Angelica, basil, catnip, chives, dill, fennel, marjoram, mint, oregano, parsley, rosemary, sage, savory, tarragon, and thyme.

Contributors

Janet Ballantyne

Janet Ballantyne began cooking at the age of 12 with her Austrian-born mother and grandmother. After college, she started a catering business and at the same time began giving cooking demonstrations on local television, which earned her a regular spot on the nationally syndicated "Joy of Gardening" TV program. Among her book credits is *The Joy of Gardening Cookbook*. Janet lives in Vermont.

Patti Barrett

No wonder Patti Barrett wanted to write the Storey book *Too Busy to Clean?* She's a very busy woman. In addition to having a new book in the works, *The Sacred Garden: Soil for the Growing Soul*, she is about to be ordained in the Episcopal Church. She will serve as an assistant priest on Nantucket, Massachusetts.

Ruth Bass

Ruth Bass loves herbs. As editor/writer of Storey's "Fresh from the Garden" series, Ruth authored *Herbal Breads, Herbal Sweets, Herbal Soups, Herbal Salads, Tomatoes Love Herbs, Onions Love Herbs, Peppers Love Herbs,* and *Mushrooms Love Herbs.* She was a longtime editor at *The Berkshire Eagle* and has written extensively for such publications as *The Boston Globe, The Cleveland Plain Dealer,* and *Yankee Magazine.* Ruth lives in western Massachusetts.

Charlene A. Braida

Charlene Braida remembers awakening each Sunday to "the redolent aroma of garlic sautéing in olive oil" as her mother began making tomato sauce for the family's traditional pasta dinner. To Charlene, that garlicky fragrance symbolizes the essence of a good meal. In her Storey book, *Glorious Garlic: A Cookbook*, she offers family favorites, old and new, "that will make your taste buds tingle with excitement." Charlene lives in New Jersey and works as an attorney.

Ricki and Robert Carroll

Say "cheese," and someone is sure to mention Ricki and Robert Carroll. Their cheesemaking career began many years ago with the purchase of two dairy goats. Founding members of the American Cheese Society, they have published articles in most of the top newspapers and magazines in the United States and wrote *Cheesemaking Made Easy* for Storey. They live in Ashfield, Massachusetts, where they own New England Cheesemaking Supply Co.

Janet Chadwick

As the title of her first book, *How to Live on Almost Nothing and Have Plenty*, suggests, Janet Chadwick is accomplished at using food wisely and well. Her other works include *The Country Journal Woodburner's Cookbook* and Storey's compendium on food preservation, *The Busy Person's Guide to Preserving Food*. Janet and her husband are retired and live in Florida.

Jane Cooper

"Some tasks, though they take more effort, offer greater rewards when done the old-fashioned way," says Jane Cooper, talking about her love of cooking on a wood-fired stove. Jane is a professional writer whose Storey book, *Woodstove Cookery*, was praised in *The Boston Globe* as telling the neophyte "how to buy a woodstove, how to set it up and fuel it, clean it and enjoy it." Jane hails from Maryland.

Carol W. Costenbader

For more than 35 years, Carol Costenbader has been growing and preserving food. Besides *The Big Book of Preserving the Harvest*, her Storey credits include *Mustards, Ketchups & Vinegars* and *Preserving Fruits & Vegetables*. Carol is founder of The Health Adventure, a teaching facility, and is a volunteer cook at a homeless shelter. She and her family divide their time between central Florida and the mountains of North Carolina.

Stephen Cresswell

As a historian and professor of history at West Virginia Wesleyan College, Stephen Cresswell has extensively researched early recipes and old-fashioned brewing techniques. His Storey book, *Homemade Root Beer, Soda, and Pop,* is a result of his research and expertise as a home brewer of soft drinks. He lives with his wife in West Virginia.

Gail Damerow

Gail Damerow got started raising livestock 30 years ago, when she bought a house that "came with chickens." She combined her career as a creative writing instructor with her research and expertise in farming to become editor of *Rural Heritage Draft Animal Magazine* and to write for Storey on animal raising and other country pursuits. Her books include *Your Goats, Guide to Raising Chickens, Fences for Pasture and Garden,* and *The Perfect Pumpkin.* Gail lives in Tennessee.

Jennifer Storey Gillis

Jennifer learned to cook at mother Martha Storey's side. A former elementary school teacher, she enjoys writing books to motivate young people to learn about nutrition and cooking. Her children's book titles include Storey's *An Apple A Day!, Green Beans & Tambourines, Hearts & Crafts,* and *In a Pumpkin Shell.* She lives in Missouri with her husband, Jack, and their children, Matthew, Sara, Charlie, and Henry.

Ken Haedrich

When it comes to maple syrup, Ken Haedrich is an unabashed fan. "I love the stuff in a big way. I love the flavor, the smell, and the color of pure maple syrup, a combination of sensual pleasures nobody has been able to capture with artificial ingredients." He wrote *The Maple Syrup Cookbook* for Storey, and he contributes to numerous magazines, including *Food & Wine, Yankee Magazine,* and *Vermont Magazine.*

Geri Harrington

The College Cookbook reflects Geri Harrington's continuing interest in easy, creative cooking. She collected and tested hundreds of recipes from more than 55 colleges and universities for the project. Geri has also written 11 other books and many articles for such magazines as *Good Housekeeping, Family Circle,* and *Women's Day.* She lives in Connecticut.

Phyllis Hobson

A true countrywoman, Phyllis Hobson is an authority on many aspects of rural living. She has written on dairymaking, livestock raising, gardening, and cooking. Her many Storey titles include *Making and Using Dried Foods, Raising a Calf for Beef, Tan Your Hide,* and *Satisfying Soups.* Phyllis is semiretired and lives in Texas.

Miriam Jacobs

Miriam Jacobs has been a recipe developer and food writer in New England for many years. She is a columnist for *Homestyle* magazine and edited *Best Recipes of Berkshire Chefs.* Her Storey title *The 10% Low-Fat Cookbook* celebrates low-fat cooking without deprivation. Miriam has three children and lives in western Massachusetts.

Ellen Foscue Johnson

"If you have a bag of flour, a source of water, a store where you can buy some yeast, and access to a stove — or, failing that, a fireplace or an outdoor fire — you can make the kind of bread that sustained the human race for several thousand years," says Ellen Foscue Johnson. The Vermont resident is a photographer and author of Storey's *The Bread Book.* She sees making bread as "a lifetime adventure."

Kelly Klober

Kelly is now market master for the East Central Missouri Farmers' Markets. His work in agriculture includes lecturing and writing, and his knowledge of livestock farming resulted in the Storey title *A Guide to Raising Pigs.* Kelly lives in Missouri.

Elizabeth Knight

Move over, Mad Hatter — Elizabeth Knight is the tea party hostess of our choice. In her Storey book *Tea with Friends,* she shares lore and methods that she has accumulated during years of running an acclaimed catering business, Celebrations! Presentations, Parties, and Creative Events. She lectures widely and is published in many major magazines. Elizabeth lives in New Jersey.

Karl F. Lutzen and Mark Stevens

These brewmaster buddies have contributed three books to Storey's collection on beermaking, *Homebrew Favorites, More Homebrew Favorites,* and *Brew Ware.* They also created the Internet public-domain recipe collections Cat's Meow I, II, and III. Mark's articles have also appeared in *All About Beer* magazine. Karl resides in Missouri; Mark and his wife live in Virginia.

Dave Miller

Author and brewing expert Dave Miller has been a brewmaster at the St. Louis Brewing Company and the Blackstone Brewery. His many publications include the Storey books *Brewing the World's Great Beers, The Complete Handbook of Home Brewing,* and *Dave Miller's Homebrewing Guide.* Dave makes his home (and lots of beer) in Tennessee.

Alexandra Nimetz, Jason Stanley, and Emeline Starr

When they collaborated for Storey on *The Healthy College Cookbook,* Alexandra, Jason, and Emeline were undergraduates at Williams College in Williamstown, Massachusetts. All three are self-taught cooks who enjoy eating for good health. They collected the recipes for the cookbook from family and friends.

Betty Oppenheimer

An experienced candlemaker, crafter, and sewer, Betty Oppenheimer has written three Storey books: *The Candlemaker's Companion, Gifts for Herb Lovers,* and *Sewing Packs, Pouches, Seats, and Sacks.* Betty is a consultant to the textile industry and was production manager for Coyote Found Candles. She lives in Washington state.

Maggie Oster

A renowned photographer, food writer, and horticulturalist, Maggie Oster is the author of more than a dozen books, including *Herbal Vinegar* and *Herb Mixtures & Spicy Blends,* which were published by Storey. Her photographs and articles have been included in many other books and magazines. She divides her time between Kentucky and Indiana.

Nancy C. Ralston and Marynor Jordan

"You can't have too many zucchinis." This could well be the motto of Nancy and Marynor; not only have they written about this ubiquitous squash in their weekly column in *The Bloomington Herald Times,* but they co-authored the acclaimed *New Zucchini Cookbook* for Storey. Nancy and Marynor live in Indiana.

Charles G. Reavis

A teacher of English and a skilled chef, Charles Reavis loves to test, develop, simplify, and update the traditional sausage-making techniques he learned from his Moravian grandfather. His Storey book, *Home Sausage Making,* includes more than 175 recipes for making and using sausage. Charles lives in Georgia.

Diana Rosen

It's always teatime for Diana. In addition to writing the Storey books *The Book of Green Tea, Steeped in Tea, Taking Time for Tea,* and *Chai, The Spice Tea of India,* she is editor of the national quarterly *Tea Talk: a newsletter on the pleasures of tea.* When not traveling the world in search of tea lore, she resides in northern California, where she is a writing coach and a consultant to tea-related businesses.

Phyllis V. Shaudys

If it pertains to herbs, Phyllis has done it. She has grown, cooked, crafted with, collected, and written about herbs for more than 40 years. Her five books include two Storey favorites, *Herbal Treasures* and *The Pleasure of Herbs*. Her articles have appeared in such publications as *Women's Day*, *The Mother Earth News*, *The Brooklyn Botanic Garden Record*, and *Flower and Garden*. Phyllis resides in Pennsylvania.

Karyn Siegel-Maier

Making safe and effective alternatives to commercial cleansing products was the motivation behind Karyn's Storey book, *The Naturally Clean Home*. An herbalist and researcher, she has written for many newspapers and magazines, including *Natural Living Today* and *Let's Live*. A mother of three, Karyn has also written *50 Simple Ways to Pamper Your Baby*. She lives in New York.

Edith Stovel and Pamela Wakefield

Edith ("DeeDee") and Pamela have shared weekend gatherings with each other's families for many years. DeeDee is an author, caterer, and a teacher of health, cooking, and nutrition. She lives in Massachusetts. Pamela is a talented cook who is well versed in entertaining large groups. She lives in New Jersey. Together they wrote the Storey book *Weekend! A Menu Cookbook for Relaxed Entertaining*. DeeDee also wrote *Picnic!* for Storey.

Maggie Stuckey

Country gardening and country cooking are twin interests of Maggie Stuckey. She has written eight books, including *The Complete Herb Book, The Complete Spice Book, Green Plants for Gray Days, 200 Tips for Growing Vegetables in the Pacific Northwest*, and *Country Tea Parties* (which she wrote for Storey). She is currently finishing a book on growing edible plants in container gardens. Maggie lives in Oregon.

Tess and Mark Szamatulski

Connecticut brewers Tess and Mark Szamatulski are a husband-and-wife team. They own a homebrew supply shop, Maltose Express, and have spent years developing recipes and techniques. Besides serving as editors of *Brew Your Own* magazine, they have put their fund of knowledge to use in the Storey title *CloneBrews*, which offers homebrewers recipes that replicate many of the world's best beers.

Stephanie Tourles

Natural Foot Care, The Herbal Body Book, Naturally Healthy Skin and *50 Simple Ways to Pamper Yourself* are the popular personal care books that Stephanie Tourles has written for Storey. Stephanie is a licensed aesthetician who creates herbal cosmetics and treatments and runs an herbal soap company, September's Sun Herbal Soap and Skincare Co., in West Hyannisport, Massachusetts.

Pattie Vargas and Rich Gulling

Mother-and-son team Pattie Vargas and Rich Gulling are avid home winemakers. They have co-authored several books on the subject, including Storey's *Cordials from Your Kitchen* and *Making Wild Wines and Meads*. Pattie is an editorial project manager at Mazer Corporation, and Rich is a pharmacy manager whose chemistry background helped them modernize their winemaking processes. They live in Ohio.

Olwen Woodier

"A" is for apple, and Olwen Woodier takes apples all the way from A to Z (as in Zucchini and Apple Soup) in her award-winning Storey publication, *The Apple Cookbook*. Gene Shalit of NBC's "Today Show" complimented her book as having "bushels of good recipes. . . . This bounty of apple ideas is a pick of the cookbook crop." Olwen lives on a farm in Virginia.

Adriana and Rochelle Zabarkes

Rochelle and Adriana Zabarkes are writers, consultants, caterers, and lovers of international cuisine. The mother-and-daughter team collaborated on the Storey title *Adriana's Spice Caravan*, a collection of exotic recipes that was a natural outgrowth of their thriving mail-order spice business of the same name. Rochelle and Adriana recently opened a retail store in New York City's Grand Central Station.

Bibliography

"The Basics." Home Wine & Beer Trade Association. (http//www.hwbta.org) (5/31/2000).

Better Homes and Gardens New Cook Book. Des Moines, Iowa: Meredith Corporation, 1996.

Brown, Kathleen. *Herbal Teas.* Pownal, Vermont: Storey Communications, 1999.

Chicago Manual of Style, The. Chicago: University of Chicago Press, 1993.

Claiborne, Craig. *The New York Times Cookbook.* New York: Harper & Row, 1990.

Conran, Terence, and Caroline Conran. *The Cook Book.* New York: Crown Publishers, 1980.

Consumer Education and Information. 2000. (http//www.fsis.usda.gov) (5/5/2000).

Cooking Resources. 1994. (http//www.globalgourmet.com) (3/13/2000).

Editors of Time-Life Books. *Breads.* Alexandria, Virginia: Time-Life Books, 1981.

———. *Candy.* Alexandria, Virginia: Time-Life Books, 1981.

———. *Classic Desserts.* Alexandria, Virginia: Time-Life Books, 1980.

———. *Preserving.* Alexandria, Virginia: Time-Life Books, 1981.

———. *Vegetables.* Alexandria, Virginia: Time-Life Books, 1979.

Emery, Carla. *Encyclopedia of Country Living.* Seattle: Sasquatch Books, 1994.

Epicurious Eating & Drinking. 2000. (http//www.food.epicurious.com) (3/13/2000).

Food and Entertaining. 1999. (http//www.ehow.com) (5/25/2000).

Fortin, François, ed. *The Visual Food Encyclopedia.* New York: Macmillan, 1996.

General Foods Kitchens. *All About Home Baking.* New York: Random House, 1960.

Gibbons, Euell. *Stalking the Healthful Herbs.* New York: David McKay Company, 1966.

Herbst, Sharon Tyler. *The Food Lover's Tiptionary.* New York: Hearst Books, 1994.

———. *The New Food Lover's Companion.* New York: Barron's Educational Series, 1995.

Kids Cooking. 1998. (http//www.familyfoodzone.com) (5/25/2000).

National Coffee Association of U.S.A. (http//www.ncausa.org) (4/6/2000).

Oster, Maggie, and Sal Gilbertie. *The Herbal Palate Cookbook.* Pownal, Vermont: Storey Communications, 1996.

Ostmann, Barbara Gibbs, and Jane L. Baker. *The Recipe Writer's Handbook.* New York: John Wiley & Sons, 1997.

Recipes of the Month. 2000. (http//www.lifescan.com) (5/25/2000).

Rombauer, Irma S., and Marion Rombauer Becker. *Joy of Cooking.* Indiananapolis: Bobbs-Merrill, 1963.

Rombauer, Irma S., Marion Rombauer Becker, and Ethan Becker. *Joy of Cooking.* New York: Scribner, 1997.

Rosso, Julee, and Sheila Lukins. *The New Basics Cookbook.* New York: Workman, 1989.

———. *The Silver Palate Cookbook.* New York: Workman, 1982.

Scott, David, and Paddy Byrne. *Seasonal Salads.* Pownal, Vermont: Storey Communications, 1986.

Sicard, Cheri. 2000. "The Basic Kitchen." Cooking School. (http//www.fabulousfoods.com) (3/13/2000).

Tips, Classes, Recipes. (http//www.kingarthurflour.com) (3/16/2000).

U.S. Department of Agriculture Home Canning Guide. 5/5/00. (http//www.fsis.usda.gov) (6/7/2000).

Westmoreland, Susan, ed. *The Good Housekeeping Step-by-Step Cookbook.* New York: Hearst Books, 1997.

Whitman, Joan, and Dolores Simon. *Recipes into Type.* New York: Harper Collins, 1993.

Credits

The following recipes and material were used and/or adapted by permission.

Glenn Andrews: From *A-106 Recipes for Gourmet Vegetables*: Purée of Jerusalem Artichokes, p. 189; Crispy Fried Squash Blossoms, p. 198; Celeriac Salad and Sweet and Sour Bok Choy, p. 207; and Creamed Morels, p. 463. From *A-111 Making Homemade Candy*: Molasses Taffy and Vinegar Candy or Taffy, p. 252; About Pulling Taffy, p. 253; Burnt Sugar Brittle and Peanut Brittle, p. 254; Vanilla Caramels, p. 255; Truffles, p. 256; and A Trio of Truffles, p. 257. From *A-112 Making and Using Flavored Vinegars*: Making Flavored Vinegars, p. 273; Blueberry Vinegar and Peach, Apricot, or Nectarine Vinegar, p. 274; Basil and Other Single-herb Vinegars, p. 275. From *A-145 Growing and Cooking with Mint*: A Proper Kentucky Derby Mint Julep, p. 290; Natural Mint Jelly, p. 303; and Mint Sorbet, p. 366. From *A-170 Growing and Using Hot Peppers*: Making a Chile Ristra, p. 395, and Hot Pepper Jelly, p. 405. From *A-172 Making European Breads*: Irish Soda Bread, p. 328. From *A-176 Salsas!*: Nectarine & Apple Salsa, p. 68; Salsa Ranchero, p. 90; Apricot Salsa, p. 215; Black Bean Salsa and Classic Red Restaurant Salsa, p. 280; and Pineapple Salsa, p. 281. From *A-183 Growing and Using Garlic*: Sautéed Zucchini with Garlic, p. 197; Garlic Purée, p. 205; Garlic Butter Garlic Bread, p. 284; Pesto, p. 306; Garlic Salt, p. 310; and Garlic Braid, p. 396. From *A-198 Basic Bread Baking*: Making Rolls, p. 109, and Anadama Batter Bread, p. 110. From *A-200 Growing & Using Dill*: Dilly of a Dip, p. 91.

Liz Anton and Beth Dooley: Berries, p. 41; Blackberry Gingerbread Waffles, Blackberry Winter, and Blueberry Cinnamon Doughnuts, p. 66; Blueberry Sour Cream Pancakes and Guidelines for Picking the Best Berries, p. 67; Berry Fool, p. 217; Fresh Cranberry Relish, p. 220; Chocolate-Dipped Strawberries, p. 257; and Cranberry Walnut Bread Pudding, p. 258.

Janet Ballantyne: From *Joy of Gardening Cookbook*: Preparing and Mixing, pp. 8–10; Tools for the Country Cook, pp. 15–20; In the Pantry, pp. 24–29 and 36–41; Crepês, p. 64; Strawberry Blintzes, p. 68; Corned Beef Parsnip Hash, p. 70; Home Sweet Home Fries, p. 71; Summer Stock, p. 76; Spring Onion Soup, p. 79; Simplest Cream Soup, p. 82; Leftover Salad Soup, p. 88; Corn Cheese

Puffs, p. 92; Savory Vegetable Turnovers, p. 94; Sweet Potato Muffins, p. 121; Frosted Lettuce Wedges, p. 123; Green Salads, p. 124; How Much Do I Need? and Seven Salad Tips, p. 125; Janet's Favorite Coleslaw, p. 126; Salads Don't Have to Be Tossed, p. 128; Corn and Tomato Salad, p. 129; Hot German Potato Salad, p. 130; Sweet Potato Tarragon Salad, p. 131; Caesar Salad, p. 140; Storing Greens, p. 141; Green Goddess Dressing, Lemon Vinaigrette, and Vinaigrette, p. 142; French-Style Dressing, p. 143; Chicken Potpie with Sugar Snaps, p. 154; About Cooking Peas, p. 190; Tarragon Carrots and Chard, p. 191; Corn in the Pot, p. 193; Succotash, p. 194; Radish Butter, p. 196; Baked Sweet Potato Sticks, p. 201; Hot Rhubarb Pudding, p. 212; Frozen Melon Sherbet and Watermelon Ice Pops, p. 216; Pumpkin Orange Cheesecake, p. 237; Italian Tomato Sauce, p. 263; Hollandaise Sauce, p. 264; and Cheese Sauce, p. 265.

Joanne Barrett: From *A-62 Cooking with Honey*: What is Honey? p. 24; Harvard Beets, p. 208; Gingerbread People, p. 245; Milk Shake, p. 359; The Flavors of Honey, p. 459; and Popcorn Balls, p. 469.

Patti Barrett: From *A-151 Container Gardening*: Vegetables in Containers, p. 497. From *Too Busy to Clean?* Kitchen Tips and Stain Removal Tricks, pp. 479–480.

Ruth Bass: From *Herbal Breads*: Banana Lemon Bread, p. 114, and Cheesy Biscuits with Thyme, p. 119. From *Herbal Salads*: Herbed Vegetable Salad and Three-Bean Salad, p. 128; Tabbouleh, p. 133; and Lemon Mint Dressing for Fruit, p. 225. From *Herbal Soups*: Fish Chowder, p. 85; Bubbie's Borscht, p. 88; Chilled Strawberry Soup, p. 89; and Cock-a-Leekie Soup, p. 325. From *Herbal Sweets*: Blueberries Romanoff, p. 218, and Rosemary Poached Pears, p. 223. From *Mushrooms Love Herbs*: Crêpes with Herbed Wild Mushrooms, p. 64; Garlicky Mushroom Spread, p. 90; and Veal Scallopine with Sage, p. 148. From *Onions Love Herbs*: Scallion Omelette with Marjoram, p. 54, and Dill Cornbread with Sausage, p. 115. From *Peppers Love Herbs*: Peppers and Sun-Dried Tomatoes with Pasta, p. 169. From *Tomatoes Love Herbs*: Tomato Omelette with Marjoram, p. 54, and Tomato Pesto Frittata, p. 56.

Marjorie Blanchard: Game Hens with Apricot Sauce, p. 156; Spicy Lentils, p. 175; Cioppino, p. 176; Plum Dessert Sauce, Nika's Plum Sauce, and Plum Purée, p. 217; Ginger Pear Sauce, p. 223; Béchamel variations, p. 264; Short Course in Sauces, p. 266; and Rémoulade Sauce, p. 267. Cream of Tomato Soup, p. 82; Spinach Soufflé, p. 191; Cabbage in Sour Cream, p. 203; Amber Onions, p. 205; Strawberry Syllabub, p. 213; Sour Cherry Cake, p. 218; Baked Apples, p. 221; and About Dandelion Greens, p. 460.

Charlene Braida: From *Glorious Garlic*: Meat, Poultry & Fish, pp. 32–35; Gazpacho, p. 89; Leeks & Sausage in Puff Pastry, p. 95; Macaroni Salad, p. 134; Moussaka, p. 148; Roast Pork and Oven-Browned Potatoes, p. 150; Pork Chops and Peaches, p. 151; Garlicky Roast Chicken, p. 152; Shrimp Scampi, p. 160; About Shrimp, p. 161; Country-Style Rabbit, p. 163; Mushroom Meat Loaf, p. 180; Gratin of Kale, p. 207; and Dandelion Salad, p. 460.

Kathleen Brown: From *A-239 An Herbalist's Guide to Growing & Using Violets*: Crystallized Violets, p. 461.

Ricki Carroll and Robert Carroll: From *Cheesemaking Made Easy*: What to Do with the Whey, p. 371; Flavored Cheddars, p. 372; and Soft Goat Cheese, p. 375.

Betty Cavage: Dressing Up Your Soup, p. 78; For Tastier Soups, p. 80; Knock-Your-Socks-Off Chili, p. 86; Pub-Style Cheese Spread, p. 93; Steak & Onion Kabobs, p. 97; Confetti Coleslaw, p. 126; Scotch Scallion Scones, p. 192; Braised Leeks, p. 203; Sautéed Leeks, p. 204; Béarnaise Sauce, p. 266; Soubise Sauce, p. 267; Onion and Mushroom Gravy, p. 269; Bourbon Barbecue Sauce, p. 277; Zesty Beer Marinade, p. 278; Shallot or Chive Butter, p. 284; and Hoppin' John, p. 345.

Janet B. Chadwick: Suggested Substitutions, pp. 6–7; Using a Microwave Oven, p. 13; Tools for the Country Cook, pp. 15–20; Seafood Newburg, p. 160; Super-Quick Turkey Divan, p. 170; Homemade Bread Mix, p. 470; and Homemade Bread, p. 470. From *The Busy Person's Guide to Preserving Food*: Freeze-Ahead Ideas, p. 26; Never-Fail Pan Gravy, p. 268; Homemade Ketchup and Ketchup without Stirring, p. 270; Canning Applesauce, p. 387; Let the Sun Do Your Drying, p. 393; Oven-Dried Tomatoes, p. 395; Drying Mushrooms, p. 396; Basic Strawberry Jam, p. 402; Grape Jelly, p. 404; and Orange Marmalade, p. 406.

Andrea Chesman: From *A-91 Favorite Pickles & Relishes*: Rhubarb Chutney, p. 212; Pickling Tips, p. 407; and Freezer Dills, p. 408. From *Pickles & Relishes*: Homemade Mustard, p. 272; Pepper Relish, p. 283; Mixed Pickles, p. 408; Cucumber-Onion Mustard Pickles, Pickled Beets, and Pickling Tips, p. 410; and Pennsylvania Chow-Chow, p. 411.

Nancy Chioffi and Gretchen Mead: From *Keeping the Harvest*: Classic Cranberry Sauce, p. 220; Pear Ginger Chutney, p. 282; Corn Relish, p. 283; Canned Tomatoes, p. 381; Getting Started with Canning, p. 382; Boiling-Water-Bath Canning, p. 384; Canning with Honey, p. 385; Pressure Canning Introduction, p. 386; Green Tomato Mincemeat, p. 388; Timetable for Pressure-Canning Vegetables, p. 389; Sauerkraut, p. 391; Drying Times, p. 394; How to Freeze and Packing and Labeling Tips, p. 397; Make Your Own Pectin, p. 402; and Watermelon Rind Pickles, p. 409.

Robert Cluett: From *A-75 Making Homemade Wine*: Herb or Dried Flower Petal Wine, p. 443.

Jane Cooper: From *Woodstove Cookery*: Cooked Cereals, p. 46; Ground Grain Cereal and Oatmeal and Apples, p. 47; Buckwheat Pancakes, p. 58; Corny Yogurt Waffles and Lightweight Waffles, p. 62; Paul's Waffles, Sour Cream Waffles, and Waffles on a Woodstove, p. 63; Summer Squash Fritters, p. 69; Baked Beans, p. 174; Creamy Broccoli Casserole, p. 179; Indian Pudding, p. 259; Rebeca's Delicious Flan, p. 261; Great Goulash, p. 318; and Apple Slaps, p. 319.

Carol W. Costenbader: From *A-197 Food Drying Techniques*: About Drying Herbs, p. 393. From *The Big Book of Preserving the Harvest*: About Freezing Dairy Products, p. 31; Southwestern Cranberry Sauce, p. 221; Canning Safety, p. 382; Preparing Food and Jars for Canning, p. 383; How to Test a Seal, p. 384; High-Acid Foods for Boiling-Water-Bath Canning, p. 385; Pressure Canning Step by Step, pp. 386–387; Tomato Sauce, p. 390; Freezing Fruits, pp. 397–398; Blanching Vegetables, p. 399; Jam, Jelly or..., p. 401; Old-Fashioned Peach Preserves, p. 402; Summer Squash Conserve, p. 403; Tomato Marmalade, p. 405; and Brined Dill Pickles, p. 407.

Jeff Cox: From *From Vines to Wines*: Optimum Serving Temperatures, p. 434.

Stephen Cresswell: From *Homemade Root Beer, Soda & Pop*: Raspberry Shrub, p. 288; Molasses Switchel, p. 288; Café Brulot, Coffee Whizzer, and Mocha Java, p. 297; Simple Eggnog, p. 339; Elderberry Champagne, p. 444; Bottling Soft Drinks and About Sassafras, p. 449; Homemade Root Beer Extract and Root Beer, p. 450; and Sarsaparilla and Sarsaparilla Soda, p. 451.

Gail Damerow: From *A Guide to Raising Chickens*: Eggs, p. 30, and How to Cut Up a Chicken, p. 415. From *The Perfect Pumpkin*: Great American Beer Pumpkin Soup, p. 80; Swiss-Style Pumpkin, p. 204; Pumpkin Pie Spice, p. 310; Pumpkin Carving and The Jack-O'-Lantern, p. 334; Traditional Pumpkin Pie, p. 337; and Skinny Puppy Pumpkin Ale, p. 436.

Mary Anna Dusablon: From *A-55 Cooking with Winter Squash and Pumpkin*: Fancy Mashed Hubbard Squash, p. 206, and Canned Winter Squash & Pumpkin, p. 390.

Wilbur F. Eastman Jr.: From *The Canning, Freezing, Curing & Smoking of Meat, Fish & Game*: Primary Cuts of Beef, p. 413; Primary Cuts of Lamb, p. 414; How to Build a Homemade Smokehouse, p. 419; and Smoking Fish, p. 420.

Editors of Garden Way Publishing: Currant Jelly (and Jam), p. 219; Candied Orange Peel, p. 226; Raspberry Vinegar, p. 274; General Presentation Tips and Packing Special Items, pp. 472–473; Small Rose Jar, p. 490; and Apple Spice Potpourri, p. 491. From *Tomatoes!*: Bacon Cheese Ball, p. 92; Barbecued Wings, p. 96; Tomato Basket, p. 137; and Fruit and Tomato Chutney, p. 282. From *A-32 Jams and Jellies*: Grape Conserve, p. 224. From *A-36 Starting Right with Bees*: What You Need to Get Started, pp. 456–459. From *Growing & Using Herbs*: Herb Chart, p. 305.

Sheryl L. Felty: From *A-61 Grow 15 Herbs for the Kitchen*: Bouquet Garni, p. 304, and Growing Herbs for the Kitchen, pp. 498–499.

Joe Fisher and Dennis Fisher: From *Brewing Made Easy*: Pale Horse Pale Ale, p. 434; Rogue Torpedo Common Beer, p. 435; and Two-Pints-Off-the-Port-Bow Porter, p. 437.

Jennifer Storey Gillis: From *An Apple A Day*: Applesauce, p. 211; Apple Pomander, p. 223; Apple Sweet, p. 245; and Chocolate Candied Apples, p. 333. From *Green Beans & Tambourines*: Tepee Bean Salad, p. 196; and Flag Cake, and Patriotic Pinwheels, p. 331. From *Hearts and Crafts*: Stained Glass Heart Cookies, p. 247, and Passion Punch, p. 289. From *In a Pumpkin Shell*: Toasted or Fried Pumpkin Seeds, p. 333.

Ken Haedrich: From *Maple Syrup Cookbook*: Maple Syrup, p. 25; A Gallon of Granola, p. 46; Cinnamon-Fried Cornmeal Mush, p. 48; Whole-Wheat Pancakes, p. 58; Jeanne's Oatmeal Pancakes, p. 60; Whole-Wheat and Hearty Corn Waffles, p. 62; Lacy Sweet Potato Breakfast Patties, p. 70; Sweet Potato, Bacon & Maple Bisque, p. 83; Ham Steaks in Rum Raisin Sauce, p. 149; Baked Bananas in Maple Rum Sauce, p. 227; Creamy Maple Mocha Pudding, p. 260; A Megabatch of Pancakes, p. 320; Applejack-Spiced Baked Apples, p. 321; and Maple Yogurt Smoothie, p. 359.

Geri Harrington: From *College Cookbook*: To Measure Accurately and Easily, p. 3; Equivalents & Substitutions, pp. 6–7; Preparing and Mixing, Stovetop Techniques, Oven Techniques, and Using an Oven, pp. 8–13; Hungarian Goulash, p. 79; Baked Pork Chops with Herbs, p. 180; Butterscotch Brownies, p. 251; Sweet

and Sour Meatballs, p. 320; Coconut Blender Pie, p. 323; and Welsh Rabbit, p. 372.

Rhonda Massingham Hart: From *A-154 Making Gingerbread Houses*: Gingerbread House, pp. 340–343.

Phyllis Hobson: Ice Cream Lingo, p. 360; Frozen Custard, p. 365; Just Like Grandma, p. 365; Cider Ice and Lemon Ice, p. 367. From *A-24 52 Great Green Tomato Recipes*: Fried Green Tomatoes, p. 187. From *A-56 Easy Game Cookery*: About That Gamey Taste, p. 162; Pheasant Baked in Foil, p. 162; Venison Stew, p. 162; How to Clean a Fish, p. 416; and Tenderizing Game, p. 417. From *A-57 Making Cheese, Butter & Yogurt*: Cheesemaking and Items for Making Cheese, p. 368; What to Do with the Whey and Cheddar Cheese, p. 371; Colby Cheese and Mozzarella Cheese, p. 372; Make Your Own Cheese Press and Romano Cheese, p. 373; Making Soft Cheese, p. 374; Neufchâtel, p. 374; Sour Milk Cottage Cheese, p. 375; Sweet-Cream Butter, p. 378; and Sour-Cream Butter, p. 379. From *A-65 Butchering Livestock at Home*: Basic Brine Cure and Curing Meats, p. 418. From *Making & Using Dried Foods*: Whole Wheat Flakes, p. 48; Carrot Cereal, p. 49; Savory Dried Peas, p. 209; Preparing Foods for Drying, p. 392; Drying Food in a Dehydrator and in a Conventional Oven, p. 392; Making Fruit Leather, p. 394; Drying Citrus Peels, p. 394; and About Rose Hips, p. 462. From *Satisfying Soups*: Phyllis's Chicken & Dumpling Stew, p. 73; Brown Stock, Chicken Broth, and Stocks, p. 74; Soup Tools, p. 75; Fish Stock and Vegetable Stock, p. 76; Family Soup, p. 77; Freezing Soups and Turkey and Mushroom Soup, p. 78; Catfish Soup, p. 81; New England Clam Chowder, p. 84; Think Soup, p. 86; Chicken Gumbo, p. 87; Sour Cherry Soup, p. 89; and Oven Lamb Stew, p. 181.

Claire Hopley: From *A-129 Making & Using Mustards*: Ballpark Mustard, p. 271; Cannon-Bullet Cooking, Honey Mustard, and Storing Homemade Mustard, p. 272; and Beer & Mustard Barbecue Sauce, p. 276–277.

Miriam Jacobs: From *The 10% Low-Fat Cookbook*: Zucchini-Parmesan Jalapeño Flatbread, p. 115; Ginger Scones, p. 117; Country Weekend Pasta Salad, p. 134; Tomatoes Stuffed with Herbed Lentils, p. 137; Turkey Cutlets with Roasted Shallot Sauce, p. 157; Broccoli Rabe Risotto; p. 172; Vegetable Barley, p. 175; Baked Peaches with Vanilla Ice Cream, p. 215; Oniony Baked Apples, p. 222; and Tomatillo Salsa, p. 280. From *A-223 Cooking with Edible Flowers*: Hibiscus Tea and Iced Hibiscus Tea, p. 295; and Flower Fritters, p. 460–461.

Ellen Foscue Johnson: From *The Bread Book*: Basics of Making Yeast Bread and Breadmaking Supplies and Equipment, p. 102; Laura's Easy, Basic, and Good White Bread, p. 103; Bread Ingredients, p. 104; Types of Bread, p. 105; Sourdough Starter and Zesty Whole Wheat Sourdough French Bread, p. 106; Triticale Bread, p. 108; Cheese Bread, p. 109; Batter Brown Bread and Substitute Ingredients, p. 110; Freezing Dough, p. 111; Yankee Grits Bread, p. 112; Whole-Wheat Granola Coffeecake, p. 116; Easy Pickin' Blueberry Drop Biscuits, p. 119; and Maple Buttermilk Muffins, p. 325.

Barbara Karoff: From *A-135 Making Quick Breads*: Your Favorite Pan, p. 112; and Basic Quick Bread and Buckwheat-Apple Bread, p. 113.

Matt Kelly: From *A-146 Perfect Grilled Meats*: Hidden Cheeseburger, p. 182, and Ginger Sauce for Ribs, p. 277. From *A-152 Perfect Grilled Vegetables*: Perfect Grilled Corn, p. 193.

Kelly Klober: From *Storey's Guide to Raising Pigs*: The Primary Cuts of Pork, p. 414.

Elizabeth Knight: From *Tea With Friends*: Set to a Tea, p. 292.

Karl F. Lutzen and Mark Stevens: From *Homebrew Favorites*: Brown Ale, p. 434, and Easy-to-Make Mead, p. 444.

Imogene McTague: From *A-32 Jams, Jellies & Preserves*: Making Homemade Jelly, pp. 400–401; Solar-Cooked Jams, p. 403; Apple Jelly, p. 404; Apple Butter and Pumpkin Butter, p. 406; and Rose Hip Jam, p. 462.

Alexander Nimetz, Jason Stanley and Emeline Starr: From *Healthy College Cookbook*: About Baking on the Lighter Side, p. 7; Tools for the Country Cook, pp. 15–20; Vegetable Chili, p. 86; Greek Salad and Tomato Basil and Mozzarella Salad, p. 127; Tuna Salad, p. 136; Taco Salad, p. 137; Beef Stroganoff, p. 147; Real Sloppy Sloppy Joe, p. 182; Burger Tips, p. 183; Tuna Melt, p. 183; Turkey Burgers, p. 183; Mashed Potatoes, p. 202; and Tomato-Mango Salsa, p. 281.

Penny Noepel: From *A-105 Fast and Easy Ways to Cook Vegetables*: Stir-Fried Celery and Carrot Strips, p. 195, and Stuffed Peppers, p. 200.

Gayle O'Donnell: From *A-150 Making Grapevine Wreaths*: Round and Full Grapevine Wreath, p. 488.

Betty Oppenheimer: From *Gifts for Herb Lovers*: Bouquet Garni Wreath, p. 483; Sachets, p. 490; and Pinecone Fire Starters, p. 491. From *Sewing Packs, Pouches, Seats & Sacks*: Grocery Bag, p. 486, and Double-Fold Bias Binding, p. 487.

Maggie Oster: From *A-142 Making Ice Cream & Frozen Yogurt*: Sugar Equivalents, p. 359; Ice Cream Making Equipment, p. 360; Making Ice Cream at Home, pp. 360–363; Butterfat Content, p. 363; Basic Vanilla Ice Cream and Vanilla Variations, p. 364; Egg Caution, p. 365; Fruit Sherbet and Sherbets and Ices, p. 366; and Basic Vanilla Yogurt and Variations, p. 367. From *Herb Mixtures & Spicy Blends*: Winter or Summer Herbed Butter Blend, p. 285; Herb Bread Blend and Salt-Free Herbal Blend, p. 306; Rosemary Black Olive Pesto, p. 307; Jamaican Blend, p. 309; Meat and Poultry Seasoning and Sweet Spice Blend, p. 310; and Pumpkin Pie Spiced Nuts, p. 471. From *Herbal Vinegar*: Red Bean and Rice Salad, p. 132; About Balsamic Treasure, p. 188; Cranberry Ketchup, p. 270; Ketchups, p. 271; and What Goes with What?, p. 275.

Dorothy Parker: From *A-115 Cooking with Potatoes*: Potato Cheese Soufflé, p. 55; Spicy Black-and-White Potato Salad, p. 131; Perfectly Baked Potatoes, p. 202; and Chestnut Potato Purée, p. 209.

Noel Perrin: From *A-51 Making Maple Syrup*: Making Maple Syrup, pp. 453–455.

Sara Pitzer: Southern Strawberry Salad, p. 139; Strawberry Rhubarb Pie and Strawberry Purée, p. 213; and Strawberry Shortcake, p. 214. From *A-77 Cooking with Dried Beans*: Dried Legumes, p. 24; Beans, p. 173; Measuring Dried Beans, p. 175; Cassoulet, p. 177; and About Dried Beans, p. 395.

Annie Proulx: From *A-47 Making the Best Apple Cider*: Common Apple Varieties for Cidermaking, p. 447; Making Apple Cider, pp. 447–448; and Boiled Cider Jelly, p. 467.

Nancy C. Ralston & Marynor Jordan: From *A-123 Great Rhubarb Recipes*: Rhubarb Punch, p. 288. From *New Zucchini Cookbook*: Squashyssoise, p. 83; Pumpkin Tempura, p. 99; Zucchini Slaw, p. 126; Butternut-Turkey Casserole, p. 178; and Zucchini-Walnut Spread, p. 467.

Charles Reavis: From *A-118 Hardwood Grilling*: Why Use Hardwood for Grilling? and East Coast Barbecued Chicken, p. 330; and Cajun-Style Grilled Swordfish, p. 350. From *Home Sausage Making*: China's Cheese and Sausage Roll, p. 96; Sausage and Rigatoni, p. 167; Paella, p. 172; Game Characteristics, p. 417; About Sausage Safety, p. 421; Basic Sausage, pp. 421–423; Chorizo, Sicilian-Style Hot or Sweet Sausage, and Country Chicken Sausage, p. 424; and Bratwurst and Old Bay Sausage, p. 425.

Bertha Reppert: From *A-161 Growing & Using Rosemary*: Patriots' Punch, p. 294.

Diana Rosen: From *Chai*: Iced Chai, Mocha Chai, Diana's Favorite Chai, and What is Chai?, p. 301. From *Steeped in Tea*: Shepherd's Pie, p. 181, and Portable Tea Spot, p. 292.

Marian Sebastiano: From *A-184 15 Herbs for Tea*: Lemon Blend Tea, p. 293, and Lavender Mint Tea, p. 294.

Althea Sexton: From *Gifts for Bird Lovers*: Votive Candleholder, p. 485, and Feed-the-Birds Ornaments, p. 488.

Phyllis V. Shaudys: From *Herbal Treasures*: Pesto, Pasta and Tomato Salad, p. 135; Barbecue Brush, p. 306; Herb & Flower Heart Wreath, p. 465; and Boursin with Fresh Herbs, p. 471. From *The Pleasure of Herbs*: Basic Herbed Omelet, p. 52; Greek Omelette, p. 53; Overnight Hearty Bean Soup, p. 79; Herbed Corn Chowder, p. 85; Sage Cheese Spread, p. 92; Crab-Cucumber Salad, p. 140; Basic Herb Vinegar Salad Dressing, p. 142; Roast Beef with Herbs, p. 146; Snow Peas with Herbs, p. 190; Citrus-Herb Cheesecake, p. 237; Bouquet Garni Vinegar and Mixed Herb Vinegar, p. 275; Herb and Fruit Juice Combinations, p. 289; and Garlic-Herb Cheese, p. 374.

Karyn Siegel-Maier: From *The Naturally Clean Home*: Fragrant Ideas, p. 477; Kitchen-Fresh Cleaner, Citrus-Sweet Dishwashing Blend, and Herbal-Clean Dishwashing Blend, p. 478; and Not Just a Pretty Scent, p. 479.

Edward C. Smith: From *The Vegetable Gardener's Bible*: About Soil-Sampling Savvy, p. 493; A Word about W-O-R-D, pp. 493–495; Dig It!, p. 495; and Key to Plants and Plan for Small Garden, p. 496.

Gwen Steege: From *101 Chocolate Chip Cookies*: Prizewinning Double Chocolate Chip Cookies, p. 248; About Baking Chocolate Chip Cookies and Chewy Chocolate Chip Cookies, p. 249; Top Hat Chocolate Chip Bars, p. 250; Substituting Cocoa, p. 256; and Double Peanut Butter Chocolate Chip Cookies, p. 323.

Edith (DeeDee) Stovel: Mediterranean Chicken Salad, p. 141; Grilled Beef Sirloin, p. 147; Baked Stuffed Fillet of Sole, p. 159; Steamed Artichokes, p. 189; Ratatouille, p. 199; Braised Turnips, p. 208; Clafouti Cherry, p. 219; Kiwi Hazelnut Meringue Cake, p. 227; and Strawberry Chiffon Pie, p. 242. From *Picnic!*: Baked Brie with Fresh Fruit, p. 94; Sunny Morning Muffins, p. 120; Red Potato Salad with Fresh Peas, p. 130; Brown Rice Salad, p. 132; Fresh Fruit Bowl Kaleidoscope, p. 138; Roast Beef Salad, p. 140; Grilled Tuna with Lime, p. 159; Garden Fresh Tomatoes with Basil and Balsamic Vinegar, p. 187; Gingerbread, p. 236; Sesame Lime Marinade, p. 278; and Take Three Corkscrews, p. 316.

Edith (DeeDee) Stovel and Pamela Wakefield: From *Weekend!*: Apple Sausage Bake, p. 45; Glorious Granola, p. 46; Creamy Scrambled Eggs, p. 50; Poached Eggs with Tomato Hash on Toasted Egg Bread, p. 51; Individual Omelettes, p. 54; Tomato

Strata and Zucchini Strata, p. 57; Orange Whole Wheat Pancakes and Power-Packed Pancakes, p. 59; Stuffed French Toast, p. 60; Orange French Toast and Overnight Oven French Toast, p. 61; Tip on Beating Egg Whites, p. 63; Big Breakfast Popover, p. 71; Shrimp & Beef Fondue, p. 96; Swiss Braided Bread, p. 107; Eternal Bran Muffins, p. 120; Hot and Cold Sesame Noodles, p. 135; Mountainous Birthday Cake, p. 232; and Peppermint Punch, p. 294.

Maggie Stuckey: From *Country Tea Parties*: Basic Scones, p. 116; Variations for Basic Scones, p. 117; Maids of Honor, p. 239; Honey Orange Butter, p. 285; How to Make a Perfect Pot, p. 291; Three Ways to Make Iced Tea, p. 292; Apple Mint Iced Tea and Herbs that Heal, p. 293; Wassail, p. 300; and About Tea Sandwiches, p. 354.

Tess and Mark Szamatulski: From *Clone Brews*: Just Like Bass Ale, p. 436.

Stephanie Tourles: From *The Herbal Body Book:* Milk Bath, p. 477, and Hand and Nail Butter and Herbal Bath Salts, p. 481.

Judy Tuttle: Applying Paint and Stenciled and Quilted Hot Pads, p. 484.

Nancy Van Leuven: Nutty Buttermilk Fish, p. 158.

Pattie Vargas and Rich Gulling: Zabaglione , p. 261; Basic Wine Cooler, p. 290; Blackberry Sangria, p. 300; Lemon Cooler, p. 427; Basic Steps in Winemaking, pp. 439–441; Grape Melomel and Peach Wine, p. 442; and Flavorings for Herb or Flower Wine, p. 443. From *A-144 Basic Homebrewing:* Brewing Equipment, p. 428. From *Cordials from Your Kitchen:* Blackberry Liqueur, p. 427; Almond Liqueur and Strawberry Liqueur, p. 445; and Aging Containers, Brandy Orange Cream, Cream Base for Liqueurs, and Liqueur or Cordial, p. 446.

Jim Wearne: From *A-144 Basic Homebrewing:* Basic Homebrew, pp. 428–434, and Basic Brewing Ingredients, p. 429.

Olwen Woodier: Homemade Pasta, p. 164; Cooking Perfect Pasta, p. 165; Traditional Lasagna, p. 166; How Much to Cook, Meatballs with Ziti, and White Clam Sauce with Thin Spaghetti, p. 168; and Types of Italian Pasta, p. 169. From *A-86 Cooking with Yogurt:* Yogurt Herb Cheese, p. 369; Basic Yogurt Recipe, Equipment for Making Yogurt, and Flavored Yogurt, p. 376; and What Went Wrong?, p. 377. From *The Apple Cookbook:* Sausage and Apple Omelette, p. 52; Apple Frittata, p. 56; The Greadeal, p. 58; Apple Pancakes, p. 60; Apple Tips and Breakfast Sausage Crêpes with Apples, p. 65; Apple Fritters, p. 69; Apple Rings and Hot Fruit, p. 99; Braised Duck, p. 157; Apple Varieties and Apple Snow, p. 222; Harvest Apple Pie, p. 238; Olwen's Apple Brown Betty, p. 243; English Custard Sauce, p. 279; Apple Cider Doughnuts, p. 332; and Apple Slices, p. 388.

Adriana and Rochelle Zabarkes: From *Adriana's Spice Caravan:* Spicy Potato Chips, p. 98; The Origins of Roast Pork, p. 151; About Roast Chicken, p. 153; Herbes de Provence, p. 304; Basic Curry Powder and Pickling Spice, p. 308; and Barbecue Rub and Crab Boil, p. 309.

Illustrations

Mike Belanger: p. 473.

Sarah Brill: p. 460.

Bethany Caskey: p. 415.

Patti Delmonte: p. 331.

Beverly Duncan: pp. 443; 448; 463 (nettles); and 496.

Judy Eliason: p. 392.

Christine Erickson: p. 437.

Brigita Fuhrmann: pp. 396; 456; 457 (beehive); 465; 483 (braiding wreath); 485 (making candleholder and templates); and 486 (finished project).

Charles Joslin: pp. 208, 274, 285, and 308.

Alison Kolesar: pp. 3; 8–21 (except for knife and cleaver page 17); 29; 52; 103; 111; 121; 147; 239; 253; 306; 317; 329; 343; 344; 362–363 (ice cream making); 375; 378 (canning jar); 379; 382–384; 386; 387; 395; 400; 401; 408; 422; 423; 431; 441; 466; 477; 489; 493; 495; 499; and 502.

Susan Berry Langsten: pp. 334, 335, and 436.

Doug Merrilees: p. 419.

Randy Mosher: pp. 430, and 435.

Doug Paisley: p. 462.

Betty Oppenheimer: pp. 486, and 487.

Carleen Powell: p. 347.

Frank Riccio: pp. 483–485 (finished projects); 488; 490; and 491.

Mary Rich: pp. 1; 6; 7; 25; 26; 28; 30; 36 (asparagus and avocado); 37 (cabbage and garlic); 38; 39 (potatoes and winter squash); 40; 43; 45; 47; 50; 53; 55; 56; 58; 59; 61; 63–65; 67 (pancakes); 68–71; 73; 75–77; 79–81; 83; 85; 87; 88; 90–92; 94; 101; 102 (flour and rolling pin); 104; 109; 112; 114; 117–119; 127; 128; 130–132; 135; 138; 141–143; 146; 150; 151; 153; 155; 156; 158; 161; 163; 167; 169; 170; 173; 174; 176–178; 180–182; 184; 187; 189 (skillet); 196; 198–200; 202; 205; 206; 212; 214; 216; 219; 220; 223; 226; 235; 237; 240; 243; 247; 251; 252; 255–257; 259; 261; 263; 265; 267; 269; 272; 277; 279; 281; 282; 284; 287; 289; 291; 293–295; 297; 298–300; 304; 307; 313; 318; 320; 322–325; 327; 330; 333; 337; 339; 345; 351; 353; 356; 360; 361; 366; 367; 369; 372; 374; 378 (butter dish); 381; 388; 393; 403; 405; 409–411; 429; 434; 450; 463 (bread); 471; 475; 480; 481; and 532.

Joanna Roy: pp. 23; 36 (artichoke); 37 (celery root and corn); 39 (summer squash and tomato); 41; 49; 54; 67 (blueberries); 102 (knife); 107; 116; 123; 124; 129; 139; 140; 148; 164; 175; 179; 183; 185; 189 (artichokes); 194; 213; 249; 264; 271; 349; 359; 363 (ice cream churn); 391; 418; 424; and 501.

Elayne Sears: pp. 137, 413, 414, 416, 417, 420, 432, 438, 439, and 442.

Laura Tedeschi: pp. 260; 278; 311; 319; 385; 444; 447; 457 (honeycomb); 459; 468; 478; and 479.

Becky Turner: p. 17 (knife and cleaver).

Index

NOTE: Page numbers in *italic* indicate illustrations; those in **boldface** indicate tables.